D1637777

A NEW
ARISTOTLE READER

EDITED BY

J. L. ACKRILL

CLARENDON PRESS · OXFORD

Oxford University Press, Great Clarendon Street, Oxford OX2 6DP
Oxford University Press is a department of the University of Oxford.
It furthers the University's objective of excellence in research, scholarship,
and education by publishing worldwide in
Oxford New York
Auckland Bangkok Buenos Aires Cape Town Chennai
Dar es Salaam Delhi Hong Kong Istanbul Karachi Kolkata
Kuala Lumpur Madrid Melbourne Mexico City Mumbai Nairobi
São Paulo Shanghai Taipei Tokyo Toronto

Oxford is a registered trade mark of Oxford University Press
in the UK and in certain other countries

Published in the United States
by Oxford University Press Inc., New York

British Library Cataloguing in Publication Data
Aristotle
A new Aristotle reader.
1. Philosophy, Ancient
I. Title   II. Ackrill, J. L.
185   B407
ISBN 0-19-875069-2
ISBN 0-19-875061-7 (Pbk)

11

Printed in Great Britain
on acid free paper by
Selwood Printing Ltd, Burgess hill

CONTENTS

Translations   vii

Aristotle's Works   x

Introduction   xi

Glossary   xiv

TEXTS

Logic   3

Natural Philosophy   79

Metaphysics   253

Practical Philosophy   361

Topics   557

List of Books   577

TRANSLATIONS

Logic

Categories   5
1–5
De Interpretatione   12
1–11
Prior Analytics   24
    I. 1–7; 27, 43^{a}25–43
    II. 21
Posterior Analytics   39
    I. 1–4, 10, 13
    II. 1–2, 8–10, 12, 19
Topics   60
    I.

Natural Philosophy

Physics   81
    I. 1–2, 5–9
    II.
    III. 1–3, 5.205^{a}7–6.207^{a}14
    IV. 4.210^{b}32–212^{a}21; 10–11
    VIII. 6; 10.267^{a}21–^{b}26

On the Heavens   132
    I. 2; 9; 10.279^{b}4–280^{a}10; 12.281^{b}3–33
    II. 12.292^{a}10–^{b}25
    III. 6

On Generation and Corruption   143
    I. 3; 4.319^{b}6–21
    II. 1.329^{a}24–^{b}5; 3.330^{a}30–^{b}6; 330^{b}31–331^{a}6; 4.331^{a}6–^{b}12; 9–11

Meteorology   158
    I. 1
    IV. 12

On the Soul   161
    I. 1; 4.408^{a}34–^{b}29
    II. except c. 7
    III. except cc. 12–13

On Memory   206
    1

On Sleep   210
2

On Dreams   214
2.459^{a}23–^{b}23, 460^{a}32–^{b}27; 3.461^{a}30–462^{a}8

On Youth and Old Age   218
3.468^{b}28–4.469^{b}20

Parts of Animals   220
   I. 1, 5
   II. 1

Movement of Animals   233
6–11

Generation of Animals   241
   I. 21.729^{b}1–II. 1.732^{a}12
   II. 1.734^{b}21–735^{a}26; 3.736^{a}24–737^{a}34
   V. 1.778^{a}16–^{b}19; 8

Metaphysics

Metaphysics *   255
   I. (*A*) 1–2
   III. (*B*) 1
   IV. (*Γ*) 1–3; 4.1005^{b}35–1006^{a}28, 1008^{b}2–1009^{a}5; 5.1009^{a}6–16, 1010^{b}1–29
   V. (*Δ*) 4–8; 29
   VI. (*E*)
   VII. (*Z*)
   VIII. (*H*)
   IX. (*Θ*)
   X. (*I*) 1; 9
   XII. (*Λ*)
   XIII. (*M*) 4–5; 10

Practical Philosophy

Nicomachean Ethics   363
   I. 1–8; 13
   II. 1–7; 9
   III.
   V. 1–2; 5.1133^{b}29–1134^{a}16; 7.1134^{b}18–1135^{a}5; 8; 9.1137^{a}5–26; 10
   VI.
   VII.
   IX. 4; 8; 9
   X.

* Books of the *Metaphysics* are often referred to by Greek capital letters, given here in brackets.

Eudemian Ethics   479
    I. 1–5
   II. 1; 6–10
VIII. 2; 3
Politics   507
    I. 1–7
  III. 1–4
 VII. 1–3; 13–15
VIII. 1–3
Poetics   540
1–15 (with omissions); 19–20

ARISTOTLE'S WORKS

This list contains all the works translated or referred to in this volume. The order is the traditional one: Logic, Natural Philosophy, Metaphysics, Practical Philosophy.

Abbreviation	Latin Title	English Title
Cat.	Categoriae	Categories
De Int.	De Interpretatione	
An. Pr.	Analytica Priora	Prior Analytics
An. Post.	Analytica Posteriora	Posterior Analytics
Top.	Topica	Topics
Soph. El.	Sophistici Elenchi	Sophistical Refutations
Phys.	Physica	Physics
	De Caelo	On the Heavens
GC	De Generatione et Corruptione	On Generation and Corruption
Meteor.	Meteorologica	Meteorology
De An.	De Anima	On the Soul
	De Sensu	On Sense
De Mem.	De Memoria	On Memory
	De Somno	On Sleep
De Insomn.	De Insomniis	On Dreams
De Iuv.	De Iuventute et Senectute	On Youth and Old Age
PA	De Partibus Animalium	Parts of Animals
MA	De Motu Animalium	Movement of Animals
GA	De Generatione Animalium	Generation of Animals
Met.	Metaphysica	Metaphysics
EN	Ethica Nicomachea	Nicomachean Ethics
EE	Ethica Eudemia	Eudemian Ethics
Pol.	Politica	Politics
Rhet.	Rhetorica	Rhetoric
Poet.	Poetica	Poetics

References to Aristotle's works may be by book and chapter, but use is also made of the numerals and letters printed in the outer margin. These derive from Bekker's 1831 edition of the text. Thus '170ᵃ13' refers to the thirteenth line of the left column on page 170 of Bekker's edition. The line-number in a translation cannot always coincide exactly with the line in the Greek.

INTRODUCTION

General Aim

The main aim of this book is to provide in a single volume reliable translations of those parts of Aristotle likely to be of most interest to students of philosophy. A secondary aim is to supply, as an aid to study, a list of key topics together with appropriate reading-lists. In what follows I shall explain briefly how I have tried to achieve these aims.

The Texts and Translations

In selecting the texts I have drawn on experience of graduate classes, and I have tried to include all the texts necessary for a careful study of most aspects of Aristotle's philosophy. Some will find here more of Aristotle than they need. I hope that they will turn this to advantage by reading more widely than they would otherwise have done.*

I have been reluctant to cut up Aristotle's works and give mere snippets. It is necessary to read an extended passage if one is to gather the context and the flow of argument, and to get an idea of Aristotle's style of philosophizing.

Some themes cannot be adequately represented in a selection such as this. I mention three. Formal logic: I have included the basic chapters on the syllogism, but a close study of Aristotle's formal logic (including his modal logic) will require reference to the *Prior Analytics* as a whole. Biology: passages of philosophical importance are to be found scattered among lengthy works of a predominantly descriptive and classificatory nature. This book includes some of the main starting-points, to tempt the student interested in the philosophical issues to read more widely in Aristotle's biological works. Political philosophy: I have included material that is of interest to every student of Aristotle's practical philosophy, but the specialist in political philosophy will naturally have to read much more of the *Politics*.

Recent translations of Aristotle have sought and often achieved a high degree of accuracy. They have tried to keep close to the text in

---

* Those approaching Aristotle for the first time will naturally require some guidance. Among suitable introductory books (included in the List of Books) are those by Ackrill, Allan, Barnes, and Lloyd.

order to put the Greekless reader as nearly as possible in the position of a reader of Greek; they have tried not to incorporate too much interpretation into their renderings. For a rough idea of Aristotle a rough but readable translation is entirely suitable; for a real understanding it will not do.

Aristotle's prose is direct, concise, and vigorous—a good vehicle for philosophical argument. But not all the works as we have them are in a revised and polished form. Some read more like lecture-notes than books ready for the publisher. Moreover, some have a relatively technical character, and employ technical terms or make use of ordinary words in special ways. For these reasons the translations of different works will themselves vary in style, from the smooth and flowing to the terse and elliptical.

The translations contained in this book are all careful and good translations. Many come from the Clarendon Aristotle series (Oxford University Press), a series of volumes specially designed to provide accurate versions for philosophical students. Several, including the long extracts from the *Nicomachean Ethics* and *Metaphysics*, come from the recently revised Oxford Aristotle translation (Princeton University Press, 1984).

One important feature of a good translation is consistency in the rendering of key terms, since philosophical questions often revolve around such terms and the reader wants to know when they are being used. Ideally some thirty or forty Greek words would be transliterated: the words 'substance', 'essence', 'being' would not appear but only '*ousia*'; instead of 'account', 'reason', 'speech', 'argument' etc. there would be '*logos*'. The nearest practicable approach to this is to use relatively few equivalents, and to provide a glossary.

The translators of different works will, however, make different choices of equivalents, partly on account of the different subject-matters, but partly also because of their various judgements as to the nuances of Greek and English words. Since a number of translators contribute to the present volume, the reader must be aware that these differences exist. In one way they will add to his difficulties; in another way they will add to his understanding—for it is in the end essential to realize that no single choice of a standard rendering (or renderings) for key philosophical terms can give *exactly* the force of the Greek. Any translator reflects Aristotle through his own mind. Reading several translators enables the student to get several perspectives instead of being confined to one only.

The main alternative renderings of some very common terms are given in the Glossary below. Individual volumes in the Clarendon Aristotle series have their own fuller glossaries. For the *Politics* and *Nicomachean Ethics* there are full glossaries in Sinclair and Saunders, and in Irwin (see List of Books).

Details of the translations used in this volume and of the texts on which they are based are given in footnotes to the translations. I have not thought it appropriate to remark on small textual changes adopted by the translators, the details of which can be found in the original volumes.

The Topics

The topics listed cover many of the main questions commonly studied, and the references supplied are offered as an aid to that study. Some of the topics are more difficult or specialized than others, and some of the books and articles listed are more difficult than others. These lists are necessarily *very* selective, and any expert will immediately be able to draw up alternative lists of equal usefulness. But I trust that there will be some teachers, and some pupils, who will find my suggestions helpful. (The order in which the items are listed is not of great significance. It is often chronological, but sometimes other considerations prevail.)

Some of the 'topics' are really sets of topics, e.g. 'Biology' or 'Political Philosophy'. Some topics are closely related to others, and I have indicated this by cross-references.

Under the topic heading I have given: references (in the conventional abbreviated form) to the main Aristotelian texts (and sometimes, in square brackets, references to secondary texts not contained in this volume); references (by author only) to books listed in the List of Books; a short list of recent articles; and a cross-reference to related topics.

GLOSSARY

aitia: cause, reason, explanation
archē: origin, starting-point, principle, first principle
aretē: virtue, excellence
eidos: form, species, sort
einai: be, exist
energeia: activity, actuality, actualization
epistēmē: knowledge, scientific knowledge, branch of knowledge, science, understanding
ergon: work, product, function, fact
genesis: becoming . . ., coming into being
homōnymos: homonymous, equivocal, ambiguous
hypokeimenon: substratum, subject, underlying thing
kata symbebēkos: accidentally, *per accidens*, incidentally, by virtue of concurrence
katēgoria: category, predicate, predication
kinēsis: change, movement
logos: utterance, statement, argument, account, definition, formula, ratio, language, reason, principle
nous: intellect, intelligence, intuition, intuitive reason, comprehension
ousia: being, substance, essence, reality
syllogismos: reasoning, calculation, inference, deduction, syllogism
telos: end, goal, fulfilment, completion
to ti ēn einai: essence, what it is to be . . .

TEXTS

Logic

CATEGORIES*

CHAPTER I

When things have only a name in common and the definition of being 1ᵃ
which corresponds to the name is different, they are called *homony-*
mous. Thus, for example, both a man and a picture are animals. These
have only a name in common and the definition of being which
corresponds to the name is different; for if one is to say what being an 5
animal is for each of them, one will give two distinct definitions.
    When things have the name in common and the definition of being
which corresponds to the name is the same, they are called *synony-*
mous. Thus, for example, both a man and an ox are animals. Each of
these is called by a common name, 'animal', and the definition of 10
being is also the same; for if one is to give the definition of each—what
being an animal is for each of them—one will give the same definition.
    When things get their name from something, with a difference of
ending, they are called *paronymous*. Thus, for example, the grammarian gets his name from grammar, the brave get theirs from bravery. 15

CHAPTER 2

Of things that are said, some involve combination while others are
said without combination. Examples of those involving combination
are 'man runs', 'man wins'; and of those without combination 'man',
'ox', 'runs', 'wins'. 20
    Of things there are: (*a*) some are *said of* a subject but are not *in* any
subject. For example, man is said of a subject, the individual man, but
is not in any subject. (*b*) Some are in a subject but are not said of any
subject. (By 'in a subject' I mean what is in something, not as a part,
and cannot exist separately from what it is in.) For example, the 25
individual knowledge-of-grammar is in a subject, the soul, but is not
said of any subject; and the individual white is in a subject, the body
(for all colour is in a body), but is not said of any subject. (*c*) Some are
both said of a subject and in a subject. For example, knowledge is in a 1ᵇ
subject, the soul, and is also said of a subject, knowledge-of-grammar.

* *Translation*: J. L. Ackrill (Clarendon Aristotle Series, 1963); *Text*: L. Minio-Paluello (Oxford Classical Texts, 1956).

(*d*) Some are neither in a subject nor said of a subject, for example, the
5   individual man or individual horse—for nothing of this sort is either in
a subject or said of a subject. Things that are individual and numerically one are, without exception, not said of any subject, but there is
nothing to prevent some of them from being in a subject—the individual knowledge-of-grammar is one of the things in a subject.

CHAPTER 3

10   Whenever one thing is predicated of another as of a subject, all things
said of what is predicated will be said of the subject also. For example,
man is predicated of the individual man, and animal of man; so animal
15   will be predicated of the individual man also—for the individual man
is both a man and an animal.

The differentiae of genera which are different and not subordinate
one to the other are themselves different in kind. For example, animal
and knowledge: footed, winged, aquatic, two-footed, are differentiae
of animal, but none of these is a differentia of knowledge; one sort of
20   knowledge does not differ from another by being two-footed. However, there is nothing to prevent genera subordinate one to the other
from having the same differentiae. For the higher are predicated of the
genera below them, so that all differentiae of the predicated genus will
be differentiae of the subject also.

CHAPTER 4

25   Of things said without any combination, each signifies either substance or quantity or qualification or a relative or where or when or
being-in-a-position or having or doing or being-affected. To give a
rough idea, examples of substance are man, horse; of quantity: four-
foot, five-foot; of qualification: white, grammatical; of a relative:
2ᵃ   double, half, larger; of where: in the Lyceum, in the market-place; of
when: yesterday, last-year; of being-in-a-position: is-lying, is-sitting;
of having: has-shoes-on, has-armour-on; of doing: cutting, burning; of
being-affected: being-cut, being-burned.

5   None of the above is said just by itself in any affirmation, but by the
combination of these with one another an affirmation is produced. For
every affirmation, it seems, is either true or false; but of things said
without any combination none is either true or false (e.g. 'man',
10   'white', 'runs', 'wins').

CHAPTER 5

A *substance*—that which is called a substance most strictly, primarily, and most of all—is that which is neither said of a subject nor in a subject, e.g. the individual man or the individual horse. The species in which the things primarily called substances are, are called *secondary* 15 *substances*, as also are the genera of these species. For example, the individual man belongs in a species, man, and animal is a genus of the species; so these—both man and animal—are called secondary substances.

It is clear from what has been said that if something is said of a subject both its name and its definition are necessarily predicated of 20 the subject. For example, man is said of a subject, the individual man, and the name is of course predicated (since you will be predicating man of the individual man), and also the definition of man will be predicated of the individual man (since the individual man is also a 25 man). Thus both the name and the definition will be predicated of the subject. But as for things which are in a subject, in most cases neither the name nor the definition is predicated of the subject. In some cases there is nothing to prevent the name from being predicated of the subject, but it is impossible for the definition to be predicated. For 30 example, white, which is in a subject (the body), is predicated of the subject; for a body is called white. But the definition of white will never be predicated of the body.

All the other things are either said of the primary substances as subjects or in them as subjects. This is clear from an examination of 35 cases. For example, animal is predicated of man and therefore also of the individual man; for were it predicated of none of the individual men it would not be predicated of man at all. Again, colour is in body 2ᵇ and therefore also in an individual body; for were it not in some individual body it would not be in body at all. Thus all the other things are either said of the primary substances as subjects or in them as 5 subjects. So if the primary substances did not exist it would be impossible for any of the other things to exist.

Of the secondary substances the species is more a substance than the genus, since it is nearer to the primary substance. For if one is to say of the primary substance what it is, it will be more informative and 10 apt to give the species than the genus. For example, it would be more informative to say of the individual man that he is a man than that he is an animal (since the one is more distinctive of the individual man

while the other is more general); and more informative to say of the
15   individual tree that it is a tree than that it is a plant. Further, it is
because the primary substances are subjects for all the other things
and all the other things are predicated of them or are in them, that they
are called substances most of all. But as the primary substances stand
to the other things, so the species stands to the genus: the species is a
20   subject for the genus (for the genera are predicated of the species but
the species are not predicated reciprocally of the genera). Hence for
this reason too the species is more a substance than the genus.

But of the species themselves—those which are not genera—one is
no more a substance than another: it is no more apt to say of the indi-
25   vidual man that he is a man than to say of the individual horse that it is
a horse. And similarly of the primary substances one is no more a
substance than another: the individual man is no more a substance
than the individual ox.

It is reasonable that, after the primary substances, their species and
genera should be the only other things called (secondary) substances.
30   For only they, of things predicated, reveal the primary substance. For
if one is to say of the individual man what he is, it will be in place to
give the species or the genus (though more informative to give man
than animal); but to give any of the other things would be out of
35   place—for example, to say 'white' or 'runs' or anything like that. So it
is reasonable that these should be the only other things called
substances. Further, it is because the primary substances are subjects
3ᵃ   for everything else that they are called substances most strictly. But as
the primary substances stand to everything else, so the species and
genera of the primary substances stand to all the rest: all the rest are
predicated of these. For if you will call the individual man gram-
5   matical it follows that you will call both a man and an animal
grammatical; and similarly in other cases.

It is a characteristic common to every substance not to be in a
subject. For a primary substance is neither said of a subject nor in a
10   subject. And as for secondary substances, it is obvious at once that
they are not in a subject. For man is said of the individual man as
subject but is not in a subject: man is not *in* the individual man.
Similarly, animal also is said of the individual man as subject but
animal is not *in* the individual man. Further, while there is nothing to
15   prevent the name of what is in a subject from being sometimes
predicated of the subject, it is impossible for the definition to be
predicated. But the definition of the secondary substances, as well as

the name, is predicated of the subject: you will predicate the definition of man of the individual man, and also that of animal. No substance, 20 therefore, is in a subject.

This is not, however, peculiar to substance; the differentia also is not in a subject. For footed and two-footed are said of man as subject but are not in a subject; neither two-footed nor footed is *in* man. Moreover, the definition of the differentia is predicated of that of 25 which the differentia is said. For example, if footed is said of man the definition of footed will also be predicated of man; for man is footed.

We need not be disturbed by any fear that we may be forced to say that the parts of a substance, being in a subject (the whole substance), 30 are not substances. For when we spoke of things *in a subject* we did not mean things belonging in something as *parts*.

It is a characteristic of substances and differentiae that all things called from them are so called synonymously. For all the predicates from them are predicated either of the individuals or of the species. 35 (For from a primary substance there is no predicate, since it is said of no subject; and as for secondary substances, the species is predicated of the individual, the genus both of the species and of the individual. Similarly, differentiae too are predicated both of the species and of the 3^b individuals.) And the primary substances admit the definition of the species and of the genera, and the species admits that of the genus; for everything said of what is predicated will be said of the subject also. 5 Similarly, both the species and the individuals admit the definition of the differentiae. But synonymous things were precisely those with both the name in common and the same definition. Hence all the things called from substances and differentiae are so called synonymously.

Every substance seems to signify a certain 'this'. As regards the 10 primary substances, it is indisputably true that each of them signifies a certain 'this'; for the thing revealed is individual and numerically one. But as regards the secondary substances, though it appears from the form of the name—when one speaks of man or animal—that a 15 secondary substance likewise signifies a certain 'this', this is not really true; rather, it signifies a certain qualification, for the subject is not, as the primary substance is, one, but man and animal are said of many things. However, it does not signify simply a certain qualification, as white does. White signifies nothing but a qualification, whereas the 20 species and the genus mark off the qualification of substance—they signify substance of a certain qualification. (One draws a wider boundary with the genus than with the species, for in speaking of animal one takes in more than in speaking of man.)

Another characteristic of substances is that there is nothing
25 contrary to them. For what would be contrary to a primary substance? For example, there is nothing contrary to an individual man, nor yet is there anything contrary to man or to animal. This, however, is not peculiar to substance but holds of many other things also, for example, of quantity. For there is nothing contrary to four-foot or to ten or to
30 anything of this kind—unless someone were to say that many is contrary to few or large to small; but still there is nothing contrary to any *definite* quantity.

Substance, it seems, does not admit of a more and a less. I do not
35 mean that one substance is not more a substance than another (we have said that it is), but that any given substance is not called more, or less, that which it is. For example, if this substance is a man, it will not be more a man or less a man either than itself or than another man. For
4ᵃ one man is not more a man than another, as one pale thing is more pale than another and one beautiful thing more beautiful than another. Again, a thing is called more, or less, such-and-such than itself; for example, the body that is pale is called more pale now than
5 before, and the one that is hot is called more, or less, hot. Substance, however, is not spoken of thus. For a man is not called more a man now than before, nor is anything else that is a substance. Thus substance does not admit of a more and a less.

10 It seems most distinctive of substance that what is numerically one and the same is able to receive contraries. In no other case could one bring forward anything, numerically one, which is able to receive contraries. For example, a colour which is numerically one and the
15 same will not be black and white, nor will numerically one and the same action be bad and good; and similarly with everything else that is not substance. A substance, however, numerically one and the same, is able to receive contraries. For example, an individual man—one and
20 the same—becomes pale at one time and dark at another, and hot and cold, and bad and good. Nothing like this is to be seen in any other case.

But perhaps someone might object and say that statements and beliefs are like this. For the same statement seems to be both true and false. Suppose, for example, that the statement that somebody is
25 sitting is true; after he has got up this same statement will be false. Similarly with beliefs. Suppose you believe truly that somebody is

sitting; after he has got up you will believe falsely if you hold the same belief about him. However, even if we were to grant this, there is still a difference in the *way* contraries are received. For in the case of substances it is by themselves changing that they are able to receive contraries. For what has become cold instead of hot, or dark instead of pale, or good instead of bad, has changed (has altered); similarly in other cases too it is by itself undergoing change that each thing is able to receive contraries. Statements and beliefs, on the other hand, themselves remain completely unchangeable in every way; it is because the *actual thing* changes that the contrary comes to belong to them. For the statement that somebody is sitting remains the same; it is because of a change in the actual thing that it comes to be true at one time and false at another. Similarly with beliefs. Hence at least the *way* in which it is able to receive contraries—through a change in itself— would be distinctive of substance, even if we were to grant that beliefs and statements are able to receive contraries. However, this is not true. For it is not because they themselves receive anything that state- ments and beliefs are said to be able to receive contraries, but because of what has happened to something else. For it is because the actual thing exists or does not exist that the statement is said to be true or false, not because it is able itself to receive contraries. No statement, in fact, or belief is changed at all by anything. So, since nothing happens in them, they are not able to receive contraries. A substance, on the other hand, is said to be able to receive contraries because it itself receives contraries. For it receives sickness and health, and paleness and darkness; and because it itself receives the various things of this kind it is said to be able to receive contraries. It is, therefore, distinc- tive of substance that what is numerically one and the same is able to receive contraries. This brings to an end our discussion of substance.

  30

  35

  4^b

  5

  10

  15

DE INTERPRETATIONE*

CHAPTER 1

16ª First we must settle what a name is and what a verb is, and then what a negation, an affirmation, a statement, and a sentence are.

Now spoken sounds are symbols of affections in the soul, and written marks symbols of spoken sounds. And just as written marks
5 are not the same for all men, neither are spoken sounds. But what these are in the first place signs of—affections of the soul—are the same for all; and what these affections are likenesses of—actual things—are also the same. These matters have been discussed in the work on the soul and do not belong to the present subject.
10 Just as some thoughts in the soul are neither true nor false while some are necessarily one or the other, so also with spoken sounds. For falsity and truth have to do with combination and separation. Thus
15 names and verbs by themselves—for instance 'man' or 'white' when nothing further is added—are like the thoughts that are without combination and separation; for so far they are neither true nor false. A sign of this is that even 'goat-stag' signifies something but not, as yet, anything true or false—unless 'is' or 'is not' is added (either simply or with reference to time).

CHAPTER 2

A *name* is a spoken sound significant by convention, without time,
20 none of whose parts is significant in separation.

For in 'Whitfield' the 'field' does not signify anything in its own right, as it does in the phrase 'white field'. Not that it is the same with complex names as with simple ones: in the latter the part is in no way
25 significant, in the former it has some force but is not significant of anything in separation, for example the 'boat' in 'pirate-boat'.

I say 'by convention' because no name is a name naturally but only when it has become a symbol. Even inarticulate noises (of beasts, for instance) do indeed reveal something, yet none of them is a name.

* *Translation*: J. L. Ackrill (Clarendon Aristotle Series, 1963); *Text*: L. Minio-Paluello (Oxford Classical Texts, 1956).

'Not man' is not a name, nor is there any correct name for it. It is   30
neither a phrase nor a negation. Let us call it an indefinite name.
'Philo's', 'to-Philo', and the like are not names but inflexions of
names. The same account holds for them as for names except that an   16ᵇ
inflexion when combined with 'is', 'was', or 'will be' is not true or false
whereas a name always is. Take, for example, 'Philo's is' or 'Philo's is
not'; so far there is nothing either true or false.   5

CHAPTER 3

A *verb* is what additionally signifies time, no part of it being significant
separately; and it is a sign of things said of something else.

It additionally signifies time: 'recovery' is a name, but 'recovers' is a
verb, because it additionally signifies something's holding *now*. And it   10
is always a sign of what holds, that is, holds of a subject.

'Does not recover' and 'does not ail' I do not call verbs. For though
they additionally signify time and always hold of something, yet there
is a difference—for which there is no name. Let us call them indefinite
verbs, because they hold indifferently of anything whether existent or   15
non-existent.

Similarly, 'recovered' and 'will-recover' are not verbs but inflexions
of verbs. They differ from the verb in that it additionally signifies the
present time, they the time outside the present.

When uttered just by itself a verb is a name and signifies
something—the speaker arrests his thought and the hearer pauses—   20
but it does not yet signify whether it is or not. For not even 'to be' or
'not to be' is a sign of the actual thing (nor if you say simply 'that which
is'); for by itself it is nothing, but it additionally signifies some
combination, which cannot be thought of without the components.   25

CHAPTER 4

A *sentence* is a significant spoken sound some part of which is significant in separation—as an expression, not as an affirmation.

I mean that 'animal', for instance, signifies something, but not that it
is or is not (though it will be an affirmation or negation if something is   30
added); the single syllables of 'animal', on the other hand, signify
nothing. Nor is the 'ice' in 'mice' significant; here it is simply a spoken
sound. In double words, as we said, a part does signify, but not in its
own right.

17ᵃ   Every sentence is significant (not as a tool but, as we said, by
convention), but not every sentence is a statement-making sentence,
but only those in which there is truth or falsity. There is not truth or
falsity in all sentences: a prayer is a sentence but is neither true nor
false. The present investigation deals with the statement-making
5   sentence; the others we can dismiss, since consideration of them
belongs rather to the study of rhetoric or poetry.

CHAPTER 5

The first single statement-making sentence is the affirmation, next is
the negation. The others are single in virtue of a connective.
Every statement-making sentence must contain a verb or an
10   inflexion of a verb. For even the definition of man is not yet a
statement-making sentence—unless 'is' or 'will be' or 'was' or something of this sort is added. (To explain why 'two-footed land animal' is
one thing and not many belongs to a different inquiry; certainly it will
not be one simply through being said all together.)
15   A single statement-making sentence is either one that reveals a
single thing or one that is single in virtue of a connective. There are
more than one if more things than one are revealed or if connectives
are lacking.
(Let us call a name or a verb simply an expression, since by saying it
one cannot reveal anything by one's utterance in such a way as to be
making a statement, whether one is answering a question or speaking
spontaneously.)
20   Of these the one is a simple statement, affirming or denying something of something, the other is compounded of simple statements and
is a kind of composite sentence.
The simple statement is a significant spoken sound about whether
something does or does not hold (in one of the divisions of time).

CHAPTER 6

25   An *affirmation* is a statement affirming something of something, a
negation is a statement denying something of something.
Now it is possible to state of what does hold that it does not hold, of
what does not hold that it does hold, of what does hold that it does
hold, and of what does not hold that it does not hold. Similarly for
30   times outside the present. So it must be possible to deny whatever

anyone has affirmed, and to affirm whatever anyone has denied. Thus it is clear that for every affirmation there is an opposite negation, and for every negation an opposite affirmation. Let us call an affirmation and a negation which are opposite a *contradiction*. I speak of statements as opposite when they affirm and deny the same thing of the same 35 thing—not homonymously, together with all other such conditions that we add to counter the troublesome objections of sophists.

CHAPTER 7

Now of actual things some are universal, others particular (I call universal that which is by its nature predicated of a number of things, and particular that which is not; man, for instance, is a universal, 17ᵇ Callias a particular). So it must sometimes be of a universal that one states that something holds or does not, sometimes of a particular. Now if one states universally of a universal that something holds or does not, there will be contrary statements (examples of what I mean 5 by 'stating universally of a universal' are 'every man is white' and 'no man is white'). But when one states something of a universal but not universally, the statements are not contrary (though what is being revealed may be contrary). Examples of what I mean by 'stating of a universal not universally' are 'a man is white' and 'a man is not white'; 10 man is a universal but it is not used universally in the statement (for 'every' does not signify the universal but that it is taken universally). It is not true to predicate a universal universally of a subject, for there cannot be an affirmation in which a universal is predicated universally 15 of a subject, for instance 'every man is every animal'.

I call an affirmation and a negation *contradictory* opposites when what one signifies universally the other signifies not universally, e.g. 'every man is white' and 'not every man is white', 'no man is white' and 'some man is white'. But I call the universal affirmation and the 20 universal negation contrary opposites, e.g. 'every man is just' and 'no man is just'. So these cannot be true together, but their opposites may both be true with respect to the same thing, e.g. 'not every man is 25 white' and 'some man is white'.

Of contradictory statements about a universal taken universally it is necessary for one or the other to be true or false; similarly if they are about particulars, e.g. 'Socrates is white' and 'Socrates is not white'. But if they are about a universal not taken universally it is not always 30 the case that one is true and the other false. For it is true to say at the same time that a man is white and that a man is not white, or that a man is noble and a man is not noble (for if base, then not noble; and if something is becoming something, then it *is* not that thing). This might seem absurd at first sight, because 'a man is not white' looks as if it signifies also at the same time that no man is white; this, however, does not signify the same, nor does it necessarily hold at the same time.

It is evident that a single affirmation has a single negation. For the negation must deny the same thing as the affirmation affirmed, and of the same thing, whether a particular or a universal (taken either universally or not universally). I mean, for example, 'Socrates is white' and 'Socrates is not white'. But if something else is denied, or the same thing is denied of something else, that will not be the opposite statement, but a different one. The opposite of 'every man is white' is 'not every man is white'; of 'some man is white', 'no man is white'; of 'a man is white', 'a man is not white'.

We have explained, then: that a single affirmation has a single negation as its contradictory opposite, and which these are; that contrary statements are different, and which these are; and that not all contradictory pairs are true or false, why this is, and when they are true or false.

CHAPTER 8

A single affirmation or negation is one which signifies one thing about one thing (whether about a universal taken universally or not), e.g. 'every man is white', 'not every man is white', 'a man is white', 'a man is not white', 'no man is white', 'some man is white'—assuming that 'white' signifies one thing.

But if one name is given to two things which do not make up one thing, there is not a single affirmation. Suppose, for example, that one gave the name 'cloak' to horse and man; 'a cloak is white' would not be a single affirmation. For to say this is no different from saying 'a horse and a man is white', and this is no different from saying 'a horse is white and a man is white'. So if this last signifies more than one thing and is more than one affirmation, clearly the first also signifies either more than one thing or nothing (because no man is a horse). Consequently it is not necessary, with these statements either, for one contradictory to be true and the other false.

CHAPTER 9

With regard to what is and what has been it is necessary for the affirmation or the negation to be true or false. And with universals　30 taken universally it is always necessary for one to be true and the other false, and with particulars too, as we have said; but with universals not spoken of universally it is not necessary. But with particulars that are going to be it is different.

For if every affirmation or negation is true or false it is necessary for everything either to be the case or not to be the case. For if one person　35 says that something will be and another denies this same thing, it is clearly necessary for one of them to be saying what is true—if every affirmation is true or false; for both will not be the case together under such circumstances. For if it is true to say that it is white or is not white, it is necessary for it to be white or not white; and if it is white or　18ᵇ is not white, then it was true to say or deny this. If it is not the case it is false, if it is false it is not the case. So it is necessary for the affirmation or the negation to be true. It follows that nothing either is or is happening, or will be or will not be, by chance or as chance has it, but　5 everything of necessity and not as chance has it (since either he who says or he who denies is saying what is true). For otherwise it might equally well happen or not happen, since what is as chance has it is no more thus than not thus, nor will it be.

Again, if it is white now it was true to say earlier that it would be　10 white; so that it was always true to say of anything that has happened that it would be so. But if it was always true to say that it was so, or would be so, it could not not be so, or not be going to be so. But if something cannot not happen it is impossible for it not to happen; and if it is impossible for something not to happen it is necessary for it to happen. Everything that will be, therefore, happens necessarily. So　15 nothing will come about as chance has it or by chance; for if by chance, not of necessity.

Nor, however, can we say that neither is true—that it neither will be nor will not be so. For, firstly, though the affirmation is false the negation is not true, and though the negation is false the affirmation, on this view, is not true. Moreover, if it is true to say that something is　20 white and large, both have to hold of it, and if true that they will hold tomorrow, they will have to hold tomorrow; and if it neither will be nor will not be the case tomorrow, then there is no 'as chance has it'. Take a sea-battle: it would *have* neither to happen nor not to happen.　25

These and others like them are the absurdities that follow if it is necessary, for every affirmation and negation either about universals spoken of universally or about particulars, that one of the opposites be
30   true and the other false, and that nothing of what happens is as chance has it, but everything is and happens of necessity. So there would be no need to deliberate or to take trouble (thinking that if we do this, this will happen, but if we do not, it will not). For there is nothing to prevent someone's having said ten thousand years beforehand that this would be the case, and another's having denied it; so that which-
35   ever of the two was true to say then, will be the case of necessity. Nor, of course, does it make any difference whether any people made the contradictory statements or not. For clearly this is how the actual things are even if someone did not affirm it and another deny it. For it is not because of the affirming or denying that it will be or will not be the case, nor is it a question of ten thousand years beforehand rather than any other time. Hence, if in the whole of time the state of things
19ᵃ   was such that one or the other was true, it was necessary for this to happen, and for the state of things always to be such that everything that happens happens of necessity. For what anyone has truly said
5   would be the case cannot not happen; and of what happens it was always true to say that it would be the case.

But what if this is impossible? For we see that what will be has an origin both in deliberation and in action, and that, in general, in things
10   that are not always actual there is the possibility of being and of not being; here both possibilities are open, both being and not being, and, consequently, both coming to be and not coming to be. Many things are obviously like this. For example, it is possible for this cloak to be cut up, and yet it will not be cut up but will wear out first. But equally,
15   its not being cut up is also possible, for it would not be the case that it wore out first unless its not being cut up were possible. So it is the same with all other events that are spoken of in terms of this kind of possibility. Clearly, therefore, not everything is or happens of necessity: some things happen as chance has it, and of the affirmation
20   and the negation neither is true rather than the other; with other things it is one rather than the other and as a rule, but still it is possible for the other to happen instead.

What is, necessarily is, when it is; and what is not, necessarily is not, when it is not. But not everything that is, necessarily is; and not every-
25   thing that is not, necessarily is not. For to say that everything that is, is of necessity, when it is, is not the same as saying unconditionally that it

is of necessity. Similarly with what is not. And the same account holds for contradictories: everything necessarily is or is not, and will be or will not be; but one cannot divide and say that one or the other is necessary. I mean, for example: it is necessary for there to be or not to 30 be a sea-battle tomorrow; but it is not necessary for a sea-battle to take place tomorrow, nor for one not to take place—though it is necessary for one to take place or not to take place. So, since statements are true according to how the actual things are, it is clear that wherever these are such as to allow of contraries as chance has it, the same necessarily holds for the contradictories also. This happens with things that are 35 not always so or are not always not so. With these it is necessary for one or the other of the contradictories to be true or false—not, however, this one or that one, but as chance has it; or for one to be true *rather* than the other, yet not *already* true or false.

Clearly, then, it is not necessary that of every affirmation and 19ᵇ opposite negation one should be true and the other false. For what holds for things that are does not hold for things that are not but may possibly be or not be; with these it is as we have said.

CHAPTER 10

Now an affirmation signifies something about something, this last 5 being either a name or a 'non-name'; and what is affirmed must be one thing about one thing. (Names and 'non-names' have already been discussed. For I do not call 'not-man' a name but an indefinite name— for what it signifies is in a way one thing, but indefinite—just as I do not call 'does not recover' a verb.) So every affirmation will contain 10 either a name and a verb or an indefinite name and a verb. Without a verb there will be no affirmation or negation. 'Is', 'will be', 'was', 'becomes', and the like are verbs according to what we laid down, since they additionally signify time. So a first affirmation and negation are: 'a man is', 'a man is not'; then, 'a not-man is', 'a not-man is not'; 15 and again, 'every man is', 'every man is not', 'every not-man is', 'every not-man is not'. For times other than the present the same account holds.

But when 'is' is predicated additionally as a third thing, there are two ways of expressing opposition. (I mean, for example, 'a man is 20 just'; here I say that the 'is' is a third component—whether name or verb—in the affirmation.) Because of this there will here be *four* cases (two of which will be related, as to order of sequence, to the

25 affirmation and negation in the way the privations are, while two will
    not). I mean that 'is' will be added either to 'just' or to 'not-just', and
    so, too, will the negation. Thus there will be four cases. What is meant
    should be clear from the following diagram:

(*a*) 'a man is just'	(*b*) 'a man is not just'
	This is the negation of (*a*).
(*d*) 'a man is not not-just'	(*c*) 'a man is not-just'
This is the negation of (*c*).	

30 'Is' and 'is not' are here added to 'just' and to 'not-just'.
    This then is how these are arranged (as is said in the *Analytics*).
    Similarly, too, if the affirmation is about the name taken universally,
    e.g.:

(*a*) 'every man is just'	(*b*) 'not every man is just'
(*d*) 'not every man is not-just'	(*c*) 'every man is not-just'

35 Here, however, it is not in the same way possible for diagonal state-
    ments to be true together, though it is possible sometimes.
    These, then, are two pairs of opposites. There are others if some-
    thing is added to 'not man' as a sort of subject, thus:

(*a*) 'a not-man is just'	(*b*) 'a not-man is not just'
(*d*) 'a not-man is not not-just'	(*c*) 'a not-man is not-just'

20ᵃ There will not be any more oppositions than these. These last are a
    group on their own separate from the others, in that they use 'not-
    man' as a name.
       In cases where 'is' does not fit (e.g. with 'recovers' or 'walks') the
5   verbs have the same effect when so placed as if 'is' were joined on, e.g.:

(*a*) 'every man walks'	(*b*) 'every man does not walk'
(*d*) 'every not-man does not walk'	(*c*) 'every not-man walks'

    Here one must not say 'not every man' but must add the 'not', the
10 negation, to 'man'. For 'every' does not signify a universal, but that it is
    taken universally. This is clear from the following:

(*a*) 'a man walks'	(*b*) 'a man does not walk'
(*d*) 'a not-man does not walk'	(*c*) 'a not-man walks'

    For these differ from the previous ones in not being universal. So
    'every' or 'no' additionally signify nothing other than that the affirma-

tion or negation is about the name taken universally. Everything else, therefore, must be added unchanged.

Since the contrary negation of 'every animal is just' is that which signifies that no animal is just, obviously these will never be true together or of the same thing, but their opposites sometimes will (e.g. 'not every animal is just' and 'some animal is just'). 'No man is just' follows from 'every man is not-just', while the opposite of this, 'not every man is not-just', follows from 'some man is just' (for there must be one). It is clear too that, with regard to particulars, if it is true, when asked something, to deny it, it is true also to affirm something. For instance: 'Is Socrates wise? No. Then Socrates is not-wise.' With universals, on the other hand, the corresponding affirmation is not true, but the negation is true. For instance: 'Is every man wise? No. Then every man is not-wise.' This is false, but 'then not every man is wise' is true; this is the opposite statement, the other is the contrary.

Names and verbs that are indefinite (and thereby opposite), such as 'not-man' and 'not-just', might be thought to be negations without a name and a verb. But they are not. For a negation must always be true or false; but one who says 'not-man'—without adding anything else—has no more said something true or false (indeed rather less so) than one who says 'man'.

'Every not-man is just' does not signify the same as any of the above, nor does its opposite, 'not every not-man is just'. But 'every not-man is not-just' signifies the same as 'no not-man is just'.

If names and verbs are transposed they still signify the same thing, e.g. 'a man is white' and 'white is a man'. For otherwise the same statement will have more than one negation, whereas we have shown that one has only one. For 'a man is white' has for negation 'a man is not white', while 'white is a man'—if it is not the same as 'a man is white'—will have for negation either 'white is not a not-man' or 'white is not a man'. But one of these is a negation of 'white is a not-man', the other of 'a man is white'. Thus there will be two negations of one statement. Clearly, then, if the name and the verb are transposed the same affirmation and negation are produced.

CHAPTER 11

To affirm or deny one thing of many, or many of one, is not *one* affirmation or negation unless the many things together make up some one thing. I do not call them one if there exists one name but there is not some one thing they make up. For example, man is perhaps an animal and two-footed and tame, yet these do make up some one thing; whereas white and man and walking do not make up one thing. So if

20 someone affirms some one thing of these it is not one affirmation; it is one spoken sound, but more than one affirmation. Similarly, if these are affirmed of one thing, that is more than one affirmation. So if a dialectical question demands as answer either the statement proposed or one side of a contradiction (the statement in fact being a side of one contradiction), there could not be *one* answer in these cases. For the

25 question itself would not be one question, even if true. These matters have been discussed in the *Topics*. (It is also clear that 'What is it?' is not a dialectical question either; for the question must give one the choice of stating whichever side of the contradiction one wishes. The

30 questioner must specify further and ask whether man is this or not this.)

Of things predicated separately some can be predicated in combination, the whole predicate as one, others cannot. What then is the difference? For of a man it is true to say two-footed separately and animal separately, and also to say them as one; similarly, white and

35 man separately, and also as one. But if someone is good and a cobbler it does not follow that he is a good cobbler. For if because each of two holds both together also hold, there will be many absurdities. For since of a man both 'white' and 'a man' are true, so also is the whole compound; again, if 'white' then the whole compound—so that he will

21ᵃ be a white white man, and so on indefinitely. Or again, we shall have 'walking white musician', and then these compounded many times over. Further, if Socrates is a man and is Socrates he will be a man Socrates; and if two-footed and a man then a two-footed man. Clearly,

5 then, one is led into many absurdities if one lays down without restriction that the compounds come about. How the matter should be put we will now explain.

Of things predicated, and things they get predicated of, those which are said accidentally, either of the same thing or of one another, will

10 not be one. For example, a man is white and musical, but 'white' and 'musical' are not one, because they are both accidental to the same thing. And even if it is true to say that the white is musical, 'musical white' will still not be one thing; for it is accidentally that the musical is white, and so 'white musical' will not be one. Nor, consequently,

15 will the cobbler who is (without qualification) good, though an animal which is two-footed will (since this is not accidental). Further, where

one of the things is contained in the other, they will not be one. This is why 'white' is not repeated and why a man is not an animal man or a two-footed man; for two-footed and animal are contained in man.

It is true to speak of the particular case even without qualification; e.g. to say that some particular man is a man or some particular white man white. Not always, though. When in what is added some opposite is contained from which a contradiction follows, it is not true but false (e.g. to call a dead man a man); but when no such opposite is contained, it is true. Or rather, when it is contained it is always not true, but when it is not, it is not always true. For example, Homer is something (say, a poet). Does it follow that he is? No, for the 'is' is predicated accidentally of Homer; for it is because he is a poet, not in its own right, that the 'is' is predicated of Homer. Thus, where predicates *both* contain no contrariety if definitions are put instead of names *and* are predicated in their own right and not accidentally, in these cases it will be true to speak of the particular thing even without qualification. It is not true to say that what is not, since it is thought about, is something that is; for what is thought about it is not that it is, but that it is not.

PRIOR ANALYTICS*

BOOK I

CHAPTER I

24ᵃ First, to state what our enquiry is about or relates to: it is about demonstration, it relates to demonstrative science. Next, we have to define the following: proposition; term; syllogism; perfect and imperfect syllogism; and then we must define: one thing's being wholly within or wholly not within another; and being predicated of
15 all, or again, of none.

A Proposition is a form of words that affirms or denies something *of* something. It will be either universal, or particular, or indesignate. By a Universal proposition I mean one saying 'applies to every one' or 'applies to none'; by a Particular proposition I mean one saying 'applies to some' or 'is inapplicable to some' or 'does not apply to every one'; by an Indesignate proposition I mean one that just says
20 something 'applies' or 'does not apply' without any 'universally' or 'in part': e.g. 'There is a single science of *contraries*' or '*Pleasure* is not a good thing'.

Demonstrative propositions differ from dialectical ones in this way: a demonstrative proposition is the taking of one side in an antiphasis [1] (somebody who is demonstrating is not enquiring but taking something to be so), whereas a dialectical proposition is enquiry related to
25 an antiphasis. But this makes no difference as regards getting a syllogism: somebody engaged either way, in demonstration or in enquiry, syllogizes on an assumption that something does or does not apply to something. Thus a syllogistic proposition is just something affirmed or denied of something, in the way just stated; if it is true, and is taken to be so because of assumptions of principles, then it is
24ᵇ demonstrative; whereas a dialectical proposition will be enquiry related to an antiphasis—from the interrogator's point of view, that is:

---

[1] An affirmation and its corresponding negation.

* *Prior Analytics* I. 1–7. *Translation*: P. T. Geach (for forthcoming volume in Clarendon Aristotle Series); *Text*: W. D. Ross (Oxford Classical Texts, 1949). *Prior Analytics* I. 27 and II. 21. *Translation*: A. J. Jenkinson, revised J. Barnes (Revised Oxford Aristotle, 1984); *Text*: W. D. Ross (Oxford Classical Texts, 1949).

from the reasoner's point of view, it will be the assumption of something that appears so and is commonly believed. (Cf. the *Topics*.) The nature of propositions, and the differences between syllogistic, demonstrative, and dialectical ones, will be rigorously stated later on; this explanation will do for now. 15

What I call a Term is something got by resolving a proposition, namely a predicate or what it is predicated of, with an 'is' added on.

A Syllogism is a form of words in which certain things are assumed and there is something other than what was assumed which necessarily follows from things' being so. By 'from' I mean 'because of'; and 20 'follows because of things' being so' means that no further proposition is needed to make the 'following' necessary. I call a syllogism Perfect when its necessity *is clear* without our having to bring in any proposition over and above the original premisses; an Imperfect syllogism is one that is not *clearly* necessary unless we introduce one or more propositions that are necessary given the initial assumptions, but were 25 not assumed as premisses.

For so-and-so to be Wholly Within such-and-such, and for such-and-such to be Predicated of Every so-and-so, is just the same. We say 'Predicated of Every' so-and-so when you cannot pick any so-and-so of which the other thing will not be said. Similarly for 'Predicated of None'.

CHAPTER 2

Every proposition says either that something applies, or that some- 25ª thing necessarily applies, or that something possibly applies. Each sort of predication contains affirmatives and negatives; and further, affirmatives and negatives alike may be universal, particular, or indesignate. 5

Plain[2] universal negative propositions necessarily allow of an interchange of their terms: e.g. if no pleasure is a good thing, then no good thing will be a pleasure either. The affirmative form too is necessarily convertible, but to a particular, not a universal: e.g. if every pleasure is a good thing, so also is some good thing a pleasure. Of plain particular 10 propositions, the affirmative form necessarily converts to a particular (e.g. if some pleasure is a good thing, some good thing is a pleasure); but the negative form does not convert necessarily (we do not get 'If

---

[2] 'Plain propositions': literally 'propositions with *applies*' (as opposed to those with *necessarily applies* or *possibly applies*).

man is inapplicable to some animal, *animal* likewise is inapplicable to some man').

Let our proposition '*A* of *B*' be a universal negative: if *A* applies to
15 no *B*, *B* likewise will apply to no *A*; for if *B* applies to some *A*, say to *C*, it will not be true that *A* applies to *B*, since *C* is one of the *B*s. If it holds for every one that *A* applies to *B*, *B* will also apply to some *A*; for if *B* applies to no *A*, *A* will also apply to no *B*; but we supposed that *A* applies to every *B*. Similarly if the proposition is particular. If
20 *A* applies to some *B*, it must hold that *B* applies to some *A*; for if not, *A* likewise will apply to no *B*. If *A* is inapplicable to some *B*, it need not be that *B* likewise is inapplicable to some *A*. Let *A* be *man*, *B*
25 *animal*; *man* does not apply to every animal, but *animal* applies to every man.

CHAPTER 3

Things will be the same way with regard to necessity-propositions: the universal negative converts to a universal, and either of the affirmatives to a particular. For if *A* necessarily applies to no *B*, *B* will
30 necessarily apply to no *A*; for if *B* possibly applies to some *A*, *A* too will possibly apply to some *B*. If *A* necessarily applies to every or to some *B*, *B* necessarily applies to some *A*; for if it did not necessarily,
35 *A* would not necessarily apply to some *B*. The particular negative does not convert, for the same reason as we mentioned before.

Next as regards possibility-propositions. The word 'possible' is said in several cases: for what *is* so, necessarily or not necessarily, and what *can be*, is said to be possible. Accordingly, in the affirmative conversions will go just as before. That is: if *A* possibly applies to
25^b every or to some *B*, *B* would possibly apply to some *A*; for if to none, then *A* would not, either, to any *B*; this was proved before. But with negatives it is not the same. However, it is similar in all negative cases where we say 'possibly' because something either necessarily does not apply or does not necessarily apply; for instance suppose one said that
5 a man is 'possibly' not a horse, or that *white* 'possibly' applies to no cloak; in the former case something necessarily does not apply, in the latter something does not necessarily apply. Here the propositions convert in the same way as before: if *horse* possibly applies to no man,
10 *man* possibly applies to no horse; and if *white* possibly applies to no cloak, *cloak* possibly applies to no white thing (since if it necessarily applies to some such, then *white* will of necessity apply to some cloak,

as was shown before). And for the particular negative likewise it is the same as before. But when 'possible' is said from things' being mostly and naturally so, and this is how we define 'possible', negative conver- 15 sions will not take place in the same way; the universal negative does not convert, the particular negative does. This will be clear when we come to speak of the possible.

For the present let us be clear on this much, besides what has been said: 'possibly applies to none' or 'is possibly inapplicable to some' is 20 *affirmative* in form; for 'is possible' is ranked with 'is', and 'is' always and universally makes an affirmative, whatever it is predicatively added to: e.g. '*is* not-good' or '*is* not-white' or in general '*is* not-thingumajig'. This too will be proved by what comes later. As regards conversions these will be just like other affirmatives. 25

CHAPTER 4

After settling these points let us now state from what and when and how any syllogistic conclusion is drawn. Demonstration is to be discussed later, syllogism must be discussed before demonstration, because syllogism is more general—a demonstration is a sort of syllogism, but not every syllogism is a demonstration. 30

When three terms have the following mutual relation: the last is wholly within the middle, and the middle is either wholly within or wholly not within the first, there must be a perfect syllogism relating the extremes. I call the Middle Term the one that is within another 35 and has another within it; in the lay-out [3] it has the middle place. I call the Extremes the term that is within another, and the term within which another is. [4] If A is predicated of every B and B of every C, A must be predicated of every C, by our previous account of *predicated of all*. Similarly if A is predicated of no B and B of every C, A will apply to 26ᵃ no C. But if the first term applies to every *middle* and the middle to no *last*, there will be no syllogism relating the extremes. For there is nothing 'necessarily following from things' being thus': the first may 5 apply to every *last* or to no *last*, so no affirmative or negative comes about necessarily; so there is nothing that 'necessarily follows from things' being thus', and no syllogism. Terms for 'applying to every': animal/man/horse. Terms for 'applying to none': animal/man/stone.

---

[3] Clearly a reference to a diagram, now lost.
[4] Each time, 'another' means the middle term.

10 Neither will there be a syllogism when the first applies to no *middle* and the middle to no *last*. Terms for 'applying': science/line/ medicine. Terms for 'not applying': science/line/unit.

Thus when the terms are in universals, it is clear when there will or will not be a syllogism in this figure; and that when there is a syllogism
15 the terms must be related as we said, and when they are thus related there is a syllogism.

Now suppose one term is in a universal, and the other in a particular relation to the other: when the universal premiss, affirmative or negative, involves the major term, and the particular premiss
20 involving the minor term is affirmative, there must be a perfect syllogism; but when the universal premiss involves the minor term, or the terms are related in any other way, there cannot be one. (I mean by the Major the term within which the middle term is; by the Minor, the term under the middle term.)

Let *A* apply to every *B* and *B* to some *C*. Given that 'being predicated of every' is what I said at the outset, *A* must apply to some
25 *C*. And if *A* applies to no *B*, and *B* to some *C*, then it must be that *A* is inapplicable to some *C*; for we have explained our use of 'predicated of none'; so there will be a perfect syllogism. Similarly if the proposition '*B* of *C*' is indesignate, so long as it is affirmative; we get the same conclusion whether the premiss is indesignate or particular.

30 If the minor term occurs in a universal premiss, affirmative or negative, there will be no syllogism, whether the other premiss, being indesignate or particular, is affirmative or negative. Suppose *A* applies, or again is inapplicable, to some *B*, and *B* applies to every *C*:
35 with the terms good/condition/prudence, *A* applies to *C*; with the terms good/condition/ignorance, *A* does not apply to *C*. Again, if *B* applies to no *C*, and *A* applies, or is inapplicable, to some *B*, or does not apply to every *B*, this way too there will be no syllogism. Terms to show this: white/horse/swan, white/horse/cow. The same terms serve if '*A* of *B*' is indesignate.

When the major term occurs in a universal premiss, affirmative or
26^b negative, and the minor term is in a particular negative, there will be no syllogism: that is, not if *A* applies to every *B* and *B* is inapplicable to some *C* (does not apply to every *C*). The reason is that the *some* to
5 which the middle term is inapplicable may have the first term going with all or with none. Suppose the terms are animal/man/white: of the white things that *man* is not predicated of, take *swan* and *snow*: *animal* is predicated of every one of the first and of none of the second, so

there is no conclusion. Again, suppose A applies to no B and B is   10
inapplicable to some C: let the terms be inanimate/man/white. Of the
white things that *man* is not predicated of, take *swan* and *snow*: *in-animate* is predicated of all of the second and none of the first.
Again, 'B is inapplicable to some C' is indeterminate; it is true both
if B applies to no C, and if B does not apply to every C because   15
inapplicable to some. If we choose terms such that B applies to no C,
there is no syllogism, as we said before. Thus it is clear that with terms
related in the way just described there will be no syllogism: otherwise
there would be one in the special case. There will be a similar proof if
the universal premiss is negative.   20
If both premisses are particular affirmative, or particular negative;
or one particular affirmative, the other particular negative; or one in-designate, the other not; or both are indesignate; in no case will there
be a syllogism. Terms to suit all cases: animal/white/horse, animal/   25
white/stone.
It is clear from what has been said that if a conclusion in this
figure is particular, the terms must be related as we said; otherwise
we never get one. Clearly, too, all syllogisms in this figure are perfect,
for all are completely made out with the original premisses. Further,   30
all forms of proposition are proved in this figure: that something
applies to every one, or to none, or to some, or not to some. I call this
the First Figure.

CHAPTER 5

When we have the same thing applying to every so-and-so and to no
such-and-such, or to every one of either, or to none of either, I call this   35
form the Second Figure; what is predicated of both I call the Middle
Term; what this is predicated of, the Extremes; the extreme lying
nearer the middle, the Major Term; the one lying further from the
middle, the Minor Term. The middle is placed outside the terms and
first in position.[5]
There is no perfect syllogism in this figure; but a syllogism is   27ᵃ
possible both with universal and with non-universal premisses. When
they are universals there will be a syllogism whenever the middle term
applies to every so-and-so and to no such-and-such, whichever side is
negative; otherwise there never is one. Thus: Let M be predicated of   5

---

[5] This reference is not to logical relations of terms, but to their places in some diagram.

no N but of every X. Since the negative converts, N will apply to no M; but M by hypothesis applied to every X; so, by our previous proof, N will apply to no X. Again: if M applies to every N and to no X, X will apply to no N. For if M applies to no X, then also X applies to no M; and M was to apply to every N; so X will apply to no N (the first figure over again), and, since the negative converts, N will apply to no X: the same conclusion as before.

These results can also be proved by a reduction *ad impossibile*.

It is clear, then, that with this relation of terms there will be a syllogism but not a perfect one; for the necessity is made out by using not merely the original premisses, but other propositions as well.

If M is predicated of every N and X, there will be no syllogism. Terms for applying: substance/animal/man; for not applying: substance/animal/number—substance being the middle term. Nor will there be one when M is predicated of no N and no X. Terms for applying: line/animal/man; for not applying: line/animal/stone. Clearly, then, if there is a syllogism with universal premisses, the terms must have the relation stated above; otherwise no necessity arises.

Now suppose the middle term is universally predicated of just one or other term. When this happens with the major term, either affirmatively or negatively, and this middle term is predicated of the minor particularly, and in the opposite way to the universal premiss (by 'the opposite way' I mean that the particular premiss is affirmative if the universal is negative, and negative if it is affirmative): then there must be a particular negative conclusion.

If M applies to no N and to some X, then N must be inapplicable to some X. For since the negative converts, N will apply to no M; but M by hypothesis applies to some X; so N will be inapplicable to some X—first figure syllogism. Again, if M applies to every N and is inapplicable to some X, N must be inapplicable to some X. For suppose N applies to every X; then if M likewise is predicated of every N, M must apply to every X; but by hypothesis M is inapplicable to some X. And if M applies to every N but not to every X, there will be a conclusion that N does not apply to every X: the same proof. If M is predicated of every X and not of every N, there will be no syllogism. Terms: animal/substance/crow, animal/white/crow. Now will there be one if M is predicated of no X but of some N. Terms for applying: animal/substance/unit; for not applying: animal/substance/science.

Thus as regards when the universal premiss is opposite in quality to the particular, we have stated when there will be and when there will   10
not be a syllogism. But when the premisses are of like form, both affirmative or both negative, there will never be a syllogism. First, let the premisses be negative and the one with the major term a universal: that is, let M apply to no N and be inapplicable to some X. Then N may apply to every X and to no X. Terms for not applying: black/   15
snow/animal; but we cannot pick terms for N's applying to every X, if M applies to some X and is inapplicable to some X; for if N applies to every X and M applies to no N, M will apply to no X, whereas by hypothesis M did apply to some X. So we cannot pick terms this way: 20
we must give a proof from the indeterminate sense of 'some'. Since it is true that M is inapplicable to some X also when it applies to none, and since with it applying to none there was no syllogism, clearly there will be none now either.

Again, let the premisses be affirmative, and the same one universal as before; that is, let M apply to every N and to some X. Then N may   25
apply to every X and to no X. Terms for applying to none: white/ swan/stone. Terms for applying to every one cannot be picked, for the same reason as before; we must give a proof from the indeterminate sense of 'some'.

Now suppose the premiss with the minor term is a universal: i.e. let M apply to every N and to some X. Then N may apply to every X and   30
to no X. Terms for applying: white/animal/crow; for not applying: white/stone/crow. If the premisses are affirmative, we get terms for not applying: white/animal/snow, and terms for applying: white/ animal/swan.

It is clear, then, that when the premisses are of like form, and one is a universal, there is never a syllogism. Nor is there one if in both   35
premisses it is to *some* that the middle term applies, or is inapplicable; or if it applies to some in one and is inapplicable to some in the other; or if in both premisses it is inapplicable to every one; or if the predication is indesignate. Terms common to all these cases: white/animal/ man, white/animal/inanimate.

From what has been said, it is clear that if the terms are related to   28ᵃ
one another as was stated above, there must be a syllogism; and that if there is a syllogism, this is how the terms have to be. Further, all the syllogisms in this figure are clearly imperfect; for all are made out with some added propositions, either necessarily implied in the given pro-   5
positions or else (with an *ad impossibile* proof) assumed hypothetically.

In this figure no conclusion reached is affirmative: all are negative, both the universals and the particulars.

CHAPTER 6

10 When one thing applies to every so-and-so and another to none, or when the two both apply to every so-and-so or both to none, I call this form the Third Figure. What both things are predicated of I call the Middle Term, and its predicates I call the Extremes; the extreme further from the middle, the Major Term; the one nearer the middle, the Minor Term. The middle term is put outside the extremes and last in position.

15 There is no perfect syllogism in this figure either; but a syllogism is possible both when the relation of the extreme terms to the middle is universal and when it is not. First, suppose it is universal. If both P and R apply to every S, P must apply to some R. For since an affirma-

20 tive proposition converts, S will apply to some R; so, since P applies to every S and S to some R, P must apply to some R; we get a first-figure syllogism. The proof can be done also by reduction *ad impossibile*; and also by *ekthesis*: if both terms P and R apply to every S, then

25 if we take one of the Ss, say N, both P and R will apply to N; so P will apply to *some R*. And if R applies to every S and P to no S there will be a syllogistic conclusion that P is inapplicable to some R: some manner of proof, by converting the premiss 'R of S'. This could also be proved

30 by an *ad impossibile*, like the last mood.

But if R applies to no S and P to every S, there will be no syllogism. Terms for 'applying': animal/horse/man; for 'not applying': animal/inanimate/man. Nor will there be a syllogism when both terms are predicated of no S. Terms for 'applying': animal/horse/inanimate;

35 terms for 'not applying' man/horse/inanimate; middle term *inanimate*.

It is clear, then, in this figure likewise when there will and when there will not be a syllogism with the terms occurring universally. When both extreme terms are affirmed, there will be a syllogistic conclusion that one term applies to *some* of the other; when they are

28ᵇ denied, there will be no conclusion. When one is denied and the other affirmed, if the major term is denied and the minor affirmed there will be a syllogistic conclusion that one extreme is inapplicable to *some* of the other: the other way round there will be no syllogism.

5 Now suppose one extreme has a universal, and the other a

particular, predicative relation to the middle. When both premisses are affirmative, there must be a syllogism, regardless of which term stands in a universal. Thus: if R applies to every S and P to some S, P must apply to some R. For since an affirmation converts, S will apply to some P; so, since R applies to every S, and S to some P, R will apply to some P, and thus P to some R. Again: if R applies to some S, and P to every S, P must apply to some R: the same method of proof. Proof by an *ad impossibile* or by *ekthesis* is also possible, as in previous cases.

Now suppose one term is affirmed and the other denied, and let the affirmative be universal. When the minor term is affirmed, there will be a syllogism. Thus: if R applies to every S and P is inapplicable to some S, then P will be inapplicable to some R; for if it applied to every R, and R applies to every S, P will also apply to every S; but it was supposed not to. There is also a proof without this reduction, if we take some S to which P does not apply. But when the major term is affirmed, there will be no syllogism. For example, suppose P applies to every S and R is inapplicable to some S. Terms for 'applying to every': inanimate/man/animal. Terms for 'applying to none' cannot be picked, if R applies to some S and is inapplicable to some S; for if P applies to every S and R to some S, P will apply to some R, whereas we were taking it to apply to no R. We must pick terms as in previous cases; since 'is inapplicable to some' is indeterminate, what applies to none is truly said to be inapplicable to some; and with R applying to no S there was no syllogism; so clearly there will be no syllogism here either.

If the negative premiss is universal, when the major term is denied and the minor affirmed there will be a syllogism. Thus: if P applies to no S and R to some S, P will be inapplicable to some R; for by converting the premiss 'R of S' we get the first figure over again. But when the minor term is denied there will be no syllogism. Terms for 'applying': animal/man/brutish; terms for 'not applying': animal/science/brutish—brutish being the middle term.

Likewise there is no syllogism when both terms are denied of the middle, one universally and one particularly. For cases where the minor term has a universal relation to the middle, we get animal/science/brutish, animal/man/brutish; where the major term has such a relation, we get as a case of 'not applying' crow/snow/white. But we cannot get a case of 'applying' if R applies to some S and is inapplicable to some; for if P applies to every R and R to some S, then also P

applies to some *S*, whereas we were taking it to apply to no *S*. The proof must proceed from the indeterminate sense of 'applies to some'.

Nor is there a syllogism if both the terms apply, or both are inapplicable, to some of the middle; nor if one applies, and one is inapplicable, to some; nor if one term applies to some, and the other does not apply to every one; nor if the premisses are indefinite. Terms
10 that serve for all cases alike: animal/man/white, animal/inanimate/white.

In this figure too, then, it is clear when there will be a syllogism and when not, and that when terms are related in the ways stated there must be a syllogism, and when there is a syllogism the terms must be so related. Moreover all syllogisms in this figure are clearly imperfect,
15 for all are made out by the use of some added propositions. Universals, affirmative or negative, clearly cannot be got by syllogism in this figure.

CHAPTER 7

Further, this clearly holds in all the figures for cases where there is no
20 syllogism formed from two premisses: if these are both affirmative or both negative, nothing at all necessarily follows from them; but when one is affirmative and the other negative, and the negative is universal, there is always a conclusion relating the minor term to the major term. E.g. if *A* applies to every or to some *B* and *B* to no *C*, by turning the
25 premisses round we get that *C* must be inapplicable to some *A*. Similarly for the other figures; by turning the premisses round we always get a syllogism.

It is further clear that replacing the particular affirmative premiss by an indesignate premiss yields the same conclusion, in all the figures.
30 It is also obvious that all the imperfect syllogisms are made out via the first figure. For all conclusions are drawn either by proof or by an *ad impossibile* move; but either way we get the first figure. If the conclusions are made out by a proof, this holds, because all conclusions were reached by conversions, and the conversions gave the first
35 figure. If the conclusions are made out by an *ad impossibile* move, the false assumption gives a first-figure syllogism. Thus, in the last figure, if both *A* and *B* apply to every *C*, *A* applies to some *B*; for if it applied to none, and *B* applies to every *C*, *A* would apply to no *C*; but it was assumed to apply to all. Similarly in other cases.

29ᵇ   In fact all syllogisms are reducible to the first-figure universal syllogisms. Second-figure syllogisms can obviously be made out by way of these, though not all in the same way; the universal syllogisms can be made out by conversion of a universal negative, the particular ones by a reduction *ad impossibile*. The first-figure particular 5 syllogisms, though they can be made out in their own right, can also be proved by a reduction *ad impossibile* via the second figure. For example: if *A* applies to every *B*, and *B* to some *C*, then *A* applies to some *C*; for if it applies to no *C* and to every *B*, *B* will apply to no *C*; 10 we know this by the second figure. The proof for the negative mood will be similar. If *A* applies to no *B* and *B* to some *C*, *A* will be inapplicable to some *C*; for if it applies to every *C*, and to no *B*, *B* will apply to no *C*; this was the middle figure. So if the syllogisms in the 15 middle figure are all reduced to the first-figure universal syllogisms, and the particular first-figure syllogisms to middle-figure syllogisms, obviously these particular syllogisms will be reduced to the first-figure universal syllogisms. In the third figure, by means of these syllogisms 20 we can directly make out the syllogisms with universal premises; syllogisms with particular premises can be made out via the particular first-figure syllogisms, which in turn were reduced to these; therefore so can the particular-premissed syllogisms of the third figure. Obviously then all syllogisms will be reduced to first-figure universal syllogisms. 25

Thus I have now stated how the syllogisms go that show something applies or does not apply; both how the syllogisms in one and the same figure go on their own account, and how the mood of different figures are related.

CHAPTER 27
. . .
Of all the things which exist some are such that they cannot be 43ᵃ predicated of anything else truly and universally, e.g. Cleon and Callias, i.e. the individual and sensible, but other things may be predicated of them (for each of these is both man and animal); and some things are themselves predicated of others, but nothing prior is predicated of them; and some are predicated of others, and yet others 30 of them, e.g. man of Callias and animal of man. It is clear then that some things are naturally not said of anything; for as a rule each sensible thing is such that it cannot be predicated of anything, save incidentally—for we sometimes say that that white object is Socrates, 35 or that that which approaches is Callias. We shall explain in another

place that there is an upward limit also to the process of predicating; for the present we must assume this. Of these it is not possible to demonstrate another predicate, save as a matter of opinion, but these may be predicated of other things. Neither can individuals be predicated of other things, though other things can be predicated of them. Whatever lies between these limits can be spoken of in both ways: they may be said of others, and others said of them. And as a rule arguments and inquiries are concerned with these things.

. . .

BOOK II

CHAPTER 21

66ᵇ It sometimes happens that just as we are deceived in the arrangement of the terms, so error may arise in our thought about them, e.g. if it is
20 possible that the same predicate should belong to more than one subject primarily, but although knowing the one, a man may forget the other and think the predicate belongs to none of it. Suppose that A belongs to B and to C in virtue of themselves, and that B and C belong to every D in the same way. If then a man thinks that A belongs to every B, and B to D, but A to no C, and C to every D, he will have
25 knowledge and ignorance of the same thing in respect of the same thing. Again if a man were to make a mistake about the members of a single series; e.g. suppose A belongs to B, B to C, and C to D, but someone thinks that A belongs to every B, but to no C: he will both
30 know that A belongs to C, and believe that it does not. Does he then actually maintain after this that what he knows, he does not believe? For he knows in a way that A belongs to C through B, knowing the particular by virtue of his universal knowledge; so that what he knows in a way, this he maintains he does not believe at all; but that is impossible.
35 In the former case, where the middle term does not belong to the same series, it is not possible to believe both the propositions with reference to each of the two middle terms: e.g. that A belongs to every B, but to no C, and both B and C belong to every D. For it turns out that the first proposition is either wholly or partially contrary. For if he believes that A belongs to everything to which B belongs, and he
67ᵃ knows that B belongs to D, then he knows that A belongs to D. Consequently if again he thinks that A belongs to nothing to which C

belongs, he does not think that *A* belongs to some of that to which *B* belongs; but if he thinks that *A* belongs to everything to which *B* belongs, and again does not think that *A* belongs to some of that to which *B* belongs, these beliefs are wholly or partially contrary.   5

In this way then it is not possible to believe; but nothing prevents a man believing one proposition of each deduction or both of one: e.g. *A* belongs to every *B*, and *B* to *D*, and again *A* belongs to no *C*. An error of this kind is similar to the error into which we fall concerning particulars: e.g. if *A* belongs to everything to which *B* belongs, and *B* to every *C*, *A* will belong to every *C*. If then a man knows that *A*   10
belongs to everything to which *B* belongs, he knows also that *A* belongs to *C*. But nothing prevents his being ignorant that *C* exists; e.g. let *A* stand for two right angles, *B* for triangle, *C* for a sensible triangle. A man might believe that *C* did not exist, though he knew that every triangle contains two right angles; consequently he will   15
know and not know the same thing at the same time. For knowing that every triangle has its angles equal to two right angles is not simple—it may obtain either by having universal knowledge or by particular. Thus by universal knowledge he knows that *C* contains two right angles, but not by particular; consequently his knowledge will not be   20
contrary to his ignorance. The argument in the *Meno*⁶ that learning is recollection may be criticized in a similar way. For it never happens that a man has foreknowledge of the particular, but in the process of induction he receives a knowledge of the particulars, as though by an act of recognition. For we know some things directly; e.g. that the   25
angles are equal to two right angles, if we see that the figure is a triangle. Similarly in all other cases.

By universal knowledge then we see the particulars, but we do not know them by the kind of knowledge which is proper to them; consequently it is possible that we may make mistakes about them, but not that we should have the knowledge and error that are contrary to one another: rather we have universal knowledge but make a mistake in regard to the particular. Similarly in the cases stated above. The   30
error in respect of the middle term is not contrary to the knowledge obtained through the deduction, nor is the belief in respect of the middle terms. Nothing prevents a man who knows both that *A* belongs to the whole of *B*, and that *B* again belongs to *C*, thinking that *A* does not belong to *C*, e.g. knowing that every mule is sterile and that   35

⁶ See Plato, *Meno* 81B–86B.

this is a mule, and thinking that this animal is with foal; for he does not know that A belongs to C, unless he considers the two things together. So it is evident that if he knows the one and does not know the other, he will fall into error. And this is the relation of universal knowledge to particular. For we know no sensible thing, once it has passed beyond the range of our senses, even if we happen to have perceived it, except by means of the universal and by possessing (but not actualizing) the proper knowledge. For knowing is spoken of in three ways: it may be either universal knowledge, or knowledge proper to the matter in hand, or actualizing such knowledge; consequently three kinds of error also are possible. Nothing then prevents a man both knowing and being mistaken about the same thing, provided that his knowledge and his error are not contrary. And this happens also to the man who knows each proposition separately and who has not previously considered the particular question. For when he believes that the mule is with foal he does not have knowledge actualized, nor on the other hand has his belief caused an error contrary to his knowledge; for the error contrary to the universal knowledge would be a deduction.

But he who believes the essence of good is the essence of bad will believe the same thing to be the essence of good and the essence of bad. Let A stand for the essence of good and B for the essence of bad, and again C for the essence of good. Since then he believes B and C identical, he will believe that C is B, and similarly that B is A; consequently that C is A. For just as we saw that if B is true of all of which C is true, and A is true of all of which B is true, and A is true of all of which B is true, A is true of C, similarly with believing. Similarly also with being; for we saw that if C is the same as B, and B as A, C is the same as A. Similarly therefore with opining. Perhaps then this is necessary if a man will grant the first point. But presumably that is false, that any one could think the essence of good to be the essence of bad (save accidentally—for it is possible to believe this in many different ways). But we must consider this matter better.

POSTERIOR ANALYTICS*

BOOK I

CHAPTER I

All teaching and all intellectual learning come about from already 71ᵃ existing knowledge. This is evident if we consider it in every case; for the mathematical sciences are acquired in this fashion, and so is each of the other arts. And similarly too with arguments—both deductive 5 and inductive arguments proceed in this way; for both produce their teaching through what we are already aware of, the former getting their premisses as from men who grasp them, the latter proving the universal through the particular's being clear. (And rhetorical arguments too persuade in the same way; for they do so either through 10 examples, which is induction, or through enthymemes, which is deduction.)

It is necessary to be already aware of things in two ways: of some things it is necessary to believe already that they are, of some one must grasp what the thing said is, and of others both—e.g. of the fact that everything is either affirmed or denied truly, one must believe that it 15 is; of the triangle, that it signifies *this*; and of the unit both (both what it signifies and that it is). For each of these is not equally clear to us.

But you can become familiar by being familiar earlier with some things but getting knowledge of the others at the very same time—i.e. of whatever happens to be under the universal of which you have knowledge. For that every triangle has angles equal to two right angles 20 was already known; but that there is a triangle in the semicircle here became familiar at the same time as the induction. (For in some cases learning occurs in this way, and the last term does not become familiar through the middle—in cases dealing with what are in fact particulars and not said of any underlying subject.)

Before the induction, or before getting a deduction, you should 25 perhaps be said to understand in a way—but in another way not. For if you did not know if it is *simpliciter*, how did you know that it has two right angles *simpliciter*? But it is clear that you understand it in *this* sense—that you understand it universally—but you do not understand

* *Translation*: J. Barnes (Clarendon Aristotle Series, 1975; Revised Oxford Aristotle, 1984); *Text*: W. D. Ross (Oxford Classical Texts, 1949).

30   it *simpliciter*. (Otherwise the puzzle in the *Meno*[1] will result; for you will learn either nothing or what you know.)

For one should not argue in the way in which some people attempt to solve it: Do you or don't you know of every pair that it is even? And when you said Yes, they brought forward some pair of which you did not think that it was, nor therefore that it was even. For they solve it by denying that people know of every pair that it is even, but only of

71ᵇ   anything of which they know that it is a pair.—Yet they know it of that which they have the demonstration about and which they got their premisses about; and they got them not about everything of which they know that it is a triangle or that it is a number, but of every number and triangle *simpliciter*. For no proposition of such a type is assumed (that

5   *what you know to be a number . . . or what you know to be rectilineal . . .*), but they are assumed as holding of every case.

But nothing, I think, prevents one from in a sense understanding and in a sense being ignorant of what one is learning; for what is absurd is not that you should know in some sense what you are learning, but that you should know it in *this* sense, i.e. in the way and sense in which you are learning it.

CHAPTER 2

We think we understand a thing *simpliciter* (and not in the sophistic

10   fashion accidentally) whenever we think we are aware both that the explanation because of which the object is is its explanation, and that it is not possible for this to be otherwise. It is clear, then, that to understand is something of this sort; for both those who do not understand and those who do understand—the former think they are themselves

15   in such a state, and those who do understand actually are. Hence that of which there is understanding *simpliciter* cannot be otherwise.

Now whether there is also another type of understanding we shall say later; but we say now that we do know through demonstration. By demonstration I mean a scientific deduction; and by scientific I mean one in virtue of which, by having it, we understand something.

20   If, then, understanding is as we posited, it is necessary for demonstrative understanding in particular to depend on things which are true and primitive and immediate and more familiar than and prior to and explanatory of the conclusion (for in this way the principles will

[1] See Plato, *Meno* 80D.

also be appropriate to what is being proved). For there will be deduction even without these conditions, but there will not be demonstration; for it will not produce understanding.

Now they must be true because one cannot understand what is not the case—e.g. that the diagonal is commensurate. And they must depend on what is primitive and non-demonstrable because otherwise you will not understand if you do not have a demonstration of them; for to understand that of which there is a demonstration non-accidentally is to have a demonstration. They must be both explanatory and more familiar and prior—explanatory because we only understand when we know the explanation; and prior, if they are explanatory, and we are already aware of them not only in the sense of grasping them but also of knowing that they are.

Things are prior and more familiar in two ways; for it is not the same to be prior by nature and prior in relation to us, nor to be more familiar and more familiar to us. I call prior and more familiar in relation to us what is nearer to perception, prior and more familiar *simpliciter* what is further away. What is most universal is furthest away, and the particulars are nearest; and these are opposite to each other.

Depending on things that are primitive is depending on appropriate principles; for I call the same thing primitive and a principle. A principle of a demonstration is an immediate proposition, and an immediate proposition is one to which there is no other prior. A proposition is the one part of a contradiction, one thing said of one; it is dialectical if it assumes indifferently either part, demonstrative if it determinately assumes the one that is true. A contradiction is an opposition which of itself excludes any intermediate; and the part of a contradiction saying something *of* something is an affirmation, the one saying something *from* something is a denial.

An immediate deductive principle I call a posit if one cannot prove it but it is not necessary for anyone who is to learn anything to grasp it; and one which it is necessary for anyone who is going to learn anything whatever to grasp, I call an axiom (for there are some such things); for we are accustomed to use this name especially of such things. A posit which assumes either of the parts of a contradiction—i.e., I mean, that something is or that something is not—I call a supposition; one without this, a definition. For a definition is a posit (for the arithmetician posits that a unit is what is quantitatively indivisible) but not a supposition (for what a unit is and that a unit is are not the same).

25   Since one should both be convinced of and know the object by
having a deduction of the sort we call a demonstration, and since this
is the case when *these* things on which the deduction depends are the
case, it is necessary not only to be already aware of the primitives
(either all or some of them) but actually to be better aware of them. For
a thing always belongs better to that thing because of which it
30   belongs—e.g. that because of which we love is better loved. Hence if
we know and are convinced because of the primitives, we both know
and are convinced of them better, since it is because of them that we
know and are convinced of what is posterior.

It is not possible to be better convinced than one is of what one
knows, of what one in façt neither knows nor is more happily disposed
toward than if one in fact knew. But this will result if someone who is
convinced because of a demonstration is not already aware of the
35   primitives, for it is necessary to be better convinced of the principles
(either all or some of them) than of the conclusion.

Anyone who is going to have understanding through demonstration
must not only be familiar with the principles and better convinced of
them than of what is being proved, but also there must be no other
72ᵇ   thing more convincing to him or more familiar among the opposites of
the principles on which a deduction of the contrary error may
depend—if anyone who understands *simpliciter* must be unpersuad-
able.

CHAPTER 3

5   Now some think that because one must understand the primitives
there is no understanding at all; others that there is, but that there are
demonstrations of everything. Neither of these views is either true or
necessary.

For the one party, supposing that one cannot understand in another
way, claim that we are led back *ad infinitum* on the grounds that we
would not understand what is posterior because of what is prior if
there are no primitives; and they argue correctly, for it is impossible to
10   go through infinitely many things. And if it comes to a stop and there
are principles, they say that these are unknowable since there is no
demonstration of them, which alone they say is understanding; but if
one cannot know the primitives, neither can what depends on them be
understood *simpliciter* or properly, but only on the supposition that
they are the case.

The other party agrees about understanding; for it, they say, occurs 15 only through demonstration. But they argue that nothing prevents there being demonstration of everything; for it is possible for the demonstration to come about in a circle and reciprocally.

But *we* say that neither is all understanding demonstrative, but in the case of the immediates it is non-demonstrable—and that this is 20 necessary is evident; for if it is necessary to understand the things which are prior and on which the demonstration depends, and it comes to a stop at some time, it is necessary for these immediates to be non-demonstrable. So as to that we argue thus; and we also say that there is not only understanding but also some principle of understanding by which we become familiar with the definitions.

And that it is impossible to demonstrate *simpliciter* in a circle is 25 clear, if demonstration must depend on what is prior and more familiar; for it is impossible for the same things at the same time to be prior and posterior to the same things—unless one is so in another way (i.e. one in relation to us, the other *simpliciter*), which induction makes familiar. But if so, knowing *simpliciter* will not have been properly 30 defined, but will be twofold. Or is the other demonstration not demonstration *simpliciter* in that it comes from about what is more familiar *to us*?

There results for those who say that demonstration is circular not only what has just been described, but also that they say nothing other than that this is the case if this is the case—and it is easy to prove 35 everything in this way. It is clear that this results if we posit three terms. (For it makes no difference to say that it bends back through many terms or through few, or through few or two.) For whenever if *A* is the case, of necessity *B* is, and if this then *C*, then if *A* is the case *C* will be the case. Thus given that if *A* is the case it is necessary that *B* is, and if this is that *A* is (for that is what being circular is)—let *A* be *C*: so to say that if *B* is the case *A* is, is to say that *C* is, and this implies 73ᵃ that if *A* is the case *C* is. But *C* is the same as *A*. Hence it results that those who assert that demonstration is circular say nothing but that if *A* is the case *A* is the case. And it is easy to prove everything in this 5 way.

Moreover, not even this is possible except in the case of things which follow one another, as properties do. Now if a single thing is laid down, it has been proved that it is never necessary that anything else should be the case (by a single thing I mean that neither if one term nor if one posit is posited . . .), but two posits are the first and 10

fewest from which it is possible, if at all, actually to deduce something. Now if *A* follows *B* and *C*, and these follow one another and *A*, in this way it is possible to prove all the postulates reciprocally in the first
15 figure, as was proved in the account of deduction. (And it was also proved that in the other figures either no deduction comes about or none about what was assumed.) But one cannot in any way prove circularly things which are not counterpredicated; hence, since there are few such things in demonstrations, it is evident that it is both empty and impossible to say that demonstration is reciprocal and that
20 because of this there can be demonstration of everything.

CHAPTER 4

Since it is impossible for that of which there is understanding *simpliciter* to be otherwise, what is understandable in virtue of demonstrative understanding will be necessary (it is demonstrative if we have it by having a demonstration). Demonstration, therefore, is deduction from what is necessary. We must therefore grasp on what
25 things and what sort of things demonstrations depend. And first let us define what we mean by 'holding of every case' and what by 'in itself' and what by 'universally'.

Now I say that something holds of every case if it does not hold in some cases and not others, nor at some times and not at others; e.g. if
30 animal holds of every man, then if it is true to call this a man, it is true to call him an animal too; and if he is now the one, he is the other too; and the same goes if there is a point in every line. Evidence: when asked if something holds of every case, we bring our objections in this way—either if in some cases it does not hold or if at some time it does not.

One thing belongs to another in itself both if it belongs to it in what
35 it is—e.g. line to triangle and point to line (for their substance depends on these and they belong in the account which says what they are)— and also if the things it belongs to themselves belong in the account which makes clear what it is—e.g. straight belongs to line and so does curved, and odd and even to number, and prime and composite, and
73^b equilateral and oblong; and for all these things there belongs in the account which says what they are in the one case line, and in the others number. And similarly in other cases too it is such things that I say belong to something in itself; and what belongs in neither way I call
5 accidental, e.g. musical or white to animal.

Again, what is not said of some other underlying subject—as what is walking is something different walking (and white), while a substance, and whatever signifies some 'this', is just what it is without being something else. Thus things which are not said of an underlying subject I call things in themselves, and those which are said of an underlying subject I call accidentals.

Again, in another way what belongs to something because of itself 10 belongs to it in itself, and what does not belong because of itself is accidental—e.g. if it lightened when he was walking, that was accidental; for it was not because of his walking that it lightened, but that, we say, was accidental. But if because of itself, then in itself—e.g. if something died while being sacrificed, it died *in* the sacrifice since it 15 died because of being sacrificed, and it was not accidental that it died while being sacrificed.

Whatever, therefore, in the case of what is understandable *simpliciter*, is said to belong to things in themselves in the sense of inhering in the predicates or of being inhered in, holds both because of themselves and from necessity. For it is not possible for them not to belong, either *simpliciter* or as regards the opposites—e.g. straight or crooked to line, and odd or even to number. For the contrary is either 20 a privation or a contradiction in the same genus—e.g. even is what is not odd among numbers, inasmuch as it follows. Hence if it is necessary to affirm or deny, it is necessary too for what belongs in itself to belong.

Now let holding of every case and in itself be defined in this fashion; 25 I call universal whatever belongs to something both of every case and in itself and as such. It is evident, therefore, that whatever is universal belongs from necessity to its objects. (To belong in itself and as such are the same thing—e.g. point and straight belong to line in itself (for they belong to it as line), and two right angles belong to triangle as 30 triangle (for the triangle is in itself equal to two right angles).)

Something holds universally whenever it is proved of a chance case and primitively; e.g. having two right angles neither holds universally of figure (yet one may prove of a figure that it has two right angles—but 35 not of a chance figure, nor does one use a chance figure in proving it; for the quadrangle is a figure but it does not have angles equal to two right angles)—and a chance isosceles does have angles equal to two right angles, but not primitively—the triangle is prior. If, then, a chance case is proved primitively to have two right angles or whatever else, it belongs universally to this primitively, and of this the 74ᵃ demonstration holds universally in itself; but of the others it holds in some fashion not in itself, nor does it hold of the isosceles universally, but with a wider extension.

76ᵃ   I call principles in each genus those which it is not possible to prove to be. Now both what the primitives and what the things dependent on them signify is assumed; but that they are must be assumed for the
35   principles and proved for the rest—e.g. we must assume what a unit or what straight and triangle signify, and that the unit and magnitude are; but we must prove that the others are.

Of the things they use in the demonstrative sciences some are proper to each science and others common—but common by analogy, since things are *useful* in so far as they bear on the genus under the science. Proper: e.g. that a line is *such-and-such*, and straight so-and-so; common: e.g. that if equals are taken from equals, the remainders are equal. But each of these is sufficient in so far as it bears on the
76ᵇ   genus; for it will produce the same result even if it is not assumed as holding of everything but only for the case of magnitudes—or, for the arithmetician, for numbers.

Proper too are the things which are assumed to be, about which the science considers what belongs to them in themselves—as e.g.
5   arithmetic is about units, and geometry is about points and lines. For they assume these to be and to be *this*. As to what are attributes of these in themselves, they assume what each signifies—e.g. arithmetic assumes what odd or even or quadrangle or cube signifies, and geometry what irrational or inflection or verging signifies—and they
10   prove that they are through the common items and from what has been demonstrated. And astronomy proceeds in the same way.

For every demonstrative science has to do with three things: what it posits to be (these form the genus of what it considers the attributes that belong to it in itself); and what are called the common axioms, the
15   primitives from which it demonstrates; and thirdly the attributes, of which it assumes what each signifies. Nothing, however, prevents some sciences from overlooking some of these—e.g. from not supposing that its genus is, if it is evident that it is (for it is not equally clear that number is and that hot and cold are), and from not assuming
20   what the attributes signify, if they are clear—just as in the case of the common items it does not assume what to take equals from equals

signifies, because it is familiar. But none the less there are by nature these three things, that about which the science proves, what it proves, and the things from which it proves.

What necessarily is the case because of itself and necessarily seems to be the case is not a supposition or a postulate. For demonstration is not addressed to external argument—but to argument in the soul—   25
since deduction is not either. For one can always object to external argument, but not always to internal argument.

Whatever a man assumes without proving it himself although it is provable—if he assumes something that seems to be the case to the learner, he supposes it (and it is a supposition not *simpliciter* but only in relation to the learner); but if he assumes the same thing when there is either no opinion present in the learner or actually a contrary one   30
present, he postulates it. And it is in this that suppositions and postulates differ; for a postulate is what is contrary to the opinion of the learner, which though it is demonstrable is assumed and used without being proved.

Now terms are not suppositions (for they are not said to be or not be   35
anything), but suppositions are among the propositions, whereas one need only grasp the terms; and suppositions are not that (unless someone will say that hearing is a supposition), but rather propositions such that, if they are the case, then by their being the case the conclusion comes about.

Nor does the geometer suppose falsehoods, as some have said, stating that one should not use a falsehood but that the geometer speaks falsely when he says that the line which is not a foot long is a foot long or that the drawn line which is not straight is straight. But the geometer does not conclude anything from there being this line which   77ᵃ
he himself has described, but from what is made clear through them.

Again, every postulate and supposition is either universal or particular; but terms are neither of these.

CHAPTER 13

Understanding the fact and the reason why differ, first in the same   78ᵃ
science—and in that in two ways: in one way, if the deduction does not come about through immediates (for the primitive explanation is   25
not assumed, but understanding of the reason why occurs in virtue of the primitive explanation); in another, if it is through immediates but not through the explanation but through the more familiar of the

converting terms. For nothing prevents the non-explanatory one of the counterpredicated terms from sometimes being more familiar, so that the demonstration will occur through this.

30   E.g. that the planets are near, through their not twinkling: let C be the planets, B not twinkling, A being near. Thus it is true to say B of C; for the planets do not twinkle. But also to say A of B; for what does not twinkle is near (let this be got through induction or through
35   perception). So it is necessary that A belongs to C; so that it has been demonstrated that the planets are near. Now this deduction is not of the reason why but of the fact; for it is not because they do not twinkle that they are near, but because they are near they do not twinkle.

But it is also possible for the latter to be proved through the former, and the demonstration will be of the reason why—e.g. let C be the
78ᵇ   planets, B being near, A not twinkling. Thus B belongs to C and A to B; so that A belongs to C. And the deduction is of the reason why; for the primitive explanation has been assumed.

Again, take the way they prove that the moon is spherical through
5   its increases—for if what increases in this way is spherical and the moon increases, it is evident that it is spherical. Now in this way the deduction of the fact comes about; but if the middle term is posited the other way about, we get the deduction of the reason why; for it is
10   not because of the increases that it is spherical, but because it is spherical it gets increases of this sort. Moon, C; spherical, B; increases, A.

But in cases in which the middle terms do not convert and the non-explanatory term is more familiar, the fact is proved but the reason why is not.

Again, in cases in which the middle is positioned outside—for in these too the demonstration is of the fact and not of the reason why; for
15   the explanation is not mentioned. E.g. why does the wall not breathe? Because it is not an animal. For if this were explanatory of breathing— i.e. if the denial is explanatory of something's not belonging, the affirmation is explanatory of its belonging (e.g. if imbalance in the hot and cold elements is explanatory of not being healthy, their balance is
20   explanatory of being healthy), and similarly too if the affirmation is explanatory of something's belonging, the denial is of its not belonging. But when things are set out in this way what we have said does not result; for not every animal breathes. The deduction of such an explanation comes about in the middle figure. E.g. let A be animal, B
25   breathing, C wall: then A belongs to every B (for everything breathing

is an animal), but to no C, so that B too belongs to no C—therefore the wall does not breathe.

Explanations of this sort resemble those which are extravagantly stated. This consists in arguing by setting the middle term too far away—e.g. Anacharsis' argument that there are no flute-girls among the Scyths, for there are no vines.

Thus with regard to the same science (and with regard to the position of the middle terms) there are these differences between the deduction of the fact and that of the reason why.

The reason why differs from the fact in another fashion, when each is considered by means of a different science. And such are those which are related to each other in such a way that the one is under the other, e.g. optics to geometry, and mechanics to solid geometry, and harmonics to arithmetic, and star-gazing to astronomy. Some of these sciences bear almost the same name—e.g. mathematical and nautical astronomy, and mathematical and acoustical harmonics. For here it is for the empirical scientists to know the fact and for the mathematical to know the reason why; for the latter have the demonstrations of the explanations, and often they do not know the fact, just as those who consider the universal often do not know some of the particulars through lack of observation.

These are those which, being something different in substance, make use of forms. For mathematics is about forms, for its objects are not said of any underlying subject—for even if geometrical objects are said of some underlying subject, still it is not *as* being said of an underlying subject that they are studied.

Related to optics as this is related to geometry, there is another science related to it—viz. the study of the rainbow; for it is for the natural scientist to know that fact, and for the student of optics—either *simpliciter* or mathematical—to know the reason why. And many even of those sciences which are not under one another are related like this—e.g. medicine to geometry; for it is for the doctor to know the fact that circular wounds heal more slowly, and for the geometer to know the reason why.

BOOK II

89ᵇ   The things we seek are equal in number to those we understand. We seek four things: the fact, the reason why, if it is, what it is.

25   For when we seek whether it is this or this, putting it into a number (e.g. whether the sun is eclipsed or not), we seek the fact. Evidence for this: on finding that it is eclipsed we stop; and if from the start we know that it is eclipsed, we do not seek whether it is. When we know the fact we seek the reason why (e.g. knowing that it is eclipsed and

30   that the earth moves, we seek the reason why it is eclipsed or why it moves).

Now while we seek these things in this way, we seek some things in another fashion—e.g. if a centaur or a god is or is not (I mean if one is or not *simpliciter* and not if one is white or not). And knowing that it is,

35   we seek what it is (e.g. so what is a god? or what is a man?).

Now what we seek and what on finding we know are these and thus many. We seek, whenever we seek the fact or if it is *simpliciter*, whether there is or is not a middle term for it; and whenever we become aware

90ᵃ   of either the fact or if it is—either partially or *simpliciter*—and again seek the reason why or what it is, then we seek what the middle term is. (I mean by the fact that it is partially and *simpliciter*—partially: Is the moon eclipsed? or is it increasing? (for in such cases we seek if it is something or is not something); *simpliciter*: if the moon or night is or is

5   not.) It results, therefore, that in all our searches we seek either if there is a middle term or what the middle term is.

For the middle term is the explanation, and in all cases that is sought. Is it eclipsed?—Is there some explanation or not? After that,

10   aware that there is one, we seek what this is. For the explanation of a substance being not this or that but *simpliciter*, or of its being not *simpliciter* but one of the things which belong to it in itself or accidentally—that is the middle term. I mean by *simpliciter* the underlying subject (e.g. moon or earth or sun or triangle) and by one of the things eclipse, equality, inequality, whether it is in the middle or not.

For in all these cases it is evident that what it is and why it is are the

same. What is an eclipse? Privation of light from the moon by the   15
earth's screening. Why is there an eclipse? or Why is the moon
eclipsed? Because the light leaves it when the earth screens it. What is
a harmony. An arithmetical ratio between high and low. Why does the
high harmonize with the low? Because an arithmetical ratio holds   20
between the high and the low. Can the high and the low harmonize?—
Is there an arithmetical ratio between them? Assuming that there is,
what then is the ratio?

That the search is for the middle term is made clear by the cases in
which the middle is perceptible. For if we have not perceived it, we   25
seek, e.g. for the eclipse, if there is one or not. But if we were on the
moon we would seek neither if it comes about nor why, but it would be
clear at the same time. For from perceiving, it would come about that
we knew the universal too. For perception tells us that it is now
screening it (for it is clear that it is now eclipsed); and from this the   30
universal would come about.

So, as we say, to know what it is is the same as to know why it is—
and that either *simpliciter* and not one of the things that belong to it, or
one of the things that belong to it, e.g. that it has two right angles, or
that it is greater or less.

CHAPTER 8

We must inquire again which of these points is correctly argued and   93ᵃ
which not correctly; and what a definition is; and whether there is in
some way demonstration and definition of what a thing is, or in no way
at all.

Since, as we said, to know what something is and to know the explanation of the fact that it is are the same—the argument for this is that   5
there is some explanation, and this is either the same thing or something else, and if it is something else it is either demonstrable or non-
demonstrable—if, then, it is something else and it is possible to
demonstrate it, it is necessary for the explanation to be a middle term
and to be proved in the first figure; for what is being proved is both
universal and affirmative.

Well, one way would be the one just examined—proving what a   10
thing is through another definition. For in the case of what a thing is, it
is necessary for the middle term to state what the thing is (and in the
case of what is proper it must be proper). Hence you will prove the one
but you will not prove the other instance of what it is to be the same

object. Now that this way will not be a demonstration was said earlier
15 (but it is a general deduction of what the thing is).

But let us say in what way a demonstration *is* possible, speaking
again from the beginning. Just as we seek the reason why when we
grasp the fact—sometimes they actually become clear together, but it
is not possible to become familiar with the reason why *before* the fact—
it is clear that similarly we cannot grasp what it is to be something
20 without grasping the fact that it is; for it is impossible to know what a
thing is if we are ignorant of whether it is. But as to whether it is,
sometimes we grasp this accidentally, and sometimes when grasping
something of the object itself—e.g. of thunder, that it is a sort of noise
of the clouds; and of eclipse, that it is a sort of privation of light; and of
man, that he is a sort of animal; and of soul, that it is something
moving itself.

25 Now in cases in which we know accidentally that a thing is,
necessarily we have no hold on what it is; for we do not even know that
it is, and to seek what it is without grasping that it is, is to seek nothing.
But in the cases in which we grasp something, it is easier. Hence in so
far as we grasp that it is, to that extent we also have some hold on what
it is.

So in cases in which we grasp something of what the thing is, let it
30 be first like this:—eclipse *A*, moon *C*, screening by the earth *B*. So to
ask whether it is eclipsed or not is to seek whether *B* is or not. And this
is no different from seeking whether there is an account of it; and if
this is, we say that that is too. (Or: of which of the contradictory pair
does the account hold—of its having two right angles or of its not
having them?)

35 When we discover it, we know at the same time the fact and the
reason why, if it is through immediates; if not, we know the fact but not
the reason why. Moon, *C*; eclipse, *A*; not being able to produce a
shadow during full moon though there is nothing evident between us,
B. Then if *B*—not being able to produce a shadow though there is
93ᵇ nothing evident between us—belongs to *C*, and *A*—being eclipsed—
to this, then it is clear *that* it is eclipsed but not yet *why*; and we know
that an eclipse is but we do not know *what* it is.

When it is clear that *A* belongs to *C*, then to seek why it belongs is
5 to seek what *B* is—whether screening or rotation of the moon or
extinction. And this is the account of the one extreme, i.e. in this case
of *A*. For an eclipse is a screening by the earth.

What is thunder? Extinction of fire in cloud. Why does it thunder?

Because the fire in the cloud is extinguished. Cloud *C*, thunder *A*, extinction of fire *B*. Thus *B* belongs to *C*, the cloud (for the fire is extinguished in it); and *A*, noise, to this; and *B* is indeed an account of *A*, the first extreme. And if again there is another middle term for this, it will be from among the remaining accounts.

We have said, then, how what a thing is is grasped and becomes familiar, hence no deduction and no demonstration of what a thing is comes about—yet it is clear through deduction and through demonstration. Hence without a demonstration you cannot become aware of what a thing is (in cases where the explanation is something else), yet there is no demonstration of it (as we said when we went through the puzzles).

CHAPTER 9

Of some things there is something else that is their explanation, of others there is not. Hence it is clear that in some cases what a thing is is immediate and a principle; and here one must suppose, or make apparent in some other way, both that they are and what they are (which the arithmetician does; for he supposes both what the unit is and that it is); but in those cases which have a middle term and for which something else is explanatory of their substance, one can, as we said, make them clear through a demonstration, but not by demonstrating what they are.

CHAPTER 10

Since a definition is said to be an account of what a thing is, it is evident that one type will be an account of what the name, or a different name-like account, signifies—e.g. what triangle signifies. And when we grasp that this is, we seek why it is; but it is difficult to grasp in this way why a thing is if we do not know that it is. The explanation of the difficulty has been stated already—that we do not even know whether it is or not, except accidentally. (An account is a unity in two ways—either by connection, like the *Iliad*, or by making one thing clear of one thing non-accidentally.)

Thus one definition of definition is the one stated; another definition is an account which makes clear why a thing is. Hence the former type of definition signifies but does not prove, whereas the latter evidently will be a sort of demonstration of what a thing is,

10

15

20

25

30

35

94ᵃ

differing in position from the demonstration. For there is a difference
between saying why it thunders and what thunder is; for in the one
case you will say: Because the fire is extinguished in the clouds. What
5   is thunder?—A noise of fire being extinguished in the clouds. Hence
the same account is put in a different way, and in *this* way it is a
continuous demonstration, in *this* way a definition.

Again, a definition of thunder is noise in the clouds; and this is a
conclusion of the demonstration of what it is.

10   The definition of immediates is an undemonstrable positing of what
they are.

One definition, therefore, is an undemonstrable account of what a
thing is; one is a deduction of what it is, differing in aspect from the
demonstration; a third is a conclusion of the demonstration of what it
is.

So it is evident from what has been said, both in what way there is a
15   demonstration of what a thing is, and in what way there is not; and in
what cases there is and in what cases there is not; and again in how
many ways something is called a definition, and in what way it proves
what a thing is and in what way it does not, and in what cases it does
and in what cases it does not; and again how it is related to demonstration and in what way it is possible for them to be of the same thing and
in what way it is not possible.

CHAPTER 12

95ᵃ   The same thing is explanatory for what is coming about and what has
come about and what will be as for what is the case (for the middle
term is explanatory)—except that for what is the case, it is the case; for
what is coming about, it is coming about; for what has come about, it
has come about; and for what will be, it will be.

E.g. why has an eclipse come about? Because the earth has come to
be in the middle. And it *is* coming about because it *is* coming to be
15   there; and it will be because it will be in the middle; and it is because it
is.

What is ice? Well, assume that it is solidified water. Water *C*; solidified, *A*; the explanatory middle term *B*—utter lack of heat. Thus *B*
belongs to *C*, and being solidified, *A*, to this. And ice is coming about
if *B* is coming about; and it has come about if it has come about; and it
20   will be if it will be.

Now what is explanatory in this way and what it is explanatory of come about together when they come about, and are the case together when they are; and similarly for having come about and going to be. But what of things that do not go together—can it be that in continuous time, as it seems to us, one should be explanatory of another? something else that has come about of the fact that this has come about, and something else that will be of the fact that this will be, and of the fact that this is coming about something that came to be before?

Well, the deduction proceeds from what has come about later (but the principle of these things is actually what has come about—and similarly in the case of what is coming about), and it does not proceed from what is earlier (e.g. since this has come about, that this has come about later). And similarly for what will be the case. For whether the time is indeterminate or determined it will not be the case that since it is true to say that this has come about it is true to say that this, the later thing, has come about. For in between it will be false to say this, when the one has already come about. And the same account also goes for what will be the case.

Neither can one deduce that since this has come about this will be. For the middle term must be coeval—something that came about for what came about, something that will be for what will be, something that is coming about for what is coming about, something that is for what is; but it is not possible for anything to be coeval with 'it has come about' and 'it will be'.

Again, the time in between can be neither determinate nor indeterminate; for it will be false to say it in between.

We must inquire what it is that holds things together so that after what *has* come about there are objects that *are* coming about. Or is it clear that what is coming about is *not* next to what has come about? For neither is what came about next to what came about; for they are limits and atomic. So just as points are not next to one another, neither are things that came about; for both are indivisible. Thus neither is what is coming about next to what has come about, for the same reason; for what is coming about is divisible, but what has come about is indivisible. So just as a line is related to a point, in the same way what is coming about is related to what has come about; for infinitely many things that have come about inhere in what is coming about.

But we must speak more clearly about this in our general account of change.

Now as to the character of the explanatory middle term when events

15 occur consecutively, let this much be assumed. For here too it is necessary for the middle and the first term to be immediate.

E.g. *A* has come about since *C* has come about (*C* has come about later, *A* before; but *C* is the principle since it is nearer to the present, which is the principle of time); and *C* has come about if *D* has come about. Thus if *D* has come about it is necessary that *A* has come 20 about; and *C* is the explanation—for if *D* came about it is necessary that *C* has come about, and if *C* has come about it is necessary that *A* has come about earlier.

If we take things in this way, will the middle term come to a stop anywhere at an immediate, or will there always be something falling in between because of the infinite nature of the past? For what has come about is not next to what has come about, as has been said. But never-25 theless it is necessary to *begin* from something that is immediate and first from the present.

The same goes too for 'it will be'. For if it is true to say that *D* will be, then necessarily it was earlier true to say that *A* will be. And *C* is explanatory of this; for if *D* will be, *C* will be earlier; and if *C* will be, 30 *A* will be earlier. And similarly the division is infinite in these cases too; for things that will be are not next to one another. But in these cases too an immediate principle must be got.

And it is like this in actual cases—if a house has come about it is necessary for stones to have been cut and to have come about. Why is this? Because it is necessary for a foundation to have come about if a 35 house has come about; and if a foundation has come about, it is necessary for stones to have come about earlier.

Again, if there is going to be a house, in the same way there will be stones earlier. It is proved similarly through the middle term; for there will be a foundation earlier.

Since we see that among the things that come about there is a sort of circular coming about, it is possible for this to be the case if the middle term and the extremes follow one another; for in these cases there is 96ᵃ conversion (this has been proved in our first chapters)[2] because the conclusions convert; and this is what being circular is.

In actual cases it appears as follows: if the earth is soaked, necessarily steam came about; and if that came about, cloud; and if 5 that came about, water: and if that came about, it is necessary for the earth to be soaked. But this was what we started from; so that it has

---

[2] See I. 3. 73ᵃ6-20.

come round in a circle—for if any whatever of them is the case, another is; and if that, another; and if that, the first.

Some things come about universally (for always and in every case either it holds or it comes about in this way), others not always but for the most part—e.g. not every male man has hair on his chin, but for the most part they do. Well, in such cases it is necessary for the middle   10
term also to hold for the most part. For if A is predicated universally of B and this universally of C, it is necessary for A to be predicated of C always and in every case; for that is what the universal is—what holds in every case and always. But it was supposed to hold for the   15
most part. Therefore it is necessary for the middle term, B, also to hold for the most part. There will be immediate principles, then, also in the case of what is for the most part, which hold or come about in this way for the most part.

CHAPTER 19

Now as for deduction and demonstration, it is evident both what each   99^b
is and how it comes about—and at the same time this goes for demonstrative understanding too (for that is the same thing). But as for the principles—how they become familiar and what is the state that becomes familiar with them—that will be clear from what follows, when we have first set down the puzzles.

Now, we have said earlier that it is not possible to understand   20
through demonstration if we are not aware of the primitive, immediate, principles. But as to knowledge of the immediates, one might puzzle both whether it is the same or not the same—whether there is understanding of each, or rather understanding of the one and some other kind of thing of the other—and also whether the states are not present in us but come about in us, or whether they are present in   25
us but escape notice.

Well, if we have them, it is absurd; for it results that we have pieces of knowledge more precise than demonstration and yet this escapes notice. But if we get them without having them earlier, how might we become familiar with them and learn them from no pre-existing knowledge? For that is impossible, as we said in the case of demonstration too. It is evidently impossible, then, both for us to have them   30
and for them to come about in us when we are ignorant and have no such state at all. Necessarily, therefore, we have some capacity, but do

not have one of a type which will be more valuable than these in respect of precision.

35 And *this* evidently belongs to all animals; for they have a connate discriminatory capacity, which is called perception. And if perception is present in them, in some animals retention of the percept comes about, but in others it does not come about. Now for those in which it does not come about, there is no knowledge outside perceiving (either none at all, or none with regard to that of which there is no retention); but for some perceivers, it is possible to grasp it in their minds. And

100ᵃ when many such things come about, then a difference comes about, so that some come to have an account from the retention of such things, and others do not.

So from perception there comes memory, as we call it, and from memory (when it occurs often in connection with the same thing),

5 experience; for memories that are many in number form a single experience. And from experience, or from the whole universal that has come to rest in the soul (the one apart from the many, whatever is one and the same in all those things), there comes a principle of skill and of understanding—of skill if it deals with how things come about, of understanding if it deals with what is the case.

10 Thus the states neither belong in us in a determinate form, nor come about from other states that are more cognitive; but they come about from perception—as in a battle when a rout occurs, if one man makes a stand another does and then another, until a position of strength is reached. And the soul is such as to be capable of undergoing this.

15 What we have just said but not said clearly, let us say again: when one of the undifferentiated things makes a stand, there is a primitive universal in the mind (for though one perceives the particular,

100ᵇ perception is of the universal—e.g. of man but not of Callias the man); again a stand is made in these, until what has no parts and is universal stands—e.g. *such-and-such* an animal stands, until animal does, and in this a stand is made in the same way. Thus it is clear that it is necessary for us to become familiar with the primitives by induction; for

5 perception too instils the universal in this way.

Since of the intellectual states by which we grasp truth some are always true and some admit falsehood (e.g. opinion and reasoning—whereas understanding and comprehension are always true), and no kind other than comprehension is more precise than understanding, and the principles of demonstrations are more familiar, and all understanding involves an account—there will not be understanding of the 10 principles; and since it is not possible for anything to be truer than understanding, except comprehension, there will be comprehension of the principles—both if we inquire from these facts and because demonstration is not a principle of demonstration so that understanding is not a principle of understanding either—so if we have no other true kind apart from understanding, comprehension will be the 15 principle of understanding. And the principle will be of the principle, and understanding as a whole will be similarly related to the whole object.

TOPICS*

BOOK I

CHAPTER I

100ᵃ   Our treatise proposes to find a line of inquiry whereby we shall be able to reason from reputable opinions about any subject presented to us, and also shall ourselves, when putting forward an argument, avoid saying anything contrary to it. First, then, we must say what deduction is, and what its varieties are, in order to grasp dialectical deduction; for this is the object of our search in the treatise before us.

25   Now a deduction is an argument in which, certain things being laid down, something other than these necessarily comes about through them. It is a demonstration, when the premisses from which the deduction starts are true and primitive, or are such that our knowledge of them has originally come through premisses which are primitive and true; and it is a dialectical deduction, if it reasons from reputable

30 opinions. Things are true and primitive which are convincing on the strength not of anything else but of themselves; for in regard to the first principles of science it is improper to ask any further for the why and wherefore of them; each of the first principles should command

100ᵇ belief in and by itself. On the other hand, those opinions are reputable which are accepted by everyone or by the majority or by the wise—i.e. by all, or by the majority, or by the most notable and reputable of them. Again, a deduction is contentious if it starts from opinions that seem to be reputable, but are not really such, or again if it merely

25 seems to reason from opinions that are or seem to be reputable. For not every opinion that seems to be reputable actually is reputable. For none of the opinions which we call reputable show their character entirely on the surface, as happens in the case of the principles of contentious arguments; for the nature of the falsity in these is obvious immediately, and for the most part even to persons with little power of

101ᵃ comprehension. So then, of the contentious deductions mentioned, the former really deserves to be called deduction, but the other should

---

* *Translation*: W. A. Pickard-Cambridge, revised J. Barnes (Revised Oxford Aristotle, 1984); *Text*: J. Brunschwig (Budé, Paris, 1967).

be called contentious deduction, but not deduction, since it appears to deduce, but does not really do so.

Further, besides all the deductions we have mentioned there are the fallacies that start from the premisses peculiar to the special sciences, as happens (for example) in the case of geometry and its sister sciences. For this form of reasoning appears to differ from the deductions mentioned above; the man who draws a false figure reasons from things that are neither true and primitive, nor yet reputable. For he does not fall within the definition: he does not assume opinions that are received either by everyone or by the majority or by the wise—that is to say, by all, or by most, or by the most reputable of them—but he conducts his deduction upon assumptions which, though appropriate to the science in question, are not true; for he effects his fallacy either by describing the semicircles wrongly or by drawing certain lines in a way in which they should not be drawn.

The foregoing must stand for an outline survey of the species of deduction. In general, in regard both to all that we have already discussed and to those which we shall discuss later, we may remark that that amount of distinction between them may serve, because it is not our purpose to give a precise definition of any of them; we merely want to describe them in outline: we consider it quite enough from the point of view of the line of inquiry before us to be able to recognize each of them in some sort of way.

CHAPTER 2

Next in order after the foregoing, we must say for how many and for what purposes the treatise is useful. They are three—intellectual training, casual encounters, and the philosophical sciences. That it is useful as a training is obvious on the face of it. The possession of a plan of inquiry will enable us more easily to argue about the subject proposed. For purposes of casual encounters, it is useful because when we have counted up the opinions held by most people, we shall meet them on the ground not of other people's convictions but of their own, shifting the ground of any argument that they appear to us to state unsoundly. For the study of the philosophical sciences it is useful, because the ability to puzzle on both sides of a subject will make us detect more easily the truth and error about the several points that arise. It has a further use in relation to the principles used in the several sciences. For it is impossible to discuss them at all from the principles proper to the particular science in hand, seeing that the principles are primitive in relation to everything else: it is through 101ᵇ reputable opinions about them that these have to be discussed, and this task belongs properly, or most appropriately, to dialectic; for dialectic is a process of criticism wherein lies the path to the principles of all inquiries.

CHAPTER 3

5 We shall be in perfect possession of the way to proceed when we are in a position like that which we occupy in regard to rhetoric and medicine and faculties of that kind; for it is not every method that the rhetorician will employ to persuade, or the doctor to heal: still, if he omits none of the available means, we shall say that his grasp of the 10 science is adequate.

CHAPTER 4

First, then, we must see of what parts our inquiry consists. Now if we were to grasp with reference to how many, and what kind of, things arguments take place, and with what materials they start, and how we are to become well supplied with these, we should have sufficiently won our goal. Now the materials with which arguments start are equal in number, and are identical, with the subjects on which deductions 15 take place. For arguments start with propositions, while the subjects on which deductions take place are problems. Now every proposition and every problem indicates either a genus or a property or an accident—for the differentia too, being generic, should be ranked together with the genus. Since, however, of what is proper to anything 20 part signifies its essence, while part does not, let us divide the proper into both the aforesaid parts, and call that part which indicates the essence a definition, while of the remainder let us adopt the terminology which is generally current about these things, and speak of it as a property. What we have said, then, makes it clear that according to our present division, the elements turn out to be four, all 25 told, namely either property or definition or genus or accident. Do not let any one suppose us to mean that each of these enunciated by itself constitutes a proposition or problem, but only that it is from these that both problems and propositions are formed. The difference between a problem and a proposition is a difference in the turn of the phrase. For if it be put in this way, 'Is two-footed terrestrial animal the definition of man?' or 'Is animal the genus of man?' the result is a proposition; but if thus, 'Is two-footed terrestrial animal the definition of man or not?' and 'Is animal the genus of man or not?' the result is a problem. Similarly too in other cases. Naturally, then, problems and propositions are equal in number; for out of every proposition you will make a problem if you change the turn of phrase.

CHAPTER 5

We must now say what are definition, property, genus, and accident. A definition is a phrase signifying a thing's essence. It is rendered in the form either of a phrase in lieu of a name, or of a phrase in lieu of another phrase; for it is sometimes possible to define the meaning of a phrase as well. People whose rendering consists of a term only, try it as they may, clearly do not render the definition of the thing in question, because a definition is always a phrase of a certain kind. One may, however, call definitory such a remark as that the beautiful is the becoming, and likewise also the question, 'Are perception and knowledge the same or different?'—for argument about definitions is mostly concerned with questions of sameness and difference. In a word we may call definitory everything that falls under the same branch of inquiry as definitions; and that all the above-mentioned examples are of this character is clear on the face of them. For if we are able to argue that two things are the same or are different, we shall be well supplied by the same turn of argument with lines of attack upon their definitions as well; for when we have shown that they are not the same we shall have demolished the definition. But the converse of this last statement does not hold; for to show that they are the same is not enough to establish a definition. To show, however, that they are not the same is enough of itself to overthrow it.

A property is something which does not indicate the essence of a thing, but yet belongs to that thing alone, and is predicated convertibly of it. Thus it is a property of man to be capable of learning grammar; for if he is a man, then he is capable of learning grammar, and if he is capable of learning grammar, he is a man. For no one calls anything a property which may possibly belong to something else, e.g. sleep in the case of man, even though at a certain time it may happen to belong to him alone. That is to say, if any such thing were actually to be called a property, it will be called not a property absolutely, but a temporary

or a relative property; for being on the right-hand side is a temporary property, while two-footed is a relative property; e.g. it is a property of man relatively to a horse and a dog. That nothing which may belong to anything else is a convertible predicate is clear; for it does not
30 necessarily follow that if something is asleep it is a man.

A genus is what is predicated in what a thing is of a number of things exhibiting differences in kind. We should treat as predicates in what a thing is all such things as it would be appropriate to mention in reply to the question, 'What is the object in question?'; as, for example, in
35 the case of man, if asked that question, it is appropriate to say 'He is an animal'. The question, 'Is one thing in the same genus as another or in a different one?' is also a generic question; for a question of that kind as well falls under the same branch of inquiry as the genus; for having argued that animal is the genus of man, and likewise also of ox, we
102ᵇ shall have argued that they are in the same genus; whereas if we show that it is the genus of the one but not of the other, we shall have argued that these things are not in the same genus.

An accident is something which, though it is none of the
5   foregoing—i.e. neither a definition nor a property nor a genus—yet belongs to the thing; and something which may either belong or not belong to any one and the self-same thing, as (e.g.) being seated may belong or not belong to some self-same thing. Likewise also whiteness; for there is nothing to prevent the same thing being at one time
10 white and at another not white. Of the definitions of accident the second is the better; for in the case of the first, anyone is bound, if he is to understand it, to know already what definition and genus and property are, whereas the second is sufficient of itself to tell us the essential nature of the thing in question. To accident are to be
15 attached also all comparisons of things together, when expressed in language that is derived in any kind of way from accident; such as, for example, the question, 'Is the honourable or the expedient preferable?' and 'Is the life of virtue or the life of self-indulgence the pleasanter?', and any other problem which may happen to be phrased in terms like these. For in all such cases the question is 'of which of the
20 two is the predicate more properly an accident?' It is clear on the face of it that there is nothing to prevent an accident from becoming a temporary or a relative property. Thus being seated is an accident, but will be a temporary property, whenever a man is the only person sitting, while if he is not the only one sitting, it is still a property relatively to those who are not sitting. So then, there is nothing to

prevent an accident from becoming both a relative and a temporary   25
property; but a property absolutely it will never be.

CHAPTER 6

We must not fail to observe that everything applicable to property and
genus and accident will be applicable to definition as well. For when
we have shown that the content of the definition fails to belong to the
subject alone, as we do in the case of a property, or that the genus
rendered in the definition is not the true genus, or that any of the   30
things mentioned in the phrase used does not belong, as would be
remarked in the case of an accident, we shall have demolished the
definition; so that, in the sense previously described, all the points we
have enumerated might in a way be called definitory. But we must not   35
on this account expect to find a single line of inquiry which will apply
universally to them all; for this is not an easy thing to find, and, even
were one found, it would be very obscure indeed, and of little service
for the treatise before us. Rather, a special plan of inquiry must be laid
down for each of the classes we have distinguished, and then, starting
from what is appropriate in each case, it will be easier to make our way   103ᵃ
right through the task before us. So then, as was said before, we must
outline a division of our subject, and other questions we must relegate
each to the particular branch to which it most naturally belongs,
speaking of them as definitory and generic questions. The questions I
mean have in effect already been assigned to their several branches.   5

CHAPTER 7

First of all we must determine the number of ways we talk of sameness.
Sameness would be generally regarded as falling, roughly speaking,
into three divisions. We generally apply the term numerically or
specifically or generically—numerically in cases where there is more
than one name but only one thing, e.g. doublet and cloak; specifically,
where there is more than one thing, but they present no differences in   10
respect of their species, as one man and another, or one horse and
another; for things like this that fall under the same species are said to
be specifically the same. Similarly, too, those things are called
generically the same which fall under the same genus, such as a horse
and a man. It might appear that the sense in which water from the
same spring is called the same water is somehow different and unlike   15

the senses mentioned above; but really such a case as this ought to be ranked in the same class with the things that in one way or another are called the same in view of unity of species. For all such things seem to be of one family and to resemble one another. For the reason why all water is said to be specifically the same as all other water is because of a certain likeness it bears to it, and the only difference in the case of water drawn from the same spring is this, that the likeness is more emphatic: that is why we do not distinguish it from the things that in one way or another are called the same in view of unity of species. It seems that things numerically one are called the same by everyone with the greatest degree of agreement. But this too is apt to be rendered in more than one sense; its most literal and primary use is found whenever the sameness is rendered by a name or definition, as when a cloak is said to be the same as a doublet, or a two-footed terrestrial animal is said to be the same as a man; a second sense is when it is rendered by a property, as when what can acquire knowledge is called the same as a man, and what naturally travels upward the same as fire; while a third use is found when it is rendered in reference to some accident, as when the creature who is sitting, or who is musical, is called the same as Socrates. For all these are meant to signify numerical unity. That what I have just said is true may be best seen where one form of appellation is substituted for another. For often when we give the order to call one of the people who are sitting down, indicating him by name, we change our description, whenever the person to whom we give the order happens not to understand us; he will, we think, understand better from some accidental feature; so we bid him call to us the man who is sitting or who is conversing—clearly supposing ourselves to be indicating the same object by its name and by its accident.

CHAPTER 8

103ᵇ   Of sameness then, as has been said, three types are to be distinguished. Now one way to confirm that the elements mentioned above are those out of which and through which and to which arguments proceed, is by induction; for if anyone were to survey propositions and problems one by one, it would be seen that each was formed either from the definition of something or from its property or from its genus or from its accident. Another way to confirm it is through deduction. For every predicate of a subject must of necessity be either convertible with its subject or not: and if it is convertible, it would be its definition or property, for if it signifies the essence, it is the definition; if not, it is a property—for this was what a property is, viz. what is predicated 10 convertibly, but does not signify the essence. If, on the other hand, it is not predicated convertibly of the thing, it either is or is not one of the terms contained in the definition of the subject; and if it is one of those terms, then it will be genus or differentia, inasmuch as the definition consists of genus and differentiae; whereas, if it is not one of those 15 terms, clearly it would be an accident, for accident was said to be what belongs to a subject without being either its definition or its genus or property.

CHAPTER 9

Next, then, we must distinguish between the categories of predication 20 in which the four above-mentioned are found. These are ten in number: What a thing is, Quantity, Quality, Relation, Place, Time, Position, State, Activity, Passivity. For the accident and genus and property and definition of anything will always be in one of these predications; for all the propositions found through these signify 25 either what something is or its quality or quantity or some one of the other types of predicate. It is clear, too, on the face of it that the man who signifies what something is signifies sometimes a substance, sometimes a quality, sometimes some one of the other types of predicate. For when a man is set before him and he says that what is set there is a man or an animal, he states what it is and signifies a 30 substance; but when a white colour is set before him and he says that what is set there is white or is a colour, he states what it is and signifies a quality. Likewise, also, if a magnitude of a cubit be set before him and he says that what is set there is a cubit or a magnitude, he will be describing what it is and signifying a quantity. Likewise, also, in the other cases; for each of these kinds of predicate, if either it be asserted 35 of itself, or its genus be asserted of it, signifies what something is; if, on the other hand, one kind of predicate is asserted of another kind, it does not signify what something is, but a quantity or a quality or one of the other kinds of predicate. Such, then, and so many, are the subjects on which arguments take place, and the materials with which they start. How we are to acquire them, and by what means we are to 104ᵃ become well supplied with them, falls next to be told.

CHAPTER 10

First, then, a definition must be given of a dialectical proposition and
5   a dialectical problem. For it is not every proposition nor yet every
problem that is to be set down as dialectical; for no one in his senses
would make a proposition of what no one holds, nor yet make a
problem of what is obvious to everybody; for the latter admits of no
doubt, while to the former no one would assent.

Now a dialectical proposition consists in asking something that is
10   reputable to all men or to most men or to the wise, i.e. either to all, or
to most, or to the most notable of these, provided it is not paradoxical;
for a man would probably assent to the view of the wise, if it be not
contrary to the opinions of most men. Dialectical propositions also
include views which are like those which are reputable; also propositions which contradict the contraries of opinions that are taken to be
15   reputable, and also all opinions that are in accordance with the
recognized arts. Thus, supposing it to be reputable that the knowledge
of contraries is the same, it might probably pass for reputable also that
the perception of contraries is the same; also, supposing it to be a
reputable opinion that there is but one single science of grammar, it
might pass for a reputable opinion that there is but one science of
flute-playing as well—and if more than one science of grammar, more
20   than one science of flute-playing as well; for all these seem to be alike
and akin. Likewise, also, propositions contradicting the contraries of
reputable opinions will pass as reputable; for if it is a reputable
opinion that one ought to do good to one's friends, it will also be a
reputable opinion that one ought not to do them harm. Here, that one
ought to do harm to one's friends is the contrary, and that one ought
25   not to do them harm is the contradictory of that contrary. Likewise
also, if one ought to do good to one's friends, one ought not to do good
to one's enemies: this too is the contradictory of the contrary—the
contrary being that one ought to do good to one's enemies. Likewise,
also, in other cases. Also, on comparison, it will look like a reputable
opinion that the contrary predicate belongs to the contrary subject:
e.g. if one ought to do good to one's friends, one ought also to do evil to
30   one's enemies. (It might appear as if doing good to one's friends were a
contrary to doing evil to one's enemies; but whether this actually is or
is not so in reality will be stated in the course of the discussion of
contraries.) Clearly also, all opinions that are in accordance with the
arts are dialectical propositions. For people are likely to assent to the

views held by those who have made a study of these things; e.g. on a   35
question of medicine they will agree with the doctor, and on a question
of geometry with the geometrician, and likewise also in other cases.

A dialectical problem is a subject of inquiry that contributes either to   104^b
choice and avoidance, or to truth and knowledge, and does that either
by itself, or as a help to the solution of some other such problem. It
must, moreover, be something on which either people hold no opinion
either way, or most people hold a contrary opinion to the wise, or the
wise to most people, or each of them among themselves. For some   5
problems it is useful to know only with a view to choice or avoidance,
e.g. whether pleasure is to be chosen or not, while some it is useful to
know merely with a view to knowledge, e.g. whether the universe is
eternal or not; others, again, are not useful in themselves for either of
these purposes, but yet help us in regard to some such problems; for
there are many things which we do not wish to know in themselves,   10
but for the sake of other things, in order that through them we may
come to know something else. Problems also include questions in
regard to which deductions conflict (the difficulty then being whether
so-and-so is so or not, there being convincing arguments for both
views); others also in regard to which we have no argument because
they are so vast, and find it difficult to give our reasons, e.g. the   15
question whether the universe is eternal or no; for into questions of
that kind too it is possible to inquire.

Problems, then, and propositions are to be defined as aforesaid. A
thesis is a paradoxical belief of some eminent philosopher; e.g. the   20
view that contradiction is impossible, as Antisthenes said; or the view
of Heraclitus that all things are in motion; or that what exists is one, as
Melissus says; for to take notice when any ordinary person expresses
views contrary to men's usual opinions would be silly. Or it may be a
view contrary to men's usual opinions about which we have an
argument, e.g. the view maintained by the sophists that what is need
not in every case either have come to be or be eternal; for a musician   25
who is a grammarian is so without ever having come to be so, or being
so eternally. For even if some do not accept this view, a man might do
so on the ground that it has an argument in its favour.

Now a thesis also is a problem, though a problem is not always a
thesis, inasmuch as some problems are such that we have no opinion   30

about them either way. That a thesis is a problem, is clear; for it
follows of necessity from what has been said that either the mass of
men disagree with the wise about the thesis, or that the one or the
other class disagree among themselves, seeing that the thesis is a
35   paradoxical belief. Practically all dialectical problems indeed are now
called theses. But it should make no difference whichever description
is used; for our object in thus distinguishing them has not been to
create a terminology, but to recognize what differences actually exist
105ª   between them.

Not every problem, nor every thesis, should be examined, but only
one which might puzzle one of those who need argument, not
punishment or perception. For people who are puzzled to know
5   whether one ought to honour the gods and love one's parents or not
need punishment, while those who are puzzled to know whether snow
is white or not need perception. The subjects should not border too
closely upon the sphere of demonstration, nor yet be too far removed
from it; for the former cases admit of no doubt, while the latter involve
difficulties too great for the art of the trainer.

CHAPTER 12

10   Having made these distinctions, we must distinguish how many
species there are of dialectical arguments. There are induction and
deduction. Now what deduction is has been said before; induction is a
passage from particulars to universals, e.g. the argument that supposing the skilled pilot is the most effective, and likewise the skilled
15   charioteer, then in general the skilled man is the best at his particular
task. Induction is more convincing and clear: it is more readily learnt
by the use of the senses, and is applicable generally to the mass of
men; but deduction is more forcible and more effective against
contradictious people.

CHAPTER 13

20   The classes, then, of things about which, and of things out of which,
arguments are constructed, are to be distinguished in the way we have
said before. The instruments whereby we are to become well supplied
with deductions are four: one, the securing of propositions; second,
the power to distinguish in how many ways an expression is used;
third, the discovery of the differences of things; fourth, the investiga-

tion of likeness. The last three, as well, are in a certain sense proposi- 25
tions; for it is possible to make a proposition corresponding to each of
them, e.g. that the desirable is either the honourable or the pleasant or
the expedient; and that sensation differs from knowledge in that the
latter may be recovered again after it has been lost, while the former
cannot; and that the relation of the healthy to health is like that of the 30
vigorous to vigour. The first proposition depends upon the use of one
term in several ways, the second upon the differences of things, the
third upon their likeness.

CHAPTER 14

Propositions should be selected in as many ways as we drew distinctions in regard to the proposition: thus one may choose the opinions 35
held by all or by most men or by the wise, i.e. by all, or most, or the
most notable of them—if they are not contrary to those that seem to be
generally held; and, again, all opinions that are in accordance with the
arts. We must make propositions also of the contradictories of 105^b
opinions contrary to those that seem to be generally held, as was laid
down before. It is useful also to make them by selecting not only those
opinions that actually are reputable, but also those that are like these,
e.g. that the perception of contraries is the same—the knowledge of
them being so—and that we see by admission of something into 5
ourselves, not by an emission; for so it is, too, in the case of the other
senses; for in hearing we admit something into ourselves, we do not
emit; and we taste in the same way. Likewise also in the other cases.
Moreover, all statements that seem to be true in all or in most cases, 10
should be taken as a principle or accepted thesis; for they are posited
by those who do not also see what exception there may be. We should
select also from the written handbooks of argument, and should draw
up sketch-lists of them upon each several kind of subject, putting them
down under separate headings, e.g. 'On Good', or 'On Life'—and that
'On Good' should deal with every form of good, beginning with the
essence. In the margin, too, one should indicate also the opinions of 15
individual thinkers, e.g. that Empedocles said that the elements of
bodies were four; for any one might assent to the saying of some
reputable authority.

Of propositions and problems there are—to comprehend the matter
in outline—three divisions; for some are ethical propositions, some 20
are on natural science, while some are logical. Propositions such as

the following are ethical: 'Ought one rather to obey one's parents or the laws, if they disagree?'; such as this are logical: 'Is the knowledge of opposites the same or not?'; while such as this are on natural science: 'Is the universe eternal or not?' Likewise also with problems. The nature of each of the aforesaid kinds of proposition is not easily rendered in a definition, but we have to try to recognize each of them by means of the familiarity attained through induction, examining them in the light of the illustrations given above.

For purposes of philosophy we must treat of these things according to their truth, but for dialectic only with an eye to opinion.

All propositions should be taken in their most universal form; then, the one should be made into many. E.g. 'The knowledge of opposites is the same'; next, 'The knowledge of contraries is the same', and 'of relative terms'. In the same way these should again be divided, as long as division is possible, e.g. the knowledge of good and evil, of white and black, of cold and hot. Likewise also in other cases.

CHAPTER 15

On the subject of propositions, the above remarks are enough. As regards the number of ways in which a term is used, we must not only treat of those terms which are used in different ways, but we must also try to render their definitions; e.g. we must not merely say that justice and courage are called good in one way, and that what conduces to vigour and what conduces to health are called so in another, but also that the former are so called because of a certain intrinsic quality they themselves have, the latter because they are productive of a certain result and not because of any intrinsic quality in themselves. Similarly also in other cases.

Whether a term is used in many ways or in one only, may be considered by the following means. First, look and see if its contrary is used in many ways, whether the discrepancy between them be one of kind or one of names. For in some cases a difference is at once displayed even in the names; e.g. the contrary of sharp in the case of a sound is flat, while in the case of a body it is dull. Clearly, then, the contrary of sharp is used in many ways, and if so, so also is sharp; for corresponding to each of the former terms the contrary will be different. For sharp will not be the same when contrary to dull and to flat, though sharp is the contrary of each. Again flat in the case of a sound has sharp as its contrary, but in the case of a body raised, so that flat is used in many ways, inasmuch as its contrary also is so used. Likewise, also, fine as applied to an animal has ugly as its contrary, but, as applied to a house, mean; so that fine is homonymous. 20

In some cases there is no discrepancy of any sort in the names used, but a difference of kind is at once obvious: e.g. in the case of clear and 25 obscure; for sound is called clear and obscure, just as colour is too. As regards the names, then, there is no discrepancy, but the difference in kind is at once obvious; for colour is not called clear in a like way to sound. This is plain also through sensation; for of things that are the same in kind we have the same sense, whereas we do not judge clear- 30 ness by the same sense in the case of sound and of colour, but in the latter case we judge by sight, in the former by hearing. Likewise also with sharp and dull in regard to flavours and bodies: here in the latter case we judge by touch, but in the former by taste. For here again there is no discrepancy in the names used, in the case either of the original terms or of their contraries; for the contrary of sharp in either case is dull. 35

Moreover, see if one use of a term has a contrary, while another has absolutely none; e.g. the pleasure of drinking has a contrary in the pain of thirst, whereas the pleasure of seeing that the diagonal is in-commensurate with the side has none, so that pleasure is used in more than one way. To love also, used of the frame of mind, has to hate as its contrary, while as used of the physical activity it has none; clearly, 106ᵇ therefore, to love is homonymous.

Further, see in regard to their intermediates, if one use has an inter-mediate, while another has none, or if both have one but not the same 5 one, as e.g. clear and obscure in the case of colours have grey as an intermediate, whereas in the case of sound they have none, or, if they have, it is muffled, as some people say that a muffled sound is inter-mediate. Clear, then, is homonymous, and likewise also obscure.

See, moreover, if some of them have more than one intermediate, while others have but one, as is the case with clear and obscure; for in 10 the case of colours there are numbers of intermediates, whereas in regard to sound there is but one, viz. muffled.

Again, in the case of the contradictory opposite, look and see if it is used in more than one way. For if it is, then the opposite of it also will 15 be used in more than one way; e.g. to fail to see is used in more than one way, viz. to fail to possess the power of sight, and to fail to put that power to active use. But if this is used in more than one way, it follows necessarily that to see also is used in more than one way; for there will

be an opposite to each way of failing to see; e.g. the opposite of failing to possess the power of sight is to possess it, while of failing to
20 put the power of sight to active use, the opposite is to put it to active use.

Moreover, examine the case of terms that are opposed as privation and possession; for if the one term is used in more than one way, then so will the remaining term: e.g. if to perceive is used in more than one way, as applied to the soul and to the body, then to be imperceptive too will be used in more than one way, as applied to the soul and to the
25 body. That the opposition between the terms now in question depends upon privation and possession is clear, since animals naturally possess each kind of perception, both as applied to the soul and as applied to the body.

Moreover, examine the inflected forms. For if 'justly' is used in
30 more than one way, the 'just', also, will be used in more than one way; for there will be a 'just' corresponding to each 'justly'; e.g. if 'justly' is used of judging according to one's own opinion, and also of judging as one ought, then 'just' also will be used in like manner. In the same way also, if 'healthy' is used in more than one way, then 'healthily' also will
35 be used in more than one way: e.g. if healthy is what produces health and what preserves health and what betokens health, then 'healthily' also will be used to mean 'in such a way as to produce' or 'preserve' or 'betoken' health. Likewise also in other cases, whenever the original term is used in more than one way, the inflexion also that is formed
107ᵃ from it will be used in more than one way, and vice versa.

Look also at the classes of the predicates signified by the term, and see if they are the same in all cases. For if they are not the same, then
5 clearly the term is homonymous: e.g. good in the case of food is what is productive of pleasure, and in the case of medicine what is productive of health, whereas as applied to the soul it is to be of a certain quality, e.g. temperate or courageous or just; and likewise also, as applied to a man. Sometimes it signifies what happens at a certain time, as (e.g.) what happens at the right time; for what happens at the right time is
10 called good. Often it signifies what is of a certain quantity, e.g. as applied to the proper amount; for the proper amount too is called good. So then good is homonymous. In the same way also clear, as applied to a body, signifies a colour, but in regard to a sound it denotes what is easy to hear. Sharp, too, is in a closely similar case; for the
15 same term does not have the same use in all its applications; for a sharp note is a swift note, as the mathematical theorists of harmony

tell us, whereas a sharp angle is one that is less than a right angle, while a sharp dagger is one cut at a sharp angle.

Look also at the genera of the objects denoted by the same name, and see if they are different without the one falling under the other, as (e.g.) donkey is both the animal and the engine. For the account of them that corresponds to the name is different; for the one will be declared to be an animal of a certain kind, and the other to be an engine of a certain kind. If, however, the genera are subordinate one to the other, there is no necessity for the accounts to be different. Thus (e.g.) animal is the genus of raven, and so is bird. Whenever therefore we say that the raven is a bird, we also say that it is a certain kind of animal, so that both the genera are predicated of it. Likewise also whenever we call the raven a winged two-footed animal, we declare it to be a bird; in this way, then, as well, both the genera are predicated of raven. But in the case of genera that are not subordinate one to the other this does not happen; for whenever we call a thing an engine, we do not call it an animal, nor vice versa.

Look also and see not only if the genera of the term before you are different without being subordinate one to the other, but also in the case of its contrary; for if its contrary is used in many ways, clearly the term before you is as well.

It is useful also to look at the definition that arises from the use of the term in combination, e.g. of a clear body and of a clear sound. For then if what is proper to each case be abstracted, the same phrase ought to remain over. This does not happen in the case of homonyms, e.g. in the cases just mentioned. For the former will be a body possessing such and such a colour, while the latter will be a sound easy to hear. Abstract, then, 'a body' and 'a sound', and the remainder in each case is not the same. It should, however, have been, had clear in each case been synonymous.

Often in the actual accounts themselves homonymy creeps in without being noticed, and for this reason the accounts also should be examined. If (e.g.) anyone describes what betokens and produces health as being in a balanced state, we must not desist but go on to examine in what sense he has used the term 'balanced' in each case, e.g. if in the latter case it means that it is of the right amount to produce health, whereas in the former it means that it is such as to betoken what kind of state prevails.

Moreover, see if the terms cannot be compared as more or less or as in like degree, as is the case (e.g.) with a clear sound and a clear

15 argument, and a sharp flavour and a sharp sound. For neither are these things said to be clear or sharp in a like degree, nor yet is the one said to be clearer or sharper than the other. Clear, then, and sharp are homonymous. For synonyms are always comparable; for they will always hold either in like manner, or else in a greater degree in one case.

Now since of genera that are different without being subordinate
20 one to the other the differentiae also are different in kind, e.g. those of animal and knowledge (for the differentiae of these are different), look and see if the items falling under the same term are differentiae of genera that are different without being subordinate one to the other, as e.g. sharp is of a sound and a body. For being sharp differentiates sound from sound, and likewise also one body from another. Sharp,
25 then, is homonymous; for it forms differentiae of genera that are different without being subordinate one to the other.

Again, see if the items falling under the same term themselves have different differentiae, e.g. colour in bodies and colour in tunes; for the
30 differentiae of colour in bodies are dispersing the eye and compressing the eye, whereas colour in melodies has not the same differentiae. Colour, then, is homonymous; for things that are the same have the same differentiae.

Moreover, since the species is never the differentia of anything, look and see if one of the items falling under the same term is a species and another a differentia, as (e.g.) clear as applied to a body is a species
35 of colour, whereas in the case of a sound it is a differentia; for one sound is differentiated from another by being clear.

CHAPTER 16

Thus when a term is used in many ways, it may be investigated by
108ᵃ these and like means. The differences which things present to each other should be examined both in the genera themselves (e.g. 'Wherein does justice differ from courage, and wisdom from temperance?'—for all these belong to the same genus); and also from one genus to another, provided they are not too far apart (e.g. 'Wherein
5 does perception differ from knowledge?'); for in the case of genera that are very far apart, the differences are entirely obvious.

CHAPTER 17

Likeness should be studied, first, in the case of things belonging to different genera, the formula being: as one is to one thing, so is another to another (e.g. as knowledge stands to the object of knowledge, so is perception related to the object of perception), or: as one is in one thing, so is another in another (e.g. as sight is in the eye, so is intellect in the soul, and as is a calm in the sea, so is windlessness in the air). Practice is more especially needed in regard to terms that are far apart; for in the case of the rest, we shall be more easily able to see the points of likeness. We should also look at things which belong to the same genus, to see if any identical attribute belongs to them all, e.g. to a man and a horse and a dog; for in so far as they have any identical attribute, in so far they are alike.

CHAPTER 18

It is useful to have examined the number of uses of a term both for clearness' sake (for a man is more likely to know what it is he asserts, if it has been made clear to him how many uses it may have), and also with a view to ensuring that our deductions shall be in accordance with the actual facts and not addressed merely to the word used. For as long as it is not clear in how many ways a term is used, it is possible that the answerer and the questioner are not directing their minds upon the same thing; whereas when once it has been made clear how many uses there are, and also upon which of them the former directs his mind when he makes his assertion, the questioner would then look ridiculous if he failed to address his argument to this. It helps us also both to avoid being misled and to mislead by fallacies; for if we know the number of uses of a term, we shall certainly never be misled by fallacy, but shall know if the questioner fails to address his argument to the same point; and when we ourselves put the questions we shall be able to mislead him, if our answerer happens not to know the number of uses of our terms. This, however, is not possible in all cases, but only when of the many uses some are true and others are false. This manner of argument, however, does not belong properly to dialectic; dialecticians should therefore by all means beware of this kind of verbal discussion, unless any one is absolutely unable to discuss the subject before him in any other way.

The discovery of differences helps us both in deductions about sameness and difference, and also in recognizing what any particular thing is. That it helps us in deductions about sameness and difference

108ᵇ is clear; for when we have discovered a difference of any kind whatever between the objects before us, we shall already have proved that they are not the same; while it helps us in recognizing what a thing is,

5 because we usually distinguish the account that is proper to the substance of each particular thing by means of the differentiae that are appropriate to it.

The examination of likeness is useful with a view both to inductive arguments and to hypothetical deductions, and also with a view to the

10 rendering of definitions. It is useful for inductive arguments, because it is by means of an induction of particulars in cases that are alike that we claim to induce the universal; for it is not easy to do this if we do not know the points of likeness. It is useful for hypothetical deductions because it is a reputable opinion that among similars what is true of one is true also of the rest. If, then, with regard to any of them we are

15 well supplied with matter for a discussion, we shall secure a preliminary admission that however it is in these cases, so it is also in the case before us; then when we have proved the former we shall have proved, on the strength of the hypothesis, the matter before us as well; for we have first made the hypothesis that however it is in these cases, so it is also in the case before us, and have then produced the demonstration. It is useful for the rendering of definitions because, if

20 we are able to see what is the same in each individual case of it, we shall be at no loss when we define it; for of the common predicates that which is most definitely predicated in what the thing is is likely to be the genus. Likewise, also, in the case of objects widely divergent, the examination of likeness is useful for purposes of definition, e.g. the

25 sameness of a calm at sea, and windlessness in the air (each being a form of rest), and of a point on a line and the unit in number (each being a principle). If, then, we render as the genus what is common to all the cases, we shall get the credit of defining not inappropriately. Definition-mongers too nearly always render them in this way; for they declare the unit to be the principle of number, and the point the

30 principle of a line. It is clear, then, that they place them in that which is common to both as their genus.

The instruments, then, whereby deductions are effected, are these; the commonplace rules, for the observance of which the aforesaid instruments are useful, are as follows.

Natural Philosophy

PHYSICS*

BOOK I

CHAPTER I

IN all disciplines in which there is systematic knowledge of things 184ᵃ
with principles, causes, or elements, it arises from a grasp of those: we
think we have knowledge of a thing when we have found its primary
causes and principles, and followed it back to its elements. Clearly, 15
then, systematic knowledge of nature must start with an attempt to
settle questions about principles.

The natural course is to proceed from what is clearer and more
knowable to us, to what is more knowable and clear by nature; for the
two are not the same. Hence we must start thus with things which are
less clear by nature, but clearer to us, and move on to things which are 20
by nature clearer and more knowable. The things which are in the first
instance clear and plain to us are rather those which are compounded.
It is only later, through an analysis of these, that we come to know
elements and principles.

That is why we should proceed from the universal to the particular.
It is the whole which is more knowable by perception, and the univer- 25
sal is a sort of whole: it embraces many things as parts. Words stand in 184ᵇ
a somewhat similar relationship to accounts. A word like 'circle' indicates a whole indiscriminately, whereas the definition of a circle
divides it into particulars. And little children at first call all men father
and all women mother, only later coming to discriminate each of
them.

CHAPTER 2

There must be either one principle or more than one. If one, it must be
either unchangeable, the view of Parmenides and Melissus, or subject 15

* Books I–II. *Translation*: W. Charlton (Clarendon Aristotle Series, 1970); *Text*:
W. D. Ross (Oxford Classical Texts, 1950). Books III–IV. *Translation*: E. Hussey
(Clarendon Aristotle Series, 1983); *Text*: W. D. Ross (Oxford Classical Texts, 1950).
Book VIII. *Translation*: R. P. Hardie and R. K. Gaye, revised J. Barnes (Revised
Oxford Aristotle, 1984); *Text*: W. D. Ross (Oxford Classical Texts, 1950).

to change, the view of the physicists, of whom some make air and others water the primary principle. If there are more principles than one, they must be either limited in number—that is, there are either two, three, four, or some such definite number of them—or unlimited.

20 In the latter case, either they are all the same kind, and differ only in shape, as Democritus held, or they are different or even opposed in species. We are here raising the same question as those who ask how many things there are: they are really inquiring about the primary constituents of things, whether they are one or several, and if several, whether they are limited or unlimited in number; so they too are inquiring into the number of principles and elements.

25 Now the question whether what is is one and unchangeable, does not belong to a discussion of nature. Just as the geometer has nothing left
185ᵃ to say to the man who does away with the principles of geometry, but must refer him to a student of something else, or of what is common to all studies, so it is when we are inquiring into principles: there will be no principle left if what is is one thing only, and one in this way. A principle must be a principle of some thing or things. Discussing
5 whether what is is one in this way, is like discussing any other thesis advanced for the sake of having a discussion, like that of Heraclitus, or the view that what is is a single man. Or like exposing a quibble, such as is latent in the arguments of both Melissus and Parmenides: for both reason invalidly from false premises, but Melissus is the duller and more obvious: grant him one absurdity and he is able to infer the
10 rest—no great achievement.

For ourselves, we may take as a basic assumption, clear from a survey of particular cases, that natural things are some or all of them subject to change. And we should not try to expose all errors, but only
15 those reached by arguing from the relevant principles; just as it is the geometer's job to refute a quadrature by means of lunes, but not one like Antipho's. Nevertheless, since, though they are not writing about nature, the Monists happen to raise difficulties pertinent to it, we would do well, perhaps, to say a little about them; for the inquiry offers scope for philosophy.

20 The most appropriate way of all to begin is to point out that things are said to be in many ways, and then ask in what way they mean that all things are one. Do they mean that there is nothing but reality, or nothing but quantity or quality? And do they mean that everything is one single reality, as it might be one single man, or one single horse, or
25 one single soul, or, if all is quality, then one single quality, like pale, or

hot, or the like? These suggestions are all very different and untenable. If there is to be reality and quality and quantity, then whether these are apart from one another or not, there will be more things than one. And if everything is quality or quantity, then whether there is also reality or not, we run into absurdity, if, indeed, impossibility can be so called. Nothing can exist separately except a reality; everything else is said of a reality as underlying thing.

Melissus says that what is is unlimited. It follows that what is is some quantity. For the unlimited is unlimited in quantity, and no reality, quality, or affection can be unlimited, except by virtue of concurrence, there being also certain quantitative things. For quantity comes into the account of the unlimited, but reality and quality do not. If, then, there is reality and quantity as well, what is is twofold and not one; if there is just reality, so far from being unlimited, it will have no magnitude at all; if it had, there would be some quantity.

Again, as things are said to be, so they are said to be one, in many ways; so let us see in what way the universe is supposed to be one. A thing is called one if it is a continuum, or if it is indivisible, and we also call things one if one and the same account is given of what the being of each would be: so, for instance, wine and the grape.

Now if the universe is continuous, the one will be many; for continua are divisible without limit. (There is a difficulty about parts and wholes, though perhaps it is a problem on its own and not relevant to the present discussion: are the parts and the whole one thing or several, and in what way are they one or several, and if several, in what way are they several? And what about the parts which are not continuous? And is each indivisibly one with the whole, since they will be the same with themselves also?)

Is the universe one, then, in that it is indivisible? Then nothing will have any quantity or quality, and what is will be neither unlimited, as Melissus says, nor limited, as Parmenides prefers. For it is limits which are indivisible, not limited things.

If, however, all things are one in account, like raiment and apparel, they will find themselves in the position of Heraclitus. The being of good and the being of bad, of good and not good, will be the same, so that good and not good, man and horse, will be the same, and the thesis under discussion will no longer be that all things are one, but that they are nothing at all. And the being of a certain quality and the being of a certain quantity will be the same.

Thinkers of the more recent past also were much agitated lest

things might turn out to be both one and many at the same time. Some,
like Lycophron, did away with the word 'is'; others sought to remodel
the language, and replace 'That man is pale' 'That man is walking', by
30   'That man pales' 'That man walks', for fear that by inserting 'is' they
would render the one many—as if things were said to be or be one in
only one way. Things, however, are many, either in account (as the
being of pale is different from the being of a musician, though the
same thing may be both: so the one is many), or by division, like the
186ᵃ   parts of a whole. At this point they got stuck, and began to admit that
the one was many; as if it were not possible for the same thing to be
both one and many, so long as the two are not opposed: a thing can be
one in possibility and in actuality.

CHAPTER 5

188ᵃ   That opposites are principles is universally agreed: by those who say
20   that the universe is one and unchanging (for Parmenides in effect
makes hot and cold principles, though he calls them fire and earth), by
those who make use of dense and rare, and by Democritus. Democritus posits the full and the empty, saying that the one is present as
that which is, and the other as that which is not; he also makes use of
position, shape, and arrangement, and these are genera of opposites:
25   position comprises above and below, in front and behind; shape comprises angular and smooth, straight and curved. Clearly, then, all in
some way agree that opposites are the principles. And that is plausible.
For the principles must come neither from one another nor from anything else, and everything else must come from them. Primary opposites fulfil these conditions: because they are primary they do not
30   come from anything else, and because they are opposite they do not
come from one another. But we must also see what emerges from
logical considerations.
Our first point must be that nothing whatever is by nature such as to
do or undergo any chance thing through the agency of any chance
thing, nor does anything come to be out of just anything, unless you
35   take a case of concurrence. For how could pale come to be out of
knowing music, unless the knowing music supervenes on the not pale
or the dark? Pale comes to be out of not pale—not, that is, out of just
188ᵇ   anything other than pale, but out of dark or something between the
two; and knowing music comes to be out of not knowing music, that is,
not out of just anything other than knowing music, but out of ignorant

of music, or something in between if there is anything in between. And a thing does not pass away into just anything in the first instance; thus the pale does not pass away into the knowing music, except by virtue of concurrence, but into the not pale, and not into any chance thing other than the pale, but into the dark or something in between. Similarly the knowing music passes away into the not knowing music, and not into any chance thing other than the knowing music, but into the ignorant of music or something in between if there is anything in between. It is the same in all other cases, since the same account holds for things which are not simple but composite, though we do not notice, because the opposed dispositions have no name. It is necessary that the united should always come to be out of disunited, and the disunited out of united, and that the united should pass away into disunion, and not just any chance disunion, but that opposed to the preceding union. And it makes no difference whether we speak of union, or arrangement, or composition: plainly the same account holds. And a house, a statue, what you please, comes to be in the same way. The house comes to be out of the not being put together but being dispersed thus of these materials, and the statue or anything else which is shaped, arises out of shapelessness. Every one of these things is an arrangement or composition.

If this is true, everything which comes to be comes to be out of, and everything which passes away passes away into, its opposite or something in between. And the things in between come out of the opposites—thus colours come out of pale and dark. So the things which come to be naturally all are or are out of opposites.

So far most thinkers are prepared to go along with us, as I said above. For they all represent their elements and what they call their principles as opposites, even if they give no reason for doing so, as though the truth itself were forcing them on. They differ among themselves in that some take pairs which are prior and some take pairs which are posterior, and some choose pairs which are more readily known with the aid of an account, and some choose pairs which are more readily known by perception: for some put forward hot and cold as the causes of coming to be, and others wet and dry, and others odd and even or strife and love, and these differ in the manner just stated. So the pairs they propose are in a way the same and different: they are different, as indeed they are generally thought to be, but by analogy the same. For they are taken from the same list, some of the opposites being wider in extent and others included under them. This is how it is

that the principles put forward are the same and different, and some
better and some worse; and some, as we said, more easily known with
5   the aid of an account, like the great and the small, and others more
easily known by perception, like the rare and the dense—for that
which is universal is more easily known in the former way, since
accounts are of what is universal, and that which is particular in the
latter, since perception is of particulars.

10   That the principles, then, must be opposites is plain.

CHAPTER 6

We must next say whether they are two, three, or more in number.

They cannot be one, since opposites are not one and the same; and
they cannot be unlimited, since if they were, what is would be
unknowable, since there is one opposition in any one kind of thing,
and reality is one such kind, and since we can get on with a limited
15   number, and it is better to use a limited, like Empedocles, than an
unlimited. Empedocles claims to do everything Anaxagoras can do
with his unlimited plurality. Further, some pairs of opposites are prior
to others, and some, like sweet and bitter, pale and dark, arise from
others, whereas principles ought to be constant.

20   That shows that they can be neither one nor unlimited in number.
But if they are limited, there is an argument for not making them only
two. For it is hard to see how density could be by nature such as to act
on rarity or vice versa, and similarly whatever the opposition: love
25   does not gather up strife and make something out of it, nor does strife
act thus with love, but both must act on a third thing distinct from
them. And some people enlist even more principles to constitute the
nature of things.

We may also run into the following difficulty if we do not posit some
additional nature to underlie the opposites. We never see opposites
30   serving as the reality of anything, and yet a principle ought not to be
something said of some underlying thing. If it is, the principle will
itself have a principle, for that which underlies is a principle, and is
thought to be prior to that which is said of it.

Again, we do not say that one reality is the opposite of another. How,
then, can a reality be constituted by things which are not realities? And
how can that which is not a reality be prior to that which is?

35   Anyone, then, who accepts both the earlier argument and this, must,
189^b if he is to preserve both, posit some third thing which underlies, as do

those who say that the universe is one single nature, such as water or fire or something between the two. The last suggestion is the most hopeful, since fire, earth, air, and water are already tangled up with oppositions. Those, then, are not without reason, who make the underlying thing different from any of these, or, if one of them, air, since that has the least perceptible differentiating features. After it comes water. Anyhow, all shape their one stuff with the opposites, with density and rarity and the more and the less; and these clearly, as I said above, are, in general terms, excess and defect. It does not seem to be at all a novel idea, that the principles of things are the one, excess and defect, though it has been put forward in different ways: earlier inquirers made the single principle passive and the pair active, whilst certain more recent thinkers prefer to turn it round and say that it is the one which is active and the pair passive.

That there are as many as three elements, then, may seem arguable to anyone guided by these and similar considerations; but at three we might draw the line. The single one is enough for being acted on; and if there are four, giving us two oppositions, we shall have to supply a further intermediate nature for each separately. Or if there are two pairs and they can produce things out of one another, one of the oppositions will be otiose. Moreover, there cannot be more than one primary opposition. Reality is a single kind of thing, so that the principles can differ only in being prior or posterior to one another, and not in kind. In any one kind there is always one opposition, and all oppositions seem to reduce to one.

That the elements, then, are neither one in number, nor more than two or three, is plain; but whether they are two or three is, as I have said, a very difficult question.

CHAPTER 7

This is how I tackle it myself. I shall be dealing first with coming to be in general, since the natural procedure is first to say what is common to all cases, and only then to consider the peculiarities of each.

When we say that one thing comes to be out of another, or that something comes to be out of something different, we may be talking either about what is simple or about what is compound. Let me explain. A man can come to be knowing music, and also the not knowing music can come to be knowing music, or the not knowing music man a man knowing music. I call the man and the not knowing music simple coming-to-be things, and the knowing music a simple thing which comes to be. When we say that the not knowing music man comes to be a knowing music man, both the coming-to-be thing and that which comes to be are compound.

5   In some of these cases we say, not just that this comes to be, but that this comes to be out of this—for instance, knowing music comes to be out of not knowing music. But not in all: knowing music does not come to be out of man, but the man comes to be knowing music.

Of what we call the simple coming-to-be things, one remains when
10   it comes to be, and the other does not. The man remains and is a man when he comes to be knowing music, but the not knowing music and the ignorant of music do not remain, either by themselves or as components.

These distinctions having been made, in all cases of coming to be, if they are looked at as I suggest, this may be taken as definite, that there must always be something underlying which is the coming-to-be
15   thing, and this, even if it is one in number, is not one in form. (By 'in form' I mean the same as 'in account'.) The being of a man is not the same as the being of ignorant of music. And the one remains and the other does not. That which is not opposed remains—the man
20   remains—but the not knowing music and the ignorant of music do not remain, and neither does the compound of the two, the ignorant of music man.

We say that something comes to be out of something, and not that something comes to be something, chiefly in connection with that which does not remain. Thus we say that knowing music comes to be out of not knowing music, but we do not say that it comes to be out of
25   man. Though we sometimes speak thus about things that do remain: we say that a statue comes to be out of bronze, not that bronze comes to be a statue. But we speak in both ways of that which comes to be out of what is opposed to it and does not remain: we say both 'this comes to be out of this' and 'this comes to be this'. Out of ignorant of music comes to be knowing music, and ignorant of music comes to be knowing music. Hence it is the same with the compound; we say both that
30   out of a man who is ignorant of music, and that a man who is ignorant of music, comes to be one who knows music.

Things are said to come to be in many ways, and some things are said, not to come to be, but to come to be something, while only realities are said simply to come to be. In the case of other things it is plain that there must be something underlying which is the coming-

to-be thing—for when a quantity, quality, relation, [time,][1] or place   35
comes to be, it is *of* an underlying thing, since it is only realities which
are not said of anything further, and all other things are of realities.   190ᵇ
But that realities too, and whatever things simply are, come to be out
of something underlying, will, if you look attentively, become plain.
There is always something which underlies, out of which the thing
comes to be, as plants and animals come to be out of seed. The things
which simply come to be do so some of them by change of shape, like a   5
statue, some by addition, like things which grow, some by subtraction,
as a Hermes comes to be out of the stone, some by composition, like a
house, some by alteration, like things which change in respect of their
matter. All things which come to be like this plainly come to be out of
underlying things.

From what has been said, then, it is clear that that which comes to   10
be is always composite, and there is one thing which comes to be, and
another which comes to be this, and the latter is twofold: either the
underlying thing, or the thing which is opposed. By that which is
opposed, I mean the ignorant of music, by that which underlies, the
man; and shapelessness, formlessness, disarray are opposed, and the   15
bronze, the stone, the gold underlie.

Plainly then if there are causes and principles of things which are
due to nature, out of which they primarily are and have come to be not
by virtue of concurrence, but each as we say when we give its reality,   20
everything comes to be out of the underlying thing and the form. For
the knowing music man is composed in a way of man and knowing
music. Analyses are into accounts of these two. So it is clear that things
which come to be come to be out of them. The underlying thing,
however, though one in number, is two in form. On the one hand there
is the man, the gold, and in general the measurable matter; this is more   25
of a this thing here, and it is not by virtue of concurrence that the thing
which comes to be comes to be from this. On the other hand there is
the lack or opposition, which is supervenient. As for the form, it is one:
it is the arrangement, or the knowledge of music, or some other thing
said of something in the same way. Hence from one angle we must say
that the principles are two, and from another that they are three; and   30
from one angle they are the opposites—as when we say that they are
the knowing music and the ignorant of music, or the hot and the cold,
or the united and the disunited—but from another angle not, for

---

[1] Excised by W. D. Ross.

opposites cannot be acted upon by one another. This difficulty too is resolved by the fact that the underlying thing is something else, and 35 that other thing is not an opposite. So in one way the principles are not more numerous than the opposites, but are, you might say, two in 191ᵃ number; but they are not two in every way, because of the diverse being which belongs to them, but three. (For the being of a man is different from the being of ignorant of music, and the being of shapeless from the being of bronze.)

How many principles there are of natural things, and in what way they are so many, has now been said. It is clear that there must be 5 something to underlie the opposites, and that the opposites must be two in number. Yet in another way that is not necessary. One of the opposites, by its absence and presence, will suffice to effect the change.

As for the underlying nature, it must be grasped by analogy. As bronze stands to a statue, or wood to a bed, or the formless before it 10 acquires a form to anything else which has a definite form, so this stands to a reality, to a this thing here, to what is. This, then is one principle, though it neither is, nor is one, in the same way as a this thing here; another principle is that of which we give the account; and there is also the opposite of this, the lack. In what way these principles 15 are two, and in what way more than two, has been said above. The theory originally was that the only principles were the opposites; then that there had to be something else to underlie them, making the principles three; on our present showing it is plain what sort of opposites are involved, how the principles stand to one another, and what the underlying thing is. Whether the form or the underlying thing has 20 the better claim to be called the reality, is still obscure; but that the principles are three, and how, and what the manner of them is, is clear. So much on how many and what the principles are.

CHAPTER 8

That this is the only way of resolving the difficulty felt by thinkers of earlier times must be our next point. The first people to philosophize 25 about the nature and truth of things got so to speak side-tracked or driven off course by inexperience, and said that nothing comes to be or passes away, because whatever comes to be must do so either out of something which is, or out of something which is not, and neither is 30 possible. What is cannot come to be, since it is already, and nothing

can come to be out of what is not, since there must be something
underlying. And thus inflating the consequences of this, they deny a
plurality of things altogether, and say that there is nothing but 'what is,
itself'.

They embraced this opinion for the reasons given. We, on the other
hand, say that it is in one way no different, that something should
come to be out of what is or is not, or that what is or is not should act   35
on or be acted on by something, or come to be any particular thing,
than that a doctor should act on or be acted on by something, or that   191ᵇ
anything should be or come to be out of a doctor. By this last we may
mean two things, so clearly it is the same when we say that something
is out of something which is, and that what is acts or is acted on. A
doctor builds a house, not as a doctor, but as a builder, and comes to
be pale, not as a doctor, but as dark. But he doctors and comes to be   5
ignorant of medicine as a doctor. Now we must properly say that a
doctor acts or is acted on, or that something comes to be out of a
doctor, only if it is as a doctor that he does or undergoes or comes to be
this. So clearly to say that something comes to be out of what is not,
is to say that it does so out of what is not, as something which is not.
They gave up through failing to draw this distinction, and from that   10
mistake passed to the greater one of supposing that nothing comes to
be or (apart from what is, itself) is, thus doing away with coming to
be altogether. We too say that nothing comes to be simply out of
what is not; but that things do come to be in a way out of what is not,
namely by virtue of concurrence. A thing can come to be out of the   15
lack, which in itself is something which is not, and is not a
constituent. This, however, makes people stare, and it is thought
impossible that anything should come to be in this way, out of what
is not.

Similarly there can be no coming to be out of what is or of what is,
except by virtue of concurrence. In that way, however, this too can
come about, just as if animal came to be out of animal and animal of a   20
particular sort out of animal of a particular sort, for instance dog out of
dog or horse out of horse. The dog would come to be, not only out of a
particular sort of animal, but out of animal; not, however, as animal,
for that belongs already. If a particular sort of animal is to come to be,
not by virtue of concurrence, it will not be out of animal, and if a particular sort of thing which is, it will not be out of thing which is; nor   25
out of thing which is not. We have already said what it means to say
that something comes to be out of what is not: it means out of what is

not, as something which is not. Further, there is no violation here of the principle that everything either is or is not.

That is one way of handling the matter; another is to point out that the same things may be spoken of either as possible or as actual. That, however, is dealt with in greater detail elsewhere.

30   So, as we have said, the difficulties are resolved, by which people were driven to do away with some of the things mentioned. For that was why the earlier thinkers too were diverted so far from the path to coming to be, passing away, and change generally; when this nature, if they had seen it, would have put them right.

CHAPTER 9

35   Others, indeed, have touched its surface, but they did not go deep enough. In the first place, they agree that it is in a general way the case
192ᵃ that a thing comes to be out of what is not, and that so far Parmenides was right. And then it appears to them that if it is one in number, it is only one in possibility, which is not at all the same thing. We for our part say that matter and lack are different, and that the one, the matter,
5   by virtue of concurrence is not, but is near to reality and a reality in a way, whilst the other, the lack, in itself is not, and is not a reality at all. According to them, on the other hand, the great and the small, whether together or separate, are what is not in the same way. So their three things and ours are completely different. They got as far as see-
10 ing that there must be an underlying nature, but they made it one. And if someone calls it a pair, viz. great and small, he is still doing the same thing, for he overlooked the other nature. The one remains, joint cause with the form of the things which come to be, as it were a
15 mother. The other half of the opposition you might often imagine, if you focus on its evil tendency, to be totally non-existent. Given that there is one thing which is divine and good and yearned for, our sug-gestion is that there is one thing which is opposite to this, and another which is by nature such as to yearn and reach out for it in accordance with its own nature. They, however, will find that the opposite is
20 reaching out for its own destruction. But the truth is that neither can the form yearn for itself, since it is in need of nothing, nor can its opposite yearn for it, since opposites are mutually destructive, but it is the matter which does the yearning. You might say that it yearns as the female for the male and as the base for the beautiful; except that it is neither base nor female, except by virtue of concurrence.

And in one way it passes away and comes to be, and in another not. 25
Considered as that in which, it does in itself pass away [for that which
passes away, the lack, is in it].[2] Considered, however, as possible, it
does not in itself pass away, but can neither be brought to be nor
destroyed. If it came to be, there would have to be something underlying, out of which, as a constituent, it came to be; that, however, is the 30
material nature itself, for by matter I mean that primary underlying
thing in each case, out of which as a constituent and not by virtue of
concurrence something comes to be; so it would have to be before it
had come to be. And if it passed away, this is what it would ultimately
arrive at, so it would have passed away before it had passed away.

As for the formal principle, whether such principles are one or
many, and of what sort or sorts they are, are questions to be treated in 35
detail in first philosophy, so we may leave them aside until we come to
that. In what follows we shall be speaking of natural forms which can
pass away.

That there are principles, then, and what and how many they are,
we may take as settled in this way. Let us now proceed, making a fresh
start.

BOOK II

CHAPTER I

SOME things are due to nature; for others there are other causes. Of 192ᵇ
the former sort are animals and their parts, plants, and simple bodies 10
like earth, fire, air, and water—for we say that these and things like
them are due to nature. All these things plainly differ from things
which are not constituted naturally: each has in itself a source of
change and staying unchanged, whether in respect of place, or growth 15
and decay, or alteration. A bed, on the other hand, or a coat, or anything else of that sort, considered as satisfying such a description, and
in so far as it is the outcome of art, has no innate tendency to change,
though considered as concurrently made of stone or earth or a mixture
of the two, and in so far as it is such, it has. This suggests that nature is 20
a sort of source and cause of change and remaining unchanged in that
to which it belongs primarily and of itself, that is, not by virtue of

---

[2] Bracketed by the translator as an intrusion into the text.

concurrence. What do I mean by that qualification? Well, a man who is a doctor might come to be a cause of health in himself. Still, in so far as he is healed he does not possess the art of medicine, but being a doctor and being healed merely concur in the same person. Were the matter otherwise, the roles would not be separable.

Similarly with other things which are made. They none of them have in themselves the source of their making, but in some cases, such as that of a house or anything else made by human hands, the source is in something else and external, whilst in others the source is in the thing, but not in the thing of itself, i.e. when the thing comes to be a cause to itself by virtue of concurrence.

Nature, then, is what has been said, and anything which has a source of this sort, has a nature. Such a thing is always a reality; for it is an underlying thing, and nature is always in an underlying thing. It is in accordance with nature, and so is anything which belongs to it of itself, as moving upwards belongs to fire—for that neither is a nature nor has a nature, but is due to nature and in accordance with nature.

We have now said what nature is and what we mean by that which is due to nature and in accordance with nature. That there is such a thing as nature, it would be ridiculous to try to show; for it is plain that many things are of the sort just described. To show what is plain by what is obscure is a sign of inability to discriminate between what is self-evident and what is not—and it is certainly possible to be so placed: a man blind from birth would have to make inferences about colours. For such people discussion must be about the words only, and nothing is understood.

Some people think that the nature and reality of a thing which is due to nature is the primary constituent present in it, something unformed in itself. Thus in a bed it would be the wood, in a statue the bronze. It is an indication of this, says Antipho, that if you bury a bed, and the decomposition gets the ability to send up a shoot, what comes up will not be a bed but wood: this seems to show that the disposition of parts customary for beds and the artistry belong only by virtue of concurrence, and that the reality is that which persists uninterruptedly while being affected in these ways. And if the particular kinds of material too are related to something else in the same way, if, for instance, bronze and gold stand thus to water, and bone and wood to earth, and so on, the thing to which they stand in this relation will be their nature and reality. Hence fire, earth, air, and water have been held to be the nature of things, some people choosing just one for this role, some several, and some making use of all. Those who fix on some such element or elements represent it or them as the entire reality, and say that other things are merely affections, states, or dispositions; and these elements are all held to be imperishable in that they do not change out of themselves, whilst other things come to be and pass away as often as you please. 25

That is one way of using the word 'nature': for the primary underlying matter in each case, of things which have in themselves a source of their movements and changes. It is also used for the shape and form which accord with a thing's account. Just as that which is in accordance with art and artificial is called art, so that which is in accordance with nature and natural is called nature. And as in the one case we would not yet say that a thing is at all in accordance with art, or that it is art, if it is a bed only in possibility, and has not yet the form of a bed, so with things constituted naturally: that which is flesh or bone only in possibility, before it acquires the form which accords with the account by which we define what flesh or bone is, does not yet have its proper nature, and is not a thing due to nature. So there is another way of speaking, according to which nature is the shape and form of things which have in themselves a source of their changes, something which is not separable except in respect of its account. Things which consist of this and the matter together, such as men, are not themselves natures, but are due to nature. 30

The form has a better claim than the matter to be called nature. For we call a thing something, when it is that thing in actuality, rather than just in possibility.

Further, men come to be from men, but not beds from beds. That is why people say that the nature of a bed is not the shape but the wood, since if it sprouts, what comes to be is wood and not a bed. But if this shows that the wood is nature, nature is form too; for men come to be from men. 10

Again, nature in the sense in which the word is used for a process proceeds towards nature. It is not like doctoring, which has as its end not the art of medicine but health. Doctoring must proceed from the art of medicine, not towards it. But the process of growth does not stand in this relation to nature: that which is growing, as such, is proceeding from something to something. What, then, is it which is growing? Not the thing it is growing out of, but the thing it is growing into. So the form is nature. 15

Things may be called form and nature in two ways, for the lack is a

20   form in a way. But whether or not there is a lack and an opposite
     involved in cases of simply coming to be, we must consider later.

                              CHAPTER 2

     Having distinguished the various things which are called nature, we
     must go on to consider how the student of mathematics differs from
     the student of nature—for natural bodies have planes, solids, lengths,
25   and points, which are the business of the mathematician. And again, is
     astronomy a branch of the study of nature, or a separate subject? It
     would be absurd if the student of nature were expected to know what
     the sun or moon is, but not to know any of the things which of them-
     selves they have supervening on them, especially as it is plain that
     those who discuss nature do also discuss the shape of the sun and
30   moon, and whether the earth and the cosmos are spherical or not.
         Both the student of nature and the mathematician deal with these
     things; but the mathematician does not consider them as boundaries
     of natural bodies. Nor does he consider things which supervene as
     supervening on such bodies. That is why he separates them; for they
35   are separable in thought from change, and it makes no difference; no
     error results. Those who talk about ideas do not notice that they too
194ᵃ are doing this: they separate physical things though they are less
     separable than the objects of mathematics. That becomes clear if you
     try to define the objects and the things which supervene in each class.
     Odd and even, straight and curved, number, line, and shape, can be
5   defined without change but flesh, bone, and man cannot. They are like
     snub nose, not like curved. The point is clear also from those branches
     of mathematics which come nearest to the study of nature, like optics,
     harmonics, and astronomy. They are in a way the reverse of geometry.
10   Geometry considers natural lines, but not as natural; optics treats of
     mathematical lines, but considers them not as mathematical but as
     natural.
         Since there are two sorts of thing called nature, form and matter,
     we should proceed as if we were inquiring what snubness is: we should
     consider things neither without their matter nor in accordance with
15   their matter. For it is certainly a problem, if there are two sorts of
     nature, which of them the student of nature is concerned with. Per-
     haps with that which consists of the two together. In that case he will
     be concerned with both. Will both, then, fall under the same study, or
     each under a different? If we had regard to the early thinkers, it might

seem that the study of nature is the study of matter, for Empedocles and Democritus touched only very superficially on form and what the being would be. But if art imitates nature, and it belongs to the same branch of knowledge to know the form and to know the matter up to a point (thus the doctor has knowledge of health, and also of bile and phlegm, the things in which health resides; and the builder knows the form of a house, and also the matter—that it is bricks and beams; and it is the same with other arts), then it belongs to the study of nature to know both sorts of nature.

Further, it belongs to the same study to know the end or what something is for, and to know whatever is for that end. Now nature is an end and what something is for. For whenever there is a definite end to a continuous change, that last thing is also what it is for; whence the comical sally in the play 'He has reached the end for which he was born'—for the end should not be just any last thing, but the best.

Indeed, the arts make their matter, that is, they either bring it into being altogether, or render it good to work with; and we use all things as if they were there for us. (For we too are ends of a sort. As was said in the *De Philosophia*, there are two sorts of thing which a thing may be said to be for.) There are two arts which control the matter and involve knowledge, the art of using, and the art which directs the making. Hence the art of using too is directive in a way, but is different in that it involves knowledge of the form, whilst the art which is directive in that it is the art of making involves knowledge of the matter. The steersman knows and prescribes what the form for a rudder is, and the carpenter knows out of what sort of wood and by what changes it will be made. In the case, then, of artefacts we make the matter for the work to be done, whilst in the case of natural objects it is there already.

Again, matter is something relative to something, for the matter varies with the form.

Up to what point, then, should the student of nature know the forms of things and what they are? Perhaps he should be like the doctor and the smith, whose knowledge of sinews and bronze extend only to what they are for; and he should confine himself to things which are separable in form, but which are in matter. For a man owes his birth to another man and to the sun. What it is which is separable, and how things are with it, it is the work of first philosophy to determine.

CHAPTER 3

These distinctions having been drawn, we must see if we can characterize and enumerate the various sorts of cause. For since the aim of
our investigation is knowledge, and we think we have knowledge of a
20   thing only when we can answer the question about it 'On account of
what?' and that is to grasp the primary cause—it is clear that we must
do this over coming to be, passing away, and all natural change; so
that, knowing their sources, we may try to bring all particular objects
of inquiry back to them.

According to one way of speaking, that out of which as a constituent
a thing comes to be is called a cause; for example, the bronze and the
25   silver and their genera would be the causes respectively of a statue and
a loving-cup. According to another, the form or model is a cause; this
is the account of what the being would be, and its genera—thus the
cause of an octave is the ratio of two to one, and more generally
number—and the parts which come into the account. Again, there is
30   the primary source of the change or the staying unchanged: for
example, the man who has deliberated is a cause, the father is a cause
of the child, and in general that which makes something of that which
is made, and that which changes something of that which is changed.
And again, a thing may be a cause as the end. That is what something
is for, as health might be what a walk is for. On account of what does
he walk? We answer 'To keep fit' and think that, in saying that, we
35   have given the cause. And anything which, the change being effected
by something else, comes to be on the way to the end, as slimness,
195ᵃ   purging, drugs, and surgical instruments come to be as means to
health: all these are for the end, but differ in that the former are works
and the latter tools.

That is a rough enumeration of the things which are called causes.
Since many different things are called causes, it follows that many dif-
5   ferent things can all be causes, and not by virtue of concurrence, of the
same thing. Thus the art of statue-making and the bronze are both
causes of a statue, and causes of it, not in so far as it is anything else,
but as a statue; they are not, however, causes in the same way, but the
latter is a cause as matter, and the former as that from which the
change proceeds. And sometimes two things are causes each of the
other; thus labour is the cause of strength, and strength of labour; not,
10   however, in the same way, but the one is a cause as the end, and the
other as source of change. And again, the same thing is the cause of

opposites. That which, by being present, is the cause of so and so, is sometimes held responsible by its absence for the opposite; thus the loss of a ship is set down to the absence of the steersman, whose presence would have been the cause of its being saved.

All the causes we have mentioned fall into four especially plain 15 groups. Letters are the cause of syllables, their matter of artefacts, fire and the like of bodies, their parts of wholes, and the hypotheses of the conclusion, as that out of which; and the one lot, the parts and so on, are causes as the underlying thing, whilst the other lot, the whole, the 20 composition, and the form, are causes as what the being would be. The seed, the doctor, the man who has deliberated, and in general the maker, are all things from which the change or staying put has its source. And there are the things which stand to the rest as their end and good; for what the other things are for tends to be best and their end. It may be taken as making no difference whether we call it good 25 or apparently good.

That, then, is how many species of cause there are. There are a good many ways in which something can be a cause, but these too may be brought under comparatively few heads. Many different things are said to be causes, and even among causes of the same species some are 30 prior and some posterior; thus the cause of health is a doctor and a man of skill, the cause of an octave is double and number, and always there are the particulars and the genera which embrace them. And some are causes as concurrent, or as the genera of these; thus the cause of a statue is in one way a sculptor and in another Polyclitus, in that being Polyclitus supervenes on the sculptor. Similarly that which 35 embraces what supervenes; thus a man, or more generally an animal, 195^{b} might be the cause of a statue. And of causes by concurrence too, some are further and some nearer, as when we might call a pale man or a musician the cause of the statue. And both proper causes and causes by virtue of concurrence may be spoken of either as able to cause or as actually causing; thus the cause of the building of a house may be 5 called a builder or a builder who is building.

Similarly with the things to which the causes stand as causes. A thing is said to stand as cause to this statue, or to a statue, or more generally to an image; or to this bronze, or to bronze, or more generally to matter. And the same with things which supervene. And a com- 10 bination, either of causes or of things to which they stand as causes, may be given, as when we say, not that the cause is Polyclitus or that it is a sculptor, but that it is the sculptor Polyclitus.

All this comes to six things, which may each be spoken of in two ways. There is the particular and the general, the concurrent and the genus to which the concurrent belongs, and these may be given singly or in combination. And any of them may be actual or possible. What difference does that make? Those causes which are particular and actual, are and are not simultaneously with the things of which they are causes. Thus there is a particular man actually doctoring as long as there is a particular man actually being healed, and a particular man actually building as long as there is a particular building actually being built. With causes which are merely possible, the same does not always hold: the builder and the house do not pass away at the same time.

As elsewhere, so here, we should look always for the topmost cause of each thing. Thus a man builds because he is a builder, and a builder builds in accordance with the art of building; the art of building, then, is the prior cause, and similarly in all cases. Again, we should look for kinds of cause for kinds of thing, and particular causes for particular things. Thus a sculptor is the cause of a statue, and this sculptor here of this statue here. And we should look for abilities as causes for things which are possible, and things actually causing for things which are being actualized.

On how many causes there are, and in what ways they are causes, let these distinctions suffice.

CHAPTER 4

Luck and the automatic[3] are reckoned as causes, and we say that many things are and come to be on account of them. We must see, then, in what way luck and the automatic fit into our causes, whether luck and the automatic are the same or different, and in general what they are.

Some people wonder even whether there are any such things or not. They say that nothing comes to be as an outcome of luck, but that there is a definite cause of everything which we say comes to be as an automatic outcome or as an outcome of luck. Thus when we say that a man as the outcome of luck came into the market-place, and found there someone he wished but did not expect to find, they claim that the cause was wishing to go and attend the market. And similarly with other things which are said to be the outcome of luck: it is always pos-

---

[3] Usually translated 'spontaneous'.

sible to find some cause for them other than luck; since if there were such a thing as luck, it would seem to be really very absurd, and one might wonder why it is that none of the sages of the past who discussed the causes connected with coming to be and passing away gave any 10 distinct account of luck; but it seems that they too thought that nothing is the outcome of luck.

Yet this too is amazing. Many things come to be, and many things are, as the outcome of luck or as an automatic outcome; and though not unaware that, as the old saw which does away with luck says, everything which comes to be can be referred back to some cause, still, 15 all men say that some things are an outcome of luck, and others not. Hence they ought to have made mention of it somehow or other. But they cannot be said even to have equated it with any of the causes they recognized, love or strife or mind or fire or the like. Either way, then, it is absurd, whether they did not think there was any such thing, or did but left it aside. Especially when they sometimes make use of it, as 20 Empedocles does when he says that air is separated out on top not invariably, but as luck will have it. At any rate he says in his *Cosmogony*: 'Thus chanced it to be running then, oft chancing otherwise.' And he says that the parts of animals mostly came to be as the outcome of luck.

There are others who make the automatic responsible for our own 25 heavens and for all the cosmic systems. They say it was an automatic outcome that the Swirl came to be, and the change which separated out and established the universe in its present arrangement. Yet this itself may excite amazement. On the one hand they hold that animals and plants neither come to be nor are as the outcome of luck, but that 30 their cause is nature or mind or something like that—for it is not as luck will have it, what comes to be from a particular seed, but an olive-tree comes to be from one sort and a man from another—but on the other hand they say that the heavens and the most divine of the things we see, came to be as an automatic outcome, without there being any such cause as animals and plants have. If that is so, that very thing is 35 worthy of attention, and it would have been well to say something 196ᵇ about it. For not only is what they say absurd in other respects, but it is still more absurd for them to say it when they see nothing in the heavens coming to be as an automatic outcome, whilst in the things which are supposed not to be the outcome of luck they see many things supervening as the outcome of luck. It might have been 5 expected to be the other way round.

There are also some who think that luck is indeed a cause, but one inscrutable to human thought, because it is divine or supernatural in character. So we must examine the automatic and luck, and see what each is, whether they are the same or different, and what their place is among the causes we have distinguished.

CHAPTER 5

10   In the first place, then, since we see some things always, and others for the most part, coming to be in the same way, it is plain that luck or its outcome is not called the cause of either of these—of that which is of necessity and always, or of that which is for the most part. But since there are other things which come to be besides these, and all men say

15   that they are the outcome of luck, plainly there is such a thing as luck and the automatic; for we know that things of this sort are the outcome of luck, and that the outcome of luck is things of this sort.

Of things which come to be, some come to be for something, and some do not. Of the former, some are in accordance with choice and some are not, but both are among things which are for something.

20   Clearly, then, also among things which are neither necessary nor for the most part, there are some to which it can belong to be for something. Anything which might be done as an outcome of thought or nature is for something. Whenever something like this comes to be by virtue of concurrence, we say that it is the outcome of luck. For as a thing is, so it can be a cause, either by itself or by virtue of concur-

25   rence. Thus that which can build is by itself the cause of a house, but that which is pale or knows music is a cause by virtue of concurrence. That which by itself is a cause is determinate, but that which is a cause by virtue of concurrence is indeterminate; for an unlimited number of things may concur in the one.

As has been said, then, whenever this happens over something

30   which comes to be for something, it is said to be an automatic outcome or the outcome of luck. (The difference between these two we shall have to determine later; for the moment this much is plain, that both are to be found among things which are for something.) Thus the man would have come for the purpose of geting back the money when his debtor was collecting contributions, if he had known; in fact, he did

35   not come for this purpose, but it happened concurrently that he came, and did what was for getting back the money. And that, though he used

197ᵃ   to go to the place neither for the most part nor necessarily. The end, the recovery, is not one of the causes in him, but it is an object of choice and an outcome of thought. And in this case the man's coming is said to be the outcome of luck, whilst if he had chosen and come for this purpose, or used to come always or for the most part, it would not be called the outcome of luck. Clearly, then, luck is a cause by virtue of concurrence in connection with those among things for something which are objects of choice. Hence thought and luck have the same field, for choice involves thought.

Necessarily, then, the causes from which an outcome of luck might come to be are indeterminate. That is why luck is thought to be an indeterminate sort of thing and inscrutable to men, and at the same time there is a way in which it might be thought that nothing comes to be as the outcome of luck. For all these things are rightly said, as might be expected. There is a way in which things come to be as the outcome of luck: they come to be by virtue of concurrence, and luck is a concurrent cause. But simply, it is the cause of nothing. As in the case of a house the cause is a builder, but by virtue of concurrence a flute-player, so in the case of the man who came and recovered the money, but did not come for that purpose, an unlimited number of things can be causes by concurrence. He might have been hoping to see someone, or litigating as plaintiff or defendant, or going to the theatre. And it is right to oppose luck to the accountable. We account for that which is always or for the most part, and luck appears in the cases apart from these. So since the causes in such cases are indeterminate, so is luck. Still, there are cases which may raise the doubt: could anything whatsoever come to be a cause of luck? For instance could the breath of the wind or the warmth of the sun be the cause of health, but not having had a haircut? For of things which are causes by virtue of concurrence, some are nearer than others.

Luck is called good when something good comes out, and bad when something bad, and it is called good fortune or bad fortune when the consequences are sizeable. Hence just to miss meeting with a great evil or good is to be lucky or unlucky, for thought treats the good or evil as already yours; what is so close seems no distance off at all. That good fortune is inconstant is also to be expected; for luck is inconstant; nothing which is the outcome of luck can be either always or for the most part.

As has been said, then, luck and the automatic are both causes by virtue of concurrence, in the field of things which are capable of coming to be neither simply nor for the most part, and of such of these as might come to be for something.

CHAPTER 6

They differ in that the automatic extends more widely. Everything which is the outcome of luck is an automatic outcome, but not every- 197b thing which is the latter is the outcome of luck. For luck and its outcome belong only to things which can be lucky and in general engage in rational activity. Hence luck must be concerned with things achievable by such activity. It is an indication of this that good fortune is thought to be the same as happiness or close to it, and happiness is a kind of rational activity: it is activity going well. So what is incapable of such activity, can do nothing as the outcome of luck.

Hence nothing done by an inanimate object, beast, or child, is the outcome of luck, since such things are not capable of choosing. Nor do good or bad fortune belong to them, unless by a resemblance, as Protarchus said that lucky are the stones from which altars are made, since they are honoured, whilst their fellows are trodden underfoot. In a way these things can undergo something as the outcome of luck, when a person engaged in activity concerning them achieves something as an outcome of luck; but otherwise not.

The automatic, on the other hand, extends to the animals other than man and to many inanimate objects. Thus we say that the horse came automatically, in that it was saved because it came, but it did not come for the purpose of being saved. And the tripod fell automatically. It was set up for someone to sit on, but it did not fall for someone to sit on. Plainly, then, in the field of things which in a general way come to be for something, if something comes to be but not for that which supervenes, and has an external cause, we say that it is an automatic outcome; and if such an outcome is for something capable of choosing and is an object of choice, we call it the outcome of luck.

An indication is the expression 'in vain', which we use when something is for something else, and what it is for does not come to be. For instance, suppose walking is for the loosening of the bowels, and a man walks without having this come to be: we say that he walked in vain and that his walk was vain, suggesting that this is what is in vain: something which is by nature such as to be for something else, when it does not accomplish that which it was for and which it is by nature such as to be for—since if someone said that he had performed his ablutions in vain because the sun did not go into eclipse, he would be ridiculous. Solar eclipses are not what washing is for. This, then, is what the automatic is like when it comes to be in vain, as the word

itself suggests. The stone did not fall for the purpose of hitting some-   30
one; it fell, then, as an automatic outcome, in that it might have fallen
through someone's agency and for hitting.

We are furthest from an outcome of luck with things which come to
be due to nature. For if something comes to be contrary to nature, we
then say not that it is the outcome of luck but rather that it is an automatic outcome. Yet it is not quite that either: the source of an auto-   35
matic outcome is external, whilst here it is internal.

What the automatic and luck are, then, and how they differ, has now   198ᵃ
been said. As for the ways in which they are causes, both are sources
from which the change originates; for they are always either things
which cause naturally or things which cause from thought—of which   5
there is an indeterminate multitude. But since the automatic and luck
are causes of things for which mind or nature might be responsible,
when something comes to be responsible for these same things by
virtue of concurrence, and since nothing which is by virtue of concurrence is prior to that which is by itself, it is clear that no cause by virtue
of concurrence is prior to that which is by itself a cause. Hence the   10
automatic and luck are posterior to both mind and nature; so however
much the automatic may be the cause of the heavens, mind and nature
are necessarily prior causes both of many other things and of this
universe.

CHAPTER 7

That there are causes, and that they are as many as we say, is clear: for
that is how many things the question 'On account of what?' embraces.   15
Either we bring it back at last to the question 'What is it?'—that happens over unchangeable things; for instance in mathematics it comes
back at last to a definition of straight or commensurable or the like. Or
to that which in the first instance effects the change; thus on account
of what did they go to war? Because of border raids. Or it is what the
thing is for: they fought for dominion. Or, in the case of things which   20
come to be, the matter.

Plainly, then, these are the causes, and this is how many they are.
They are four, and the student of nature should know about them all,
and it will be his method, when stating on account of what, to get back
to them all: the matter, the form, the thing which effects the change,
and what the thing is for.

The last three often coincide. What a thing is, and what it is for, are   25

one and the same, and that from which the change originates is the same in form as these. Thus a man gives birth to a man, and so it is in general with things which are themselves changed in changing other things—and things which are not so changed fall beyond the study of nature. They have no change or source of change in themselves when they change other things, but are unchangeable. Hence there are three
30 separate studies: one of things which are unchangeable, one of things which are changed but cannot pass away, and one of things which can pass away.

So in answering the question 'On account of what?' we bring it back to the matter, and to what the thing is, and to what first effected the change. People usually investigate the causes of coming to be thus:
35 they see what comes after what, and what first acted or was acted on, and go on seeking what comes next. But there are two sources of natural change, of which one is not natural, since it has no source of
198ᵇ change in itself. Anything which changes something else without itself being changed is of this latter sort; for instance, that which is completely unchangeable and the first thing of all, and a thing's form or what it is, for that is its end and what it is for. Since, then, nature is for
5 something, this cause too should be known, and we should state on account of what in every way: that this out of this necessarily (i.e. out of this simply, or out of this for the most part); and if so-and-so is to be (as the conclusion out of the premisses); and that this would be what the being would be; and because better thus—better not simply, but in relation to the reality of the thing concerned.

CHAPTER 8

10 We must first give reasons for including nature among causes which are for something, and then turn to the necessary, and see how it is present in that which is natural. For everyone brings things back to this cause, saying that because the hot is by nature such as to be thus, and similarly the cold and everything else of that sort, therefore these things of necessity come to be and are. For if they mention any other
15 cause, as one does love and strife and another mind, they just touch on it and then goodbye.

The problem thus arises: why should we suppose that nature acts for something and because it is better? Why should not everything be like the rain? Zeus does not send the rain in order to make the corn grow: it comes of necessity. The stuff which has been drawn up is bound to cool, and having cooled, turn to water and come down. It is merely concurrent that, this having happened, the corn grows. Similarly, if someone's corn rots on the threshing-floor, it does not rain for this purpose, that the corn may rot, but that came about concurrently. What, then, is to stop parts in nature too from being like this—the front teeth of necessity growing sharp and suitable for biting, and the back teeth broad and serviceable for chewing the food, not coming to be *for* this, but by coincidence? And similarly with the other parts in which the 'for something' seems to be present. So when all turned out just as if they had come to be for something, then the things, suitably constituted as an automatic outcome, survived; when not, they died, and die, as Empedocles says of the man-headed calves.

This, or something like it, is the account which might give us pause. It is impossible, however, that this should be how things are. The things mentioned, and all things which are due to nature, come to be as they do always or for the most part, and nothing which is the outcome of luck or an automatic outcome does that. We do not think that it is the outcome of luck or coincidence that there is a lot of rain in winter, but only if there is a lot of rain in August; nor that there are heatwaves in August, but only if there is a heatwave in winter. If, then, things seem to be either a coincidental outcome or for something, and the things we are discussing cannot be either a coincidental or an automatic outcome, they must be for something. But all such things are due to nature, as the authors of the view under discussion themselves admit. The 'for something', then, is present in things which are and come to be due to nature.

Again, where there is an end, the successive things which go before are done for it. As things are done, so they are by nature such as to be, and as they are by nature such as to be, so they are done, if there is no impediment. Things are done for something. Therefore they are by nature such as to be for something. Thus if a house were one of the things wh h come to be due to nature, it would come to be just as it now does by the agency of art; and if things which are due to nature came to be not only due to nature but also due to art, they would come to be just as they are by nature. The one, then, is for the other. In general, art either imitates the works of nature or completes that which nature is unable to bring to completion. If, then, that which is in accordance with art is for something, clearly so is that which is in accordance with nature. The relation of that which comes after to that which goes before is the same in both.

20   The point is most obvious if you look at those animals other than
men, which make things not by art, and without carrying out inquiries
or deliberation. Spiders, ants, and the like have led people to wonder
how they accomplish what they do, if not by mind. Descend a little
25   further, and you will find things coming to be which conduce to an
end even in plants, for instance leaves for the protection of fruit. If,
then, the swallow's act in making its nest is both due to nature and for
something, and the spider's in making its web, and the plant's in producing leaves for its fruit, and roots not up but down for nourishment,
30   plainly this sort of cause is present in things which are and come to be
due to nature. And since nature is twofold, nature as matter and nature
as form, and the latter is an end, and everything else is for the end, the
cause as that for which must be the latter.

Mistakes occur even in that which is in accordance with art. Men
who possess the art of writing have written incorrectly, doctors have
35   administered the wrong medicine. So clearly the same is possible also
in that which is in accordance with nature. If it sometimes happens
199^b   over things which are in accordance with art, that that which goes
right is for something, and that which goes wrong is attempted for
something but miscarries, it may be the same with things which are
natural, and monsters may be boss shots at that which is for some-
5   thing. When things were originally being constituted, man-headed
calves, if they were unable to reach a certain limit and end, came to be
as a result of a defect in some principle, as they now do as the result of
defective seed.

Again, seed must come first, and not the animal straight off, and the
'omnigenous protoplast' was seed.

10   Again, the 'for something' is present in plants too, though it is less
articulate. Was it the case, then, that as there were man-headed calves,
so there were olive-headed vinelets in the vegetable kingdom? Or is
that absurd? But there should have been, if that is how it was with
animals.

Again, coming to be among seeds too would have had to be as luck
15   would have it. But a person who says that does away with nature and
things due to it altogether. A thing is due to nature, if it arrives, by a
continuous process of change, starting from some principle in itself, at
some end. Each principle gives rise, not to the same thing in all cases,
nor to any chance thing, but always to something proceeding towards
the same thing, if there is no impediment. What something is for, and
20   what is for that, can also come to be as the outcome of luck, as when we

say that the family friend came as the outcome of luck and paid the ransom before departing, if he behaved as if he had come for that purpose but had not in fact come for that purpose. That is by virtue of concurrence (for luck is a cause by virtue of concurrence, as we said above); but when a certain thing comes to be always or for the most part, it is not a concurrent happening, nor the outcome of luck. Now 25 with that which is natural it is always thus if there is no impediment.

It is absurd not to think that a thing comes to be for something unless the thing which effects the change is seen to have deliberated. Art too does not deliberate. If the art of shipbuilding were present in wood, it would act in the same way as nature; so if the 'for something' 30 is present in art, it is present in nature too. The point is clearest when someone doctors himself: nature is like that.

That nature is a cause, then, and a cause in this way, for something, is plain.

CHAPTER 9

Is that which is of necessity, of necessity only on some hypothesis, or can it also be simply of necessity? The general view is that things come 35 to be of necessity, in the way in which a man might think that a city 200ᵃ wall came to be of necessity, if he thought that since heavy things are by nature such as to sink down, and light to rise to the surface, the stones and foundations go down, the earth goes above them because it is lighter, and the posts go on top because they are lightest of all. Now 5 without these things no city wall would have come to be; still, it was not on account of them, except as matter, that it came to be, but for the protection and preservation of certain things. Similarly with anything else in which the 'for something' is present: without things which have a necessary nature it could not be, but it is, not on account of them, except in the way in which a thing is on account of its matter, but for something. Thus on account of what is a saw like this? That this may 10 be, and for this. It is impossible, however, that this thing which it is for should come to be, unless it is made of iron. It is necessary, then, that it should be made of iron, if there is to be a saw, and its work is to be done. The necessary, then, is necessary on some hypothesis, and not as an end: the necessary is in the matter, the 'that for which' in the account.

The necessary appears in mathematics and in the things which 15 come to be in accordance with nature, in a parallel fashion. Because the straight is so and so, it is necessary that a triangle should have angles together equal to two right angles, and not the other way round. Still, if triangles did not have angles together equal to two right angles, we should have no straight lines. With things which come to be for something the case is reversed: if the end will be or is, that which comes before will be or is; and if we do not have it, then just as in mathematics, if we do not have the conclusion, we shall not have the starting-point, so here we shall not have the end or that for which. That too is a starting-point, not of the practical activity, but of the reasoning. (In mathematics too the starting-point is of the reasoning, since there is no practical activity there.) So if there is to be a house, it is necessary that these things should come to be or be present, and in general it is necessary that there should be the matter which is for something, e.g. the bricks and stones if there is to be a house. Nevertheless, the end is not on account of these things except as matter, nor on account of them will it come into being. In general, if they, for instance the stones or the iron, are not present, there will be no house or saw; just as in mathematics there will not be the starting-points if the triangle does not have angles together equal to two right angles.

Plainly, then, the necessary in things which are natural is that which is given as the matter, and the changes it undergoes. The student of nature should state both causes, but particularly the cause which is what the thing is for; for that is responsible for the matter, whilst the matter is not responsible for the end. And the end is that for which, and the start is from the definition and the account; and just as in the case of things which are in accordance with art, since this is the sort of thing a house is, this and that must of necessity come to be and be present, or since this is what health is, this and that must come to be of necessity and be present: so if this is what a man is, then so and so, and if so and so, then such and such.

Perhaps the necessary enters even into the account. Suppose the work of sawing is defined as a certain sort of division: that will not be, unless the saw has teeth of a certain sort, and there will not be teeth like that, if it is not made of iron. For even in the account there are parts which stand to it as matter.

BOOK III

CHAPTER 1

Since nature is a principle of change and alteration, and our inquiry is 200ᵇ about nature, it must not escape us what change is: for if it is not known, it must be that nature is not known either. And after making an analysis of change, we must try to inquire in the same way about 15 the subjects next in order. Change is thought to be something continuous, and the infinite is the first thing that presents itself to view in the continuous (which is why those who try to define the continuous often find themselves making use of the definition of the infinite as an auxiliary, the supposition being that what is divisible *ad* 20 *infinitum* is continuous). Further, it is thought that there cannot be change without place and void and time. So it is clear that, both for these reasons, and because they are common to everything and universal, we must give a treatment of each of these subjects, as a preliminary to further inquiry (for the consideration of specialities is subsequent to that of things that are common)—beginning, as we said, 25 with change.

Things are—some only actually, some potentially and actually— either a 'this'; or so much; or of such a kind, and likewise they are in the other categories of that-which-is. (Of the relative, one kind is said in respect of excess and of deficiency, another in respect of the active and the passive, and, in general, in respect of that which is productive 30 of change and that which is changeable. For that which is productive of change, is so *in* that which is changeable, and that which is changeable is so *by the agency* of that which is productive of change.) There is no change apart from actual things; for whatever alters always does so in respect either of substance, or of quantity, or of qualification, or of place, and there is, as we assert, nothing to be found as a common item 35 superior to these, which is neither a 'this' nor a quantity nor a qualifi- 201ᵃ cation nor any of the other occupants of categories; and so there is no change or alteration either of anything apart from the things mentioned, because nothing *is*, apart from the things mentioned. But each occupant of a category is present in everything in two ways, e.g. the 'this' (one case of it is the form, the other is the privation); and in respect of qualification (one case is *white* and the other *black*); and in 5 respect of quantity (one case is *complete* and the other *incomplete*). So too in respect of locomotion, one case is *above*, the other is *below*, or one case is *light*, the other is *heavy*. So that there are just as many species of change and alteration as of that-which-is.

10   There being a distinction, in respect of each kind of being, between being actually and being potentially, the actuality of that which potentially is, *qua* such, is change. For example: the actuality of what admits of qualitative change, *qua* admitting of qualitative change, is qualitative change; of what admits of increase and decrease (there is no common term to cover both), it is increase and decrease; of what admits of coming-to-be and ceasing-to-be, it is coming-to-be and ceasing-to-be; of what admits of locomotion, it is locomotion. That

15   this is change is clear from the following: when that which is buildable is in actuality, in the respect in which we call it such, it is being built, and this is the process of building; and similarly with learning and healing and rolling and jumping and maturing and growing old.

Since some things are the same things both actually and potentially,

20   not at the same time or not in the same part, but, e.g., hot in actuality, cold in potentiality—from this it already follows that many things will act and be acted upon mutually. For everything of this kind will be at the same time both active and passive. So too, then, that which produces change naturally will itself be changeable; for everything of that

25   kind is itself changed when it produces change. Some even think that everything that produces change is itself changed; however, the truth about that will become clear from other considerations—in fact, there is something that produces change and is not changeable.

The actuality, then, of what is potentially—when being in actuality it is operating, not *qua* itself but *qua* changeable—is change. I mean

30   '*qua*' thus: the bronze is potentially a statue, but yet it is not the actuality of bronze *qua* bronze that is change. For it is not the same thing to be bronze and to be potentially something: if indeed it were, without qualification and by definition, the same thing, then the actuality of the bronze, *qua* bronze, would be change, but, as has been said, it is not the same thing. The case is clear with opposites: to be capable of

35   being healthy and to be capable of being sick are different—otherwise being sick and being healthy would be the same thing—but the under-

201ᵇ   lying subject, that which is healthy and that which is diseased, be it moisture or blood, is one and the same. Since then it is not the same thing, just as *colour* is not the same as *visible thing*, it is manifest that the actuality of the potential, *qua* potential, is change.

5   That change is this, and that change occurs just when the actuality is this actuality, and neither before nor after, is clear; for it is possible

for each thing to operate at one time and not at another, e.g. the build-able, and the operation of the buildable, *qua* buildable, is the process of building. For the operation is either the process of building or the 10 house; but when the house is, the buildable no longer is; but to get built is what the buildable does, so that the process of building must be the operation. And the process of building is a kind of change. But now the same argument will apply in the case of the other changes as 15 well.

CHAPTER 2

That this is a good account is clear also from what others say about change, and from the fact that it is not easy to define it in any other way. In the first place, one would not be able to put change and altera-tion into another genus; and, again, it is clear when we consider how some people treat it, asserting that change is difference and inequality 20 and that which is not—it is not necessary for any of these things to change, either different things or unequal things or things which are not; nor, even, does alteration take place into or from these things more than it does into or from their opposites. The reason why they assign change to these things is that change is thought to be something indefinite, and the principles in the second column of correlated 25 opposites are indefinite because they are privative; none of them is a 'this' or is of such a kind, nor belongs to one of the other categories. And the reason why change is thought to be indefinite is that it is not possible to assign it either to the potentiality of things that are, nor yet to their operation: for neither that which it is possible may be a quan- 30 tity, nor that which is a quantity in operation, necessarily changes, and besides change does seem to be a kind of operation, but an incomplete one—the reason being that the potential, of which it is the operation, is incomplete. This, then, is why it is difficult to grasp what it is; for it is necessary to assign it either to privation or to potentiality or to simple operation, but none of these is obviously admissible. There remains, 35 then, the way that has been stated, that it *is* a kind of operation, but an operation such as we said, which is difficult to spot but of which the 202ᵃ existence is possible.

As was said, everything that produces change is also changed, if it is potentially changeable and its not being changed is rest (the not being changed of that which admits of change is rest). For to operate on 5 this, *qua* such, is just what it is to produce change, and this it does by

Physics

contact, so that it will at the same time also be acted upon. That which produces change will always carry some form, either 'this' or 'of such a kind' or 'so much', which will be the principle of, and responsible for, the change, when it produces change—e.g. what is actually a human being makes, out of that which is potentially a human being, a human being.

CHAPTER 3

Again—a point which makes difficulty—it is manifest that the change is in that which is changeable. For it is the actuality of this, brought about by that which is productive of change. Yet the operation of that which is productive of change, also, is not other—there must in fact be an actuality of both—for it is productive of change by its being capable of so doing, and it produces change by its operation, but it is such as to operate on what is changeable; so that the operation of both is one in the same way as it is the same interval from 1 to 2 as from 2 to 1, and as the uphill and the downhill—these are one, yet their definition is not one, and similarly with that which produces and undergoes change.

This presents a difficulty of a formal kind. It is perhaps necessary that there should be some operation of that which is active and of that which is passive: the one is an acting-upon, the other is a being-acted-upon, and the product and end of the one is a product of action, and of the other a modification. Since then both of the operations are changes, if they are different, what are they in? Either they are both in that which is acted upon and changes; or the acting-upon is in that which acts, the being-acted-upon in that which is acted upon (if one has to call this too an acting-upon, it is so by homonymy). But if this is the case, the change will be in that which produces change, since the same argument applies to that which produces and that which undergoes change: so that either everything that produces change will change; or having change it will not change. But if both are in that which changes and is acted upon, the acting-upon *and* the being-acted-upon, and the teaching and the learning are, being two, in the learner, then in the first place it will not be true that the operation of each thing is present in each thing; and again, it is absurd that it should change by *two* changes at the same time: what two qualitative changes will there be of one thing to one form? This is impossible. Suppose then that the operation will be one. But it is unreasonable that there should be one and the same operation of two things different in form. And if teaching and learning are the same thing, and acting-upon and being-acted-upon, then to teach will be the same thing as to learn, and to act upon as to be acted upon, so that it will be necessary that every teacher learns and everyone that acts upon is acted upon.

Or can it be that: it is *not* absurd that the operation of one thing should be in another (for teaching is the operation of that which is disposed to teach, but it is *on* something, and not cut off, but is of this on this); and there is, also, nothing to prevent the operation of two things being one and the same, not as the same in being, but in the way that what potentially is is related to what is operating, and it is also not necessary that the teacher learns, even if to act upon and to be acted upon are the same thing, provided they are not the same in the sense that the definition that gives the 'what it was to be' is one (as with 'raiment' and 'clothing'), but in the sense in which the road from Thebes to Athens is the same as the road from Athens to Thebes, as was said earlier? For it is not the case that all the same things are present in things that are the same in any sense whatever, but only of those of which the being is the same. And, in any case, even if teaching is the same thing as learning, to learn is not therefore the same thing as to teach, just as, even if two things separated by an interval have one interval between them, to be distant in the direction from A to B is not one and the same thing as to be distant in the direction from B to A. But speaking generally, the teaching is not the same, in the primary sense, as the learning, nor the acting-upon as the being-acted-upon, but that in which these things are present, namely the change, is the same as the being acted upon; for to be the operation of A in B, and to be the operation of B by the agency of A, are different in definition.

It has been said, then, what change is, both generally and in particular, for it is not unclear how each of the kinds of it will be defined: qualitative change, for example, is the actuality of that which admits of qualitative change, *qua* admitting of qualitative change. [To put it in an even more familiar way, the actuality of what is potentially such as to act and such as to be acted upon, *qua* such (both without qualification and again in each particular case), is either building or healing.][4] And an account will be given in the same way about each of the other kinds of change.

---

[4] Bracketed by the translator as an intrusion into the text.

CHAPTER 5
...

205ᵃ That, in general it is impossible for there to be an infinite body, perceptible by sense, is clear from the following. Every thing perceptible
10 by sense is such as to be naturally somewhere, and each such thing has
a certain place, and the same place for a portion of it as for the whole of
it: e.g. for the whole of the earth and a single clod, and for fire and a
spark. Hence, if the infinite body is homogeneous, it will be immobile
or it will always be in motion. Yet this is impossible. For what will be
down rather than up, or anywhere whatever? I mean, for example: if
15 there were a lump of the infinite body, where will that be in motion or
where will it be at rest, since the place of the body of the same kind is
infinite? Will it then occupy the whole of the place? How could it? So
what sort of being at rest or what motion will it have, and where? Will
it be at rest everywhere? In that case it will not be moved. Or will it be
in motion everywhere? In that case it will not come to a halt. But if the
20 whole is not homogeneous, the places too will be different. And in the
first place the body of the whole will not be one, except by being in
contact. Next, these components will in form either be finite, or infinite in number. But they cannot be finite, for if the whole is infinite
some will be infinite and some not (e.g. fire or water will be infinite);
25 but such a thing destroys the opposites. But if they are infinite in number and simple, the places will be infinite in number too and the
elements will be infinite in number. So if this is impossible, and the
places are finite, the whole is too. (For it is impossible that the place
and the body should not fit, since neither is the place as a whole larger
30 than the possible size of the body (at the same time, the body will not
even be infinite any more), nor is the body larger than the place; for
otherwise there will either be void or a body with no natural where-
abouts. It was for this reason that none of the natural philosophers
made fire or earth the one infinite body, but either water or air or that
which is intermediate between them, because each of fire and earth
35 has clearly a determinate place, but these others are ambiguous
between up and down.)
205ᵇ   Anaxagoras talks oddly about the infinite's being at rest; he says that
the infinite keeps itself still, and that this is because it is in itself, since
no other thing surrounds it; as if a thing's nature were to be there,
5 wherever it is. But this is not true: a thing may be somewhere because
forced to be there, and not where it is naturally. So, however true it
may be that the whole is not in motion (what is kept still by itself and is

in itself must be immobile), it is still necessary to say why it is not in its nature to be moved. It is not sufficient to leave the matter with this statement; for it might be that it had, not moving, nowhere else to   10 move to, yet there was nothing to prevent its being by nature such as to move. After all the earth does not move either, nor, if it were infinite, but held back by the centre, would it do so; but it would stay still at the centre, not because there is nowhere where it will be moved to, but because it is by nature such as to do so. Yet one might say that it kept itself still. If, then, this is not the reason even in the case of the earth, if that were infinite, but the reason is that it has weight, and what has   15 weight stays still at the centre, and the earth is at the centre; in the same way, the infinite would stay still in itself for some other reason and not because it is infinite and keeps itself still. At the same time it is clear that any part whatever of the infinite would have to stay still; for, just as the infinite stays still in itself, keeping itself still, so too if any part whatever is taken, that will stay still in itself. For the places of the   20 whole and of the part are of the same form—e.g. of the whole of the earth and a clod, below, and of the whole of fire and a spark, above. So that, if the place of the infinite is that which is in itself, the place of a part is the same; hence it will stay still in itself.

In general, it is manifest that it is impossible to say at the same time that there is an infinite body and that there is some natural place for   25 bodies, if every body perceptible by sense has either heaviness or lightness and, if it is heavy, has a natural motion to the centre, and if it is light, upwards. For this must be so of the infinite too: but it is impossible, both for all of it to have either heavy or light as properties and for half of it to have each of the two. How will you divide it? And how, of what is infinite, can there be an above and a below, or an   30 extreme and a centre? Again, every body perceptible by sense is in place, and the kinds and varieties of place are: above, below, forward, backward, right, and left. These are not determined only relatively to us, and conventionally; they are so in the universe itself. But they can-   35 not exist in the infinite. And in general, if there cannot be an infinite   206ᵃ place, and every body is in a place, there cannot be an infinite body. Yet what is somewhere is in a place, and what is in a place is some-where. If then, the infinite cannot even be any quantity—for then it will be some particular quantity, e.g. of two or three cubits; that is what 'quantity' means—so too that which is in place is so because it is some-   5 where, and that is either above or below or in some other of the six dimensions, and of each of these there is some limit. It is manifest, then, from these considerations that there is in actual operation no infinite body.

CHAPTER 6

But if there is, unqualifiedly, no infinite, it is clear that many impos-
10 sible things result. For there will be a beginning and end of time, and
magnitudes will not be divisible into magnitudes, and number will not
be infinite. Now when the alternatives have been distinguished thus
and it seems that neither is possible, an arbitrator is needed and it is
clear that in a sense the infinite is and in a sense it is not. 'To be', then,
may mean 'to be potentially' or 'to be actually'; and the infinite is
15 either in addition or in division. It has been stated that magnitude is
not in actual operation infinite; but it *is* infinite in division—it is not
hard to refute indivisible lines—so that it remains for the infinite to be
potentially. (We must not take 'potentially' here in the same way as
20 that in which, if it is possible for this to be a statue, it actually will be a
statue, and suppose that there is an infinite which will be in actual
operation.) Since 'to be' has many senses, just as the day is, and the
contest is, by the constant occurring of one thing after another, so too
with the infinite. (In these cases too there is 'potentially' and 'in actual
operation': the Olympic games *are*, both in the sense of the contest's
being able to occur and in the sense of its occurring.) But the infinite's
25 being is shown in one way in the case of time and the human race, and
in another in the case of division of magnitudes. In general, the infinite is in virtue of one thing's constantly being taken after another—
each thing taken is finite, but it is always one followed by another; but
206ᵇ in magnitudes what was taken persists, in the case of time and the race
of men the things taken cease to be, yet so that the series does not give
out.

The infinite by addition is in a sense the same as the infinite by division. For in that which is finite by addition there is an inversely corre-
5 sponding process: to see it as being divided *ad infinitum* will be at the
same time to see it as being added to a definite amount. For if, in a
finite magnitude, one takes a definite amount and takes in addition
always in the same proportion, (but not taking a magnitude which is
the same particular one) one will not traverse the finite magnitude; but
10 if one increases the proportion so that one always takes in the same
particular magnitude, one will traverse it, because every finite quantity is exhausted by any definite quantity whatever.

The infinite, then, is in no other way, but is in this way, potentially and by way of reduction (and actually too, in the sense in which we say that the day and the games are). It is potentially, in the way in which matter is, and not in itself, as the finite is. The infinite by addition, too, is potentially in this way; this infinite, we say, is in a way the same thing as the infinite by division. For it will always be possible to take something which is outside—though it will not exceed every definite quantity and will always be smaller. To be infinite so as to exceed every definite quantity by addition is not possible even potentially unless there is something which is actually infinite, accidentally, as the natural philosophers say that the body outside the world-system, of which the substance is air or some other such thing, is infinite. But if it is not possible for there to be a perceptible body which is actually infinite in this sense, it is manifest that there cannot be one even potentially infinite by addition, except in the way that has been stated, in inverse correspondence to the division-process. (Even Plato, for this reason, made two infinites, because there seems to be an excess and a going-to-infinity both in extent and in reduction; but, having made two, he does not make use of them, for in Plato's numbers neither the infinite by reduction is present, the unit being a minimum, nor the infinite in extent, because he makes number end with the number ten.)

It turns out that the infinite is the opposite of what people say it is: it is not that of which no part is outside, but that of which some part is always outside. (An indication is this: people call rings infinite too if they have no hoop, because it is always possible to take something outside, and they talk so because of a certain similarity, though not using the primary sense—for *that*, this property must be present and also one must never take the same thing as before and this is not so in the case of the circle, where only the next thing is always different from its predecessor.) So, that is infinite, of which it is always possible to take some part outside, when we take according to quantity. But that of which no part is outside, is complete and whole: that is how we define 'whole', as meaning that of which no part is absent—e.g. a whole man or a whole box. And as what is whole in a particular case, so is that which is whole in the primary sense: it is that of which no part is outside. (That outside which absence is, is not all, whatever may be absent.) ('Whole' and 'complete' are either exactly the same or very close in their nature. Nothing is complete unless it has an end, and an end is a limit.)

BOOK IV

CHAPTER 4

210^b   What place is, should become manifest in the following way. Let us
assume about it all the things that are thought truly to belong to it in
respect of itself. We require, then, that place should be the first thing
211^a   surrounding that of which it is the place; and not anything pertaining
to the object; that the primary place should be neither less nor
greater (than the object); that it should be left behind by each object
when the object moves and be separable from it; further, that every
place should have 'above' and 'below'; and that each body should
5   naturally move to and remain in its proper places, and this it must do
either above or below. It is from these, that we take to be true, that the
rest of the inquiry must proceed. We must try to make inquiry in such
a way that the 'what-is-it' is provided; and so that the problems are
solved; the things that are thought to be present in place are in fact
10   present; finally, the reason for the difficulty and for the problems
about it is manifest; this is the best way of demonstrating anything.

First it should be noticed that place would not be a subject for
inquiry if there were not change in respect of place. This too is chiefly
why we think that the heavens are in place, because they are always in
change. This change divides into locomotion, increase and decrease;
15   for in increase and decrease too something moves, and what formerly
was there changes position in turn into a smaller or a larger. What is
changed is so in actual operation in itself; or accidentally; and what
are changed accidentally are either what can in themselves be
20   changed: e.g. the parts of the body and the nail in the boat; or things
that cannot be changed in themselves but are always changed accidentally—e.g. whiteness and knowledge; these alter their place in the
sense that that in which they are present does so.

Now we say we are in the heavens as in a place, because we are in
25   the air and it is in the heavens; and in the air—not the *whole* air, but it
is because of the limit of it that surrounds us that we say we are in the
air (if the *whole* air were our place, a thing would not in every case be
equal to its place, but it *is* thought to be equal; this kind of place is the
primary place in which it is). So when that which surrounds is not
divided from, but continuous with, the thing surrounded, the latter is
30   said to be in the former not as in a place but as the part is in the whole;
but when that which surrounds is divided from and in contact with the

things surrounded, the latter is in the extreme of the surrounding thing first; and this extreme is neither a part of that which is in it, nor is it greater than the extension of the thing surrounded but equal to it, since the extremes of things which are in contact are in the same spot. And if the thing surrounded is continuous it is moved not *in* the sur-   35 rounding thing but with it; if it is divided, it is moved *in* the latter— just as much, whether or not the surrounding thing is itself moved.   211ᵇ

Now it is already manifest from these points what place is. Roughly,   5 there are four things, some one of which place must be: form, or matter, or some extension (that which is between the extremes), or the extremes, if there is no extension apart from the magnitude of the body which comes to be in the place. But that it is not possible for it to be three of these, is manifest.   10

It is because it surrounds that form is thought to be place, for the extremes of what surrounds and of what is surrounded are in the same spot. They are both limits, but not of the same thing: the form is a limit of the object, and the place of the surrounding body.

And because the thing surrounded and divided off often moves about while the surrounding thing remains (e.g. water leaves a vessel),   15 what is in between is thought to be something, on the supposition that there is some extension over and above the body which changes position. (But that is not so: what happens is that whatever body it may chance to be, of those that change position and are such as to be in contact, comes in.) If there were some extension which was what was naturally there and static, then there would be infinitely many places   20 in the same spot. For, when the water and the air change position, all the parts will do the same thing in the whole as all the water does in the vessel, and at the same time the place will be moving about; so that the place will have another place and there will be many places together. (But the place of the part, in which it moves when the whole   25 vessel changes position, is not different but the same: for the air and the water (or the parts of the water) replace each other in the place in which they are, not in the place which they are coming to be in; *that* latter place is a part of the place which is the place of the whole world.)

Matter, too, might be thought to be place, if one considered the case of something at rest and not separated but continuous. For just as, if it   30 changes qualitatively, there is something which now is white but once was black, and now is hard but once was soft (this is why we say there is matter), so too place is thought to be because of this kind of pheno-menon, except that *that* (matter's being thought to be) is because what

35   was air is now water, while place is thought to be because where there
212ᵃ   was air, there now is water. But, as was said earlier, matter is neither
      separable from the object, nor does it surround it, while place has both
      properties.

          If, then, place is none of the three, neither the form nor the matter
      nor some extension which is always present and different from the
      extension of the object that changes position, it must be that place is
5   the remaining one of the four, the limit of the surrounding body, at
      which it is in contact with that which is surrounded. (By 'that which is
      surrounded' I mean that *body*, that which is changeable by locomo-
      tion.) Place is thought to be something profound and difficult to grasp,
      both because the matter and the form, in addition, appear involved in
10   it, and because of the fact that change of position of a moving body
      occurs within a surrounding body which is at rest; for from this it
      appears to be possible that there is an extension in between which is
      something other than the magnitudes which move. Air, too, helps to
      some extent to give this impression by appearing to be incorporeal;
      place seems to be not only the limits of the vessel but also that which is
      in between, which is considered as being void.

          Just as the vessel is a place which can be carried around, so place is
15   a vessel which cannot be moved around. So when something moves
      inside something which is moving and the thing inside moves about
      (e.g. a boat in a river), the surrounding thing functions for it as a vessel
      rather than as a place; place is meant to be unchangeable, so that it is
      the whole river, rather, that is the place, because as a whole it is
20   unchangeable. (So that is what place is: the first unchangeable limit of
      that which surrounds.)

CHAPTER 10

          After what has been said, the next thing is to inquire into time. First, it
30   is well to go through the problems about it, using the untechnical
      arguments as well as technical ones: whether it is among things that
      are or things that are not, and then what its nature is.

          That it either is not at all or only scarcely and dimly is, might be
      suspected from the following considerations. Some of it has been and
      is not, some of it is to be and is not yet. From these both infinite time
218ᵃ   and any arbitrary time are composed. But it would seem to be impos-
      sible that what is composed of things that are not should participate in
      being. Further, it is necessary that, of everything that is resoluble into

parts, if it is, either all the parts or some of them should be when it is. But of time, while it is resoluble into parts, some parts have been, some are to be, and none is. The now is not a part, for a part measures the whole, and the whole must be composed of the parts, but time is not thought to be composed of nows. Again, it is not easy to see whether the now, which appears to be the boundary between past and future, remains always one and the same or is different from time to time. If it is always different, and if no two distinct parts of things that are in time are simultaneous—except those of which one includes the other, as the greater time includes the smaller—and if the now which is not but which previously was must have ceased to be at some time, then the nows too will not be simultaneous, and it must always be the case that the previous now has ceased-to-be. Now, that it has ceased-to-be in itself is not possible, because then it is; but it cannot be that the former now has ceased to be in another now, either. For we take it that it is impossible for the nows to be adjoining one another, as it is for a point to be adjoining a point; so, since the now has not ceased to be in the next now but in some other one, it will be simultaneously in the nows in between, which are infinitely many; but this is impossible. Yet it is not possible either that the same now should always persist. For nothing that is divisible and finite has only one limit, whether it is continuous in one direction or in more than one. But the now is a limit, and it is possible to take a finite time. Again, if to be together in time and neither before nor after, is to be in the one and the same now, and if both previous and subsequent nows are in this present now, then events of a thousand years ago will be simultaneous with those of today and none will be either previous or subsequent to any other.

Let this much, then, be our examination of difficulties about the properties of time. As to what time is and what its nature is, this is left equally unclear by the recorded opinions of earlier thinkers and by our own previous discussions. Some say it is the change of the universe, some the celestial sphere itself. Yet of the celestial revolution even a part is a time, though it has not a revolution. (The part considered is a part of a revolution, but not a revolution.) Again, if there were more than one world, time would equally be the change of any one whatever of them, so that there would be many times simultaneously. The sphere of the universe was thought to be time, by those who said it was, because everything is both in time and in the sphere of the universe; but this assertion is too simple-minded for us to consider the impossibilities it contains.

Since time is above all thought to be change, and a kind of altera-
10   tion, this is what must be examined. Now the alteration and change of
anything is only in the thing that is altering, or wherever the thing that
is being changed and altering may chance to be; but time is equally
everywhere and with everything. Again, alteration may be faster or
slower, but not time; what is slow and what is fast is defined by time,
15   fast being that which changes much in a short time, slow that which
changes little in a long time. But time is not defined by time, whether
by its being so much or by its being of such a kind. It is manifest, then,
that time is not change (let it make no difference to us, at present,
20   whether we say 'change' or 'alteration').

CHAPTER 11

And yet time is not apart from alteration, either. When we ourselves
do not alter in our mind or do not notice that we alter, then it does not
seem to us that any time has passed, just as it does not seem so to the
fabled sleepers in the sanctuary of the heroes in Sardinia, when they
25   wake up; they join up the later now to the earlier, and make it one,
omitting what is in between because of failure to perceive it. So, just
as, if the now were not different but one and the same, there would be
no time, in the same way, even when the now *is* different but is not
noticed to be different, what is in between does not seem to be any
30   time. If, then, when we do not mark off any alteration, but the soul
seems to remain in one indivisible, it happens as a consequence that
we do not think there was any time, and if when we do perceive and
mark off an alteration, then we do say that some time has passed, then
it is manifest that there is no time apart from change and alteration. It
is manifest, then, that time neither is change nor is apart from change,
219ᵃ and since we are looking for what time is we must start from this fact,
and find what aspect of change it is. We perceive change and time
together: even if it is dark and we are not acted upon through the body,
5   but there is some change in the soul, it immediately seems to us that
some time has passed together with the change. Moreover, whenever
some time seems to have passed, some change seems to have occurred
together with it. So that time is either change or some aspect of
change; and since it is not change, it must be some aspect of change.
10   Now since what changes changes from something to something,
and every magnitude is continuous, the change follows the magnitude:
it is because the magnitude is continuous that the change is too. And it

is because the change is that the time is. (For the time always seems to
have been of the same amount as the change.)

Now the before and after is in place primarily; there, it is by conven-   15
tion. But since the before and after is in magnitude, it must also be in
change, by analogy with what there is there. But in time, too, the
before and after is present, because the one always follows the other of
them. The before and after in change is, in respect of what makes it   20
what it is, change; but its being is different and is not change.

But time, too, we become acquainted with when we mark off
change, marking it off by the before and after, and we say that time has
passed when we get a perception of the before and after in change. We   25
mark off change by taking them to be different things, and some other
thing between them; for whenever we conceive of the limits as other
than the middle, and the soul says that the nows are two, one before
and one after, then it is and this it is that we say time is. (What is
marked off by the now is thought to be time: let this be taken as true.)
So whenever we perceive the now as one, and not either as before and   30
after in the change, or as the same but pertaining to something which
is before and after, no time seems to have passed, because no change
seems to have occurred either. But whenever we do perceive the
before and after, then we speak of time.

For that is what time is: number of change in respect of the before   219ᵇ
and after. So time is not change but is that in respect of which change
has a number. An indication: we discern the greater and the less by
number, and greater and less change by time; hence time is a kind of   5
number. But number is so called in two ways: we call number both
that which is counted and countable, and that by which we count.
Time is that which is counted and not that by which we count. (That
by which we count is different from that which is counted.)

Just as the change is always other and other, so the time is too,
though the whole time in sum is the same. For the now is the same X,   10
whatever X it may be which makes it what it is; but its being is not the
same. It is the now that measures time, considered as before and after.
The now is in a way the same, and in a way not the same: considered as
being at different stages, it is different—that is what it is for it to be a
now—but whatever it is that makes it a now is the same. For change
follows magnitude, as was said, and time, we assert, follows change. As   15
it is with the point, then, so it is with the moving thing, by which we
become acquainted with change and the before and after in it. The
moving thing is, in respect of what makes it what it is, the same (as the

point is, so is a stone or something else of that sort); but in definition it is different, in the way in which the sophists assume that being Coriscus-in-the-Lyceum is different from being Coriscus-in-the-market-place. That, then, is different by being in different places, and the now follows the moving thing as time does change. For it is by the moving thing that we become acquainted with the before and after in change, and the before and after, considered as countable, is the now. Here too, then, whatever it is that makes it the now is the same—it is the before and after in change. But its being is different: the now is the before and after, considered as countable. Moreover, it is this that is most familiar; for the change too is known by that which changes, and the motion by the moving thing, because the moving thing is a 'this', but the change is not. So the now is in a way the same always, and in a way not the same, since the moving thing too is so.

It is manifest too that, if time were not, the now would not be either, and if the now were not, time would not be. For just as the moving thing and the motion go together, so too do the number of the moving thing and the number of the motion. Time is the number of the motion, and the now is, as the moving thing is, like a unit of number.

Moreover, time is both continuous, by virtue of the now, and divided at the now—this too follows the motion and the moving thing. For the change and the motion too are one by virtue of the moving thing, because that is one (not one X, whatever X it may be that makes it what it is—for then it might leave a gap—but one in definition). And this bounds the change before and after. This too in a sense follows the point: the point, too, both makes the length continuous and bounds it, being the beginning of one and the end of another. But when one takes it in this way, treating the one point as two, one must come to a halt, if the same point is to be both beginning and end. But the now is always different, because the moving thing changes. Hence time is a number, not as a number of the same point, in that it is beginning and end, but rather in the way in which the extremes are the number of the line—and not as the parts of the line are, both because of what has been said (one will treat the middle point as two, so that there will be rest as a result), and further because it is manifest that the now is no portion of time, nor is the division a portion of the change, any more than the point is of the line (it is the two lines that are portions of the one). So, considered as a limit, the now is not time but is accidentally so, while, considered as counting, it is a number. (For

limits are of that alone of which they are limits, but the number of
these horses, the ten, is elsewhere too.)

It is manifest then that time is a number of change in respect of the
before and after, and is continuous, for it is a number of what is con-   25
tinuous.

BOOK VIII

CHAPTER 6

Since there must always be motion without intermission, there must   258ᵇ
necessarily be something eternal, whether one or many, that first
imparts motion, and this first mover must be unmoved. Now the question whether each of the things that are unmoved but impart motion is
eternal is irrelevant to our present argument; but the following considerations will make it clear that there must necessarily be some such
thing, which, while it has the capacity of moving something else, is
itself unmoved and exempt from all change, both unqualified and   15
accidental. Let us suppose, if you will, that in the case of certain things
it is possible for them at different times to be and not to be, without
any process of becoming and perishing (in fact it would seem to be
necessary, if a thing that has not parts at one time is and at another
time is not, that any such thing should without undergoing any change
at one time be and at another time not be). And let us further suppose   20
it possible that some principles that are unmoved but capable of
imparting motion at one time are and at another time are not. Even so,
this cannot be true of *all* such principles, since there must clearly be
something that *causes* things that move themselves at one time to be
and at another not to be. For, since nothing that has not parts can be in
motion, everything which moves itself must have magnitude, though   25
nothing that we have said makes this necessarily true of every mover.
So the fact that some things become and others perish, and that this is
so continuously, cannot be caused by any one of those things that,
though they are unmoved, do not always exist; nor again some be
caused by some and others by others. The eternity and continuity of the
process cannot be caused either by any one of them singly or by the   30
sum of them, because this causal relation must be eternal and necessary, whereas the sum of these movers is infinite and they do not all
exist together. It is clear, then, that though there may be countless

259ᵃ instances of the perishing of movers unmoved, and though many
things that move themselves perish and are succeeded by others that
come into being, and though one thing that is unmoved moves one
thing while another moves another, nevertheless there is something
that comprehends them all, and that as something apart from each one
of them, and this it is that is the cause of the fact that some things are
5 and others are not and of the continuous process of change; and this
causes the motion of the other movers, while they are the causes of the
motion of other things. Motion, then, being eternal, the first mover, if
there is but one, will be eternal also; if there are more than one, there
will be a plurality of such eternal movers. We ought, however, to
suppose that there is one rather than many, and a finite rather than an
infinite number. When the consequences of either assumption are the
10 same, we should always assume that things are finite rather than infinite in number, since in things constituted by nature that which is
finite and that which is better ought, if possible, to be present rather
than the reverse; and here it is sufficient to assume only one mover,
the first of unmoved things, which being eternal will be the principle
of motion to everything else.

The following argument also makes it evident that the first mover
15 must be something that is one and eternal. We have shown that there
must always be motion. That being so, motion must be continuous,
because what is always is continuous, whereas what is in succession is
not continuous. But further, if motion is continuous, it is one; and it is
one only if the mover and the moved are each of them one, since in the
event of a thing's being moved now by one thing and now by another
the whole motion will not be continuous but successive.

20 Moreover a conviction that there is a first unmoved something may
be reached not only from the foregoing arguments, but also by considering again the principles operative in movers. Now it is evident
that among existing things there are some that are sometimes in
motion and sometimes at rest. This fact has served to make it clear
that it is not true either that all things are in motion or that all things
are at rest or that some things are always at rest and the remainder
always in motion: on this matter proof is supplied by things that fluc-
25 tuate between the two and have the capacity of being sometimes in
motion and sometimes at rest. The existence of things of this kind is
clear to all; but we wish to explain also the nature of each of the other
two kinds and show that there are some things that are always
unmoved and some things that are always in motion. In the course of

our argument directed to this end we established the fact that everything that is in motion is moved by something, and that the mover is   30
either unmoved or in motion, and that, if it is in motion, it is moved at
each stage either by itself or by something else; and so we proceeded
to the position that of things that are moved, the principle of things
that are in motion is that which moves itself, and the principle of the   259^b
whole series is the unmoved. Further it is evident from actual observation that there are things that have the characteristic of moving themselves, e.g. the animal kingdom and the whole class of living things.
This being so, then, the view was suggested that perhaps it may be
possible for motion to come to be in a thing without having been in
existence at all before, because we see this actually occurring in   5
animals: they are unmoved at one time and then again they are in
motion, as it seems. We must grasp the fact, therefore, that animals
move themselves only with one kind of motion, and that this is not
strictly originated by them. The cause of it is not derived from the
animal itself: there are other natural motions in animals, which they
do not experience through their own instrumentality, e.g. increase,
decrease, and respiration: these are experienced by every animal while   10
it is at rest and not in motion in respect of the motion set up by its own
agency; here the motion is caused by the environment and by many
things that enter into the animal: thus in some cases the cause is nourishment—when it is being digested animals sleep, and when it is being
distributed they awake and move themselves, the first principle of this
motion being thus originally derived from outside. Therefore animals
are not always in continuous motion by their own agency: it is something else that moves them, itself being in motion and changing as it   15
comes into relation with each several thing that moves itself. (Moreover in all these things the first mover and cause of their self-motions
is itself moved by itself, though in an accidental sense: that is to say,
the body changes its place, so that that which is in the body changes its
place also and moves itself by leverage.) Hence we may be sure that if a   20
thing belongs to the class of unmoved things which move themselves
accidentally, it is impossible that it should cause continuous motion.
So the necessity that there should be motion continuously requires
that there should be a first mover that is unmoved even accidentally, if,
as we have said, there is to be in the world of things an unceasing and   25
undying motion, and the world is to remain self-contained and within
the same limits; for if the principle is permanent, the universe must
also be permanent, since it is continuous with the principle. (We must

distinguish, however, between accidental motion of a thing by itself
and such motion by something else, the former being confined to
30   perishable things, whereas the latter belongs also to certain principles
of heavenly bodies, of all those, that is to say, that experience more
than one locomotion.)

And further, if there is always something of this nature, a mover that
is itself unmoved and eternal, then that which is first moved by it must
260ᵃ   also be eternal. Indeed this is clear also from the consideration that
there would otherwise be no becoming and perishing and no change
of any kind in other things, if there were nothing in motion to move
them; for the motion imparted by the unmoved will always be
imparted in the same way and be one and the same, since the unmoved
5   does not itself change in relation to that which is moved by it. But that
which is moved by something that, though it is in motion, is moved
directly by the unmoved stands in varying relations to the things that it
moves, so that the motion that it causes will not be always the same: by
reason of the fact that it occupies contrary positions or assumes contrary forms it will produce contrary motions in each several thing that
10   it moves and will cause it to be at one time at rest and at another time
in motion.

The foregoing argument, then, has served to clear up the point
about which we raised a difficulty at the outset—why is it that instead
of all things being either in motion or at rest, or some things being
always in motion and the remainder always at rest, there are things
that are sometimes in motion and sometimes not? The cause of this is
15   now plain: it is because, while some things are moved by an eternal
unmoved mover and are therefore always in motion, other things are
moved by something that is in motion and changing, so that they too
must change. But the unmoved mover, as has been said, since it
remains simple and unvarying and in the same state, will cause motion
that is one and simple.

CHAPTER 10

. . .

267ᵃ   Since there must be continuous motion in the world of things, and this
is a single motion, and a single motion must be a motion of a magnitude (for that which is without magnitude cannot be in motion), and of
a single magnitude moved by a single mover (for otherwise there will
not be continuous motion but a consecutive series of separate
25   motions), then if the mover is a single thing, it is either in motion or

unmoved: if, then, it is in motion, it will have to keep pace with that which it moves and itself be in process of change, and it will also have to be moved by something: so we have a series that must come to an end, and a point will be reached at which motion is imparted by something that is unmoved. Thus we have a mover that has no need to change along with that which it moves but will be able to cause motion always (for the causing of motion under these conditions involves no effort); and this motion alone is regular, or at least it is so in a higher degree than any other, since the mover is never subject to any change. So, too, in order that the motion may continue to be of the same character, the moved must not be subject to change in relation to it. So it must occupy either the centre or the circumference, since these are the principles. But the things nearest the mover are those whose motion is quickest, and in this case it is the motion of the circumference that is the quickest: therefore the mover occupies the circumference.

There is a difficulty in supposing it to be possible for anything that is in motion to cause motion continuously and not merely in the way in which it is caused by something repeatedly pushing (in which case the continuity amounts to no more than successiveness). Such a mover must either itself continue to push or pull or perform both these actions, or else the action must be taken up by something else and be passed on from one mover to another (the process that we described before as occurring in the case of things thrown, since the air, being divisible, is a mover in virtue of the fact that different parts of the air are moved one after another); and in either case the motion cannot be a single motion, but only a consecutive series of motions. The only continuous motion, then, is that which is caused by the unmoved mover; for it remains always invariable, so that its relation to that which it moves remains also invariable and continuous.

Now that these points are settled, it is clear that the first unmoved mover cannot have any magnitude. For if it has magnitude, this must be either a finite or an infinite magnitude. Now we have already proved in our course on physics that there cannot be an infinite magnitude; and we have now proved that it is impossible for a finite magnitude to have an infinite force, and also that it is impossible for a thing to be moved by a finite magnitude during an infinite time. But the first mover causes a motion that is eternal and causes it during an infinite time. It is clear, therefore, that it is indivisible and is without parts and without magnitude.

267ᵇ

5

10

15

20

25

ON THE HEAVENS*

BOOK I

CHAPTER 2

268ᵇ The question as to the nature of the whole, whether it is infinite in size or limited in its total mass, is a matter for subsequent inquiry. We will now speak of those parts of the whole which are specifically distinct.

15 Let us take this as our starting-point. All natural bodies and magnitudes we hold to be, as such, capable of locomotion; for nature, we say, is their principle of movement. But all movement that is in place, all locomotion, as we term it, is either straight or circular or a combination of these two which are the only simple movements. And the

20 reason is that these two, the straight and the circular line, are the only simple magnitudes. Now revolution about the centre is circular motion, while the upward and downward movements are in a straight line, 'upward' meaning motion away from the centre, and 'downward' motion towards it. All simple motion, then, must be motion either away from or towards or about the centre. This seems to be in exact

25 accord with what we said above: as body found its completion in three dimensions, so its movement completes itself in three forms.

Bodies are either simple or compounded of such; and by simple bodies I mean those which possess a principle of movement in their own nature, such as fire and earth with their kinds, and whatever is akin to them. Necessarily, then, movements also will be either simple

269ᵃ or in some sort compound—simple in the case of the simple bodies, compound in that of the composite—and the motion is according to the prevailing element. Supposing, then, that there is such a thing as simple movement, and that circular movement is simple, and that both movement of a simple body is simple and simple movement is of

5 a simple body (for if it is movement of a compound it will be in virtue of a prevailing element), then there must necessarily be some simple body which moves naturally and in virtue of its own nature with a circular movement. By constraint, of course, it may be brought to

* *Translation*: J. L. Stocks, revised J. Barnes (Revised Oxford Aristotle, 1984); *Text*: D. J. Allan (Oxford Classical Texts, 1936).

move with the motion of something else different from itself, but it cannot so move naturally, since there is one sort of movement natural to each of the simple bodies. Again, if the unnatural movement is the contrary of the natural and a thing can have no more than one contrary, it will follow that circular movement, being a simple motion, must be unnatural, if it is not natural, to the body moved. If then the body whose movement is circular is fire or some other element, its natural motion must be the contrary of the circular motion. But a single thing has a single contrary; and upward and downward motion are the contraries of one another. If, on the other hand, the body moving with this circular motion which is unnatural to it is something different from the elements, there will be some other motion which is natural to it. But this cannot be. For if the natural motion is upward, it will be fire or air, and if downward, water or earth. Further, this circular motion is necessarily primary. For the complete is naturally prior to the incomplete, and the circle is a complete thing. This cannot be said of any straight line:—not of an infinite line; for then it would have a limit and an end; nor of any finite line; for in every case there is something beyond it, since any finite line can be extended. And so, since the prior movement belongs to the body which is naturally prior, and circular movement is prior to straight, and movement in a straight line belongs to simple bodies—fire moving straight upward and earthy bodies straight downward towards the centre—since this is so, it follows that circular movement also must be the movement of some simple body. For the movement of composite bodies is, as we said, determined by that simple body which prevails in the composition. From this it is clear that there is in nature some bodily substance other than the formations we know, prior to them all and more divine than they. Or again, we may take it that all movement is either natural or unnatural, and that the movement which is unnatural to one body is natural to another—as, for instance, is the case with the upward and downward movements, which are natural and unnatural to fire and earth respectively. It necessarily follows that circular movement, being unnatural to these bodies, is the natural movement of some other. Further, if, on the one hand, circular movement is *natural* to something, it must surely be some simple and primary body which naturally moves with a natural circular motion, as fire moves up and earth down. If, on the other hand, the movement of the rotating bodies about the centre is *unnatural*, it would be remarkable and indeed quite inconceivable that this movement alone should be continuous and eternal, given that it is unnatural. At any rate the evidence of all other cases goes to show that it is the unnatural which quickest passes away.

10 And so, if, as some say, the body so moved is fire, this movement is just as unnatural to it as downward movement; for anyone can see that fire moves in a straight line away from the centre. On all these grounds, therefore, we may infer with confidence that there is something beyond the bodies that are about us on this earth, different and separ-

15 ate from them; and that the superior glory of its nature is proportionate to its distance from this world of ours.

CHAPTER 9

277^b We must show not only that the heaven is one, but also that more than one heaven is impossible, and, further, that, as exempt from decay and generation, the heaven is eternal. We may begin by rehearsing the puzzles. From one point of view it might seem impossible that the

30 heaven should be one and unique, since in all formations and products whether of nature or of art we can distinguish the shape in itself and the shape in combination with matter. For instance the form of the

278^a sphere is one thing and the gold or bronze sphere another; the shape of the circle again is one thing, the bronze or wooden circle another. For when we state the essential nature of the sphere or circle we do not include in the formula gold or bronze, because they do not belong to its substance; but if we are speaking of the copper or gold sphere we

5 do include them. We still make the distinction even if we cannot conceive or apprehend any other example beside the particular thing. This may, of course, sometimes be the case: it might be, for instance, that only one circle could be found; yet none the less the difference will remain between its being a circle and its being this particular circle, the one being form, the other form in matter, i.e. a particular thing. Now

10 since the heaven is perceptible it must be regarded as a particular; for everything that is perceptible subsists, as we know, in matter. But if it is a particular, there will be a distinction between being this heaven and being a heaven without qualification. There is a difference, then, between this heaven and a heaven without qualification; the second is form and shape, the first form in combination with matter; and any

15 shape or form has, or may have, more than one particular instance.

On the supposition of Forms such as some assert, this must be the case, and equally on the view that no such entity has a separate existence. For in every case in which the substance is in matter it is a fact of observation that the particulars of like form are several or infinite in number. Hence there either are, or may be, more heavens than one. 20 On these grounds, then, it might be inferred either that there are or that there might be several heavens. We must, however, return and ask how much of this argument is correct and how much not.

Now it is quite right to say that the formula of the shape apart from the matter must be different from that of the shape in the matter, and we may allow this to be true. We are not, however, therefore compelled to assert a plurality of worlds. Such a plurality is in fact impos- 25 sible if this world contains the entirety of matter, as in fact it does. But perhaps our contention can be made clearer in this way. Suppose aquilinity to be curvature in the nose or flesh, and flesh to be the matter of aquilinity. Suppose, further, that all flesh came together into 30 a single whole of flesh endowed with this aquiline quality. Then neither would there be, nor could there arise, any other thing that was aquiline. Similarly, suppose flesh and bones to be the matter of man, and suppose a man to be created of all flesh and all bones in indissoluble union. The possibility of another man would be removed. Whatever case you took it would be the same. The general rule is this: 278ᵇ a thing whose substance resides in a substratum of matter can never come into being in the absence of all matter. Now the heaven is certainly a particular and a material thing; if however it is composed not of a p̄art but of the whole of matter, then though being a heaven and 5 being this heaven are still distinct, yet there is no other heaven, and no possibility of others being made, because all the matter is already included in this. It remains, then, only to prove that it is composed of all natural perceptible body.

First, however, we must explain what we mean by 'heaven' and in 10 how many ways we use the word, in order to make clearer the object of our inquiry. In one sense, then, we call 'heaven' the substance of the extreme circumference of the whole, or that natural body whose place is at the extreme circumference. We recognize habitually a special right to the name 'heaven' in the extremity or upper region, which we take to be the seat of all that is divine. In another sense, we use this 15 name for the body continuous with the extreme circumference, which contains the moon, the sun, and some of the stars; these we say are 'in the heaven'.

In yet another sense we give the name to all body included within the extreme circumference, since we habitually call the whole or total- 20 ity 'the heaven'. The word, then, is used in three senses.

Now the whole included within the extreme circumference must be composed of *all* physical and sensible body, because there neither is, nor can come into being, any body outside the heaven. For if there is a natural body outside the extreme circumference it must be either a simple or a composite body, and its position must be either natural or unnatural. But it cannot be any of the simple bodies. For it has been shown that that which moves in a circle cannot change its place. And it cannot be that which moves from the centre or that which lies lowest. *Naturally* they could not be there, since their proper places are elsewhere; and if these are there *unnaturally*, the exterior place will be natural to some other body, since a place which is unnatural to one body must be natural to another; but we saw that there is no other body besides these. Then it is not possible that any simple body should be outside the heaven. But, if no simple body, neither can any mixed body be there; for the presence of the simple body is involved in the presence of the mixture. Further, neither can any body come into that place; for it will do so either naturally or unnaturally, and will be either simple or composite; so that the same argument will apply, since it makes no difference whether the question is 'Is it there?' or 'Can it come to be there?' From our arguments then it is evident not only that there is not, but also that there could never come to be, any bodily mass whatever outside the circumference. For the world as a whole includes *all* its appropriate matter, which is, as we saw, natural perceptible body. So that neither are there now, nor have there ever been, nor can there ever be formed more heavens than one, but this heaven of ours is one and unique and complete.

It is therefore evident that there is also no place or void or time outside the heaven. For in every place body can be present; and void is said to be that in which the presence of body, though not actual, is possible; and time is the number of movement. But in the absence of natural body there is no movement, and outside the heaven, as we have shown, body neither exists nor can come to exist. It is clear then that there is neither place, nor void, nor time, outside the heaven. Hence whatever is there, is of such a nature as not to occupy any place, nor does time age it; nor is there any change in any of the things which lie beyond the outermost motion; they continue through their entire duration unalterable and unmodified, living the best and most self-sufficient of lives. As a matter of fact, this word 'duration' possessed a divine significance for the ancients; for the fulfilment which includes the period of life of any creature, outside of which no natural develop-

ment can fall, has been called its duration. On the same principle the 25
fulfilment of the whole heaven, the fulfilment which includes all time
and infinity, is duration—a name based upon the fact that it *is*
always[1]—being immortal and divine. From it derive the being and life
which other things, some more or less articulately but others feebly,
enjoy. So, too, in its discussions concerning the divine, popular philo- 30
sophy often propounds the view that whatever is divine, whatever is
primary and supreme, is necessarily unchangeable. This fact confirms
what we have said. For there is nothing else stronger than it to move it—
since that would be more divine—and it has no defect and lacks none
of its proper excellences. Its unceasing movement, then, is also
reasonable, since everything ceases to move when it comes to its 279[b]
proper place, but the body whose path is the circle has one and the
same place for starting-point and goal.

CHAPTER 10

Having established these distinctions, we may now proceed to the
question whether the heaven is ungenerated or generated, indestruct- 5
ible or destructible. Let us start with a review of the theories of other
thinkers; for the proofs of a theory are difficulties for the contrary
theory. Besides, those who have first heard the pleas of our adver-
saries will be more likely to credit the assertions which we are going to
make. We shall be less open to the charge of procuring judgement by 10
default. To give a satisfactory decision as to the truth it is necessary to
be rather an arbitrator than a party to the dispute.

That the world was generated all are agreed, but, generation over,
some say that it is eternal, others say that it is destructible like any 15
other natural formation. Others again, with Empedocles of Acragas
and Heraclitus of Ephesus, believe that it alternates, being sometimes
as it is now and sometimes different and in a process of destruction,
and that this continues without end.

Now to assert that it was generated and yet is eternal is to assert the
impossible; for we cannot reasonably attribute to anything any characteristics but those which observation detects in many or all instances.
But in this case the facts point the other way: generated things are seen 20
always to be destroyed. Further, a thing whose present state had no
beginning and which could not have been other than it was at any

---

[1] The word translated 'duration' derives from a phrase meaning 'always existing'.

previous moment throughout its entire duration, cannot possibly be changed. For there will have to be some cause of change, and if this had been present earlier it would have been possible for that which
25 could not be otherwise to be otherwise. Suppose that the world was formed out of elements which were formerly otherwise. Then if their condition was always so and could not have been otherwise, the world could never have come into being. And if the world did come into being, then, clearly, their condition must have been capable of change and not eternal: after combination therefore they will be dispersed, just as in the past after dispersion they came into combination, and
30 this process either has been or could have been, indefinitely repeated. But if this is so, the world cannot be indestructible, and it does not matter whether the change of condition has actually occurred or remains a possibility.

Some of those who hold that the world, though indestructible, was yet generated, try to support their case by a parallel which is illusory. They say that in their statements about its generation they are doing what geometricians do when they construct their figures, not implying that the universe really had a beginning, but for didactic reasons facili-
280ᵃ tating understanding by exhibiting the object, like the figure, as in course of formation. The two cases, as we said, are not parallel; for, in the construction of the figure, when the various steps are completed the same figure forthwith results; but in these other demonstrations
5 what results is not the same. Indeed it cannot be so; for antecedent and consequent, as assumed, are in contradiction. The ordered, it is said, arose out of the unordered; and the same thing cannot be at the same time both ordered and unordered; there must be a process and a lapse of time separating the two states. In the figure, on the other hand,
10 there is no temporal separation. It is clear that the universe cannot be at once eternal and generated.

. . .

CHAPTER 12

281ᵇ Let us take our start from this point. The impossible and the false have not the same significance. One use of 'impossible' and 'possible', and
5 'false' and 'true', is hypothetical. It is impossible, for instance, on a certain hypothesis that the triangle should have its angles equal to two right angles, and on another the diagonal is commensurable. But there are also things possible and impossible, false and true, absolutely. Now it is one thing to be absolutely false, and another thing to be

absolutely impossible. To say that you are standing when you are not
standing is to assert a falsehood, but not an impossibility. Similarly to   10
say that a man who is playing the harp, but not singing, is singing, is to
say what is false but not impossible. To say, however, that you are at
once standing and sitting, or that the diagonal is commensurable, is to
say what is not only false but also impossible. Thus it is not the same
thing to make a false and to make an impossible hypothesis; and from
the impossible hypothesis impossible results follow. A man has, it is   15
true, the capacity at once of sitting and standing, because when he
possesses the one he also possesses the other; but it does not follow
that he can at the same time sit and stand, but at different times. But if
a thing has for infinite time more than one capacity, another time is
impossible and the times must coincide. Thus if anything which exists
for infinite time is destructible, it will have the capacity of not being.   20
Now if it exists for infinite time let this capacity be actualized; and it
will be in actuality at once existent and non-existent. Thus a false conclusion would follow because a false assumption was made; but if what
was assumed had not been impossible its consequence would not have
been impossible.

Anything then which always exists is absolutely imperishable. It is   25
also ungenerated, since if it was generated it will have the power of not
being for some time. For as that which formerly was, but now is not,
or is capable at some future time of not being, is destructible, so that
which is capable of formerly not having been is generated. But in the
case of that which always is, there is no time for such a capacity of not
being, whether the supposed time is finite or infinite; for its capacity   30
of being must include the finite time since it covers infinite time.

It is therefore impossible that one and the same thing should be
capable of always existing and of always not-existing.

BOOK II

CHAPTER 12

. . .
A second difficulty which may with equal justice be raised is this. Why   292ᵃ
is it that the primary motion includes such a multitude of stars that
their whole array seems to defy counting,while of the other stars each
one is separated off, and in no case do we find two or more attached to
the same motion?

On these questions it is well that we should seek to increase our
15 understanding, though we have but little to go upon, and are placed at
so great a distance from the facts in question. Nevertheless if we base
our consideration on such things, we shall not find this difficulty by
any means insoluble. We think of the stars as mere bodies, and as units
20 with a serial order indeed but entirely inanimate; but we should rather
conceive them as enjoying life and action. On this view the facts cease
to appear surprising. For it is plausible that the best-conditioned of all
things should have its good without action, that that which is nearest
to it should achieve it by little and simple action, and that which is
further removed by a complexity of actions, just as with men's bodies
25 one is in good condition without exercise at all, another after a short
walk, while another requires running and wrestling and hard training,
and there are yet others who however hard they worked themselves
could never secure this good, but only some substitute for it. To
succeed often or in many things is difficult. For instance, to throw ten
thousand Chians[2] with the dice would be impossible, but to throw one
30 or two is comparatively easy. In action, again, when A has to be done
to get B, B to get C, and C to get D, one step or two present little
difficulty, but as the series extends the difficulty grows. We must,
then, think of the action of the stars as similar to that of animals and
292ᵇ plants. For on our earth it is man that has the greatest variety of
actions—for there are many goods that man can secure; hence his
actions are various and directed to ends beyond them—while the
5 perfectly conditioned has no need of action, since it is itself the end,
and action always requires two terms, end and means. The lower
animals have less variety of action than man; and plants perhaps have
little action and of one kind only. For either they have but one
attainable good (as indeed man has), or, if several, each contributes
directly to their ultimate good. One thing then has and enjoys the
10 ultimate good, other things attain to it, one immediately by few steps,
another by many, while yet another does not even attempt to secure it
but is satisfied to reach a point not far removed from that consummation. Thus, taking health as the end, there will be one thing
that always possesses health, others that attain it, one by reducing
flesh, another by running and thus reducing flesh, another by taking
15 steps to enable himself to run, thus further increasing the number of
movements, while another cannot attain health itself, but only

_____
² Double ones.

running or reduction of flesh, so that one or other of these is for such a being the end. For while it is clearly best for any being to attain the real end, yet, if that cannot be, the nearer it is to the best the better will be its state. It is for this reason that the earth moves not at all and the bodies near to it with few movements. For they do not attain the final end, but only come as near to it as their share in the divine principle permits. But the first heaven finds it immediately with a single movement, and the bodies intermediate between the first and last heavens attain it indeed, but at the cost of a multiplicity of movement.

20

BOOK III

CHAPTER 6

First we must inquire whether the elements are eternal or subject to generation and destruction; for when this question had been answered their number and character will be manifest. In the first place, they cannot be eternal. It is a matter of observation that fire, water, and every simple body undergo a process of analysis, which must either continue infinitely or stop somewhere. Suppose it infinite. Then the time occupied by the process will be infinite, and also that occupied by the reverse process of synthesis. For the processes of analysis and synthesis succeed one another in the various parts. It will follow that there are two infinite times which are mutually exclusive, the time occupied by the synthesis, which is infinite, being preceded by the period of analysis. There are thus two mutually exclusive infinites, which is impossible. Suppose, on the other hand, that the analysis stops somewhere. Then the body at which it stops will be either atomic or, as Empedocles seems to have intended, a divisible body which will yet never be divided. The foregoing arguments show that it cannot be an atom; but neither can it be a divisible body which analysis will never reach. For a smaller body is more easily destroyed than a larger; and a destructive process which succeeds in destroying, that is, in resolving into smaller bodies, a body of some size, cannot reasonably be expected to fail with the smaller body. Now in fire we observe a destruction of two kinds: it is destroyed by its contrary when it is quenched, and by itself when it dies out. But the effect is produced by a greater quantity upon a lesser, and the more quickly the smaller it is.

304^{b}

25

30

305^{a}

5

10

The elements of bodies must therefore be subject to destruction and generation.

Since they are generated, they must be generated either from something incorporeal or from a body, and if from a body, either from one another or from something else. The theory which generates them from something incorporeal requires a separate void. For everything that comes to be comes to be in something, and that in which the generation takes place must either be incorporeal or possess body; and if it has body, there will be two bodies in the same place at the same time, viz. that which is coming to be and that which was previously there, while if it is incorporeal, there must be a separate void. But we have already shown that this is impossible. But, on the other hand, it is equally impossible that the elements should be generated from some kind of body. That would involve a body distinct from the elements and prior to them. But if this body possesses weight or lightness, it will be one of the elements; and if it has no tendency to movement, it will be an immovable or mathematical entity, and therefore not in a place at all. A place in which a thing is at rest is a place in which it might move, either by constraint, i.e. unnaturally, or in the absence of constraint, i.e. naturally. If, then, it is in a place and somewhere, it will be one of the elements; and if it is not in a place, nothing can come from it, since that which comes into being and that out of which it comes must needs be together. The elements therefore cannot be generated from something incorporeal nor from a body which is not an element, and the only remaining possibility is that they are generated from one another.

ON GENERATION AND CORRUPTION*

BOOK I

CHAPTER 3

Having settled these matters we must first consider whether there is 317ᵃ
anything which comes to be *simpliciter* and perishes, or whether strictly
speaking there is nothing which does so, but it is always a case of
coming to be something from being something. What I mean is, for
example, coming to be well from being ill and ill from being well, or
small from big and big from small, and all the other cases following 35
this pattern. For coming to be *simpliciter* would involve something's 317ᵇ
coming to be from not being *simpliciter*, so that it would be true to say
that not being belongs to some things: coming to be something is from
not being something, e.g. from not being white or not being beautiful,
whereas coming to be *simpliciter* is from not being *simpliciter*. 5

Simpliciter can signify either what is first in each category of being or
what is universal and includes everything. If the former, generation of
substance will be from what is not substance; but where neither substance nor individuality belongs, neither, of course, does any of the
other categories, e.g. quality, quantity, or place, for that would mean
affections existing in separation from substances. If, on the other 10
hand, 'not being *simpliciter*' means not being generally, this will
amount to a universal denial of everything, so that that which comes to
be must needs come to be from nothing.

The dilemmas that arise concerning these matters and their solu-
tions have been set out at greater length elsewhere, but it should now
again be said by way of summary that in one way it is from what is not
that a thing comes to be *simpliciter*, though in another way it is always 15
from what is; for that which is potentially but is not actually must
necessarily pre-exist, being described in both these ways. But even
when these distinctions have been made, there remains a question of
remarkable difficulty, which we must take up once again, namely, how
is coming to be *simpliciter* possible, whether from what is potentially or

---

* *Translation*: C. J. F. Williams (Clarendon Aristotle Series, 1982); *Text*: H. H.
Joachim (Oxford, 1922).

20   some other way. One might well wonder whether there is coming to be
of substance and the individual, as opposed to quality, quantity, and
place (and the same question arises in the case of ceasing to be). For if
something comes to be, clearly there will exist potentially, not
actually, some substance from which the coming to be will arise and
25   into which that which ceases to be has to change. Now will any of the
others belong to this actually? What I mean is: Will that which is only
potentially individual and existent, but neither individual nor existent
simpliciter, have any quality or quantity or place? If it has none of these,
but all of them potentially, that which in this sense is not will consequently be separable, and further, the principal and perpetual fear of
30   the early philosophers will be realized, namely, the coming to be of
something from nothing previously existing. But if being individual
and a substance are not going to belong to it while some of the other
things we have mentioned are, the affections will, as we have
remarked, be separable from the substances.

We ought, then, to work at these problems as much as possible, and
also enquire what is the cause of there always being generation, both
35   generation *simpliciter* and the partial sort of generation. Given that
318ª there is one cause from which we say movement begins, and another
which is matter, it is the latter sort of cause that we must speak about.
For the former has already been spoken about in the treatise on movement, where we said that there is that which is throughout time
5   unmoved and that which is always in motion: the former of these, the
unmoved principle, it is the task of that other and prior philosophy to
clarify; the latter, that which moves the other things through being
continually moved, we shall treat of later, and determine which thing
of this sort of those we call particular is the cause. Now, however, let
us discuss the cause which is placed in the class of matter. It is because
10   of this that corruption and generation never disappear from nature.
For maybe at the same time as this becomes clear, so will the solution
to the dilemma we were faced with just now as to the correct way of
speaking also about corruption and generation *simpliciter*.

Enough of a dilemma is in fact involved in the question what is the
cause of the continued succession of generation, if that which perishes
disappears into the non-existent and the non-existent is nothing (for
the non-existent is neither something nor suchlike nor so big nor
15   somewhere). If some one of the things which exist is always disappear-
ing, why has not the universe been entirely spent and taken its depar-
ture long ago, if, that is, there was only a limited quantity of matter for

the generation of each of the things coming into being? For it is certainly not because the matter of generation is infinite that it does not give out. That is impossible, since nothing is actually infinite, but only 20 potentially, as subject to division; so the only possible inexhaustible generation would be due to something smaller always coming into existence—but in fact this is not what we see.

Is it, then, because the corruption of one thing is the generation of another and vice versa, that the change is necessarily unceasing? 25

As far as concerns the existence of generation and corruption alike in the case of each of the things which are, this explanation should be considered sufficient for them all. But why some things are said to come to be and to cease to be *simpliciter* and others not *simpliciter* needs further consideration, if indeed one and the same thing is both the generation of *A* and the perishing of *B* and vice versa. Some account of this is needed. For we say on occasion that now something 30 is perishing *simpliciter*, not merely that *B* is perishing, and that *this* is a case of generation *simpliciter*, and *that* of corruption. Again, this comes to be something without coming to be *simpliciter*: we say that a person who learns comes to be knowledgeable, not that he comes to be *simpliciter*. We often make a distinction by saying that some things signify 35 a particular individual and others do not. The account that is needed 318ᵇ is a consequence of this.

For there is a difference between the things into which the changing object changes: for instance, it may be that the way that leads to a fire is a coming to be *simpliciter*, but a perishing of something, say earth; whereas the coming to be of earth is a coming to be something, not 5 coming to be *simpliciter*, but a perishing *simpliciter*, say of fire. Thus Parmenides speaks of two, saying that that which is and that which is not are fire and earth, respectively. It makes no difference whether we postulate this particular pair or another like it: what we are after is the manner of the change, not its matter. The way which leads to that which is not *simpliciter* is corruption *simpliciter*: that which leads to 10 what is *simpliciter* is generation *simpliciter*. In whatever terms the distinction is made, whether in terms of earth and fire or of some other pair, one of the pair will be that which is, the other that which is not. This, then, is one way in which generation and corruption *simpliciter* will differ from those which are not *simpliciter*. Another way is by the character of the matter involved. If the distinguishing characteristics of the matter signify individuality to a greater degree, the matter itself 15 is to a greater degree substance; if they signify privation, non-being.

For example if heat is a positive characteristic and a form, but cold a privation, earth and fire differ in accordance with these distinguishing characteristics.

The common view is rather that the difference is in terms of the per-
20   ceptible and the imperceptible: when the change is to perceptible matter they say that generation occurs, when to matter that is not apparent, corruption. They distinguish what is and what is not by their perceiving or not perceiving it, in the same way as the knowable is what is and the unknowable what is not, for perception has the force of knowledge. Just as they hold that their own life and being consists in
25   perceiving or being able to perceive, so, they think, does that of things. In a sense they are on to something true, though what they actually say is untrue. Coming to be *simpliciter* and perishing come out differently on the common view and on the correct view. By the standard of per- ception wind and air are to a lesser degree, so they accordingly say that the things which perish *simpliciter* perish by changing into these, and
30   that things come into being when they change into what is tangible, i.e. earth. In fact, however, wind and air are individual and identifiable with form to a greater extent than earth.

We have now stated the reason why there is such a thing as genera- tion *simpliciter*, which is the corruption of something, and such a thing as corruption *simpliciter*, which is the generation of something: it is due
35   to a difference of matter either in respect of its being substance or not being substance, or in respect of its being more or less so, or because
319ᵃ   in the one case the matter from which or to which the change takes place is more perceptible and in the other case less perceptible. The reason why some things are said to come to be *simpliciter*, others only to come to be something, not in virtue of the generation of one from
5   another in the manner we have just been describing—for all that has so far been determined is why, when every instance of corruption is the generation of something else, we do not attribute 'coming to be' and 'ceasing to be' impartially to the things which change into one another; but the problem that was mentioned later was not this, but
10   why that which learns is not said to come to be *simpliciter* but to come to be knowledgeable, whereas that which is born *is* said to come to be—*this* distinction is made in terms of the categories. For some things signify an individual, some a quality, some a quantity. So those which do not signify substance are not said to come to be *simpliciter* but to come to be something. For all that, in every category alike we talk of generation in connection with just one of the two columns; for

instance, in substance if it is 'fire', but not if it is 'earth', and in quality 15
if it is 'knowledgeable', but not if it is 'ignorant'.

We have thus dealt with the fact that some things come to be *simpliciter* and others not, both in general and amongst substances themselves. We have also stated why the substratum is cause, as matter, of the continuous occurrence of generation: namely, because it is able to change from one contrary to another, and because the generation of one thing in the case of substances is always the corruption of another 20 and the corruption of one thing the generation of another.

Furthermore, neither is there any need to puzzle over the question why there is generation although things are always perishing. For just as they say that something ceases to be *simpliciter* when it passes into imperceptibility and not-being, so they say that a thing comes to be from not being when it comes to be from being imperceptible. So 25 whether or not the substratum is something, things come to be from not being. Thus it is equally from what is not that things come to be and into what is not that things perish. It is only natural, then, that it does not give out; for generation is the corruption of what is not and corruption the generation of what is not.

However, a doubt might be raised whether this thing which is not 30 *simpliciter* is one of the pair of contraries—earth, the heavy element, for instance, as what is not, and fire, the light element, as what is—or whether, on the contrary, earth too is what is, whilst what is not is the matter that belongs equally to earth and fire. Again, is the matter of each of these different? Or would that mean that they did not come into being from each other or from their contraries (for it is to these 319ᵇ that the contraries belong, namely, to fire, earth, water, and air)? Or is there one way in which the matter is the same and another in which it is different? For the substratum, whatever it may be is the same, but the being is not the same. So much, then, for these questions. 5

CHAPTER 4

We must now explain the difference between generation and alteration, since we say that these changes are different from one another. The substratum is one thing and the affection whose nature is to be predicated of the substratum another, and either of them can change. So it is alteration when the substratum remains, being something per- 10 ceptible, but change occurs in the affections which belong to it, whether these are contraries or intermediates. For example, the body is well then ill, but remains the same body; the bronze is now round, now a thing with corners, but remains the same. When, however, the whole changes without anything perceptible remaining as the same substratum, but the way the seed changes entirely into blood, water into air, or air entirely into water, then, when we have this sort of thing, it is a case of generation (and corruption of something else); particularly if the change takes place from what is imperceptible to what is perceptible either by touch or by all the senses, as when water is generated or corrupts into air, since air is—near enough—imperceptible.

BOOK II

CHAPTER I

Our view is that there is a matter of the perceptible bodies, but that this is not separable but is always together with a contrariety, from which the so-called 'elements' come to be. A more precise account of them has been given elsewhere. Nevertheless, since this *is* the way in which the primary bodies are from the matter, we must give an account of these also, regarding, certainly, as a principle that is really first, the matter which, though inseparable, does underlie the contraries (for neither is the hot matter for the cold nor the latter for the hot, but the substratum is matter for them both); so first that which is perceptible body in potentiality is principle, and secondly the contrarieties (I mean, for example, heat and cold), and only thirdly fire and water and the like. For these change into one another, and it is not as Empedocles and others say (for there would be no alteration); but the contrarieties do not change. But none the less even so we must discuss what and how many of them are principles of body. The others posit them and make use of them but have nothing to say about why these are they, or this many.

CHAPTER 3

Since the elements are four in number, and of the four the pairings are six, but it is not in the nature of contraries to be paired with one another (it is impossible for one and the same thing to be both hot and cold, or, again, wet and dry), obviously the pairings of the elements

will be four in number: hot and dry, and wet and hot; and, again, cold
and dry, and cold and wet. And they are attached correspondingly to
the apparently simple bodies, fire, air, water, and earth. For fire is hot   330ᵇ
and dry, air hot and wet (for air is something like steam), water cold
and wet, and earth cold and dry. So it is in a rational way that the dif-   5
ferentiae are allotted to the primary bodies, and the number of them
corresponds.

The simple bodies being four in number, two each belong to each of
the two places: fire and air belong to that which moves towards the
boundary, earth and air to that which moves towards the middle. Fire
and earth are the extremes and the purest; water and air are the means
and more mixed. Two of them are contrary to the other two, respect-   331ᵃ
ively: water is contrary to fire, earth to air, because they are constituted
by the contrary affections. All the same, being four, each belongs *sim-*
pliciter to one of the affections: earth belongs to dry rather than to cold,
water to cold rather than to wet, air to wet rather than to hot, and fire   5
to hot rather than to dry.

CHAPTER 4

Since it has been settled earlier that generation for the simple bodies is
from one to another, and since, moreover, it is apparent even to perception that they come to be (for otherwise there would be no alteration, for alteration is in respect of the affections of tangible objects), we
must now discuss the way in which they change into one another, and   10
whether every one can come to be from every other one, or whether
this is possible for some but impossible for the others.

It is in fact clear that all are by nature able to change into each other.
For generation is to contraries and from contraries, and the elements
all have contrariety with each other on account of their differentiae   15
being contraries. For some both are contraries, e.g. fire and water (for
the one is dry and hot, the other wet and cold), for others only one is,
e.g. air and water (for the one is wet and hot, the other wet and cold).
So in general it is clear that it is natural for every one to come to be   20
from every other; and consequently it is not difficult to see in each
case taken individually how it happens. For, while they will all come
from each other, they will differ from each other in that with some it is
faster, with others slower, and with some it is easier, with others more
difficult. The change is fast in the case of those which have   25

counterparts relative to one another, slow in the case of those which lack them, because it is easier for one thing to change than for many. For example, from fire there will be air if one of its properties changes, the former having been hot and dry whilst the latter is hot and wet, so
30 that if the dryness is conquered by wetness there will be air. Again, from air there will be water if the heat is conquered by cold, the former having been hot and wet, the latter cold and wet, so that if the heat changes there will be water. In the same way there will be earth from
35 water and fire from earth. For both have counterparts relative to both:
331ᵇ water is wet and cold, earth cold and dry, so that if the wetness is conquered there will be earth; and again, since fire is dry and hot, whereas earth is cold and dry, if the cold is destroyed there will be fire from earth. Clearly, therefore, the generation of the simple bodies will be cyclical, and this is the easiest way in which change can take place—on
5 account of the presence of counterparts in consecutive pairs of elements. Although it is possible for water to come to be from fire, and earth from air, and again fire and air from water and earth, it is more difficult because more things have to change. If there is to be fire from water both the cold and the wetness have to be destroyed, and again if
10 air from earth both the cold and the dryness have to be destroyed. In the same way if there is to be water and earth from fire and air both things have to change.

CHAPTER 9

335ᵃ But since there are some things which come to be and perish, and since generation does in fact occur in the place around the middle
25 body, we must say, concerning all generation alike, how many principles there are of it and what they are. We shall in this way be able more easily to study particular cases, namely, when we have first obtained a grasp of the things which are universal.

The principles are equal in number and identical in kind to those which hold in the case of the eternal and primary beings: one of them is by way of matter and one by way of form. And the third principle
30 must also exist, for the other two are not adequate for making things come to be any more than in the case of the primary beings.

The cause by way of matter of things which come to be is that which is capable of being and not being. For some things of necessity are, i.e. the eternal things, and some things of necessity are not (of these the
35 one class cannot not be, the other cannot be, since it is not possible for

them to be otherwise, contrary to necessity); some things, however, are   335^b
capable both of being and of not being—which is what that which
comes to be and perishes is. For this is at one time and at another is
not. So generation and corruption belong necessarily to what is capable of being and not being. That is why it is the cause by way of matter   5
of things which come to be: the cause by way of 'that for the sake of
which' is the shape or form, and this is the definition of the essence of
each thing.

To these, however, must be added the third cause, which every
philosopher dreams of but none actually mentions. Some thought that
the nature of the forms is an adequate cause for coming to be. And this
is the view of Socrates in the *Phaedo*. (He, you remember, after   10
blaming everyone else for saying nothing to the point, adopts the
hypothesis that, of things that are, some are forms and some partake of
the forms, and that everything is said to be in virtue of the form, to
come to be in virtue of receiving a share of it and to perish in virtue of
losing it; so if this is true, the forms, he thinks, are necessarily the
causes of both generation and corruption.) For others, it is the matter   15
itself; for it is from this that movement arises. But neither party gives
the correct account. For if the forms are causes, why do they not
always generate things continuously rather than sometimes doing so
and sometimes not, since both the forms and the things which partake
in them are always there? Furthermore, in some cases we observe
something else being the cause: it is the doctor who induces health   20
and the knowledgeable man knowledge, despite the existence of both
health itself and knowledge and those who partake in it; and it is the
same in all the other cases where something is performed in virtue of a
capacity.

If, on the other hand, someone were to say that it was the matter
which generated things on account of movement, what he said would
be more scientific than that just described. For that which alters a   25
thing, or changes its shape, is more truly the cause of generation; and
generally we are accustomed to describe as the producer, both in the
case of things which occur in nature and of those which result from
skill, that thing, whatever it may be, which has to do with movement.
Nevertheless, what these people have to say is also incorrect. For it is
the property of matter to be acted upon and to be moved, whereas
causing movement and acting belongs to another capacity. This is   30
obviously the case with things which come to be through skill and
those which come to be through nature: the water does not itself

produce an animal out of itself, nor the wood a bed—it is skill which does this. So these people are for this reason incorrect in their account, and because they leave aside what is more strictly the cause; for they
35   take away the essence and the form.

Moreover, the capacities they attribute to the bodies, in virtue of
336ᵃ   which they make things come to be, are too instrumental, since they eliminate the formal cause. For since, according to them, the nature of the hot is to segregate and that of the cold to gather together, and that of each of the others is either to act or to be acted upon, they say that
5   out of these and by their means everything else comes to be and is destroyed. In fact, however, it is apparent that even fire itself is moved and acted upon. Again, what they do is rather like someone assigning the responsibility for things' coming to be to the saw and the various tools: for, necessarily, it is only if someone is sawing that something is
10   being divided, and it is only if someone is planing that something is being made smooth; and it is the same in the other cases. So, however much fire acts and causes movement, the question how it causes movement remains something which they do not go on to consider, nor that it is worse than the tools.

We have spoken in general about the causes before, and have now dealt with matter and form.

CHAPTER 10

Next, since it has been proved that movement by way of locomotion is
15   eternal, generation also, these things being so, must take place continuously; for the locomotion will produce the generation perpetually by bringing near and then removing the generating body. At the same time it is clear that what was said earlier was well said, namely, calling
20   locomotion and not generation the first of the changes. For it is much more reasonable to suppose that what is, is the cause of coming to be for what is not, than that what is not, is the cause of being for what is. Now that which is changing its place is, but that which is coming to be is not. That is why locomotion is in fact prior to generation.

Since it has been assumed, and indeed proved, that things are subject to continuous generation and corruption, and since we hold that
25   locomotion is the cause of coming to be, it is obvious that, if the locomotion is one, it will not be possible for both generation and corruption to occur, on account of their being contraries (for it is the nature of that which is the same and remains in the same state always

to produce the same effects, so either there will always be generation
or corruption); but the movements must be more than one, and contraries, in virtue either of direction or irregularity, since contraries 30
have contraries as their causes.

For this reason it is not the primary locomotion which is the cause
of generation and corruption, but that in the inclined circle. For in this
latter there is both continuity and being moved with two movements;
for, if there is always to be continuous generation and corruption, 336ᵇ
there has always to be, on the one hand, something being moved so
that these changes may not fail, and, on the other hand, two movements, to prevent there being only one of the two results. So the
locomotion of the whole is the cause of the continuity, whilst the inclination is the cause of the approach and retreat. For this results in its
coming to be further away at one time and nearer at another, and since
the distance is unequal the movement will be irregular. So, if it gener- 5
ates by approaching and being near, this same thing destroys by
retreating and coming to be further away; and if it generates by
repeatedly approaching, it also destroys by repeatedly retreating. For
contraries have contraries as their causes, and the corruption and the
generation that occur in nature take place in equal time. 10

This is why the times and the lives of all sorts of things have a
number which defines them. All things have order, and every time and
life is measured by a period, though not the same for all, but a smaller
for some and a longer for others. The period, i.e. the measure, is a year
for some, more for others, less for others. 15

There are things obvious even to perception which are in agreement with this reasoning of ours; for we see that while the sun is
approaching there is generation, but while it is retreating, diminution,
and each of these in equal time. For the times of the corruption and
the generation which occur in nature are equal. Often, however, it
happens that things perish in a shorter time on account of the 20
mingling of things with one another. For, matter being irregular and
not everywhere the same, the comings to be of things are also necessarily irregular, some fast, some slower. So it comes about as a result of
the generation of these things that corruption occurs of others.

As we have said, generation and corruption will always be continuous and, owing to the cause we have mentioned, will never fail. This 25
happens with good reason; for we say that nature in all cases desires
what is better, and that being is better than not being (it has been said
elsewhere how many senses there are in which we use 'be'), and this

30   cannot exist in all things since some are too far removed from the
principle. Accordingly God has filled up the whole in the only way
that remained by making generation perpetual. This was the way to
connect being together as much as possible, since coming to be continually and generation are the nearest things there are to being.

The cause of this, as has frequently been said, is circular locomo-
337ª tion, since this alone is continuous. That is why even the other things
which change into each other in respect of their affections and
capacities, as do the simple bodies, are imitating circular locomotion.
For when air comes to be from water and fire from air and water back
again from the fire, we say that generation has come round in a circle
because it has turned round and come back again. So even locomotion
in a straight line is continuous in that it imitates circular motion.

At the same time from this something which people have found
puzzling becomes clear, namely, why, when each of the bodies is
10   moving to its proper place, the bodies have not in an infinite time
separated out. The cause of this in fact is their change into one
another. If each remained in its own place and was not changed by its
neighbour, they would by now have separated out. They change, then,
because of the double locomotion; and because they change, none of
15   them can remain in any of the places assigned.

It is clear, then, from what has been said that there is such a thing as
generation and corruption, and owing to what cause, and what the
generable and corruptible is. But since something must be the mover,
if there is going to be movement, as has been said in previous works;
and if there is movement always, there must always be something to
20   move it; and if it is continuous, the mover must be one and the same
thing, immovable, ungenerated, and unalterable, and if the circular
movements are more than one, more than one, but all necessarily in
some way under a single principle. Because time is continuous, move-
25   ment must be continuous, given that it is impossible there should be
time without movement; time, then, is the number of a particular continuous movement, of circular movement therefore, as was determined in our introductory work. Is the movement continuous in virtue
of the continuity of the thing moved or the continuity of that in respect
of which it is moved, e.g. its place or some affection of it? Obviously in
30   virtue of that of the thing moved. (For how could an affection be continuous otherwise than in virtue of the continuity of the thing to which
it belongs? If, however, it is also in virtue of that in respect of which,
this belongs only to place, since it has a certain size.) Of things moved,

only that which is moved in a circle is continuous so as to be always continuous with itself. This, then, is what produces continuous movement, the body which travels in a circle, and its movement produces time.

CHAPTER 11

In the case of things which are moved continuously by way of generation or of alteration, or of change in general, we see that which is successively and comes to be *this* after *this* without any intermission.   35
Accordingly we must consider whether there is anything which of   337^b
necessity will be, or whether there is no such thing but all are capable of not coming to be.

That some are is obvious, and the difference between 'it will be' and 'it is going to be' is a direct consequence of this; for that of which it is true to say that it will be is something of which it must be true to say   5
some time that it is, but that of which it is now true to say that it is going to be—there is nothing to prevent *that* not coming to be: a person who is going to take a walk may not take a walk. More generally, since some things that are, are capable also of not being, there will also, clearly, be things coming to be that are like that, i.e. their coming to be will not take place of necessity.

Are they all, then, like this? Or not, some being such that it is neces-   10
sary *simpliciter* for them to come to be, and just as in the case of being there are some incapable of not being and some capable of it, so in the case of coming to be? For example, it is necessary, after all, that there should come to be solstices and impossible that it should not be possible.

Granted that the coming to be of something earlier is necessary if a later thing is to be, e.g. if a house, then foundations, and if foundations, then clay: does it follow that if there have come to be founda-   15
tions a house must necessarily come to be? Or can we not yet say this, unless it is necessary *simpliciter* that the latter itself come to be? In this case, if foundations have come to be, it is also necessary that a house come to be; for such was the relationship of the earlier thing to the later, namely, that if there is to be the latter, necessarily there will be the former, earlier, thing. If, accordingly, it is necessary for the later   20
one to come to be, it is necessary also for the earlier one, and if the earlier one comes to be, it is accordingly necessary for the later one to do so—but not because of the earlier one, but because it was assumed

that it was necessary it should exist. So in those cases where it is necessary for the later one to exist there is conversion, and it is always 25 necessary, if the earlier has come to be, that the later one should also come to be.

If, then, it proceeds to infinity downwards, it will not be necessary *simpliciter* for *this* (one of the later ones) to come to be, but only conditionally; for there will always have to be some further thing in front of it on account of which it is necessary for *it* to come to be; so, given that the infinite has no principle, there will be no first member on account of which it will be necessary for it to come to be.

Nor, on the other hand, will it be true, in the case of a finite series, 30 to say of *that* that it is necessary *simpliciter* for it to come to be—a house, for example, when the foundations come to be. For when they come to be, if it is not necessary for *that* always to come to be, it will follow that something is always the case which is capable of not always being the case. But 'always' must belong to the coming to be, if its 35 coming to be is necessary. For 'necessarily' and 'always' go together 338ᵃ (since what necessarily is, cannot not be), so that if it is necessarily, it is eternal, and if it is eternal, it is necessarily. If, therefore, the coming to be is necessary, the coming to be of this thing is eternal, and if eternal, necessary.

So if the coming to be of something is necessary *simpliciter*, it is bound to come back in a circle and return on itself. For the coming to 5 be is bound to be either finite or not, and if not, in a straight line or in a circle. Of these, if it is to be eternal, it cannot be in a straight line on account of there being no sort of principle (neither of members of the series going downwards, taken as it were from the future, nor upwards, as it were from the past); but it has to have a principle, without being 10 finite, and be eternal. That is why it has to be in a circle.

So there is bound to be conversion: if *this* comes to be necessarily, then the earlier, and again, if *that*, then the later comes to be necessarily. This moreover, always takes place continuously, since it makes no difference to this whether we say that it proceeds through two or 15 many stages. So that which is necessary *simpliciter* exists in movement and generation in a circle; and if it is in a circle, it is necessary for each one to come to be and to have come to be; and if necessary, the generation of these things is in a circle.

This is reasonable, because on quite other grounds movement in a circle, i.e. that of the heavens, has been shown to be eternal—namely, that those things come to be and will be of necessity which are the

movements that belong to this and which are because of it. If that
which is moved in a circle moves something continually, the move-   338^b
ment of these things must also be in a circle. For example, the locomotion above it being in a circle, the sun moves in *this* way, and since it
moves in *that* way, the seasons because of it come to be in a circle and
return upon themselves, and since these come to be in this way, the
things affected by them do so in their turn.   5

Some things, then, are obviously like this; water and air, for
instance, come to be in a circle, and if there is a cloud it is bound to
rain and if it rains there is bound also to be a cloud. Men and animals,
on the other hand, do not return on themselves in such a way that the
same one comes to be again (since there was no necessity, given that
your father came to be, that you should have come to be, only that he   10
should have, given that you did), and it seems that this generation is in
a straight line. Why is there this difference? This again is where the
investigation begins: do all things return on themselves in the same
way, or not, but rather some in number and some only in form? It is
obvious that those whose substance, i.e. what is moved, is imperishable will be the same in number, since movement follows the thing
moved, but those whose substance is, on the contrary, perishable must   15
necessarily return on themselves in form, not in number. That is why
water from air and air from water is the same in form, not in number;
but if these too are the same in number, still they are not things whose
substance comes to be, the sort, namely, that is capable of not being.

METEOROLOGY*

BOOK I

CHAPTER I

338ᵃ We have already discussed the first causes of nature, and all natural motion, also the stars ordered in the motion of the heavens, and the corporeal elements—enumerating and specifying them and showing how they change into one another—and becoming and perishing in general. There remains for consideration a part of this inquiry which all our predecessors called meteorology. It is concerned with events 338ᵇ that are natural, though their order is less perfect than that of the first of the elements of bodies. They take place in the region nearest to the motion of the stars. Such are the milky way, and comets, and the movement of meteors. It studies also all the affections we may call common to air and water, and the kinds and parts of the earth and the affections of its parts. These throw light on the causes of winds and 339ᵃ earthquakes and all the consequences of their motions. Of these things some puzzle us, while others admit of explanation in some degree. Further, the inquiry is concerned with the falling of thunderbolts and with whirlwinds and fire-winds, and further, the recurrent affections 5 produced in these same bodies by concretion. When the inquiry into these matters is concluded let us consider what account we can give, in accordance with the method we have followed, of animals and plants, both generally and in detail. When that has been done we may say that the whole of our original undertaking will have been carried out.

10 After this introduction let us begin by discussing our immediate subject.

BOOK IV

CHAPTER 12·

389ᵇ Having explained all this we must describe the nature of flesh, bone, and the other homogeneous bodies severally.

* *Translation*: E. W. Webster, revised J. Barnes (Revised Oxford Aristotle, 1984); *Text*: F. H. Fobes (Cambridge, Mass., 1918).

Our account of the formation of the homogeneous bodies has given us the elements out of which they are compounded and the classes into which they fall, and has made it clear to which class each of those bodies belongs. The homogeneous bodies are made up of the elements, and all the works of nature in turn of the homogeneous bodies as matter. All the homogeneous bodies consist of the elements described, as matter, but their essence is determined by their definition. The fact is always clearer in the case of the later products, of those, in fact, that are instruments, as it were, and have an end: it is clearer, for instance, that a dead man is a man only in name. And so the hand of a dead man, too, will in the same way be a hand in name only, just as stone flutes might still be called flutes; for these too, seem to be instruments of a kind. But in the case of flesh and bone the fact is not so clear to see, and in that of fire and water even less. For the end is least obvious there where matter predominates most. If you take the extremes, matter is pure matter and the essence is pure definition; but the bodies intermediate between the two are related to each in proportion as they are near to either. For each of these elements has an end and is not water or fire in any and every condition of itself, just as flesh is not flesh nor viscera viscera, and the same is true in a higher degree with face and hand. What a thing is is always determined by its function: a thing really is itself when it can perform its function; an eye, for instance, when it can see. When a thing cannot do so it is that thing only in name, like a dead eye or one made of stone, just as a wooden saw is no more a saw than one in a picture. The same, then, is true of flesh, except that its function is less clear than that of the tongue. So, too, with fire; but its function is perhaps even harder to specify by physical inquiry than that of flesh. The parts of plants, and inanimate bodies like copper and silver, are in the same case. They all are what they are in virtue of a certain power of action or passion—just like flesh and sinew. But we cannot state their definitions accurately, and so it is not easy to tell when they are really there and when they are not unless the body is thoroughly corrupted and its shape only remains. So ancient corpses suddenly become ashes in the grave and very old fruit preserves its shape only but not its sensible qualities; so, too, with the solids that form from milk.

Now heat and cold and the motions they set up as the bodies are solidified by the hot and the cold are sufficient to form all such parts as are the homogeneous bodies, flesh, bone, hair, sinew, and the rest. For they are all of them differentiated by the various qualities enumerated

above, tension, ductility, fragmentability, hardness, softness, and the rest of them: all of which are derived from the hot and the cold and the mixture of their motions. But no one would go as far as to consider
10   them sufficient in the case of the non-homogeneous parts (like the head, the hand, or the foot) which these homogeneous parts go to make up. Cold and heat and their motion would be admitted to account for the formation of copper or silver, but not for that of a saw, a bowl, or a box. So here, save that in the examples given the cause is art, but in the non-homogeneous bodies nature or some other cause.
15   Since, then, we know to what class each of the homogeneous bodies belongs, we must now find what each of them is, i.e. what is blood, flesh, semen, and the rest? For we know the cause of a thing and its definition when we know either its matter or its definition—and best when we know both these factors of its generation and destruction, and also the source of the origin of its motion.
20   After the homogeneous bodies have been explained we must consider the non-homogeneous too, and lastly the bodies made up of these, such as man, plants, and the rest.

ON THE SOUL*

BOOK I

CHAPTER I

Knowledge we regard as a fine and worthwhile thing, and one kind as 402ᵃ
more so than another either in virtue of its accuracy or in virtue of its
being concerned with superior and more remarkable things. On both
these grounds we should with reason place the study of the soul in the
first rank. It would seem, also, that an acquaintance with it makes a
great contribution to truth as a whole, and especially to the study of 5
nature; for the soul is as it were the first principle of animal life. We
seek to inquire into and ascertain both its nature and its essence, and
after that all the attributes belonging to it; of these some are thought to
be properties peculiar to the soul, while others are thought to belong
because of it to animals also.

But in every respect and in every way it is the most difficult of things 10
to attain any conviction about it. For, since the inquiry is common to
many other things too—I mean that concerning essence and what a
thing is—it might perhaps be thought that there is one procedure in
the case of all those things for which we wish to ascertain the essence,
just as there *is*, demonstration, for the incidental properties; so that we 15
ought to look for this procedure. But if there is not one common
procedure for dealing with what a thing is, the undertaking will be still
more difficult; for we shall have to establish what is the way to proceed
in each case. And if it is evident whether this consists in demonstration 20
or division or some other procedure, there will still be many puzzles
and uncertainties as to what starting-points we must use in our
inquiry; for different subjects, e.g. numbers and planes, have different
first principles.

First surely we must determine in which of the genera the soul is
and what it is; I mean whether it is a particular thing and substance or
quality or quantity or some other of the categories which have been 25
distinguished. And secondly we must determine whether it is one of

* *Translation*: D. W. Hamlyn (Clarendon Aristotle Series, 1968); *Text*: W. D. Ross
(Oxford Classical Texts, 1956).

those things which are in potentiality or whether it is rather a kind of actuality; for this makes no small difference. And we must inquire also if it is divisible or indivisible and whether every soul is of like kind or not; and if not of like kind, whether differing in species or genus.

For as things are, people who speak and inquire about the soul seem to study the human soul only. But we must take care not to overlook the question whether there is one definition of the soul, as of animal, or whether there is a different one for each, as of horse, dog, man, and god, the universal animal being either nothing or secondary; and it would be similar for any other common predicate.

Furthermore, if there are not many souls but only parts, should we inquire into the whole soul or its parts? It is difficult too to decide which of these are really different from each other, and whether we must inquire into the parts first or their functions, e.g. thinking or the intellect, and perceiving or that which can perceive; and similarly for the rest also. And if the functions come first, the question might be raised whether we should inquire into the corresponding objects before these, e.g. the object of perception before that which can perceive, and the object of thought before the intellect.

It seems that not only is ascertaining what a thing is useful for a consideration of the reasons for the attributes which follow upon essences (as in mathematics ascertaining what straight and curved or line and surface are is useful for seeing to how many right angles the angles of a triangle are equal), but also conversely the attributes contribute a great part to the knowledge of what a thing is; for when we are able to give an account of either all or most of the attributes as they appear to us, then we shall be able to speak best about the essence too; for the starting-point of every demonstration is what a thing is, so that, for those definitions which do not enable us to ascertain the attributes nor even make it easy to guess about this, it is clear that they have all been stated dialectically and to no purpose.

There is also the problem whether the properties of the soul are all common also to that which has it or whether they are peculiar to the soul itself; for it is necessary to deal with this, though it is not easy. It appears that in most cases the soul is not affected nor does it act apart from the body, e.g. in being angry, being confident, wanting, and perceiving in general; although thinking looks most like being peculiar to the soul. But if this too is a form of imagination or does not exist apart from imagination, it would not be possible even for this to exist apart from the body.

If then there is any of the functions or affections of the soul which is   10
peculiar to it, it will be possible for it to be separated from the body.
But if there is nothing peculiar to it, it will not be separable, but it will
be like the straight, to which, *qua* straight, many properties belong,
e.g. it will touch a bronze sphere at a point, although the straight if
separated will not so touch; for it is inseparable, if it is always found   15
with some body.

It seems that all the affections of the soul involve the body—passion,
gentleness, fear, pity, confidence, and, further, joy, and both loving
and hating; for at the same time as these the body is affected in a certain way. This is shown by the fact that sometimes when severe and
manifest sufferings befall us we are not provoked to exasperation or   20
fear, while at other times we are moved by small and imperceptible
sufferings when the body is aroused and is as it is when it is in anger.
This is even further evident; for men may come to have the affections
of the frightened although nothing frightening is taking place.

If this is so, it is clear that the affections of the soul are principles   25
involving matter. Hence their definitions are such as 'Being angry is a
particular movement of a body of such and such a kind, or a part or
potentiality of it, as a result of this thing and for the sake of that'. And
for these reasons an inquiry concerning the soul, either every soul or
this kind of soul, is at once the province of the student of nature.

But the student of nature and the dialectician would define each of
these differently, e.g. what anger is. For the latter would define it as a   30
desire for retaliation or something of the sort, the former as the boiling
of the blood and hot stuff round the heart. Of these, the one gives the
matter, the other the form and principle. For this is the principle of the
thing, but it must be in a matter of such and such a kind if it is to be.   403^b
Thus the principle of a house is, say, that it is a covering to prevent
destruction by winds, rain, and heat, but someone else will say that a
house is stones, bricks, and timber, and another again that it is the
form in them for the sake of these other things.   5

Which of these, then, is the student of nature? Is it the one who is
concerned with the matter, but is ignorant of the principle, or the one
who is concerned with the principle only? Or is it rather the one who
is concerned with the product of both? Who then is each of the others?
Or is there no particular person who is concerned with the properties   10
of matter which are not separable nor treated as separable, while the
student of nature is concerned with everything which is a function or
affection of such-and-such a body and such-and-such a matter?

Anything not of this kind is the concern of someone else, and in some cases of a craftsman perhaps, e.g. a carpenter or doctor. The properties which are not separable, but which are not treated as properties of such-and-such a body but in abstraction, are the concern of the mathematician. Those which are treated as separable are the concern of the 'first philosopher'.

Let us return to the point from which our discussion began. We were saying that the affections of the soul are, at any rate in so far as they are such as passion and fear, inseparable in this way from the natural matter of the animals in which they occur, and not in the same way as a line or surface.

CHAPTER 4

. . .

There will be greater reason for raising the question whether the soul is moved, on consideration of the following. We say that the soul is grieved, rejoices, is confident, and afraid, and again is angry, perceives, and thinks. And all these seem to be movements. One might conclude from this that the soul itself is moved; but this is not necessary.

Even if it is indeed the case that being grieved, rejoicing, and thinking are movements, that each of them consists in being moved, and that the movement is due to the soul, e.g. that being angry and being afraid consist in the heart's being moved in a particular way and that thinking is a movement either of this perhaps or of some other part, and that some of these happen because of movements in place and others because of movements constituting alteration (what sort and how is a matter for a separate discussion)—then to say that the soul is angry is as if one were to say that the soul weaves or builds. For it is surely better not to say that the soul pities, learns, or thinks, but that the man does these with his soul; and this not because the movement takes place in it, but because sometimes it reaches as far as it or at other times comes from it; e.g. perception starts from particular things, while recollection starts from the soul itself and extends to movements or persistent states in the sense-organs.

The intellect seems to be born in us as a kind of substance and not to be destroyed. For it would be destroyed if at all by the feebleness of old age, while as things are what happens is similar to what happens in the case of the sense-organs. For, if an old man acquired an eye of a certain kind, he would see as well as even a young man. Hence old age is not due to the soul's being affected in a certain way, but to this happening to that which the soul is in, as is the case in drunkenness and disease.

Thus thought and contemplation decay because something else within is destroyed, while thought is in itself unaffected. But thinking and loving or hating are not affections of that, but of the individual thing which has it, in so far as it does. Hence when this too is destroyed we neither remember nor love; for these did not belong to that, but to the composite thing which has perished. But the intellect is surely something more divine and is unaffected. 25

. . .

BOOK II

CHAPTER I

Enough has been said of the views about the soul which have been handed down by our predecessors. Let us start again, as it were from the beginning, and try to determine what the soul is and what would be its most comprehensive definition. 412ª 5

Now we speak of one particular kind of existent things as substance, and under this heading we so speak of one thing *qua* matter, which in itself is not a particular, another *qua* shape and form, in virtue of which it is then spoken of as a particular, and a third *qua* the product of these two. And matter is potentiality, while form is actuality—and that in two ways, first as knowledge is, and second as contemplation is. 10

It is bodies especially which are thought to be substances, and of these especially natural bodies; for these are sources of the rest. Of natural bodies, some have life and some do not; and it is self-nourishment, growth, and decay that we speak of as life. Hence, every natural body which partakes of life will be a substance, and substance of a composite kind. 15

Since it is indeed a body of such a kind (for it is one having life), the soul will not be body; for the body is not something predicated of a subject, but exists rather as subject and matter. The soul must, then, be substance *qua* form of a natural body which has life potentially. Substance is actuality. The soul, therefore, will be the actuality of a body of this kind. 20

But actuality is so spoken of in two ways, first as knowledge is and second as contemplation is. It is clear then that the soul is actuality as

knowledge is; for both sleep and waking depend on the existence of
25   soul, and waking is analogous to contemplation, and sleep to the possession but not the exercise of knowledge. In the same individual,
knowledge is in origin prior. Hence the soul is the first actuality of a
natural body which has life potentially.

Whatever has organs will be a body of this kind. Even the parts of
plants are organs, although extremely simple ones, e.g. the leaf is a
412ᵇ   covering for the pod, and the pod for the fruit; while roots are analogous to the mouth, for both take in food.

If then we are to speak of something common to every soul, it will be
the first actuality of a natural body which has organs. Hence too we
5   should not ask whether the soul and body are one, any more than
whether the wax and the impression are one, or in general whether the
matter of each thing and that of which it is the matter are one. For,
while unity and being are so spoken of in many ways, that which is
most properly so spoken of is the actuality.

10   It has then been stated in general what the soul is; for it is
substance, that corresponding to the principle of a thing. And this is
'what it is for it to be what it was' for a body of such a kind. Compare
the following: if an instrument, e.g. an axe, were a natural body, then
its substance would be what it is to be an axe, and this would be its
soul; if this were removed it would no longer be an axe, except
15   homonymously. But as it is it is an axe; for it is not of this kind of body
that the soul is 'what it is for it to be what it was' and the principle, but
of a certain kind of natural body having within itself a source of
movement and rest.

We must consider what has been said in relation to the parts of the
body also. For, if the eye were an animal, sight would be its soul; for
20   this is an eye's substance—that corresponding to its principle. The eye
is matter for sight, and if this fails it is no longer an eye, except
homonymously, just like an eye in stone or a painted eye. We must
now apply to the whole living body that which applies to the part; for
as the part is to the part, so analogously is perception as a whole to the
whole perceptive body as such.

25   It is not that which has lost its soul which is potentially such as to
live, but that which possesses it. Seeds and fruit are potentially bodies
of this kind.

Just, then, as the cutting and the seeing, so too is the waking state
actuality, while the soul is like sight and the potentiality of the instru-
413ᵃ   ment; the body is that which is this potentially. But just as the pupil

and sight make up an eye, so in this case the soul and body make up an animal.

That, therefore, the soul or certain parts of it, if it is divisible, cannot be separated from the body is quite clear; for in some cases the 5 actuality is of the parts themselves. Not that anything prevents at any rate *some* parts from being separable, because of their being actualities of no body. Furthermore, it is not clear whether the soul is the actuality of the body in the way that the sailor is of the ship. Let this suffice as a rough definition and sketch about the soul. 10

CHAPTER 2

Since it is from things which are obscure but more obvious that we arrive at that which is clear and more intelligible in respect of the principle involved, we must try again in this way to treat of the soul; for a defining statement should not only make clear the fact, as the majority of definitions do, but it should also contain and reveal the 15 reason for it. As things are, the statements of the definitions are like conclusions. For example, what is squaring? The construction of an equilateral rectangle equal to one which is not equilateral. But such a definition is a statement of the conclusion; whereas one who says that squaring is the discovery of the mean proportional states the reason for the circumstance.

We say, then, making a beginning of our inquiry, that that which has 20 soul is distinguished from that which has not by life. But life is so spoken of in many ways, and we say that a thing lives if but one of the following is present—intellect, perception, movement and rest in respect of place, and furthermore the movement involved in nutrition, and both decay and growth.

For this reason all plants too are thought to live; for they evidently 25 have in them such a potentiality and first principle, through which they come to grow and decay in opposite directions. For they do not grow upwards without growing downwards, but they grow in both directions alike and in every direction—this being so of all that are constantly nourished and continue to live, as long as they are able to 30 receive nourishment. This form of life can exist apart from the others, but the others cannot exist apart from it in mortal creatures. This is obvious in the case of plants; for they have no other potentiality of soul.

It is, then, because of this first principle that living things have life. 413^b

But it is because of sense-perception first of all that they will be animals, for even those things which do not move or change their place, but which do have sense-perception, we speak of as animals and not merely as living.

First of all in perception all animals have touch. Just as the nutritive
5   faculty can exist apart from touch and from all sense-perception, so touch can exist apart from the other senses. We speak of as nutritive that part of the soul in which even plants share; all animals clearly have the sense of touch. The reason for each of these circumstances
10 we shall state later.

For the present let it be enough to say only that the soul is the source of the things above mentioned and is determined by them—by the faculties of nutrition, perception, thought, and movement. Whether each of these is a soul or a part of a soul, and if a part, whether it is such as to be distinct in definition only or also in place,
15 are questions to which it is not hard to find answers in some cases, although others present difficulty.

For, just as in the case of plants some clearly live when divided and separated from each other, the soul in them being actually one in actuality in each plant, though potentially many, so we see this hap-
20 pening also in other varieties of soul in the case of insects when they are cut in two; for each of the parts has sense-perception and motion in respect of place, and if sense-perception, then also imagination and desire. For where there is sense-perception, there is also both pain and pleasure, and where these, there is of necessity also wanting.

Concerning the intellect and the potentiality for contemplation the
25 situation is not so far clear, but it seems to be a different kind of soul, and this alone can exist separately, as the everlasting can from the perishable.

But it is clear from these things that the remaining parts of the soul are not separable, as some say; although that they are different in definition is clear. For being able to perceive and being able to believe
30 are different, since perceiving too is different from believing; and likewise with each of the other parts which have been mentioned.

Moreover, some animals have all these, others only some of them, and others again one alone, and this will furnish distinctions between animals; what is the reason for this we must consider later. Very much
414ᵉ the same is the case with the senses; for some animals have them all, others only some, and others again one only, the most necessary one, touch.

That by means of which we live and perceive is so spoken of in two ways, as is that by means of which we know (we so speak in the one case of knowledge, in the other of soul, for by means of each of these we say we know). Similarly, we are healthy in the first place by means of health and in the second by means of a part of the body or even the whole. Now, of these knowledge and health are shape and a kind of form and principle, and as it were activity of the recipient, in the one case of that which is capable of knowing, in the other of that which is capable of health (for the activity of those things which are capable of acting appears to take place in that which is affected and disposed). Now the soul is that by means of which, primarily, we live and perceive and think. Hence it will be a kind of principle and form, and not matter or subject.

Substance is so spoken of in three ways, as we have said, and of these cases one is form, another matter, and the third the product of the two; and of these matter is potentiality and form actuality. And since the product of the two is an ensouled thing, the body is not the actuality of soul, but the latter is the actuality of a certain kind of body.

And for this reason those have the right conception who believe that the soul does not exist without a body and yet is not itself a kind of body. For it is not a body, but something which belongs to a body, and for this reason exists in a body, and in a body of such-and-such a kind. Not as our predecessors supposed, when they fitted it to a body without any further determination of what body and of what kind, although it is clear that one chance thing does not receive another. In our way it happens just as reason demands. For the actuality of each thing comes naturally about in that which is already such potentially and in its appropriate matter. From all this it is clear that the soul is a kind of actuality and principle of that which has the potentiality to be such.

CHAPTER 3

Of the potentialities of the soul which have been mentioned, some existing things have them all, as we have said, others some of them, and certain of them only one. The potentialities which we mentioned are those for nutrition, sense-perception, desire, movement in respect of place, and thought.

Plants have the nutritive faculty only; other creatures have both this and the faculty of sense-perception. And if that of sense-perception, then that of desire also; for desire comprises wanting, passion, and

wishing: all animals have at least one of the senses, touch, and for that which has sense-perception there is both pleasure and pain and both the pleasant and the painful: and where there are these, there is also
5   wanting: for this is a desire for that which is pleasant.

Furthermore, they have a sense concerned with food; for touch is such a sense; for all living things are nourished by dry and moist and hot and cold things, and touch is the sense for these and only inciden-
10   tally of the other objects of perception; for sound and colour and smell contribute nothing to nourishment, while flavour is one of the objects of touch. Hunger and thirst are forms of wanting, hunger is wanting the dry and hot, thirst wanting the moist and cold; and flavour is, as it were, a kind of seasoning of these. We must make clear about these
15   matters later, but for now let us say this much, that those living things which have touch also have desire.

The situation with regard to imagination is obscure and must be con-sidered later. Some things have in addition the faculty of movement in respect of place, and others, e.g. men and anything else which is similar or superior to man, have that of thought and intellect.
20   It is clear, then, that it is in the same way as with figure that there will be one definition of soul; for in the former case there is no figure over and above the triangle and the others which follow it in order, nor in the latter case is there soul over and above those mentioned. Even in the case of figures there could be produced a common definition, which will fit all of them but which will not be peculiar to any one. Similarly too with the kinds of soul mentioned.
25   For this reason it is foolish to seek both in these cases and in others for a common definition, which will be a definition peculiar to no actually existing thing and will not correspond to the proper indivis-ible species, to the neglect of one which will.

The circumstances with regard to soul are similar to the situation over figures; for in the case both of figures and of things which have
30   soul that which is prior always exists potentially in what follows in order, e.g. the triangle in the quadrilateral on the one hand, and the nutritive faculty in that of perception on the other. Hence we must inquire in each case what is the soul of each thing, what is that of a plant, and what is that of a man or a beast.

For what reason they are so arranged in order of succession must be
415ᵃ considered. For without the nutritive faculty there does not exist that of perception; but the nutritive faculty is found apart from that of per-ception in plants. Again, without the faculty of touch none of the other

senses exists, but touch exists without the others; for many animals 5
have neither sight nor hearing nor sense of smell. And of those which
can perceive, some have the faculty of movement in respect of place,
while others have not. Finally and most rarely, they have reason and
thought; for those perishable creatures which have reason have all the
rest, but not all those which have each of the others have reason. But 10
some do not even have imagination, while others live by this alone.
The contemplative intellect requires a separate discussion. That the
account, therefore, appropriate for each of these is most appropriate
for the soul also is clear.

CHAPTER 4

Anyone who is going to engage in inquiry about these must grasp what 15
each of them is and then proceed to investigate what follows and the
rest. But if we must say what each of them is, e.g. what is the faculty of
thought or of perception or of nutrition, we must again first say what
thinking and perceiving are; for activities and actions are in respect of
definition prior to their potentialities. And if this is so, and if again, 20
prior to them, we should have considered their correlative objects,
then we should for the same reason determine first about them, e.g.
about nourishment and the objects of perception and thought.

Hence, we must first speak about nourishment and reproduction;
for the nutritive soul belongs also to the other living things and is the
first and most commonly possessed potentiality of the soul, in virtue of 25
which they all have life. Its functions are reproduction and the use of
food; for it is the most natural function in living things, such as are
perfect and not mutilated or produced by generation, to produce
another thing like themselves—an animal to produce an animal, a
plant a plant—in order that they may partake of the everlasting and
divine in so far as they can; for all desire that, and for the sake of that 415ᵇ
they do whatever they do in accordance with nature. (But that for the
sake of which is twofold—the purpose for which and the beneficiary
for whom.) Since, then, they cannot share in the everlasting and
divine by continuous existence, because no perishable thing can
persist numerically one and the same, they share in them in so far as 5
each can, some more and some less; and what persists is not the
thing itself but something like itself, not one in number but one in
species.

The soul is the cause and first principle of the living body. But these

are so spoken of in many ways, and similarly the soul is cause in the
10   three ways distinguished; for the soul is cause as being that from which
the movement is itself derived, as that for the sake of which it occurs,
and as the essence of bodies which are ensouled.

That it is so as essence is clear; for essence is the cause of existence
for all things, and for living things it is living that is existing, and the
cause and first principle of this is the soul. Furthermore, the actuality
is the principle of that which is such potentially.

15   And it is clear that the soul is cause also as that for the sake of which.
For just as the intellect acts for the sake of something, in the same way
also does nature, and this something is its end. Of this sort is the soul
in animals in accordance with nature; for all natural bodies are instruments for soul, and just as it is with those of animals so it is with those
of plants also, showing that they exist for the sake of soul. But that for
20   the sake of which is so spoken of in two ways, the purpose for which
and the beneficiary for whom.

Moreover, soul is also that from which motion in respect of place is
first derived; but not all living things have this potentiality. Alteration
and growth also occur in virtue of soul; for perception is thought to be
25   a kind of alteration, and nothing perceives which does not partake of
soul. And the situation is similar with growth and decay; for nothing
decays or grows naturally unless it is nourished, and nothing is nourished which does not share in life.

Empedocles did not speak well when he added this, that growth
takes place in plants, when they root themselves downwards because
416ᵃ   earth naturally moves in this direction, and when they grow upwards
because fire moves in that way. For he does not have a good understanding of up and down (for up and down are not the same for all
things as they are for the universe, but the roots of plants are as the
head in animals, if we are to speak of organs as different or the same in
5   virtue of their functions). In addition to this, what is it that holds
together the fire and the earth, given that they tend in opposite directions? For they will be torn apart, unless there is something to prevent
them; but if there is, then this is the soul and the cause of growth and
nourishment.

Some think that it is the nature of fire which is the cause quite
10   simply of nourishment and growth; for it appears that it alone of
bodies is nourished and grows. For this reason one might suppose that
in both plants and animals it is this which does the work. It is in a way
a contributory cause, but not the cause simply; rather it is the soul

which is this. For the growth of fire is unlimited while there is some- 15
thing to be burnt, but in all things which are naturally constituted
there is a limit and a proportion both for size and for growth; and these
belong to soul, but not to fire, and to principle rather than to matter.

Since it is the same potentiality of the soul which is nutritive and
reproductive, we must first determine the facts about nutrition; for it 20
is distinguished in relation to the other potentialities by this function.
It is thought that one thing is food for its contrary, though not in all
cases, but wherever contraries receive not only generation from each
other but also growth; for many things come to be from each other, but
not all are quantities, e.g. the healthy comes to be from the sick. Not
even those which do receive growth from each other seem to consti- 25
tute food for each other in the same way; but water is food for fire,
while fire does not feed water. It seems, then, that it is especially in the
simple bodies that one thing is food, the other the thing fed.

But there is a difficulty here; for some say that the like is fed by like, 30
as is the case with growth, while others, as we have said, think the
reverse, that one thing is fed by its contrary, since the like is unaffected
by like whereas food changes and is digested; and in all cases change is
to the opposite or to an intermediate state. Furthermore, food is
affected by that which is fed, but not the latter by the food, just as the 416ᵇ
carpenter is not affected by his material, but the latter by him; the carpenter changes merely from idleness to activity.

It makes a difference whether the food is the last thing which is
added or the first. But if both are food, but the one undigested and the
other digested, it would be possible to speak of food in both ways; in so 5
far as the food is undigested, the opposite is fed by opposite, in so far
as it is digested, the like by like. So that it is clear that in a way both
speak rightly and not rightly.

But since nothing is fed which does not partake of life, that which is
fed would be the ensouled body, *qua* ensouled, so that nourishment 10
too is relative to that which is ensouled, and this not accidentally.

But being food and being capable of producing growth are different; for it is in so far as the ensouled thing is something having quantity that food is capable of producing growth, but it is in so far as it is a
particular and a substance that it is food. For the ensouled thing maintains its substance and exists as long as it is fed; and it can bring about 15
the generation not of that which is fed, but of something like it; for its
substance is already in existence, and nothing generates itself, but
rather maintains itself. Hence this first principle of the soul is a

potentiality such as to maintain its possessor as such, while food pre-
pares it for activity; for this reason, if deprived of food it cannot exist.

20   Since there are three things, that which is fed, that with which it is
fed, and that which feeds, that which feeds is the primary soul, that
which is fed is the body which has this, and that with which it is fed is
the food.

Since it is right to call all things after their end, and the end is to
generate something like oneself, the primary soul will be that which
can generate something like itself.

25   That with which one feeds is twofold, just as that with which one
steers is, i.e. both the hand and the rudder, the one moving and being
moved, the other being moved only. Now it is necessary that all food
should be capable of being digested, and it is heat which effects the
digestion; hence every ensouled thing has heat. What nourishment is

30   has now been stated in outline; but we must elucidate it later in the
appropriate work.

CHAPTER 5

Now that these matters have been determined let us discusss generally
the whole of perception. Perception consists in being moved and
affected, as has been said; for it is thought to be a kind of alteration.

35   Some say too that the like is affected by like. How this is possible or
417ᵃ   impossible we have stated in our general account of acting and being
affected.

There is a problem why perception of the senses themselves does
not occur, and why they do not give rise to perception without there
being any external objects, although there is in them fire, earth, and
the other elements, of which, either in themselves or in respect of their
accidents, there is perception. It is clear, then, that the faculty of

5   sense-perception does not exist by way of activity but by way of potentiality only; for this reason the perception does not occur, just as fuel
does not burn in and through itself without something that can burn it;
otherwise it would burn itself and would need no actually existing fire.

Since we speak of perceiving in two ways (for we speak of that which

10   potentially hears and sees as hearing and seeing, even if it happens to
be asleep, as well as of that which is actually doing these things); perception too will be so spoken of in two ways, the one as in potentiality,
the other as in actuality. Similarly with the object of perception too,
one will be potentially, the other actually.

First then let us speak as if being affected, being moved, and acting are the same thing; for indeed movement is a kind of activity, although an incomplete one, as has been said elsewhere. And everything is affected and moved by something which is capable of bringing this about and is in actuality. For this reason, in one way, as we said, a thing is affected by like, and in another by unlike; for it is the unlike which is affected, although when it has been affected it is like.

But we must make distinctions concerning potentiality and actuality; for at the moment we are speaking of them in an unqualified way. For there are knowers in that we should speak of a man as a knower because man is one of those who are knowers and have knowledge; then there are knowers in that we speak straightaway of the man who has knowledge of grammar as a knower. (Each of these has a capacity but not in the same way—the one because his kind, his stuff, is of this sort, the other because he can if he so wishes contemplate, as long as nothing external prevents him.) There is thirdly the man who is already contemplating, the man who is actually and in the proper sense knowing this particular A. Thus, both the first two, being potential knowers, become actual knowers, but the one by being altered through learning and frequent changes from an opposite disposition, the other by passing in another way from the state of having arithmetical or grammatical knowledge without exercising it to its exercise.

Being affected is not a single thing either; it is first a kind of destruction of something by its contrary, and second it is rather the preservation of that which is so potentially by that which is so actually and is like it in the way that a potentiality may be like an actuality. For that which has knowledge comes to contemplate, and this is either not an alteration (for the development of the thing is into itself and into actuality) or a different kind of alteration. For this reason it is not right to say that something which understands is altered when it understands, any more than a builder when he builds. The leading of a thinking and understanding thing, therefore, from being potentially such to actuality should not be called teaching, but should have another name; while that which, starting from being potentially such, learns and acquires knowledge by the agency of that which is actually such and is able to teach either should not be said to be affected, as has been said, or else we should say that there are two kinds of alteration, one a change to conditions of privation, the other to a thing's dispositions and nature.

The first change in that which can perceive is brought about by the

15

20

25

30

417^b

5

10

15

parent, and when it is born it already has sense-perception in the same
way as it has knowledge. Actual sense-perception is so spoken of in the
same way as contemplation; but there is a difference in that in sense-
20   perception the things which are able to produce the activity are external, i.e. the objects of sight and hearing, and similarly for the rest of the
objects of perception. The reason is that actual perception is of particulars, while knowledge is of universals; and these are somehow in
the soul itself. For this reason it is open to us to think when we wish,
25   but perceiving is not similarly open to us; for there must be the object
of perception. The situation is similar with sciences dealing with
objects of perception, and for the same reason, that objects of perception are particular and external things.

But there will be an opportunity later to clarify these matters; for the
30   present let it be enough to have determined this much—that, while
that which is spoken of as potential is not a single thing, one thing
being so spoken of as we should speak of a boy as a potential general,
another as we should so speak of an adult, it is in the latter way with
418ᵃ   that which can perceive. But since the difference between the two has
no name, although it has been determined that they are different and
how they are so, we must use 'to be affected' and 'to be altered' as
though they were the proper words.

That which can perceive is, as we have said, potentially such as the
object of perception already is actually. It is not like the object, then,
5   when it is being affected by it, but once it has been affected it becomes
like it and is such as it is.

CHAPTER 6

We must speak first of the objects of perception in relation to each
sense. But objects of perception are so spoken of in three ways; of
these we say that we perceive two in themselves, and one incidentally.
10   Of the two, one is special to each sense, the other common to all.

I call special-object whatever cannot be perceived by another sense,
and about which it is impossible to be deceived; e.g. sight has colour,
hearing sound, and taste flavour, while touch has many varieties of
object. But at any rate each judges about these, and is not deceived as
to the fact that there is colour or sound, but rather as to what or where
15   the coloured thing is or as to what or where the object which sounds is.

Such then are spoken of as special to each, while those that are
spoken of as common are movement, rest, number, figure, size; for

such as these are not special to any, but common to all. For certain movements are perceptible by both touch and sight.

An object of perception is spoken of as incidental, e.g. if the white thing were the son of Diares; for you perceive this incidentally, since this which you perceive is incidental to the white thing. Hence too you are not affected by the object of perception as such.

Of the objects which are perceived in themselves it is the special-objects which are objects of perception properly, and it is to these that the essence of each sense is naturally relative.

CHAPTER 8

Let us now first determine the facts about sound and hearing. Sound exists in two ways; for there is sound which is something in actuality, and sound which is so potentially. For some things we say do not have a sound, e.g. sponge or wool, while others do, e.g. bronze and anything solid and smooth, because they can make a sound, that is they can produce an actual sound between themselves and the organ of hearing.

Actual sound is always of something in relation to something and in something; for it is a blow which produces it. For this reason it is impossible for there to be sound when there is only one thing; for the striker and the thing struck are different. Hence the thing which makes the sound does so in relation to something; and a blow cannot occur without movement. But, as we have said, sound is not the striking of any chance thing; for wool produces no sound if it is struck, but bronze does, and any smooth and hollow object. Bronze does so because it is smooth, while hollow objects produce many blows after the first by reverberation, that which is set in motion being unable to escape.

Furthermore, sound is heard in air, and also in water although less so, but it is not the air or the water which is responsible for the sound; rather, there must be solid objects striking against each other and against the air. This happens when the air remains after being struck and is not dispersed. For this reason it makes a sound if it is struck quickly and forcibly; for the movement of the striker must be too quick for the air to disperse, just as if one were to strike a blow at a heap or whirl of sand in rapid motion.

An echo occurs when the air is made to bounce back like a ball from air which has become a single mass on acount of a container which has limited it and prevented it from dispersing. It is likely that an echo

Marginal line numbers: 20, 25, 419^b, 5, 10, 15, 20, 25

always occurs, although not a distinct one, since the same thing surely happens with sound as with light too; for light is always reflected (otherwise there would not be light everywhere, but there would be darkness outside the area lit by the sun), but it is not reflected as it is from water, or bronze, or any other smooth object, so as to produce a shadow, by which we delimit the light.

The void is rightly said to be responsible for hearing. For the air is thought to be a void, and it is this which produces hearing, when it is moved as a single, continuous mass. But, because of its lack of coherence, it makes no noise, unless that which is struck is smooth. Then the air becomes a single mass at the same time, because of the surface of the object; for a smooth object has a single surface.

It is, then, that which can move air which is single because continuous as far as the organ of hearing which can produce sound. Air is naturally one with the organ of hearing; and because this is in air, the air inside is moved when that outside is moved. For this reason the animal does not hear with every part of it, nor does the air penetrate everywhere; for it is not everywhere that the part which will be set in motion and made to sound has air. The air itself is soundless because it is easily dispersed; but when it is prevented from dispersing, its movement is sound. The air inside the ears has been walled up inside so as to be immovable, in order that it may accurately perceive all the varieties of movement. That is why we hear in water too, because the water does not penetrate into the very air which is naturally one with the ear; nor even into the ear, because of its convolutions. When this does happen, there is no hearing; nor is there if the tympanum membrane is injured, just as with the cornea of the eye [when it is injured]. Further, an indication of whether we hear or not is provided by whether there is always an echoing sound in the ear, as in a horn; for the air in the ears is always moving with a movement of its own. But sound is something external and not private to the ear. And that is why they say that we hear by means of what is empty and rsonant, because we hear by means of that which has air confined within it.

Is it the thing struck or the striker which makes the sound? Or is it indeed both, but in different ways? For sound is the movement of that which can be moved in the way in which things rebound from smooth surfaces when someone strikes them. Thus, not everything, as has been said, makes a noise when it is struck or striking something, e.g. if a needle strikes another; but the object struck must be of even surface, so that the air may rebound and vibrate as a mass.

The differences between things which sound are revealed in the actual sound; for just as colours are not seen without light, so sharp and flat in pitch are not perceived without sound. These are so spoken of by transference from tangible objects; for that which is sharp moves the sense to a great extent in a little time, while that which is flat moves 30 it little in much time. Not that the sharp is quick and the flat slow, but the movement in the one case is such because of speed, in the other because of slowness. There seems to be an analogy with the sharp and 420ᵇ blunt in the case of touch; for the sharp as it were stabs, while the blunt as it were thrusts, because the one produces motion in a short time, the other in a long, so that the one is incidentally quick, the other slow.

So much for our account of sound. Voice is a particular sound made 5 by something with a soul; for nothing which does not have a soul has a voice, although such things may be said, by way of likeness, to have a voice, e.g. the pipe, lyre, and any other things which lack a soul but have variation in pitch, melody, and articulation; there is a likeness here because voice too has these properties. But many animals do not have a voice, e.g. those which are bloodless as well as fish among those 10 which do have blood. And this is reasonable enough, since sound is a particular movement of air. But those fishes which are said to have a voice, e.g. those in the Achelous, make a sound with their gills or some such part; but voice is sound made by an animal and not with any chance part of its body.

But since everything which makes a sound does so because something strikes something else in something else again, and this last is air, it is reasonable that the only creatures to have voice should be 15 those which take in air. For nature then uses the air breathed in for two functions; just as it uses the tongue for both tasting and articulation, and of these tasting is essential (and so is found in a greater number of creatures), while expression is for the sake of well-being, so also nature uses breath both to maintain the inner warmth, as some- 20 thing essential (the reason will be stated elsewhere), and also to produce voice so that there may be well-being.

The organ of breathing is the throat, and that for which this part exists is the lung; for it is through this part that land animals have more warmth than other creatures. It is also primarily the region round the heart which needs breath. Hence the air must pass in when 25 it is breathed in.

So, the striking of the inbreathed air upon what is called the wind-pipe due to the soul in these parts constitutes voice. For, as we have

said, not every sound made by an animal is voice (for it is possible to
30 make a sound also with the tongue or as in coughing); but that which
does the striking must have a soul and there must be a certain imagination (for voice is a particular sound which has meaning, and not one
merely of the inbreathed air, as a cough is; rather it is with this air that
421ᵃ the animal strikes the air in the windpipe against the windpipe itself).
An indication of this is the fact that we cannot use the voice when
breathing in or out, but only when holding the breath; for one who
holds his breath produces the motion by its means. It is clear too why
fish have no voice; for they have no throat. They do not have this part
5 because they do not take in air or breathe in. The reason for this
requires separate discussion.

CHAPTER 9

It is less easy to determine the nature of smell and the object of smell
than that of the things already mentioned; for it is not so clear what
sort of thing smell is as it is with sound or colour. The reason for this is
10 that this sense is, in our case, not accurate but is worse than with many
animals; for man can smell things only poorly, and he perceives none
of the objects of smell unless they are painful or pleasant, because the
sense-organ is not accurate. It is reasonable to suppose that it is in this
way too that hard-eyed animals perceive colours, and that the varieties
of colour are not distinct for them, except in so far as they do or do not
15 inspire fear. So too is the human race with regard to smells.
For it seems that smell has an analogy with taste, and the forms of
flavour are in a similar position to those of smell, but in our case taste
is more accurate because it is a form of touch, and it is this sense which
is most accurate in man; for in the others he is inferior to many
20 animals, but in respect of touch he is accurate above all others. For
this reason he is also the most intelligent of animals. An indication of
this is the fact that in the human race natural ability and the lack of it
depend on this sense-organ and on no other; for people with hard
flesh are poorly endowed with thought, while those with soft flesh are
25 well endowed.
Just as flavours are sweet or bitter, so are smells. But some things
have a corresponding smell and taste (I mean, for example, sweet
smell and sweet taste) while other things have an opposite smell and
taste. Similarly too a smell may be pungent, bitter, sharp, or oily. But,
30 as we have said, because smells are not very distinct, as flavours are,

they have taken their names from the latter in virtue of a resemblance in the things; for sweet smell belongs to saffron and honey and bitter to thyme and such like, and similarly in the other cases.

421ᵇ

Smell is like hearing and each of the other senses, in that as hearing is of the audible and inaudible, and sight of the visible and invisible, so smell is of the odorous and inodorous. Some things are inodorous because it is impossible that they should have a smell at all, others because they have a little and faint smell. The tasteless also is so spoken of similarly.

5

Smell too takes place through a medium, such as air or water; for water-animals too seem to perceive smell, whether they have or do not have blood, just as those which live in the air; for some of these, drawn by the smell, seek for their food from a great distance.

10

Hence there appears to be a problem, if all creatures have smell in the same way, yet man smells when inhaling but not when, instead of inhaling, he is exhaling or holding his breath, no matter whether the object is distant or near, or even if it is placed on the nostril. Also, that what is placed upon the sense-organ itself should be imperceptible is common to all animals, but the inability to perceive without inhaling is peculiar to men; this is clear from experiment. So that the bloodless animals, since they do not inhale, would seem to have another sense apart from those spoken of. But that is impossible, since they perceive smell; for, the perception of the odorous, whether it be foul or fragrant, is smell. Moreover, they are evidently destroyed by the same strong odours as man is, e.g. bitumen, sulphur, and the like. They must, then, smell but without inhaling.

15

20

25

It seems that in man this sense-organ differs from that of the other animals, just as his eyes differ from those of the hard-eyed animals— for his eyes have eyelids, as a screen and sheath, as it were, and he cannot see without moving or raising them. But the hard-eyed animals have nothing of this sort, but see straightaway what takes place in the transparent. In the same way, therefore, the sense-organ of smell is in some creatures uncovered, like the eye, while in those which take in air it has a covering, which is removed when they inhale, owing to the dilatation of the veins and passages. And for this reason those animals which inhale do not smell in water; for in order to smell they must first inhale, and it is impossible to do this in water. Smell belongs to what is dry, just as flavour does to what is wet, and the sense-organ of smell is potentially of such a kind.

30

422ᵃ

5

CHAPTER 10

The object of taste is a form of the tangible; and this is the reason why
10   it is not perceptible through the medium of any foreign body; for no
more is it so with touch. And the body in which the flavour resides, the
object of taste, is in moisture as its matter; and this is a tangible thing.
Hence even if we live in water we should perceive a sweet object
thrown into it; but the perception would not have come to us through a
medium but because of the mixture of the object with the moisture,
15   just as in a drink. But colour is not seen in this way as the result of
admixture, nor through effluences. There is nothing, then, here corresponding to a medium; but just as the object of sight is colour, so that
of taste is flavour. Nothing produces the perception of flavour without
moisture, but it must have moisture actually or potentially, as is the
case with salt; for it is easily dissolved and acts as a solvent on the
tongue.
20   Sight is of both the visible and the invisible (for darkness is invisible, and sight judges of this too), and further of that which is excess-
ively bright (for this is invisible but in a different way from darkness).
Similarly too hearing is of sound and silence, the one being audible,
the other inaudible, and also of very loud sound as sight is of what is
25   very bright (for just as a faint sound is inaudible so in a way is a loud
and violent sound). And one thing is spoken of as invisible quite
generally, like the impossible in other cases, while another is so
spoken of if it is its nature to have the relevant quality but it fails to
have it or has it imperfectly, parallel to the footless or kernel-less. So
30   too taste is of the tasteable and the tasteless, the latter being that which
has little or poor flavour or is destructive of taste. But the primary distinction seems to be between the drinkable and undrinkable (for both
are a form of taste, but the latter is bad and destructive, while the
former is natural); and the drinkable is an object common to touch and
taste.
422ᵇ   Since the tasteable is moist, its sense-organ too must be neither
actually moist nor incapable of being moistened. For taste is affected
by the tasteable, *qua* tasteable. The sense-organ of taste, therefore,
which is capable of being moistened while being preserved intact, but
which is not itself moist, must be moistened. An indication of this is
5   the fact that the tongue does not perceive either when it is very dry or
when it is too wet; for in the latter case there is a contact with the
moisture which is there first, just as when someone first tastes a strong

flavour and then tastes another, and as to sick people all things seem bitter because they perceive them with a tongue full of moisture of that kind.

The kinds of flavour, as in the case of colours, are, when simple, 10 opposites: the sweet and the bitter; next to the one the oily and to the other the salt; and between these the pungent, the rough, the astringent, and the sharp. These seem to be just about all the varieties of flavour. Consequently, that which can taste is potentially such, while 15 that which makes it so actually is the object of taste.

CHAPTER 11

Concerning the tangible and touch the same account may be given; for if touch is not one sense but many, then the objects perceptible by touch must also be many. It is a problem whether it is many or one and also what is the sense-organ for that which can perceive by touch, 20 whether it is the flesh and what is analogous to this in other creatures, or whether it is not, but the flesh is the medium, while the primary sense-organ is something else which is internal. For every sense seems to be concerned with one pair of opposites, sight with white and black, hearing with high and low pitch, and taste with bitter and sweet; but in 25 the object of touch there are many pairs of opposites, hot and cold, dry and wet, rough and smooth, and so on for the rest. There is *a* solution to this problem at any rate—that there are many pairs of opposites in the case of the other senses also, e.g. in vocal sound there is not only high and low pitch, but also loudness and softness, and smoothness 30 and roughness of voice, and so on. There are other differences of this kind in the case of colour too. But what the one thing is which is the subject for touch as sound is for hearing is not clear.

As to whether the sense-organ for touch is internal or whether it is not this but the flesh directly, no inference can be drawn, it seems, from 423ᵃ the fact that perception occurs simultaneously with contact. For even as things are, if someone were to make a sort of membrane and stretch it round the flesh, it would communicate the sensation in the same way immediately when touched; and yet it is clear that the sense-organ would not be in this; and if this were to become naturally attached, the 5 sensation would pass through it still more quickly. Hence, the part of the body which is of this kind seems to be to us as the air would be if it were naturally attached to us all round; for we should then have thought that we perceived sound, colour, and smell by virtue of a single

thing, and that sight, hearing, and smell were a single sense. But as
10   things are, because that through which the movements occur is separated from us, the sense-organs mentioned are manifestly different. But
in the case of touch, this is, as things are, unclear; for the ensouled
body cannot be composed of air or of water, for it must be something
solid. The remaining alternative is that it is a mixture of earth and
15   these, as flesh and what is analogous to it tends to be; hence, the body
must be the naturally adhering medium for that which can perceive by
touch, and its perceptions take place through it, manifold as they are.
That they are manifold is made clear through touch in the case of the
tongue; for it perceives all tangible objects with the same part as that
with which it perceives flavour. If, then, the rest of the flesh perceived
20   flavour, taste and touch would seem to be one and the same sense. But
as things are they are two, because they are not interchangeable.

One might raise a problem here. Every body has depth, and that is
the third dimension, and if between two bodies there exists a third it is
not possible for them to touch each other. That which is moist or wet
25   is not independent of body, but must be water or have water in it.
Those things which touch each other in water must, since their
extremities are not dry, have water between them, with which their
extremities are full. If this is true, it is impossible for one thing to
touch another in water, and similarly in air also (for air is related to
30   things in it as water is to things in water, although we are more liable
not to notice this, just as animals which live in water fail to notice
423ᵇ   whether the things which touch each other are wet). Does, then, the
perception of everything take place similarly, or is it different for different things, just as it is now thought that taste and touch act by contact, while the other senses act from a distance?

But this is not the case; rather we perceive the hard and the soft
5   through other things also, just as we do that which can sound, the
visible, and the odorous. But the latter are perceived from a distance,
the former from close at hand, and for this reason the fact escapes our
notice; since we perceive all things surely through a medium, but in
these cases we fail to notice. Yet, as we said earlier too, even if we perceived all objects of touch through a membrane without noticing that
10   it separated us from them, we should be in the same position as we are
now when in water or in air; for as things are we suppose that we touch
the objects themselves and that nothing is through a medium.

But there is a difference between the object of touch and those of
sight and hearing, since we perceive them because the medium acts on

us, while we perceive objects of touch not through the agency of the medium but simultaneously with the medium, like a man who is struck through his shield; for it is not that the shield is first struck and then strikes the man, but what happens is that both are struck simultaneously.

It seems in general that just as air and water are to sight, hearing, and smell, so the flesh and the tongue are to their sense-organ as each of those is. And neither in the one case nor in the other would perception occur when contact is made with the sense-organ itself, e.g. if someone were to put a white body on the surface of the eye. From this it is clear that that which can perceive the object of touch is internal. For then the same thing would happen as in the other cases; for we do not perceive what is placed on the sense-organ, but we do perceive what is placed upon the flesh. Hence the flesh is the medium for that which can perceive by touch.

It is the distinctive qualities of body, *qua* body, which are tangible. The qualities which I speak of as distinctive are those which determine the elements, hot and cold, dry and wet, of which we have spoken earlier in our account of the elements. Their sense-organ, that of touch, in which the sense called touch primarily resides, is the part which is potentially such as they are. For perceiving is a form of being affected; hence, that which acts makes that part, which is potentially as it is, such as it is itself actually.

For this reason we do not perceive anything which is equally hot or cold, or hard or soft, but rather excesses of these, the sense being a sort of mean between the opposites present in objects of perception. And that is why it judges objects of perception. For the mean is capable of judging; for it becomes to each extreme in turn the other extreme. And just as that which is to perceive white and black must be neither of them actually, although both potentially (and similarly too for the other senses), so in the case of touch that which is to perceive such must be neither hot nor cold.

Again, just as sight was in a way of both the visible and the invisible, and just as the other senses too were similarly concerned with opposites, so too touch is of the tangible and the intangible; and the intangible is that which has to a very small degree the distinguishing characteristic of things which are tangible, as is the case with air, and also those tangible things which are in excess, as are those which are destructive. The situation with respect to each of the senses, then, has been stated in outline.

CHAPTER 12

In general, with regard to all sense-perception, we must take it that the sense is that which can receive perceptible forms without their matter,
20 as wax receives the imprint of the ring without the iron or gold, and it takes the imprint which is of gold or bronze, but not *qua* gold or bronze. Similarly too in each case the sense is affected by that which has colour or flavour or sound, but by these not in so far as they are what each of them is spoken of as being, but in so far as they are things of a certain kind and in accordance with their principle. The primary
25 sense-organ is that in which such a potentiality resides. These are then the same, although what it is for them to be such is not the same. For that which perceives must be a particular extended magnitude, while what it is to be able to perceive and the sense are surely not magnitudes, but rather a certain principle and potentiality of that thing.

It is clear from all this too why excess in the objects of perception
30 destroys the sense-organs (for if the movement is too violent for the sense-organ its principle is destroyed—and this we saw the sense to be—just as the consonance and pitch of the strings are destroyed when they are struck too violently). It is also clear why plants do not perceive, although they have a part of the soul and are affected by tangible
424ᵇ objects; for they are cooled and warmed. The reason is that they do not have a mean, nor a first principle of a kind such as to receive the forms of objects of perception; rather they are affected by the matter as well.

Someone might raise the question whether that which cannot smell might be affected by smell, or that which cannot see by colour; and
5 similarly in the other cases. If the object of smell is smell, then smell must produce, if anything, smelling; hence nothing which is unable to smell can be affected by smell (and the same account applies to the other cases), nor can any of those things which can perceive be so affected except in so far as each is capable of perceiving. This is clear
10 at the same time from the following too. Neither light and darkness nor sound nor smell does anything to bodies, but rather the things that they are in, e.g. it is the air accompanying the thunderbolt which splits the wood. But tangible objects and flavours do affect bodies; for otherwise by what could soulless things be affected and altered? Will those other objects, too, then, affect them? Or is it the case that not every
15 body is affected by smell and sound, and those which are affected are indeterminate and inconstant, like air (for air smells, as if it had been

affected)? What then is smelling apart from being affected? Or is smelling also perceiving, whereas the air when affected quickly becomes an object of perception?

BOOK III

CHAPTER 1

That there is no other sense apart from the five (and by these I mean sight, hearing, smell, taste, and touch) one might be convinced by the following considerations. We have even now perception of everything of which touch is the sense (for all the qualities of the tangible, *qua* tangible, are perceptible to us by touch). Also, if we lack any sense we must also lack a sense-organ. Again, all the things which we perceive through direct contact are perceptible by touch, which we in fact have, while all those which we perceive through media and not by direct contact are perceptible by means of the elements (I mean, for example, air and water). And the situation is such that if two things different in kind from each other are perceptible through one thing, then whoever has a sense-organ of this kind must be capable of perceiving both (e.g. if the sense-organ is composed of air, and air is required both for sound and for colour); while if there is more than one medium for the same object, e.g. both air and water for colour (for both are transparent), then he who has one of these alone will perceive whatever is perceptible through both. Now, sense-organs are composed of two of these elements only, air and water (for the pupil of the eye is composed of water, the organ of hearing of air, and the organ of smell of one or other of these), while fire either belongs to none of them or is common to all (for nothing is capable of perceiving without warmth), and earth either belongs to none of them or is a constituent specially and above all of that of touch. So there would remain no sense-organ apart from those of water and air, and these some animals possess even now. It may be inferred then that all the senses are possessed by those animals which are neither imperfect nor maimed (for even the mole apparently has eyes under the skin); hence, unless there is some other body and a property possessed by none of the bodies existing here and now, no sense can be left out.

Nor again is it possible for there to be any special sense-organ for the common-objects, which we perceive by each sense incidentally,

424^b

25

30

425^a

5

10

15

i.e. movement, rest, figure, magnitude, number, and unity; for we perceive all these through movement, e.g. magnitude through movement (hence also figure, for figure is a particular form of magnitude), what is at rest through absence of movement, number through negation of continuity and also by the special-objects; for each sense
20 perceives one thing. Hence it is clear that it is impossible for there to be a special sense for any of these, e.g. movement. For in that case it would be as we now perceive the sweet by sight; and this we do because we in fact have a perception of both, as a result of which we recognize them at the same time when they fall together. (Otherwise we should perceive them in no other way than incidentally, as we
25 perceive the son of Cleon not because he is the son of Cleon but because he is white, and the white object happens to be the son of Cleon.) But for the common-objects we have even now a common sense, not incidentally; there is, then, no special sense for them; for if so we should not perceive them otherwise than as stated.
30   The senses perceive each other's special-objects incidentally, not in so far as they are themselves but in so far as they form a unity, when sense-perception simultaneously takes place in respect of the same
425ᵇ object, e.g. in respect of bile that it is bitter and yellow (for it is not the task of any further perception at any rate to say that both are one); hence too one may be deceived, and if something is yellow, one may think that it is bile.
   One might ask for what purpose we have several senses and not one
5 only. Is it perhaps in order that the common-objects which accompany the special-objects, e.g. movement, magnitude, and number, may be less likely to escape our notice? For if there were sight alone, and this was of white, they would be more likely to escape our notice and all things would seem to be the same because colour and magnitude invariably accompany each other. But as things are, since the
10 common-objects are present in the objects of another sense too, this makes it clear that each of them is distinct.

CHAPTER 2

Since we perceive that we see and hear, it must either be by sight that one perceives that one sees or by another sense. But in that case there will be the same sense for sight and for its object, colour. So that either there will be two senses for the same thing or the sense itself will be the one for itself.

Again, if the sense concerned with sight were indeed different from 15 sight, either there will be an infinite regress or there will be some sense which is concerned with itself; so that we had best admit this of the first in the series.

But this presents a difficulty; for if to perceive by sight is to see, and if one sees colour or that which possesses colour, then, if one is to see that which sees, that which sees primarily will have colour. It is clear 20 then that to perceive by sight is not a single thing; for even when we do not see, it is by sight that we judge both darkness and light, though not in the same way. Moreover, even that which sees is in a way coloured; for each sense-organ is receptive of the object of perception without its matter. That is why perceptions and imaginings remain in the sense-organs even when the objects of perception are gone. 25

The activity of the object of perception and of the sense is one and the same, although what it is for them to be such is not the same. I mean, for example, the actual sound and the actual hearing; for it is possible to have hearing and not to hear, and that which has sound is not always sounding. But when that which can hear is active, and that 30 which can sound is sounding, then the actual hearing takes place at the same time as the actual sound, and one might call these, the one 426ᵃ listening, the other sounding.

If then movement, i.e. acting, is in that which is acted upon, both the sound and hearing as actual must be in that which is potentially hearing; for the activity of that which can act and produce movement takes place in that which is affected; for this reason it is not necessary 5 for that which produces movement to be itself moved. The activity of that which can sound is sound or sounding, while that of that which can hear is hearing or listening; for hearing is twofold, and so is sound.

The same account applies also to the other senses and objects of perception. For just as both acting and being affected are in that which 10 is affected and not in that which acts, so both the activity of the object of perception and that of that which can perceive are in that which can perceive. But in some cases they have a name, e.g. sounding and listening, while in others one or the other has no name; for, the activity of sight is spoken of as seeing, but that of colour has no name, while that of that which can taste is tasting, but that of flavour has no name.

Since the activity of the object of perception and of that which can 15 perceive is one, though what it is for them to be such is not the same, the hearing and sound which are so spoken of must be simultaneously destroyed and simultaneously preserved, and so too for flavour and

On the Soul

taste, and the rest similarly; but this is not necessary for those which
20 are spoken of as potential. But the earlier philosophers of nature did
not state the matter well, thinking that there is without sight nothing
white nor black, nor flavour without tasting. For in one way they were
right but in another wrong; for since perception and the object of
perception are so spoken of in two ways, as potential and as actual, the
statement holds of the latter, but it does not hold of the former. But
25 they spoke undiscriminatingly concerning things which are so spoken
of *not* undiscriminatingly.

If voice is a kind of consonance, and voice and hearing are in a way
one, and if consonance is a proportion, then hearing must also be a
30 kind of proportion. And it is for this reason too that either excess,
whether high or low pitch, destroys hearing; and in the same way in
flavours excess destroys taste, and in colours the too bright or dark
426ᵇ destroys sight, and so too in smelling with strong smell, whether sweet
or bitter, since the sense is a kind of proportion. For this reason too
things are pleasant when brought pure and unmixed to the proportion,
e.g. the high-pitched, sweet, or salt, for they are pleasant then; but in
5 general a mixture, a consonance, is more pleasant than either high or
low pitch. The sense is a proportion; and objects in excess dissolve or
destroy it.

Each sense, therefore, is concerned with the subject perceived by it,
being present in the sense-organ, *qua* sense-organ, and it judges the
10 varieties of the subject perceived by it, e.g. sight for white and black,
and taste for sweet and bitter; and similarly for the other senses too.
Since we judge both white and sweet and each of the objects of
perception by reference to each other, by what do we perceive also
that they differ? This must indeed be by perception; for they are
15 objects of perception. From this it is clear also that flesh is not the
ultimate sense-organ; for if it were it would be necessary for that
which judges to judge when it is itself touched.

Nor indeed is it possible to judge by separate means that sweet is
different from white, but both must be evident to one thing—for otherwise, even if I perceived one thing and you another, it would be
20 evident that they were different from each other. Rather one thing
must assert that they are different; for sweet is different from white.
The same thing then asserts this; hence, as it asserts so it both thinks
and perceives. That, therefore, it is not possible to judge separate
things by separate means is clear.

And that it is not possible either at separate times is clear from the

following. For just as it is the same thing which asserts that good and 25
bad are different, so also when it asserts that the one and the other are
different the time when is not incidental (I mean as, for example, when
I say now that they are different, but not that they are different now);
but it so asserts both now and that they are different now; all at the
same time, therefore. Hence, it is undivided and does this in an
undivided time.

But yet it is impossible for the same thing to be moved simultaneously with opposite motions, in so far as it is indivisible, and in an 30
indivisible time. For if something is sweet it moves perception or
thought in one way, while the bitter moves it in the opposed way, while 427ª
white moves it quite differently. Is, then, that which judges at the same
time both numerically indivisible and undivided, while divided in
what it is for it to be such? It is indeed in one way that which is divided
which perceives divided objects, but in another way it is this *qua*
indivisible; for in what it is for it to be such it is divided, while it is
indivisible in place and number. Or is this impossible? For the same 5
indivisible thing may be both opposites potentially, although it is not
so in what it is for it to be such, but it becomes divided when
actualized; and it is not possible for it to be simultaneously white and
black, so that it cannot also be affected simultaneously by forms of
these, if perception and thought are of this kind.

But it is like what some call a point, which is both indivisible and 10
divisible in so far as it is one and two. That which judges, therefore, is
one and judges at one time in so far as it is indivisible, but in so far as it
is divisible it simultaneously uses the same point twice. In so far then
as it uses the boundary-point twice it judges two separate things in a
way separately; in so far as it uses it as one it judges one thing and at
one time.

So much then by way of discussion about the first principle in virtue 15
of which we say that an animal is capable of perceiving.

CHAPTER 3

There are two distinguishing characteristics by which people mainly
define the soul: motion in respect of place; and thinking, understanding, and perceiving. Thinking and understanding are thought to 20
be like a form of perceiving (for in both of these the soul judges and
recognizes some existing thing). Indeed the ancients say that

understanding and perceiving are the same. Empedocles for instance said 'Wisdom increases for men according to what is present to them' and elsewhere 'Whence different thoughts continually present them-
25 selves to them'. And Homer's 'Such is the mind of men' means the same thing too. For all these take thinking to be corporeal, like perceiving, and both perceiving and understanding to be of like by like, as we explained in our initial discussion. (Yet they should at the
427ᵇ same time have said something about error, for this is more charac-teristic of animals and the soul spends more time in this state; hence on their view either all appearances must be true, as some say, or error must be a contact with the unlike, for this is the opposite of
5 recognizing like by like. But error about opposites—like knowledge of them—seems to be the same thing.) That perceiving and understand-ing, therefore, are not the same is clear. For all animals have the former, but few the latter. Nor again is thinking, in which one can be right and wrong (right thinking being understanding, knowledge, and
10 true belief, wrong the opposite of these)—nor is this the same as perceiving. For the perception of the special-objects is always true and is found in all animals, whereas it is possible to think falsely also, and thinking is found in no animal in which there is not also reason;
15 for imagination is different from both perception and thought, and this does not occur without perception, nor supposal without it.

That imagination is not the same kind of thinking as supposal is clear. For the former is up to us when we wish (for it is possible to produce something before our eyes, as those do who set things out in
20 mnemonic systems and form images of them); but believing is not up to us, for it must be either true or false. Moreover, when we believe that something is terrible or alarming we are immediately affected correspondingly, and similarly if it is something encouraging; but in the case of the imagination we are just as if we saw the terrible or encouraging things in a picture.
25 There are also varieties of supposal itself—knowledge, belief, understanding, and their opposites; but the difference between these must be left for another discussion.

As for thought, since it is different from perceiving and seems to include on the one hand imagination and on the other supposal, we must determine about imagination before going on to discuss the
428ᵃ other. Now if imagination is that in virtue of which we say that an image occurs to us and not as we speak of it metaphorically, is it one of those potentialities or dispositions in virtue of which we judge and are

correct or incorrect? Such are perception, belief, knowledge, and intellect.

Now, that it is not perception is clear from the following. Perception   5
is either a potentiality like sight or an activity like seeing; but something can appear to us when neither of these is present, e.g. things in dreams. Secondly, perception is always present but not imagination. But if they were the same in actuality it would be possible for all beasts to have imagination; and it seems that this is not so, e.g. the ant or bee,   10
and the grub. Next, perceptions are always true, while imaginings are for the most part false. Further, it is not when we are exercising our senses accurately with regard to objects of perception that we say that this appears to us to be a man, but rather when we do not perceive it distinctly; and then it may be either true or false. And, as we said   15
before, sights appear to us even with the eyes closed.

Nor again will imagination be any of those things which are always correct, e.g. knowledge or intellect; for imagination can be false also. It remains, then, to see if it is belief; for belief may be either true or false. But conviction follows on belief (for it is not possible to believe things   20
without being convinced of them); and while no beast has conviction, many have imagination. Furthermore every belief implies conviction, conviction implies being persuaded, and persuasion implies reason; some beasts have imagination, but none reason.

It is clear, therefore, that imagination will be neither belief together with perception, nor belief through perception, nor a blend of belief   25
and perception, both on these grounds and because it is clear that on that view the belief will have as object nothing else but that which, if it exists, is the object of the perception too. I mean that it will be the blend of the belief in white and the perception of white that will be imagination; for it will surely not come about from the belief in the   30
good and the perception of white. Something's appearing to us will then be believing what one perceives and not incidentally. But things   428ᵇ
can also appear falsely, when we have at the same time a true supposition about them; e.g. the sun appears a foot across, although we believe it to be bigger than the inhabited world. So it follows on this view either that we shall have abandoned the true belief that we had,   5
although the circumstances remain as they were, and we have not forgotten it or been persuaded to the contrary, or, if we still have it, the same one must be both true and false. But it could become false only if the circumstances changed without our noticing. Imagination, then, is not any one of these things nor is it formed from them.

10   But since it is possible when one thing is moved for another to be moved by it, and since imagination is thought to be a kind of movement and not to occur apart from sense-perception but only in things which perceive and with respect to those things of which there is perception, since too it is possible for movement to occur as the result of the activity of perception, and this must be like the perception—this

15   movement cannot exist apart from sense-perception or in things which do not perceive; and in respect of it, it is possible for its possessor to do and be affected by many things, and it may be both true and false.

This happens for the following reasons: Perception of the special-objects is true or is liable to falsity to the least possible extent.

20   Secondly there is the perception that those things which are incidental to these objects of perception are so; and here now it is possible to be in error, for we are not mistaken on the point that there is white, but about whether the white object is this thing or another we may be mistaken. Thirdly there is perception of the common-objects which follow upon the incidental-objects to which the special-objects belong (I mean, for example, movement and magnitude); and it is about these that it is most possible to be in error in sense-perception.

25   The movement which comes about as a result of the activity of sense-perception will differ in so far as it comes from these three kinds of perception. The first is true as long as perception is present, while the others may be false whether it is present or absent, and especially when the object of perception is far off.

30   If, then, nothing else has the stated characteristics except imagination, and this is what was said, imagination will be a movement taking

429ᵃ   place as a result of actual sense-perception. And since sight is sense-perception *par excellence*, the name for imagination (*phantasia*) is taken from light (*phaos*), because without light it is not possible to see. And because imaginations persist and are similar to perceptions, animals

5   do many things in accordance with them, some because they lack reason, viz. beasts, and others because their reason is sometimes obscured by passion, disease, or sleep, viz. men. As to what imagination is, then, and why, let this suffice.

CHAPTER 4

10   In respect of that part of the soul by which the soul both knows and understands, whether this is distinct or not distinct spatially but only

in definition, we must inquire what distinguishing characteristic it has, and how thinking ever comes about.

Now, if thinking is akin to perceiving, it must be either being affected in some way by the object of thought or something else of this kind. It must then be unaffected, but capable of receiving the form, and potentially such as it, although not identical with it; and as that which is capable of perceiving is to the objects of perception, so must be the intellect similarly to its objects.

It must, then, since it thinks all things, be unmixed, as Anaxagoras says, in order that it may rule, that is in order that it may know; for the intrusion of anything foreign to it hinders and obstructs it; hence too, it must have no other nature than this, that it is potential. That part of the soul, then, called intellect (and I speak of as intellect that by which the soul thinks and supposes) is actually none of existing things before it thinks. Hence, too, it is reasonable that it should not be mixed with the body; for in that case it would come to be of a certain kind, either cold or hot, or it would even have an organ like the faculty of perception; but as things are it has none. Those who say, then, that the soul is a place of forms speak well, except that it is not the whole soul but that which can think, and it is not actually but potentially the forms.

That the ways in which the faculties of sense-perception and intellect are unaffected are not the same is clear from reference to the sense-organs and the sense. For the sense is not capable of perceiving when the object of perception has been too intense, e.g. it cannot perceive sound after loud sounds, nor see or smell after strong colours or smells. But when the intellect thinks something especially fit for thought, it thinks inferior things not less but rather more. For the faculty of sense-perception is not independent of the body, whereas the intellect is distinct. When the intellect has become each thing in the way that one who actually knows is said to do so (and this happens when he can exercise his capacity by himself), it exists potentially even then in a way, although not in the same way as before it learned or discovered; and then it can think by itself.

Since a magnitude and what it is to be a magnitude are different, and water and what it is to be water (and so too for many other things, but not for all; for in some cases they are the same), we judge what it is to be flesh and flesh itself either by means of something different or by the same thing differently disposed. For flesh does not exist apart from matter, but like the snub it is a this in a this. It is, then, with the faculty of sense-perception that we judge the hot and the cold and those things of which flesh is a certain proportion. But it is by something else, either something distinct or something which is to the former as a bent line is related to itself when straightened out, that we judge what it is to be flesh.

Again, in the case of those things which exist in abstraction, the straight corresponds to the snub, for it involves extension; but 'what it is for it to be what it was', if what it is to be straight and the straight are
20   different, is something else; let it be duality. We judge it, then, by something different or by the same thing differently disposed. In general, then, as things are distinct from matter, so it is too with what concerns the intellect.

Given that the intellect is something simple and unaffected, and that it has nothing in common with anything else, as Anaxagoras says,
25   someone might raise these questions: how will it think, if thinking is being affected in some way (for it is in so far as two things have something in common that the one is thought to act and the other to be affected)? And can it itself also be thought? For either everything else will have intellect, if it can itself be thought without this being through anything else and if what can be thought is identical in form, or it will have something mixed in it which makes it capable of being thought as the other things are.

Now, being affected in virtue of something common has been dis-
30   cussed before—to the effect that the intellect is in a way potentially the objects of thought, although it is actually nothing before it thinks;
430ᵃ   potentially in the same way as there is writing on a tablet on which nothing actually written exists; that is what happens in the case of the intellect. And it is itself an object of thought, just as its objects are. For, in the case of those things which have no matter, that which thinks and that which is thought are the same; for contemplative knowledge and
5   that which is known in that way are the same. The reason why it does not always think we must consider. In those things which have matter each of the objects of thought is present potentially. Hence, *they* will not have intellect in them (for intellect is a potentiality for being such things without their matter), while *it* will have what can be thought in it.

CHAPTER 5

10   Since in the whole of nature there is something which is matter to each kind of thing (and this is what is potentially all of them), while on the

other hand there is something else which is their cause and is productive by producing them all—these being related as an art to its material—so there must also be these differences in the soul. And there is an intellect which is of this kind by becoming all things, and 15 there is another which is so by producing all things, as a kind of disposition, like light, does; for in a way light too makes colours which are potential into actual colours. And this intellect is distinct, unaffected, and unmixed, being in essence activity.

For that which acts is always superior to that which is affected, and the first principle to the matter. Actual knowledge is identical with its 20 object; but potential knowledge is prior in time in the individual but not prior even in time in general; and it is not the case that it sometimes thinks and at other times not. In separation it is just what it is, and this alone is immortal and eternal. (But we do not remember because this is unaffected, whereas the passive intellect is perishable, 25 and without this thinks nothing.)[1]

CHAPTER 6

The thinking of undivided objects is among those things about which there is no falsity. Where there is both falsity and truth, there is already a combination of thoughts as forming a unity—as Empedocles said 'where in many cases heads grew without necks' and were then joined together by Love—so too these things, previously separate, are 30 combined, e.g. the incommensurable and the diagonal; and if the thinking is concerned with things that have been or will be, then time 430^b is thought of in addition and combined in the thought. For falsity always depends upon a combination; for even if someone says that white is non-white he combines white and non-white. It is possible to say that these are all divisions too. But at any rate, it is not only that Cleon is white that is false or true but also that he was or will be. And 5 that which produces a unity is in each case the intellect.

Since the undivided is twofold, either potentially or actually, nothing prevents one thinking of the undivided when one thinks of a length (for this is actually undivided), and that in an undivided time; for the time is divided and undivided in a similar way to the length. It is not possible to say what one was thinking of in each half time; for 10

---

[1] Or: 'In separation it is just what it is, and this alone is immortal and eternal (but we do not remember, because while this is unaffected the passive intellect is perishable); and without this nothing thinks.'

these do not exist, except potentially, if the whole is not divided. But if one thinks of each of the halves separately, then one divides the time also simultaneously; and then it is as if they were lengths themselves. But if one thinks of the whole as made up of both halves, then one does 15 so in time made up of both halves.

That which is thought and the time in which it is thought are divided incidentally and not as those things were, although they are undivided as they were; for there is in these too something undivided, although surely not separate, which makes the time and the length unities. And this exists similarly in everything which is continuous, 20 both time and length.

That which is undivided not quantitatively but in form one thinks of in an undivided time and with an undivided part of the soul.

The point and every division, and that which is in this way undivided, are made known as privation is. And the same account applies to the other cases, e.g. how one recognizes evil or black; for one recognizes them in a way by their opposites. That which recognizes must be its object potentially, and the latter must be in it. But if 25 there is anything which has no opposite, then this will know itself and is activity and distinct.

Every assertion says something of something, as too does denial, and is true or false. But not every thought is such; that of what a thing is in respect of 'what it is for it to be what it was' is true, and does not say something of something. But just as the seeing of a special-object 30 is true, while the seeing whether the white thing is a man or not is not always true, so it is with those things which are without matter.

CHAPTER 7

431ᵃ Actual knowledge is identical with its object. But potential knowledge is prior in time in the individual, but not prior even in time in general; for all things that come to be are derived from that which is actually.

It is clear that the object of perception makes that which can perceive, actively so instead of potentially so; for it is not affected or 5 altered. Hence this is a different form from movement; for movement is an activity of the incomplete, while activity proper is different, the activity of the complete.

Perceiving, then, is like mere assertion and thought; when something is pleasant or painful, the soul pursues or avoids it, as it were 10 asserting or denying it; and to feel pleasure or pain is to be active with the perceptive mean towards the good or bad as such. Avoidance and desire, as actual, are the same thing, and that which can desire and that which can avoid are not different either from each other or from that which can perceive; but what it is for them to be such is different. To the thinking soul images serve as sense-perceptions. And when it asserts or denies good or bad, it avoids or pursues it. Hence the soul 15 never thinks without an image.

And just as the air makes the pupil such and such, and this in turn something else, and the organ of hearing likewise, and the last thing in the series is one thing, and a single mean, although what it is for it to be such is plural . . .

What it is by which one determines the difference between sweet 20 and hot has been stated already, but we must say also the following. It is one thing, but it is so as a boundary is, and these things, being one by analogy and number, are each to each as those are to each other; for what difference does it make to ask how one judges those things which are not of the same kind or those which are opposites, like white and black? Now let it be the case that as A, white, is to B, black, so C is to 25 D; so that it holds *alternando* too.[2] Now if CD were to belong to one thing, then it would be the case, as for AB too, that they would be one and the same, although what it is for them to be such is not the same— and similarly for those others. And the same account would apply if A were sweet and B white. 431[b]

That which can think, therefore, thinks the forms in images, and just as in those what is to be pursued and avoided is determined for it, so, apart from sense-perception, when it is concerned with images, it is moved, e.g. perceiving that the beacon is alight you recognize when 5 you see it moving that it belongs to the enemy, but sometimes you calculate on the basis of images or thoughts in the soul, as if seeing, and plan what is going to happen in relation to present affairs. And when one says, as there, that something is pleasant or painful, so here one avoids or pursues—and so in action generally. That which is apart 10 from action too, the true and the false, are in the same genus as the good and bad; but they differ, the first being absolute, the second relative to someone.

Those things which are spoken of as in abstraction one thinks of just as, if one thought actually of the snub, not *qua* snub, but separately *qua* hollow, one would think of it apart from the flesh in

---

[2] I.e., as A is to C, so B is to D.

15 which the hollow exists—one thinks of mathematical entities which
are not separate, as separate, when one thinks of them.

In general, the intellect in activity is its objects. Whether or not it is
possible for the intellect to think of any objects which are separate
from spatial magnitude when it is itself not so separate must be
considered later.

CHAPTER 8

20 Now, summing up what has been said about the soul, let us say again
that the soul is in a way all existing things; for existing things are either
objects of perception or objects of thought, and knowledge is in a way
the objects of knowledge and perception the objects of perception.
How this is so we must inquire.

Knowledge and perception are divided to correspond to their
25 objects, the potential to the potential, the actual to the actual. In the
soul that which can perceive and that which can know are potentially
these things, the one the object of knowledge, the other the object of
perception. These must be either the things themselves or their forms.
Not the things themselves; for it is not the stone which is in the soul,
432ª but its form. Hence the soul is as the hand is; for the hand is a tool of
tools, and the intellect is a form of forms and sense a form of objects of
perception.

Since there is no actual thing which has separate existence, apart
from, as it seems, magnitudes which are objects of perception, the
objects of thought are included among the forms which are objects of
5 perception, both those that are spoken of as in abstraction and those
which are dispositions and affections of objects of perception. And for
this reason unless one perceived things one would not learn or understand anything, and when one contemplates one must simultaneously
contemplate an image; for images are like sense-perceptions, except
10 that they are without matter. But imagination is different from
assertion and denial; for truth and falsity involve a combination of
thoughts. But what distinguishes the first thoughts from images?
Surely neither these nor any other thoughts will *be* images, but they
will not exist without images.

CHAPTER 9

15 The soul of animals has been defined by reference to two potentialities, that concerned with judgement, which is the function of thought

and sense-perception, and secondly that for producing movement in respect of place. Let so much suffice about perception and the intellect; we must now inquire what it is in the soul which produces movement, whether it is one part of it separate either spatially or in definition, or whether it is the whole soul, and if it is one part, whether it is a special part in addition to those usually spoken of and those which we have mentioned, or whether it is one of these. 20

A problem arises straightaway, in what way we should speak of parts of the soul and how many there are. For in one way there seem to be an indefinite number and not only those which some mention in distinguishing them—the parts concerned with reasoning, passion, and wanting, or according to others the rational and irrational parts; for in virtue of the distinguishing characteristics by which they distinguish these parts, there will clearly be other parts too with a greater disparity between them than these, those which we have already discussed, the nutritive, which belongs both to plants and to all animals, and the perceptive, which could not easily be set down as either irrational or rational. There is again the part concerned with the imagination, which is different from all of them in what it is for it to be such, although with which of them it is identical or non-identical presents a great problem, if we are to posit separate parts of the soul. In addition to these there is the part concerned with desire, which would seem to be different from all both in definition and in potentiality. And it would be absurd surely to split this up; for in the part concerned with reasoning there will be wishing, and in the irrational part wanting and passion; and if the soul is tripartite there will be desire in each part. 25 30 432^b 5

To come then to the point with which our discussion is now concerned, what is it that moves the animal in respect of place? For, movement in respect of growth and decay, which all have, would seem to be produced by what all have, the faculties of generation and nutrition. We must inquire also later concerning breathing in and out, and sleep and waking; for these too present great difficulty. 10

But as for movement in respect of place, we must inquire what it is that produces in the animal the movement involved in travelling. That, then, it is not the nutritive potentiality is clear; for this movement is always for the sake of something and involves imagination and desire; for nothing which is not desiring or avoiding something moves unless as the result of force. Besides, plants would then be capable of movement and they would have some part instrumental for this kind of movement. 15

Similarly it is not the faculty of sense-perception either; for there
20   are many animals which have sense-perception but are stationary and
unmoving throughout. If, then, nature does nothing without reason
and never fails in anything that is necessary, except in creatures which
are maimed or imperfect, while the animals of this kind are perfect
and not maimed (an indication being that they can reproduce them-
25   selves and have a maturity and a decline)—then it follows too that they
would have parts instrumental for travelling.

Nor is it the part concerned with reasoning and what is called the
intellect that produces the movement; for the contemplative intellect
contemplates nothing practicable, and says nothing about what is to
be avoided and pursued, while the movement always belongs to one
who is avoiding or pursuing something. But even when it contem-
30   plates something of the kind, it does not straight away command
avoidance or pursuit, e.g. it often thinks of something fearful or
pleasant, but it does not command fear, although the heart is moved,
or, if the object is pleasant, some other part.

433ᵃ   Again, even if the intellect enjoins us and thought tells us to avoid or
pursue something, we are not moved, but we act in accordance with
our wants, as the incontinent man does. And in general we see that the
man who has the art of healing does not always heal, this implying that
5   there is something else which is responsible for action in accordance
with knowledge and not knowledge itself. Nor is desire responsible for
this movement; for continent people, even when they desire and want
things, do not do those things for which they have the desire, but they
follow reason.

CHAPTER 10

It is at any rate clear that these two produce movement, either desire
10   or intellect, if we set down the imagination as a kind of thought; for
many follow their imaginations against their knowledge, and in the
other animals thought and reasoning do not exist, although imagination does. Both of these, therefore, can produce movement in respect
of place, intellect and desire, but intellect which reasons for the sake of
something and is practical; and it differs from the contemplative
15   intellect in respect of the end. Every desire too is for the sake of something; for the object of desire is the starting-point for the practical
intellect, and the final step is the starting-point for action.

Hence it is reasonable that these two appear the sources of movement, desire and practical thought. For the object of desire produces movement, and, because of this, thought produces movement, because the object of desire is its starting-point. And when the imagination produces movement it does not do so without desire. Thus there is one thing which produces movement, the faculty of desire. For if there were two things which produced movement, intellect and desire, they would do so in virtue of some common form; but as things are, the intellect does not appear to produce movement without desire (for wishing is a form of desire, and when one is moved in accordance with reasoning, one is moved in accordance with one's wish too), and desire produces movement even contrary to reasoning; for wanting is a form of desire.

Intellect then is always right; but desire and imagination are both right and not right. Hence it is always the object of desire which produces movement, but this is either the good or the apparent good; not every good but the practicable good. And it is that which can also be otherwise that is practicable.

Now, that it is this account of potentiality of the soul—the one called desire, that produces movement is clear. But for those who divide the soul into parts, if they divide and distinguish them according to potentialities, it transpires that there are many parts, the nutritive, perceptive, thinking, deliberative, and furthermore that concerned with desire; for these differ more from each other than do the parts concerned with wanting and passion.

But desires arise which are opposed to each other, and this happens when reason and wants are opposed, and it takes place in creatures which have a perception of time (for the intellect bids us resist on account of the future, while our wants bid us act on account of what is immediate; for what is immediately pleasant seems both absolutely pleasant and absolutely good because we do not see the future). Hence that which produces movement will be one in kind, the faculty of desire as such—and first of all the object of desire (for this produces movement without being moved, by being thought of or imagined)— though numerically there will be more than one thing which produces movement.

There are three things, one that which produces movement, second that whereby it does so, and third again that which is moved, and that which produces movement is twofold, that which is unmoved and that which produces movement and is moved. That which is unmoved is the practical good, and that which produces movement and is moved

is the faculty of desire (for that which is moved is moved in so far as it desires, and desire as actual is a form of movement), while that which is moved is the animal; and the instrument by which desire produces movement is then something bodily. Hence it must be investigated
20   among the functions common to body and soul.

To speak in summary fashion for the present—that which produces movement instrumentally is found where a beginning and an end are the same, e.g. in the hinge-joint; for there the convex and the concave are respectively the end and the beginning of movement (which is why the one is at rest while the other moves), the two being different
25   in definition, but spatially inseparable. For everything is moved by pushing and pulling; hence, as in a wheel, one point must remain fixed and the movement must begin from this. In general, therefore, as we have said, in so far as the animal is capable of desire so far is it capable of moving itself; and it is not capable of desire without imagination. And all imagination is either concerned with reasoning
30   or perception. In the latter then the other animals share also.

CHAPTER II

We must consider also what it is that produces movement in the
434ᵃ imperfect animals which have perception by touch only—whether they can have imagination and wants, or not. For they evidently have pain and pleasure, and if these they must have wants also. But how could they have imagination? Or is it that just as they are moved indeterminately, so also they have these things, but indeterminately?
5   Imagination concerned with perception, as we have said, is found in the other animals also, but that concerned with deliberation in those which are capable of reasoning (for the decision whether to do this or that is already a task for reasoning; and one must measure by a single standard; for one pursues what is superior; so that one has the ability to make one image out of many).
10   The reason why these animals are thought not to have beliefs is that they do not have beliefs derived from inference. Hence desire does not imply the deliberative faculty. Sometimes it overcomes and moves a wish; sometimes the latter does this to the former, like a ball, one desire overcoming the other, when incontinence occurs. But by nature
15   the higher is always predominant and effective; so that three motions are thereby involved. But the faculty of knowledge is not moved but remains constant.

Since the one supposition and proposition is universal and the other is particular (the one saying that such-and-such a man ought to do such-and-such a thing, while the other says that this then is such-and-such a thing, and I am such-and-such a man), then either it is the latter opinion, not the universal one, which produces movement, or it is both, but the first is more static while the other is not. 20

ON MEMORY*

CHAPTER 1

449^b In discussing memory and remembering, it is necessary to say what
they are, and how their occurrence is to be explained, and to which
5   part of the soul this affection, and recollecting, belong. For it is not the
same people who are good at remembering and at recollecting.
Rather, for the most part, slow people are better at remembering,
while those who are quick and learn well are better at recollecting.

First, then, one must consider what sort of things the objects of
10   memory are, for this often leads people astray. For it is not possible to
remember the future, which is instead an object of judgement and
prediction. (There might even be a predictive science, as some people
say divination is.) Nor is memory of the present; rather, perception is,
for by perception we know neither the future nor the past, but only the
15   present. But memory is of the past. No one would say he was remembering what was present, when it was present, e.g. this white
thing when he was seeing it; nor would he say he was remembering the
object of his theorizing when he was in the act of theorizing and thinking. Rather he says simply that he is perceiving the one, and exercising
scientific knowledge of the other. But when a person possesses
scientific knowledge and perception without actually exercising them,
20   under these conditions he remembers in the one case that he learned
or theorized, in the other that he heard, or saw, or something of the
kind. For whenever someone is actively engaged in remembering, he
always says in his soul in this way that he heard, or perceived, or
thought this before.

Therefore memory is not perception or conception, but a state or
25   affection connected with one of these, when time has elapsed. There is
no memory of the present at the present, as has been said. But perception is of the present, prediction of the future, and memory of the past.
And this is why all memory involves time. So only animals which
perceive time remember, and they do so by means of that with which
they perceive.

---

*   *Translation*: R. Sorabji (London, 1972); *Text*: W. D. Ross (Oxford, 1955).

An account has already been given of imagination in the discussion   30
of the soul, and it is not possible to think without an image. For the
same effect occurs in thinking as in drawing a diagram. For in the   450ᵃ
latter case, though we do not make any use of the fact that the size of
the triangle is determinate, we none the less draw it with a determinate
size. And similarly someone who is thinking, even if he is not thinking
of something with a size, places something with a size before his eyes,
but thinks of it not as having a size. If its nature is that of things which   5
have a size, but not a determinate one, he places before his eyes something with a determinate size, but thinks of it simply as having size.
Now the reason why it is not possible to think of anything without
continuity, nor of things not in time without time, is another story. But
it is necessary that magnitude and change should be known by the   10
same means as time. And an image is an affection belonging to the
common sense. So it is apparent that knowledge of these is due to the
primary perceptive part. Memory, even the memory of objects of
thought, is not without an image. So memory will belong to thought in
virtue of an incidental association, but in its own right to the primary
perceptive part.

And this is why some other animals too have memory, and not only   15
men and those animals that have judgement or intelligence. But if
memory were one of the thinking parts, not many of the other animals
would have it, and perhaps no mortal animals would, since even as it
is, they do not all have memory, because they do not all have perception of time. For, as we said before, when someone is actively
engaged in memory, he perceives in addition that he saw this, or heard   20
it, or learned it earlier; and earlier and later are in time.

It is apparent, then, to which part of the soul memory belongs,
namely the same part as that to which imagination belongs. And it is
the objects of imagination that are remembered in their own right,
whereas things that are not grasped without imagination are remembered in virtue of an incidental association.   25

One might be puzzled how, when the affection is present but the
thing is absent, what is not present is ever remembered. For it is clear
that one must think of the affection, which is produced by means of
perception in the soul and in that part of the body which contains the
soul, as being like a sort of picture, the having of which we say is   30
memory. For the change that occurs marks in a sort of imprint, as it
were, of the sense-image, as people do who seal things with signet
rings.

(And this is also why memory does not occur in those who are
450ᵇ subject to a lot of movement, because of some trouble or because of
their time of life, just as if the change and the seal were falling on
running water. In others, because of wearing down, as in the old parts
of buildings, and because of the hardness of what receives the affec-
5 tion, the imprint is not produced. And this is why the very young and
the old have poor memory, since they are in a state of flux, the former
because they are growing, the latter because they are wasting away.
Similarly the very quick and the very slow are also obviously neither of
them good at remembering. For the former are too fluid, the latter too
10 hard. Therefore with the former the image does not remain in the soul,
while with the latter it does not take hold.)

But then, if this is the sort of thing that happens with memory, does
one remember this affection, or the thing from which it was produced?
For if the former, we would remember nothing absent; but if the latter,
15 how is it that while perceiving the affection we remember the absent
thing which we are not perceiving? And if it is like an imprint or
drawing in us, why should the perception of this be the memory of a
different thing, rather than of the affection itself? For one who is
exercising his memory contemplates this affection and perceives this.
How therefore will he remember what is not present? For at that rate
one could also see and hear what is not present.

20 Or is there a way in which this is possible and happens? For the
figure drawn on a panel is both a figure and a copy, and while being
one and the same, it is both, even though the being of the two is not the
same. And one can contemplate it both as a figure and as a copy. In the
same way one must also conceive the image in us to be something in its
25 own right and to be of another thing. In so far, then, as it is something
in its own right, it is an object of contemplation or an image. But in so
far as it is of another thing, it is a sort of copy and a reminder. So again
when the change connected with the other thing is active, if the soul
perceives the image as something in its own right, it appears to come
to one as a thought or image. But if one contemplates the image as
30 being of another thing, and (just as in the case of the drawing) as a
copy, and as of Coriscus, when one hasn't seen Coriscus, then (not
only in the case of the drawing is the experience of so contemplating it
different from when one contemplates it as a drawn figure; but also) in
451ᵃ the case of the soul, the one image occurs simply as a thought, the
other, because it is a copy (as in the case of the drawing), is a reminder.

And for this reason, when changes like this are produced in our soul as a result of former perception, we sometimes do not know whether this is happening in accordance with the previous perception, and are in doubt whether it is memory or not.

At other times it happens that we have a thought and recollect that we heard or saw something earlier. This happens when one changes from contemplating the image as the thing that it is to contemplating it as being of something else.

The contrary also happens, as it did to Antipheron of Oreus and other mad people. For they used to speak of their images as things that had occurred and as if they were remembering them. This happens whenever someone contemplates what is not a copy as if it were.

Exercises safeguard memory by reminding one. And this is nothing other than contemplating something frequently as a copy and not as a thing in its own right.

Now, it has been said what memory and remembering are, namely the having of an image regarded as a copy of that of which it is an image, and to which part in us memory belongs, namely the primary perceptive part and that with which we perceive time.

ON SLEEP*

455ª   We must now proceed to inquire into the cause why one sleeps and wakes, and into the particular nature of the sense-perception, or sense-perceptions, if there be several, on which these affections
5   depend. Since, then, some animals possess all the modes of sense-perception, and some not all, not, for example, sight, while all possess touch and taste, except such animals as are imperfectly developed, a class of which we have already treated in our work on the soul; and since an animal when asleep is unable to exercise, straightforwardly, any sensory faculty whatever, it follows that in the
10   state called sleep the same affection must extend to all the senses; because, if it attaches itself to one of them but not to another, then an animal while asleep may perceive with the latter; but this is impossible.

   Now, since every sense has something special and also something common; special, as, e.g., seeing is to the sense of sight, hearing to the
15   auditory sense, and so on with the other senses severally; while all are accompanied by a common power, in virtue whereof a person perceives that he sees or hears (for, assuredly, it is not by *sight* that one sees that he sees; and it is not by taste, or sight, or both together that one discerns, and can discern that sweet things are different from
20   white things, but by a part common to all the organs of sense; for there is one sensory function, and the controlling sensory organ is one, though differing as a faculty of perception in relation to each genus, e.g., sound or colour); and since this subsists in association chiefly with the faculty of touch (for this can exist apart from all the other organs of sense, but none of them can exist apart from it—a subject of
25   which we have treated in our speculations concerning the soul); it is therefore evident that waking and sleeping are an affection of this. This explains why they belong to all animals; for touch alone belongs to all.

---

* *Translation*: J. I. Beare, revised J. Barnes (Revised Oxford Aristotle, 1984); *Text*: W. D. Ross (Oxford, 1955).

For if sleeping were caused by the senses having all undergone
some affection, it would be strange that these senses, for which it is
neither necessary nor in a manner possible to be active simultaneously, should necessarily all go idle and become motionless 30
simultaneously. For the contrary, viz. that they should not rest
simultaneously, would have been more reasonably anticipated. But,
according to the explanation just given, all is quite clear regarding
those also. For, when the sense organ which controls all the others, 455ᵇ
and to which all the others are tributary, has been in some way
affected, it is necessary that these others should be all affected at the
same time, whereas, if one of these becomes powerless, there is no
necessity for it to do so.

It is indeed evident from many considerations that sleep does not
consist in the mere fact that the senses do not function or that one does
not employ them, nor even in the inability to exercise the sense-
perceptions; for such is what happens in cases of swooning. A swoon 5
means just such impotence of perception, and certain other cases of
unconsciousness also are of this nature. Moreover, persons who have
the blood-vessels in the neck compressed become insensible. But
sleep supervenes when such incapacity of exercise has neither arisen
in some chance organ of sense, nor from some chance cause, but
when, as has been just stated, it has its seat in the primary organ with
which one perceives objects in general. For when this has become 10
powerless all the other sensory organs also must lack power to
perceive; but when one of them has become powerless, it is not
necessary for this also to lose its power.

We must next state the cause to which sleep is due, and its quality as
an affection. Now, since there are several types of cause (for we say
that that for the sake of which, and that whence the origin of motion 15
comes, and the matter, and the account, are all causes), in the first
place, then, as we assert that nature operates for the sake of an end,
and that this end is a good; and that to every creature which is
endowed by nature with the power to move, but cannot with pleasure
to itself move always and continuously, rest is necessary and bene- 20
ficial; and since, taught by truth itself, men apply to sleep this meta-
phorical term, calling it a rest: we conclude that its end is the
conservation of animals. But the waking state is the goal, since the
exercise of sense-perception or of thought is the goal for all beings to
which either of these appertains; inasmuch as these are best, and the
goal is what is best. Again, sleep belongs of necessity to each animal. I 25

use the term 'necessity' in its conditional sense, meaning that if an animal is to exist and have its own proper nature, it must have certain endowments; and, if these are to belong to it, certain others likewise must belong to it.

The next question to be discussed is that of the kind of movement or action, taking place within their bodies, from which the affection of waking or sleeping arises in animals. Now, we must assume that the causes of this affection in all other animals are identical with, or analogous to, those which operate in sanguineous animals; and that the causes operating in sanguineous animals generally are identical with those operating in man. Hence we must consider them all on this basis. Now, it has been determined already in another work that sense-perception in animals originates in the same part in which movement originates. This is one of three determinate places, viz. that which lies midway between the head and the abdomen. This in sanguineous animals is the region of the heart; for all sanguineous animals have a heart; and from this it is that both motion and the controlling sense-perception originate. Now, as regards movement, it is obvious that the origin of breathing and of the cooling process generally takes its rise there; and it is with a view to the conservation of the heat in this part that nature has provided respiration and the process of being cooled by moisture. Of this *per se* we shall treat hereafter. In bloodless animals, and insects, and such as do not respire, the connatural spirit is seen puffed up and subsiding in the part which is in them analogous. This is clearly observable in the holoptera such as wasps and bees; also in flies and such creatures. And since to move anything, or do anything, is impossible without strength, and holding the breath produces strength—in creatures which inhale, the holding of that breath which comes from without, but in creatures which do not respire, of that which is connatural (which explains why winged insects, when they move, are perceived to make a humming noise, due to the friction of the connatural spirit colliding with the diaphragm of the holoptera); and since every animal moves if some sense-perception, either internal or external, occurs in the primary organ of sense, accordingly if sleeping and waking are affections of this organ, the place in which and the organ in which sleep and waking originate, is evident.

Some persons move in their sleep, and perform many acts like waking acts, but not without an image or an exercise of sense-perception; for a dream is in a certain way a sense-impression. But of them we have to speak later on. Why it is that persons when aroused remember their dreams, but do not remember these acts which are like waking acts, has been explained in the work on *Problems*.

25

ON DREAMS*

CHAPTER 2

459ᵃ We can best consider the nature of the dream and the manner in which
it originates by regarding it in the light of the circumstances attending
25 sleep. The objects of sense-perception corresponding to each sensory
organ produce sense-perception in us, and the affection due to their
operation is present in the organs of sense not only when the perceptions are actualized, but even when they have departed.

What happens in these cases may be compared with what happens
in the case of projectiles moving in space. For in the case of these the
movement continues even when that which set up the movement is no
30 longer in contact. For that which set them in motion moved a certain
portion of air, and this, in turn, being moved excites motion in another
portion; and so it is in this way that the bodies, whether in air or in
liquids, continue moving, until they come to a standstill.

459ᵇ This we must likewise assume to happen in the case of qualitative
change; for that part which has been heated by something hot, heats
the part next to it, and this propagates the affection onwards to the
starting-point. This must therefore happen in sense-perception, since
actual perceiving is a qualitative change. This explains why the
affection continues in the sensory organs, both in their deeper and in
their more superficial parts, not merely while they are actually
5 engaged in perceiving, but even after they have ceased to do so. That
they do this, indeed, is obvious in cases where we continue for some
time engaged in a particular form of perception; for then, when we
shift the scene of our perceptive activity, the previous affection
remains; for instance, when we have turned our gaze from sunlight
10 into darkness. For the result of this is that one sees nothing, owing to
the motion excited by the light still subsisting in our eyes. Also, when
we have looked for a long while at one colour, e.g. at white or green,
that to which we next transfer our gaze appears to be of the same
colour. Again if, after having looked at the sun or some other brilliant
object, we close the eyes, then, if we watch carefully, it appears in a
15 straight line with the direction of vision (whatever this may be), at first

* *Translation*: J. I. Beare, revised J. Barnes (Revised Oxford Aristotle, 1984); *Text*:
W. D. Ross (Oxford, 1955).

its own colour; then it changes to crimson, next to purple, until it becomes black and disappears. And also when persons turn away from looking at objects in motion, e.g. rivers, and especially those which flow very rapidly, things really at rest are then seen as moving; and persons become deaf after hearing loud noises, and after smelling very strong odours their power of smelling is impaired; and similarly in other cases. These phenomena manifestly take place in the way above described.

In order to answer our original question, let us now, therefore, assume one proposition, which is clear from what precedes, viz. that even when the external object of perception has departed, the impressions it has made persist, and are themselves objects of perception; and let us assume, besides, that we are easily deceived respecting the operations of sense-perception when we are excited by emotions, and different persons according to their different emotions; for example, the coward when excited by fear, the amorous person by amorous desire; so that, with but little resemblance to go upon, the former thinks he sees his foes approaching, the latter, that he sees the object of his desire; and the more deeply one is under the influence of the emotion, the less similarity is required to give rise to these impressions. Thus, too, both in fits of anger, and also in all states of appetite, all men become easily deceived, and more so the more their emotions are excited. This is the reason too why persons in the delirium of fever sometimes think they see animals on their walls because of the faint resemblance to animals of the markings thereon when put together in patterns; and this sometimes corresponds with the emotional states of the sufferers, in such a way that, if the latter be not very ill, they know well enough that it is an illusion; but if the illness is more severe they actually move according to the appearances. The cause of these occurrences is that the faculty in virtue of which the controlling sense judges is not identical with that in virtue of which images come before the mind. A proof of this is, that the sun presents itself as only a foot in diameter, though often something else gainsays the imagination. Again, when the fingers are crossed, one object seesm to be two; but yet we deny that it is two; for sight is more authoritative than touch. Yet, if touch stood alone, we should actually have pronounced the one object to be two. The ground of such false judgments is that any appearances whatever present themselves, not only when its object moves a sense, but also

when the sense by itself alone is moved, provided only it be moved in
25   the same manner as it is by the object. For example, to persons sailing
past the land seems to move, when it is really the eye that is being
moved by something else.

CHAPTER 3
. . .

For it is owing to the fact that the movement which reaches the source
of sense comes from the sensory organs, that one even when awake
461ᵇ   believes himself to see, or hear, or otherwise perceive; just as it is from
a belief that the organ of sight is being stimulated, though in reality not
so stimulated, that we sometimes declare ourselves to see, or that,
from the fact that touch announces two movements, we think that the
one object is two. For, as a rule, the governing sense affirms the report
of each particular sense, unless another particular sense, more
authoritative, makes a contradictory report. In every case an appear-
5   ance presents itself, but what appears does not in every case seem real,
unless when the deciding faculty is inhibited, or does not move with its
proper motion. Moreover, as we said that different men are subject to
illusions, each according to the different emotion present in him, so it
is that the sleeper, owing to sleep, and to the movements then going on
in his sensory organs, as well as to the other facts of the sensory
10   process, is liable to illusion, so that what has little similarity to
something appears to be the thing itself. For when one is asleep, in
proportion as most of the blood sinks inwards, so the internal movements, some potential, others actual, accompany it inwards. They are
so related that, if anything moves the blood, some one sensory movement will emerge from it, while if this perishes another will take its
place; while to one another also they are related in the same way as the
15   artificial frogs in water which rise to the surface as the salt becomes
dissolved. The residuary movements are like these: they are within the
soul potentially, but actualize themselves only when the impediment
to their doing so has been relaxed; and according as they are thus set
free, they begin to move in the blood which remains in the sensory
organs, and which is now but scanty, and take on likenesses after the
manner of cloud-shapes, which in their rapid metamorphoses one
20   compares now to human beings and a moment afterwards to centaurs.
Each of them is however, as has been said, the remnant of a sensory
impression taken when sense was actualizing itself; and when this, the
true impression, has departed, its remnant is still there, and it is

correct to say of it, that though not actually Coriscus, it is like Coriscus. When the person was actually perceiving, his controlling and judging sensory faculty did not call it Coriscus, but, prompted by this, called the genuine person yonder Coriscus. Accordingly, that 25 which, when actually perceiving, says this (unless completely inhibited by the blood), now, as though it were perceiving, is moved by the movements persisting in the sense-organs, and that which is like the thing seems to it to be the thing itself; and the effect of sleep is so great that it causes this mistake to pass unnoticed. Accordingly, just as if a finger be pressed under the eyeball without being observed, one object will not only present two visual images, but will create an 462ᵃ opinion of its being two objects; while if it be observed, the presentation will be the same, but the same opinion will not be formed of it; exactly so it is in states of sleep: if the sleeper perceives that he is asleep, and is conscious of the sleeping state during which the perception comes before his mind, it presents itself still, but something within him speaks to this effect: 'the image of Coriscus presents itself, but the real Coriscus is not present'; for often, when one is asleep, 5 there is something in the soul which declares that what then presents itself is but a dream. If, however, he is not aware of being asleep, there is nothing which will contradict the testimony of the bare presentation.

. . .

ON YOUTH AND OLD AGE*

. . .

468ᵇ Likewise in sanguineous animals the heart is the first organ developed; this is evident from what has been observed in those cases
30 where observation of their growth is possible. Hence in bloodless animals also what corresponds to the heart must develop first. We have already asserted in our treatise on the parts of animals that it is from the heart that the veins issue, and that in sanguineous animals
469ᵃ the blood is the final nutriment from which the members are formed. Hence it is clear that there is one function in nutrition which the mouth has the faculty of performing, and a different one appertaining to the stomach. But it is the heart that has supreme control, exercising an additional completing function. Hence in sanguineous animals the
5 source both of the sensitive and the nutritive soul must be in the heart, for the functions relative to nutrition exercised by the other parts are ancillary to the activity of the heart. It is the part of the dominating organ to achieve the final result, as of the physician's efforts to be directed towards health, and not to be occupied with subordinate offices.
10 Certainly, however, all sanguineous animals have the supreme organ of the sense-faculties in the heart, for it is here that we must look for the common sensorium belonging to all the sense-organs. These in two cases, taste and touch, can be clearly seen to extend to the heart, and hence the others also must lead to it, for in it the other organs may
15 possibly initiate changes, whereas with the upper region of the body taste and touch have no connection. Apart from these considerations, if the life is always located in this part, evidently the principle of sensation must be situated there too, for it is *qua* animal that a body is said to be a living thing, and it is called animal because endowed with sensation. Elsewhere in other works we have stated the reasons why
20 some of the sense-organs are, as is evident, connected with the heart, while others are situated in the head. (It is this fact that causes some people to think that it is in virtue of the brain that the function of perception belongs to animals.)

* *Translation*: J. I. Beare, revised J. Barnes (Revised Oxford Aristotle, 1984); *Text*: W. D. Ross (Oxford, 1955).

CHAPTER 4

Thus if, on the one hand, we look to the observed facts, what we have said makes it clear that the source of the sensitive soul, together with that connected with growth and nutrition, is situated in this organ and 25 in the central one of the three divisions of the body. But it follows by reason also; for we see that in every case, when several paths are open, Nature always chooses the best. Now if both principles are located in the midst of the substance, the two parts of the body, viz. that which 30 elaborates and that which receives the nutriment in its final form will best perform their appropriate function; for the soul will then be close to each, and the central situation which it will, as such, occupy is the position of a dominating power.

Further, that which employs an instrument and the instrument it 469ᵇ employs must be distinct both in capacity and, if possible, in location, just as the flute and that which plays it—the hand—are diverse. Thus if animal is defined by the possession of sensitive soul, this principle must in the sanguineous animals be in the heart, and, in the bloodless ones, in the corresponding part of their body. But in animals all the 5 members and the whole body possess some connate natural heat, and hence when alive they are observed to be warm, but when dead and deprived of life they are the opposite. Indeed, the source of this warmth must be in the heart in sanguineous animals, and in the case of 10 bloodless animals in the corresponding organ, for, though all parts of the body by means of their natural heat work upon and concoct the nutriment, the governing organ takes the chief share in this process. Hence, even when the other members become cold, life remains; but when the warmth here is quenched, death always ensues, because the 15 source of heat in all the other members depends on this, and the soul is, as it were, set aglow with fire in this part, which in sanguineous animals is the heart and in the bloodless order the analogous member. Hence, of necessity, life must be simultaneous with the maintenance of heat, and what we call death is its destruction. 20

PARTS OF ANIMALS*

BOOK I

CHAPTER I

639ᵃ In relation to every study and investigation, humbler or more valuable alike, there appear to be two kinds of proficiency. One can properly be called knowledge of the subject, the other as it were a sort of educated-
5 ness. For it is characteristic of an educated man to be able to judge successfully what is properly expounded and what is not. This in fact is the kind of man that we think the generally educated man is, and by being educated we mean being able to do just this—except that in his case we consider one and the same man capable of judging about
10 practically everything, whereas we consider another capable in some limited field; for there may be another who is qualified in the same way as the former, but only in respect of part.

Clearly therefore the inquiry about nature, too, must possess certain principles of the kind to which one will refer in appraising the method of demonstration, apart from the question how the truth has it,
15 whether thus or otherwise.

I mean, for example, should one take each *being* singly and clarify its nature independently, making individual studies of, say, man or lion or ox and so on, or should one first posit the attributes common to all in respect of something common? For many of the same attributes
20 belong to many different kinds of animal, for example sleep, breathing, growth, wasting, death, and any other affections and conditions of this sort (for at present we are not in a position to speak of them with clarity and precision). If we do speak of the animals severally, it is plain that we shall often be saying the same things about many of
25 them. For each of the above attributes belongs to both horses and dogs and men, so that if one refers to each of their attributes one will have to speak repeatedly about the same ones—all that are the same in different species of animal while having no differentia themselves. On

---

* Book I. *Translation*: D. M. Balme (Clarendon Aristotle Series, 1972); *Text*: I. Becker (Berlin, 1831). Book II. *Translation*: W. Ogle, revised J. Barnes (Revised Oxford Aristotle, 1984); *Text*: A. L. Peck (Loeb Library, 1937).

the other hand there are no doubt others which, although they have   30
the same designation, differ by the specific differentia. Animal
locomotion, for example, is evidently not one in species, for there are   639ᵇ
differences between flying, swimming, walking, and creeping. Therefore we must not overlook the question how the examination should
be made, that is whether one should first survey common general
attributes and then later the peculiar ones, or take them individually   5
straight away. At present this has not been clarified. Nor has the next
question:

Should the natural philosopher, like the mathematicians when they
demonstrate astronomy, first survey the appearances in regard to the
animals and their parts in each case, and only then go on to state the   10
because-of-what (i.e. the causes), or should he proceed in some other
way?

And further, since we see more than one cause in connection with
coming-to-be in nature, for example the cause *for the sake of which* as
well as the cause *from which comes the beginning of the movement*, we must
be clear about these too, as to which sort of cause is naturally first and
which second.

First is evidently the one we call *for the sake of something*. For this is   15
the definition, and the definition is the beginning alike in things
composed according to an art and in things composed naturally. It is
after defining health or house, either mentally or perceptually, that the
doctor and the builder respectively expound the definitions and the
causes of each thing they do and why it must be done thus. And the *for
the sake of which* and the good exist to a greater degree in the works of   20
nature than in those of art.

The *necessary* cause is not present in all natural things in the same
way. Nearly everyone tries to reduce explanations to it, not having distinguished in how many ways the necessary is spoken of.

The *absolutely necessary* is present in what is eternal, but it is the
hypothetically necessary that is present in everything that comes to be, as   25
it is in the artefacts such as a house and anything else of that sort. It is
necessary that such-and-such matter be present if there is to be a
house or some other end; and first this thing must come to be and be
moved, then this, and so on successively as far as the end and that for
the sake of which each thing comes to be and is. It is the same with   30
things that come to be naturally.

But the mode of demonstration, i.e. the mode of necessity, differs as   640ᵃ
between natural science and the theoretical sciences. (We have

discussed the latter elsewhere.) For the latter begin from what is, the
5   former from what will be: 'Because health or man is such, it is
necessary that this be or come to be'—not 'Because this is or has come
to be, that or necessity is or will be'. Nor can one link together the
necessity in such a demonstration for ever, so as to say 'Because this is,
therefore that is'. (These matters too have been clarified elsewhere; we
have explained where necessity is present, where it is reciprocal, and
for what reason.)

10   Another question not to be overlooked is whether it is appropriate
to speak, as the earlier scientists did, of the way in which each thing
naturally *comes to be* rather than of the way in which it *is*. There is an
important difference here.

It seems right that, even in dealing with coming-to-be, our starting-
point should be the same as we said before; first to take the
15   appearances in respect of each kind, and only then to go on to speak of
their causes. For in house-building too it is more the case that *these*
things take place because the form of the house is *such*, than that the
house is such because it comes to be in this way. For coming-to-be is
for the sake of being, not being for the sake of coming-to-be. Hence
20   Empedocles was wrong in saying that many attributes belong to
animals because it happened so in their coming-to-be, for instance
that their backbone is such because it happened to get broken by
bending. He failed to recognize, first, that the seed previously
constituted must already possess this sort of capability, and secondly
that its producer was prior not only in definition but in time; for it is
25   the man that generates a man, and therefore it is because *that* man is
such that *this* man's coming-to-be happens so.

The same applies to things that seem to come to be spontaneously,
as it does also to artificial things; for in some cases the same things as
come to be from an art also come to be spontaneously, for example
30   health. Now there are some things whose producing agent pre-exists
resembling them, for example the art of making statues: for they do not
come to be spontaneously. And the art is the definition of the work
without the matter. And so it is with chance products: as the art has it,
so they come to be.

Hence we should if possible say that because this is what it is to be a
man, therefore he has these things; for he cannot be without these
35   parts. Failing that, we should get as near as possible to it: we should
640^b either say altogether that it cannot be otherwise, or that it is at least
good thus. And these follow. And because he is such a thing, his

coming-to-be necessarily happens so and is such. And that is why this part comes to be first, and then this. And this is the way we should speak of everything that is composed naturally.

Now those who in ancient times were the first to philosophize about nature were thinking about the material origin and that sort of cause— what and what kind of thing is matter, how does the universe come to be out of it, and with what cause of movement (such as strife or love or mind or spontaneity), assuming that the underlying matter has a certain kind of nature by necessity—fire a hot nature and earth a cold one, the former light and the latter heavy. For this is how they generate the universe. And they speak similarly of the coming-to-be of the animals and plants: they say, for example, that when the water flowed in the body a hollow stomach came to be, together with all the receptacles of food and residue, and when the breath made its way through, the nostrils were forced open. But the air and the water are the bodies' matter; for it is out of such bodies that they all construct nature. But if the existence of man and the animals and their parts is natural, we must have to say of each part—of flesh, bone, blood, and all the homoeomerous parts, and similarly of the non-homoeomerous such as face, hand, foot—in virtue of what, and in respect of what sort of capability, each is such as it is. For it is not enough to say what it is made of, for example of fire or of earth. If we were speaking of a bed or some such thing, we should be trying to define its form rather than its matter such as the metal or timber—or if not the form, at least the matter of the composite whole. For a bed is a *this in this*, or a *this such*, so that we should have to speak also of its shape and of what sort of thing it is in respect of its form. For its nature in respect of conformation is more important than its material nature.

But now if each animal and part existed by virtue of shape and colour, Democritus might be right; for this seems to be his assumption. At any rate he says it is clear to everybody what sort of thing man is in conformation, suggesting that he is known by shape and colour. Yet the dead man too has the same conformation of shape, but nevertheless is not a man. Moreover there cannot be a hand in any and every state, such as metal or wood, except homonymously like the doctor in the picture. For it will not be able to do its own work any more than stone flutes or the painted doctor can do theirs. In the same way none of the dead man's parts is such a part any longer, for example eye or hand. Therefore his statement is too simple: it is like a carpenter speaking about a wooden hand. For that is how the writers on nature

state the coming-to-be and causes of the shape: they say by what
powers things were fashioned. But no doubt the carpenter will say
adze or drill where the other says air and earth—except that the
carpenter's account will be better, for it will not be enough for him just
to say that after the tool struck this became hollow and that became
flat, but he will say why he made the blow so, and for the sake of what,
giving the reason—so that it should come to have such or such a
conformation. Clearly therefore their account is wrong. They ought to
say that the animal is *such*, and to speak about that—what it is and
what kind of a thing, and the same with each of its parts, just as in
speaking of the form of the bed.

Now if this is soul, or part of soul, or not without soul (at any rate
when soul has gone there is no longer an animal, nor does any of its
parts remain the same except in shape alone, like those turned to stone
in the fable)—if then this is so, it will be for the natural philosopher to
speak and know about soul (if not about all soul, then about just this
part in virtue of which the animal is *such*); he will both say what the
soul is (or just this part of it) and speak about the attributes that belong
to the animal in virtue of its soul's being such. He must do so
especially because nature is spoken of in two ways: in one way it is
nature as matter, in the other it is nature as being. And the latter is also
nature as moving cause and as end. And such, in the animal, is either
its whole soul or some part of it. So in this way the student of nature
will actually have to speak more about soul than about the matter, in
proportion as it is more due to soul that the matter is nature than the
other way round. For the timber too is bed and stool in that it is
potentially these.

The question may arise, in view of what has just been said, as to
whether it belongs to natural science to speak about all soul or about
some. For if about all, then no philosophy is left outside natural
science. For the intellect has the intelligibles as its object. So natural
science would seek to know about everything; for it belongs to the
same science to study intellect and the intelligible, if indeed they are
correlative and if all correlatives are the object of the same study, just
as it does with perception and the perceptibles.

The answer is that not all of the soul is an origin of movement, nor
are all of its parts. Growth is originated by the same part as in plants,
alteration by the perceptive part, and locomotion by some other part
but not by the intellective; for locomotion is present in other animals
too, but thought in none. Clearly therefore not all soul is to be spoken

about; for not all soul is nature, but some part of it, either one part or   10
several.

A further reason why none of the abstract objects can be studied by
natural science is that nature does everything *for the sake of* something.
For as in the artefacts there is the art, so in things themselves there is
evident another such origin and cause, which we grasp from the   15
universe just as we grasp the hot and the cold. This is why it is more
likely that the heavens have been brought into being by such a cause, if
they have come into being, than the animals that are mortal. At any
rate the ordered and the defined is far more apparent in the heavenly
bodies than about us, while the inconstant and random is more
apparent about the mortal bodies. Yet there are those who say that   20
although each animal exists and came to be naturally, the heavens
were constituted in this way by chance and spontaneity—in which
there is not a sign of chance and disorder.

But we commonly say that 'this is for the sake of that' wherever
there is apparent some end which the movement reaches if nothing   25
stands in the way. So it is evident that something of this sort exists (and
it is precisely what we call *nature*). For what comes to be from each
seed is certainly not the product of chance, but *this* comes from *this*;
nor does any chance seed come from any chance body. The seed, then,
is the origin and productive agent of what comes out of it. For these
are natural: at any rate they grow naturally out of this. Yet still prior to   30
this is that of which it is the seed; for the seed is a coming-to-be, but the
end is a being. And still prior to both is that from which the seed is. For
it is the seed in two ways, of that *out of* which it is and of that *of* which it
is: it is the seed of that from which it came, e.g. a horse, and of that
which will be out of it, e.g. a mule, not however in the same way but of   35
each in the way we said. Further, the seed is potentially something;
and we know how potentiality is related to actuality.   642ᵃ

There are then these two causes, the *for-the-sake-of-which* and the
of-necessity—for many things come to be because of necessity. Perhaps
the question might arise as to what kind of necessity is meant by those
who say 'of necessity'. For neither of the two modes defined in our   5
philosophical treatises can be present. In things that have coming-to-
be, however, there is the third kind. For we say that food is a necessary
thing not according to either of those modes but in that it is impossible
to be without it. This is as it were *ex hypothesi*. For just as there is a
necessity that the axe be hard, since one must cut with it, and, if hard,   10
that it be of bronze or iron, so too since the body is an instrument (for

each of its parts is for the sake of something, and so is the body as a whole), therefore there is a necessity that it be *such* a thing and made of *such* things if that end is to be.

15   Clearly then there are two ways of causing, and our account should if possible arrive at both, or failing that at least try to make this clear; and all who fail to state this give virtually no account of nature. For nature is an origin more than matter is. Occasionally even Empedocles stumbles
20   on it, led by the truth itself, and is compelled to say that the being and nature of a thing is its definition. For example, in expounding what bone is he does not say it is a particular one of the elements, nor two or three, nor all, but a definition of their mixture; clearly therefore flesh too and every other such part exists in the same way.

25   The reason why previous generations did not arrive at this way is that they lacked the notion of what-it-is-to-be and the defining of the being. Although Democritus was the first to touch upon it, it was not as something necessary to the study of nature but because he was carried away by the facts themselves. In Socrates' time, although this
30   interest grew, the inquiry into nature ceased, and those who philosophized turned aside to the study of practical virtue and political science.

Exposition should be as follows: for example, breathing exists for the sake of *this*, while *that* comes to be of necessity because of *those*. Necessity signifies sometimes that if there is to be *that* for the sake of which, *these* must necessarily be present; and sometimes that this is
35   their state and nature. For the hot necessarily goes out and comes in again when it meets resistance, and the air must flow in; so much is
642ᵇ   already necessitated. And when the inner hot beats back, in the cooling occurs the inflow of the outside air and the outflow.

CHAPTER 5

644ᵇ   Of all beings naturally composed, some are ungenerated and imperishable for the whole of eternity, but others are subject to coming-to-be and perishing. It has come about that in relation to the
25   former, which possess value—indeed divinity—the studies we can make are less, because both the starting-points of the inquiry and the things we long to know about present extremely few appearances to observation. We are better equipped to acquire knowledge about the perishable plants and animals because they grow beside us: much can
30   be learned about each existing kind if one is willing to take sufficient

pains. Both studies have their attractions. Though we grasp only a little of the former, yet because the information is valuable we gain more pleasure than from everything around us, just as a small and random glimpse of those we love pleases us more than seeing many other things large and in detail. But the latter, because the information about them is better and more plentiful, take the advantage in knowledge. Also, because they are closer to us and belong more to our nature, they have their own compensations in comparison with the philosophy concerned with the divine things. And since we have completed the account of our views concerning these, it remains to speak about animal nature, omitting nothing if possible whether of lesser or greater value. For even in the study of animals unattractive to the senses, the nature that fashioned them offers immeasurable pleasures in the same way to those who can learn the causes and are naturally lovers of wisdom. It would be unreasonable, indeed absurd, to enjoy studying their representations on the grounds that we thereby study the art that fashioned them (painting or sculpture), but not to welcome still more the study of the actual things composed by nature, at least when we can survey their causes. Therefore we must avoid a childish distaste for examining the less valued animals. For in all natural things there is something wonderful. And just as Heraclitus is said to have spoken to the visitors, who were wanting to meet him but stopped as they were approaching when they saw him warming himself at the oven—he kept telling them to come in and not worry, 'for there are gods here too'—so we should approach the inquiry about each animal without aversion, knowing that in all of them there is something natural and beautiful. For the non-random, the *for-something's-sake*, is present in the works of nature most of all, and the end for which they have been composed or have come to be occupies the place of the beautiful. If anyone has thought the study of the other animals valueless, he should think the same about himself; for one cannot without considerable distaste view the parts that compose the human kind, such as blood, flesh, bones, veins, and the like. Just as in any discussion of parts or equipment we must not think that it is the matter to which attention is being directed or which is the object of the discussion, but rather the conformation as a whole (a house, for example, rather than bricks, mortar, and timber), in the same way we must think that a discussion of nature is about the composition and the being as a whole, not about parts that can never occur in separation from the being they belong to.

645^b It is necessary first to divide off, in relation to each kind, the attributes that belong essentially to all the animals, and then to try to divide off their causes. Now we have said before that many belong in
5 common to many animals, some simply (for example feet, feathers, scales, and affections too in the same way), but others analogously. (By 'analogously' I mean that some have lungs while others have not lungs but something else instead which is to them what lungs are to the former; and some have blood while others have the analogous part
10 that possesses the same capability as blood does for the blooded.) To speak separately about each particular will, as we said before, often result in repetition when we speak of every attribute: the same ones belong to many. Let this then be determined so.

Since every instrument is for the sake of something, and each bodily
15 part is for the sake of something, and what they are for the sake of is an activity, it is plain that the body too as a whole is composed for the sake of a full activity. For sawing has not come to be for the sake of the saw, but the saw for the sawing; for sawing is a kind of using. Consequently the body too is in a way for the sake of the soul, and the parts
20 are for the sake of the functions in relation to which each has naturally grown. Therefore we must first state the activities, both those common to all and those that are generic and those that are specific. (I call them common when they belong to all animals, generic when they belong to animals whose differences among each other are seen to be in degree.
25 For example, I speak generically of 'bird' but specifically of 'man' and of every animal that has no differentia in respect of its general definition. What they have in common some have by analogy, some generically, some specifically.)

Now where activities are for the sake of other activities, clearly the parts of which they are the activities are set apart in the same way as
30 the activities. Similarly if some activities are prior and exist as the end of others, each part whose activity is such will have the same priority. And thirdly, the things whose existence necessitates attributes. (By 'affections and activities' I mean generation, growth, coition, waking,
35 sleep, locomotion, and all other such attributes of animals. By 'parts' I mean nose, eye, and the face as a whole, each of which is called a
646^a member; and it is the same with the other parts.)

So much then for the manner of the investigation. And we should try to state the causes in respect both of the common and of the peculiar attributes, beginning, in the way that we have made clear, first with what is first.

BOOK II

CHAPTER I

The nature and the number of the parts of which animals are severally   646ᵃ
composed are matters which have already been set forth in detail in
the book of *Histories* about animals. We have now to inquire what are   10
the causes that in each case have determined this composition, a
subject quite distinct from that dealt with in the *Histories*.

Now there are three degrees of composition; and of these the first in
order, as all will allow, is composition out of what some call the
elements, such as earth, air, water, fire. Perhaps, however, it would be
more accurate to say composition out of the elementary forces; nor   15
indeed out of all of these, as said elsewhere in previous treatises. For
wet and dry, hot and cold, form the material of all composite bodies;
and all other differences are secondary to these, such differences, that
is, as heaviness or lightness, density or rarity, roughness or smooth-   20
ness, and any other such properties of bodies as there may be. The
second degree of composition is that by which the homogeneous parts
of animals, such as bone, flesh, and the like, are constituted out of the
primary substances. The third and last stage is the composition which
forms the heterogeneous parts, such as face, hand, and the rest.

Now the order of development and the order of substance are   25
always the inverse of each other. For that which is posterior in the
order of development is antecedent in the order of nature, and that is
genetically last which in nature is first.

(That this is so is manifest by induction; for a house does not exist
for the sake of bricks and stones, but these materials for the sake of the
house; and the same is the case with the materials of other bodies. And
the same thing can be shown by argument. For generation is a process   30
from something to something, from a principle to a principle—from
the primary efficient cause, which is something already endowed with
a certain nature, to some definite form or similar end; for man
generates man, and plant generates plant, in each case out of the   35
underlying material.)

In order of time, then, the material and the generative process must   646ᵇ
necessarily be anterior; but in logical order the substance and form of
each being precedes the material. This is evident if one only tries to
define the process of formation. For the definition of house-building   5
includes that of the house; but the definition of the house does not

include that of house-building; and the same is true of all other
productions. So that it must necessarily be that the elementary
material exists for the sake of the homogeneous parts, seeing that these
are genetically posterior to it, just as the heterogeneous parts are
posterior genetically to them. For these heterogeneous parts have
reached the end and goal, having the third degree of composition, in
10 which development often attains its final term.

Animals, then, are composed of homogeneous parts, and are also
composed of heterogeneous parts. The former, however, exist for the
sake of the latter. For the active functions and operations of the body
are carried on by these; that is, by the heterogeneous parts, such as
the eye, the nostril, the whole face, the fingers, the hand, and the
15 whole arm. But inasmuch as there is a great variety in the functions
and motions not only of the whole animal but also of the individual
organs, it is necessary that the substances out of which these are
composed shall present a diversity of powers. For some purposes
softness is advantageous, for others hardness; some parts must be
capable of extension, others of flexion. Such powers, then, are
20 distributed separately to the different homogeneous parts, one being
soft another hard, one wet another dry, one viscous another brittle;
whereas each of the heterogeneous parts presents a combination of
multifarious powers. For the hand, to take an example, requires one
power to enable it to effect pressure, and another for simple
25 prehension. For this reason the instrumental parts of the body are
compounded out of bones, sinews, flesh, and the like, but not these
latter out of the former.

So far, then, as has yet been stated, the relations between these two
orders of parts are determined by a final cause. We have, however, to
inquire whether necessity may not also have a share in the matter; and
it must be admitted that these mutual relations could not from the very
30 beginning have possibly been other than they are. For heterogeneous
parts can be made up out of homogeneous parts, either from a
plurality of them, or from a single one, as is the case with some of the
viscera which, varying in configuration, are yet, to speak broadly,
formed from a single homogeneous substance; but that homogeneous
substances should be formed out of a combination of heterogeneous
parts is clearly an impossibility—for then a homogeneous thing would
consist of many heterogeneous things. For these causes, then, some
647ª parts of animals are simple and homogeneous, while others are
composite and heterogeneous; and dividing the parts into the instru-

mental and the sensitive, each one of the former is, as before said, heterogeneous, and each one of the latter homogeneous. For each sense is confined to a single order of sensibles, and its organ must be such as to admit that order. But that which is endowed with a property potentially is acted on by that which has the like property actually, so that the two are the same in kind, and if the latter is single so also is the former. Thus it is that while no physiologists ever dream of saying of the hand or face or other such part that one is earth, another water, another fire, they couple each separate sense-organ with a separate element, asserting this one to be air and that other to be fire.

Sensation, then, is confined to the simple or homogeneous parts. But, as might reasonably be expected, the organ of touch, though still homogeneous, is yet the least simple of all the sense-organs. For touch more than any other sense appears to be correlated to several distinct kinds of objects, and to recognize more than one category of contrasts, heat and cold, for instance, dry and wet, and other similar oppositions. Accordingly, the organ which deals with these varied objects is of all the sense-organs the most corporeal, being either the flesh, or the substance which in some animals takes the place of flesh.

Now as there cannot possibly be an animal without sensation, it follows as a necessary consequence that every animal must have some homogeneous parts; for these alone are capable of sensation, the heterogeneous parts serving for the active functions. Again, as the sensory faculty, the motor faculty, and the nutritive faculty are all lodged in one and the same part of the body, as was stated in a former treatise, it is necessary that the part which is the primary seat of these principles shall on the one hand, in its character of general sensory recipient, be one of the simple parts; and on the other hand shall, in its motor and active character, be one of the heterogeneous parts. For this reason it is the heart which in sanguineous animals constitutes this central part, and in bloodless animals it is that which takes the place of a heart. For the heart, like the other viscera, divides into homogeneous parts; but it is at the same time heterogeneous in virtue of its definite configuration. And the same is true of the other so-called viscera, which are indeed formed from the same material as the heart. For all these viscera have a sanguineous character owing to their being situated upon vascular ducts and branches. For just as a stream of water deposits mud, so the various viscera, the heart excepted, are, as it were, deposits from the stream of blood in the vessels. And as to the heart, the very starting-point of the vessels, and the actual seat of the

5

10

15

20

25

30

647ᵇ

5 force by which the blood is first fabricated, it is as one would naturally expect, constituted out of the selfsame nutriment which it originates. Such, then, are the reasons why the viscera are of sanguineous aspect: and why in one point of view they are homogeneous, in another heterogeneous.

MOVEMENT OF ANIMALS*

CHAPTER 6

Now whether the soul is moved or not, and, if it is moved, how it is 700^b
moved, has already been discussed in our work on the soul. Since all 5
lifeless things are moved by something else, and since we have set
forth in our work on first philosophy our views concerning how the
first and eternally moved is moved, and how the first mover imparts
motion, it remains for us to consider how the soul moves the body, and 10
what is the origin of an animal's motion. For if we exclude the motion
of the universe, living creatures are responsible for the motion of
everything else, except such things as are moved by each other
through striking against each other. Hence all their movements have a
limit; for so do the motions of living creatures. For all animals both
impart movement and are moved for the sake of something, so that this 15
is the limit to all their movement: the thing for-the-sake-of-which.
Now we see that the movers of the animal are reasoning and *phantasia*[1]
and choice and wish and appetite. And all of these can be reduced to
thought and desire. For both *phantasia* and sense-perception hold the
same place as thought, since all are concerned with making distinc- 20
tions—though they differ from each other in ways we have discussed
elsewhere. Wish and spiritedness and appetite are all desire, and
choice shares both in reasoning and in desire. So that the first mover is
the object of desire and also of thought; not, however, every object of
thought, but the end in the sphere of things that can be done. So it is a 25
good of this sort that imparts movement, not everything noble. For in
so far as something else is done for the sake of this, and in so far as it is
an end of things that are for the sake of something else, thus far it
imparts movement. And we must suppose that the apparent good
ranks as a good, and so does the pleasant (since it is an apparent good).
So it is clear that the movement of the eternally moved by the eternal 30
mover is in one respect similar to that of any animal, but in another
respect dissimilar; hence the first is moved eternally, but the movement of animals has a limit. But the eternally noble and that which is
truly and primarily good, and not good at one time but not at another,

---

* *Translation and text*: M. C. Nussbaum (Princeton, 1978).
[1] Usually translated 'imagination'.

is too divine and too honourable to be relative to anything else. The first mover, then, imparts movement without being moved, and desire and the faculty of desire impart movement while being themselves 701ᵃ moved. But it is not necessary for the last of the things that are moved to move anything. And from this it is obvious, too, that it is reasonable that movement from place to place is the last of the movements in things subject to becoming. For the animal moves and progresses in virtue of desire or choice, when some alteration has taken place in 5 accordance with sense-perception or *phantasia*.

CHAPTER 7

But how does it happen that thinking is sometimes accompanied by action and sometimes not, sometimes by motion, and sometimes not? It looks as if almost the same thing happens as in the case of reasoning and making inferences about unchanging objects. But in that case the 10 end is a speculative proposition (for whenever one thinks the two premises, one thinks and puts together the conclusion), whereas here the conclusion which results from the two premises is the action. For example, whenever someone thinks that every man should take walks, and that he is a man, at once he takes a walk. Or if he thinks that no 15 man should take a walk now, and that he is a man, at once he remains at rest. And he does both of these things, if nothing prevents or compels him. I should make something good; a house is something good. At once he makes a house. I need covering; a cloak is a covering. I need a cloak. What I need, I have to make; I need a cloak. I have to make a cloak. And the conclusion, the 'I have to make a cloak', is an 20 action. And he acts from a starting-point. If there is to be a cloak, there must necessarily be this first, and if this, this. And this he does at once. Now, that the action is the conclusion, is clear. And as for the premisses of action, they are of two kinds—through the good and 25 through the possible.

But as sometimes happens when we ask dialectical questions, so here reason does not stop and consider at all the second of the two premisses, the obvious one. For example, if taking walks is good for a man, it does not waste time considering that he is a man. Hence whatever we do without calculating, we do quickly. For whenever a 30 creature is actually using sense-perception or *phantasia* or thought towards the thing for-the-sake-of-which, he does at once what he desires. For the activity of the desire takes the place of questioning or

thinking. 'I have to drink', says appetite. 'Here's drink', says sense-perception or *phantasia* or thought. At once he drinks. This, then, is the way that animals are impelled to move and act: the proximate   35
reason for movement is desire, and this comes to be either through sense-perception or through *phantasia* and thought. With creatures that desire to act, it is sometimes from appetite or spiritedness and sometimes from wish that they make or act.   701ᵇ

The movement of animals is like that of automatic puppets, which are set moving when a small motion occurs: the cables are released and the pegs strike against one another; and like that of the little cart (for the child riding in it pushes it straight forward, and yet it moves in a circle because it has wheels of unequal size: for the smaller acts like a   5
centre, as happens in the case of the cylinders). For they have functioning parts that are of the same kind: the sinews and bones. The latter are like the pegs and the iron in our example, the sinews like the cables. When these are released and slackened the creature moves. Now in the puppets and carts no alteration takes place, since if the   10
inner wheels were to become smaller and again larger, the movement would still be circular. But in the animal the same part has the capacity to become both larger and smaller and to change its shape, as the parts expand because of heat and contract again because of cold,   15
and alter. Alteration is caused by *phantasiai* and sense-perceptions and ideas. For sense-perceptions are at once a kind of alteration, and *phantasia* and thinking have the power of the actual things. For it turns out that the form conceived of the pleasant or fearful is like the actual   20
thing itself. That is why we shudder and are frightened just thinking of something. All these are affections and alterations; and when bodily parts are altered some become larger, some smaller. It is not difficult to see that a small change occurring in an origin sets up great and   25
numerous differences at a distance—just as, if the rudder shifts a hair's breadth, the shift in the prow is considerable. Further, when, under the influence of heat or cold or some other similar affection, an alteration is produced in the region of the heart, even if it is only in an imperceptibly small part of it, it produces a considerable difference in   30
the body, causing blushing and pallor, as well as shuddering, trembling, and their opposites.

CHAPTER 8

Now the origin of motion is, as we have said, the object of pursuit or
avoidance in the sphere of action. Of necessity the thought and
phantasia of these are accompanied by heating and chilling. For the
35   painful is avoided and the pleasant pursued, and the painful and the
pleasant are nearly always accompanied by chilling and heating
702ᵃ   (although we do not notice this when it happens in a small part).
This is clear from the passions. For feelings of confidence, fears,
sexual excitement, and other bodily affections, painful and pleasant,
are accompanied by heating or chilling, in some cases of a part, in
5   others of the whole body. Memory and anticipation, using things of
this kind as likenesses, are now to a lesser degree, now to a greater,
responsible for the same things. Hence it is with good reason that
the inner regions and those around the origins of the organic
members are fashioned as they are, so as to change from solid to
10   liquid and from liquid to solid, from soft to hard and vice versa.
Since these processes happen this way, and since the passive and
active have the nature which we have often ascribed to them, then
whenever it happens that there are both active and passive elements,
and neither falls short in any respect of the account we give of them,
15   at once one acts and the other is acted upon. That is why it is pretty
much at the same time that the creature thinks it should move
forward and moves, unless something else impedes it. For the
affections suitably prepare the organic parts, desire the affections,
and *phantasia* the desire; and *phantasia* comes about either through
20   thought or through sense-perception. The rapidity and simultaneity
result from the fact that the active and passive are naturally relative
to each other.

That which first moves the animal must necessarily be in some
origin. We have said that a joint is the origin for one part and the end
of the other; hence nature uses it sometimes as one, sometimes as two.
For whenever movement starts from there, one of the end-points must
25   necessarily remain at rest, and the other be moved—for we have said
already that the mover must support itself against something at rest.
Accordingly, the extremity of the forearm is moved without imparting
movement, while in the elbow-joint the one part, which lies in the
whole segment that is being moved, is moved, but there must also be
30   something unmoved; which is what we mean by saying that it is
potentially one point, but becomes actually two. So if the forearm were

the animal, somewhere in this joint would be the movement-imparting origin of the soul.

But since it is possible for some lifeless thing to have this same relation to the hand, as, for example, if someone should move a staff in his hand, it is clear that the soul would not be in either of the end-points—neither in the end-point of what is moved, nor in the other   35
origin (for the stick has both an origin and an end-point with reference to the hand). So for this reason, if the movement-imparting origin   702ᵇ
from the soul is not also in the staff, it is not in the hand either. For the extremity of the hand stands in the same relation to the wrist, and so does this part to the elbow. It makes no difference whether the part is attached to the body by growth or not; the staff is like a separable limb.   5
So the soul must not be in any origin that is the end of something else, not even if there is something else more external than that—as, e.g., the origin of the extremity of the stick is in the hand, and that of the extremity of the hand in the wrist. And if it is not even in the hand,   10
because it is still higher up, neither is the origin in this higher place: for while the elbow remains at rest, all below it is moved as a continuous whole.

CHAPTER 9

Since the left and right sides are similarly formed, and these opposites can be moved simultaneously, so that it is impossible for the left to be moved in virtue of the right's remaining at rest, and vice versa, and since the origin is always in something higher than both, the origin of   15
the movement-imparting soul must necessarily be in the middle. For of both extremes the middle is the limit. And it is similarly related to motions from above and below—e.g., those from the head—and also to those proceeding from the spine in creatures which have a spine. And it is reasonable that this should be so: for we say that the faculty of   20
sense-perception, too, is there. So that when, because of sense-perception, the area around the origin is altered and changes, the adjacent parts change also, expanding and contracting, so that by these means animal motion necessarily comes about. And the middle section of the body is potentially one, but of necessity becomes more   25
than one in actuality. For the limbs can be set in motion simultaneously from the origin, and while one is at rest the other is in motion. Suppose, for example that in the figure *ABC B* is moved, and *A* imparts movement. But there must, however, be something at rest,

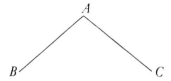

30   if one is to be moved and the other to impart movement. Then *A*,
though potentially one, becomes two in actuality, so that it must be not
a point but some magnitude. Again, *C* may be moved simultaneously
with *B*, so that both of the origins in *A* must of necessity impart movement while being moved. Then there must be something else besides
these that imparts motion but is not moved. Otherwise the extremities
35   or origins in *A* would support themselves against each other when
movement takes place, just like men who stand back to back and move
their legs. There must be some one thing that moves them both, and
703ᵃ   this is the soul, which is distinct from a spatial magnitude of this kind,
though it is in it.

CHAPTER 10

According to the account that gives the reason for motion, desire is the
5   middle, which imparts movement being moved. But in living bodies
there must be some body of this kind. Now that which is moved but
does not by nature initiate movement can be affected by an external
power, but a mover must of necessity have some power and strength. It
is clear that all animals have connate *pneuma*[2] and derive their
10   strength from this. (How the connate *pneuma* is maintained we have
explained elsewhere.) This seems to bear a relation to the origin of
life-activities that is similar to that which the point in the joints, the
one which imparts movement and is moved, has to the unmoved. And
since the origin is for some animals situated in the heart, for some in
15   an analogous part, it is clear that the connate *pneuma* is also there.
(Whether the *pneuma* is always the same or is always changing must be
discussed elsewhere, for the same question arises about the other
parts as well.) And it is obviously well disposed by nature to impart
movement and supply strength. Now the functions of movement are
20   pushing and pulling, so the tool of movement has to be capable of
expanding and contracting. And this is just the nature of the *pneuma*.

---

² 'Breath', 'spirit'.

For it contracts and expands without constraint, and is able to pull and push for the same reason; and it has weight by comparison with the fiery and lightness by comparison with its opposite. Whatever is going to impart motion without undergoing alteration must be of this 25 kind. For the natural bodies overcome one another according to their predominance: the light is overcome and kept down by the heavier, and the heavy kept up by the lighter.

We have said what the part is in virtue of whose motion the soul imparts movement, and what the reason is. We should consider the organization of an animal to resemble that of a city well-governed by 30 laws. For once order is established in a city, there is no need of a separate monarch to preside over every activity; each man does his own work as assigned, and one thing follows another because of habit. In animals this same thing happens because of nature: specifically 35 because each part of them, since they are so ordered, is naturally disposed to do its own task. There is, then, no need of soul in each part: it is in some governing origin of the body, and other parts live because they are naturally attached, and do their tasks because of 703ᵇ nature.

CHAPTER II

We have now explained how animals move with voluntary motions, and for what reasons. But they also display involuntary movements in some of their parts, and more often non-voluntary movements. By 5 involuntary I mean such movements as those of the heart and the penis; for often these are moved when something appears, but without the command of thought. By non-voluntary, movements such as sleep and waking and respiration, and all the others of this kind; for neither *phantasia* nor desire is, strictly speaking, in control of any of these. But 10 since the animal must necessarily undergo natural alteration, and since when the parts are altered some grow and some waste away, so that at once it moves and undergoes the changes that naturally succeed one another (heatings and chillings, both those from without and those which occur naturally within, being responsible for the 15 movements)—for this reason the irrational movements, too, of the above-mentioned parts occur when an alteration has taken place. For thought and *phantasia*, as we explained earlier, present that which produces the affections, in that they present the forms of the objects 20 that produce them. Now these parts exhibit these motions most conspicuously, since each of them is like a separate living creature. In the case of the heart, the reason for this is clear: in it are the origins of the senses. And there is evidence that the generative part, too, is of this

25 kind: for the force of the semen comes forth from it like a kind of living creature. Furthermore, it is quite reasonable that movements are set up in the origin by the parts and in the parts by the origin, and so reach one another. Let A be the origin. Then the movements from each

30 letter in the diagram we have drawn arrive at the origin, and from the origin as it moves and changes (since it is potentially many) the movement of B goes to B, that of C to C, that of both to both. But from B to C it goes by going first from B to A, as to an origin, then from A to C,

35 as from an origin. As for the fact that as a result of the same thoughts there is sometimes an irrational movement in the parts, sometimes not, the reason for this is that sometimes the passive matter is present

704ᵃ in the right quantity and quality, and sometimes not.

704ᵇ We have now discussed the reasons for the parts of each animal, the soul, and also sense-perception, sleep, memory, and movement in general. It remains to speak of generation.

GENERATION OF ANIMALS*

BOOK I

CHAPTER 21

How is it that the male contributes to generation, and how is the seed   729^b
from the male a cause of what is produced? Is it by being present
within and by being immediately a part of the body that is being
produced, mingling with the matter from the female? Or does the body   5
of the seed not participate, but only the capability and movement that
is in it? For it is the latter that is the agent, while that which becomes
constituted and takes the shape is the remainder of the female residue.
This is evident both according to reason and on the facts. For, considering it generally, we do not see one thing being produced *out of*   10
agent and patient in the sense that the agent is present within the
product, nor indeed (to generalize) *out of* mover and moved. But now
the female *qua* female is the patient, while the male *qua* male is the
agent and is that from which comes the beginning of the movement.
So that if we take the extremes of each, whereby the one is agent and   15
mover while the other is patient and moved, the one thing being
produced is not *out of* these except in the way that the bed is out of the
carpenter and wood or the sphere out of the wax and the form. Clearly
then it is not necessary that something should come away from the
male; and if something does come away, it does not follow that the   20
offspring is made out of it as out of something present within, but only
as out of mover and form, in the way that the cured invalid is the
product of the medical art.

On the facts too, what happens agrees with this argument. For this
is why certain males, even though they couple with the females, are
seen to put no part into the female, but on the contrary the female is
seen to put a part into the male, as is the case in certain insects. For the   25
effect that the seed, in those that emit, brings about in the female, is

* Books I–II. *Translation*: D. M. Balme (Clarendon Aristotle Series, 1972); *Text*:
H. J. Drossaart-Lulofs (Oxford Classical Texts, 1965). Book V. *Translation*: A. Platt,
revised J. Barnes (Revised Oxford Aristotle, 1984); *Text*: H. J. Drossaart-Lulofs (Oxford
Classical Texts, 1965).

brought about in these insects by the heat and capability in the animal itself when the female brings into it the part that is receptive of the residue. This is also why such animals are joined for a long time, but
30   when separated generate quickly. For they remain coupled until they have constituted the matter in the way that semen does; but after separating they emit the foetus quickly because they generate an unperfected offspring; for all of this sort produce grubs.

But what occurs in birds and in the oviparous kind of fishes is the
35   best evidence that the seed does not come from all the parts, and that
730ᵃ the male does not emit any part such as will remain present within the offspring, but generates an animal merely by the capability in the semen, just as we said of insects in which the female puts a part into
5   the male. For if a hen is gestating wind-eggs and is then mated before the egg has changed from being entirely yellow to turning white, the eggs become fertile instead of wind-eggs; and if it is mated with a second cock while the egg is still yellow, the chicks turn out to be of
10   the same kind in every respect as the second cock. This is why some who are concerned with the highly bred birds act in this way, changing the first and subsequent matings. It implies that the seed is not mixed in and present within, and that it did not come from every part; for it would have come from both cocks, so that the same parts would have
15   been contained twice. But by its capability the male seed puts the matter and nutriment that is in the female into a particular kind of state. The seed that came in later can do this by heating and concocting, since the egg takes nutriment so long as it is increasing in size. The same occurs in the generation of the oviparous fishes too. When
20   the female has laid the eggs, the male sprinkles the semen over them; those that it reaches become fertile, but those that it does not are infertile, implying that the male's contribution to the animals is not quantitative but qualitative.

It is clear then from what has been said that, in those animals that
25   emit seed, the seed does not come from every part; and that the female does not contribute in the same way as the male to the generation of the offspring that are constituted, but the male contributes a source of movement and the female the matter. This is why the female does not generate by itself; for it needs a source and something to provide
30   movement and definition (though of course in certain animals, for example hens, nature can generate up to a point; for these do constitute, but the products are unperfected, the so-called wind-eggs).

CHAPTER 22

It is also why the generation of the offspring takes place in the female: neither the male itself nor the female emits the semen into the male, but both contribute into the female that which is produced from them, 35
because it is the female that contains the matter out of which the 730ᵇ
product is fashioned. And some matter must be present immediately, already collected, out of which the foetus is constituted in the first place; other matter must continually be added so that what is being gestated may grow. Therefore birth must take place in the female; for 5
the carpenter too is close by the timber, the potter is by the clay, and in general every act of working-upon and proximate movement takes place by the matter, for example building takes place in what is being built.

One may also grasp from these examples how the male contributes to generation. For not every male emits seed, and in those that do emit 10
it the seed is no part of the foetus that is produced, just as nothing comes away from the carpenter to the matter of the timber, nor is there any part of carpentry in the product, but the shape and the form are produced *from* the carpenter *through* the movement *in* the matter. His 15
soul (in which is the form) and his knowledge move his hands or some other part in a movement of a particular kind—different when their product is different, the same when it is the same—the hands move the tools, and the tools move the matter. Similarly the male's nature, in those that emit seed, uses the seed as a tool containing movement in 20
actuality, just as in the productions of an art the tools are in movement; for the movement of the art is in a way in them. Those then that emit seed contribute in this way to generation. But those that do not 25
emit, where the female inserts some part of itself into the male, act like one bringing the matter to the craftsman. For because of the weakness of such males their nature is not capable of acting through other means, but even when it applies itself direct the movements have barely enough strength; it acts like modellers, not carpenters, since it fashions the thing being constituted not by touching it through some- 30
thing else but directly by using its own parts.

CHAPTER 23

Now in all animals that have locomotion the female is separated from the male: female is one animal and male is another, but they are the 35

same in form (for example, each is a man or a horse). But in the plants
731ᵃ these capabilities are mingled and the female is not separated from the
male. This is why they generate out of themselves and emit not semen
but a foetus, what we call seeds. This is well said by Empedocles in his
poem:

5   Thus do tall trees bear eggs: first olive-trees ...

For the egg is a foetus, and the animal is produced out of part of it
while the remainder is nutriment; the growing plant too is produced
out of part of the seed, while the remainder becomes nutriment for the
10   shoot and the first root. In a way the same happens also in those
animals that have the male and the female separated. For when they
are due to generate they become unseparated, as in plants, and their
nature wants to become one; this indeed is visibly evident when they
15   unite and couple, that both become a single animal. It is natural for
those that do not emit seed to remain joined for a long time until they
have constituted the foetus, for example the insects that couple; but
others, for example the blooded animals, remain only until they have
discharged some part that the male introduces, which will take further
time to constitute the foetus. The former remain connected for some
20   part of a day; in the latter the semen takes several days to constitute the
foetus, but they separate when they have emitted such semen. Animals
are just like divided plants, as though one were to take plants apart
whenever they bear seed and were to separate them into the male and
female that are present within.

25   Nature fashions all this reasonably. For plants have no other
function or activity in their being except the generation of seed, so that
since this is done through the coupling of male and female nature has
arranged them together by mingling them; that is why male and female
30   are inseparate in the plants. But the animal's function is not only to
generate (for that is common to all living things), but also they all
participate in some sort of cognition, some of them in more, some in
less, some in very little at all. For they have perception, and perception
is a sort of cognition. Its value or lack of value in our eyes differs
35   greatly according as we compare it with intelligence or with the
731ᵇ soulless kind of things. Compared with being intelligent, merely to
participate in touch and taste seems like nothing; but compared with
plant or stone it seems wonderful. One would welcome even this share
of cognition, rather than lie dead and non-existent. It is by perception
5   that animals differ from things that are merely alive. But since it must

also be alive, if it is an animal, when it is due to accomplish the function of the living thing it then couples and unites and becomes as if it were a plant, as we said. But the testacean animals, which are between animals and plants, through being in both kinds perform the function of neither. For as plants they do not have male and female and do not generate into another, while as animals they do not bear fruit out of themselves as plants do, but are constituted and generated out of a certain earthy and wet compound.

BOOK II

CHAPTER 1

It has been stated previously that the female and the male are sources of generation, and what is their capability and the definition of their being. As for the reason why the one becomes and is female and the other male—that it is due to necessity and the proximate mover and a certain sort of matter, our argument must try to explain as it proceeds. But that it is for the better, and due to the cause *for the sake of something*, derives from a prior principle.

For since some existing things are eternal and divine, while the others are capable both of being and of not being, and since the good and the divine is always according to its own nature a cause of the better in things that are capable, while the non-eternal is capable both of being and of partaking in both the worse and the better, and since soul is a better thing than body, and the ensouled than the soulless because of the soul, and being than not being, and living than not living,—for these reasons there is generation of animals. For since the nature of such a kind cannot be eternal, that which comes into being is eternal in the way that is possible for it. Now it is not possible in number (for the being of existing things is in the particular, and if this were such it would be an eternal) but it is possible in form. That is why there is always a kind—of men and of animals and of plants.

Since their source is the male and female, it must be for the sake of generation that male and female exist in those that have them. But the proximate moving cause (in which is present the definition and the form) is better and more divine in its nature than the matter; and it is better that the more excellent be separated from the worse. Because of this the male is separated from the female wherever possible and as far as possible. . . .

734^b   Everything produced naturally or by an art is produced *by* a thing existing actually *out of* what is potentially of that sort. Now the seed,

25   and the movement and source which it contains, are such that as the movement ceases each part is produced having soul. For it is not face nor flesh unless it has soul: after their death it will be equivocal to say that one is a face and the other flesh, as it would be if they were made of stone or wood. The homoeomerous parts and the instrumental parts are produced simultaneously. We would not say that an axe or other instrument was made by fire alone: no more would we say it of

30   hand or foot. The same applies to flesh, for it too has a certain function. Now heat and cold would make them hard and soft and tough and brittle, with all other such affections that belong to the parts containing soul, but would not go so far as giving them the definition

35   in virtue of which the one is now flesh and the other bone: that is due to the movement derived from the generator, which is *actually* what the thing out of which the product comes is *potentially*. It is the same

735^a   with things produced according to an art. Heat and cold make the iron hard and soft, but the *sword* is made by the instruments' movement which contains a definition belonging to the art. For the art is source and form of the product, but in another thing; but the movement of nature is in the thing itself, being derived from another nature which contains the form actualized.

5   And has the seed soul or not? The same reasoning applies to it as to the parts. For there can be no soul in anything except in that of which it is in fact the soul, nor can there be a part unless it has some soul (except homonymously, like a dead man's eye). Clearly therefore it

10   does have soul and exists—potentially. But it is possible to be relatively nearer and further in potentiality, as the geometer asleep is further than the one awake, and the latter than the one studying.

Now this generative process is not caused by any of its parts, but by that which proximately moved it from outside. For nothing generates itself. But once it has been produced, it proceeds to increase itself.

15   Therefore some first thing is produced, not everything at once. And the first thing to be produced must be that which contains the source of increase; for all alike, whether plant or animal, possess this, the nutritive. (And this is what is generative of another like oneself; for that is the function of every naturally perfected thing, both animal and

plant.) It must be so, because once a body has been produced it must be increased. Therefore although it was generated by that which is 20 synonymous (a man by a man), it is increased by means of itself. It itself must be something, therefore, if it causes increase. Now if it is one particular thing, and this is first, it must be the first to be produced. Consequently if the heart is the first to be produced in certain animals (and the part analogous to it in those that do not have a heart), the source must be from the heart in those that have one, and 25 from the analogous part in the others.

CHAPTER 3

If, in the case of those that emit semen into the female, that which 736ᵃ enters is no part of the foetus produced, where is its bodily part 25 diverted, if it is true that it works through the capability that is within it? We must make clear (i) whether that which is constituted in the female takes over anything from that which enters, or nothing; (ii) concerning soul in virtue of which it is called an animal (it is animal in 30 virtue of the perceptive part of the soul), whether it is present within the seed and the foetus or not, and where it comes from. One could not class the foetus as soulless, in every way devoid of life; for the seeds and foetuses of animals are no less alive than plants, and are fertile up 35 to a point. It is plain enough that they have nutritive soul (and why they must obtain this first is evident from what we have made clear elsewhere concerning soul), but as they progress they have also the 736ᵇ perceptive soul in virtue of which they are animal. For they do not become simultaneously animal and man, or animal and horse, and so on; for the end is the last to be produced, and the end of each animal's generation is that which is peculiar to it. This is why the question of intellect—when and how and from where it is acquired by those that 5 partake in this source—is especially difficult, and we must try hard to grasp it according to our capabilities and to the extent that is possible.

Now seeds and foetuses which are not yet separate must clearly be classed as possessing the nutritive soul *potentially*, but not *actually* 10 until they are drawing in their food like the separated foetuses and are performing the function of this sort of soul; for at first all such seem to live a plant's life. And what we say of the perceptive and intellective souls should clearly conform with that; for all souls must be possessed 15 potentially before actually.

And either they must all be produced in the body without existing

beforehand, or they must all pre-exist, or some must but not others; and they must be produced in the matter either without having entered in the male's seed, or having come from there; and in the male
20   they must either all be produced from outside, or none from outside, or some but not others.

Now it is evident from the following that they cannot all pre-exist: all principles whose actuality is bodily are clearly unable to be present without body (for example, walking without feet). Hence too they
25   cannot enter from outside. For they can neither enter by themselves, since they have no separate existence, nor enter in a body; for the seed is a residue produced by a change in the nutriment. It remains then that the intellect alone enters additionally from outside and alone is divine; for bodily actuality is in no way associated with its actuality.
30   Now the capability of all soul seems to be associated with a body different from and more divine than the so-called elements; and as the souls differ from each other in value and lack of value, so too this sort of nature differs. For within the seed of everything there is present that
35   which makes the seeds to be fertile, the so-called hot. This is not fire or that sort of capability, but the *pneuma* enclosed within the seed and within the foamy part, and more precisely the nature in the *pneuma*,
737ᵃ   being analogous to the element of the stars. This is why fire generates no animal, and none is seen to be constituted in things subjected to fire, whether wet things or dry. But the heat of the sun and the heat of animals do generate—not only the heat conveyed through the seed,
5   but also if there is some other residue of their nature, even this too contains a vital source. Such things make it plain that the heat in animals neither is fire nor has its origin from fire.

But the body of the semen, in which there also comes the portion of soul-source—partly separate from body in all those in which some-
10   thing divine is included (and such is what we call intellect) and partly inseparate—this body of the semen dissolves and evaporates, having a fluid and watery nature. That is why one should not look for it always to come out again, nor to be any part of the constituted form, any more than the curdling-juice which sets the milk: it too changes and is no
15   part of the mass that is being constituted.

Since the seed is residue, and is being moved in the same movement
20   as that with which the body grows when the final nutriment is being particularized, when it comes into the uterus it constitutes and moves the female's residue in the same movement in which it itself is actually moving. For that too is residue and contains all the parts potentially,

though none actually. It even contains potentially the sort of parts
whereby there is a difference between male and female. For just as the   25
offspring of deformed animals are sometimes deformed and sometimes not, so that of a female is sometimes female and sometimes not—
but male. For the female is as it were a male deformed, and the menses
are seed but not pure seed; for it lacks one thing only, the source of the
soul. This is why in all animals that produce wind-eggs the egg that is   30
being constituted has the parts of both, but has not the source, and
therefore does not become ensouled; for the source is brought in by
the male's seed. But once it has acquired such a source, the female's
residue becomes a foetus.

BOOK V

CHAPTER I

We must now investigate the qualities by which the parts of animals   778ᵃ
differ. I mean such qualities of the parts as blueness and blackness of
the eyes, height and depth of pitch in the voice, and differences in   20
colour and in hair or feathers. Some such qualities are found to
characterize the whole of a kind of animals sometimes, while in other
kinds they occur at random, as is especially the case in man. Further,
in connection with the changes in the time of life, all animals are alike
in some points, but are opposed in others as in the case of the voice
and the colour of the hair, for some do not grow grey visibly in old age,   25
while man is subject to this more than any other animal. And some of
these affections appear immediately after birth, while others become
plain as age advances or in old age.

Now we must no longer suppose that the cause of these and all such
phenomena is the same. For whenever things are not the product of   30
nature in general nor yet characteristic of each separate kind, then
none of these things is such as it is or is so developed for the sake of
anything. The eye for instance exists for a final cause, but it is not blue
for a final cause unless this condition be characteristic of the kind of
animal. In fact in some cases this condition has no connection with the
account of the animal's essence, but we must refer the causes to the
material and the motive principle on the view that these things come   778ᵇ
into being by necessity. For, as we said originally at the outset of our
discussion, when we are dealing with definite and ordered products of

nature, we must not say that each *is* of a certain quality because it *becomes* so, rather that they *become* so and so because they *are* so and
5   so, for the process of becoming attends upon being and is for the sake of being, not vice versa.

Past students of nature, however, took the opposite view. The reason for this is that they did not see that the causes were numerous, but only saw the material and efficient and did not distinguish even
10 these, while they made no inquiry at all into the formal and final causes.

Everything then exists for a final cause, and all those things which are included in the definition of each animal, or which either are for the sake of some end or are ends in themselves, come into being both through this cause and the rest. But when we come to those things which come into being without falling under the heads just
15 mentioned, their cause must be sought in the movement or process of coming into being, on the view that the differences which mark them arise in the actual formation of the animal. An eye, for instance, the animal must have of necessity (for an animal is supposed to be of such a sort), but an eye of a particular kind it will have of necessity in another sense, not the sense mentioned just above, because it is its nature to act or be acted on in this or that way.

. . .

CHAPTER 8

788ᵇ With regard to the teeth it has been stated previously that they do not exist for a single purpose nor for the same purpose in all animals, but
5   in some for nutrition, in others also for fighting and for vocal speech. We must, however, consider it not alien to the discussion of generation to inquire into the reason why the front teeth are formed first and the grinders later, and why the latter are not shed but the former are shed and grow again.

10 Democritus has spoken of these questions but not well, for he assigns the cause too generally without investigating the facts in all cases. He says that the early teeth are shed because they are formed in animals too early, for it is when animals are practically in their prime that they grow according to nature, and suckling is the cause he
15 assigns for their being found too early. Yet the pig also suckles but does not shed his teeth, and, further, all the saw-toothed animals suckle, but some of them do not shed any teeth except the canines, e.g.

lions. This mistake, then, was due to his speaking generally without examining what happens in all cases; but this is what we ought to do, for any one who makes any general statement must speak of all the particular cases.

Now we assume, basing our assumption upon what we see, that   20
nature never fails nor does anything in vain so far as is possible in each case. And it is necessary, if an animal is to obtain food after the time of taking milk is over, that it should have instruments for the treatment of the food. If, then, as Democritus says, this happened about the time of   25
reaching maturity, nature would fail in something possible for her to do. And, besides, the operation of nature would be contrary to nature, for what is done by violence is contrary to nature, and it is by violence tht he says the formation of the first teeth is brought about. That this view then is not true is plain from these and other similar considerations.

Now these teeth are developed before the flat teeth, in the first place   30
because their function is earlier (for dividing comes before crushing, and the flat teeth are for crushing, the others for dividing), in the second place because the smaller is naturally developed quicker than the larger, even if both start together, and these teeth are smaller in size than the grinders, because the bone of the jaw is flat in that part   789ᵃ
but narrow towards the mouth. From the greater part, therefore, must flow more nutriment to form the teeth, and from the narrower part less.

The act of sucking in itself contributes nothing to the formation of the teeth, but the heat of the milk makes them appear more quickly. A proof of this is that even in suckling animals those young which enjoy   5
hotter milk grow their teeth quicker, heat being conducive to growth.

They are shed, after they have been formed, partly because it is better so (for what is sharp is soon blunted, so that a fresh relay is needed for the work, whereas the flat teeth cannot be blunted but are only smoothed in time by wearing down), partly from necessity   10
because, while the roots of the grinders are fixed where the jaw is flat and the bone strong, those of the front teeth are in a thin part, so that they are weak and easily moved. They grow again because they are shed while the bone is still growing and the animal is still young enough to grow teeth. A proof of this is that even the flat teeth grow for   15
a long time, the last of them cutting the gum at about twenty years of age; indeed in some cases the last teeth have been grown in quite old age. This is because there is much nutriment in the broad part of the

789ᵇ bones, whereas the front part being thin soon reaches perfection and no residual matter is found in it, the nutriment being consumed in its own growth.

Democritus, however, neglecting the final cause, reduces to necessity all the operations of nature. Now they are necessary, it is true, but yet they are for a final cause and for the sake of what is best in 5 each case. Thus nothing prevents the teeth from being formed and being shed in this way; but it is not on account of these causes but on account of the end; these are causes in the sense of being the moving and efficient instruments and the material. So it is reasonable that nature should perform most of her operations using breath as an instrument, for as some instruments serve many uses in the arts, e.g. 10 the hammer and anvil in the smith's art, so does breath in things formed by nature. But to say that necessity is the cause is much as if we should think that the water has been drawn off from a dropsical patient on account of the lancet alone, not on account of health, for the 15 sake of which the lancet made the incision.

We have thus spoken of teeth, saying why some are shed and grow again, and others not, and generally for what cause they are formed. And we have spoken of the other affections of the parts which are found to occur not for any final end but of necessity and on account of 20 the motive cause.

Metaphysics

METAPHYSICS*

BOOK I (A)

CHAPTER I

All men by nature desire to know. An indication of this is the delight   980ᵃ
we take in our senses; for even apart from their usefulness they are
loved for themselves; and above all others the sense of sight. For not
only with a view to action, but even when we are not going to do
anything, we prefer sight to almost everything else. The reason is that   25
this, most of all the senses, makes us know and brings to light many
differences between things.

By nature animals are born with the faculty of sensation, and from
sensation memory is produced in some of them, though not in others.
And therefore the former are more intelligent and apt at learning than   980ᵇ
those which cannot remember; those which are incapable of hearing
sounds are intelligent though they cannot be taught, e.g. the bee, and
any other race of animals that may be like it; and those which besides
memory have this sense of hearing, can be taught.   25

The animals other than man live by appearances and memories,
and have but little of connected experience; but the human race lives
also by art and reasonings. And from memory experience is produced
in men; for many memories of the same thing produce finally the
capacity for a single experience. Experience seems to be very similar   981ᵃ
to science and art, but really science and art come to men *through*
experience; for 'experience made art', as Polus says, 'but inexperience   5
luck'. And art arises, when from many notions gained by experience
one universal judgement about similar objects is produced. For to
have a judgement that when Callias was ill of this disease this did him
good, and similarly in the case of Socrates and in many individual

* Books I and III. *Translation*: W. D. Ross, revised J. Barnes (Revised Oxford
Aristotle, 1984); *Text*: W. D. Ross (Oxford, 1924). Books IV–VI. *Translation*: C. A.
Kirwan Clarendon Aristotle Series, 1971); *Text*: W. Jaeger (Oxford Classical Texts,
1957). Books VII–XII. *Translation*: W. D. Ross, revised J. Barnes (Revised Oxford
Aristotle, 1984); *Text*: W. D. Ross (Oxford, 1924). Book XIII. *Translation*: J. Annas
(Clarendon Aristotle Series, 1976); *Text* W. Jaeger (Oxford Classical Texts, 1957).

cases, is a matter of experience; but to judge that it has done good to
10   all persons of a certain constitution, marked off in one class, when they
were ill of this disease, e.g. to phlegmatic or bilious people when
burning with fever,—this is a matter of art.

With a view to action experience seems in no respect inferior to art,
and we even see men of experience succeeding more than those who
15   have theory without experience. The reason is that experience is
knowledge of individuals, art of universals, and actions and productions are all concerned with the individual; for the physician does
not cure a man, except in an incidental way, but Callias or Socrates or
20   some other called by some such individual name, who happens to be a
man. If, then, a man has theory without experience, and knows the
universal but does not know the individual included in this, he will
often fail to cure; for it is the individual that is to be cured. But yet we
think that *knowledge* and *understanding* belong to art rather than to
25   experience, and we suppose artists to be wiser than men of experience
(which implies that wisdom depends in all cases rather on knowledge);
and this because the former know the cause, but the latter do not. For
men of experience know that the thing is so, but do not know why,
while the others know the 'why' and the cause. Hence we think that
30   the master-workers in each craft are more honourable and know in a
truer sense and are wiser than the manual workers, because they know
the causes of the things that are done (we think the manual workers are
981ᵇ   like certain lifeless things which act indeed, but act without knowing
what they do, as fire burns,—but while the lifeless things perform each
of their functions by a natural tendency, the labourers perform them
through habit); thus we view them as being wiser not in virtue of being
5   able to act, but of having the theory for themselves and knowing the
causes. And in general it is a sign of the man who knows, that he can
teach, and therefore we think art more truly knowledge than experience is; for artists can teach, and men of mere experience cannot.
10   Again, we do not regard any of the senses as wisdom; yet surely
these give the most authoritative knowledge of particulars. But they do
not tell us the 'why' of anything—e.g. why fire is hot; they only say that
it is hot.

At first he who invented any art that went beyond the common
15   perceptions of man was naturally admired by men, not only because
there was something useful in the inventions, but because he was
thought wise and superior to the rest. But as more arts were invented,
and some were directed to the necessities of life, others to its re-

creation, the inventors of the latter were always regarded as wiser than the inventors of the former, because their branches of knowledge did not aim at utility. Hence when all such inventions were already estab- 20
lished, the sciences which do not aim at giving pleasure or at the necessities of life were discovered, and first in the places where men first began to have leisure. This is why the mathematical arts were founded in Egypt; for there the priestly caste was allowed to be at leisure.

We have said in the *Ethics* what the difference is between art and 25
science and the other kindred faculties; but the point of our present discussion is this, that all men suppose what is called wisdom to deal with the first causes and the principles of things. This is why, as has been said before, the man of experience is thought to be wiser than the 30
possessors of any perception whatever, the artist wiser than the men of experience, the master-worker than the mechanic, and the theoretical kinds of knowledge to be more of the nature of wisdom than the 982ᵃ
productive. Clearly then wisdom is knowledge about certain causes and principles.

CHAPTER 2

Since we are seeking this knowledge, we must inquire of what kind are the causes and the principles, the knowledge of which is wisdom. If we 5
were to take the notions we have about the wise man, this might perhaps make the answer more evident. We suppose first, then, that the wise man knows all things, as far as possible, although he has not knowledge of each of them individually; secondly, that he who can learn things that are difficult, and not easy for man to know, is wise 10
(sense-perception is common to all, and therefore easy and no mark of wisdom); again, he who is more exact and more capable of teaching the causes is wiser, in every branch of knowledge; and of the sciences, also, that which is desirable on its own account and for the sake of knowing it is more of the nature of wisdom than that which is desirable 15
on account of its results, and the superior science is more of the nature of wisdom than the ancillary; for the wise man must not be ordered but must order, and he must not obey another, but the less wise must obey *him*.

Such and so many are the notions, then, which we have about 20
wisdom and the wise. Now of these characteristics that of knowing all things must belong to him who has in the highest degree universal

knowledge; for he knows in a sense all the subordinate objects. And these things, the most universal, are on the whole the hardest for men 25 to know; for they are furthest from the senses. And the most exact of the sciences are those which deal most with first principles; for those which involve fewer principles are more exact than those which involve additional principles, e.g. arithmetic than geometry. But the science which investigates causes is also more capable of teaching, for the people who teach are those who tell the causes of each thing. And 30 understanding and knowledge pursued for their own sake are found most in the knowledge of that which is most knowable; for he who chooses to know for the sake of knowing will choose most readily that which is most truly knowledge, and such is the knowledge of that 982ᵇ which is most knowable; and the first principles and the causes are most knowable; for by reason of these, and from these, all other things are known, but these are not known by means of the things sub- 5 ordinate to them. And the science which knows to what end each thing must be done is the most authoritative of the sciences, and more authoritative than any ancillary science; and this end is the good in each class, and in general the supreme good in the whole of nature. Judged by all the tests we have mentioned, then, the name in question falls to the same science; this must be a science that investigates the first principles and causes; for the good, i.e. that for the sake of which, 10 is one of the causes.

That it is not a science of production is clear even from the history of the earliest philosophers. For it is owing to their wonder that men both now begin and at first began to philosophize; they wondered originally at the obvious difficulties, then advanced little by little and 15 stated difficulties about the greater matters, e.g. about the phenomena of the moon and those of the sun and the stars, and about the genesis of the universe. And a man who is puzzled and wonders thinks himself ignorant (whence even the lover of myth is in a sense a lover of 20 wisdom, for myth is composed of wonders); therefore since they philosophized in order to escape from ignorance, evidently they were pursuing science in order to know, and not for any utilitarian end. And this is confirmed by the facts; for it was when almost all the necessities of life and the things that make for comfort and recreation were 25 present, that such knowledge began to be sought. Evidently then we do not seek it for the sake of any other advantage; but as the man is free, we say, who exists for himself and not for another, so we pursue this as the only free science, for it alone exists for itself.

Hence the possession of it might be justly regarded as beyond human power; for in many ways human nature is in bondage, so that according to Simonides 'God alone can have this privilege', and it is unfitting that man should not be content to seek the knowledge that is suited to him. If, then, there is something in what the poets say, and jealousy is natural to the divine power, it would probably occur in this case above all, and all who excelled in this knowledge would be unfortunate. But the divine power cannot be jealous (indeed, according to the proverb, 'bards tell many a lie'), nor should any science be thought more honourable than one of this sort. For the most divine science is also most honourable; and this science alone is, in two ways, most divine. For the science which it would be most meet for God to have is a divine science, and so is any science that deals with divine objects; and this science alone has both these qualities; for God is thought to be among the causes of all things and to be a first principle, and such a science either God alone can have, or God above all others. All the sciences, indeed, are more necessary than this, but none is better.

Yet the acquisition of it must in a sense end in something which is the opposite of our original inquiries. For all men begin, as we said, by wondering that the matter is so (as in the case of automatic marionettes or the solstices or the incommensurability of the diagonal of a square with the side; for it seems wonderful to all men who have not yet perceived the explanation that there is a thing which cannot be measured even by the smallest unit). But we must end in the contrary and, according to the proverb, the better state, as is the case in these instances when men learn the cause; for there is nothing which would surprise a geometer so much as if the diagonal turned out to be commensurable.

We have stated, then, what is the nature of the science we are searching for, and what is the mark which our search and our whole investigation must reach.

BOOK III (B)

CHAPTER I

We must, with a view to the science which we are seeking, first recount the subjects that should be first discussed. These include both the other opinions that some have held on certain points, and any points besides these that happen to have been overlooked. For those who wish to get clear of difficulties it is advantageous to state the difficulties well; for the subsequent free play of thought implies the solution of the previous difficulties, and it is not possible to untie a 30 knot which one does not know. But the difficulty of our thinking points to a knot in the object; for in so far as our thought is in difficulties, it is in like case with those who are tied up; for in either case it is impossible to go forward. Therefore one should have surveyed all the difficulties beforehand, both for the reasons we have stated and 35 because people who inquire without first stating the difficulties are like those who do not know where they have to go; besides, a man does not otherwise know even whether he has found what he is looking 995ᵇ for or not; for the end is not clear to such a man, while to him who has first discussed the difficulties it is clear. Further, he who has heard all the contending arguments, as if they were the parties to a case, must be in a better position for judging.

5 The first problem concerns the subject which we discussed in our prefatory remarks. It is this—whether the investigation of the causes belongs to one or to more sciences, and, if to one, whether this should survey only the first principles of substance, or also the principles on which all men base their proofs, e.g. whether it is possible at the same 10 time to assert and deny one and the same thing or not, and all other such questions. And if the science in question deals with substance, whether *our* science deals with all substances, or more than one, and if more, whether all are akin, or some of them must be called forms of wisdom and the others something else. And this itself is also one of the things that must be discussed—whether sensible substances 15 alone should be said to exist or others also besides them, and whether these others are of one kind or there are several classes of substances, as is supposed by those who believe both in Forms and in mathematical objects intermediate between these and sensible things. We must inquire, then, as we say, into these questions, and also whether our investigation is concerned only with substances or also with the 20 essential attributes of substances. Further, with regard to the same and other and like and unlike and contrariety, and with regard to prior and posterior and all other such terms, about which the dialecticians try to inquire, starting their investigation from reputable premises 25 only,—whose business is it to inquire into all these? Further, we must discuss the essential attributes of these themselves; and we must ask

not only what each of these is, but also whether one thing always has one contrary. Again, whether the principles and elements of things are the *classes*, or the *parts* present in each thing into which it is divided; and if they are the classes, whether they are the classes that are predicated proximately of the individuals, or the highest classes, e.g. whether animal or man is the first principle and the more independent   30 of the individual instance? And we must inquire and discuss especially whether there is, besides the matter, any thing that is a cause in itself or not, and whether this can exist apart or not, and whether it is one or more in number. Once more, is there something apart from the concrete thing (by the concrete thing I mean the matter with some-   35 thing predicated of it), or is there nothing apart, or is there something in some cases though not in others, and what sort of cases are these? Again we ask whether the principles are limited in number or in kind,   996ᵃ both those in the formulae and those in the substratum; and whether the principles of perishable and of imperishable things are the same or different; and whether they are all imperishable or those of perishable things are perishable. Further, there is the question which is hardest   5 of all and most perplexing, whether unity and being, as the Pythago-reans and Plato said, are not attributes of something else but are the substance of existing things, or this is not the case, but the substratum is something else,—as Empedocles says, love; as someone else says, fire; while one says water and one air. Again we ask whether the prin-ciples are universal or like individual things, and whether they exist   10 potentially or actually; further, whether they are potential or actual in any other sense than in reference to movement; for these questions also would present much difficulty. Further, whether numbers and lines and figures and points are a kind of substance or not, and if they are substances whether they are separate from sensible things or   15 present in them? With regard to all these matters not only is it hard to get possession of the truth, but it is not easy even to think out the difficulties well.

BOOK IV (Γ)

CHAPTER I

There is a discipline which studies that which is *qua* thing-that-is and   1003ᵃ those things that hold good of this in its own right. That is not the same as any of what are called the special disciplines. For none of the others examines universally that which is *qua* thing-that-is, but all select some part of it and study what is coincidental concerning that; as for instance the mathematical disciplines. But since we are seeking origins, i.e. the most extreme causes, it is plain that these are necessarily a particular nature's in its own right. If therefore these origins were also sought by those seeking the elements of the things-that-are, the elements too are necessarily of that which is *qua* thing-that-is, not coincidentally. Hence we also have to find the first causes of that which is *qua* thing-that-is.

CHAPTER 2

That which *is* may be so called in several ways, but with reference to one thing, i.e. one particular nature, not homonymously. Just as that which is healthy all has reference to health (either from its preserving, or producing, or being a sign of health, or because recipient of it); and that which is medical has reference to medical art (either it is called medical from possessing medical art, or from being naturally suited to it, or from being an exercise of medical art)—and we shall find other things called what they are in ways similar to these: just so that which *is* may also be so called in several ways, but all with reference to one origin. For some are called things that are because they are substances; some because they are affections of a substance; some because they are a route to a substance, or destructions, or lacks, or qualities, or productive, or generative of a substance or of things called what they are with reference to substance; or denials of one of these or of a substance (that is why we assert that even what is not *is* a thing that is not).

Therefore, just as everything that is healthy falls to one discipline, this is equally so in the other cases too. For it falls to one discipline to study not only things called what they are by virtue of one thing, but also things called what they are with reference to one nature; indeed in a certain sense the latter too are called what they are by virtue of one thing. Plainly, therefore, it also falls to one discipline to study the things that are *qua* things-that-are.

In every case the fundamental concern of a discipline is with its primary object, i.e. that on which the others depend and to which they owe their being called what they are. So if this thing is substance, the philosopher will need to have the principles and causes of substances.

Every one genus falls to one perception and discipline; as for instance all spoken sounds are studied by grammar, which is one 20 discipline. Hence it also falls to generically one discipline to study all the forms of that which is *qua* thing-that-is, and the forms of those forms.

Suppose it true, then, that that which *is* and that which is *one* are the same thing—i.e. one nature— in that each follows from the other as origin and cause do, not as being indicated by one formula (though it 25 makes no difference even if we believe them like that—indeed it helps). For one man and a man that is and a man are the same thing; and nothing different is indicated by the reduplication in wording of 'he is one man' and 'he is one man that is' (it is plain that there is no distinction in the processes of coming to be or destruction); and equally 30 in the case of that which is one. It follows obviously that the addition indicates the same thing in these cases, and that which is one is nothing different apart from that which is. Again, each thing's substance *is* one non-coincidentally; equally, it is also just what a certain kind of thing-that-is is. It follows that there are as many forms of thing-that-is as of thing-that-is-one; and what these are (I mean 35 such things as *the same* and *similar* and others of that kind) falls to be studied by generically the same discipline. Practically all contraries 1004ᵃ derive from this origin; but we must take them as having been studied in the 'Selection of Contraries'.

And there are as many parts of philosophy as there are substances; so that it is necessary that there be among them a first and a next. For 5 that which *is* divides directly into genera; hence the disciplines too will follow these. For the philosopher is like the mathematician, as he is called; for that also has parts, a primary and a secondary discipline and others successively within mathematics.

Since opposites fall to be studied by one discipline, and the *one* is opposed to *plurality* (the reason why the denial and lack of a thing fall 10 to be studied by one discipline is that the one thing of which they are the denial or lack is studied in both cases. For we either say baldly that that thing does not hold good, or of a certain genus; in the latter case, then, some differentia is added to the one, apart from what is there in the denial. For the denial is the thing's absence, but in the case of the 15 lack a certain nature comes in too as the subject of which the lack is stated)—since the one is opposed to plurality, it follows that it also falls to the discipline mentioned to make intelligible the opposites of the things mentioned, both that which is *other* and *dissimilar* and

unequal, and everything else called what it is either by virtue of one of
20 these or by virtue of plurality and the one. Among these is *contrariety*, since contrariety is a kind of difference, and difference is otherness. It follows that since the one is so called in several ways, these things also will be called what they are in several ways. Nevertheless it falls to one discipline to make all of them intelligible; for it will fall to another not if they are called what they are in several ways but only if the formulae
25 are connected neither by virtue of one thing nor by a reference to one thing.

Since everything is connected to that which is primary (as for instance, anything called one to the primary one—and the same can be asserted to hold also of *the same* and *other* and *contraries*), it follows that after dividing the number of ways in which each thing may be called what it is, we have to display, with reference to what is primary in each predication, in *what* way it is so called with reference to that; for some
30 things will be so called from possessing it, some from producing it, others in other such ways.

It is obvious, therefore, that it falls to one discipline to discuss these things and substance (that was one of the perplexities we listed); and it
1004ᵇ falls to the philosopher to be capable of studying all of them. For if not the philosopher, who will it be who investigates whether Socrates and Socrates sitting down are the same thing, or whether one is contrary to one, or what the contrary is and in how many ways it is so called; and
5 equally with the other questions of that kind? Therefore, since these things are in their own right affections of that which is one *qua* one and of that which is *qua* thing-that-is, not *qua* numbers or lines or fire, plainly it falls to that discipline to make intelligible both what they are and the things coincidental to them; and those who examine these questions are at fault not because they are not philosophizing, but
10 because substance is prior, and of substance they have no comprehension. For just as there are affections distinctive of number *qua* number—as for instance oddness, evenness, commensurability, equality, excess, deficiency—and these hold good of numbers both in their own right and with reference to one another (and equally there are others distinctive of things solid, changeless, changeable, weight-
15 less, and possessing weight); so too certain things are distinctive of that which is *qua* thing-that-is, and these are the things about which it falls to the philosopher to investigate the truth.

It is a sign of this that dialecticians and sophists assume the same guise as the philosopher. Sophistic is only imagined to be science.

Dialecticians discuss everthing, and that which *is* is common to every- 20
thing; but it is plain that they do so because that is proper to
philosophy. Sophistic and dialectic do indeed range over the same
genus as philosophy, but differ from it in the one case by the type of
capacity, in the other by the life chosen; dialectic probes where 25
philosophy seeks understanding, and sophistic is imagined to be
science but is not really.

Again, every contrary on one side of the table is a lack, and all of
them reduce to that which is and that which is not, and to one and
plurality (as for instance keeping-the-same is on the side of the one,
change on the side of plurality). Practically everyone agrees that the
things-that-are, and substance, are composed out of contraries: at any 30
rate, everyone describes the origins of things as contraries, whether
odd and even or hot and cold or limit and limitless or love and strife,
and it is obvious that all the others also reduce to the one and plurality
(we must take the reduction for granted), and the origins proposed by 1005ᵃ
others also find their place without exception under these genera. It is
therefore obvious from this too that it falls to one discipline to study
that which is *qua* thing-that-is. For all things either are or are made up
of contraries, and contraries originate in the one and plurality. The
latter fall to one discipline, whether or not they are called what they 5
are by virtue of one thing. Doubtless the truth is that they are not;
nevertheless, even if that which is one is so called in several ways, the
others will be so called with reference to the first; and equally so will
contraries. (This is so, even if that which is, or that which is one, is not
universal, i.e. the same in every case, or separable; doubtless they are 10
not, but some of them are related to one thing, others form a
succession.) This also explains why it does not fall to the geometer to
study the question what is the *contrary*, or *complete*, or *one*, or *thing-
that-is*, or *the same*, or *other*, except on the basis of a hypothesis.

It is therefore plain: that it falls to one discipline to study that which
is *qua* thing-that-is, and those things that hold good of it *qua* thing-
that-is; and that the same discipline undertakes the study not only of 15
substances but of whatever holds good of them also, both the things
mentioned and *prior* and *posterior* and *genus* and *form* and *whole* and
part and the others of that kind.

CHAPTER 3

We have to say whether it falls to one, or a different, discipline to deal
20   with the things which in mathematics are termed axioms, and with
substance. It is indeed obvious that the investigation of these too falls
to one discipline, and that the philosopher's; for they hold good of
every thing-that-is and not of a certain genus, separate and distinct
from the others. Everyone uses them, it is true; because they are of that
25   which is *qua* thing-that-is, and each genus is a thing-that-is. But
everyone uses them just so far as is sufficient for him, that is, so far as
the genus extends about which he is carrying out demonstrations.
Since it is plain that they hold good of all things *qua* things-that-*are*
(for that is what all things have in common), it follows that their study
too falls to him who makes intelligible that which is *qua* thing-that-is.
This explains why none of those who conduct specialized investiga-
30   tions endeavour to say anything about them, as to whether or not they
are true. Geometers and arithmeticians do not; some students of
nature do, but that is not surprising, since they alone have considered
that they were investigating the whole of nature, i.e. that which is. But
since there is someone still further above the student of nature (for
35   nature is one particular genus of thing-that-is), the investigation of
these things also must fall to him who studies what is universal, and
primary substance. The study of nature is also a science, but not
1005^b primary.
The endeavours of some of those who discuss their truth, as to how
they ought to be accepted, are due to lack of training in analytics. The
5   student ought to come ready equipped with knowledge of these things,
not seek it while listening.
Plainly, therefore, it falls to the philosopher, i.e. the student of what
is characteristic of all substance, also to investigate the principles of
trains of reasoning.
It is appropriate for him who has the best understanding about each
10   genus to be able to state the firmest principles of that actual subject,
and hence, when his subject is the things-that-are *qua* things-that are,
to state the firmest principles of everything: and this man is the
philosopher. A principle about which it is impossible to be in error is
firmest of all. For a principle of that kind is necessarily the most
intelligible, since everyone makes mistakes on matters about which he
15   does not have understanding; and is non-hypothetical, since what is
necessarily part of the equipment of one who apprehends any of the

things-that-are is not a hypothesis, and what one necessarily understands who understands anything is necessarily part of the equipment
he comes with. It is plain, then, that a principle of that kind is firmest
of all.

We have next to state what principle this is. *For the same thing to hold
good and not to hold good simultaneously of the same thing and in the same respect*   20
is impossible (given any further specifications which might be added
against the dialectical difficulties).

This, then, is the firmest of all principles, for it fits the specification
stated. For it is impossible for anyone to believe that the same thing is
and is not, as some consider Heraclitus said—for it is not necessary   25
that the things one says one should also believe. But if it is not possible
for contraries to hold good of the same thing simultaneously (given
that the customary specifications are added to this proposition too),
and the opinion contrary to an opinion is that of the contradictory,
then obviously it is impossible for the same person to believe simul-   30
taneously that the same thing is and is not; for anyone who made that
error would be holding contrary opinions simultaneously. That is why
all those who demonstrate go back to this opinion in the end: it is, in
the nature of things, the principle of all the other axioms also.

CHAPTER 4

There are those who, as we said, both themselves assert that it is   35
possible for the same thing to be and not to be, and assert that it is   1006ᵃ
possible to believe so. Many even of writers on nature make use of this
statement. But we have just accepted that it is impossible to be and not
be simultaneously, and we have shown by means of this that it is the   5
firmest of all principles. Some, owing to lack of training, actually ask
that it be demonstrated: for it is lack of training not to recognize of
which things demonstration ought to be sought, and of which not. For
in general it is impossible that there should be demonstration of
everything, since it would go on to infinity so that not even so would it
be demonstration. But if there are some things of which demonstra-   10
tion ought not to be sought, they could not say what they regard as a
principle more fully of that kind.

But even this can be demonstrated to be impossible, in the manner
of a refutation, if only the disputant says something. If he says nothing,
it is ridiculous to look for a statement in response to one who has a
statement of nothing, in so far as he has not; such a person, in so far as   15

he is such, is similar to a vegetable. By 'demonstrating in the manner
of a refutation' I mean something different from demonstrating,
because in demonstrating one might be thought to beg the original
question, but if someone else is cause of such a thing it must be refutation and not demonstration. In response to every case of that kind the
20 original step is not to ask him to state something either to be or not to
be (for that might well be believed to beg what was originally at issue),
but at least to signify something both to himself and to someone else;
for that is necessary if he is to say anything. For if he does not, there
would be no statement for such a person, either in response to himself
or to anyone else. But if he does offer this, there will be demonstration,
25 for there will already be something definite. But the cause is not he
who demonstrates but he who submits; for eliminating statement he
submits to statement. Again, anyone who agrees to this has agreed that
something is true independently of demonstration. . . .

1008ᵇ Again, are we to say that he who believes that things are in a certain
state, or are not, is in error, while he who believes both has the truth?
For if he has the truth, what can be meant by saying that the nature of
5   things-that-are is of that kind? If he does not have the truth, but has
more truth than the one who believes the former way, then the things-
that-are would already be in some state, and that would be true and
not simultaneously also not true. But if everyone equally both is in
error and states the truth, there will be nothing for such a person to
10 speak or say; for he simultaneously says this and not this. And if a man
believes nothing, but considers it equally so and not so, how would his
state be different from a vegetable's?
    From which it is also quite obvious that nobody actually is in that
condition, neither those who state this thesis nor anybody else. For
why does anyone walk to Megara rather than stay where he is, when he
15 considers that he should walk there? Why does he not proceed one
morning straight into a well or over a precipice, if there is one about:
instead of evidently taking care to avoid doing so, as one who does not
consider that falling in is equally a good thing and not a good thing? It
is consequently plain that he believes that one thing is better, another
not better. And if so, he must also believe that one thing is a man and
20 another not a man, one thing sweet and another not sweet. For he
neither seeks nor believes everything indifferently when, considering
that it is better to drink water and see a man, he thereupon seeks to do
so; and yet he ought to, if the same thing were equally a man and not a

man. But just as we said, there is nobody who does not evidently take   25
care to avoid some things and not others; so that it seems that everyone holds some beliefs baldly, if not about everything then about what
is better and worse. And if this is not knowledge but opinion, one
would have to be all the more anxious about the truth, as a sick man is
more anxious about his health than one who is healthy. For indeed a
man who holds an opinion is in an unhealthy condition with regard to   30
the truth, compared with one who has knowledge.

Again, however much everything is so-and-so and not so-and-so, at
least the more and the less are present in the nature of things-that-are.
For we would not assert that two and three are *equally* even, or that
one who considered that four things were five and one who considered
that they were a thousand were *equally* in error. So if they are not   35
equally, it is plain that one of them is less, so that he has more truth. So
if what is more is nearer, there must be something true which the more   1009ᵃ
true view is nearer. And even if that is not so, at least there is already
something more firm and more truthlike, and we should be rid of the
unadulterated thesis which would prevent us from having anything   5
definite in our thinking.

CHAPTER 5

From the same opinion also derives the thesis of Protagoras, and it is
necessary that both either are or are not the case equally. For if everything that is thought or imagined is true, it is necessary that everything
should be simultaneously true and false; for many people have   10
mutually contrary beliefs, and regard those whose opinions are not the
same as their own as in error, so that it is necessary that the same thing
should both be and not be. And if the latter, it is necessary that what is
thought to be should all be true; for those who are in error and those
who have the truth hold mutually opposite opinions, and so, if that is
the state of things-that-are, all will have the truth. It is plain, then, that   15
both theses derive from the same thinking. . . .

As for truth, to show that not everything that is imagined is true: first,   1010ᵇ
even if perception, at least of what is special, is not false, still imagination is not the same thing as perception. Next, one may legitimately be
surprised that they should find perplexing the question whether   5
magnitudes and colours are such as they are imagined by those who
are at a distance or those who are near, and by the healthy or the sick;

or whether what is imagined by the weak or the strong is heavier; or
whether what is imagined by the sleeping or the waking is true. For it
10   is obvious that they do not really consider it so: at any rate if someone
in Libya believes himself one night in Athens, he does not set off for
the Odeon. Again, as for the future, as Plato also says, the opinions of a
doctor and an ignorant man are surely not equally authoritative, as for
instance on the question whether someone is or is not going to be
healthy.
15   Again, in the case of our perceptions themselves the perception of
what is alien and special, or of what is neighbouring and what is its
own, are not equally authoritative, but in the case of colour it is sight,
not taste, and in the case of flavour taste, not sight; and each of these
never asserts about the same thing in the same time that it is simultaneously so-and-so and not so-and-so.
20   Nor, even in another time, was there dispute about the affection,
but only about that in which the affection coincides; I mean for
instance that the same wine might be thought sweet at one time and
not sweet at another, if there is an alteration either in it or in the body;
but the sweet such as it is, when it is, has never yet altered, and one
25   always has the truth about it, and anything that is going to be sweet is
such of necessity. Yet this is eliminated by all these theses—just as
nothing has a substance, so too nothing is of necessity. For it is not
possible that what is necessary should be thus and otherwise, so that if
30   anything is of necessity it will not be both thus and not thus.

BOOK V (Δ)

CHAPTER 4

1014^b   We call *nature*, in one sense, the coming to be of things that *grow*, as if
one were to pronounce the *u* in '*phusis*' long; in another, the first
constituent out of which a growing thing grows; again, what makes the
primary change in any naturally existing thing a constituent of the
20   thing *qua* itself. All things are said to grow which gain enlargement
through another thing by contact and assimilation or (as with
embryos) adhesion. Assimilation differs from contact, for in the latter
case there is no necessity for any other thing apart from contact, while
in the case of things assimilated there is some one thing, the same in
25   both, which makes them assimilated instead of in contact, and makes

them one in respect of continuity and quantity, though not in respect of qualification.

Again, that out of which a naturally existing thing first is or comes to be, and which is unstructured and not subject to loss of its own capacity, is called a nature, as for instance bronze is called the nature of a statue and of bronze artefacts, wood of wooden ones, and equally 30 in the other cases; for each is made out of these, the first matter being conserved. It is in this sense that the elements of naturally existing things are also asserted to be their nature (some mentioning fire, some earth, some air, some water, others something else of that kind, and 35 others some or all of these).

In another sense again, the substance of naturally existing things is called their nature, as for instance those who say that a thing's primary composition is its nature, or as Empedocles says: 1015ᵃ

> None has a nature of the things that are;
> There is but mixture and exchange of things
> Mixed; but nature's name men fix on them.

This explains why, with things that exist or come to be naturally, although that out of which it is their nature to be or come to be is already present, we still do not assert that they possess their nature if they do not possess their form and shape. What is made up of both of 5 these, then, exists *naturally*, as for instance animals and their parts. The nature is both the first matter (and this in two ways, either first relative to the thing itself or first in general, as for instance with works of bronze the bronze is first relative to themselves but in general it is perhaps water, if all meltables are water), and the form and substance, 10 that is, the fulfilment of their coming to be. By transference from this case, all substance in general has come to be called nature, because nature is also a kind of substance.

Of all those mentioned, then, the nature which is primary and fundamentally so called is the substance of those things that possess an origin of change in themselves *qua* themselves. For matter is called 15 nature from being recipient of this, and comings to be and growth from being changes arising from it. And the origin of change of naturally existing things is this, being a constituent in a way (either potentially or in complete reality).

CHAPTER 5

20 We call *necessary* that without which, as a joint-cause, it is not possible
to live, as for instance breathing and nourishment are necessary for an
animal, because it is incapable of existing without them; and anything
without which it is not possible for good to exist or come to be, or for
bad to be discarded or got rid of, as for instance drinking medicine is
25 necessary so as not to be ill, and sailing to Aegina so as to get money.
    Again, that which is compulsory, and compulsion; that is, what
obstructs and thwarts an inclination or choice. For what is compulsory
is called necessary, which is why it is also disagreeable, as Evenus
asserts,

No necessary deed
But has an irksome nature,

30 and compulsion is a kind of necessity, as Sophocles says,

Compulsion does necessitate I do this;

and necessity is, rightly, thought of as not open to persuasion, for it is
contrary to that change which is in accordance with choice and
reasoning.
    Again, when it is not possible for a thing to be otherwise, we assert
35 that it is necessary for it to be so. Indeed the others are all in some way
called necessary by virtue of this. For what is compulsory is called
1015ᵇ necessary either to do or to suffer when it is not possible to follow
inclination on account of that which compels, necessity being that on
account of which it is not possible to do otherwise; and the same is
true in the case of the joint-causes of living and of good, for when it is
not possible that in the one case good and in the other case living
5 should exist without certain things, those things are necessary and that
cause is a kind of necessity. Again, demonstration is among the things
that are necessary, because it is not possible for a thing to be otherwise
if it has been demonstrated baldly; the cause of this is the initial
premisses, if the things from which the reasoning proceeds are
incapable of being otherwise.
10 With some things, then, another thing is the cause of their being
necessary; with others nothing is, but on account of them other things
are of necessity. It follows that the primary, and fundamentally,
necessary thing is that which is simple; for it is not possible that this
should be in more than one state, nor therefore thus and otherwise—

for it would thereby be in more than one state. Consequently, if there
are certain invariable and changeless things, there is nothing com-　15
pulsory or unnatural in them.

CHAPTER 6

Things are called *one* either coincidentally or in their own right:
coincidentally as for instance Coriscus and the artistic and artistic
Coriscus (for it is the same thing to say 'Coriscus and the artistic' and
'artistic Coriscus'), and the artistic and the just and artistic and just　20
Coriscus. For all these are called one coincidentally, the just and the
artistic because they coincide in one substance, the artistic and
Coriscus because one coincides in the other. Equally the artistic
Coriscus is in a certain sense one with Coriscus because one of the
parts in the formula coincides in the other, I mean the artistic in　25
Coriscus; and the artistic Coriscus with just Coriscus because a part of
each coincides in the same one thing. The same is true if the coincidental is spoken of in the case of a genus or in the case of the
names of something universal, as for instance that a man and an　30
artistic man are the same thing; for it is either because the artistic
coincides in what is one substance, the man, or because both coincide
in a certain particular thing, as for instance Coriscus (except that they
do not both hold good in the same manner, but one doubtless as a
genus and in the substance, the other as a state or affection of the
substance). Everything called one coincidentally, then, is so called in　35
this sense.

Of things called one in their own right, some are so called from
being continuous, as for instance a bundle from its tie and planks of　1016ᵃ
wood from their glue; and a line, even if bent, is called one if it is continuous, as is each part of the body, as for instance a leg and an arm.
But among these what is naturally continuous is more one than what
is artificially so. We call continuous that whose change in its own right　5
is one and cannot be otherwise; and a change is one when indivisible,
and indivisible in respect of time. Whatever is one not by contact is
continuous in its own right; for if you put planks in contact with one
another you will not assert that these are one plank or body or
anything else continuous. Continuous things in general, then, are
called one even if they have a bend, but still more those that have no　10
bend, as for instance the shin or thigh more than the leg because it is
possible for a change of the leg not to be one change. Also a straight

line is more one than a bent line; the line that is bent and has an angle we call both one and not one, because it is possible for a change to be made in it both all at once and not all at once, but that in a straight line is always made all at once and no part having magnitude is at rest while another changes, as happens with the bent line.

In another sense again, a thing is called one from its subject's being undifferentiated in form, and it is undifferentiated if its form is perceptually indivisible. And the subject is either the first or the last relative to the final state; for wine is called one and so is water, in that they are indivisible in respect of form, and juices (as for instance oil and wine) and meltables are all called one because the ultimate subject of all of them is the same—for all these things are water or air.

Things are also called one whose genus is one, being differentiated by opposite differentiae; and these are all called one because the genus which is the subject of their differentiae is one (as for instance a horse, a man, and a dog are one something because all animals)—in much the same sense, indeed, as the things whose matter is one. These things are sometimes called one in this way, but sometimes the genus above is called the same, if they are the last forms of the genus—that which is further above these; as for instance the isosceles and the equilateral are one and the same figure because both triangles, but they are not the same triangles.

Again, things are called one when the formula saying what it is to be is indivisible relative to another formula which indicates the actual thing (for taken by itself every formula is divisible). For in this way what has grown and is diminishing is one, because its formula is one, as is that of the form in the case of planes. In general when the conception which conceives what it is to be certain things is indivisible and cannot separate them in time or place or formula, they are most of all one, and those that are substances most of all among these. (For whenever things are without division, they are universally called one in that respect in which they are without it, as for instance if they are without division *qua* man they are one man, if *qua* animal one animal, if *qua* magnitude one magnitude.)

While most things, then, are called one from either doing or possessing or being affected by or being related to some other thing that is one, the things called one in the primary way are those whose substance is one, and one either in continuity or in form or in formula; for things which either are non-continuous or do not have one form or do not have one formula we in fact reckon as more than one thing.

Again, although in a way we assert that anything whatever is one which is a quantity and continuous, in a way we do not if it is not some kind of whole, that is, if it does not possess one form; as for instance if we observed the parts of a shoe put together anyhow we should not so readily assert that they were one (unless on account of their con- 15 tinuity), but only if they were put together in such a way as to be a shoe and thereby possess some one form. That is why a circular line is of all lines most one, because it is whole and complete.

To be one is to be a kind of origin of number; for a first measure is an origin, for what first makes each genus intelligible to us is its first measure. The origin, therefore, of our acquaintance with each kind of 20 thing is that which is one. But that which is one is not the same thing in every genus; for it may be here a quarter-tone, there a vowel or mute, and another thing in the case of weight, and something else in the case of change. But in every case that which is one is indivisible either in quantity or in form. Now what is indivisible in respect of quantity in 25 all dimensions is called a unit if it has no position, a point if it has position, and what is divisible in respect of quantity in one dimension is a line, in two a plane, in all three a body. In the reverse order, what is divisible in two dimensions is a plane, in one dimension a line, and what is divisible in no dimensions in respect of quantity is a point and unit, the unit being without position, the point with position. 30

Again, some things are one in respect of number, some in respect of form, some in respect of genus, some in respect of analogy: in number things whose matter is one, in form things whose formula is one, in genus things whose figure of predication is the same, in respect of analogy any things related as are two further things. In 35 every case the earlier imply the later, as for instance what is one in number is also one in form but what is one in form is not all in number, and whatever is one in form is all one in genus but what is 1017ᵃ in genus is not all in form; it is, however, in analogy, but what is in analogy is not all in genus.

It is obvious that what is *many* will be so called in opposite ways to what is one. For some things will be many from being non-continuous, some from possessing matter (either the first or the last) which is 5 divisible in respect of form, some from having more than one formula saying what it is to be.

CHAPTER 7

That which *is* may be so called either coincidentally or in its own right: coincidentally, as for instance we assert someone just to *be* artistic, and a man artistic, and someone artistic a man; in much the
10 same way as we say that someone artistic builds, because being artistic coincides in a housebuilder or a housebuilder in someone artistic (for 'that this is this' signifies 'that in this this coincides'). And so it is in the cases mentioned; for when we say that a man is artistic and someone
15 artistic a man, or that someone pale is artistic or the latter pale, in the one case it is because both coincide in the same thing and in the other because it coincides in a thing-that-is; while the artistic is a man because the artistic coincides in the latter (it is in this way that the not-pale is said to *be*, because what it coincides in *is*). Things said to *be*
20 coincidentally, then, are so said in this way: either because both hold good of the same thing-that-is, or because the former holds good of a thing-that-is, or because the thing itself, of which that of which it is itself predicated holds good, is.

All things which signify the figures of predication are said to *be* in their own right; for 'to be' signifies in the same number of ways as they
25 are said. Since, therefore, among things predicated some signify what a thing is, some a qualification, some a quantity, some a relative, some doing or being affected, some where, some when, 'to be' signifies the same thing as each of these. For there is no difference between 'a man *is* one that keeps-healthy' and 'a man keeps-healthy' or between 'a
30 man *is* one that walks, or cuts' and 'a man walks, or cuts', and equally in the other cases.

Again, 'to be' and 'is' signify that a thing is true, and 'not to be' that it is not true but a falsehood, equally in the case of affirmation and of denial; as for instance that Socrates *is* artistic, that this is true, or that
35 Socrates *is* not-pale, that it is true; and 'a diagonal *is not* commensurable' that it is a falsehood.

1017^{b} Again, 'to be' and 'that which is' signify those of the things mentioned which *are* potentially and those which *are* in complete reality; for both that which sees potentially and that which sees in complete reality we assert to *be* a thing-that-sees, and in the same way
5 both that which is capable of using knowledge and that which is using it we assert to know, and both that of which rest already holds good and that which is capable of being-at-rest we assert to be-at-rest. Equally in the case of substances also; for both the idol in the stone

and the half of a line and the grain which is not yet ripe we assert to *be*. When a thing is or is not yet *capable* must be defined elsewhere.

CHAPTER 8

We call a *substance* both simple bodies, as for instance earth and fire   10
and water and everything of that kind, and bodies in general and the things constituted out of them—animals and deities and the parts of these; all these are called substance because they are not said of a subject but the rest are said of them:

in another sense, any constituent of such things (the things not said   15
of a subject) which is cause of their being, as for instance the soul in the case of an animal:

again, those constituent parts of such things which define and signify a this and with whose elimination the whole thing is eliminated, as for instance the body with the plane's (as some assert) and the plane with the line's; in general it is thought by some that   20
number is of this kind, on the grounds that when it is eliminated there is nothing, and it defines everything.

Again, what it is to be, the formula of which is a definition, is also called each thing's substance.

It follows, then, that a substance is so called in two senses: both the ultimate subject, which is not further said of anything else; and whatever, being a this, is also separable (such is each thing's shape and   25
form).

CHAPTER 29

We call a *falsehood*, in one sense, what is a falsehood as an *actual thing*:   1024ᵇ
and this sometimes from the thing's being not compounded, or incapable of being compounded, as we say of a diagonal's being commensurable or of your sitting down—for one of these is a false-   20
hood always, the other sometimes (for in this way these things are not things-that-are); sometimes anything which, while being a thing-that-is, is nevertheless characteristically imagined either not to be such as it is or to be something that is not, as for instance a sketch, and dreams— for these are something, but not what they impose on us to imagine they are. These, then, are the ways in which actual things are called false, either from their not themselves being or from their giving rise to   25
an imagination of something that is not.

A false *formula* is, *qua* false, of things that are not, and that is why
every formula is false of something other than that of which it is true,
as for instance that of a circle is false of a triangle. Each thing has, in
one way, one formula, that of what it is to be; in another way it has

30   many, since both it and it affected (as for instance Socrates and artistic
Socrates) are in a way the same thing. A false formula is, taken baldly,
the formula of nothing. That is why Antisthenes naïvely considered
that nothing can legitimately be described except by its own proper
formula, one to one; an opinion from which it resulted that there is no
such thing as contradiction, nor even practically as falsity. But there is

35   such a thing as describing each thing not only by its own formula but
also by another's; this may be done altogether falsely, but also in a way

1025ᵃ   truly, as eight is double, by the formula of two.

Apart from these ways of calling things false, a false *man* is one who
uses such formulae recklessly and deliberately, not on any other
account than their own, and who imposes such formulae on other

5   people; just as we assert that actual things are false when they impose a
false imagination. This explains what is misleading about the
argument in the *Hippias* that the same man is false and true. For it
takes for false the man who is *capable* of falsity (and that is he who
knows, the wise man); and again it takes for better the man who does

10   wrong *willingly*. The latter falsehood is got by induction: for a man
who limps willingly is superior to one who does so unwillingly
(meaning by limping pretending, since if he were willingly *lame* he
would doubtless be inferior, as in the moral case).

BOOK VI (E)

CHAPTER I

1025ᵇ   We are seeking the origins and the causes of the things-that-are, and
plainly of them *qua* things-that-are. For there is a particular cause of

5   health and of fitness, and there are origins and elements and causes of
the objects of mathematics, and in general every thinking, or thought-
partaking, discipline deals with causes and origins, more or less
precise. But all these disciplines delimit a particular thing-that-is—a
particular genus—and treat of it, not of that which *is* baldly or *qua*

10   thing-that-is. Nor do they produce any statement of what it is; but
starting from that—having either indicated it to the senses or found a

hypothesis as to what it is—they proceed from that to demonstrate, either more or less rigorously, the things that hold good in its own right of the genus with which they are dealing. For that reason it is obvious that from such an induction there is no demonstration of substance, i.e. of what a thing is, but some other manner of indicating it. 15
Equally, neither is anything said as to whether the genus of which they treat is or is not, because it falls to the same thinking to indicate both what a thing is and whether it is.

But since physics is one of the disciplines dealing with a particular genus of thing-that-is (for it deals with the sort of substance in which 20
the origin of change and of keeping-the-same is in itself), it is plain that this discipline is neither practical nor productive. For in the case of the producible the origin is in the producer—either intelligence or art or capacity of some kind; and in the case of the doable it is in the doer—choice: for the doable and the choosable are the same. It follows that, if all thinking is either practical or productive or theoretical, that 25
concerned with nature must be of a theoretical kind, but a kind which studies such of the things-that-are as are capable of being changed, and substance as in a formula for the most part, yet not separable substance.

We must pay attention to the manner of a thing's formula, i.e. of what it is to be that thing; since the inquiry will get nowhere otherwise. 30
Among things defined, i.e. those which are *what* something is, some are like the snub, others like the concave, and the difference between these is that in the snub matter is implicit—for the snub is a concave *nose*—whereas concavity is independent of perceptible matter. So if every naturally existing thing is called what it is in the same way as the snub, for instance nose, eye, face, flesh, bone, and animal as a whole, 1026ᵃ
and leaf, root, bark, and plant as a whole—for the formulae of none of them are independent of change but always include matter—the manner in which we need to investigate and define what a thing is in the case of naturally existing things is plain.

It is plain too that it falls to the student of nature to study a certain 5
kind of soul, namely any which is not independent of matter.

All this makes it obvious, then, that the study of nature is theoretical. But mathematics is also theoretical. On the other hand, it is not immediately plain whether the objects of mathematics are changeless and separable, even though it is plain that some mathematics studies its objects *qua* changeless and *qua* separable. However, if there is any- 10
thing invariable and changeless and separable, it is obvious that

acquaintance with it falls to a theoretical discipline, not, however, to the study of nature (which deals with certain changeable things) nor indeed to mathematics, but to something prior to both. For the study of nature deals with things that are separable but not changeless, while

15 certain parts of mathematics deal with things which, though changeless, are doubtless not separable but as in matter. But the primary discipline will deal also with things separable and changeless.

All causes are necessarily invariable; but these are especially so, for they are the causes of the divinities obvious to us.

It follows that there must be three kinds of theoretical philosophy,
20 mathematical, natural, and theological; for it is not hard to see that if the divine is present anywhere, it is present in this kind of nature. Of these the most estimable ought to deal with the most estimable genus. The theoretical are to be preferred, then, among the other disciplines, and this among the theoretical.

For one might be perplexed as to whether the primary philosophy
25 really is universal, or deals with a particular genus and one particular nature. For not even mathematics is all of a piece in this respect, geometry and astronomy being concerned with a particular nature, while universal mathematics is common to all. If then there is no other substance apart from those constituted naturally, the discipline concerned with nature would be primary. But if there is some change-
30 less substance, this is prior and is primary philosophy, and universal in this way, because primary; and it would fall to it to study that which is *qua* thing-that-is, both what it is and the things that hold good of it *qua* thing-that-is.

CHAPTER 2

But that which *is*, when baldly so called, may be so called in several ways. One of them was that which is coincidentally, another that
35 which is as true (and that which is not, that which is as falsehood). Apart from these there are the figures of predication, as for instance what a thing is, how qualified, of what quantity, where, when, and any-
1026ᵇ thing else that signifies in this sense; again apart from all these, that which is potentially and actually.

Since that which is may be so called, then, in several ways, it has first to be stated that there is no study that deals with that which is coincidentally. A sign of this is its neglect in every discipline, practical, productive, and theoretical. For one who produces a house
5

does not produce all the things which coincide in the house that is coming to be, for they are infinite. For there is nothing to prevent the house he has produced being pleasing to some, harmful to others, beneficial to others, and different from virtually everything that is; but the discipline of housebuilding is not productive of any of these things. In the same manner, a geometer does not study what is in this way coincidental to his figures, nor whether a triangle and a triangle possessing two right angles are different. This result is reasonable, for the coincidental is like a mere name. Hence Plato was in a way not wrong to classify sophistic as dealing with what is not. For the sophists' arguments are concerned, one might almost say, more than anything with the coincidental: whether artistic and literate, or artistic Coriscus and Coriscus, are different or the same thing; and whether everything that is, but not always, has come to be, so that if someone, being artistic, has come to be literate, he has also, being literate, come to be artistic—with all the other arguments of that kind. For what is coincidental is obviously close to what is not, as is plain also from arguments such as this: that with things-that-are in another sense there is a process of coming to be and destruction, but with things that are coincidentally there is not.

We ought nevertheless further to state, as far as possible, the nature of the coincidental and the cause why it is; for at the same time it will doubtless also be plain why no discipline deals with it. Since, then, among the things-that-are some are in the same state always and of necessity (not necessity in the sense of compulsion but what we call so from the impossibility of being otherwise), others not of necessity or always but for the most part, this is the origin and this the cause of the existence of the coincidental: for what is neither always nor for the most part, that we assert to be coincidental; as for instance if there is cold stormy weather in the dog days, we assert that that is a coincidence, but not if there is stifling heat, because the one is always or for the most part, the other not; and it is coincidence that a man is pale, for that is neither always nor for the most part, but he is not an animal coincidentally; and it is coincidental that a housebuilder heals somebody, because it is characteristic of a doctor, not a housebuilder, to do that, but it was a coincidence that the housebuilder was a doctor; and a cook, aiming to give pleasure, might produce health in somebody, but not by virtue of his culinary art—hence it was a coincidence, we assert, and in a way he produces it, but baldly not.

For of some of them other things are sometimes the things that produce them; of others there is no definite art or capacity. For of things that are or come to be coincidentally the cause is also co-incidentally.

It follows that since not everything is of necessity and always a thing-that-is or a thing coming to be, most things being so for the most
10 part, it is necessary that there be that which is coincidentally; as for instance someone pale is neither always nor for the most part artistic, and when this comes to be he will be so coincidentally—otherwise everything will be of necessity.

It follows that the matter that is capable of being otherwise than it is for the most part, is cause of the coincidental.

15 We have to take *this* as our original question: is there nothing which is neither always nor for the most part? or is this impossible? Con-sequently there are, apart from these, chance, i.e. coincidental, things.

But does it hold good of some things to be for the most part but of none to be always? Or are some things invariable? These things will have to be investigated later.

20 But it is obvious that no discipline deals with the coincidental; for every discipline deals either with that which is always or with that which is for the most part. How else could one learn, or teach another? For a thing has to be defined either by that which is always or by that which is for the most part: as for instance that for the most part the fever-patient benefits from honey-water. But the exception—when he
25 does not, as for instance at new moon—cannot be stated; for that which is at new moon is also either always or for the most part. But the coincidental is an exception to that.

We have stated, then, what the concidental is and the cause why it is, and that no discipline deals with it.

CHAPTER 3

It is obvious that there are origins and causes that are able to come to
30 be and to be destroyed without being in process of coming to be and being destroyed. For otherwise everything will be of necessity, if what-ever is in process of coming to be and being destroyed necessarily has some cause non-coincidentally.

Will *this* be or not? It will if *this* comes to be, but not otherwise; and that if something else does. And in this way it is plain that as time is
1027ᵇ continually subtracted from a limited period of time, we shall come to the present. Thus:

> this man will die by violence if he goes out,
> and that if he gets thirsty,
> and that if something else.

In this way we shall come to what holds good now, or to something that has come to be. For instance:

> ... if he gets thirsty,
> and that if he is eating something salty.

But this last either holds good or else does not; so of necessity he will 5 die or not die. Equally, if one jumps over to what has come to be, the same argument applies; for that—I mean what has come to be—is already a constituent of something. Consequently, everything that will be will be of necessity, e.g. that he who is living dies; for something has already come to be, as for instance opposites in the same thing. But 10 whether by disease or violence is not yet necessary, but will be if *this* comes to be. It is consequently plain that it runs as far as some origin, but this no further to anything else; the origin of whatever may chance will therefore be this, and nothing else is the cause of its coming to be.

But what kind of origin and what kind of cause such a reduction leads to, whether to matter or to what a thing is for or to what effects a 15 change, needs to be investigated fully.

CHAPTER 4

So much for that which *is* coincidentally; it has been sufficiently distinguished. That which is as true and that which is not as falsehood are concerned with composition and division and, taken together, 20 with the apportionment of a contradiction. For truth has the affirmation in the case of what is compounded and the denial in the case of what is divided, while a falsehood has the contradictory of this apportionment. (How we come to conceive things together or separately is another question—by together and separately I mean not in succession but so as to make up some one thing.)

For falsehood and truth are not in actual things (the good, for 25 example, being true and the bad *eo ipso* a falsehood), but in thought; though in the case of simples, i.e. what things are, not in thought either. What needs study with regard to that which is and is not in this way will have to be investigated later. But since the combination and 30 the division are in thought, not in actual things, and that which *is* in this way is a different thing-that-is from those which are in the fundamental way (for the thought connects or divides either what a thing is, or how qualified, or of what quantity or whatever else it may be), we may leave on one side that which is as coincidental and that which is as true. For the cause of the one is indefinite and of the other 1028ᵃ is a certain affection of thought, and both are concerned with the remaining genus of thing-that-is and do not indicate the existence of any extra nature of thing-that-is.

So we may leave them aside, and investigate the causes and origins of that which is itself, *qua* thing-that-is.

5 (In our chapters distinguishing the number of ways in which various things are called what they are, it was obvious that that which is may be so called in several ways.)

BOOK VII (Z)

CHAPTER I

1028ᵃ There are several senses in which a thing may be said to be, as we pointed out previously in our book on the various senses of words; for in one sense it means what a thing is or a 'this', and in another sense it means that a thing is of a certain quality or quantity or has some such predicate asserted of it. While 'being' has all these senses, obviously that which is primarily is the 'what', which indicates the 15 substance of the thing. For when we say of what quality a thing is, we say that it is good or beautiful, but not that it is three cubits long or that it is a man; but when we say *what* it is, we do not say 'white' or 'hot' or 'three cubits long', but 'man' or 'God'. And all other things are said to be because they are, some of them, quantities of that which *is* in this primary sense, others qualities of it, others affections of it, and others 20 some other determination of it. And so one might raise the question whether 'to walk' and 'to be healthy' and 'to sit' signify in each case something that is, and similarly in any other case of this sort; for none of them is either self-subsistent or capable of being separated from substance, but rather, if anything, it is that which walks or is seated or 25 is healthy that is an existent thing. Now these are seen to be more real because there is something definite which underlies them; and this is the substance or individual, which is implied in such a predicate; for 'good' or 'sitting' are not used without this. Clearly then it is in virtue

of this category that each of the others *is*. Therefore that which is
primarily and *is* simply (not is something) must be substance.   30
    Now there are several senses in which a thing is said to be primary;
but substance is primary in every sense—in formula, in order of
knowledge, in time. For of the other categories none can exist independently, but only substance. And in formula also this is primary;   35
for in the formula of each term the formula of its substance must be
present. And we think we know each thing most fully, when we know   1028ᵇ
what it is, e.g. what man is or what fire is, rather than when we know its
quality, its quantity, or where it is; since we know each of these things
also, only when we know *what* the quantity or the quality *is*.
    And indeed the question which, both now and of old, has always
been raised, and always been the subject of doubt, viz. what being is, is
just the question, what is substance? For it is this that some assert to be   5
one, others more than one, and that some assert to be limited in
number, other unlimited. And so we also must consider chiefly and
primarily and almost exclusively what that is which *is* in this sense.

CHAPTER 2

Substance is thought to belong most obviously to bodies; and so we
say that both animals and plants and their parts are substances, and so   10
are natural bodies such as fire and water and earth and everything of
the sort, and all things that are parts of these or composed of these
(either of parts or of the whole bodies), e.g. the heaven and its parts,
stars and moon and sun. But whether these alone are substances, or
there are also others, or only some of these, or some of these and some
other things are substances, or none of these but only some other   15
things, must be considered. Some think the limits of body, i.e. surface,
line, point, and unit, are substances, and more so than body or the
solid. Further, some do not think there is anything substantial besides
sensible things, but others think there are eternal substances which
are more in number and more real, e.g. Plato posited two kinds of
substance—the Forms and the objects of mathematics—as well as a   20
third kind, viz. the substance of sensible bodies. And Speusippus
made still more kinds of substance, beginning with the One, and
making principles for each kind of substance, one for numbers,
another for spatial magnitudes, and then another for the soul; and in
this way he multiplies the kinds of substance. And some say Forms
and numbers have the same nature, and other things come after them,   25

e.g. lines and planes, until we come to the substance of the heavens and to sensible bodies.

Regarding these matters, then, we must inquire which of the common statements are right and which are not right, and what things are substances, and whether there are or are not any besides sensible substances, and how sensible substances exist, and whether there is a
30   separable substance (and if so why and how) or there is no substance separable from sensible substances; and we must first sketch the nature of substance.

CHAPTER 3

The word 'substance' is applied, if not in more senses, still at least to four main objects: for both the essence and the universal and the genus
35   are thought to be the substance of each thing, and fourthly the substratum. Now the substratum is that of which other things are predicated, while it is itself not predicated of anything else. And so we must first determine the nature of this; for that which underlies a thing
1029ᵃ   primarily is thought to be in the truest sense its substance. And in one sense matter is said to be of the nature of substratum, in another, shape, and in a third sense, the compound of these. By the matter I mean, for instance, the bronze, by the shape the plan of its form, and
5   by the compound of these (the concrete thing) the statue. Therefore if the form is prior to the matter and more real, it will be prior to the compound also for the same reason.

We have now outlined the nature of substance, showing that it is that which is not predicated of a subject, but of which all else is predicated. But we must not merely state the matter thus; for this is not enough. The statement itself is obscure, and further, on this view,
10   *matter* becomes substance. For if this is not substance, it is beyond us to say what else is. When all else is taken away evidently nothing but matter remains. For of the other elements some are affections, products, and capacities of bodies, while length, breadth, and depth are quantities and not substances. For a quantity is not a substance;
15   but the substance is rather that to which these belong primarily. But when length and breadth and depth are taken away we see nothing left except that which is bounded by these, whatever it be; so that to those who consider the question thus matter alone must seem to be sub-
20   stance. By matter I mean that which in itself is neither a particular thing nor of a certain quantity nor assigned to any other of the

categories by which being is determined. For there is something of which each of these is predicated, so that its being is different from that of each of the predicates; for the predicates other than substance are predicated of substance, while substance is predicated of matter. Therefore the ultimate substratum is of itself neither a particular thing nor of a particular quantity nor otherwise positively characterized; nor 25 yet negatively, for negations also will belong to it only by accident.

For those who adopt this point of view, then, it follows that matter is substance. But this is impossible; for both separability and individuality are thought to belong chiefly to substance. And so form and the compound of form and matter would be thought to be substance, rather than matter. The substance compounded of both, i.e. of matter 30 and shape, may be dismissed; for it is posterior and its nature is obvious. And matter also is in a sense manifest. But we must inquire into the third kind of substance; for this is the most difficult.

It is agreed that there are some substances among sensible things, so that we must look first among these. For it is an advantage to 1029^b advance to that which is more intelligible. For learning proceeds for all in this way—through that which is less intelligible by nature to that which is more intelligible; and just as in conduct our work is to start 5 from what is good for each and make what is good in itself good for each, so it is our work to start from what is more intelligble to oneself and make what is intelligible by nature intelligible to oneself. Now what is intelligible and primary for particular sets of people is often intelligible to a very small extent, and has little or nothing of reality. But yet one must start from that which is barely intelligible but 10 intelligible to oneself, and try to understand what is intelligible in itself, passing, as has been said, by way of those very things which one understands.

CHAPTER 4

Since at the start we distinguished the various marks by which we 1 determine substance, and one of these was thought to be the essence, we must investigate this. And first let us say something about it in the abstract. The essence of each thing is what it is said to be in virtue of 13 itself. For being you is not being musical; for you are not musical in virtue of yourself. What, then, you are in virtue of yourself is your 15 essence.

But not the whole of this is the essence of a thing; not that which

something is in virtue of itself in the way in which a surface is white, because being a surface is not being white. But again the combination of both—being a white surface—is not the essence of surface. Why? Because 'surface' itself is repeated. The formula, therefore, in which the term itself is not present but its meaning is expressed, this is the
20   formula of the essence of each thing. Therefore if to be a white surface is to be a smooth surface, to be white and to be smooth are one and the same.

But since there are compounds of substance with the other categories (for there is a substrate for each category, e.g. for quality, quantity, time, place, and motion), we must inquire whether there is a
25   formula of the essence of each of them, i.e. whether to these compounds also there belongs an essence, e.g. to white man. Let the compound be denoted by 'cloak'. What is being a cloak? But, it may be said, this also is not said of something in its own right. We reply that there are two ways in which a predicate may fail to be true of a subject in its own right, and one of these results from addition, and the other
30   not. *One* kind of predicate is not said of a thing in its own right because the term that is being defined is added to something else, e.g. if in defining the essence of white one were to state the formula of white *man*; *another* because something else is added to it, e.g. if 'cloak' meant
1030ᵃ   white man, and one were to define cloak as white; white man is white indeed, but its essence is not to be white. But is being a cloak an essence at all? Probably not. For the essence is what something is; but when one thing is said of another, that is not what a 'this' is, e.g. white
5   man is not what a 'this' is, since being a 'this' belongs only to substances. Therefore there is an essence only of those things whose formula is a definition. But we have a definition not where we have a word and a formula identical in meaning (for in that case all formulae would be definitions; for there will be some name for any formula whatever, so that even the *Iliad* would be a definition), but where there is a
10   formula of something primary; and primary things are those which do not involve one thing's being said of another. Nothing, then, which is not a species of a genus will have an *essence*—only species will have it, for in these the subject is not thought to participate in the attribute and
15   to have it as an affection, nor to have it by accident; but for everything else as well, if it has a name, there will be a formula of its meaning— viz. that this attribute belongs to this subject; or instead of a simple formula we shall be able to give a more accurate one; but there will be no definition nor essence.

But after all, 'definition', like 'what a thing is', has several meanings: 'what a thing is' in one sense means substance and a 'this', in another one or other of the predicates, quantity, quality, and the like. For as 'is' is predicable of all things, not however in the same sense, but of one sort of thing primarily and of others in a secondary way, so too the 'what' belongs simply to substance, but in a limited sense to the other categories. For even of a quality we might ask what it is, so that a quality also is a 'what',—not simply, however, but just as, in the case of that which is not, some say, in the abstract, that that which is not *is*— not *is* simply, but *is* non-existent. So too with a quality.

Now we must inquire how we should express ourselves on each point, but still more how the facts actually stand. And so now also since it is evident what language we use, essence will belong, just as the 'what' does, primarily and in the simple sense to substance, and in a secondary way to the other categories also,—not essence simply, but the essence of a quality or of a quantity. For it must be either homonymously that we say these *are*, or by making qualifications and abstractions (in the way in which that which is not known may be said to be known),—the truth being that we use the word neither homonymously nor in the same sense, but just as we apply the word 'medical' when there is a *reference* to one and the same thing, not *meaning* one and the same thing, nor yet speaking homonymously; for a patient and an operation and an instrument are called medical neither homonymously nor in virtue of one thing, but with reference to one thing. But it does not matter in which of the two ways one likes to describe the facts; this is evident, that definition and essence in the primary and simple sense belong to substances. Still they belong to other things as well in a similar way, but not primarily. For if we suppose this it does not follow that there is a definition of every word which means the same as any formula; it must mean the same as a particular kind of formula; and this condition is satisfied if it is a formula of something which is one, not by continuity like the *Iliad* or the things that are one by being bound together, but in one of the main senses of 'one' which answer to the senses of 'is'; now 'that which is' in one sense denotes a 'this', in another quantity, in another quality. And so there can be a formula or definition of white man, but not in the sense in which there is a definition either of white or of a substance.

CHAPTER 5

It is a difficult question, if one denies that a formula with an addition is
15   a definition, whether any of the things that are not simple but coupled
will be definable. For we *must* explain them by an addition. E.g. there
is the nose, and concavity, and snubness, which is compounded out of
the two by the presence of the one in the other, and it is not by
accident that the nose has the attribute either of concavity or of
snubness, but in virtue of its nature; nor do they attach to it as white-
20   ness does to Callias, or to man (because Callias, who happens to be a
man, is white), but rather as 'male' attaches to animal and 'equal' to
quantity, and as everything else which is said of something in its own
right. And such attributes are those in which is involved either the
formula or the *name* of the subject of the particular attribute, and
which cannot be explained without this; e.g. white can be explained
25   apart from man, but not female apart from animal. Therefore there is
either no essence and definition of any of these things, or if there is, it
is in another sense, as we have said.

But there is also a second difficulty about them. For if snub nose
and concave nose are the same thing, snub and concave will be the
same thing; but if snub and concave are not the same (because it is
impossible to speak of snubness apart from the thing of which, in its
own right, it is an attribute, for snubness is concavity *in the nose*), either
30   it is impossible properly to say 'snub nose' or the same thing will have
been said twice, concave nose nose; for snub nose will be concave nose
nose. And so it is absurd that such things should have an essence; if
they have, there will be an infinite regress; for in snub nose yet another
nose will be involved.

1031ᵃ   Clearly then only substance is definable. For if the other categories
also are definable, it must be by addition, e.g. the odd, for it cannot be
defined apart from number; nor can female be defined apart from
animal. (When I say 'by addition' I mean the expressions in which we
5   have to say the same thing twice, as in these instances.) And if this is
true, coupled terms also, like 'odd number', will not be definable (but
this escapes our notice because our formulae are not accurate). But if
these also are definable, either it is in some other way or, as we said,
definition and essence must be said to have more than one sense.
10   Therefore in one sense nothing will have a definition and nothing will
have an essence, except substances, but in another sense other things
will have them. Clearly, then, definition is the formula of the essence,

and essence must belong to substances either alone or chiefly and primarily and in the unqualified sense.

CHAPTER 6

We must inquire whether each thing and its essence are the same or different. This is of some use for the inquiry concerning substance; for each thing is thought to be not different from its substance, and the essence is said to be the substance of each thing.

Now in the case of things with accidental attributes the two would be generally thought to be different, e.g. white man would be thought to be different from the essence of white man. For if they are the same, the essence of man and that of white man are also the same; for a man and a white man are the same, as people say, so that the essence of white man and that of man would be also the same. But probably it is not necessary that things with accidental attributes should be the same. For the extreme terms are not in the same way the same.— Perhaps *this* might be thought to follow, that the extreme terms, the accidents, should turn out to be the same, e.g. the essence of white and that of musical; but this is not actually thought to be the case.

But in the case of so-called self-subsistent things, is a thing necessarily the same as its essence? E.g. if there are some substances which have no other substances nor entities prior to them—substances such as some assert the Ideas to be? If the essence of good is to be different from the Idea of good, and the essence of animal from the Idea of animal, and the essence of being from the Idea of being, there will, firstly, be other substances and entities and Ideas besides those which are asserted, and, secondly, these others will be prior substances if the essence is substance. And if the posterior substances are severed from one another, there will be no knowledge of the ones and the others will have no being. (By 'severed' I mean, if the Idea of good has not the essence of good, and the latter has not the property of being good.) For there is knowledge of each thing only when we know its essence. And the case is the same for other things as for the good; so that if the essence of good is not good, neither will the essence of being be, nor the essence of unity be one. And all essences alike exist or none of them does; so that if the essence of being is not, neither will any of the others be. Again, that which has not the property of being good is not good. The good, then, must be one with the essence of good, and the beautiful with the essence of beauty, and so with all things which

15

20

25

30

1031^b

5

10

do not depend on something else but are self-subsistent and primary. For it is enough if they are this, even if there are no Forms; and

15 perhaps all the more if there are Forms.—At the same time it is clear that if there are Ideas such as some people say there are, the substratum of them will not be substance; for these must be substances, and not predicable of a substratum; for if they were they would exist only by being participated in.—Each thing then and its essence are one and the same in no merely accidental way, as is evident both from the preceding arguments and because to *know* each thing, at least, is to

20 know its essence, so that even by the exhibition of instances it becomes clear that both must be one.

(But of an accidental term, e.g. 'the musical' or 'the white', since it has two meanings, it is not true to say that it itself is identical with its

25 essence; for both that to which the accidental quality belongs, and the accidental quality, are white, so that in a sense the accident and its essence are the same, and in a sense they are not; for the essence of white is not the same as the man or the white man, but it is the same as the attribute white.)

The absurdity of the separation would appear also if one were to assign a name to each of the essences; for there would be another

30 essence besides the original one; e.g. to the essence of horse there will belong a second essence. Yet why should not some things be their essences from the start, since essence is substance? But not only are a

1032ᵃ thing and its essence one, but the formula of them is also the same, as is clear even from what has been said; for it is not by accident that the essence of one, and the one, are one. Further, if they were different, the process would go on to infinity; for we should have the essence of one, and the one, so that in their case also the same infinite regress would be found. Clearly, then, each primary and self-subsistent thing

5 is one and the same as its essence.

Now the sophistical objections to this position, and the question whether Socrates and to be Socrates are the same thing, are obviously answered in the same way; for there is no difference either in the standpoint from which the question would be asked, or in that from which one could answer it successfully. We have explained, then, in

10 what sense each thing is the same as its essence and in what sense it is not.

CHAPTER 7

Of things that come to be some come to be by nature, some by art, some spontaneously. Now everything that comes to be comes to be by the agency of something and from something and comes to be something. And the something which I say it comes to be may be found in any category; it may come to be either a 'this' or of some quantity or of some quality or somewhere.

Now natural comings to be are the comings to be of those things which come to be by nature; and that out of which they come to be is what we call matter; and that by which they come to be is something which exists naturally; and the something which they come to be is a man or a plant or one of the things of this kind, which we say are substances if anything is. All things that come to be either by nature or by art have matter, for each of them is capable both of being and of not being, and this capacity is the matter in each. And, in general, both that from which they are produced is nature, and the type according to which they are produced is nature (for that which is produced, e.g. a plant or an animal, has a nature), and so is that by which they are produced—the so-called 'formal' nature, which is specifically the same as the nature of the thing produced (though it is in another individual); for man begets man.

Thus, then, are natural products produced; all other productions are called 'makings'. And all makings proceed either from art or from a capacity or from thought. Some of them happen also spontaneously or by chance just as natural products sometimes do; for there also the same things sometimes are produced without seed as well as from seed. Concerning these cases, then, we must inquire later, but from art proceed the things of which the form is in the soul. (By form i mean the essence of each thing and its primary substance.) For even contraries have in a sense the same form; for the substance of a privation is the opposite substance, e.g. health is the substance of disease; for it is by its absence that disease exists; and health is the formula and the knowledge in the soul. The healthy subject, then, is produced as the result of the following train of thought; since *this* is health, if the subject is to be healthy *this* must first be present, e.g. a uniform state of body, and if this is to be present, there must be heat; and the physician goes on thinking thus until he brings the matter to a final step which he himself can take. Then the process from this point onward, i.e. the process towards health, is called a 'making'. Therefore

15

20

25

30

1032^b

5

10

it follows that in a sense health comes from health and house from house, that with matter from that without matter; for the medical art and the building art are the form of health and of the house; and I call
15 the essence substance without matter. Of productions and movements one part is called thinking and the other making,—that which proceeds from the starting-point and the form is thinking, and that which proceeds from the final step of the thinking is making. And each of the intermediate steps is taken in the same way. I mean, for instance, if the subject is to be healthy his bodily state must be made uniform. What
20 then does being made uniform imply? This or that. And this depends on his being made warm. What does this imply? Something else. And this something is present potentially; and what is present potentially is already in the physician's power.

The active principle then and the starting-point for the process of becoming healthy is, if it happens by art, the form in the soul, and if spontaneously, it is that, whatever it is, which is the starting-point of his making for the man who makes by art, as in healing the starting-
25 point is perhaps the production of warmth, and this the physician produces by rubbing. Warmth in the body, then, is either a part of health or is followed (either directly or through several intermediate steps) by something which is a part of health; and this, viz. that which produces the part, is the last step, and so are, e.g. the stones a part of the house, and so in all other cases.

30 Therefore, as we say, it is impossible that anything should be produced if there were nothing before. Obviously then some part of the result will pre-exist of necessity; for the matter is a part; for this is present in the process and it is this that becomes something. But do
1033ª some also of the elements in the *formula* pre-exist? Well, we describe in both ways what bronze circles are; we describe both the matter by saying it is bronze, and the form by saying that it is such and such a figure; and figure is the proximate genus in which it is placed. The
5 bronze circle, then, has its matter *in its formula*.

And as for that out of which as matter they are produced, some things are said, when they have been produced, to be not it but of it, e.g. the statue is not stone but of stone. But though what becomes healthy is a man, a man is not what the healthy product is said to come from. The reason is that though a thing comes both from its privation and from its substratum, which we call its matter (e.g. what becomes
10 healthy is both a man and an invalid), it is said to come rather from its privation (e.g. it is from an invalid rather than from a man that a healthy

subject is produced). And so the healthy subject is not said to *be* an invalid, but to be a man, and a healthy man. But as for the things whose privation is obscure and nameless, e.g. in bronze the privation of a particular shape or in bricks and timber the privation of arrange- 15 ment as a house, the thing is thought to be produced *from* these materials, as in the former case the healthy man is produced *from* an invalid. And so, as there also a thing is not said to be that from which it comes, here the statue is not said to be wood but is said by a verbal change to be not wood but wooden, not bronze but of bronze, not stone but of stone, and the house is said to be not bricks but of bricks (since we should not say without qualification, if we looked at things carefully, even that a statue is produced from wood or a house from 20 bricks, because its coming to be implies change in that from which it comes, and not permanence). For this reason, then, we use this way of speaking.

CHAPTER 8

Since anything which is produced is produced by something (and this I call the starting-point of the production), and from something (and 25 let this be taken to be not the privation but the matter; for the meanings we attach to these have already been distinguished), and since something is produced (and this is either a sphere or a circle or whatever else it may chance to be), just as we do not make the sub-stratum—the bronze—so we do not make the sphere, except inciden-tally, because the bronze sphere is a sphere and we make the former. 30 For to make a 'this' is to make a 'this' out of the general substratum. I mean that to make the bronze round is not to make the round or the sphere, but something else, i.e. to produce this form in something else. For if we make the form, we must make it out of something else; for 1033ᵇ this was assumed. E.g. we make a bronze sphere; and that in the sense that out of this, which is bronze, we make this other, which is a sphere. If, then, we make the sphere itself, clearly we must make it in the same way, and the processes of making will regress to infinity. Obviously then the form also, or whatever we ought to call the shape of the 5 sensible thing, is not produced, nor does production relate to it,— i.e. the essence is not produced; for this is that which is made to be in something else by art or by nature or by some capacity. But that there is a *bronze sphere*, this we make. For we make it out of bronze and the sphere; we bring the form into this particular matter, and the result is a

10   bronze sphere. But if the essence of sphere in general is produced, something must be produced out of something. For the product will always have to be divisible, and one part must be this and another that, I mean the one must be matter and the other form. If then a sphere is the figure whose circumference is at all points equidistant from the

15   centre, part of this will be the medium in which the thing made will be, and part will be in that medium, and the whole will be the thing produced, which corresponds to the bronze sphere. It is obvious then from what has been said that the thing, in the sense of form or substance, is not produced, but the concrete thing which gets its name from this is produced, and that in everything which comes to be matter is present, and one part of the thing is matter and the other form.

20   Is there then a sphere apart from the individual spheres or a house apart from the bricks? Rather we may say that no 'this' would ever have been coming to be, if this had been so. The 'form' however means the 'such', and is not a 'this'—a definite thing; but the artist makes, or the father generates, a 'such' out of a 'this'; and when it has been generated, it is a 'this such'. And the whole 'this', Callias or Socrates, is analogous

25   to this bronze sphere, but man and animal to bronze sphere in general. Obviously then the cause which consists of the Forms (taken in the sense in which some maintain the existence of the Forms, i.e. if they are something apart from the individuals) is useless with regard both to comings-to-be and to substances; and the Forms need not, for this reason at least, be self-subsistent substances. In some cases it is even

30   obvious that the producer is of the same kind as the produced (not, however, the same nor one in number, but in form), e.g. in the case of natural products (for man produces man), unless something happens contrary to nature, e.g. the production of a mule by a horse. And even these cases are similar; for that which would be found to be common to horse and ass, the genus next above them, has not received a name,

1034ᵃ   but it would doubtless be both, as the mule is both. Obviously, therefore, it is quite unnecessary to set up a Form as a pattern (for we should have looked for Forms in these cases if any; for these are substances if anything is so); the begetter is adequate to the making of

5   the product and to the causing of the form in the matter. And when we have the whole, such and such a form in this flesh and in these bones, this is Callias or Socrates; and they are different in virtue of their matter (for that is different), but the same in form; for their form is indivisible.

The question might be raised, why some things are produced spontaneously as well as by art, e.g. health, while others are not, e.g. a house. The reason is that in some cases the matter which determines the production in the making and producing of any work of art, and in which a part of the product is present, is such as to be set in motion by itself and in some cases is not of this nature, and of the former kind some can move itself in the particular way required, while other matter is incapable of this; for many things can be set in motion by themselves but not in some particular way, e.g. that of dancing. The things then whose matter is of this sort, e.g. stones, cannot be moved in the particular way required, except by something else, but in another way they can move themselves; and so it is with fire. Therefore some things cannot exist apart from some one who has the art of making them, while others can exist without such a person; for motion can be started by these things which have not the art but can move of themselves, i.e. either by *other* things which have not the art or by a part of the product itself.

And it is clear also from what has been said that in a sense everything is produced from another individual which shares its name (natural products are so produced), or a part of itself which shares its name (e.g. the house produced by reason is produced from a house; for the art of building is the form of the house), or something which contains a part of it,—if we exclude things produced by accident. For what directly and of itself causes the production is a part of the product. The heat in the movement causes heat in the body, and this is either health, or a part of health, or is followed by a part of health or by health itself. And so it is said to cause health, because it produces that on which health follows.

Therefore substance is the starting-point of all production, as of deduction. It is from the 'what' that deductions start; and from it also we now find processes of production to start. And things which are formed by nature are in the same case as these products of art. For the seed produces them as the artist produces the works of art; for it has the form potentially, and that from which the seed comes has in a sense the same name as the offspring—only in a sense, for we must not expect all cases to have exactly the same name, as in the production of human being from human being; for a woman also can be produced by a man—unless there is a deformity: that is why it is not from a mule that a mule is produced. The natural things which (like some artificial objects) can be produced spontaneously are those whose matter can

5 be moved even by itself in the way in which the seed usually moves it; but those things which have not such matter cannot be produced except by parents.

But not only regarding substance does our argument prove that its form does not come to be, but the argument applies to all the primary

10 classes alike, i.e. quantity, quality, and the other categories. For as the bronze sphere comes to be, but not the sphere nor the bronze, and so too in the case of bronze itself, if it comes to be (for the matter and the form must always exist before), so is it as regards both 'what' and quality and quantity and the other categories likewise; for the quality

15 does not come to be, but the wood of that quality, and the quantity does not come to be, but the wood or the animal of that size. But we may learn from these instances a peculiarity of substance, that there must exist beforehand another actual substance which produces it, e.g. an animal if an animal is produced; but it is not necessary that a quality or quantity should pre-exist otherwise than potentially.

CHAPTER 10

20 Since a definition is a formula, and every formula has parts, and as the formula is to the thing, so is the part of the formula to the part of the thing, we are already faced by the question whether the formula of the parts must be present in the formula of the whole or not. For in some cases the formulae of the parts are seen to be present, and in some not.

25 The formula of the circle does not include that of the segments, but that of the syllable includes that of the letters; yet the circle is divided into segments as the syllable is into letters.—And further if the parts are prior to the whole, and the acute angle is a part of the right angle and the finger a part of the animal, the acute angle will be prior to the

30 right angle and the finger to the man. But the latter are thought to be prior; for in formula the parts are explained by reference to them, and in virtue also of their power of existing apart from the parts the wholes are prior.

Perhaps we should rather say that 'part' is used in several senses. One of these is 'that which measures another thing in respect of quantity'. But let this sense be set aside; let us inquire about the parts of which *substance* consists. If then matter is one thing, form another,

1035ᵃ the compound of these a third, and both the matter and the form and the compound are substance, even the matter is in a sense called part of a thing, while in a sense *it* is not, but only the elements of which the formula of the form consists. E.g. flesh (for this is the matter in which it $\quad$ 5 is produced) is not a part of concavity, but of snubness it is a part; and the bronze is a part of the particular statue, but not of the statue as form. (For each thing must be referred to by naming its form, and as having form, but never by naming its material aspect as such.) And so the formula of the circle does not include that of the segments, but the formula of the syllable includes that of the letters; for the letters are $\quad$ 10 parts of the formula of the form, and not matter, but the segments are parts, in the sense of matter, on which the form supervenes; yet they are nearer the form than the bronze is when roundness is produced in bronze. But in a sense not even every kind of letter will be present in the formula of the syllable, e.g. particular waxen letters or the letters as $\quad$ 15 sounds in the air; for these also are part of the syllable only in the sense that they are its perceptible matter. For even if the line when divided passes away into its halves, or the man into bones and muscles and flesh, it does not follow that they are composed of these as parts of their substance, but rather as matter; and these are parts of the $\quad$ 20 concrete thing, but not of the form, i.e. of that to which the formula refers; and therefore they will not be in the formulae either. Therefore of some things the formula of such parts will be present, but in others it must not be present, where the formula does not refer to the concrete object. For it is for this reason that some things have as their constituent principles parts into which they pass away, while some $\quad$ 25 have not. Those things in which the form and the matter are taken together, e.g. the snub, or the bronze circle, pass away into these material parts, and the matter is a part of them; but those things which do not involve matter but are without matter, and whose formulae are formulae of the form only, do not pass away,—either not at all or at any $\quad$ 30 rate not in this way. Therefore these materials are principles and parts of the concrete things, while of the form they are neither parts nor principles. And therefore the clay statue is resolved into clay and the ball into bronze and Callias into flesh and bones, and again the circle into its segments; for there is a sense of 'circle' in which it involves matter. For 'circle' is used homonymously, meaning both the circle in $\quad$ 1035^{b} general and the individual circle, because there is no name proper to the individuals.

The truth has really now been stated, but still let us state it yet more clearly, taking up the question again. The parts of the formula, into $\quad$ 5 which the formula is divided, are prior to it, either all or some of them. The formula of the right angle, however, does not include the formula of the acute, but the formula of the acute includes that of the right angle; for he who defines the acute uses the right angle; for the acute is less than a right angle. The circle and the semicircle also are in a like relation; for the semicircle is defined by the circle; and so is the finger by the whole body, for a finger is such-and-such a part of a man. Therefore the parts which are of the nature of matter and into which as its matter a thing is divided, are posterior; but those which are parts of the formula, and of the substance according to its formula, are prior, either all or some of them. And since the soul of animals (for this is the substance of living beings) is their substance according to the formula, i.e. the form and the essence of a body of a certain kind (at least we shall define each part, if we define it well, not without reference to its function, and this cannot belong to it without perception), therefore the parts of soul are prior, either all or some of them, to the concrete animal, and similarly in each case of a concrete whole; and the body and its parts are posterior to this its substance, and it is not the substance but the concrete thing that is divided into these parts as its matter. To the concrete thing these are in a sense prior, but in a sense they are not. For they cannot even exist if severed from the whole; for it is not a finger in *any* state that is the finger of a living thing, but the dead finger is a finger only homonymously. Some parts are neither prior nor posterior to the whole, i.e. those which are most important and in which the formula, i.e. the substance, is immediately present, e.g. perhaps the heart or the brain; for it does not matter which of the two has this quality. But man and horse and terms which are thus applied to individuals, but universally, are not substance but something composed of this particular formula and this particular matter treated as universal; but when we come to the individual, Socrates is composed of ultimate individual matter; and similarly in all other cases.

A part may be a part either of the form (i.e. the essence), or of the compound of the form and the matter, or of the matter itself. But only the parts of the form are parts of the formula, and the formula is of the universal; for being a circle is the same as the circle, and being a soul is the same as the soul. But when we come to the concrete thing, e.g. *this* circle, i.e. one of the individual circles, whether sensible or intelligible (I mean by intelligible circles the mathematical, and by sensible circles those of bronze and of wood), of these there is no definition, but they are known by the aid of thought or perception; and when they go out of our actual consciousness it is not clear whether they exist or not; but they are always stated and cognized by means of the universal formula. But matter is unknowable in itself. And some matter is sensible and some intelligible, sensible matter being for instance bronze and wood and all matter that is changeable, and intelligible 10 matter being that which is present in sensible things not *qua* sensible, i.e. in the objects of mathematics. We have stated, then, how whole and part, and prior and posterior, are related.

When any one asks whether the right angle and the circle and the animal are prior to that into which they are divided and of which they 15 consist, i.e. the parts, we must meet the inquiry by saying that the question cannot be answered simply. For if the soul is the animal or the living thing, or the soul of each individual is the individual itself, and being a circle is the circle, and being a right angle and the essence of the right angle is the right angle, then the whole in one sense must be called posterior to the part in one sense, i.e. to the parts included in the formula and to the parts of the individual right angle (for both the 20 material right angle which is made of bronze, and that which is formed by individual lines, are posterior to their parts); while the immaterial right angle is posterior to the parts included in the formula, but prior to those included in the particular instance. But the question must not be answered simply. If, however, the soul is something different and is not identical with the animal, even so some parts must be called prior and others must not, as has been said. 25

CHAPTER 11

The question is naturally raised, what sort of parts belong to the form and what sort not to the form, but to the concrete thing. Yet if this is not plain it is not possible to define anything; for definition is of the universal and of the form. If then it is not evident which of the parts are of the nature of matter and which are not, neither will the formula of the thing be evident. In the case of things which are found to occur in 30 specifically different materials, as a circle may exist in bronze or stone or wood, it seems plain that these, the bronze or the stone, are no part of the essence of the circle, since it is found apart from them. Of things which are *not* seen to exist apart, there is no reason why the same may not be true, e.g. even if all circles that had ever been seen were of bronze (for none the less the bronze would be no part of the form); but 1036ᵇ it is hard to effect this severance in thought. E.g. the form of man is always found in flesh and bones and parts of this kind; are these then

5   also parts of the form and the formula? No, they are matter; but because man is not found also in other matters we are unable to effect the severance.

Since this is thought to be possible, but it is not clear *when* it is the case, some are in doubt even in the case of the circle and the triangle,

10   thinking that it is not right to define these by lines and by continuous space, but that all these are to the circle or the triangle as flesh or bones are to man, and bronze or stone to the statue; and they bring all things to numbers, and they say the formula of line is that of two. And *of those* who assert the Ideas some make two the line itself, and others

15   make it the form of the line; for in some cases they say the Form and that of which it is the Form are the same, e.g. two and the Form of two; but in the case of line they say this is no longer so.

It follows then that there is one Form for many things whose Form is evidently different (a conclusion which confronted the Pythagoreans also); and that it is possible to make one thing the very Form of

20   all, and to hold that the others are not Forms; but thus all things will be one.

Now we have stated that the question of definitions contains some difficulty, and why this is so. Therefore to bring all things thus to Forms and to eliminate the matter is useless labour; for some things surely are a particular form in a particular matter, or particular things in a particular state. And the comparison which Socrates the younger

25   used to make in the case of animal is not good; for it leads away from *the truth, and makes one suppose that man can possibly exist without* his parts, as the circle can without the bronze. But the case is not similar; for an animal is something perceptible, and it is not possible to define it without reference to movement—nor, therefore, without

30   reference to the parts and to their being in a certain state. For it is not a hand in *any* state that is a part of man, but the hand which can fulfil its work, which therefore must be alive; if it is not alive it is not a part.

Regarding the objects of mathematics, why are the formulae of the parts not parts of the formulae of wholes, e.g. why are not the formulae of the semicircles parts of the formula of the circle? It cannot be said, 'because these parts are perceptible things'; for they are not. But perhaps this makes no difference; for even some things which are not

1037ᵃ perceptible must have matter; for there is some matter in everything which is not an essence and a bare form but a 'this'. The semicircles, then, will be parts, not of the universal circle, but of the individual circles, as has been said before; for while one kind of matter is perceptible, there is another which is intelligible.

It is clear also that the soul is the primary substance and the body is   5
matter, and man or animal is the compound of both taken universally; and Socrates or Coriscus, if even the soul of Socrates is Socrates, is taken in two ways (for some mean by such a term the soul, and others mean the concrete thing), but if he is simply this particular soul and this particular body, the individual is analogous to the universal.

Whether there is, apart from the matter of such substances, any   10
other substance, and one should look for some substance other than these, e.g. numbers or something of the sort, must be considered later. For it is for the sake of this that we are trying to determine the nature of perceptible substances, since in a sense the inquiry about perceptible substances is the work of natural science, i.e. of second   15
philosophy; for the natural scientist must not only know about the matter, but also about the substance in the sense of the formula, and even more than about the other. And in the case of definitions, how the elements in the formula are parts of the definition, and why the definition is one formula (for clearly the thing is one, but in virtue of *what* is the thing one, although it has parts?)—this must be considered later.   20

What the essence is and in what sense it is independent, has been stated universally in a way which is true of every case, and also why the formula of the essence of some things contains the parts of the thing defined, while that of others does not; and we have stated that in the formula of the substance the material parts will not be present (for they are not even parts of the substance in that sense, but of the   25
concrete substance; but of this there is in a sense a formula, and in a sense there is not; for there is no formula of it with its matter, for this is indefinite, but there is a formula of it with reference to its primary substance—e.g. in the case of man the formula of the soul—, for the substance is the indwelling form, from which along with the matter the so-called concrete substance is derived; e.g. concavity is a form of this   30
sort, for from this and the nose arise snub nose and snubness); but in the concrete substance, e.g. a snub nose or Callias, the matter also will be present. And we have stated that the essence and the individual thing are in some cases the same; i.e. in the case of primary substances,   1037ᵇ
e.g. curvature and the essence of curvature, if this is primary. (By a primary substance I mean one which does not imply the presence of something in something else, i.e. in a substrate which acts as matter.)

5 But things which are of the nature of matter or of wholes which
include matter, are not the same as their essences, nor are accidental
unities like that of Socrates and musical; for these are the same only by
accident.

CHAPTER 12

Now let us treat first of definition, in so far as we have not treated of it
10 in the *Analytics*; for the problem stated in them is useful for our
inquiries concerning substance. I mean this problem:—wherein
consists the unity of that, the formula of which we call a definition, as
for instance in the case of man, two-footed animal; for let this be the
formula of man. Why, then, is this one, and not many, viz. animal *and*
two-footed? For in the case of 'man' and 'white' there is a plurality
15 when one term does not belong to the other, but a unity when it does
belong and the subject, man, has a certain attribute; for then a unity is
produced and we have the white man. In the present case, on the other
hand, one does not share in the other; the genus is not thought to share
in its differentiae; for then the same thing would share in contraries;
20 for the differentiae by which the genus is divided are contrary. And
even if the genus does share in them, the same argument applies, since
the differentiae present in man are many, e.g. endowed with feet, two-
footed, featherless. Why are these one and not many? Not because
they are present in one thing; for on this principle a unity can be made
out of any set of attributes. But surely all the attributes in the defini-
25 tion *must* be one; for the definition is a single formula and a formula of
substance, so that it must be a formula of some one thing; for substance means a 'one' and a 'this', as we maintain.
We must first inquire about definitions arising out of divisions.
30 There is nothing in the definition except the first-named genus and
the differentiae. The other genera are the first genus and along with
this the differentiae that are taken with it, e.g. the first may be animal,
the next animal which is two-footed, and again animal which is two-
footed and featherless, and similarly if the definition includes more
1038ª terms. And in general it makes no difference whether it includes many
or few terms,—nor, therefore, whether it includes few or simply two;
and of the two the one is differentia and the other genus, e.g. in 'two-
footed animal' 'animal' is genus, and the other is differentia. If then
5 the genus absolutely does not exist apart from the species which it as
genus includes, or if it exists but exists as matter (for the voice is genus

and matter, but its differentiae make the species, i.e. the letters, out of it), clearly the definition is the formula which comprises the differentiae.

But it is also necessary in division to take the differentia of the differentia; e.g. endowed with feet is a differentia of animal; again we must know the differentia of animal endowed with feet *qua* endowed with feet. Therefore we must not say, if we are to speak rightly, that of that which is endowed with feet one part has feathers and one is featherless; if we say this we say it through incapacity; we must divide it into cloven-footed or not-cloven; for these are differentiae in the foot; cloven-footedness is a form of footedness. And we always want to go on so till we come to the species that contain no differences. And then there will be as many kinds of foot as there are differentiae, and the kinds of animals endowed with feet will be equal in number to the differentiae. If then this is so, clearly the *last* differentia will be the substance of the thing and its definition, since it is not right to state the same things more than once in our definitions; for it is superfluous. And this does happen; for when we say 'animal which is endowed with feet, and two-footed' we have said nothing other than 'animal having feet, having two feet'; and if we divide this by the proper division, we shall be saying the same thing many times—as many times as there are differentiae.

If then a differentia of a differentia be taken at each step, one differentia—the last—will be the form and the substance; but if we divide according to accidental qualities, e.g. if we were to divide that which is endowed with feet into the white and the black, there will be as many differentiae as there are processes of division. Therefore it is plain that the definition is the formula which contains the differentiae, or, according to the right method, the last of these. This would be evident, if we were to change the order of such definitions, e.g. that of man, saying 'animal which is two-footed and endowed with feet'; for 'endowed with feet' is superfluous when 'two-footed' has been said. But order is no part of the substance; for how are we to think the one element posterior and the other prior? Regarding the definitions, then, which arise out of divisions, let this much be taken as stated in the first place as to their nature.

CHAPTER 13

1038ᵇ Let us again return to the subject of our inquiry, which is substance. As the substrate and the essence and the compound of these are called substance, so also is the universal. About two of these we have spoken;

5 about the essence and about the substrate, of which we have said that it underlies in two senses, either being a 'this'—which is the way in which an animal underlies its attributes—, or as the matter underlies the complete reality. The universal also is thought by some to be in the fullest sense a cause, and a principle; therefore let us attack the discussion of this point also. For it seems impossible that any universal term should be the name of a substance. For primary substance is that

10 kind of substance which is peculiar to an individual, which does not belong to anything else; but the universal is common, since that is called universal which naturally belongs to more than one thing. Of which individual then will this be the substance? Either of all or of none. But it cannot be the substance of all; and if it is to be the substance of one, this one will be the others also; for things whose substance is one and whose essence is one are themselves also one.

15 Further, substance means that which is not predicable of a subject, but the universal is predicable of some subjects always.

But perhaps the universal, while it cannot be substance in the way in which the essence is so, can be present in this, e.g. animal can be present in man and horse. Then clearly there is a formula of the universal. And it makes no difference even if there is not a formula of

20 everything that is in the substance; for none the less the universal will be the substance of something. Man is the substance of the individual man in whom it is present; therefore the same will happen again, for a substance, e.g. animal, must be the substance of that in which it is present as something peculiar to it. And further it is impossible and absurd that the 'this', i.e. the substance, if it consists of parts, should

25 not consist of substances nor of what is a 'this', but of quality; for that which is not substance, i.e. the quality, will then be prior to substance and to the 'this'. Which is impossible; for neither in formula nor in time nor in coming to be can the affections be prior to the substance; for then they would be separable from it. Further, in Socrates there will be a substance in a substance, so that he will be the substance of

30 two things. And in general it follows, if man and such things are substances, that none of the elements in their formulae is the substance of anything, nor does it exist apart from the species or in

anything else; I mean, for instance, that no animal exists apart from the particular animals, nor does any other of the elements present in formulae exist apart.

If, then, we view the matter from these standpoints, it is plain that no universal attribute is a substance, and this is plain also from the fact 1039ᵃ that no common predicate indicates a 'this', but rather a 'such'. If not, many difficulties follow and especially the 'third man'.

The conclusion is evident also from the following consideration— that a substance cannot consist of substances present in it actually (for things that are thus actually two are never actually one, though if they 5 are *potentially* two, they can be one, e.g. the double line consists of two halves—potentially; for the *actualization* of the halves divides them from one another; therefore if the substance is one, it will not consist of substances present in it); and according to the argument which Democritus states rightly; he says one thing cannot come from two nor 10 two from one; for he identifies his indivisible magnitudes with substances. It is clear therefore that the same will hold good of number, if number is a synthesis of units, as is said by some; for two is either not one, or there is no unit present in it actually.

The consequence of this view involves a difficulty. If no substance can consist of universals because a universal indicates a 'such', not a 15 'this', and if no composite substance can be composed of actual substances, every substance would be incomposite, so that there would not even be a formula of any substance. But it is thought by all and has been previously stated that it is either only, or primarily, substance that can be defined; yet now it seems that not even 20 substance can. There cannot, then, be a definition of anything; or rather in a sense there can be, and in a sense there cannot. And what we say will be plainer from what follows.

CHAPTER 14

It is clear also from these very facts what consequences confront those who say the Ideas are substances and can exist apart, and at the same 25 time make the Form consist of the genus and the differentiae. For if the Forms exist and animal is present in man and horse, it is either one and the same in number, or different. (In formula it is clearly one; for he who states the formula unfolds the same formula in either case.) If there is a man-in-himself who is a 'this' and exists apart, the parts of 30 which he consists, e.g. animal and two-footed, must indicate a 'this' and be things existing apart and substances; therefore animal too must be of this sort.

Now if animal, which is in the horse and in man, is one and the same, as you are one and the same with yourself, how will the one in things that exist apart be one, and how will this animal escape being divided even from itself?

Further, if it is to share in two-footed and many-footed, an impossible conclusion follows; for contrary attributes will belong at the same time to it although it is one and a this. If it does not, what is the relation implied when one says the animal is two-footed or has feet? But perhaps these are put together and are in contact, or are mixed. Yet all these are absurd.

But suppose the Form to be different in each species. Then there will be practically an infinite number of things whose *substance* is animal; for it is not by accident that man has animal for one of its elements. Further, animal-in-itself will be many. For the animal in each species will be the substance of the species; for it is not dependent on anything else; if it were, that other would be an element in man, i.e. would be the genus of man. And further all the elements of which man is composed will be Ideas. Now nothing can be the Idea of one thing and the substance of another; this is impossible. Each, then, of the Ideas present in the species of animals will be the ideal animal. Further, from what will these Ideas be derived; how will they be derived from the ideal animal? Or how can an Idea of animal whose essence is simply animal exist apart from the ideal animal? Further, in the case of sensible things both these consequences and others still more absurd follow. If, then, these consequences are impossible, clearly there are not Forms of sensible things in the sense in which some maintain their existence.

CHAPTER 15

Since substance is of two kinds, the concrete thing and the formula (I mean that one kind of substance is the formula taken with the matter, while another kind is the formula in its generality), substances in the former sense are capable of destruction (for they are capable also of generation), but there is no destruction of the formula in the sense that it is ever in course of being destroyed; for there is no generation of it (the being of house is not generated, but only the being of *this* house), but without generation and destruction formulae are and are not; for it has been shown that no one produces nor makes these. For this reason, also, there is neither definition nor demonstration of sensible individual substances, because they have matter whose nature is such that they are capable both of being and of not being; for which reason all the individual instances of them are destructible. If then demonstration is of necessary truths and definition involves knowledge, and if, just as knowledge cannot be sometimes knowledge and sometimes ignorance, but the state which varies thus is opinion, so too demonstration and definition cannot vary thus, but it is opinion that deals with that which can be otherwise than as it is, clearly there can neither be definition nor demonstration of sensible individuals. For perishing things are obscure to those who have knowledge of them, when they have passed from our perception; and though the formulae remain in the soul unchanged, there will no longer be either definition or demonstration. Therefore when one of those who aim at definition defines any individual, he must recognize that his definition may always be overthrown; for it is not possible to define such things.

Nor is it possible to define any Idea. For the Idea is, as its supporters say, an individual, and can exist apart; and the formula must consist of words; and he who defines must not invent a word (for it would be unknown), but the established words are common to each of a number of things; these then must apply to something besides the thing defined; e.g. if one were defining you, he would say 'an animal which is lean' or 'white', or something else which will apply also to some one other than you. If anyone were to say that perhaps all the attributes taken apart may belong to many subjects, but together they belong only to this one, we must reply firstly that they belong also to both the elements, e.g. two-footed animal belongs to animal and to the two-footed. And where the elements are eternal this is even necessary, since the elements are prior to and parts of the compound; what is more, they can also exist apart, if 'man' can exist apart. For either neither or both can. If, then, neither can, the genus will not exist apart from the species; but if it does, the differentia will also. Secondly, we must reply that they are prior in being; and things which are prior to others are not destroyed when the others are.

Again, if the Ideas consist of Ideas (as they must, since elements are simpler than the compound), it will be further necessary that the elements of which the Idea consists, e.g. animal and two-footed, should be predicated of many subjects. If not, how will they be known? For there will then be an Idea which cannot be predicated of more subjects than one. But this is not thought possible—every Idea is thought to be capable of being shared.

As has been said, then, people do not realize that it is impossible to define in the case of eternal things, especially those which are unique, like the sun or the moon. For they err not only by adding attributes after whose removal the sun would still exist, e.g. 'going round the earth' or 'night-hidden' (for from their view it follows that if it stands still or is visible, it will no longer be the sun; but it is strange if this is so; for the 'sun' means a certain *substance*); but also by the mention of attributes which can belong to another subject; e.g. if another thing with the stated attributes comes into existence, clearly it will be a sun; the formula therefore is general. But the sun was supposed to be an individual, like Cleon or Socrates. Why does not one of the supporters of the Ideas produce a definition of an Idea? It would become clear, if they tried, that what has now been said is true.

CHAPTER 16

Evidently even of the things that are thought to be substances, most are only potentialities,—e.g. the parts of animals (for none of them exists separately; and when they *are* separated, then they too exist, all of them, merely as matter) and earth and fire and air; for none of them is one, but they are like a heap before it is fused by heat and some one thing is made out of the bits. One might suppose especially that the parts of living things and the corresponding parts of the soul are both, i.e. exist both actually and potentially, because they have sources of movement in something in their joints; for which reason some animals live when divided. Yet all the parts must exist only potentially, when they are one and continuous by nature,—not by force or even by growing together, for such a phenomenon is an abnormality.

Since the term 'unity' is used like the term 'being', and the substance of that which is one is one, and things whose substance is numerically one are numerically one, evidently neither unity nor being can be the substance of things, just as being an element or a principle cannot be the substance, but we seek *what* the principle is, that we may refer the thing to something more intelligible. Now of these things being and unity are more substantial than principle or element or cause, but not even the former are substance, since in general nothing that is common is substance; for substance does not belong to anything but to itself and to that which has it, of which it is the substance. Further, that which is one cannot be in many things at the 25 same time, but that which is common is present in many things at the same time; so that clearly no universal exists apart from the individuals.

But those who say the Forms exist, in one respect are right, in saying the Forms exist apart, if they are substances; but in another respect they are not right, because they say the one *in* many is a Form. The reason for their doing this is that they cannot say what are the 30 substances of this sort, the imperishable substances which exist apart from the individual and sensible substances. They make them, then, the same in kind as the perishable things (for this kind of substance we know)—man himself and the horse itself, adding to the sensible things the word 'itself'. Yet even if we had not seen the stars, none the less, I suppose, would there be eternal substances besides those which we 1041ᵃ knew; so that now also if we do not know what eternal substances there are, yet it is doubtless necessary that some should exist. Clearly, then, no universal term is the name of a substance, and no substance is composed of substances. 5

CHAPTER 17

We should say what, and what sort of thing, substance is, taking another starting-point; for perhaps from this we shall get a clear view also of that substance which exists apart from sensible substances. Since, then, substance is a principle and a cause, let us a⎽⎽ck it from this standpoint. The 'why' is always sought in this form—'why does 10 one thing attach to another?' For to inquire why the musical man is a musical man, is either to inquire—as we have said—why the man is musical, or it is something else. Now 'why a thing is itself' is doubtless a meaningless inquiry; for the fact or the existence of the thing must 15 already be evident (e.g. that the moon is eclipsed), but the fact that a thing is itself is the single formula and the single cause in all such questions as why the man is man, or the musical musical, unless one were to say that each thing is inseparable from itself, and its being one just meant this. This, however, is common to all things and is a short and easy way with the question. But we *can* inquire why man is an animal of 20 such and such a nature. Here, then, we are evidently not inquiring why he who is a man is a man. We are inquiring, then, why something is predicable of something; that it is predicable must be clear; for if not, the inquiry is an inquiry into nothing. E.g. why does it thunder?—why

25 is sound produced in the clouds? Thus the inquiry is about the predication of one thing of another. And why are certain things, i.e. stones and bricks, a house? Plainly we are seeking the cause. And this is the essence (to speak abstractly), which in some cases is that for the sake of which, e.g. perhaps in the case of a house or a bed, and in some
30 cases is the first mover; for this also is a cause. But while the efficient cause is sought in the case of genesis and destruction, the final cause is sought in the case of being also.

The object of the inquiry is most overlooked where one term is not
1041ᵇ expressly predicated of another (e.g. when we inquire why man is), because we do not distinguish and do not say definitely 'why do these parts form this whole?' But we must distinguish the elements before we begin to inquire; if not, it is not clear whether the inquiry is significant or unmeaning. Since we must know the existence of the
5 thing and it must be given, clearly the question is *why* the matter is some individual thing, e.g. why are these materials a house? Because that which was the essence of a house is present. And why is this individual thing, or this body in this state, a man? Therefore what we seek is the cause, i.e. the form, by reason of which the matter is some definite thing; and this is the substance of the thing. Evidently, then, in the case of simple things no inquiry nor teaching is possible; but we
10 must inquire into them in a different way.

As regards that which is compounded out of something so that the whole is one—not like a heap, however, but like a syllable,—the syllable is not its elements, *ba* is not the same as *b* and *a*, nor is flesh fire and earth; for when they are dissolved the wholes, i.e. the flesh and
15 the syllable, no longer exist, but the elements of the syllable exist, and so do fire and earth. The syllable, then, is something—not only its elements (the vowel and the consonant) but also something else; and the flesh is not only fire and earth or the hot and the cold, but also something else. Since, then, that something must be either an element
20 or composed of elements, if it is an element the same argument will again apply; for flesh will consist of this and fire and earth and something still further, so that the process will go on to infinity; while if it is a compound, clearly it will be a compound not of one but of many (or else it will itself be that one), so that again in this case we can use the
25 same argument as in the case of flesh or of the syllable. But it would seem that this is something, and not an element, and that it is the cause which makes *this* thing flesh and *that* a syllable. And similarly in all other cases. And this is the substance of each thing; for this is the

primary cause of its being; and since, while some things are not
substances, as many as are substances are formed naturally and by   30
nature, their substance would seem to be this nature, which is not an
element but a principle. An *element* is that into which a thing is divided
and which is present in it as matter, e.g. *a* and *b* are the elements of the
syllable.

BOOK VIII (H)

CHAPTER 1

We must draw our conclusions from what has been said, and sum up   1042ᵃ
our results, and put the finishing touch to our inquiry. We have said
that the causes, principles, and elements of substances are the object   5
of our search. And some substances are recognized by all thinkers, but
some have been advocated by particular schools. Those generally
recognized are the natural substances, i.e. fire, earth, water, air, etc.,
the simple bodies; secondly, plants and their parts, and animals and
the parts of animals; and finally the heavens and the parts of the   10
heavens. Some particular schools say that Forms and the objects of
mathematics are substances. And it follows from our arguments that
there are other substances, the essence and the substratum. Again, in
another way the genus seems more substantial than the species, and
the universal than the particulars. And with the universal and the
genus the Ideas are connected; it is in virtue of the same argument that   15
they are thought to be substances. And since the essence is substance,
and the definition is a formula of the essence, for this reason we have
discussed definition and essential predication. Since the definition is a
formula, and a formula has parts, we had to consider with respect to
the notion of part, what are parts of the substance and what are not,   20
and whether the same things are also parts of the definition. Further,
then, neither the universal nor the genus is a substance; we must
inquire later into the Ideas and the objects of mathematics; for some
say these exist apart from sensible substances.

But now let us resume the discussion of the generally recognized
substances. These are the sensible substances, and sensible sub-   25
stances all have matter. The substratum is substance, and this is in one
sense the matter (and by matter I mean that which, not being a 'this'
actually, is potentially a 'this'), and in another sense the formula or

form (which being a 'this' can be separately formulated), and thirdly
30   the complex of matter and form, which alone is generated and
destroyed, and is, without qualification, capable of separate existence;
for of substances in the sense of formulae some are separable and
some are not.

But clearly matter also is substance; for in all the opposite changes
that occur there is something which underlies the changes, e.g. in
respect of place that which is now here and again elsewhere, and in
35   respect of increase that which is now of one size and again less or
greater, and in respect of alteration that which is now healthy and
1042ᵇ   again diseased; and similarly in respect of substance there is something that is now being generated and again being destroyed, and now
underlies the process as a 'this' and again underlies it as the privation
of positive character. In this last change the others are involved. But in
5   either one or two of the others this is not involved; for it is not
necessary if a thing has matter for change of place that it should also
have matter for generation and destruction.

CHAPTER 2

The difference between becoming in the unqualified sense and
becoming in a qualified sense has been stated in the *Physics*. Since the
substance which exists as substratum and as matter is generally
recognized, and this is that which exists potentially, it remains for us
10   to say what is the substance, in the sense of *actuality*, of sensible things.
Democritus seems to think there are three kinds of difference between
things; the underlying body, the matter, is one and the same, but they
differ either in rhythm, i.e. shape, or in turning, i.e. position, or in
15   inter-contact, i.e order. But evidently there are many differences; for
instance, some things are characterized by the mode of composition of
their matter, e.g. the things formed by mixture, such as honey-water;
and others by being bound together, e.g. a bundle; and others by being
glued together, e.g. a book; and others by being nailed together, e.g. a
casket; and others in more than one of these ways; and others by
20   position, e.g. the threshold and the lintel (for these differ by being
placed in a certain way); and others by time, e.g. dinner and breakfast;
and others by place, e.g. the winds; and others by the affections proper
to sensible things, e.g. hardness and softness, density and rarity,
dryness and wetness; and some things by some of these qualities,
25   others by them all, and in general some by excess and some by defect.

Clearly then the word 'is' has just as many meanings; a thing is a threshold because it lies in such-and-such a position, and its being means its lying in that position, while being ice means having been solidified in such-and-such a way. And the being of some things will be defined by *all* these qualities, because some parts of them are mixed, others are fused, others are bound together, others are solidified, and others possess the other differentiae; e.g. the hand or 30 the foot. We must grasp, then, the kinds of differentiae (for these will be the principles of the being of things), e.g. the things characterized by the more and the less, or by the dense and the rare, and by other such qualities; for all these are characterized by excess and defect. 35 And everything that is characterized by shape or by smoothness and roughness, is determined by the straight and the curved. And for other things their being will mean their being mixed, and their not being will mean the opposite. It is clear then from these facts that if its substance 1043ᵃ is the cause of each thing's being, we must seek in these differentiae the cause of the being of each of these things. Now none of these differentiae is substance, even when coupled with matter, yet in each there is something analogous to substance; and as in substances that 5 which is predicated of the matter is the actuality itself, in all other definitions also it is what most resembles full actuality. E.g. if we had to define a threshold, we should say 'wood or stone in such-and-such a position', and a house we should define as 'bricks and timbers in such-and-such a position' (or we may name that for the sake of which as well in some cases), and if we define ice we say 'water frozen or solidified in such-and-such a way', and harmony is 'such-and-such a blending of 10 high and low'; and similarly in all other cases.

Obviously then the actuality or the formula is different when the matter is different; for in some cases it is the juxtaposition, in others the mixing, and in others some other of the attributes we have named. And so, in defining, those who define a house as stones, bricks, and timbers, are speaking of the potential house, for these are the matter; 15 but those who define it as a covering for bodies and chattels, or add some other similar differentia, speak of the actuality; and those who combine both of these speak of the third kind of substance, which is composed of matter and form. For the formula that gives the differentiae seems to be an account of the form and the actuality, while 20 that which gives the components is rather an account of the matter. And the same is true with regard to the definitions which Archytas used to accept; for they are accounts of the combined form and matter.

E.g. what is still weather? Absence of motion in a large extent of air; air is the matter, and absence of motion is the actuality and substance. What is a calm? Smoothness of sea; the material substratum is the sea, 25 and the actuality or form is smoothness. It is obvious then, from what has been said, what sensible substance is and how it exists—one kind of it as matter, another as form or actuality; while the third kind is that which is composed of these two.

CHAPTER 3

We must not forget that sometimes it is not clear whether a name 30 means the composite substance, or the actuality or form, e.g. whether 'house' is a sign for the composite thing, 'a covering consisting of bricks and stones laid thus and thus', or for the actuality or form, 'a covering', and whether a line is twoness in length or twoness, and whether an animal is a soul in a body or a soul. For soul is the 35 substance or actuality of some body. 'Animal' might indeed be applied to both, not as being defined by one formula, but as being applied by reference to one thing. But this question, while important for another purpose, is of no importance for the inquiry into sensible substance; 1043ᵇ for the essence certainly attaches to the form and the actuality. For soul and to be soul are the same, but to be man and man are not the same, unless indeed the soul is to be called man; and thus on one interpretation the thing is the same as its essence, and on another it is not.

5 If we consider we find that the syllable is not produced by the letters and juxtaposition, nor is the house bricks and juxtaposition. And this is right; for the juxtaposition or mixing is not produced by those things of which it is the juxtaposition or mixing. And the same is true in the other cases, e.g. if the threshold is characterized by its position, the position is not produced by the threshold, but rather the latter is 10 produced by the former. Nor is man animal and biped, but there must be something besides these, if these are matter,—something which is neither an element in the whole nor produced by an element, but is the substance, which people eliminate and state the matter. If then this is the cause of the thing's being, and if the cause of its being is its substance, they cannot be stating the substance itself.

15 This, then, must either be eternal or it must be destructible without being ever in course of being destroyed, and must have come to be without ever being in course of coming to be. But it has been proved

and explained elsewhere that no one makes or generates the form, but it is a 'this' that is made, i.e. the complex of form and matter that is generated. Whether the substances of destructible things can exist apart, is not yet at all clear; except that obviously that is impossible in some cases—in the case of things which cannot exist apart from the individual instances, e.g. house or utensil. Perhaps neither these things themselves, nor any of the other things which are not formed by nature, are substances at all; for one might say that the nature in natural objects is the only substance to be found in destructible things.

Therefore the difficulty which was raised by the school of Antisthenes and other such uneducated people has a certain appropriateness. They argued that the 'what' cannot be defined (for the definition is a lengthy formula); but of what *sort* a thing, e.g. silver, is, they thought it possible to explain, not saying what it is but that it is like tin. Therefore one kind of substance can be defined and formulated, i.e. the composite kind, whether it be the object of sense or of reason; but the primary parts of which this consists cannot be defined, since a definitory formula predicates something of something, and one part of the definition must play the part of matter and the other that of form.

It is also obvious that, if all substances are in a sense numbers, they are so in this sense and not, as some say, as numbers of units. For definition is a sort of number; for it is divisible, and into indivisible parts (for definitory formulae are not infinite), and number also is of this nature. And as, when one of the parts of which a number consists has been taken from or added to the number, it is no longer the same number, but a different one, even if it is the very smallest part that has been taken away or added, so the definition and the essence will no longer remain when anything has been taken away or added. And the number must have something in virtue of which it is one thing, while our opponents cannot say if it is one (for either it is not one but a sort of heap, or if it is, we ought to say what it is that makes one out of many); and the definition is one, but similarly they cannot say what makes *it* one. And this is natural; for the same reason is applicable, and substance is one in the sense which we have explained, and not, as some say, by being a sort of unit or point; each is a complete reality and a definite nature. And as number does not admit of the more and the less, neither does substance, in the sense of form, but if any substance does, it is only the substance which involves matter. Let this then suffice for an account of the generation and destruction of so-called substances—in what sense it is possible and in what sense impossible—and of the reduction of things to number.

CHAPTER 4

15 Regarding material substance we must not forget that even if all things have the same primary constituent or constituents, and if the same matter serves as starting-point for their generation, yet there is a matter proper to each, e.g. the sweet or the fat for phlegm, and the bitter, or something else, for bile; though perhaps these have the same

20 constituent. And there come to be several matters for the same thing, when the one matter is matter for the other, e.g. phlegm comes from the fat and from the sweet, if the fat comes from the sweet; and it comes from bile by analysis of the bile into its ultimate matter. For one thing comes from another in two senses, either because it will be found at a later stage of development, or because it is produced if the other is analysed into its original constituents. When the matter is one,

25 different things may be produced owing to difference in the moving cause, e.g. from wood may be made both a chest and a bed. But *some* different things must have their matter different, e.g. a saw could not be made of wood, nor is this in the power of the moving cause; for it could not make a saw of wool or of wood. But if, as a matter of fact, the

30 same thing can be made of different material, clearly the art, i.e. the moving principle, is the same; for if both the matter and the moving principle were different, the product would be too.

When one inquires what is the cause, one should, as causes are spoken of in several senses, state all the possible causes. E.g what is the material cause of man? The menstrual fluid. What is the moving cause? The *semen*. The formal cause? His essence. The final cause?

1044^b His end. But perhaps the latter two are the same.—We must state the *proximate* causes. What is the material cause? Not fire or earth, but the matter peculiar to the thing.

Regarding *generable* natural substances, *if* the causes are really these and of this number and we have to learn the causes, we must

5 inquire thus, if we are to inquire rightly. But in the case of natural but *eternal* substances another account must be given. For perhaps some have no matter, or not matter of this sort but only such as can be moved in respect of place. Nor does matter belong to those things which exist by nature but are not substances; their substratum is the

10 *substance*. E.g. what is the cause of an eclipse? What is its matter?

There is none; the *moon* is that which suffers eclipse. What is the moving cause which extinguishes the light? The earth. The final cause perhaps does not exist. The formal principle is the definitory formula, but this is obscure if it does not include the cause. E.g. what is eclipse? Deprivation of light. But if we add 'by interposition of the earth', this is the formula which includes the cause. In the case of sleep it is not clear what it is that proximately has this affection. Surely the animal, it will be said. Yes, but the animal in virtue of what, i.e. what is the proximate subject? The heart or some other part. Next, by what is it produced? Next, what is the affection—that of the proximate subject, not of the whole animal? Shall we say that it is immobility of such-and-such a kind? Yes, but to what process in the proximate subject is this due?

CHAPTER 5

Since some things are and are not, without coming to be and ceasing to be, e.g. points, if they can be said to *be*, and in general forms (for it is not white that comes to be, but the wood comes to be white, if everything that comes to be comes from something and comes to be something), not all contraries can come from one another, but it is in different senses that a white man comes from a black man, and white comes from black. Nor has everything matter, but only those things which come to be and change into one another. Those things which, without ever being in course of changing, are or are not, have no matter.

There is difficulty in the question how the matter of each thing is related to its contrary states. E.g. if the body is potentially healthy, and disease is contrary to health, is it potentially both? And is water potentially wine and vinegar? We answer that it is the matter of one in virtue of its positive state and its form, and of the other in virtue of the privation of its positive state and the corruption of it contrary to its nature. It is also hard to say why wine is not said to be the matter of vinegar nor potentially vinegar (though vinegar is produced from it), and why the living man is not said to be potentially dead. In fact they are not, but the corruptions in question are accidental, and it is the matter of the animal that is itself in virtue of its corruption the potency and matter of a corpse, and it is water that is the matter of vinegar. For the one comes from the other as night from day. And *all* things which change thus into one another must be reduced to their matter, e.g. if from a corpse is produced an animal, the corpse is first reduced to its matter, and only then becomes an animal; and vinegar is first reduced to water, and only then becomes wine.

CHAPTER 6

To return to the difficulty which has been stated with respect to definitions and numbers, what is the cause of the unity of each of them? In the case of all things which have several parts and in which the whole is not, as it were, a mere heap, but the totality is something besides the parts, there is a cause of unity; for as regards material things contact is the cause in some cases, and in others viscosity or some other such quality. And a definition is a formula which is one not by being connected together, like the *Iliad*, but by dealing with one object.—What then is it that makes man one; why is he one and not many, e.g. both animal and biped, especially if there are, as some say, an ideal animal and an ideal biped? Why are not those Ideas the ideal man, so that men would exist by participation not in man, nor in one Idea, but in two, animal and biped? And in general man would be not one but more than one thing, animal and biped.

Clearly, then, if people proceed thus in their usual manner of definition and speech, they cannot explain and solve the difficulty. But if, as we say, one element is matter and another is form, and one is potentially and the other actually, the question will no longer be thought a difficulty. For this difficulty is the same as would arise if 'round bronze' were the definition of cloak; for this name would be a sign of the definitory formula, so that the question is, what is the cause of the unity of round and bronze? The difficulty disappears, because the one is matter, the other form. What then is the cause of this—the reason why that which was potentially is actually,—what except, in the case of things which are generated, the agent? For there is no other reason why the potential sphere becomes actually a sphere, but this was the essence of each. Of matter some is the object of reason, some of sense, and part of the formula is always matter and part is actuality, e.g. the circle is a figure which is plane. But of the things which have no matter, either for reason or for sense, each is by its nature essentially a kind of unity, as it is essentially a kind of being—a 'this', a quality, or a quantity. And so neither 'existent' nor 'one' is present in definitions, and an essence is by its very nature a kind of unity as it is a kind of being. This is why none of these has any reason outside itself for being one, nor for being a kind of being; for each is by its nature a kind of being and a kind of unity, not as being in the genus 'being' or 'one' nor in the sense that being and unity can exist apart from particulars.

Owing to the difficulty about unity some speak of participation, and raise the question, what is the cause of participation and what is it to participate; and others speak of communion, as Lycophron says   10 knowledge is a communion of knowing with the soul; and others say life is a composition or connection of soul and body. Yet the same account applies to all cases; for being healthy will be either a communion or a connection or a composition of soul and health, and the fact that the bronze is a triangle will be a composition of bronze and triangle, and the fact that a thing is white will be a composition of   15 surface and whiteness.—The reason is that people look for a unifying formula, and a difference, between potentiality and actuality. But, as has been said, the proximate matter and the form are one and the same thing, the one potentially, the other actually. Therefore to ask the cause of their being one is like asking the cause of unity in general; for   20 each thing is a unity, and the potential and the actual are somehow one. Therefore there is no other cause here unless there is something which caused the movement from potentiality into actuality. And all things which have *no* matter are *without qualification* essentially unities.

BOOK IX (Θ)

CHAPTER 1

We have treated of that which *is* primarily and to which all the other categories of being are referred—i.e. of substance. For it is in virtue of the formula of substance that the others are said to be—quantity and   30 quality and the like; for all will be found to contain the formula of substance, as we said in the first part of our work. And since 'being' is in one way divided into 'what', quality, and quantity, and is in another way distinguished in respect of potentiality and fulfilment, and of function, let us discuss potentiality and fulfilment. First let us explain   35 potentiality in the strictest sense, which is, however, not the most useful for our present purpose. For potentiality and actuality extend further than the mere sphere of motion. But when we have spoken of   1046ᵃ this first kind, we shall in our discussions of actuality explain the other kinds of potentiality.

5   We have pointed out elsewhere that 'potentiality' and the word 'can' have several senses. Of these we may neglect all the potentialities that are so called homonymously. For some are called so by analogy, as in geometry; and we say things can be or cannot be because in some definite way they are or are not.

But all potentialities that conform to the same type are starting-
10   points, and are called potentialities in reference to one primary kind, which is a starting-point of change in another thing or in the thing itself *qua* other. For one kind is a potentiality for being acted on, i.e. the principle in the very thing acted on, which makes it capable of being changed and acted on by another thing or by itself regarded as other; and another kind is a state of insusceptibility to change for the worse and to destruction by another thing or by the thing itself *qua* other, i.e. by a principle of change. In all these definitions is contained
15   the formula of potentiality in the primary sense.—And again these so-called potentialities are potentialities either of acting merely or of being acted on, or of acting or being acted on *well*, so that even in the formulae of the latter the formulae of the prior kinds of potentiality are somehow contained.

Obviously, then, in a sense the potentiality of acting and of being acted on is one (for a thing may be capable either because it can be
20   acted on or because something else can be acted on by it), but in a sense the potentialities are different. For the one is in the thing acted on; it is because it contains a certain motive principle, and because even the matter is a motive principle, that the thing acted on is acted on, one thing by one, another by another; for that which is oily is
25   inflammable, and that which yields in a particular way can be crushed; and similarly in all other cases. But the other potentiality is in the agent, e.g. heat and the art of building are present, one in that which can produce heat and the other in the man who can build. And so in so far as a thing is an organic unity, it cannot be acted on by itself; for it is one and not two different things. And want of potentiality, or power-
30   lessness, is the privation which is contrary to potentiality of this sort, so that every potentiality belongs to the same subject and refers to the same process as a corresponding want of potentiality. Privation has several senses; for it means that which has not a certain quality and that which might naturally have it but has not got it, either in general or when it might naturally have it, and either in some particular way,

e.g. when it *completely* fails to have it, or when it in any degree fails to have it. And in certain cases if things which naturally have a quality lose it by violence, we say they suffer privation. 35

CHAPTER 2

Since some such principles are present in soulless things, and others in things possessed of soul, and in soul and in the rational part of the 1046^b soul, clearly some potentialities will be non-rational and some will be accompanied by reason. This is why all arts, i.e. all productive forms of knowledge, are potentialities; they are principles of change in another thing or in the artist himself considered as other.

And each of those which are accompanied by reason is alike capable 5 of contrary effects, but one non-rational power produces one effect; e.g. the hot is capable only of heating, but the medical art can produce both disease and health. The reason is that science is a rational formula, and the same rational formula explains a thing and its privation, only not in the same way; and in a sense it applies to both, but in a sense it applies rather to the positive fact. Therefore such 10 sciences must deal with contraries, but with one in virtue of their own nature and with the other not in virtue of their nature; for the rational formula applies to one object in virtue of that object's nature, and to the other, in a sense, accidentally. For it is by denial and removal that it explains the contrary; for the contrary is the primary privation, and this is the entire removal of the positive term. Now since on the one 15 hand contraries do not occur in the same thing, but on the other hand science is a potentiality which depends on the possession of a rational formula, and the soul possesses a principle of movement; therefore, on the one hand, the healthy produces only health and what can heat only heat and what can cool only cold, but the scientific man, on the other hand, produces both the contrary effects. For there is a rational formula which applies to both, though not in the same way, and it is in 20 a soul which possesses a principle of movement; so that the soul will start both processes from the same principle, applying them to the same object. And so the things whose potentiality is according to a rational formula act contrariwise to the things whose potentiality is non-rational; for the products of the former are included under one principle, the rational formula.

It is obvious also that the potentiality of merely doing a thing or 25 having it done to one is implied in that of doing it or having it done *well*, but the latter is not always implied in the former; for he who does a thing well must do it, but he who does it merely need not do it well.

CHAPTER 3

There are some who say, as the Megaric school does, that a thing can act only when it is acting, and when it is not acting it cannot act, e.g. he who is not building cannot build, but only he who is building, when he is building; and so in all other cases. It is not hard to see the absurdities that attend this view.

For it is clear that on this view a man will not be a builder unless he is building (for to be a builder is to be able to build), and so with the other arts. If, then, it is impossible to have such arts if one has not at some time learnt and acquired them, and it is then impossible not to have them if one has not sometime lost them (either by forgetfulness or by some accident or by time; for it cannot be by the destruction of the object itself, for that lasts for ever), a man will not have the art when he has ceased to use it, and yet he may immediately build again; how then will he have got the art? And similarly with regard to lifeless things; nothing will be either cold or hot or sweet or perceptible at all if people are not perceiving it; so that the upholders of this view will have to maintain the doctrine of Protagoras. But, indeed, nothing will even have perception if it is not perceiving, i.e. exercising its perception. If, then, that is blind which has not sight though it would naturally have it, when it would naturally have it and when it still exists, the same people will be blind many times in the day—and deaf too.

Again, if that which is deprived of potentiality is incapable, that which is not happening will be incapable of happening; but he who says of that which is incapable of happening that it is or will be will say what is untrue; for this is what incapacity meant. Therefore these views do away with both movement and becoming. For that which stands will always stand, and that which sits will always sit; if it is sitting it will not get up; for that which cannot get up will be incapable of getting up. But we cannot say this, so that evidently potentiality and actuality are different; but these views make potentiality and actuality the same, so that it is no small thing they are seeking to annihilate.

Therefore it is possible that a thing may be capable of being and yet not be, and capable of not being and yet be, and similarly with the other kinds of predicate; it may be capable of walking and yet not walk, or

capable of not walking and yet walk. And a thing is capable of doing something if there is nothing impossible in its having the actuality of that of which it is said to have the capacity. I mean for instance, if a   25
thing is capable of sitting and it is open to it to sit, there will be nothing impossible in its actually sitting; and similarly if it is capable of being moved or moving, or of standing or making to stand, or of being or coming to be, or of not being or not coming to be.

The word 'actuality', which we connect with fulfilment, has, strictly   30
speaking, been extended from movements to other things; for actuality in the strict sense is identified with movement. And so people do not assign movement to non-existent things, though they do assign some other predicates. E.g. they say that non-existent things are objects of thought and desire, but not that they are moved; and this because, while they do not actually exist, they would have to exist actually if they were moved. For of non-existent things some exist potentially;   1047ᵇ
but they do not *exist*, because they do not exist in fulfilment.

CHAPTER 4

If what we have described is the possible or a consequence of the possible, evidently it cannot be true to say 'this is capable of being but will not be',—a view which leads to the conclusion that there is   5
nothing incapable of being. Suppose, for instance, that a man (one who did not understand the meaning of 'incapable of being') were to say that the diagonal of the square is capable of being measured but will not be measured, because a thing may be capable of being or coming to be, and yet not be or be about to be. But from the premisses this necessarily follows, that if we actually suppose that which is not,   10
but is capable of being, to be or to have come to be, there will be nothing impossible in this; but the result *will* be impossible, for the actual measuring of the diagonal is impossible. For the false and the impossible are not the same; that you are standing now is false, but not impossible.

At the same time it is clear that if, when A is, B must be, then, when   15
A is possible, B also must be possible. For if B need not be possible, there is nothing to prevent its not being possible. Now let A be supposed possible. Then, when A is possible, nothing impossible would follow if A were supposed to be; and then B must of course be. But we supposed B to be impossible. Let it be impossible, then. If,   20
then, B is impossible, A also must be so. But A was supposed

possible; therefore *B* also is possible. If, then, *A* is possible, *B* also
will be possible, if they were so related that if *A* is, *B* must be. If, then,
25   *A* and *B* being thus related, *B* is not possible on this condition, *A* and
B will not be related as was supposed. And if when *A* is possible, *B*
must be possible, then if *A* is, *B* must also be. For to say that *B* must
be possible, if *A* is possible, means that if *A* is both at the time when
and in the way in which it was supposed capable of being, *B* also must
30   then and in that way be.

                                   CHAPTER 5

As all potentialities are either innate, like the senses, or come by
practice, like the power of playing the flute, or by learning, like that of
the arts, those which come by practice or by rational formula we must
35   acquire by previous exercise, but this is not necessary with those
which are not of this nature and which imply passivity.
1048ᵃ   Since that which is capable is capable of something and at some
time and in some way—with all the other qualifications which must be
present in the definiton—, and since some things can work according
to a rational formula and their potentialities involve a formula, while
other things are non-rational and their potentialities are non-rational,
and the former potentialities must be in a living thing, while the latter
5   can be both in the living and in the lifeless; as regards potentialities of
the latter kind, when the agent and the patient meet in the way appropriate to the potentiality in question, the one must act and the other be
acted on, but with the former kind this is not necessary. For the non-
rational potentialities are all productive of one effect each, but the
rational produce contrary effects, so that they would produce contrary
effects at the same time; but this is impossible. That which decides,
10   then, must be something else; I mean by this, desire or choice. For
whichever of two things the animal desires decisively, it will do, when
it is in the circumstances appropriate to the potentiality in question
and meets the passive object. Therefore everything which has a
rational potentiality, when it desires that for which it has a potentiality
and in the circumstances in which it has it, must do this. And it has the
15   potentiality in question when the passive object is present and is in a
certain state; if not it will not be able to act. To add the qualification 'if
nothing external prevents it' is not further necessary; for it has the
potentiality in so far as this is a potentiality of acting, and it is this not
in all circumstances but on certain conditions, among which will be

the exclusion of external hindrances; for these are barred by some of
the positive qualifications. And so even if one has a rational wish, or an   20
appetite, to do two things or contrary things at the same time, one
cannot do them; for it is not on these terms that one has the potentiality for them, nor is it a potentiality for doing both at the same time,
since one will do just the things which it is a potentiality for doing.

CHAPTER 6

Since we have treated of the kind of potentiality which is related to   25
movement, let us discuss actuality, what and what sort of thing it is. In
the course of our analysis it will also become clear, with regard to the
potential, that we not only ascribe potentiality to that whose nature it
is to move something else, either without qualification or in some
particular way, but also use the word in another sense, in the pursuit of
which we have discussed these previous senses. Actuality means the   30
existence of the thing, not in the way which we express by 'potentially';
we say that potentially, for instance, a statue of Hermes is in the block
of wood and the half-line is in the whole, because it might be
separated out, and even the man who is not studying we call a man of
science, if he is capable of studying. Otherwise, actually. Our meaning
can be seen in the particular cases by induction, and we must not seek   35
a definition of everything but be content to grasp the analogy,—that as
that which is building is to that which is capable of building, so is the   1048[b]
waking to the sleeping, and that which is seeing to that which has its
eyes shut but has sight, and that which is shaped out of the matter to
the matter, and that which has been wrought to the unwrought. Let
actuality be defined by one member of this antithesis, and the   5
potential by the other. But all things are not said in the *same sense* to
exist actually, but only by analogy—as A is in B or to B, C is in D or to
D; for some are as movement to potentiality, and the others as
substance to some sort of matter.

The infinite and the void and all similar things are said to exist   10
potentially and actually in a different sense from that in which many
other things are said so to exist, e.g. that which sees or walks or is seen.
For of the latter class these predicates can at some time be truly
asserted without qualification; for the seen is so called sometimes
because it is being seen, sometimes because it is capable of being seen.
But the infinite does not exist potentially in the sense that it will ever
actually have separate existence; its separateness is only in knowledge.   15

For the fact that division never ceases to be possible gives the result that this actuality exists potentially, but not that it exists separately.

Since of the actions which have a limit none is an end but all are relative to the end, e.g. the process of making thin is of this sort, and the things themselves when one is making them thin are in movement
20 in this way (i.e. without being already that at which the movement aims), this is not an action or at least not a complete one (for it is not an end); but that in which the end is present is an action. E.g. at the same time we are seeing and have seen, are understanding and have understood, are thinking and have thought: but it is not true that at the same time we are learning and have learnt, or are being cured and have been
25 cured. At the same time we are living well and have lived well, and are happy and have been happy. If not, the process would have had sometime to cease, as the process of making thin ceases: but, as it is, it does not cease; we are living and have lived. Of these processes, then, we must call the one set movements, and the other actualities. For every movement is incomplete—making thin, learning, walking, building;
30 these are movements, and incomplete movements. For it is not true that at the same time we are walking and have walked, or are building and have built, or are coming to be and have come to be—it is a different thing that is being moved and that has been moved, and that is moving and that has moved; but it is the same thing that at the same time has seen and is seeing, or is thinking and has thought. The latter sort of process, then, I call an actuality, and the former a movement.

CHAPTER 7

35 What and what sort of thing the actual is may be taken as explained by these and similar considerations. But we must distinguish when a
1049ᵃ thing is potentially and when it is not; for it is not at any and every time. E.g. is *earth* potentially a man? No—but rather when it has already become *seed*, and perhaps not even then, as not everything can be healed by the medical art or by chance, but there is a certain kind of thing which is capable of it, and only this is potentially healthy. And
5 the definition of that which as a result of *thought* comes to be in fulfilment from having been potentially is that when it has been wished it comes to pass if nothing external hinders it, while the condition on the other side—viz. in that which is healed—is that nothing in it hinders the result. Similarly there is potentially a house, if nothing in the thing acted on—i.e. in the matter—prevents it from becoming a house, and if

there is nothing which must be added or taken away or changed; this is   10
potentially a house, and the same is true of all other things for which
the source of their becoming is external. And in the cases in which the
source of the becoming is in the very thing which suffers change, that
thing is potentially whatever things will be, through itself, if nothing
external hinders it. E.g. the seed is not yet potentially a man; for it
must further undergo a change in a foreign medium. But when
through its own motive principle it has already got such and such   15
attributes, in this state it is already potentially a man; while in the
former state it needs another principle, just as earth is not yet
potentially a statue, for it must change in order to become bronze.

It seems that when we call a thing not something else but 'of' that
something (e.g a casket is not wood but of wood, and wood is not earth   20
but made of earth, and again perhaps in the same way earth is not
something else but made of that something), that something is always
potentially (in the full sense of that word) the thing which comes after
it in this series. E.g. a casket is not earthen nor earth, but wooden; for
wood is potentially a casket and is the matter of a casket, wood in
general of a casket in general, and this particular wood of this
particular casket. And if there is a first thing, which no longer is called   25
after something else, and said to be of it, this is prime matter; e.g. if
earth is airy and air is not fire but fiery, fire then is prime matter, not
being a 'this'. For the subject and substratum differ by being or not
being a 'this'; the substratum of *accidents* is an individual such as a
man, i.e. body and soul, while the accident is something like musical   30
or white. (The subject is called, when music is implanted in it, not
music but musical, and the man is not whiteness but white, and not
ambulation or movement but walking or moving—as in the above
examples of 'of' something.) Wherever this is so, then, the ultimate
subject is a substance; but when this is not so but the predicate is a   35
form or a 'this', the ultimate subject is matter and material substance.
And it is only right that the 'of' something locution should be used
with reference both to the matter and to the accidents; for both are
indeterminates. We have stated, then, when a thing is to be said to be   1049^b
potentially and when it is not.

CHAPTER 8

We have distinguished the various senses of 'prior', and it is clear that
actuality is prior to potentiality. And I mean by potentiality not only   5

that definite kind which is said to be a principle of change in another thing or in the thing itself regarded as other, but in general every principle of movement or of rest. For nature also is in the same genus as potentiality; for it is a principle of movement—not, however, in something else but in the thing itself *qua* itself. To all such potentiality, then, actuality is prior both in formula and in substance; and in time it is prior in one sense, and in another not.

Clearly it is prior in formula; for that which is in the primary sense potential is potential because it is possible for it to become actual, e.g. I mean by 'capable of building' that which can build, and by 'capable of seeing' that which can see, and by 'visible' that which can be seen. And the same account applies to all other cases, so that the formula and the knowledge of the one must precede the knowledge of the other.

In time it is prior in this sense: the actual member of a species is prior to the potential member of the same species, though the individual is potential before it is actual. I mean that the matter and the seed and that which is capable of seeing, which are potentially a man and corn and seeing, but not yet actually so, are prior in time to this particular man who now exists actually, and to the corn and to the seeing subject; but they are posterior in time to other actually existing things, from which they were produced. For from the potential the actual is always produced by an actual thing, e.g. man by man, musician by musician; there is always a first mover, and the mover already exists actually. We have said in our account of substance that everything that is produced is something produced from something and by something, and is the same in species as it.

This is why it is thought impossible to be a builder if one has built nothing or a harpist if one has never played the harp; for he who learns to play the harp learns to play it by playing it, and all other learners do similarly. And thence arose the sophistical quibble, that one who does not know a science will be doing that which is the object of the science; for he who is learning it does not know it. But since, of that which is coming to be, some part must have come to be, and, of that which, in general, is changing, some part must have changed (this is shown in the treatise on movement), he who is learning must, it would seem, know some part of the science. It is surely clear, then, in this way, that the actuality is in this sense also, viz. in order of becoming and of time, prior to the potentiality.

But it is also prior in substance; firstly, because the things that are posterior to becoming are prior in form and in substance, e.g. man is prior to boy and human being to seed; for the one already has its form, and the other has not. Secondly, because everything that comes to be moves towards a principle, i.e. an end. For that for the sake of which a thing is, is its principle, and the becoming is for the sake of the end; and the actuality is the end, and it is for the sake of this that the potentiality is acquired. For animals do not see in order that they may have sight, but they have sight that they may see. And similarly men have the art of building that they may build, and theoretical science that they may theorize; but they do not theorize that they may have theoretical science, except those who are learning by practice; and these do not theorize except in a limited sense, or else they have no need to theorize. Further, matter exists in a potential state, just because it may attain to its form; and when it exists *actually*, then it is in its form.

And the same holds good in cases in which the end is a movement, as well as in all others. Therefore as teachers think they have achieved their end when they have exhibited the pupil at work, so also does nature. For if this is not the case, we shall have Pauson's Hermes over again; for it will be hard to say about the knowledge, as about the statue, whether it is within or without. For the action is the end, and the actuality is the action. And so even the *word* 'actuality' is derived from 'action', and points to the fulfilment.

And while in some cases the exercise is the ultimate thing (e.g. in sight the ultimate thing is seeing, and no other product besides this results from sight), but from some things a product follows (e.g. from the art of building there results a house as well as the act of building), yet none the less the act is in the former case the end and in the latter more of an end than the mere potentiality is. For the act of building is in the thing that is being built, and comes to be—and is—at the same time as the house.

Where, then, the result is something apart from the exercise, the actuality is in the thing that is being made, e.g. the act of building is in the thing that is being built and that of weaving in the thing that is being woven, and similarly in all other cases, and in general the movement is in the thing that is being moved; but when there is no product apart from the actuality, the actuality is in the agents, e.g. the act of seeing is in the seeing subject and that of theorizing in the theorizing subject and the life is in the soul (and therefore well-being also; for it is a certain kind of life). Obviously, therefore, the substance or form is actuality. From this argument it is obvious that actuality is prior in substance to potentiality; and as we have said, one actuality always precedes another in time right back to the actuality of the eternal prime mover.

But actuality is prior in a higher sense also; for eternal things are prior in substance to perishable things, and no eternal thing exists potentially. The reason is this. Every potentiality is at one and the same time a potentiality for the opposite; for, while that which is not capable of being present in a subject cannot be present, everything that is capable of being may possibly not be actual. That, then, which is capable of being may either be or not be; the same thing, then, is capable both of being and of not being. And that which is capable of not being may possibly not be; and that which may possibly not be is perishable, either without qualification, or in the precise sense in which it is said that it possibly may not be, i.e. either in respect of place or quantity or quality; 'without qualification' means 'in substance'. Nothing, then, which is without qualification imperishable is without qualification potentially (though there is nothing to prevent its being potentially in some respect, e.g. potentially of a certain quality or in a certain place); imperishable things, then, exist actually. Nor can anything which is of *necessity* be potential; yet these things are primary; for if these did not exist, nothing would exist. Nor does eternal movement, if there be such, exist potentially; and, if there is an eternal mover, it is not potentially in motion (except in respect of 'whence' and 'whither'; there is nothing to prevent its having matter for this). Therefore the sun and the stars and the whole heaven are ever active, and there is no fear that they may sometime stand still, as the natural philosophers fear they may. Nor do they tire in this activity; for movement does not imply for them, as it does for perishable things, the potentiality for opposites, so that the continuity of the movement should be laborious; for it is that kind of substance which is matter and potentiality, not actuality, that causes this.

Imperishable things are imitated by those that are involved in change, e.g. earth and fire. For these also are ever active; for they have their movement of themselves and in themselves. But the other potentialities, according to the distinction we have drawn above, are all potentialities for opposites; for that which can move another in this way can also move it not in this way, i.e. if it acts according to a rational formula. But the same *non-rational* potentialities can produce opposite results only by their presence or absence.

If, then, there are any entities or substances such as the dialecticians   35
say the Ideas are, there must be something much more scientific than
the Idea of science and something more mobile than the Idea of move-   1051ᵃ
ment; for these will be more of the nature of actualities, while the Ideas
are potentialities for these. Obviously, then, actuality is prior both to
potentiality and to every principle of change.

CHAPTER 9

That the good actuality is better and more valuable than the good
potentiality is evident from the following argument. Everything of   5
which we say that it can do something, is alike capable of contraries,
e.g. that of which we say that it can be healthy is the same as that which
can be ill, and has both potentialities at once; for one and the same
potentiality is a potentiality for health and illness, for rest and motion,
for building and throwing down, for being built and being thrown   10
down. The capacity for contraries is present at the same time; but
contraries cannot be present at the same time, and the actualities also
cannot be present at the same time, e.g. health and illness. Therefore
one of them must be the good, but the capacity is both the contraries
alike, or neither; the actuality, then, is better. And in the case of bad   15
things, the end or actuality must be worse than the potentiality; for
that which can is both contraries alike.

Clearly, then, the bad does not exist apart from bad things; for the
bad is in its nature posterior to the potentiality. And therefore we may
also say that in the things which are from the beginning, i.e. in eternal
things, there is nothing bad, nothing defective, nothing perverted (for   20
perversion is something bad).

It is by actualization also that geometrical relations are discovered;
for it is by dividing the given figures that people discover them. If they
had been already divided, the relations would have been obvious; but as
it is the divisions are present only potentially. Why are the angles of
the triangle equal to two right angles? Because the angles about one
point are equal to two right angles. If, then, the line parallel to the side   25
had been already drawn, the theorem would have been evident to anyone as soon as he saw the figure. Why is the angle in a semicircle in all
cases a right angle? Because if three lines are equal—the two which
form the base, and the perpendicular from the centre—the conclusion
is evident at a glance to one who knows this premiss.

Obviously, therefore, the potentially existing relations are discovered

30   by being brought to actuality (the reason being that thinking is the
actuality of thought); so that potentiality is discovered from
actuality (and therefore it is by an act of construction that people
acquire the knowledge), though the single actuality is later in
generation.

CHAPTER 10

The terms 'being' and 'non-being' are employed firstly with reference
to the categories, and secondly with reference to the potentiality or
1051ᵇ   actuality of these or their opposites, while being and non-being in the
strictest sense are truth and falsity. The condition of this in the objects
is their being combined or separated, so that he who thinks the
separated to be separated and the combined to be combined has the
truth, while he whose thought is in a state contrary to that of the
5   objects is in error. This being so, when is what is called truth or falsity
present, and when is it not? We must consider what we mean by these
terms. It is not because we think that you are white, that you *are* white,
but because you are white we who say this have the truth. If, then,
some things are always combined and cannot be separated, and others
10   are always separated and cannot be combined, while others are
capable either of combination or of separation, being is being
combined and one, and not being is being not combined but more
than one; regarding contingent facts, then, the same opinion or the
same statement comes to be false and true, and it is possible at one
15   time to have the truth and at another to be in error; but regarding
things that cannot be otherwise opinions are not at one time true and
at another false; but the same opinions are always true or always false.

With regard to *incomposites*, what is being or not being, and truth or
falsity? A thing of this sort is not composite, so as to be when it is
compounded, and not to be if it is separated, like the white wood or
20   the incommensurability of the diagonal; nor will truth and falsity be
still present in the same way as in the previous cases. In fact, as truth is
not the same in these cases, so also being is not the same; but truth or
falsity is as follows—contact and assertion are truth (assertion not
being the same as affirmation), and ignorance is non-contact. For it is
25   not possible to be in *error* regarding the question what a thing is, save
in an accidental sense; and the same holds good regarding non-
composite substances (for it is not possible to be in error about them).
And they all exist actually, not potentially; for otherwise they would

come to be and cease to be; but, as it is, being itself does not come to
be (nor cease to be); for if it did it would have to come out of some-   30
thing. About the things, then, which are essences and exist in actuality,
it is not possible to be in error, but only to think them or not to think
them. Inquiry about their 'what' takes the form of asking whether they
are of such-and-such a nature or not.

As regards being in the sense of truth and not being in the sense of
falsity, in one case there is truth if the subject and the attribute are
really combined, and falsity if they are not combined; in the other
case, if the object is existent it exists in a particular way, and if it does
not exist in this way it does not exist at all; and truth means thinking   1052ᵃ
these objects, and falsity does not exist, nor error, but only
ignorance,—and not an ignorance which is like blindness; for blindness is akin to a total absence of the faculty of thinking.

It is evident also that about unchangeable things there can be no
error in respect of time, if we assume them to be unchangeable. E.g. if   5
we suppose that the triangle does not change, we shall not suppose
that at one time its angles are equal to two right angles while at another
time they are not (for that would imply change). It is possible,
however, to suppose that one member of such a class has a certain
attribute and another has not, e.g. while we may suppose that no even
number is prime, we may suppose that some are and some are not. But
regarding a single number not even this form of error is possible; for
we cannot in this case suppose that one instance has an attribute and   10
another has not; but whether our judgement be true or false, it is
implied that the fact is eternal.

BOOK X (I)

CHAPTER I

We have said previously, in our distinction of the various meanings of   1052ᵃ
words, that 'one' has several meanings; while it is used in many senses,   15
the things that are primarily and of their own nature and not accidentally called one may be summarized under four heads. (1) There is the
continuous, either in general, or especially that which is continuous by
nature and not by contact nor by bonds; and of these, those thing have   20
more unity and are prior, whose movement is more indivisible and
simpler. (2) That which is a whole and has a certain shape and form is

one in a still higher degree; and especially if a thing is of this sort by nature, and not by force like the things which are unified by glue or nails or by being tied together, i.e. if it has in itself something which is the cause of its continuity. A thing is of this sort because its movement is one and indivisible in place and time; so that evidently if a thing has by nature a principle of movement that is of the first kind (i.e. local movement) and the first in that kind (i.e. circular movement), this is in the primary sense one extended thing. The things, then, which are in this way one are either continuous or whole, and the other things that are one are those whose formula is one. Of this sort are the things the thought of which is one, i.e. those the thought of which is indivisible; and it is indivisible if the thing is indivisible in kind or in number. (3) In number, then, the individual is indivisible, and (4) in kind, that which in intelligibility and in knowledge is indivisible, so that that which causes substances to be one must be one in the primary sense. 'One', then, has all these meanings—the naturally continuous, the whole, the individual, and the universal. And all these are one because in some cases the movement, in others the thought or the formula, is indivisible.

But it must be observed that the questions, what sort of things are said to be one, and on the other hand what it is to be one and what is the formula of it, should not be assumed to be the same. 'One' has all these meanings, and each of those things to which one of these kinds of unity belongs will be one; but 'to be one' will sometimes mean being one of these things, and sometimes something else, which is even nearer to the *word* 'one', while these things approximate to its force. This is also true of 'element' or 'cause', if one had both to specify the things of which it is predicable and to give the definition of the word. For in a sense fire is an element (and doubtless 'the indefinite' or something else of the sort is by its own nature an element), but in a sense it is not; for it is not the same thing to be fire and to be an element, but while as a particular thing with a nature of its own fire is an element, the name 'element' means that it has this attribute, that there is something which is made of it as a primary constituent. And so with 'cause' and 'one' and all such terms. For this reason to be one is to be indivisible (being essentially a 'this' and capable of existing apart either in place or in form or thought); or perhaps to be whole and indivisible; but it is especially to be the first measure of a kind, and above all of quantity; for it is from this that it has been extended to the other categories. For measure is that by which quantity is known; and quantity *qua* quantity is known either by a 'one' or by a number, and all number is known by a 'one'. Therefore all quantity *qua* quantity is known by the one, and that by which quantities are primarily known is the one itself; and so the one is the starting-point of number *qua* number. And hence in the other classes too 'measure' means that by which each is first known, and the measure of each is a 'one'—in length, in breadth, in depth, in weight, in speed. (Weight and speed are common to both contraries; for each of them has two meanings,— 'weight' means both that which has any amount of gravity and that which has an excess of gravity, and 'speed' both that which has any amount of movement and that which has an excess of movement; for even the slow has a certain speed and the light a certain weight.)

In all these, then, the measure and starting-point is something one and indivisible, since even in lines we treat as indivisible the line a foot long. For everywhere we seek as the measure something one and indivisible; and this is that which is simple either in quality or in quantity. Now where it is thought impossible to take away or to add, there the measure is exact. Hence that of number is most exact; for we posit the unit as absolutely indivisible; and in all other cases we imitate this sort of measure. For in the case of a furlong or a talent or of anything large any addition or subtraction might more easily escape our notice than in the case of something smaller; so that the first thing from which, as far as our perception goes, nothing can be subtracted, all men make the measure, whether of liquids or of solids, whether of weight or of size; and they think they know the quantity when they know it by means of this measure. And they know movement too by the simple movement and the quickest; for this occupies least time. And therefore in astronomy a 'one' of this sort is the starting-point and measure (for they assume the movement of the heavens to be uniform and the quickest, and judge the others by reference to it), and in music the quarter-tone (because it is the least interval) and in speech the letter. And all these are one in this sense—not that 'one' is something predicable in the same sense of all of these, but in the sense we have mentioned.

But the measure is not always one in number—sometimes there are several; e.g. the quarter-tones (not to the ear, but as determined by the ratios) are two, and the articulate sounds by which we measure are more than one, and the diagonal of the square and its side are measured by two quantities, and so are all spatial magnitudes. Thus, then, the one is the measure of all things, because we come to know

the elements in the substance by dividing the things either in respect
20   of quantity or in respect of kind. The one is indivisible just because the
first of each class of things is indivisible. But it is not in the same way
that every 'one' is indivisible, e.g. a foot and a unit; the latter is
absolutely indivisible, while the former must be placed among things
which are undivided in perception, as has been said already,—for
doubtless every continuous thing is divisible.

The measure is always homogeneous with the thing measured; the
25   measure of spatial magnitudes is a spatial magnitude, and in particular
that of length is a length, that of breadth a breadth, that of articulate
sounds an articulate sound, that of weight a weight, that of units a unit.
(For we must state the matter so, and not say that the measure of
numbers is a number; we ought indeed to say this if we were to use the
corresponding form of·words, but the supposition does not really
correspond—it is as if one supposed that the measure of units is units,
30   and not a unit, for a number is a plurality of units.)

Knowledge also, and perception, we call the measure of things, for
the same reason, because we know something by them,—while as a
matter of fact they are measured rather than measure other things. But
it is with us as if someone else measured us and we came to know how
big we are by seeing that he applied the cubit-measure a certain
number of times to us. But Protagoras says man is the measure of all
1053ᵇ   things, meaning really the man who knows or the man who perceives,
and these because they have respectively knowledge and perception,
which we say are the measures of objects. They are saying nothing,
then, while appearing to be saying something remarkable. Evidently,
then, being one in the strictest sense, if we define it according to the
5   meaning of the word, is a measure, and especially of quantity, and
secondly of quality. And some things will be one if they are indivisible
in quantity, and others if they are indivisible in quality; therefore that
which is one is indivisible, either absolutely or *qua* one.

CHAPTER 9

1058ᵃ   One might raise the question, why woman does not differ from man in
30   species, female and male being contrary, and their difference being a
contrariety; and why a female and a male animal are not different in
species, though this difference belongs to animal in virtue of its own
nature, and not as whiteness or blackness does; both female and male
belong to it *qua* animal. This question is almost the same as the ques-

tion why one contrariety makes things different in species and another   35
does not, e.g. 'with feet' and 'with wings' do, but whiteness and blackness do not. Perhaps it is because the former are modifications
peculiar to the genus, and the latter are less so. And since one element
is formula and one is matter, contrarieties which are in the formula
make a difference in species, but those which are in the compound   1058ᵇ
material thing do not make one. Therefore whiteness in a man, or
blackness, does not make one, nor is there a difference in species
between the white man and the black man, not even if each of them be   5
denoted by one word. For man plays the part of matter, and matter
does not create a difference; for it does not make individual men
species of man, though the flesh and the bones of which this man and
that man consist are other. The compound thing is other, but not other
in species, because in the formula there is no contrariety, and man is
the ultimate indivisible kind. Callias is formula together with matter;   10
white man, then, is so also, because Callias is white; man, then, is
white only incidentally. Nor do a brazen and a wooden circle differ in
species; and if a brazen triangle and a wooden circle differ in species,
it is not because of the matter, but because there is a contrariety in the
formula. But does the matter not make things other in species, when it   15
is other in a certain way, or is there a sense in which it does? For why is
this horse other than this man in species, although their matter is
included with their formulae? Doubtless because there is a contrariety
in the *formula*. For while there is a contrariety also between white man
and black horse, and it is a contrariety in species, it does not depend
on the whiteness of the one and the blackness of the other, since even   20
if both had been white, yet they would have been other in species. And
male and female are indeed modifications peculiar to animal, not
however in virtue of its substance but in the matter, i.e. the body. This
is why the same seed becomes female or male by being acted on in a
certain way. We have stated, then, what it is to be other in species, and
why some things differ in species and others do not.   25

BOOK XII (Λ)

CHAPTER 1

Substance is the subject of our inquiry; for the principles and the   1069ᵃ
causes we are seeking are those of substances. For if the universe is of

20 the nature of a whole, substance is its first part; and if it coheres by virtue of succession, on this view also substance is first, and is succeeded by quality, and then by quantity. At the same time these latter are not even beings in the unqualified sense, but are quantities and movements—or else even the not-white and the not-straight would be; at least we say even these *are*, e.g. 'there is a not-white'. Further, none of the others can exist apart. And the old philosophers 25 also in effect testify to this; for it was of substance that they sought the principles and elements and causes. The thinkers of the present day tend to rank universals as substances (for genera are universals, and these they tend to describe as principles and substances, owing to the abstract nature of their inquiry); but the old thinkers ranked particular things as substances, e.g. fire and earth, but not what is common to both, body.

30   There are three kinds of substance—one that is sensible (of which one subdivision is eternal and another is perishable, and which all recognize, as comprising e.g. plants and animals)—of this we must grasp the elements, whether one or many; and another that is immovable, and this certain thinkers assert to be capable of existing apart, some dividing it into two, others combining the Forms and the objects 35 of mathematics into one class, and others believing only in the mathematical part of this class. The former two kinds of substance are 1069ᵇ the subject of natural science (for they imply movement); but the third kind belongs to another science, if there is no principle common to it and to the other kinds.

Sensible substance is changeable. Now if change proceeds from 5 opposites or from intermediate points, and not from all opposites (for the voice is not-white) but from the contrary, there must be something underlying which changes into the contrary state; for the contraries do not change.

CHAPTER 2

Further, something persists, but the contrary does not persist; there is then, some third thing besides the contraries, viz. the matter. Now since changes are of four kinds—either in respect of the essence or of the quality or of the quantity or of the place, and change in respect of 10 the 'this' is simple generation and destruction, and change in quantity is increase and diminution, and change in respect of an affection is alteration, and change in place is motion, changes will be from given states into those contrary to them in these several respects. The matter, then, which changes must be capable of both states. And since things are said to be in two ways, everything changes from that which is potentially to that which is actually, e.g. from the potentially white to the actually white, and similarly in the case of increase and diminution. Therefore not only can a thing come to be, incidentally, out of that which is not, but also all things come to be out of that which is, but is potentially, and is not actually. And this is the 'One' of Anaxagoras; for instead of 'all things were together' and the 'Mixture' of Empedocles and Anaximander and the account given by Democritus, it is better to say all things were together potentially but not actually. Therefore these thinkers seem to have had some notion of matter.

Now all things that change have matter, but different matter; and of eternal things those which are not generable but are movable in space have matter—not matter for generation, however, but for motion from one place to another.

(One might raise the question from what sort of non-being generation proceeds; for things are said not to be in three ways.)

If, then, a thing exists potentially, still it is not potentially any and every thing, but different things come from different things; nor is it satisfactory to say that all things were together; for they differ in their matter, since otherwise why did an infinity of things come to be, and not one thing? For Reason is one, so that if matter also is one, that must have come to be in actuality which the matter was in potentiality. The causes and the principles, then, are three, two being the pair of contraries of which one is formula and form and the other is privation, and the third being the matter.

CHAPTER 3

Next we must observe that neither the matter nor the form comes to be—i.e. the proximate matter and form. For everything that changes is something and is changed by something and into something. That by which it is changed is the primary mover; that which is changed, the matter; that into which it is changed, the form. The process, then, will go on to infinity, if not only the bronze comes to be round but also the round or the bronze comes to be; therefore there must be a stop at some point.

Next we must observe that each substance comes into being out of something synonymous. (Natural objects and other things are substances.) For things come into being either by art or by nature or by chance or by spontaneity. Now art is a principle of movement in something other than the thing moved, nature is a principle in the thing itself (for man begets man), and the other causes are privations of these two.

There are three kinds of substance—the matter, which is a 'this' by 10 being perceived (for all things that are characterized by contact and not by organic unity are matter and substratum); the nature, a 'this' and a state that it moves towards; and again, thirdly, the particular substance which is composed of these two, e.g. Socrates or Callias. Now in some cases the 'this' does not exist apart from the composite substance, e.g. the form of house does not so exist, unless the art of 15 building exists apart (nor is there generation and destruction of these forms, but it is in another way that the house apart from its matter, and health, and all things of art, exist and do not exist); but if it does it is only in the case of natural objects. And so Plato was not far wrong when he said that there are as many Forms as there are kinds of natural things (if there are Forms at all),—though not of such things as 20 fire, flesh, head; for all these are matter, and the last matter is the matter of that which is in the fullest sense substance. The moving causes exist as things preceding the effects, but causes in the sense of formulae are simultaneous with their effects. For when a man is healthy, then health also exists; and the shape of a bronze sphere exists at the same time as the bronze sphere. But we must examine whether 25 any form also survives afterwards. For in some cases this may be so, e.g. the soul may be of this sort—not all soul but the reason; for doubtless it is impossible that *all* soul should survive. Evidently then there is no necessity, on this ground at least, for the existence of the Ideas. For man is begotten by man, each individual by an individual; 30 and similarly in the arts; for the medical art is the formula of health.

CHAPTER 4

The causes and the principles of different things are in a sense different, but in a sense, if one speaks universally and analogically, they are the same for all. For we might raise the question whether the principles and elements are different or the same for substances and for relatives, and similarly in the case of each of the categories. But it is 35 paradoxical that they should be the same for all. For then from the same elements will proceed relatives and substances. What then will

this common element be? For there is nothing common to and distinct   1070^b
from substance and the other things which are predicated; but the
element is prior to the things of which it is an element. But again
substance is not an element of relatives, nor is any of these an element
of substance. Further, how can all things have the same elements? For
none of the elements can be the same as that which is composed of the   5
elements, e.g. *b* or *a* cannot be the same as *ba*. (None, therefore, of the
intelligibles, e.g. unity or being, is an element; for these are predicable
of each of the compounds as well.) None of the elements then would
be either a substance or a relative; but it must be one or other. All
things then have not the same elements.

Or, as we put it, in a sense they have and in a sense they have not;   10
e.g. perhaps the elements of perceptible bodies are, as *form*, the hot,
and in another sense the cold, which is the *privation*; and, as *matter*,
that which directly and of itself is potentially these; and both these are
substances and also the things composed of these, of which these are
the principles (i.e. any unity which is produced out of the hot and the
cold, e.g. flesh or bone); for the product must be different from the   15
elements. These things then have the same elements and principles,
but different things have different elements; and if we put the matter
thus, all things have not the same elements, but analogically they have;
i.e. one might say that there are three principles—the form, the
privation, and the matter. But each of these is different for each class,
e.g. in colour they are white, black, and surface. Again, there is light,   20
darkness, and air; and out of these are produced day and night.

Since not only the elements present in a thing are causes, but also
something external, i.e. the moving cause, clearly while principle and
element are different both are causes, and principle is divided into
these two kinds; and that which moves a thing or makes it rest is a
principle and a substance. Therefore analogically there are three   25
elements, and four causes and principles; but the elements are
different in different things, and the primary moving cause is different
for different things. Health, disease, body; the moving cause is the
medical art. Form, disorder of a particular kind, bricks; the moving
cause is the building art. And since the moving cause in the case of
natural things is for man (e.g.) man, and in the products of thought it is   30
the form or its contrary, there are in a sense three causes, while in a
sense there are four. For the medical art is in some sense health, and
the building art is the form of the house, and man begets man; further,
besides these there is that which as first of all things moves all things.   35

CHAPTER 5

Some things can exist apart and some cannot, and it is the former that
1071ᵃ are substances. And therefore all things have the same causes,
because, without substances, affections and movements do not exist.
Further, these causes will probably be soul and body, or reason and
desire and body.

And in yet another way, analogically identical things are principles,
5 i.e. actuality and potency; but these also are not only different for
different things but also apply in different senses to them. For in some
cases the same thing exists at one time actually and at another
potentially, e.g. wine or flesh or man. (And these too fall under the
above-named causes. For the form exists actually, if it can exist apart,
and so does the complex of form and matter, and the privation, e.g.
10 darkness or the diseased. But the matter exists potentially; for this is
that which can become both the actual things.) But the distinction of
actuality and potentiality applies differently to cases where the matter
is not the same, in which cases the form also is not the same but
different; e.g. the cause of man is the elements in man (viz. fire and
earth as matter, and the peculiar form), and the external cause,
15 whatever it is, e.g. the father, and besides these the sun and its oblique
course, which are neither matter nor form nor privation nor of the
same species with man, but moving causes.

Further, one must observe that some causes can be expressed in
universal terms, and some cannot. The primary principles of all things
are the actual primary 'this' and another thing which exists potentially.
The universal causes, then, of which we spoke do not *exist*. For the
20 *individual* is the source of the individuals. For while man is the cause
of man universally, there *is* no universal man; but Peleus is the cause
of Achilles, and your father of you, and this particular *b* of this
particular *ba*, though *b* in general is the cause of *ba* taken without
qualification.

Again, if the causes of substances are causes of everything, still
25 different things have different causes and elements, as was said; the
causes of things that are not in the same class, e.g. of colours, sounds,
substances, and quantities, are different except in an analogical sense;
and those of things in the same species are different, not in species,
but in the sense that the causes of different individuals are different,
your matter and form and moving cause being different from mine,
while in their universal formula they are the same. And if we inquire

what are the principles or elements of substances and relations and   30
qualities—whether they are the same or different, clearly when the
terms 'principle' and 'element' are used in several senses the principles and elements of all are the same, but when the senses are distinguished the causes are not the same but different, except that in a
special sense the causes of all are the same. They are in a special sense
the same, i.e. by analogy, because matter, form, privation, and the
moving cause are common to all things; and the causes of substances
may be treated as causes of all things in this sense, that when they are
removed all things are removed; further, that which is first in respect   35
of fulfilment is the cause of all things. But in another sense there are
different first causes, viz. all the contraries which are neither stated as
classes nor spoken of in several ways; and, further, the matters of
different things are different. We have stated, then, what are the prin-   1071ᵇ
ciples of sensible things and how many they are, and in what sense
they are the same and in what sense different.

CHAPTER 6

Since there were three kinds of substance, two of them natural and one
unmovable, regarding the latter we must assert that it is necessary that
there should be an eternal unmovable substance. For substances are   5
the first of existing things, and if they are all destructible, all things are
destructible. But it is impossible that movement should either come
into being or cease to be; for it must always have existed. Nor can time
come into being or cease to be; for there could not be a before and an
after if time did not exist. Movement also is continuous, then, in the
sense in which time is; for time is either the same thing as movement   10
or an attribute of movement. And there is no continuous movement
except movement in place, and of this only that which is circular is
continuous.

But if there is something which is capable of moving things or
acting on them, but is not actually doing so, there will not be movement; for that which has a capacity need not exercise it. Nothing, then,
is gained even if we suppose eternal substances, as the believers in the
Forms do, unless there is to be in them some principle which can   15
cause movement; and even this is not enough, nor is another
substance besides the Forms enough; for if it does not *act*, there will
be no movement. Further, even if it acts, this will not be enough, if its
substance is potentiality; for there will not be *eternal* movement; for

that which is potentially may possibly not be. There must, then, be
20   such a principle, whose very substance is actuality. Further, then,
these substances must be without matter; for they must be eternal, at
least if anything else is eternal. Therefore they must be actuality.

Yet there is a difficulty; for it is thought that everything that acts is
able to act, but that not everything that is able to act acts, so that the
potentiality is prior. But if this is so, nothing at all will exist; for it is
25   possible for things to be capable of existing but not yet to exist. Yet if
we follow the mythologists who generate the world from night, or the
natural philosophers who say that all things were together, the same
impossible result ensues. For how will there be movement, if there is
30   no actual cause? Matter will surely not move itself—the carpenter's art
must act on it; nor will the menstrual fluids nor the earth set themselves in motion, but the seeds and the semen must act on them.

This is why some suppose eternal actuality—e.g. Leucippus and
Plato; for they say there is always movement. But why and what this
movement is they do not say, nor, if the world moves in this way or
that, do they tell us the cause of its doing so. Now nothing is moved at
35   random, but there must always be something present, e.g. as a matter
of fact a thing moves in one way by nature, and in another by force or
through the influence of thought or something else. Further, what sort
of movement is primary? This makes a vast difference. But again
Plato, at least, cannot even say what it is that he sometimes supposes
1072ᵃ   to be the source of movement—that which moves itself; for the *soul* is
later, and simultaneous with the heavens, according to his account. To
suppose potentiality prior to actuality, then, is in a sense right, and in a
sense not; and we have specified these senses.

5   That actuality is prior is testified by Anaxagoras (for his Reason is
actuality) and by Empedocles in his doctrine of love and strife, and by
those who say that there is always movement, e.g. Leucippus.

Therefore chaos or night did not exist for an infinite time, but the
same things have always existed (either passing through a cycle of
changes or in some other way), since actuality is prior to potentiality.
If, then, there is a constant cycle, something must always remain,
10   acting in the same way. And if there is to be generation and destruction, there must be something else which is always acting in different
ways. This must, then, act in one way in virtue of itself, and in another
in virtue of something else—either of a third agent, therefore, or of the
first. But it must be in virtue of the first. For otherwise this again
15   causes the motion both of the third agent and of the second. Therefore

it is better to say the first. For it was the cause of eternal movement; and something else is the cause of variety, and evidently both together are the cause of eternal variety. This, accordingly, is the character which the motions actually exhibit. What need then is there to seek for other principles?

CHAPTER 7

Since this is a possible account of the matter, and if it were not true, the world would have proceeded out of night and 'all things together' and out of non-being, these difficulties may be taken as solved. There is, then, something which is always moved with an unceasing motion, which is motion in a circle; and this is plain not in theory only but in fact. Therefore the first heavens must be eternal. There is therefore also something which moves them. And since that which is moved and moves is intermediate, there is a mover which moves without being moved, being eternal, substance, and actuality. And the object of desire and the object of thought move in this way; they move without being moved. The primary objects of desire and of thought are the same. For the apparent good is the object of appetite, and the real good is the primary object of wish. But desire is consequent on opinion rather than opinion on desire; for the thinking is the starting-point. And thought is moved by the object of thought, and one side of the list of opposites is in itself the object of thought; and in this, substance is first, and in substance, that which is simple and exists actually. (The one and the simple are not the same; for 'one' means a measure, but 'simple' means that the thing itself has a certain nature.) But the good, also, and that which is in itself desirable are on this same side of the list; and the first in any class is always best, or analogous to the best.

That that for the sake of which is found among the unmovables is shown by making a distinction; for that for the sake of which is both that *for* which and that *towards* which, and of these the one is unmovable and the other is not. Thus it produces motion by being loved, and it moves the other moving things. Now if something is moved it is capable of being otherwise than as it is. Therefore if the actuality of the heavens is primary motion, then in so far as they are in motion, in *this* respect they are capable of being otherwise,—in place, even if not in substance. But since there is something which moves while itself unmoved, existing actually, this can in no way be otherwise

20

25

30

35

1072^b

5

than as it is. For motion in space is the first of the kinds of change, and motion in a circle the first kind of spatial motion; and this the first mover *produces*. The first mover, then, of necessity exists; and in so far as it is necessary, it is good, and in this sense a first principle. For the necessary has all these senses—that which is necessary perforce because it is contrary to impulse, that without which the good is impossible, and that which cannot be otherwise but is *absolutely* necessary.

On such a principle, then, depend the heavens and the world of nature. And its life is such as the best which we enjoy, and enjoy for but a short time. For it is ever in this state (which we cannot be), since its actuality is also pleasure. (And therefore waking, perception, and thinking are most pleasant, and hopes and memories are so because of their reference to these.) And thought in itself deals with that which is best in itself, and that which is thought in the fullest sense with that which is best in the fullest sense. And thought thinks itself because it shares the nature of the object of thought; for it becomes an object of thought in coming into contact with and thinking its objects, so that thought and object of thought are the same. For that which is *capable* of receiving the object of thought, i.e. the substance, is thought. And it is *active* when it *possesses* this object. Therefore the latter rather than the former is the divine element which thought seems to contain, and the act of contemplation is what is most pleasant and best. If, then, God is always in that good state in which we sometimes are, this compels our wonder; and if in a better this compels it yet more. And God *is* in a better state. And life also belongs to God; for the actuality of thought is life, and God is that actuality; and God's essential actuality is life most good and eternal. We say therefore that God is a living being, eternal, most good, so that life and duration continuous and eternal belong to God; for this *is* God.

Those who suppose, as the Pythagoreans and Speusippus do, that supreme beauty and goodness are not present in the beginning, because the beginnings both of plants and of animals are *causes*, but beauty and completeness are in the *effects* of these, are wrong in their opinion. For the seed comes from other individuals which are prior and complete, and the first thing is not seed but the complete being, e.g. we must say that before the seed there is a man,—not the man produced from the seed, but another from whom the seed comes.

It is clear then from what has been said that there is a substance which is eternal and unmovable and separate from sensible things. It has been shown also that this substance cannot have any magnitude, but is without parts and indivisible. For it produces movement through infinite time, but nothing finite has infinite power. And, while every magnitude is either infinite or finite, it cannot, for the above reason, have finite magnitude, and it cannot have infinite magnitude 10 because there is no infinite magnitude at all. But it is also clear that it is impassive and unalterable; for all the other changes are posterior to change of place. It is clear, then, why the first mover has these attributes.

CHAPTER 8

We must not ignore the question whether we have to suppose one such substance or more than one, and if the latter, how many; we must 15 also mention, regarding the opinions expressed by others, that they have said nothing that can even be clearly stated about the number of the substances. For the theory of Ideas has no special discussion of the subject; for those who believe in Ideas say the Ideas are numbers, and they speak of numbers now as unlimited, now as limited by the 20 number 10; but as for the reason why there should be just so many numbers, nothing is said with any demonstrative exactness.

We however must discuss the subject, starting from the presuppositions and distinctions we have mentioned. The first principle or primary being is not movable either in itself or accidentally, but produces the primary eternal and single movement. And since that 25 which is moved must be moved by something, and the first mover must be in itself unmovable, and eternal movement must be produced by something eternal and a single movement by a single thing, and since we see that besides the simple spatial movement of the universe, which we say the first and unmovable substance produces, there are 30 other spatial movements—those of the planets—which are eternal (for the body which moves in a circle is eternal and unresting; we have proved these points in the *Physics*), each of *these* movements also must be caused by a substance unmovable in itself and eternal. For the nature of the stars is eternal, being a kind of substance, and the mover 35 is eternal and prior to the moved, and that which is prior to a substance must be a substance. Evidently, then, there must be substances which are of the same number as the movements of the stars, and in their nature eternal, and in themselves unmovable, and without magnitude, for the reason before mentioned. 1073^{b}

That the movers are substances, then, and that one of these is first and another second according to the same order as the movements of the stars, is evident. But in the number of movements we reach a problem which must be treated from the standpoint of that one of the mathematical sciences which is most akin to philosophy—viz. of astronomy; for this science speculates about substance which is perceptible but eternal, but the other mathematical sciences, i.e. arithmetic and geometry, treat of no substance. That the movements are more numerous than the bodies that are moved, is evident to those who have given even moderate attention to the matter, for each of the planets has more than one movement. But as to the actual number of these movements, we now—to give some notion of the subject—quote what some of the mathematicians say, that our thought may have some definite number to grasp; but, for the rest, we must partly investigate for ourselves, partly learn from other investigators, and if those who study this subject form an opinion contrary to what we have now stated, we must esteem both parties indeed, but follow the more accurate.

Eudoxus supposed that the motion of the sun or of the moon involves, in either case, three spheres, of which the first is the sphere of the fixed stars, and the second moves in the circle which runs along the middle of the zodiac, and the third in the circle which is inclined across the breadth of the zodiac; but the circle in which the moon moves is inclined at a greater angle than that in which the sun moves. And the motion of the planets involves, in each case, four spheres, and of these also the first and second are the same as the first two mentioned above (for the sphere of the fixed stars is that which moves all the other spheres, and that which is placed beneath this and has its movement in the circle which bisects the zodiac is common to all), but the *poles* of the third sphere of each planet are in the circle which bisects the zodiac, and the motion of the fourth sphere is in the circle which is inclined at an angle to the equator of the third sphere; and the poles of the third sphere are different for the other planets, but those of Venus and Mercury are the same.

Callippus made the position of the spheres the same as Eudoxus did, but while he assigned the same number as Eudoxus did to Jupiter and to Saturn, he thought two more spheres should be added to the sun and two to the moon, if we were to explain the phenomena, and one more to each of the other planets.

1074ª   But it is necessary, if all the spheres combined are to explain the phenomena, that for each of the planets there should be other spheres (one fewer than those hitherto assigned) which counteract those already mentioned and bring back to the same position the first sphere of the star which in each case is situated below the star in question; for only thus can all the forces at work produce the motion of the planets. Since, then, the spheres by which the planets themselves are moved are eight and twenty-five, and of these only those by which the lowest-situated planet is moved need not be counteracted, the spheres which counteract those of the first two planets will be six in number, and the spheres which counteract those of the next four planets will be sixteen, and the number of all the spheres—those which move the planets and those which counteract these—will be fifty-five. And if one were not to add to the moon and to the sun the movements we mentioned, all the spheres will be forty-nine in number.

Let this then be taken as the number of the spheres, so that the unmovable substances and principles may reasonably be taken as just so many; the assertion of *necessity* must be left to more powerful thinkers.

If there can be no spatial movement which does not conduce to the moving of a star, and if further every being and every substance which is immune from change and in virtue of itself has attained to the best must be considered an end, there can be no other being apart from these we have named, but this must be the number of the substances. For if there are others, they will cause change as being an end of movement; but there *cannot* be other movements besides those mentioned. And it is reasonable to infer this from a consideration of the bodies that are moved; for if everything that moves is for the sake of that which is moved, and every movement belongs to something that is moved, no movement can be for the sake of itself or of another movement, but all movements must be for the sake of the stars. For if a movement is to be for the sake of a movement, this latter also will have to be for the sake of something else; so that since there cannot be an infinite regress, the end of every movement will be one of the divine bodies which move through the heaven.

Evidently there is but one heaven. For if there are many heavens as there are many men, the moving principles, of which each heaven will have one, will be one in form but in number many. But all things that are many in number have matter. (For one and the same formula applies to *many* things, e.g. the formula of man; but Socrates is *one*.) But the primary essence has not matter; for it is fulfilment. So the

unmovable first mover is one both in formula and in number; therefore also that which is moved always and continuously is one alone;
therefore there is one heaven alone.

1074ᵇ Our forefathers in the most remote ages have handed down to us
their posterity a tradition, in the form of a myth, that these substances
are gods and that the divine encloses the whole of nature. The rest of
the tradition has been added later in mythical form with a view to the
5 persuasion of the multitude and to its legal and utilitarian expediency;
they say these gods are in the form of men or like some of the other
animals, and they say other things consequent on and similar to these
which we have mentioned. But if we were to separate the first point
from these additions and take it alone—that they thought the first
substances to be gods—we must regard this as an inspired utterance,
10 and reflect that, while probably each art and science has often been
developed as far as possible and has again perished, these opinions
have been preserved like relics until the present. Only thus far, then, is
the opinion of our ancestors and our earliest predecessors clear to us.

CHAPTER 9

15 The nature of the divine thought involves certain problems; for while
thought is held to be the most divine of phenomena, the question what
it must be in order to have that character involves difficulties. For if it
thinks nothing, what is there here of dignity? It is just like one who
sleeps. And if it thinks, but this depends on something else, then (as
that which is its substance is not the act of thinking, but a capacity) it
20 cannot be the best substance; for it is through thinking that its value
belongs to it. Further, whether its substance is the faculty of thought
or the act of thinking, what does it think? Either itself or something
else; and if something else, either the same always or something
different. Does it matter, then, or not, whether it thinks the good or
any chance thing? Are there not some things about which it is
25 incredible that it should think? Evidently, then, it thinks that which is
most divine and precious, and it does not change; for change would be
change for the worse, and this would be already a movement. First,
then, if it is not the act of thinking but a capacity, it would be reasonable to suppose that the continuity of its thinking is wearisome to it.
30 Secondly, there would evidently be something else more precious
than thought, viz. that which is thought. For both thinking and the act
of thought will belong even to one who has the worst of thoughts.

Therefore if this ought to be avoided (and it ought, for there are even some things which it is better not to see than to see), the act of thinking cannot be the best of things. Therefore it must be itself that thought thinks (since it is the most excellent of things), and its thinking is a thinking on thinking.

But evidently knowledge and perception and opinion and under- 35 standing have always something else as their object, and themselves only by the way. Further, if thinking and being thought are different, in respect of which does goodness belong to thought? For being an act of thinking and being an object of thought are not the same. We answer that in some cases the knowledge is the object. In the productive 1075ᵃ sciences (if we abstract from the matter) the substance in the sense of essence, and in the theoretical sciences the formula or the act of think-ing, *is* the object. As, then, thought and the object of thought are not different in the case of things that have not matter, they will be the same, i.e. the thinking will be one with the object of its thought.

A further question is left—whether the object of the thought is 5 composite; for if it were, thought would change in passing from part to part of the whole. We answer that everything which has not matter is indivisible. As human thought, or rather the thought of composite objects, is in a certain period of time (for it does not possess the good at this moment or at that, but its best, being something *different* from it, is attained only in a whole period of time), so throughout eternity is the thought which has *itself* for its object. 10

CHAPTER 10

We must consider also in which of two ways the nature of the universe contains the good or the highest good, whether as something separate and by itself, or as the order of the parts. Probably in both ways, as an army does. For the good is found both in the order and in the leader, and more in the latter; for he does not depend on the order but it depends on him. And all things are ordered together somehow, but 15 not all alike,—both fishes and fowls and plants; and the world is not such that one thing has nothing to do with another, but they are connected. For all are ordered together to one end. (But it is as in a house, where the freemen are least at liberty to act as they will, but all things or most things are already ordained for them, while the slaves 20 and the beasts do little for the common good, and for the most part live at random; for this is the sort of principle that constitutes the nature of each.) I mean, for instance, that all must at least come to be dissolved into their elements, and there are other functions similarly in which all share for the good of the whole.

25   We must not fail to observe how many impossible or paradoxical results confront those who hold different views from our own, and what are the views of the subtler thinkers, and which views are attended by fewest difficulties. All make all things out of contraries. But neither 'all things' nor 'out of contraries' is right; nor do they tell
30   us how the things in which the contraries are present can be made out of the contraries; for contraries are not affected by one another. Now for us this difficulty is solved naturally by the fact that there is a third factor. These thinkers however make one of the two contraries matter; this is done for instance by those who make the unequal matter for the equal, or the many matter for the one. But this also is refuted in the same way; for the matter which is one is contrary to nothing. Further,
35   all things, except the one, will, on the view we are criticizing, partake of evil; for the bad is itself one of the two elements. But the other school does not treat the good and the bad even as principles; yet in all things the good is in the highest degree a principle. The school we first mentioned is right in saying that it is a principle, but *how* the good is a
1075ᵇ   principle they do not say—whether as end or as mover or as form.

Empedocles also has a paradoxical view; for he identifies the good with love. But this is a principle both as mover (for it brings things together) and as matter (for it is part of the mixture). Now even if it happens that the same thing is a principle both as matter and as
5   mover, still *being* them is not the same. In which respect then is love a principle? It is paradoxical also that strife should be imperishable; strife is for him the nature of the bad.

Anaxagoras makes the good a motive principle; for thought moves things, but moves them for the sake of something, which must be some-
10   thing other than it, except according to *our* way of stating the case; for the medical art *is* in a sense health. It is paradoxical also not to suppose a contrary to the good, i.e. to thought. But all who speak of the contraries make no use of the contraries, unless we bring their views into shape. And why some things are perishable and others imperishable, no one tells us; for they make all existing things out of the same
15   principles. Further, some make existing things out of the non-existent; and others to avoid the necessity of this make all things one.

Further, why should there always be becoming, and what is the cause of becoming?—this no one tells us. And those who suppose two principles must suppose another, a superior principle, and so must those who believe in the Forms; for why did things come to participate, or why do they participate, in the Forms? And all other thinkers are confronted by the necessary consequence that there is something contrary to Wisdom, i.e. to the highest knowledge; but *we* 20 are not. For there is nothing contrary to that which is primary (for all contraries have matter and are potentially); and the ignorance which is contrary would lead us to a contrary object; but what is primary has no contrary.

Again, if besides sensible things no others exist, there will be no first principle, no order, no becoming, no heavenly bodies, but each prin- 25 ciple will have a principle before it, as in the account of the mythologists and all the natural philosophers. But if the Forms or the numbers are to exist, they will be causes of nothing; or if not that, at least not of movement.

Further, how is extension, i.e. a continuum, to be produced out of unextended parts? For number will not, either as mover or as form, 30 produce a continuum. But again there cannot be any contrary that is also a productive or moving principle; for it would be possible for it not to be. Or at least its action would be posterior to its capacity. The world then would not be eternal. But it is; one of these premises, then, must be denied. And we have said how this must be done. Further, in virtue of what the numbers, or the soul and the body, or in general the 35 form and the thing, are one—of this no one tells us anything; nor can any one tell, unless he says, as we do, that the mover makes them one. And those who say mathematical number is first and go on to generate one kind of substance after another and give different principles for each, make the substance of the universe a series of episodes (for one 1076ᵃ substance has no influence on another by its existence or nonexistence), and they give us many principles; but the world must not be governed badly. 'The rule of many is not good; let there be one ruler' (Homer, *Iliad* II 204).

BOOK XIII (M)

CHAPTER 4

As for mathematical objects, then, so much must suffice—that they 1078ᵇ really exist and the way in which they really exist, and the way in which they are prior and that in which they are prior. Now as regards Forms, we must first examine just the theory of the Form, not connecting it at 10 all with the nature of numbers, but just as the people who first said that there were Forms understood it at the outset.

The theory of Forms occurred to the people who stated it because as regards truth they were convinced by the Heraclitean arguments that all perceptible things are always in flux, so that if there is to be 15 knowledge of anything, or understanding, there must be some other, permanent kinds of thing over and above perceptible things, because there is no knowledge of things in flux.

Now Socrates gave his attention to virtues of character, and tried in connection with them to give general definitions. He was the first to do so, for among the natural scientists Democritus touched on this 20 only slightly and defined the hot and the cold, after a fashion, while the Pythagoreans had already done so in the case of a few things whose definitions they reduced to numbers, e.g. what opportunity is, or the just, or marriage. But it was natural for Socrates to try to find what a thing is, because he was trying to reason formally, and the starting-point of formal reasoning is what a thing is. For at that time there was 25 not yet the dialectical power to enable people to consider opposites apart from what a thing is, and whether the same branch of knowledge deals with contraries; for there are just two things one might fairly ascribe to Socrates, arguments from particular to general, and general definitions, both being concerned with the starting-point of knowl-30 edge.—Well, Socrates did not take the universals to be separate, nor the definitions, but *they* [the Platonists] made them separate, and called such entities Forms.

So it followed for them almost by the same argument that there are Forms of everything to which we apply general terms, rather as if someone who wanted to count things thought that he would not be 35 able to do so while there were only a few, but made more before counting them. For the Forms are, one may say, more numerous than 1079ª perceptible particulars (though it was in seeking causes for the latter that they went on from them to Forms), because in each case there is, over and above the real objects, something else with the same name, both for things around us and for eternal things.

5   Besides, none of the ways of proving that there are Forms is decisive. Some do not logically imply their conclusion; others produce Forms of things of which they do not think there are Forms. According to the arguments from the branches of knowledge there will be

Forms of everything of which there is a branch of knowledge; according to the One over Many there will be Forms even of negations; according to the Thought of what Perished there will be Forms of perishable things, since we have a kind of image of them. Besides, among the most precise arguments some produce Forms of relatives, of which they deny that there is an independent class, and others involve the Third Man. Altogether, the arguments for Forms do away with things whose existence the believers in Forms put before the existence of Forms; for the result is that it is not the two that is primary but number, and the relative prior to that, the relative being prior to the independent—not to mention all the ways in which people who have followed up the theory of Forms contradict the principles.

Besides, given their argument for the existence of Forms, there will be Forms not only of actual objects but of many other things too, because there is a single concept not only for a real object but also in the case of things that are not objects, and there are branches of knowledge for things other than objects. And thousands of other such problems result. By necessity and according to the theory, if Forms can be participated in then there must be Forms only of real objects, since they are not participated in accidentally; a Form must be participated in in so far as it is not said of a subject. I mean, for example, if something participates in the original Double, the same thing participates in eternal, but only accidentally, since the Double is, accidentally, eternal. So Forms will be real objects. But the same terms signify being an object yonder as do so here. Otherwise what will be the point of saying that there is something over and above these objects (the One over Many)? If Forms and particulars have the same form, there will be something common (for why is two one and the same in the case of perishable twos and of the many but eternal twos, any more than in the case of the original Two and a particular two?). But if the form is not the same, they will be merely homonymous, as if one were to call Callias and a block of wood 'man', having observed nothing in common between them.

If we are to suppose that in other respects the common definitions fit the Forms, for instance, plane figure and the other parts of the definition in the case of the original Circle, but that *what it is* must be added, then we should consider whether this is not completely vacuous. To what will it be added, to centre or to plane, or to all of them? All the elements in its reality are Forms, e.g. animal and two-footed. Besides, clearly there will have to be such a thing as Original,

10 just like plane, some sort of entity which will be present in all the
Forms as their genus.

CHAPTER 5

Most of all one might puzzle over what on earth Forms contribute
either to eternal perceptible objects or to those that come into being
and pass away. They are not causes of movement, nor of any change in
15 them.

But neither are they any help toward knowledge of the other things
(they are not their reality, or they would have been in them) nor
towards their being what they are, not being present in their
participants. If they were, they might perhaps seem to be causes, as
white is of a thing's being white, by being mixed in. But this account,
20 given first by Anaxagoras and later by Eudoxus in his discussions, and
by some others, is very simple to upset; it is easy to collect many
absurdities against such a theory.

But nor can other things come 'from' the Forms in any ordinary way
of speaking.

25 Saying that they are paradigms and that other things participate in
them is vacuous, use of poetic metaphor. What is it that works looking
towards the Forms?

And anything can both exist and come into existence without having
been copied from something else, so that someone like Socrates could
come into being whether Socrates exists or not; and clearly it is the
30 same even if Socrates were eternal.

And there will be several paradigms (and so Forms) of the same
thing, e.g. Animal and Two-footed will be paradigms of man, at the
same time as the original Man.

Besides, Forms are paradigms not only of perceptible things but
also of themselves, e.g. the genus is the paradigm of the forms of the
35 genus. So the same thing will be both paradigm and likeness.

Besides, it would seem impossible for a thing's reality to exist
separately from the thing whose reality it is; so how could Forms exist
1080ᵃ separately, if they are the reality of things?

In the *Phaedo* it is put this way: Forms are causes both of being and
of coming into being. Yet even if Forms exist there is still no coming
into being unless there is something to start things moving; and many
5 other things come into being, like a house or a ring, of which they say
there are no Forms. So clearly those things of which they do say there

are Forms can also be and come into being because of causes like those of things just mentioned, and not because of Forms.

So as regards Forms one can collect many objections like those considered, both in this way and by more formal and precise argu- 10 ments.

CHAPTER 10

Let us now discuss an issue which contains a problem both for those 1086ᵇ who believe in Forms and for those who do not, and has already been mentioned at the start in the *Discussion of Problems*. If one does not take 15 real objects to be separate, in the way in which individual existing things are said to be separate, one will do away with reality as we want to describe it. But if one does take real objects to be separate, how is one to take their elements and principles?

(*a*) If they are individual and not universal, then (i) there will be as 20 many existing things as elements, and (ii) the elements will not be knowable.

(i) Suppose syllables in speech are real objects and their elements [letters] are elements of real objects. Then there must be only one *BA* and one of each other syllable, since they are not universal and the same in form; each is one in number and a particular and not the same 25 in name as any other. (Besides, they do take it that the original is in each case one.) But if this is true of the syllables, it is true of their letters [elements]; so there will not be more than one *A*, nor more than one of any letter [element], by the same argument which shows that there cannot be more than one of the same syllable. But if this is the 30 case, there will be nothing else existing over and above the elements, only the elements.

(ii) Again, the elements will not be knowable, because they are not universal, while knowledge is of universals. This is clear from proofs and definitions; we cannot validly reason that this triangle has its angles equal to two right angles, unless every triangle has its angles equal to two right angles; nor that this man is an animal, unless every 35 man is an animal.

(*b*) But if the principles *are* universal, either the real objects that come from them are universal, or objects that are not real will be prior 1087ᵃ to those that are. For a universal is not a real object, but an element or principle is universal, and an element or principle is prior to the things whose element or principle it is.

All this, then, is a natural result when they make Forms out of
5   elements and also claim that there is a single separate entity over and
above the real objects that have the same form. But there is nothing to
stop there being many *A*s and *B*s (as with elements of speech) without
there being an original *A* and an original *B* over and above the many;
and if so then as far as this is concerned there will be infinitely many
similar syllables.

10   The fact that all knowledge is universal, so that the principles of
existing things must be universal and not separate real objects,
contains the greatest problem among those mentioned, but none the
less the statement is true in one way but not in another. Knowledge,
15   like knowing, is of two kinds, one potential, one actual. Potentiality,
being (as matter) universal and indefinite, is of what is universal and
indefinite, but actuality, being definite, is of something definite, and
being individual, is of an individual. It is only incidentally that sight
20   sees universal colour, because this individual colour which it sees is *a*
colour; and the grammarian's object of study, this individual *A*, is *an*
A. If principles must be universal, so must what comes from them be
universal, just as in proofs; but if this is so nothing will be separate or a
25   real object. Anyway clearly knowledge is in one way universal and in
another not.

Practical Philosophy

NICOMACHEAN ETHICS*

BOOK I

CHAPTER 1

Every art and every inquiry, and similarly every action and choice, is   1094ᵃ
thought to aim at some good; and for this reason the good has rightly
been declared to be that at which all things aim. But a certain difference
is found among ends; some are activities, others are products apart from
the activities that produce them. Where there are ends apart from the
actions, it is the nature of the products to be better than the activities.   5
Now, as there are many actions, arts, and sciences, their ends also are
many; the end of the medical art is health, that of shipbuilding a vessel,
that of strategy victory, that of economics wealth. But where such arts
fall under a single capacity—as bridle-making and the other arts con-   10
cerned with the equipment of horses fall under the art of riding, and this
and every military action under strategy, in the same way other arts fall
under yet others—in all of these the ends of the master arts are to be
preferred to all the subordinate ends; for it is for the sake of the former   15
that the latter are pursued. It makes no difference whether the activities
themselves are the ends of the actions, or something else apart from the
activities, as in the case of the sciences just mentioned.

CHAPTER 2

If, then, there is some end of the things we do, which we desire for its
own sake (everything else being desired for the sake of this), and if we do
not choose everything for the sake of something else (for at that rate the   20
process would go on to infinity, so that our desire would be empty and
vain), clearly this must be the good and the chief good. Will not the
knowledge of it, then, have a great influence on life? Shall we not, like
archers who have a mark to aim at, be more likely to hit upon what we
should? If so, we must try, in outline at least, to determine what it is, and   25

Translation: W. D. Ross (and J. O. Urmson), revised J. Barnes (Revised Oxford
Aristotle, 1984); *Text*: I. Bywater (Oxford Classical Texts, 1894).

of which of the sciences or capacities it is the object. It would seem to belong to the most authoritative art and that which is most truly the master art. And politics appears to be of this nature; for it is this that ordains which of the sciences should be studied in a state, and which 1094^b each class of citizens should learn and up to what point they should learn them; and we see even the most highly esteemed of capacities to fall under this, e.g. strategy, economics, rhetoric; now, since politics 5 uses the rest of the sciences, and since, again, it legislates as to what we are to do and what we are to abstain from, the end of this science must include those of the others, so that this end must be the good for man. For even if the end is the same for a single man and for a state, that of the state seems at all events something greater and more complete both to attain and to preserve; for though it is worth while to attain the end 10 merely for one man, it is finer and more godlike to attain it for a nation or for city-states. These, then, are the ends at which our inquiry, being concerned with politics, aims.

CHAPTER 3

Our discussion will be adequate if it has as much clearness as the subject-matter admits of; for precision is not to be sought for alike in all discussions, any more than in all the products of the crafts. Now fine and just actions, which political science investigates, exhibit much 15 variety and fluctuation, so that they may be thought to exist only by convention, and not by nature. And goods also exhibit a similar fluctuation because they bring harm to many people; for before now men have been undone by reason of their wealth, and others by reason of their courage. We must be content, then, in speaking of such subjects and 20 with such premises to indicate the truth roughly and in outline, and in speaking about things which are only for the most part true and with premises of the same kind to reach conclusions that are no better. In the same spirit, therefore, should each of our statements be *received*; for it is the mark of an educated man to look for precision in each class of 25 things just so far as the nature of the subject admits: it is evidently equally foolish to accept probable reasoning from a mathematician and to demand from a rhetorician demonstrative proofs.

Now each man judges well the things he knows, and of these he is a good judge. And so the man who has been educated in a subject is a good 1095^a judge of that subject, and the man who has received an all-round education is a good judge in general. Hence a young man is not a proper hearer of lectures on political science; for he is inexperienced in the actions that occur in life, but its discussions start from these and are about these; and, further, since he tends to follow his passions, his study will be vain and unprofitable, because the end aimed at is not knowledge 5 but action. And it makes no difference whether he is young in years or youthful in character; the defect does not depend on time, but on his living and pursuing each successive object as passion directs. For to such persons, as to the incontinent, knowledge brings no profit; but to those who desire and act in accordance with a rational principle 10 knowledge about such matters will be of great benefit.

These remarks about the student, the way in which out statements should be received, and the purpose of the inquiry, may be taken as our preface.

CHAPTER 4

Let us resume our inquiry and state, in view of the fact that all knowledge and choice aims at some good, what it is that we say political 15 science aims at and what is the highest of all goods achievable by action. Verbally there is very general agreement; for both the general run of men and people of superior refinement say that it is happiness, and identify living well and faring well with being happy; but with regard to what happiness is they differ, and the many do not give the same 20 account as the wise. For the former think it is some plain and obvious thing, like pleasure, wealth, or honour; they differ, however, from one another—and often even the same man identifies things, with health when he is ill, with wealth when he is poor; but, conscious of their ignor- 25 ance, they admire those who proclaim some great thing that is above their comprehension. Now some thought that apart from these many goods there is another which is good in itself and causes the goodness of all these as well. To examine all the opinions that have been held would no doubt be somewhat fruitless: it is enough to examine those that are most prevalent or that seem to have some reason in their favour. 30

Let us not fail to notice, however, that there is a difference between arguments from and those to the first principles. For Plato, too, was right in raising this question and asking, as he used to do, 'are we on the way from or to the first principles?' There is a difference, as there is in a racecourse between the course from the judges to the turning-point and 1095^{b} the way back. For, while we must begin with what is familiar, things are so in two ways—some to us, some without qualification. Presumably, then, *we* must begin with things familiar to *us*. Hence anyone who is to listen intelligently to lectures about what is noble and just and, generally, about the subjects of political science must have been brought up in good habits. For the facts are the starting-point, and if they are sufficiently plain to him, he will not need the reason as well; and the man who has been well brought up has or can easily get starting-points. And as for him who neither has nor can get them, let him hear the words of Hesiod:

Far best is he who knows all things himself;
Good, he that hearkens when men counsel right;
But he who neither knows, nor lays to heart
Another's wisdom, is a useless wight.

CHAPTER 5

Let us, however, resume our discussion from the point at which we digressed. To judge from the lives that men lead, most men, and men of the most vulgar type, seem (not without some reason) to identify the good, or happiness, with pleasure; which is the reason why they love the life of enjoyment. For there are, we may say, three prominent types of life—that just mentioned, the political, and thirdly the contemplative life. Now the mass of mankind are evidently quite slavish in their tastes, preferring a life suitable to beasts, but they get some reason for their view from the fact that many of those in high places share the tastes of Sardanapallus. But people of superior refinement and of active disposition identify happiness with honour; for this is, roughly speaking, the end of the political life. But it seems too superficial to be what we are looking for, since it is thought to depend on those who bestow honour rather than on him who receives it, but the good we divine to be something of one's own and not easily taken from one. Further, men seem to pursue honour in order that they may be assured of their merit; at least it is by men of practical wisdom that they seek to be honoured, and among those who know them, and on the ground of their excellence; clearly, then, according to them, at any rate, excellence is better. And perhaps one might even suppose this to be, rather than honour, the end of the political life. But even this appears somewhat incomplete; for possession of excellence seems actually compatible with being asleep, or with lifelong inactivity, and, further, with the greatest sufferings and misfortunes; but a man who was living so no one would call happy, unless he were maintaining a thesis at all costs. But enough of this; for the subject has been sufficiently treated even in ordinary discussions. Third comes the contemplative life, which we shall consider later.   5

The life of money-making is one undertaken under compulsion, and wealth is evidently not the good we are seeking; for it is merely useful and for the sake of something else. And so one might rather take the aforenamed objects to be ends; for they are loved for themselves. But it is evident that not even these are ends—although many arguments have been thrown away in support of them. Let us then dismiss them.   10

CHAPTER 6

We had perhaps better consider the universal good and discuss thoroughly what is meant by it, although such an inquiry is made an uphill one by the fact that the Forms have been introduced by friends of our own. Yet it would perhaps be thought to be better, indeed to be our duty, for the sake of maintaining the truth even to destroy what touches us closely, especially as we are philosophers; for, while both are dear,   15
piety requires us to honour truth above our friends.

The men who introduced this doctrine did not posit Ideas of classes within which they recognized priority and posteriority (which is the reason why they did not maintain the existence of an Idea embracing all numbers); but things are called good both in the category of substance and in that of quality and in that of relation, and that which is *per se*, i.e.   20
substance, is prior in nature to the relative (for the latter is like an off-shoot and accident of what is); so that there could not be a common Idea set over all these goods. Further, since things are said to be good in as many ways as they are said to be (for things are called good both in the category of substance, as God and reason, and in quality, e.g. the virtues,   25
and in quantity, e.g. that which is moderate, and in relation, e.g. the useful, and in time, e.g. the right opportunity, and in place, e.g. the right locality and the like), clearly the good cannot be something universally present in all cases and single; for then it would not have been predicated in all the categories but in one only. Further, since of the things answering to one Idea there is one science, there would have been   30
one science of all the goods; but as it is there are many sciences even of the things that fall under one category, e.g. of opportunity (for opportunity in war is studied by strategy and in disease by medicine), and the moderate in food is studied by medicine and in exercise by the science of gymnastics. And one might ask the question, what in the

world they *mean* by 'a thing itself', if in man himself and in a particular
1096ᵇ man the account of man is one and the same. For in so far as they are
men, they will in no respect differ; and if this is so, neither will there be a
difference in so far as they are good. But again it will not be good any the
more for being eternal, since that which lasts long is no whiter than that
which perishes in a day. The Pythagoreans seem to give a more
5 plausible account of the good, when they place the one in the column of
goods; and it is they that Speusippus seems to have followed.

   But let us discuss these matters elsewhere; an objection to what we
have said, however, may be discerned in the fact that the Platonists have
10 not been speaking about *all* goods, and that the goods that are pursued
and loved for themselves are called good by reference to a single Form,
while those which tend to produce or to preserve these somehow or to
prevent their contraries are called so by reference to these, and in a
different sense. Clearly, then, goods must be spoken of in two ways, and
some must be good in themselves, the others by reason of these. Let us
15 separate, then, things good in themselves from things useful, and
consider whether the former are called good by reference to a single
Idea. What sort of goods would one call good in themselves? Is it those
that are pursued even when isolated from others, such as intelligence,
sight, and certain pleasures and honours? Certainly, if we pursue these
also for the sake of something else, yet one would place them among
20 things good in themselves. Or is nothing other than the Idea good in
itself? In that case the Form will be empty. But if the things we have
named are also things good in themselves, the account of the good will
have to appear as something identical in them all, as that of whiteness is
identical in snow and in white lead. But of honour, wisdom, and
pleasure, just in respect of their goodness, the accounts are distinct and
25 diverse. The good, therefore, is not something common answering to
one Idea.

   But then in what way are things called good? They do not seem to be
like the things that only chance to have the same name. Are goods one,
then, by being derived from one good or by all contributing to one good,
or are they rather one by analogy? Certainly as sight is in the body, so is
reason in the soul, and so on in other cases. But perhaps these subjects
30 had better be dismissed for the present; for perfect precision about them
would be more appropriate to another branch of philosophy. And
similarly with regard to the Idea; even if there is some one good which is
universally predicable of goods or is capable of separate and independent existence, clearly it could not be achieved or attained by

man; but we are now seeking something attainable. Perhaps, however, someone might think it worth while to have knowledge of it with a view to the goods that *are* attainable and achievable; for having this as a sort of pattern we shall know better the goods that are good for us, and if we know them shall attain them. This argument has some plausibility, but seems to clash with the procedure of the sciences; for all of these, though they aim at some good and seek to supply the deficiency of it, leave on one side the knowledge of *the* good. Yet that all the exponents of the arts should be ignorant of, and should not even seek, so great an aid is not probable. It is hard, too, to see how a weaver or a carpenter will be benefited in regard to his own craft by knowing this 'good itself', or how the man who has viewed the Idea itself will be a better doctor or general thereby. For a doctor seems not even to study health in this way, but the health of man, or perhaps rather the health of a particular man; for it is individuals that he is healing. But enough of these topics.

1097ᵃ

CHAPTER 7

Let us again return to the good we are seeking, and ask what it can be. It seems different in different actions and arts; it is different in medicine, in strategy, and in the other arts likewise. What then is the good of each? Surely that for whose sake everything else is done. In medicine this is health, in strategy victory, in architecture a house, in any other sphere something else, and in every action and choice the end; for it is for the sake of this that all men do whatever else they do. Therefore, if there is an end for all that we do, this will be the good achievable by action, and if there are more than one, these will be the goods achievable by action.

So the argument has by a different course reached the same point; but we must try to state this even more clearly. Since there are evidently more than one end, and we choose some of these (e.g. wealth, flutes, and in general instruments) for the sake of something else, clearly not all ends are complete ends; but the chief good is evidently something complete. Therefore, if there is only one complete end, this will be what we are seeking, and if there are more than one, the most complete of these will be what we are seeking. Now we call that which is in itself worthy of pursuit more complete than that which is worthy of pursuit for the sake of something else, and that which is never desirable for the sake of something else more complete than the things that are desirable both in themselves and for the sake of that other thing, and therefore we call complete without qualification that which is always desirable in itself and never for the sake of something else.

Now such a thing happiness, above all else, is held to be; for this we choose always for itself and never for the sake of something else, but honour, pleasure, reason, and every excellence we choose indeed for themselves (for if nothing resulted from them we should still choose each of them), but we choose them also for the sake of happiness, judging that through them we shall be happy. Happiness, on the other hand, no one chooses for the sake of these, nor, in general, for anything other than itself.

From the point of view of self-sufficiency the same result seems to follow; for the complete good is thought to be self-sufficient. Now by self-sufficient we do not mean that which is sufficient for a man by himself, for one who lives a solitary life, but also for parents, children, wife, and in general for his friends and fellow citizens, since man is sociable by nature. But some limit must be set to this; for if we extend our requirement to ancestors and descendants and friends' friends we are in for an infinite series. Let us examine this question, however, on another occasion; the self-sufficient we now define as that which when isolated makes life desirable and lacking in nothing; and such we think happiness to be; and further we think it most desirable of all things, without being counted as one good thing among others—if it were so counted it would clearly be made more desirable by the addition of even the least of goods; for that which is added becomes an excess of goods, and of goods the greater is always more desirable. Happiness, then, is something complete and self-sufficient, and is the end of action.

Presumably, however, to say that happiness is the chief good seems a platitude, and a clearer account of what it is is still desired. This might perhaps be given, if we could first ascertain the function of man. For just as for a flute-player, a sculptor, or any artist, and, in general, for all things that have a function or activity, the good and the 'well' is thought to reside in the function, so would it seem to be for man, if he has a function. Have the carpenter, then, and the tanner certain functions or activities, and has man none? Is he naturally functionless? Or as eye, hand, foot, and in general each of the parts evidently has a function, may one lay it down that man similarly has a function apart from all these? What then can this be? Life seems to be common even to plants, but we are seeking what is peculiar to man. Let us exclude, therefore, the life of nutrition and growth. Next there would be a life of perception, but *it* also seems to be common even to the horse, the ox, and every animal.

There remains, then, an active life of the element that has a rational principle (of this, one part has such a principle in the sense of being obedient to one, the other in the sense of possessing one and exercising 5 thought); and as this too can be taken in two ways, we must state that life in the sense of activity is what we mean; for this seems to be the more proper sense of the term. Now if the function of man is an activity of soul in accordance with, or not without, rational principle, and if we say a so-and-so and a good so-and-so have a function which is the same in kind, e.g. a lyre-player and a good lyre-player, and so without qualification in 10 all cases, eminence in respect of excellence being added to the function (for the function of a lyre-player is to play the lyre, and that of a good lyre-player is to do so well): if this is the case, [and we state the function of man to be a certain kind of life, and this to be an activity or actions of the soul implying a rational principle, and the function of a good man to be the good and noble performance of these, and if any action is well performed when it is performed in accordance with the appropriate 15 excellence: if this is the case,][1] human good turns out to be activity of soul in conformity with excellence, and if there are more than one excellence, in conformity with the best and most complete.

But we must add 'in a complete life'. For one swallow does not make a summer, nor does one day; and so too one day, or a short time, does not make a man blessed and happy.

Let this serve as an outline of the good; for we must presumably first 20 sketch it roughly, and then later fill in the details. But it would seem that any one is capable of carrying on and articulating what has once been well outlined, and that time is a good discoverer or partner in such a work; to which facts the advances of the arts are due; for anyone can add what is lacking. And we must also remember what has been said before, 25 and not look for precision in all things alike, but in each class of things such as accords with the subject-matter, and so much as is appropriate to the inquiry. For a carpenter and a geometer look for right angles in different ways; the former does so in so far as the right angle is useful for 30 his work, while the latter inquires what it is or what sort of thing it is; for he is a spectator of the truth. We must act in the same way, then, in all other matters as well, that our main task may not be subordinated to minor questions. Nor must we demand the cause in all matters alike; it is 1098b enough in some cases that the *fact* be well established, as in the case of the first principles; the fact is a primary thing or first principle. Now of first principles we see some by induction, some by perception, some by a

[1] Excised by Bywater.

certain habituation, and others too in other ways. But each set of principles we must try to investigate in the natural way, and we must take
pains to determine them correctly, since they have a great influence on
what follows. For the beginning is thought to be more than half of the
whole, and many of the questions we ask are cleared up by it.

CHAPTER 8

We must consider it, however, in the light not only of our conclusion
and our premisses, but also of what is commonly said about it; for with a
true view all the facts harmonize, but with a false one they soon clash.
Now goods have been divided into three classes, and some are
described as external, others as relating to soul or to body; and we call
those that relate to soul most properly and truly goods. But we are
positing actions and activities relating to soul. Therefore our account
must be sound, at least according to this view, which is an old one and
agreed on by philosophers. It is correct also in that we identify the end
with certain actions and activities; for thus it falls among goods of the
soul and not among external goods. Another belief which harmonizes
with our account is that the happy man lives well and fares well; for we
have practically defined happiness as a sort of living and faring well.
The characteristics that are looked for in happiness seem also, all of
them, to belong to what we have defined happiness as being. For some
identify happiness with excellence, some with practical wisdom,
others with a kind of philosophic wisdom, others with these, or one of
these, accompanied by pleasure or not without pleasure; while others
include also external prosperity. Now some of these views have been
held by many men and men of old, others by a few persons; and it is
not probable that either of these should be entirely mistaken, but
rather that they should be right in at least some one respect or even in
most respects.

With those who identify happiness with excellence or some one
excellence our account is in harmony; for to excellence belongs activity
in accordance with excellence. But it makes, perhaps, no small
difference whether we place the chief good in possession or in use, in
state or in activity. For the state may exist without producing any good
result, as in a man who is asleep or in some way quite inactive, but the
activity cannot; for one who has the activity will of necessity be acting,
and acting well. And as in the Olympic Games it is not the most beautiful
and the strongest that are crowned but those who compete (for it is some

of these that are victorious), so those who act rightly win the noble and
good things in life.

Their life is also in itself pleasant. For pleasure is a state of soul, and to
each man that which he is said to be a lover of is pleasant; e.g. not only is
a horse pleasant to the lover of horses, and a spectacle to the lover of
sights, but also in the same way just acts are pleasant to the lover of
justice and in general excellent acts to the lover of excellence. Now for
most men their pleasures are in conflict with one another because these
are not by nature pleasant, but the lovers of what is noble find pleasant
the things that are by nature pleasant; and excellent actions are such, so
that these are pleasant for such men as well as in their own nature. Their
life, therefore, has no further need of pleasure as a sort of adventitious
charm, but has its pleasure in itself. For, besides what we have said, the
man who does not rejoice in noble actions is not good at all; for no
one would call a man just who did not enjoy acting justly, nor any man
liberal who did not enjoy liberal actions; and similarly in all other cases.
If this is so, excellent actions must be in themselves pleasant. But they
are also *good* and *noble*, and have each of these attributes in the highest
degree, since the good man judges well about these attributes and he
judges in the way we have described. Happiness then is the best,
noblest, and most pleasant thing, and these attributes are not severed as
in the inscription at Delos—

> Most noble is that which is justest, and best is health;
> But pleasantest is it to win what we love.

For all these properties belong to the best activities; and these, or one—
the best—of these, we identify with happiness.

Yet evidently, as we said, it needs the external goods as well; for it is
impossible, or not easy, to do noble acts without the proper equipment.
In many actions we use friends and riches and political power as instruments; and there are some things the lack of which takes the lustre from
blessedness, as good birth, satisfactory children, beauty; for the man
who is very ugly in appearance or ill-born or solitary and childless is
hardly happy, and perhaps a man would be still less so if he had
thoroughly bad children or friends or had lost good children or friends
by death. As we said, then, happiness seems to need this sort of
prosperity in addition; for which reason some identify happiness with
good fortune, though others identify it with excellence.

CHAPTER 13

1102ª Since happiness is an activity of soul in accordance with complete
excellence, we must consider the nature of excellence; for perhaps we
shall thus see better the nature of happiness. The true student of
politics, too, is thought to have studied this above all things; for he
wishes to make his fellow citizens good and obedient to the laws. As an
10 example of this we have the lawgivers of the Cretans and the Spartans,
and any others of the kind that there may have been. And if this inquiry
belongs to political science, clearly the pursuit of it will be in
accordance with our original plan. But clearly the excellence we must
15 study is human excellence; for the good we were seeking was human
good and the happiness human happiness. By human excellence we
mean not that of the body but that of the soul; and happiness also we call
an activity of soul. But if this is so, clearly the student of politics must
know somehow the facts about soul, as the man who is to heal the eyes
20 must know about the whole body also; and all the more since politics is
more prized and better than medicine; but even among doctors the best
educated spend much labour on acquiring knowledge of the body. The
student of politics, then, must study the soul, and must study it with
these objects in view, and do so just to the extent which is sufficient for
the questions we are discussing; for further precision is perhaps some-
25 thing more laborious than our purposes require.

Some things are said about it, adequately enough, even in the discussions outside our school, and we must use these; e.g. that one element in
the soul is irrational and one has a rational principle. Whether these are
30 separated as the parts of the body or of anything divisible are, or are
distinct by definition but by nature inseparable, like convex and
concave in the circumference of a circle, does not affect the present
question.

Of the irrational element one division seems to be widely distributed,
and vegetative in its nature, I mean that which causes nutrition and
1102ᵇ growth; for it is this kind of power of the soul that one must assign to all
nurslings and to embryos, and this same power to full-grown creatures;
this is more reasonable than to assign some different power to them.
Now the excellence of this seems to be common to all and not
specifically human; for this part or faculty seems to function most in
5 sleep, while goodness and badness are least manifest in sleep (whence
comes the saying that the happy are not better off than the wretched for
half their lives; and this happens naturally enough, since sleep is an

inactivity of the soul in that respect in which it is called good or bad), unless perhaps to a small extent some of the movements actually penetrate, and in this respect the dreams of good men are better than those of ordinary people. Enough of this subject, however; let us leave the nutritive faculty alone, since it has by its nature no share in human excellence.

There seems to be also another irrational element in the soul—one which in a sense, however, shares in a rational principle. For we praise the reason of the continent man and of the incontinent, and the part of their soul that has reason, since it urges them aright and towards the best objects; but there is found in them also another natural element beside reason, which fights against and resists it. For exactly as paralysed limbs when we choose to move them to the right turn on the contrary to the left, so is it with the soul; the impulses of incontinent people move in contrary directions. But while in the body we see that which moves astray, in the soul we do not. No doubt, however, we must none the less suppose that in the soul too there is something beside reason, resisting and opposing it. In what sense it is distinct from the other elements does not concern us. Now even this seems to have a share in reason, as we said; at any rate in the continent man it obeys reason—and presumably in the temperate and brave man it is still more obedient; for in them it speaks, on all matters, with the same voice as reason.

Therefore the irrational element also appears to be twofold. For the vegetative element in no way shares in reason, but the appetitive and in general the desiring element in a sense shares in it, in so far as it listens to and obeys it; this is the sense in which we speak of paying heed to one's father or one's friends, not that in which we speak of 'the rational' in mathematics.[2] That the irrational element is in some sense persuaded by reason is indicated also by the giving of advice and by all reproof and exhortation. And if this element also must be said to have reason, that which has reason also will be twofold, one subdivision having it in the strict sense and in itself, and the other having a tendency to obey as one does one's father.

Excellence too is distinguished into kinds in accordance with this difference; for we say that some excellences are intellectual and others moral,[3] philosophic wisdom and understanding and practical wisdom

10

15

20

25

30

1103ᵃ

5

---

[2] The Greek term means (i) 'possess reason', (ii) 'pay heed to', 'obey', (iii) 'be rational' (in the mathematical sense).

[3] 'Moral', here and hereafter, is used in the archaic sense of 'pertaining to character or *mores*'.

being intellectual, liberality and temperance moral. For in speaking about a man's character we do not say that he is wise or has understanding but that he is good-tempered or temperate; yet we praise the wise man also with respect to his state; and of states we call those which merit
10 praise excellences.

BOOK II

CHAPTER I

Excellence, then, being of two kinds, intellectual and moral, intellectual
15 excellence in the main owes both its birth and its growth to teaching (for which reason it requires experience and time), while moral excellence comes about as a result of habit, whence also its name is one that is formed by a slight variation from the word for 'habit'.[4] From this it is also plain that none of the moral excellences arises in us by nature; for
20 nothing that exists by nature can form a habit contrary to its nature. For instance the stone which by nature moves downwards cannot be habituated to move upwards, not even if one tries to train it by throwing it up ten thousand times; nor can fire be habituated to move downwards, nor can anything else that by nature behaves in one way be trained to behave in another. Neither by nature, then, nor contrary to nature do excellences arise in us; rather we are adapted by nature to receive them,
25 and are made perfect by habit.

Again, of all the things that come to us by nature we first acquire the potentiality and later exhibit the activity (this is plain in the case of the senses; for it was not by often seeing or often hearing that we got these senses, but on the contrary we had them before we used them, and did
30 not come to have them by using them); but excellences we get by first exercising them, as also happens in the case of the arts as well. For the things we have to learn before we can do, we learn by doing, e.g. men become builders by building and lyre-players by playing the lyre; so too
1103ᵇ we become just by doing just acts, temperate by doing temperate acts, brave by doing brave acts.

This is confirmed by what happens in states; for legislators make the citizens good by forming habits in them, and this is the wish of every legislator; and those who do not effect it miss their mark, and it is in this
5 that a good constitution differs from a bad one.

---

⁴ The Greek words for character and habit are almost identical.

Again, it is from the same causes and by the same means that every excellence is both produced and destroyed, and similarly every art; for it is from playing the lyre that both good and bad lyre-players are produced. And the corresponding statement is true of builders and of all the rest; men will be good or bad builders as a result of building well 10 or badly. For if this were not so, there would have been no need of a teacher, but all men would have been born good or bad at their craft. This, then, is the case with the excellences also; by doing the acts that we do in our transactions with other men we become just or unjust, and by 15 doing the acts that we do in presence of danger, and being habituated to feel fear or confidence, we become brave or cowardly. The same is true of appetites and feelings of anger; some men become temperate and good-tempered, others self-indulgent and irascible, by behaving in one way or the other in the appropriate circumstances. Thus, in one word, 20 states arise out of like activities. This is why the activities we exhibit must be of a certain kind; it is because the states correspond to the differences between these. It makes no small difference, then, whether we form habits of one kind or of another from our very youth; it makes a very great difference, or rather *all* the difference. 25

CHAPTER 2

Since, then, the present inquiry does not aim at theoretical knowledge like the others (for we are inquiring not in order to know what excellence is, but in order to become good, since otherwise our inquiry would have been of no use), we must examine the nature of actions, namely how we 30 ought to do them; for these determine also the nature of the states that are produced, as we have said. Now, that we must act according to right reason is a common principle and must be assumed—it will be discussed later, both what it is, and how it is related to the other excellences. But this must be agreed upon beforehand, that the whole 1104ᵃ account of matters of conduct must be given in outline and not precisely, as we said at the very beginning that the accounts we demand must be in accordance with the subject-matter; matters concerned with conduct and questions of what is good for us have no fixity, any more than matters of health. The general account being of this nature, the 5 account of particular cases is yet more lacking in exactness; for they do not fall under any art or set of precepts, but the agents themselves must in each case consider what is appropriate to the occasion, as happens also in the art of medicine or of navigation.

10   But though our present account is of this nature we must give what help we can. First, then, let us consider this, that it is the nature of such things to be destroyed by defect and excess, as we see in the case of strength and of health (for to gain light on things imperceptible we must use the evidence of sensible things); both excessive and defec-
15   tive exercise destroy the strength, and similarly drink or food which is above or below a certain amount destroys the health, while that which is proportionate both produces and increases and preserves it. So too is it, then, in the case of temperance and courage and the other excellences.
20   For the man who flies from and fears everything and does not stand his ground against anything becomes a coward, and the man who fears nothing at all but goes to meet every danger becomes rash; and similarly the man who indulges in every pleasure and abstains from none becomes self-indulgent, while the man who shuns every pleasure, as boors do, becomes in a way insensible; temperance and
25   courage, then, are destroyed by excess and defect, and preserved by the mean.

But not only are the sources and causes of their origination and growth the same as those of their destruction, but also the sphere of their
30   activity will be the same; for this is also true of the things which are more evident to sense, e.g. of strength; it is produced by taking much food and undergoing much exertion, and it is the strong man that will be most able to do these things. So too is it with the excellences; by abstaining from pleasures we become temperate, and it is when we have become so that we are most able to abstain from them; and similarly too in the case
1104ᵇ   of courage; for by being habituated to despise things that are terrible and to stand our ground against them we become brave, and it is when we have become so that we shall be most able to stand our ground against them.

CHAPTER 3

We must take as a sign of states the pleasure or pain that supervenes on
5   acts; for the man who abstains from bodily pleasures and delights in this very fact is temperate, while the man who is annoyed at it is self-indulgent, and he who stands his ground against things that are terrible and delights in this or at least is not pained is brave, while the man who is pained is a coward. For moral excellence is concerned with pleasures
10   and pains; it is on account of pleasure that we do bad things, and on

account of pain that we abstain from noble ones. Hence we ought to have been brought up in a particular way from our very youth, as Plato says, so as both to delight in and to be pained by the things that we ought; for this is the right education.

Again, if the excellences are concerned with actions and passions, and every passion and every action is accompanied by pleasure and pain, for this reason also excellence will be concerned with pleasures and pains. This is indicated also by the fact that punishment is inflicted by these means; for it is a kind of cure, and it is the nature of cures to be effected by contraries.

Again, as we said but lately, every state of soul has a nature relative to and concerned with the kind of things by which it tends to be made worse or better; but it is by reason of pleasures and pains that men become bad, by pursuing and avoiding these—either the pleasures and pains they ought not or when they ought not or as they ought not, or by going wrong in one of the other similar ways that reason can distinguish. Hence men even define the excellences as certain states of impassivity and rest; not well, however, because they speak absolutely, and do not say 'as one ought' and 'as one ought not' and 'when one ought or ought not', and the other things that may be added. We assume, then, that this kind of excellence tends to do what is best with regard to pleasures and pains, and badness does the contrary.

The following facts also may show us that they are concerned with these same things. There being three objects of choice and three of avoidance, the noble, the advantageous, the pleasant, and their contraries, the base, the injurious, the painful, about all of these the good man tends to go right and the bad man to go wrong, and especially about pleasure; for this is common to the animals, and also it accompanies all objects of choice; for even the noble and the advantageous appear pleasant.

Again, it has grown up with us all from our infancy; this is why it is difficult to rub off this passion, ingrained as it is in our life. And we measure even our actions, some of us more and others less, by pleasure and pain. For this reason, then, our whole inquiry must be about these; for to feel delight and pain rightly or wrongly has no small effect on our actions.

Again, it is harder to fight with pleasure than with anger, to use Heraclitus' phrase, but both art and excellence are always concerned with what is harder; for even the good is better when it is harder. Therefore for this reason also the whole concern both of excellence and of

15

20

25

30

1105ᵃ

5

10

political science is with pleasures and pains; for the man who uses these well will be good, he who uses them badly bad.

That excellence, then, is concerned with pleasures and pains, and that by the acts from which it arises it is both increased and, if they are
15 done differently, destroyed, and that the acts from which it arose are those in which it actualizes itself—let this be taken as said.

CHAPTER 4

The question might be asked, what we mean by saying that we must become just by doing just acts, and temperate by doing temperate acts;
20 for if men do just and temperate acts, they are already just and temperate, exactly as, if they do what is grammatical or musical they are proficient in grammar and music.

Or is this not true even of the arts? It is possible to do something grammatical either by chance or under the guidance of another. A man will be proficient in grammar, then, only when he has both done some-
25 thing grammatical and done it grammatically; and this means doing it in accordance with the grammatical knowledge in himself.

Again, the case of the arts and that of the excellences are not similar; for the products of the arts have their goodness in themselves, so that it is enough that they should have a certain character, but if the acts that are in accordance with the excellences have themselves a certain character it does not follow that they are done justly or temperately. The
30 agent also must be in a certain condition when he does them; in the first place he must have knowledge, secondly he must choose the acts, and choose them for their own sakes, and thirdly his action must proceed from a firm and unchangeable character. These are not reckoned in as
1105^b conditions of the possession of the arts, except the bare knowledge; but as a condition of the possession of the excellences, knowledge has little or no weight, while the other conditions count not for a little but for everything, i.e. the very conditions which result from often doing just and temperate acts.

5 Actions, then, are called just and temperate when they are such as the just or the temperate man would do; but it is not the man who does these that is just and temperate, but the man who also does them *as* just and temperate men do them. It is well said, then, that it is by doing just acts that the just man is produced, and by doing temperate acts the
10 temperate man; without doing these no one would have even a prospect of becoming good.

But most people do not do these, but take refuge in theory and think they are being philosophers and will become good in this way, behaving somewhat like patients who listen attentively to their doctors, but do none of the things they are ordered to do. As the latter will not be made well in body by such a course of treatment, the former will not be made well in soul by such a course of philosophy. 15

CHAPTER 5

Next we must consider what excellence is. Since things that are found in the soul are of three kinds—passions, faculties, states—excellence must be one of these. By passions I mean appetite, anger, fear, confidence, envy, joy, love, hatred, longing, emulation, pity, and in general the feelings that are accompanied by pleasure or pain; by faculties the things in virtue of which we are said to be capable of feeling these, e.g. of becoming angry or being pained or feeling pity; by states the things in virtue of which we stand well or badly with reference to the passions, e.g. with reference to anger we stand badly if we feel it violently or too weakly, and well if we feel it moderately; and similarly with reference to the other passions. 20 25

Now neither the excellences nor the vices are *passions*, because we are not called good or bad on the ground of our passions, but are so called on the ground of our excellences and our vices, and because we are neither praised nor blamed for our passions (for the man who feels fear or anger is not praised, nor is the man who simply feels anger blamed, but the man who feels it in a certain way), but for our excellences and our vices we *are* praised or blamed. 30 1106ᵃ

Again, we feel anger and fear without choice, but the excellences are choices or involve choice. Further, in respect of the passions we are said to be moved, but in respect of the excellences and the vices we are said not to be moved but to be disposed in a particular way. 5

For these reasons also they are not *faculties*; for we are neither called good nor bad, nor praised nor blamed, for the simple capacity of feeling the passions; again, we have the faculties by nature, but we are not made good or bad by nature; we have spoken of this before. 10

If, then, the excellences are neither passions nor faculties, all that remains is that they should be *states*.

Thus we have stated what excellence is in respect of its genus.

CHAPTER 6

We must, however, not only describe it as a state, but also say what sort
15   of state it is. We may remark, then, that every excellence both brings into
good condition the thing of which it is the excellence and makes the
work of that thing be done well; e.g. the excellence of the eye makes both
the eye and its work good; for it is by the excellence of the eye that we see
well. Similarly the excellence of the horse makes a horse both good in
20   itself and good at running and at carrying its rider and at awaiting the
attack of the enemy. Therefore, if this is true in every case, the
excellence of man also will be the state which makes a man good and
which makes him do his own work well.

How this is to happen we have stated already, but it will be made plain
25   also by the following consideration of the nature of excellence. In everything that is continuous and divisible it is possible to take more, less, or
an equal amount, and that either in terms of the thing itself or relatively
to us; and the equal is an intermediate between excess and defect. By the
intermediate in the object I mean that which is equidistant from each of
30   the extremes, which is one and the same for all men; by the intermediate
relatively to us that which is neither too much nor too little—and this is
not one, nor the same for all. For instance, if ten is many and two is few,
six is intermediate, taken in terms of the object; for it exceeds and is
exceeded by an equal amount; this is intermediate according to
35   arithmetical proportion. But the intermediate relatively to us is not to be
taken so; if ten pounds are too much for a particular person to eat and
1106^b two too little, it does not follow that the trainer will order six pounds; for
this also is perhaps too much for the person who is to take it, or too
little—too little for Milo, too much for the beginner in athletic exercises.
The same it true of running and wrestling. Thus a master of any art
5   avoids excess and defect, but seeks the intermediate and chooses this—
the intermediate not in the object but relatively to us.

If it is thus, then, that every art does its work well—by looking to the
intermediate and judging its works by this standard (so that we often say
10   of good works of art that it is not possible either to take away or to add
anything, implying that excess and defect destroy the goodness of works
of art, while the mean preserves it; and good artists, as we say, look to
this in their work), and if, further, excellence is more exact and better
than any art, as nature also is, then it must have the quality of aiming at
15   the intermediate. I mean moral excellence; for it is this that is concerned
with passions and actions, and in these there is excess, defect, and the

intermediate. For instance, both fear and confidence and appetite and anger and pity and in general pleasure and pain may be felt both too much and too little, and in both cases not well; but to feel them at the right times, with reference to the right objects, towards the right people, with the right aim, and in the right way, is what is both intermediate and best, and this is characteristic of excellence. Similarly with regard to actions also there is excess, defect, and the intermediate. Now excellence is concerned with passions and actions, in which excess is a form of failure, and so is defect, while the intermediate is praised and is a form of success; and both these things are characteristics of excellence. Therefore excellence is a kind of mean, since it aims at what is intermediate.

Again, it is possible to fail in many ways (for evil belongs to the class of the unlimited, as the Pythagoreans conjectured, and good to that of the limited), while to succeed is possible only in one way (for which reason one is easy and the other difficult—to miss the mark easy, to hit it difficult); for these reasons also, then, excess and defect are characteristic of vice, and the mean of excellence;

For men are good in but one way, but bad in many.

Excellence, then, is a state concerned with choice, lying in a mean relative to us, this being determined by reason and in the way in which the man of practical wisdom would determine it. Now it is a mean between two vices, that which depends on excess and that which depends on defect; and again it is a mean because the vices respectively fall short of or exceed what is right in both passions and actions, while excellence both finds and chooses that which is intermediate. Hence in respect of its substance and the account which states its essence it is a mean, with regard to what is best and right it is an extreme.

But not every action nor every passion admits of a mean; for some have names that already imply badness, e.g. spite, shamelessness, envy, and in the case of actions adultery, theft, murder; for all of these and suchlike things imply by their names that they are themselves bad, and not the excesses or deficiencies of them. It is not possible, then, ever to be right with regard to them; one must always be wrong. Nor does goodness or badness with regard to such things depend on committing adultery with the right woman, at the right time, and in the right way, but simply to do any of them is to go wrong. It would be equally absurd, then, to expect that in unjust, cowardly, and self-indulgent action there should be a mean, an excess, and a deficiency; for at that rate there would be a mean of excess and of deficiency, an excess of excess, and a

deficiency of deficiency. But as there is no excess and deficiency of temperance and courage because what is intermediate is in a sense an extreme, so too of the actions we have mentioned there is no mean nor
25 any excess and deficiency, but however they are done they are wrong; for in general there is neither a mean of excess and deficiency, nor excess and deficiency of a mean.

CHAPTER 7

We must, however, not only make this general statement, but also apply it to the individual facts. For among statements about conduct those
30 which are general apply more widely, but those which are particular are more true, since conduct has to do with individual cases, and our statements must harmonize with the facts in these cases. We may take these cases from the diagram. With regard to feelings of fear and confidence courage is the mean; of the people who exceed, he who exceeds in fear-
1107ᵇ lessness has no name (many of the states have no name), while the man who exceeds in confidence is rash, and he who exceeds in fear and falls short in confidence is a coward. With regard to pleasures and pains—
5 not all of them and not so much with regard to the pains—the mean is temperance, the excess self-indulgence. Persons deficient with regard to the pleasures are not often found; hence such persons also have received no name. But let us call them 'insensible'.

With regard to giving and taking of money the mean is liberality, the
10 excess and the defect prodigality and meanness. They exceed and fall short in contrary ways to one another: the prodigal exceeds in spending and falls short in taking, while the mean man exceeds in taking and falls short in spending. (At present we are giving a mere outline or summary,
15 and are satisfied with this; later these states will be more exactly determined.) With regard to money there are also other dispositions—a mean, magnificence (for the magnificent man differs from the liberal man; the former deals with large sums, the latter with small ones), an
20 excess, tastelessness and vulgarity, and a deficiency, niggardliness; these differ from the states opposed to liberality, and the mode of their difference will be stated later.

With regard to honour and dishonour the mean is proper pride, the excess is known as a sort of empty vanity, and the deficiency is undue
25 humility; and as we said liberality was related to magnificence, differing from it by dealing with small sums, so there is a state similarly related to proper pride, being concerned with small honours while that is con-

cerned with great. For it is possible to desire small honours as one ought, and more than one ought, and less, and the man who exceeds in his desires is called ambitious, the man who falls short unambitious, while the intermediate person has no name. The dispositions also are nameless, except that that of the ambitious man is called ambition. Hence the people who are at the extremes lay claim to the middle place; and we ourselves sometimes call the intermediate person ambitious and sometimes unambitious, and sometimes praise the ambitious man and sometimes the unambitious. The reason of our doing this will be stated in what follows; but now let us speak of the remaining states according to the method which has been indicated.

With regard to anger also there is an excess, a deficiency, and a mean. Although they can scarcely be said to have names, yet since we call the intermediate person good-tempered let us call the mean good temper; of the persons at the extremes let the one who exceeds be called irascible, and his vice irascibility, and the man who falls short an inirascible sort of person, and the deficiency inirascibility.

There are also three other means, which have a certain likeness to one another, but differ from one another: for they are all concerned with intercourse in words and actions, but differ in that one is concerned with truth in this sphere, the other two with pleasantness; and of this one kind is exhibited in giving amusement, the other in all the circumstances of life. We must therefore speak of these too, that we may the better see that in all things the mean is praiseworthy, and the extremes neither praiseworthy nor right, but worthy of blame. Now most of these states also have no names, but we must try, as in the other cases, to invent names ourselves so that we may be clear and easy to follow. With regard to truth, then, the intermediate is a truthful sort of person and the mean may be called truthfulness, while the pretence which exaggerates is boastfulness and the person characterized by it a boaster, and that which understates is mock modesty and the person characterized by it mock-modest. With regard to pleasantness in the giving of amusement the intermediate person is ready-witted and the disposition ready wit, the excess is buffoonery and the person characterized by it a buffoon, while the man who falls short is a sort of boor and his state is boorishness. With regard to the remaining kind of pleasantness, that which is exhibited in life in general, the man who is pleasant in the right way is friendly and the mean is friendliness, while the man who exceeds is an obsequious person if he has no end in view, a flatterer if he is aiming at his own advantage, and the man who falls

30

1108ᵃ

5

10

15

20

25

30   short and is unpleasant in all circumstances is a quarrelsome and
surly sort of person.

There are also means in the passions and concerned with the
passions; since shame is not an excellence, and yet praise is extended to
the modest man. For even in these matters one man is said to be
intermediate, and another to exceed, as for instance the bashful man
who is ashamed of everything; while he who falls short or is not ashamed
of anything at all is shameless, and the intermediate person is modest.

1108ᵇ   Righteous indignation is a mean between envy and spite, and these
states are concerned with the pain and pleasure that are felt at the
fortunes of our neighbours; the man who is characterized by righteous
indignation is pained at undeserved good fortune, the envious man,
going beyond him, is pained at all good fortune, and the spiteful man

5   falls so far short of being pained that he even rejoices. But these states
there will be an opportunity of describing elsewhere; with regard to
justice, since it has not one simple meaning, we shall, after describing
the other states, distinguish its two kinds and say how each of them is a

10   mean; and similarly we shall treat also of the rational excellences.

CHAPTER 9

1109ᵃ   That moral excellence is a mean, then, and in what sense it is so, and that
it is a mean between two vices, the one involving excess, the other
deficiency, and that it is such because its character is to aim at what is
intermediate in passions and in actions, has been sufficiently stated.
Hence also it is no easy task to be good. For in everything it is no easy

25   task to find the middle, e.g. to find the middle of a circle is not for
everyone but for him who knows; so, too, anyone can get angry—that is
easy—or give or spend money; but to do this to the right person, to the
right extent, at the right time, with the right aim, and in the right way,
that is not for everyone, nor is it easy; that is why goodness is both rare
and laudable and noble.

30   Hence he who aims at the intermediate must first depart from what is
the more contrary to it, as Calypso advises—

Hold the ship out beyond that surf and spray. (*Odyssey* XII 219.)

For of the extremes one is more erroneous, one less so; therefore, since
to hit the mean is hard in the extreme, we must as a second best, as
people say, take the least of the evils; and this will be done best in the

1109ᵇ   way we describe.

But we must consider the things towards which we ourselves also are easily carried away; for some of us tend to one thing, some to another; and this will be recognizable from the pleasure and the pain we feel. We must drag ourselves away to the contrary extreme; for we shall get into   5
the intermediate state by drawing well away from error, as people do in straightening sticks that are bent.

Now in everything the pleasant or pleasure is most to be guarded against; for we do not judge it impartially. We ought, then, to feel towards pleasure as the elders of the people felt towards Helen, and in   10
all circumstances repeat their saying; for if we dismiss pleasure thus we are less likely to go astray. It is by doing this, then, (to sum the matter up) that we shall best be able to hit the mean.

But this is no doubt difficult, and especially in individual cases; for it is not easy to detemine both how and with whom and on what provoca-   15
tion and how long one should be angry; for we too sometimes praise those who fall short and call them good-tempered, but sometimes we praise those who get angry and call them manly. The man, however who deviates little from goodness is not blamed, whether he do so in the direction of the more or of the less, but only the man who deviates more widely; for *he* does not fail to be noticed. But up to what point and to   20
what extent a man must deviate before he becomes blameworthy it is not easy to determine by reasoning, any more than anything else that is perceived by the senses; such things depend on particular facts, and the decision rests with perception. So much, then, makes it plain that the intermediate state is in all things to be praised, but that we must incline sometimes towards the excess, sometimes towards the deficiency; for so   25
shall we most easily hit the mean and what is right.

BOOK III

CHAPTER I

Since excellence is concerned with passions and actions, and on   30
voluntary passions and actions praise and blame are bestowed, on those that are involuntary forgiveness, and sometimes also pity, to distinguish the voluntary and the involuntary is presumably necessary for those who are studying excellence and useful also for legislators with a view to the assigning both of honours and of punishments.

Those things, then, are thought involuntary, which take place under

1110ᵃ compulsion or owing to ignorance; and that is compulsory of which the moving principle is outside, being a principle in which nothing is contributed by the person who acts or is acted upon, e.g. if he were to be carried somewhere by a wind, or by men who had him in their power.

    But with regard to the things that are done from fear of greater evils or
5 for some noble object (e.g. if a tyrant were to order one to do something base, having one's parents and children in his power, and if one did the action they were to be saved, but otherwise would be put to death), it may be debated whether such actions are involuntary or voluntary. Something of the sort happens also with regard to the throwing of goods overboard in a storm; for in the abstract no one throws goods away
10 voluntarily, but on condition of its securing the safety of himself and his crew any sensible man does so. Such actions, then, are mixed, but are more like voluntary actions; for they are worthy of choice at the time when they are done, and the end of an action is relative to the occasion. Both the terms, then, 'voluntary' and 'involuntary', must be used with reference to the moment of action. Now the man acts voluntarily; for the
15 principle that moves the instrumental parts of the body in such actions is in him, and the things of which the moving principle is in a man himself are in his power to do or not to do. Such actions, therefore, are voluntary, but in the abstract perhaps involuntary; for no one would choose any such act in itself.

20   For such actions men are sometimes even praised, when they endure something base or painful in return for great and noble objects gained; in the opposite case they are blamed, since to endure the greatest indignities for no noble end or for a trifling end is the mark of an inferior person. On some actions praise indeed is not bestowed, but forgiveness is, when one does what he ought not under pressure which overstrains
25 human nature and which no one could withstand. But some acts, perhaps, we cannot be forced to do, but ought rather to face death after the most fearful sufferings; for the things that forced Euripides' Alcmaeon to slay his mother seem absurd. It is difficult sometimes to determine what should be chosen at what cost, and what should be
30 endured in return for what gain, and yet more difficult to abide by our decisions; for as a rule what is expected is painful, and what we are forced to do is base, whence praise and blame are bestowed on those who have been compelled or have not.

1110ᵇ   What sort of acts, then, should be called compulsory? We answer that without qualification actions are so when the cause is in the external circumstances and the agent contributes nothing. But the things that in themselves are involuntary, but now and in return for these gains are worthy of choice, and whose moving principle is in the agent, are in themselves involuntary, but now and in return for these gains voluntary. They are more like voluntary acts; for actions are in the class of particulars, and the particular acts here are voluntary. What sort of things are to be chosen in return for what it is not easy to state; for there are many differences in the particular cases.

But if someone were to say that pleasant and noble objects have a compelling power, forcing us from without, all acts would be for him compulsory; for it is for these objects that all men do everything they do. And those who act under compulsion and unwillingly act with pain, but those who do acts for their pleasantness and nobility do them with pleasure; it is absurd to make external circumstances responsible, and not oneself, as being easily caught by such attractions for base acts. The compulsory, then, seems to be that whose moving principle is outside, the person compelled contributing nothing.

Everything that is done by reason of ignorance is *non*-voluntary; it is only what produces pain and regret that is *in*voluntary. For the man who has done something owing to ignorance, and feels not the least vexation at his action, has not acted voluntarily, since he did not know what he was doing, nor yet involuntarily, since he is not pained. Of people, then, who act by reason of ignorance he who regrets is thought an involuntary agent, and the man who does not regret may, since he is different, be called a non-voluntary agent; for, since he differs from the other, it is better that he should have a name of his own.

Acting by reason of ignorance seems also to be different from acting *in* ignorance; for the man who is drunk or in a rage is thought to act as a result not of ignorance but of one of the causes mentioned, yet not knowingly but in ignorance.

Now every wicked man is ignorant of what he ought to do and what he ought to abstain from, and error of this kind makes men unjust and in general bad; but the term 'involuntary' tends to be used not if a man is ignorant of what is to his advantage—for it is not ignorance in choice that makes action involuntary (it makes men wicked), nor ignorance of the universal (for *that* men are *blamed*), but ignorance of particular circumstances of the action and the objects with which it is concerned. For it is on these that both pity and forgiveness depend, since the person who is ignorant of any of these acts involuntarily.

Perhaps it is just as well, therefore, to determine their nature and number. A man may be ignorant, then, of who he is, what he is doing,

what or whom he is acting on, and sometimes also what (e.g. what
5   instrument) he is doing it with, and to what end (e.g. for safety), and how
he is doing it (e.g. whether gently or violently). Now of all of these no one
could be ignorant unless he were mad, and evidently also he could not
be ignorant of the agent; for how could he not know himself? But of what
he is doing a man might be ignorant, as for instance people say 'it
slipped out of their mouths as they were speaking', or 'they did not know
10   it was a secret', as Aeschylus said of the mysteries, or a man might say he
'let it go off when he merely wanted to show its working', as the man did
with the catapult. Again, one might think one's son was an enemy, as
Merope did, or that a pointed spear had a button on it, or that a stone
was pumice-stone; or one might give a man a draught to save him and
really kill him; or one might want to touch a man, as people do in
15   sparring, and really strike him. The ignorance may relate, then, to any of
these things, i.e. of the circumstances of the action, and the man who
was ignorant of any of these is thought to have acted involuntarily, and
especially if he was ignorant on the most important points; and these are
thought to be what he is doing and with what aim. Further, the doing of
20   an act that is called involuntary in virtue of ignorance of this sort must be
painful and involve regret.

   Since that which is done under compulsion or by reason of ignorance
is involuntary, the voluntary would seem to be that of which the moving
principle is in the agent himself, he being aware of the particular
25   circumstances of the action. Presumably acts done by reason of anger or
appetite are not rightly called involuntary. For in the first place, on that
showing none of the other animals will act voluntarily, nor will children;
and secondly, is it meant that we do not do voluntarily *any* of the acts
that are due to appetite or anger, or that we do the noble acts voluntarily
and the base acts involuntarily? Is not this absurd, when one and the
same thing is the cause? But it would surely be odd to describe as
30   involuntary the things one ought to desire; and we ought both to be
angry at certain things and to have an appetite for certain things, e.g. for
health and for learning. Also what is involuntary is thought to be painful,
but what is in accordance with appetite is thought to be pleasant. Again,
what is the difference in respect of involuntariness between errors
committed upon calculation and those committed in anger? Both are to
1111^b be avoided, but the irrational passions are thought not less human than
reason is, and therefore also the actions which proceed from anger or
appetite are the man's actions. It would be odd, then, to treat them as
involuntary.

CHAPTER 2

Both the voluntary and the involuntary having been delimited, we must next discuss choice; for it is thought to be most closely bound up with 5 excellence and to discriminate characters better than actions do.

Choice, then, seems to be voluntary, but not the same thing as the voluntary; the latter extends more widely. For both children and the other animals share in voluntary action, but not in choice, and acts done on the spur of the moment we describe as voluntary, but not as chosen. 10

Those who say it is appetite or anger or wish or a kind of opinion do not seem to be right. For choice is not common to irrational creatures as well, but appetite and anger are. Again, the incontinent man acts with appetite, but not with choice; while the continent man on the contrary acts with choice, but not with appetite. Again, appetite is contrary to 15 choice, but not appetite to appetite. Again, appetite relates to the pleasant and the painful, choice neither to the painful nor to the pleasant.

Still less is it anger; for acts due to anger are thought to be less than any other objects of choice.

But neither is it wish, though it seems near to it; for choice cannot 20 relate to impossibles, and if anyone said he chose them he would be thought silly; but there may be a wish even for impossibles, e.g. for immortality. And wish may relate to things that could in no way be brought about by one's own efforts, e.g. that a particular actor or athlete should win in a competition; but no one chooses such things, but only the things that he thinks could be brought about by his own efforts. 25 Again, wish relates rather to the end, choice to what contributes to the end; for instance, we wish to be healthy, but we choose the acts which will make us healthy, and we wish to be happy and say we do, but we cannot well say we choose to be so; for, in general, choice seems to relate to the things that are in our own power. 30

For this reason, too, it cannot be opinion; for opinion is thought to relate to all kinds of things, no less to eternal things and impossible things than to things in our own power; and it is distinguished by its falsity or truth, not by its badness or goodness, while choice is distinguished rather by these.

Now with opinion in general perhaps no one really says it is identical. 1112ᵃ But it is not identical even with any kind of opinion; for by choosing what is good or bad we are men of a certain character, which we are not by holding certain opinions. And we choose to get or avoid something good or bad, but we have opinions about what a thing is or whom it is good for or how it is good for him; we can hardly be said to opine to get or 5 avoid anything. And choice is praised for being related to the right object rather than for being rightly related to it, opinion for being truly related to its object. And we choose what we best know to be good, but we opine what we do not know at all; and it is not the same people that are thought to make the best choices and to have the best opinions, but 10 some are thought to have fairly good opinions, but by reason of vice to choose what they should not. If opinion precedes choice or accompanies it, that makes no difference; for it is not this that we are considering, but whether it is *identical* with some kind of opinion.

What, then, or what kind of thing is it, since it is none of the things we have mentioned? It seems to be voluntary, but not all that is voluntary 15 seems to be an object of choice. Is it, then, what has been decided on by previous deliberation? For choice involves reason and thought. Even the name seems to suggest that it is what is chosen before other things.

CHAPTER 3

Do we deliberate about everything, and is everything a possible subject of deliberation, or is deliberation impossible about some things? We 20 ought presumably to call not what a fool or a madman would deliberate about, but what a sensible man would deliberate about, a subject of deliberation. Now about eternal things no one deliberates, e.g. about the universe or the incommensurability of the diagonal and the side of a square. But no more do we deliberate about the things that involve movement but always happen in the same way, whether of necessity or 25 by nature or from any other cause, e.g. the solstices and the risings of the stars; nor about things that happen now in one way, now in another, e.g. droughts and rains; nor about chance events, like the finding of treasure. But we do not deliberate even about all human affairs; for instance, no Spartan deliberates about the best constitution for the 30 Scythians. For none of these things can be brought about by our own efforts.

We deliberate about things that are in our power and can be done; and these are in fact what is left. For nature, necessity, and chance are thought to be causes, and also thought and everything that depends on man. Now every class of men deliberates about the things that can be done by their own efforts. And in the case of exact and self-contained 1112ᵇ sciences there is no deliberation, e.g. about the letters of the alphabet (for we have no doubt how they should be written); but the things that are brought about by our own efforts, but not always in the same way, are the things about which we deliberate, e.g. questions of medical treatment or of money-making. And we do so more in the case of the art of navigation than in that of gymnastics, inasmuch as it has been less exactly worked out, and again about other things in the same ratio, and more also in the case of the arts than in that of the sciences; for we have more doubt about the former. Deliberation is concerned with things that happen in a certain way for the most part, but in which the event is obscure, and with things in which it is indeterminate. We call in others to aid us in deliberation on important questions, distrusting ourselves as not being equal to deciding.

We deliberate not about ends but about what contributes to ends. For a doctor does not deliberate whether he shall heal, nor an orator whether he shall convince, nor a statesman whether he shall produce law and order, nor does anyone else deliberate about his end. Having set the end they consider how and by what means it is to be attained; and if it seems to be produced by several means they consider by which it is most easily and best produced, while if it is achieved by one only they consider how it will be achieved by this and by what means *this* will be achieved, till they come to the first cause, which in the order of discovery is last. For the person who deliberates seems to inquire and analyse in the way described as though he were analysing a geometrical construction (not all inquiry appears to be deliberation—for instance mathematical inquiries—but all deliberation is inquiry), and what is last in the order of analysis seems to be first in the order of becoming. And if we come on an impossibility, we give up the search, e.g. if we need money and this cannot be got; but if a thing appears possible we try to do it. By 'possible' things I mean things that might be brought about by our own efforts; and these in a sense include things that can be brought about by the efforts of our friends, since the moving principle is in ourselves. The subject of investigation is sometimes the instruments, sometimes the use of them; and similarly in the other cases—sometimes the means, sometimes the mode of using it or the means of bringing it about. It seems, then, as has been said, that man is a moving principle of actions; now deliberation is about the things to be done by the agent himself, and actions are for the sake of things other than themselves. For the end cannot be a subject of deliberation, but only what contributes to the ends; nor indeed can the particular facts be a subject of it, as whether this is bread or has been baked as it should; for these are matters of perception. If we are to be always deliberating, we shall have to go on to infinity.

The same thing is deliberated upon and is chosen, except that the object of choice is already determinate, since it is that which has been
5   decided upon as a result of deliberation that is the object of choice. For every one ceases to inquire how he is to act when he has brought the moving principle back to himself and to the ruling part of himself; for this is what chooses. This is plain also from the ancient constitutions, which Homer represented; for the kings announced their choices to the
10 people. The object of choice being one of the things in our own power which is desired after deliberation, choice will be deliberate desire of things in our own power; for when we have decided as a result of deliberation, we desire in accordance with our deliberation.

We may take it, then, that we have described choice in outline, and stated the nature of its objects and the fact that it is concerned with what contributes to the ends.

CHAPTER 4

15 That *wish* is for the end has already been stated; some think it is for the good, others for the apparent good. Now those who say that the good is the object of wish must admit in consequence that that which the man who does not choose aright wishes for is not an object of wish (for if it is to be so, it must also be good; but it was, if it so happened, bad); while
20 those who say the apparent good is the object of wish must admit that there is no natural object of wish, but only what seems so to each man. Now different things appear so to different people, and, if it so happens, even contrary things.

If these consequences are unpleasing, are we to say that absolutely and in truth the good is the object of wish, but for each person the
25 apparent good; that that which is in truth an object of wish is an object of wish to the good man, while any chance thing may be so to the bad man, as in the case of bodies also the things that are in truth wholesome are wholesome for bodies which are in good condition, while for those that are diseased other things are wholesome—or bitter or sweet or hot or
30 heavy, and so on; since the good man judges each class of things rightly, and in each the truth appears to him? For each state of character has its own ideas of the noble and the pleasant, and perhaps the good man differs from others most by seeing the truth in each class of things, being as it were the norm and measure of them. In most things the error seems

to be due to pleasure; for it appears a good when it is not. We therefore choose the pleasant as a good, and avoid pain as an evil.

CHAPTER 5

The end, then, being what we wish for, the things contributing to the end what we deliberate about and choose, actions concerning the latter must be according to choice and voluntary. Now the exercise of the excellences is concerned with these. Therefore excellence also is in our own power, and so too vice. For where it is in our power to act it is also in our power not to act, and vice versa; so that, if to act, where this is noble, is in our power, not to act, which will be base, will also be in our power, and if not to act, where this is noble, is in our power, to act, which will be base, will also be in our power. Now if it is in our power to do noble or base acts, and likewise in our power not to do them, and this was what being good or bad meant, then it is in our power to be virtuous or vicious.

The saying that 'no one is voluntarily wicked or involuntarily blessed' seems to be partly false and partly true; for no one is involuntarily blessed, but wickedness *is* voluntary. Or else we shall have to dispute what has just been said, at any rate, and deny that man is a moving principle or begetter of his actions as of children. But if these facts are evident and we cannot refer actions to moving principles other than those in ourselves, the acts whose moving principles are in us must themselves also be in our power and voluntary.

Witness seems to be borne to this both by individuals in their private capacity and by legislators themselves; for these punish and take vengeance on those who do wicked acts (unless they have acted under compulsion or as a result of ignorance for which they are not themselves responsible), while they honour those who do noble acts, as though they meant to encourage the latter and deter the former. But no one is encouraged to do the things that are neither in our power nor voluntary; it is assumed that there is no gain in being persuaded not to be hot or in pain or hungry or the like, since we shall experience these feelings none the less. Indeed, we punish a man for his very ignorance, if he is thought responsible for the ignorance, as when penalties are doubled in the case of drunkenness; for the moving principle is in the man himself, since he had the power of not getting drunk and his getting drunk was the cause of his ignorance. And we punish those who are ignorant of anything in the laws that they ought to know and that is not difficult, and so too in the case of anything else that they are thought to be ignorant of through carelessness; we assume that it is in their power not to be ignorant, since they have the power of taking care.

But perhaps a man is the kind of man not to take care. Still they are themselves by their slack lives responsible for becoming men of that
5　kind, and men are themselves responsible for being unjust or self-indulgent, in that they cheat or spend their time in drinking bouts and the like; for it is activities exercised on particular objects that make the corresponding character. This is plain from the case of people training for any contest or action; they practise the activity the whole time. Now not to know that it is from the exercise of activities on particular objects
10　that states of character are produced is the mark of a thoroughly senseless person. Again, it is irrational to suppose that a man who acts unjustly does not wish to be unjust or a man who acts self-indulgently to be self-indulgent. But if without being ignorant a man does the things which will make him unjust, he will be unjust voluntarily. Yet it does not follow that if he wishes he will cease to be
15　unjust and will be just. For neither does the man who is ill become well on those terms—although he may, perhaps, be ill voluntarily, through living incontinently and disobeying his doctors. In that case it was *then* open to him not to be ill, but not now, when he has thrown away his chance, just as when you have let a stone go it is too late to recover it; but yet it was in your power to throw it, since the
20　moving principle was in you. So, too, to the unjust and to the self-indulgent man it was open at the beginning not to become men of this kind, and so they are such voluntarily; but now that they have become so it is not possible for them not to be so.

But not only are the vices of the soul voluntary, but those of the body also for some men, whom we accordingly blame; while no one blames those who are ugly by nature, we blame those who are so owing to want of exercise and care. So it is, too, with respect to weakness and infirmity;
25　no one would reproach a man blind from birth or by disease or from a blow, but rather pity him, while everyone would blame a man who was blind from alcoholism or some other form of self-indulgence. Of vices of the body, then, those in our own power are blamed, those not in our
30　power are not. And if this be so, in the other cases also the vices that are blamed must be in our own power.

Now someone may say that all men aim at the apparent good, but
1114ᵇ　have no control over the appearance; but the end appears to each man in a form answering to his character. We reply that if each man is somehow responsible for the state he is in, he will also be himself somehow

responsible for how things appear to him; but if not, no one is responsible for his own evildoing, but everyone does evil acts through ignorance of the end, thinking that by these he will get what is best, and the aiming at the end is not self-chosen but one must be born with an eye, as it were, by which to judge rightly and choose what is truly good, and he is well endowed by nature who is well endowed with this. For it is what is greatest and most noble, and what we cannot get or learn from another, but must have just such as it was when given us at birth, and to be well and nobly endowed with this will be complete and true natural endowment. If this is true, then, how will excellence be more voluntary than vice? To both men alike, the good and the bad, the end appears and is fixed by nature or however it may be, and it is by referring everything else to this that men do whatever they do.

Whether, then, it is not by nature that the end appears to each man such as it does appear, but something also depends on him, or the end is natural but because the good man does the rest voluntarily excellence is voluntary, vice also will be none the less voluntary; for in the case of the bad man there is equally present that which depends on himself in his actions even if not in his end. If, then, as is asserted, the excellences are voluntary (for we are ourselves somehow part-causes of our states of character, and it is by being persons of a certain kind that we assume the end to be so-and-so), the vices also will be voluntary; for the same is true of them.

With regard to the excellences in *general* we have stated their genus in outline, viz. that they are means and that they are states, and that they tend by their own nature to the doing of the acts by which they are produced, and that they are in our power and voluntary, and act as right reason prescribes. But actions and states are not voluntary in the same way; for we are masters of our actions from the beginning right to the end, if we know the particular facts, but though we control the beginning of our states the gradual progress is not obvious, any more than it is in illnesses; because it was in our power, however, to act in this way or not in this way, therefore the states are voluntary.

Let us take up the several excellences, however, and say which they are and what sort of things they are concerned with and how they are concerned with them; at the same time it will become plain how many they are. And first let us speak of courage.

CHAPTER 6

That it is a mean with regard to fear and confidence has already been made evident; and plainly the things we fear are terrible things, and these are, to speak without qualification, evils; for which reason people

10 even define fear as expectation of evil. Now we fear all evils, e.g. disgrace, poverty, disease, friendlessness, death, but the brave man is not thought to be concerned with all; for to fear some things is even right and noble, and it is base not to fear them—e.g. disgrace; he who fears this is good and modest, and he who does not is shameless. He is, however,

15 by some people called brave, by an extension of the word; for he has in him something which is like the brave man, since the brave man also is a fearless person. Poverty and disease we perhaps ought not to fear, nor in general the things that do not proceed from vice and are not due to a man himself. But not even the man who is fearless of these is brave. Yet we apply the word to him also in virtue of a similarity; for some who in the

20 dangers of war are cowards are liberal and are confident in face of the loss of money. Nor is a man a coward if he fears insult to his wife and children or envy or anything of the kind; nor brave if he is confident when he is about to be flogged. With what sort of terrible things, then, is the brave man concerned? Surely with the greatest; for no one is more

25 likely than he to stand his ground against what is dreadful. Now death is the most terrible of all things; for it is the end, and nothing is thought to be any longer either good or bad for the dead. But the brave man would not seem to be concerned even with death in *all* circumstances, e.g. at sea or in disease. In what circumstances, then? Surely in the noblest.

30 Now such deaths are those in battle; for these take place in the greatest and noblest danger. And this agrees with the ways in which honours are bestowed in city-states and at the courts of monarchs. Properly, then, he will be called brave who is fearless in face of a noble death, and of all emergencies that involve death; and the emergencies of war are in the highest degree of this kind. Yet at sea also, and in disease, the brave man

1115ᵇ is fearless, but not in the same way as the seamen; for he has given up hope for safety, and is disliking the thought of death in this shape, while they are hopeful because of their experience. At the same time, we show courage in situations where there is the opportunity of showing prowess

5 or where death is noble; but in these forms of death neither of these conditions is fulfilled.

CHAPTER 7

What is terrible is not the same for all men; but we say there are things
terrible even beyond human strength. These, then, are terrible to
everyone—at least to every sensible man; but the terrible things that are
not beyond human strength differ in magnitude and degree, and so too   10
do the things that inspire confidence. Now the brave man is as dauntless
as man may be. Therefore, while he will fear even the things that are not
beyond human strength, he will fear them as he ought and as reason
directs, and he will face them for the sake of what is noble; for this is the
end of excellence. But it is possible to fear these more, or less, and again
to fear things that are not terrible as if they were. Of the faults that are   15
committed one consists in fearing what one should not, another in
fearing as we should not, another in fearing when we should not, and so
on; and so too with respect to the things that inspire confidence. The
man, then, who faces and who fears the right things and with the right
aim, in the right way and at the right time, and who feels confidence
under the corresponding conditions, is brave; for the brave man feels
and acts according to the merits of the case and in whatever way reason   20
directs. Now the end of every activity is conformity to the corresponding
state. This is true, therefore, of the brave man as well as of others. But
courage is noble. Therefore the end also is noble; for each thing is
defined by its end. Therefore it is for a noble end that the brave man
endures and acts as courage directs.

Of those who go to excess he who exceeds in fearlessness has no
name (we have said previously that many states have no names), but he   25
would be a sort of madman or insensible person if he feared nothing,
neither earthquakes nor the waves, as they say the Celts do not; while
the man who exceeds in confidence about what really is terrible is
rash. The rash man, however, is also thought to be boastful and only a
pretender to courage; at all events, as the brave man *is* with regard to   30
what is terrible, so the rash man wishes to *appear*; and so he imitates
him in situations where he can. Hence also most of them are a mixture
of rashness and cowardice; for, while in these situations they display
confidence, they do not hold their ground against what is really
terrible. The man who exceeds in fear is a coward; for he fears both
what he ought not and as he ought not, and all the similar character-
izations attach to him. He is lacking also in confidence; but he is more   1116ᵃ
conspicuous for his excess of fear in painful situations. The coward,
then, is a despairing sort of person; for he fears everything. The brave

man, on the other hand, has the opposite disposition; for confidence is
5   the mark of a hopeful disposition. The coward, the rash man, and the
brave man, then, are concerned with the same objects but are differently disposed towards them; for the first two exceed and fall short,
while the third holds the middle, which is the right, position; and rash
men are precipitate, and wish for dangers beforehand but draw back
when they are in them, while brave men are keen in the moment of
action, but quiet beforehand.

10   As we have said, then, courage is a mean with respect to things that
inspire confidence or fear, in the circumstances that have been stated;
and it chooses or endures things because it is noble to do so, or because
it is base not to do so. But to die to escape from poverty or love or
anything painful is not the mark of a brave man, but rather of a coward;
for it is softness to fly from what is troublesome, and such a man endures
15   death not because it is noble but to fly from evil.

CHAPTER 8

Courage, then, is something of this sort, but the name is also applied to
five other kinds. (1) First comes political courage; for this is most like
true courage. Citizens seem to face dangers because of the penalties
imposed by the laws and the reproaches they would otherwise incur,
and because of the honours they win by such action; and therefore those
20   peoples seem to be bravest among whom cowards are held in dishonour
and brave men in honour. This is the kind of courage that Homer
depicts, e.g. in Diomede and in Hector:

> First will Polydamas be to heap reproach on me then;

and

25   For Hector one day 'mid the Trojans shall utter his vaulting harangue:
'Afraid was Tydeides, and fled from my face'

This kind of courage is most like that which we described earlier,
because it is due to excellence; for it is due to shame and to desire of a
noble object (i.e. honour) and avoidance of disgrace, which is ignoble.
30   One might rank in the same class even those who are compelled by their
rulers; but they are inferior, inasmuch as they act not from shame but
from fear, and to avoid not what is disgraceful but what is painful; for
their masters compel them, as Hector does:

But if I shall spy any dastard that cowers far from the fight,
Vainly will such an one hope to escape from the dogs.   35

And those who give them their posts, and beat them if they retreat, do the same, and so do those who draw them up with trenches or something   1116^b of the sort behind them; all of these apply compulsion. But one ought to be brave not under compulsion but because it is noble to be so.

(2) Experience with regard to particular facts is also thought to be courage; this is indeed the reason why Socrates thought courage was   5 knowledge. Other people exhibit this quality in other dangers, and soldiers exhibit it in the dangers of war; for there seem to be many empty alarms in war, of which these have had the most comprehensive experience; therefore they seem brave, because the others do not know the nature of the facts. Again, their experience make them most capable of doing without being done to, since they can use their arms and have the   10 kind that are likely to be best both for doing and for not being done to; therefore they fight like armed men against unarmed or like trained athletes against amateurs; for in such contests too it is not the bravest men that fight best, but those who are strongest and have their bodies in the best condition. Soldiers turn cowards, however, when the danger   15 puts too great a strain on them and they are inferior in numbers and equipment; for they are the first to fly, while citizen-forces die at their posts, as in fact happened at the temple of Hermes. For to the latter flight is disgraceful and death is preferable to safety on those terms;   20 while the former from the very beginning faced the danger on the assumption that they were stronger, and when they know the facts they fly, fearing death more than disgrace; but the brave man is not that sort of person.

(3) Passion also is sometimes reckoned as courage; those who act from passion, like wild beasts rushing at those who have wounded them,   25 are thought to be brave, because brave men also are passionate; for passion above all things is eager to rush on danger, and hence Homer's 'put strength into his passion' and 'aroused their spirit and passion' and 'bitter spirit in his nostrils' and 'his blood boiled'. For all such expressions seem to indicate the stirring and onset of passion. Now   30 brave men act for the sake of the noble, but passion aids them; while wild beasts act under the influence of pain; for they attack because they have been wounded or because they are afraid, since if they are in a forest they do not come near one. Thus they are not brave because, driven by pain and passion, they rush on danger without foreseeing any of the perils,   35

since at that rate even asses would be brave when they are hungry; for
1117ᵃ blows will not drive them from their food; and lust also makes adulterers
do many daring things. The courage that is due to passion seems to be
5   the most natural, and to be courage if choice and aim be added.

Men, then, as well as beasts, suffer pain when they are angry, and are
pleased when they exact their revenge; those who fight for these
reasons, however, are pugnacious but not brave; for they do not act for
the sake of the noble nor as reason directs, but from feeling; they have,
however, something akin to courage.

10   (4) Nor are sanguine people brave; for they are confident in danger
only because they have conquered often and against many foes. Yet they
closely resemble brave men, because both are confident; but brave man
are confident for the reasons stated earlier, while these are so because
they think they are the strongest and can suffer nothing. (Drunken men
also behave in this way; they become sanguine.) When their adventures
15   do not succeed, however, they run away; but it was the mark of a brave
man to face things that are, and seem, terrible for a man, because it is
noble to do so and disgraceful not to do so. Hence also it is thought the
mark of a braver man to be fearless and undisturbed in sudden alarms
than to be so in those that are foreseen; for it must have proceeded more
20   from a state of character, because less from preparation; for acts that are
foreseen may be chosen by calculation and reason, but sudden actions
are in accordance with one's state of character.

(5) People who are ignorant also appear brave, and they are not far
removed from those of a sanguine temper, but are inferior inasmuch as
they have no self-reliance while these have. Hence also the sanguine
25   hold their ground for a time; but those who have been deceived fly if they
know or suspect that things are different, as happened to the Argives
when they fell in with the Spartans and took them for Sicyonians.

CHAPTER 9

We have, then, described the character both of brave men and of those
who are thought to be brave.

Though courage is concerned with confidence and fear, it is not
30   concerned with both alike, but more with the things that inspire fear; for
he who is undisturbed in face of these and bears himself as he should
towards these is more truly brave than the man who does so towards the
things that inspire confidence. It is for facing what is painful, then, as
has been said, that men are called brave. Hence also courage involves

pain, and is justly praised; for it is harder to face what is painful than to abstain from what is pleasant. Yet the end which courage sets before it would seem to be pleasant, but to be concealed by the attending circumstances, as happens also in athletic contests; for the end at which boxers aim is pleasant—the crown and the honours—but the blows they take are distressing to flesh and blood, and painful, and so is their whole exertion; and because the blows and the exertions are many the end, which is but small, appears to have nothing pleasant in it. And so, if the case of courage is similar, death and wounds will be painful to the brave man and against his will, but he will face them because it is noble to do so or because it is base not to do so. And the more he is possessed of excellence in its entirety and the happier he is, the more he will be pained at the thought of death; for life is best worth living for such a man, and he is knowingly losing the greatest goods, and this is painful. But he is none the less brave, and perhaps all the more so, because he chooses noble deeds of war at that cost. It is not the case, then, with all the excellences that the exercise of them is pleasant, except in so far as it reaches its end. But it is quite possible that the best soldiers may be not men of this sort but those who are less brave but have no other good; for these are ready to face danger, and they sell their life for trifling gains.

So much, then, for courage; it is not difficult to grasp its nature in outline, at any rate, from what has been said.

CHAPTER 10

After courage let us speak of temperance; for these seem to be the excellences of the irrational parts. We have said that temperance is a mean with regard to pleasures (for it is less, and not in the same way, concerned with pains); self-indulgence also is manifested in the same sphere. Now, therefore, let us determine with what sort of pleasures they are concerned. We may assume the distinction between bodily pleasures and those of the soul, such as love of honour and love of learning; for the lover of each of these delights in that of which he is a lover, the body being in no way affected, but rather the mind; but men who are concerned with such pleasures are called neither temperate nor self-indulgent. Nor, again, are those who are concerned with the other pleasures that are not bodily; for those who are fond of hearing and telling stories and who spend their days on anything that turns up are called gossips, but not self-indulgent, nor are those who are pained at the loss of money or of friends.

1117^b

5

10

15

20

25

30

1118^a

Temperance must be concerned with bodily pleasures, but not all even of these; for those who delight in objects of vision, such as colours and shapes and painting, are called neither temperate nor self-indulgent; yet it would seem possible to delight even in these either as one should or to excess or to a deficient degree.

And so too is it with objects or heaing; no one calls those who delight extravagantly in music or acting self-indulgent, nor those who do so as they ought temperate.

Nor do we apply these names to those who delight in odour, unless it be incidentally; we do not call those self-indulgent who delight in the odour of apples or roses or incense, but rather those who delight in the odour of unguents or of dainty dishes; for self-indulgent people delight in these because these remind them of the objects of their appetite. And one may see even other people, when they are hungry, delighting in the smell of food; but to delight in this kind of thing is the mark of the self-indulgent man; for these are objects of appetite to him.

Nor is there in animals other than man any pleasure connected with these senses except incidentally. For dogs do not delight in the scent of hares, but in the eating of them, but the scent told them the hares were there; nor does the lion delight in the lowing of the ox, but in eating it; but he perceived by the lowing that it was near, and therefore appears to delight in the lowing; and similarly he does not delight because he sees a stag or a wild goat, but because he is going to make a meal of it. Temperance and self-indulgence, however, are concerned with the kind of pleasures that the other animals share in, which therefore appear slavish and brutish; these are touch and taste. But even of taste they appear to make little or no use; for the business of taste is the discriminating of flavours, which is done by wine-tasters and people who season dishes; but they hardly take pleasure in making these discriminations, or at least self-indulgent people do not, but in the actual enjoyment, which in all cases comes through touch, both in the case of food and in that of drink and in that of sexual intercourse. This is why a certain gourmand prayed that his throat might become longer than a crane's, implying that it was the contact that he took pleasure in.

Thus the sense with which self-indulgence is connected is the most widely shared of the senses; and self-indulgence would seem to be justly a matter of reproach, because it attaches to us not as men but as animals. To delight in such things, then, and to love them above all others, is brutish. For even of the pleasures of touch the most liberal have been eliminated, e.g. those produced in the gymnasium by rubbing and by the consequent heat; for the contact characteristic of the self-indulgent man does not affect the whole body but only certain parts.

CHAPTER 11

Of the appetites some seem to be common, others to be peculiar to individuals and acquired; e.g. the appetite for food is natural, since everyone who is without it craves for food or drink, and sometimes for both, and for love also (as Homer says) if he is young and lusty; but not everyone craves for this or that kind of nourishment or love, nor for the same things. Hence such craving appears to be our very own. Yet it has of course something natural about it; for different things are pleasant to different kinds of people, and some things are more pleasant to everyone than chance objects. Now in the natural appetites few go wrong, and only in one direction, that of excess; for to eat or drink whatever offers itself till one is surfeited is to exceed the natural amount, since natural appetite is the replenishment of one's deficiency. Hence these people are called belly-gods, this implying that they fill their belly beyond what is right. It is people of entirely slavish character that become like this. But with regard to the pleasures peculiar to individuals many people go wrong and in many ways. For while the people who are fond of so and so are so called because they delight either in the wrong things, or more than most people do, or in the wrong way, the self-indulgent exceed in all three ways; they both delight in some things that they ought not to delight in (since they are hateful), and if one ought to delight in some of the things they delight in, they do so more than one ought and more than most men do.

Plainly, then, excess with regard to pleasures is self-indulgence and is culpable; with regard to pains one is not, as in the case of courage, called temperate for facing them or self-indulgent for not doing so, but the self-indulgent man is so called because he is pained more than he ought to be at not getting pleasant things (even his pain being caused by pleasure), and the temperate man is so called because he is not pained at the absence of what is pleasant and at his abstinence from it.

The self-indulgent man, then, craves for all pleasant things or those that are most pleasant, and is led by his appetite to choose these at the cost of everything else; hence he is pained both when he fails to get them and when he is craving for them (for appetite involves pain); but it seems absurd to be pained for the sake of pleasure. People who fall short with regard to pleasures and delight in them less than they should are hardly

found; for such insensibility is not human. Even the other animals distinguish different kinds of food and enjoy some and not others; and if there is anyone who finds nothing pleasant and nothing more attractive
10   than anything else, he must be something quite different from a man; this sort of person has not received a name because he hardly occurs. The temperate man occupies a middle position with regard to these objects. For he neither enjoys the things that the self-indulgent man enjoys most—but rather dislikes them—nor in general the things that he should not, nor anything of this sort to excess, nor does he feel pain or craving when they are absent, or does so only to a moderate degree, and
15   not more than he should, nor when he should not, and so on; but the things that, being pleasant, make for health or for good condition, he will desire moderately and as he should, and also other pleasant things if they are not hindrances to these ends, or contrary to what is noble, or beyond his means. For he who neglects these conditions loves such pleasures more than they are worth, but the temperate man is not that
20   sort of person, but the sort of person that right reason prescribes.

CHAPTER 12

Self-indulgence is more like a voluntary state than cowardice. For the former is actuated by pleasure, the latter by pain, of which the one is to be chosen and the other to be avoided; and pain upsets and destroys the nature of the person who feels it, while pleasure does nothing of the sort. Therefore self-indulgence is more voluntary. Hence also it is more
25   a matter of reproach; for it is easier to become accustomed to its objects, since there are many things of this sort in life, and the process of habituation to them is free from danger, while with terrible objects the reverse is the case. But cowardice would seem to be voluntary in a different degree from its particular manifestations; for it is itself painless, but in these we are upset by pain, so that we even throw down
30   our arms and disgrace ourselves in other ways; hence our acts are even thought to be done under compulsion. For the self-indulgent man, on the other hand, the particular acts are voluntary (for he does them with craving and desire), but the whole state is less so; for no one craves to be self-indulgent.

The name self-indulgence is applied also to childish faults; for they
1119^b   bear a certain resemblance to what we have been considering. Which is called after which makes no difference to our present purpose; plainly, however, the later is called after the earlier. The transference of the

name seems not a bad one; for that which desires what is base and which develops quickly ought to be kept in a chastened condition,[5] and these characteristics belong above all to appetite and to the child, since children in fact live at the beck and call of appetite, and it is in them that the desire for what is pleasant is strongest. If, then, it is not going to be obedient and subject to the ruling principle, it will go to great lengths; for in an irrational being the desire for pleasure is insatiable and tries every source of gratification, and the exercise of appetite increases its innate force, and if appetites are strong and violent they even expel the power of calculation. Hence they should be moderate and few, and should in no way oppose reason—and this is what we call an obedient and chastened state—and as the child should live according to the direction of his tutor, so the appetitive element should live according to reason. Hence the appetitive element in a temperate man should harmonize with reason; for the noble is the mark at which both aim, and the temperate man craves for the things he ought, as he ought, and when he ought; and this is what reason directs.

Here we conclude our account of temperance.

BOOK V

CHAPTER I

With regard to justice and injustice we must consider what kind of actions they are concerned with, what sort of mean justice is, and between what extremes the just act is intermediate. Our investigation shall follow the same course as the preceding discussions.

We see that all men mean by justice that kind of state which makes people disposed to do what is just and makes them act justly and wish for what is just; and similarly by injustice that state which makes them act unjustly and wish for what is unjust. Let us too, then, first lay this down as a rough sketch. For the same is not true of the sciences and the faculties as of states. For it seems that the same faculty or science deals with contraries; but a state of character which is one of two contraries does *not* produce the contrary results; e.g. as a result of health we do not do what is the opposite of healthy, but only what is healthy; for we say a man walks healthily, when he walks as a healthy man would.

---

[5] The Greek word for 'self-indulgent' is connected with that for 'chasten', 'punish'.

Now often one contrary state is recognized from its contrary, and often states are recognized from the subjects that exhibit them; for if

20 good condition is known, bad condition also becomes known, and good condition is known from the things that are in good condition, and they from it. If good condition is firmness of flesh, it is necessary both that bad condition should be flabbiness of flesh and that the wholesome should be that which causes firmness in flesh. And it follows for the most

25 part that if one contrary is ambiguous the other also will be ambiguous; e.g. if 'just' is so, that 'unjust' will be so too.

Now 'justice' and 'injustice' seem to be ambiguous, but because the homonymy is close, it escapes notice and is not obvious as it is, comparatively, when the meanings are far apart, e.g. (for here the difference in outward form is great) as the homonymy in the use of *kleis*

30 for the collar-bone of an animal and for that with which we lock a door. Let us then ascertain the different ways in which a man may be said to be unjust. Both the lawless man and the grasping and unequal man are thought to be unjust, so that evidently both the law-abiding and the

1129ᵇ equal man will be just. The just, then, is the lawful and the equal, the unjust the unlawful and the unequal.

Since the unjust man is grasping, he must be concerned with goods—not all goods, but those with which prosperity and adversity have to do, which taken absolutely are always good, but for a particular person

5 are not always good. (Men pray for and pursue the same things; but they should not, but should pray that the things that are good absolutely may also be good for them, and should choose the things that are good for them.) The unjust man does not always choose the greater, but also the less—in the case of things bad absolutely; but because the lesser evil is itself thought to be in a sense good, and

10 graspingness is directed at the good, therefore he is thought to be grasping. And he is unequal; for this contains and is common to both.

Since the lawless man was seen to be unjust and the law-abiding man just, evidently all lawful acts are in a sense just acts; for the acts laid down by the legislative art are lawful, and each of these, we say, is just.

15 Now the laws in their enactments on all subjects aim at the common advantage either of all or of the best or of those who hold power, or something of the sort; so that in one sense we call those acts just that tend to produce and preserve happiness and its components for the political society. And the law bids us do both the acts of a brave man (e.g.

20 not to desert our post or take to flight or throw away our arms), and those of a temperate man (e.g. not to commit adultery or outrage), and those of

a good-tempered man (e.g. not to strike another or speak evil), and similarly with regard to the other excellences and forms of wickedness, commanding some acts and forbidding others; and the rightly-framed 25 law does this rightly, and the hastily conceived one less well.

This form of justice, then is complete excellence—not absolutely, but in relation to others. And therefore justice is often thought to be the greatest of excellences and 'neither evening nor morning star' is so wonderful; and proverbially 'in justice is every excellence comprehended'. And it is complete excellence in its fullest sense, because it is 30 the actual exercise of complete excellence. It is complete because he who possesses it can exercise his excellence towards others too and not merely by himself; for many men can exercise excellence in their own affairs, but not in their relations to others. This is why the saying of 1130ᵃ Bias is thought to be true, that 'rule will show the man'; for a ruler is necessarily in relation to other men and a member of a society. For this same reason justice, alone of the excellences, is thought to be another's good, because it is related to others; for it does what is advantageous to another, either a ruler or a partner. Now the worst man is he who 5 exercises his wickedness both towards himself and towards his friends, and the best man is not he who exercises his excellence towards himself but he who exercises it towards another; for this is a difficult task. Justice in this sense, then, is not part of excellence but excellence entire, nor is the contrary injustice a part of vice but vice entire. What the difference is 10 between excellence and justice in this sense is plain from what we have said; they are the same but being them is not the same; what, as a relation to others, is justice is, as a certain kind of state without qualification, excellence.

CHAPTER 2

But at all events what we are investigating is the justice which is a *part* of excellence; for there is a justice of this kind, as we maintain. Similarly it 15 is with injustice in the particular sense that we are concerned.

That there is such a thing is indicated by the fact that while the man who exhibits in action the other forms of wickedness acts unjustly but not graspingly (e.g. the man who throws away his shield through cowardice or speaks harshly through bad temper or fails to help a friend with money through meanness), when a man acts graspingly he often exhibits none of these vices,—no, nor all together, but certainly wicked- 20 ness of some kind (for we blame him) and injustice. There is, then, another kind of injustice which is a part of injustice in the wide sense, and something unjust which answers to a part of what is unjust in the wide sense of contrary to the law. Again, if one man commits adultery for the sake of gain and makes money by it, while another does so at the bidding of appetite though he loses money and is penalized for it, the latter would be held to be self-indulgent rather than grasping while the former is unjust, but not self-indulgent; evidently, therefore, he is unjust by reason of his making gain by his act. Again, all other unjust acts are ascribed invariably to some particular kind of wickedness, e.g. adultery to self-indulgence, the desertion of a comrade in battle to cowardice, physical violence to anger; but if a man makes gain, his action is ascribed to no form of wickedness but injustice. Evidently, therefore, there is apart from injustice in the wide sense another, particular, injustice which shares the name and nature of the first, because its definition falls within the same genus; for the force of both lies in a relation to others but the one is concerned with honour or money or safety—or that which includes all these, if we had a single name for it—and its motive is the pleasure that arises from gain; while the other is concerned with all the objects with which the good man is concerned.

It is clear, then, that there is more than one kind of justice, and that there is one which is distinct from excellence entire; we must try to grasp what and what sort of thing it is.

The unjust has been divided into the unlawful and the unequal, and the just into the lawful and the equal. To the unlawful answers the afore-mentioned sort of injustice. But since the unequal and the unlawful are not the same, but are different as a part is from its whole (for all that is unequal is unlawful, but not all that is unlawful is unequal), the unjust and injustice are not the same as but different from the former kind, as part from whole; for injustice in this sense is a part of injustice in the wide sense, and similarly justice in the one sense of justice in the other. Therefore we must speak also about particular justice and particular injustice, and similarly about the just and the unjust. The justice, then, which answers to the whole of excellence and the corresponding in-justice, one being the exercise of excellence as a whole, and the other that of vice as a whole towards others, we may leave on one side. And how the just and the unjust which answer to these are to be distinguished is evident; for practically the majority of the acts commanded by the law are those which are prescribed from the point of view of excellence taken as a whole; for the law bids us practise every

excellence and forbids us to practise any vice. And the things that tend   25
to produce excellence taken as a whole are those of the acts prescribed
with a view to education for the common good. But with regard to the
education of the individual as such, which makes him without qualification a good man, we must determine later whether this is the function of
the political art or of another; for perhaps it is not the same in every case
to be a good man and a good citizen.

Of particular justice and that which is just in the corresponding   30
sense, one kind is that which is manifested in distributions of honour or
money or the other things that fall to be divided among those who have a
share in the constitution (for in these it is possible for one man to have a
share either unequal or equal to that of another), and another kind is that
which plays a rectifying part in transactions. Of this there are two   1131ª
divisions; of transactions some are voluntary and others involuntary—
voluntary such transactions as sale, purchase, usury, pledging, lending,
depositing, letting (they are called voluntary because the origin of these   5
transactions is voluntary), while of the involuntary some are clandes-
tine, such as theft, adultery, poisoning, procuring, enticement of slaves,
assassination, false witness, and others are violent, such as assault,
imprisonment, murder, robbery with violence, mutilation, abuse,
insult.

CHAPTER 5

We have now defined the unjust and the just. These having been   1133ᵇ
marked off from each other, it is plain that just action is intermediate   30
between acting unjustly and being justly treated; for the one is to have
too much and the other to have too little. Justice is a kind of mean, but
not in the same way as the other excellences, but because it relates to an
intermediate amount, while injustice relates to the extremes. And
justice is that in virtue of which the just man is said to be a doer, by   1134ª
choice, of that which is just, and one who will distribute either between
himself and another or between two others not so as to give more of what
is desirable to himself and less to his neighbour (and conversely with
what is harmful), but so as to give what is equal in accordance with   5
proportion; and similarly in distributing between two other persons.
Injustice on the other hand is similarly related to the unjust, which is
excess and defect, contrary to proportion, of the useful or hurtful. For
which reason injustice is excess and defect, viz. because it is productive
of excess and defect—in one's own case excess of what is in its own

10   nature useful and defect of what is hurtful, while in the case of others it is
      as a whole like what it is in one's own case, but proportion may be
      violated in either direction. In the unjust act to have too little is to be
      unjustly treated; to have too much is to act unjustly.

15   Let this be taken as our account of the nature of justice and injustice,
      and similarly of the just and the unjust in general.

CHAPTER 7

1134ᵇ   Of political justice part is natural, part legal,—natural, that which every-
      where has the same force and does not exist by people's thinking this or
20   that; legal, that which is originally indifferent, but when it has been laid
      down is not indifferent, e.g. that a prisoner's ransom shall be a mina, or
      that a goat and not two sheep shall be sacrificed, and again all the laws
      that are passed for particular cases, e.g. that sacrifice shall be made in
      honour of Brasidas, and the provisions of decrees. Now some think that
      all justice is of this sort, because that which is by nature is unchangeable
25   and has everywhere the same force (as fire burns both here and in
      Persia), while they see change in the things recognized as just. This,
      however, is not true in this unqualified way, but is true in a sense; or
      rather, with the gods it is perhaps not true at all, while with us there is
      something that is just even by nature, yet all of it changeable; but still
30   some is by nature, some not by nature. It is evident which sort of thing,
      among things capable of being otherwise, is by nature, and which is not
      but is legal and conventional, assuming that both are equally change-
      able. And in all other things the same distinction will apply; by nature
      the right hand is stronger, yet it is possible that all men should come to
1135ᵃ   be ambidextrous. The things which are just by virtue of convention and
      expediency are like measures; for wine and corn measures are not
      everywhere equal, but larger in wholesale and smaller in retail markets.
      Similarly, the things which are just not by nature but by human enact-
      ment are not everywhere the same, since constitutions also are not the
5   same, though there is but one which is everywhere by nature the best.
      . . .

CHAPTER 8

15   Acts just and unjust being as we have described them, a man acts
      unjustly or justly whenever he does such acts voluntarily; when in-
      voluntarily, he acts neither unjustly nor justly except in an incidental

way; for he does things which happen to be just or unjust. Whether an act is or is not one of injustice (or of justice) is determined by its voluntariness or involuntariness; for when it is voluntary it is blamed, and at the same time is then an act of injustice; so that there will be things that are unjust but not yet acts of injustice, if voluntariness be not present as well. By the voluntary I mean, as has been said before, any of the things in a man's own power which he does with knowledge, i.e. not in ignorance either of the person acted on or of the instrument used or of the end that will be attained (e.g. whom he is striking, with what, and to what end), each such act being done not incidentally nor under compulsion (e.g. if you take my hand and strike someone else with it, I do not act voluntarily; for the act was not in my power). The person struck may be the striker's father, and the striker may know that it is a man or one of the persons present, but not know that it is his father; a similar distinction may be made in the case of the end, and with regard to the whole action. Therefore that which is done in ignorance, or though not done in ignorance is not in the agent's power, or is done under compulsion, is involuntary (for many natural processes, also, we knowingly both perform and experience, none of which is either voluntary or involuntary; e.g. growing old or dying). But in the case of unjust and just acts alike the injustice or justice may be only incidental; for a man might return a deposit unwillingly and from fear, and then he must not be said either to do what is just or to act justly, except in an incidental way. Similarly the man who under compulsion and unwillingly fails to return the deposit must be said to act unjustly, and to do what is unjust, only incidentally. Of voluntary acts we do some by choice, others not by choice; by choice those which we do after deliberation, not by choice those which we do without previous deliberation. Thus there are three kinds of injury in transactions; those done in ignorance are *mistakes* when the person acted on, the act, the instrument, or the end is other than the agent supposed; the agent thought either that he was not hitting any one or that he was not hitting with this missile or not hitting this person or to this end, but a result followed other than that which he thought likely (e.g. he threw not with intent to wound but only to prick), or the person hit or the missile was other than he supposed. Now when the injury takes place contrary to reasonable expectation, it is a *misadventure*. When it is not contrary to reasonable expectation but does not imply vice, it is a *mistake* (for a man makes a mistake when the ignorance originates in him, but is the victim of accident when its origin lies outside him). When he acts with

20   knowledge but not after deliberation, it is an *act of injustice*—e.g. the acts due to anger or to other passions necessary or natural to man; for when men do such harmful and mistaken acts they act unjustly, and the acts are acts of injustice, but this does not imply that the doers are

25   unjust or wicked; for the injury is not due to vice. But when a man acts from choice, he is an *unjust man* and a vicious man.

Hence acts proceeding from anger are rightly judged not to be done of malice aforethought; for it is not the man who acts in anger but he who enraged him that starts the mischief. Again, the matter in dispute is not whether the thing happened or not, but its justice; for it is apparent injustice that occasions anger. For they do not dispute the occurrence of

30   the act—as in commercial transactions where one of the two parties *must* be vicious—unless they do so owing to forgetfulness; but, agreeing about the fact, they dispute on which side justice lies (whereas a man who has deliberately injured another cannot help knowing that he has done so), so that the one thinks he is being treated unjustly and the other disagrees.

1136ᵃ   But if a man harms another by choice, he acts unjustly; and *these* are the acts of injustice which imply that the doer is an unjust man, provided that the act violates proportion or equality. Similarly, a man *is just* when he acts justly by choice; but he *acts justly* if he merely acts voluntarily.

5   Of involuntary acts some are forgivable, others not. For the mistakes which men make not only in ignorance but also from ignorance are forgivable, while those which men do not from ignorance but (though they do them *in* ignorance) owing to a passion which is neither natural nor such as man is liable to, are not forgivable.

CHAPTER 9

. . .

1137ᵃ   Men think that acting unjustly is in their power, and therefore that being just is easy. But it is not; to lie with one's neighbour's wife, to wound another, to deliver a bribe, is easy and in our power, but to do these things as a result of a certain state of character is neither easy nor in our power. Similarly to know what is just and what is unjust requires, men

10   think, no great wisdom, because it is not hard to understand the matters dealt with by the laws (though these are not the things that are just, except incidentally); but how actions must be done and distributions effected in order to be just, to know *this* is a greater achievement than knowing what is good for the health; though even there, while it is easy to know that honey, wine, hellebore, cautery, and the use of the knife are

so, to know how, to whom, and when they should be applied with a view $_{15}$ to producing health, is no less an achievement than that of being a physician. Again, for this reason men think that acting unjustly is characteristic of the just man no less than of the unjust, because he would be not less but even more capable of doing each of these acts; for he could lie with a woman or wound a neighbour; and the brave man $_{20}$ could throw away his shield and turn to flight in this direction or in that. But to play the coward or to act unjustly consists not in doing these things, except incidentally, but in doing them as the result of a certain state of character, just as to practise medicine and to heal consists not in applying or not applying the knife, in using or not using medicines, but $_{25}$ in doing so in a certain way.

. . .

CHAPTER 10

Our next subject is equity and the equitable, and their respective $_{30}$ relations to justice and the just. For on examination they appear to be neither absolutely the same nor generically different; and while we sometimes praise what is equitable and the equitable man (so that we apply the name by way of praise even to instances of the other virtues, instead of 'good', meaning by 'more equitable' that a thing is better), at 1137^{b} other times, when we reason it out, it seems strange if the equitable, being something different from the just, is yet praiseworthy; for either the just or the equitable is not good, if they are different; or, if both are $_{5}$ good, they are the same.

These, then, are pretty much the considerations that give rise to the problem about the equitable; they are all in a sense correct and not opposed to one another; for the equitable, though it is better than one kind of justice, yet is just, and it is not as being a different class of thing that it is better than the just. The same thing, then, is just and equitable, and while both are good the equitable is superior. What creates the $_{10}$ problem is that the equitable is just, but not the legally just but a correction of legal justice. The reason is that all law is universal but about some things it is not possible to make a universal statement which will be correct. In those cases, then, in which it is necessary to speak universally, but not possible to do so correctly, the law takes the usual case, $_{15}$ though it is not ignorant of the possibility of error. And it is none the less correct; for the error is not in the law nor in the legislator but in the nature of the thing, since the matter of practical affairs is of this kind

20   from the start. When the law speaks universally, then, and a case arises
      on it which is not covered by the universal statement, then it is right,
      when the legislator fails us and has erred by over-simplicity, to correct
      the omission—to say what the legislator himself would have said had he
      been present, and would have put into his law if he had known. Hence
25   the equitable is just, and better than one kind of justice—not better than
      absolute justice but better than the error that arises from the absolute-
      ness of the statement. And this is the nature of the equitable, a correc-
      tion of law where it is defective owing to its universality. In fact this is the
      reason why all things are not determined by law, viz. that about some
      things it is impossible to lay down a law, so that a decree is needed. For
30   when the thing is indefinite the rule also is indefinite, like the lead rule
      used in making the Lesbian moulding; the rule adapts itself to the shape
      of the stone and is not rigid, and so too the decree is adapted to the facts.
          It is plain, then, what the equitable is, and that it is just and is better
      than one kind of justice. It is evident also from this who the equitable
      man is; the man who chooses and does such acts, and is no stickler for
      justice in a bad sense but tends to take less than his share though he has
1138ᵃ the law on his side, is equitable, and this state is equity, which is a sort of
      justice, and not a different state.

BOOK VI

CHAPTER I

1138ᵇ Since we have previously said that one ought to choose that which is
      intermediate, not the excess nor the defect, and that the intermediate
20   is determined by the dictates of reason, let us discuss this. In all the
      states we have mentioned, as in all other matters, there is a mark to
      which the man who possesses reason looks, and heightens or relaxes
      his activity accordingly, and there is a standard which determines the
      mean states which we say are intermediate between excess and defect,
25   being in accordance with right reason. But such a statement, though
      true, is by no means illuminating; for in all other pursuits which are
      objects of knowledge it is indeed true to say that we must not exert
      ourselves nor relax our efforts too much or too little, but to an
      intermediate extent and as right reason dictates; but if a man had only
30   this knowledge he would be none the wiser—e.g. we should not know
      what sort of medicines to apply to our body if someone were to say 'all

those which the medical art prescribes, and which agree with the practice of one who possesses the art'. Hence it is necessary with regard to the states of the soul also not only that this true statement should be made, but also that it should be determined what right reason is and what is the standard that fixes it.

We divided the excellences of the soul and said that some are excellences of character and others of intellect. Now we have discussed the moral excellences; with regard to the others let us express our view as follows, beginning with some remarks about the soul. We said before that there are two parts of the soul—that which possesses reason and that which is irrational; let us now draw a similar distinction within the part which possesses reason. And let it be assumed that there are two parts which possess reason—one by which we contemplate the kind of things whose principles cannot be otherwise, and one by which we contemplate variable things; for where objects differ in kind the part of the soul answering to each of the two is different in kind, since it is in virtue of a certain likeness and kinship with their objects that they have the knowledge they have. Let one of these parts be called the scientific and the other the calculative; for to deliberate and to calculate are the same thing, but no one deliberates about what cannot be otherwise. Therefore the calculative is one part of the faculty which possesses reason. We must, then, learn what is the best state of each of these two parts; for this is the excellence of each.

1139ᵃ

5

10

15

CHAPTER 2

The excellence of a thing is relative to its proper function. Now there are three things in the soul which control action and truth—sensation, thought, desire.

Of these sensation originates no action; this is plain from the fact that beasts have sensation but no share in action.

What affirmation and negation are in thinking, pursuit and avoidance are in desire; so that since moral excellence is a state concerned with choice, and choice is deliberate desire, therefore both the reasoning must be true and the desire right, if the choice is to be good, and the latter must pursue just what the former asserts. Now this kind of intellect and of truth is practical; of the intellect which is contemplative, not practical nor productive, the good and the bad state are truth and falsity (for this is the function of everything intellectual); while of

20

25

30 the part which is practical and intellectual the good state is truth in
agreement with right desire.

The origin of action—its efficient, not its final cause—is choice, and
that of choice is desire and reasoning with a view to an end. This is
why choice cannot exist either without thought and intellect or without a moral state; for good action and its opposite cannot exist without
35 a combination of intellect and character. Intellect itself, however,
moves nothing, but only the intellect which aims at an end and is prac-
1139ᵇ tical; for this rules the productive intellect as well, since every one who
makes makes for an end, and that which is made is not an end in the
unqualified sense (but only relative to something, i.e. of something)—
only that which is *done* is that; for good action is an end, and desire
aims at this. Hence choice is either desiderative thought or intellectual
desire, and such an origin of action is a man.

5 (Nothing that is past is an object of choice, for example no one
chooses to have sacked Troy; for no one *deliberates* about the past, but
about what is future and contingent, while what is past is not capable
of not having taken place; hence Agathon is right in saying

10   For this alone is lacking even to God,
To make undone things that have once been done.)

The function of both the intellectual parts, then, is truth. Therefore
the states that are most strictly those in respect of which each of these
parts will reach truth are the excellences of the two parts.

CHAPTER 3

Let us begin, then, from the beginning, and discuss these states once
15 more. Let it be assumed that the states by virtue of which the soul
possesses truth by way of affirmation or denial are five in number: art,
knowledge, practical wisdom, philosophic wisdom, comprehension;⁶
for belief and opinion may be mistaken.

Now what *knowledge* is, if we are to speak exactly and not follow
20 mere similarities, is plain from what follows. We all suppose that what
we know is not capable of being otherwise; of things capable of being
otherwise we do not know, when they have passed outside our
observation, whether they exist or not. Therefore the object of
knowledge is of necessity. Therefore it is eternal; for things that are of
necessity in the unqualified sense are all eternal; and things that are

⁶ *Nous*, often rendered by 'intuitive reason'.

eternal are ungenerated and imperishable. Again, every science is   25
thought to be capable of being taught, and its object of being learned.
And all teaching starts from what is already known, as we maintain in
the *Analytics* also; for it proceeds sometimes through induction and
sometimes by deduction. Now induction is of first principles and of
the universal, and deduction proceeds *from* universals. There are
therefore principles from which deduction proceeds, which are not   30
reached by deduction; it is therefore by induction that they are
acquired. Knowledge, then, is a state of capacity to demonstrate, and
has the other limiting characteristics which we specify in the *Analytics*;
for it is when a man believes in a certain way and the principles are
known to him that he has knowledge, since if they are not better
known to him than the conclusion, he will have his knowledge only   35
incidentally.

Let this, then, be taken as our account of knowledge.

CHAPTER 4

Among things that can be otherwise are included both things made   1140ᵃ
and things done; making and acting are different (for their nature we
treat even the discussions outside our school as reliable); so that the
reasoned state of capacity to act is different from the reasoned state of
capacity to make. Nor are they included one in the other; for neither is   5
acting making nor is making acting. Now since building is an art and is
essentially a reasoned state of capacity to make, and there is neither
any art that is not such a state nor any such state that is not an art, *art* is
identical with a state of capacity to make, involving a true course of   10
reasoning. All art is concerned with coming into being, i.e. with
contriving and considering how something may come into being
which is capable of either being or not being, and whose origin is in
the maker and not in the thing made; for art is concerned neither with
things that are, or come into being, by necessity, nor with things that
do so in accordance with nature (since these have their origin in them-   15
selves). Making and acting being different, art must be a matter of
making, not of acting. And in a sense chance and art are concerned
with the same objects; as Agathon says, 'art loves chance and chance
loves art'. Art, then, as has been said, is a state concerned with making,   20
involving a true course of reasoning, and lack of art on the contrary is a
state concerned with making, involving a false course of reasoning;
both are concerned with what can be otherwise.

CHAPTER 5

Regarding *practical wisdom* we shall get at the truth by considering who
25   are the persons we credit with it. Now it is thought to be a mark of a
man of practical wisdom to be able to deliberate well about what is
good and expedient for himself, not in some particular respect, e.g.
about what sorts of thing conduce to health or to strength, but about
what sorts of thing conduce to the good life in general. This is shown
by the fact that we credit men with practical wisdom in some particular respect when they have calculated well with a view to some
30   good end which is one of those that are not the object of any art. Thus
in general the man who is capable of deliberating has practical
wisdom. Now no one deliberates about things that cannot be otherwise nor about things that it is impossible for him to do. Therefore,
since knowledge involves demonstration, but there is no demonstration of things whose first principles can be otherwise (for all such
1140^b   things might actually be otherwise), and since it is impossible to
deliberate about things that are of necessity, practical wisdom cannot
be knowledge or art; not knowledge because that which can be done
is capable of being otherwise, not art because action and making are
different kinds of thing. It remains, then, that it is a true and reasoned
5   state of capacity to act with regard to the things that are good or bad
for man. For while making has an end other than itself, action cannot;
for good action itself is its end. It is for this reason that we think
Pericles and men like him have practical wisdom, viz. because they
can see what is good for themselves and what is good for men in
10   general; we consider that those can do this who are good at managing
households or states. (This is why we call temperance by this name;
we imply that it preserves one's practical wisdom.[7] Now what it
preserves is a belief of the kind we have described. For it is not any and
every belief that pleasant and painful objects destroy and pervert, e.g.
the belief that the triangle has or has not its angles equal to two right
15   angles, but only beliefs about what is to be done. For the principles of
the things that are done consist in that for the sake of which they are to
be done; but the man who has been ruined by pleasure or pain forthwith fails to see any such principle—to see that for the sake of this or
because of this he ought to choose and do whatever he chooses and
does; for vice is destructive of the principle.)

---

[7] The Greek word for 'temperance' is connected with the expression translated
'preserving one's practical wisdom'.

Practical wisdom, then, must be a reasoned and true state of 20
capacity to act with regard to human goods. But further, while there is
such a thing as excellence in art, there is no such thing as excellence
in practical wisdom; and in art he who errs willingly is preferable, but
in practical wisdom, as in the excellences, he is the reverse. Plainly,
then, practical wisdom is an excellence and not an art. There being 25
two parts of the soul that possess reason, it must be the excellence of
one of the two, i.e. of that part which forms opinions; for opinion is
about what can be otherwise, and so is practical wisdom. But yet it is
not only a reasoned state; this is shown by the fact that a state of that
sort may be forgotten but practical wisdom cannot. 30

CHAPTER 6

Knowledge is belief about things that are universal and necessary, and
there are principles of everything that is demonstrated and of all
knowledge (for knowledge involves reasoning). This being so, the first
principle of what is known cannot be an object of knowledge, of art, or
of practical wisdom; for that which can be known can be demonstrated, and art and practical wisdom deal with things that can be 1141ª
otherwise. Nor are these first principles the objects of wisdom, for it is
a mark of the wise man to have *demonstration* about some things. If,
then, the states by which we have truth and are never deceived about
things that cannot—or can—be otherwise are knowledge, practical
wisdom, philosophic wisdom, and comprehension, and it cannot be 5
any of the three (i.e. practical wisdom, scientific knowledge, or philosophic wisdom), the remaining alternative is that it is comprehension
that grasps the first principles.

CHAPTER 7

Wisdom in the arts we ascribe to their most finished exponents, e.g. to
Phidias as a sculptor and to Polyclitus as a maker of statues, and here 10
we mean nothing by wisdom except excellence in art; but we think
that some people are wise in general, not in some particular field or in
any other limited respect, as Homer says in the *Margites*,

> Him did the gods make neither a digger nor yet a ploughman 15
> Nor wise in anything else.

Therefore wisdom must plainly be the most finished of the forms of
knowledge. It follows that the wise man must not only know what

follows from the first principles, but must also possess truth about the
first principles. Therefore wisdom must be comprehension combined
with knowledge—knowledge of the highest objects which has received
as it were its proper completion.

20   For it would be strange to think that the art of politics, or practical
wisdom, is the best knowledge, since man is not the best thing in the
world. Now if what is healthy or good is different for men and for
fishes, but what is white or straight is always the same, any one would
say that what is wise is the same but what is practically wise is
25   different; for it is to that which observes well the various matters
concerning itself that one ascribes practical wisdom, and it is to this
that one will entrust such matters. This is why we say that some even
of the lower animals have practical wisdom, viz. those which are found
to have a power of foresight with regard to their own life. It is evident
also that wisdom and the art of politics cannot be the same; for if the
30   state of mind concerned with a man's own interests is to be called
wisdom, there will be many wisdoms; there will not be one concerned
with the good of all animals (any more than there is one art of
medicine for all existing things), but a different wisdom about the
good of each species.

But if the argument be that man is the best of the animals, this
makes no difference; for there are other things much more divine in
1141ᵇ   their nature even than man, e.g., most conspicuously, the bodies of
which the heavens are framed. From what has been said it is plain,
then, that wisdom is knowledge, combined with comprehension, of
the things that are highest by nature. This is why we say Anaxagoras,
Thales, and men like them have wisdom but not practical wisdom,
5   when we see them ignorant of what is to their own advantage, and why
we say that they know things that are remarkable, admirable, difficult,
and divine, but useless; viz. because it is not human goods that they
seek.

Practical wisdom on the other hand is concerned with things
human and things about which it is possible to deliberate; for we say
this is above all the work of the man of practical wisdom, to deliberate
10   well, but no one deliberates about things that cannot be otherwise, nor
about things which have not an end, and that a good that can be
brought about by action. The man who is without qualification good at
deliberating is the man who is capable of aiming in accordance with
calculation at the best for man of things attainable by action. Nor is
15   practical wisdom concerned with universals only—it must also

recognize the particulars; for it is practical, and practice is concerned with particulars. This is why some who do not know, and especially those who have experience, are more practical than others who know; for if a man knew that light meats are digestible and wholesome, but did not know which sorts of meat are light, he would not produce health, but the man who knows that chicken is wholesome is more   20 likely to produce health.

Now practical wisdom is concerned with action; therefore one should have both forms of it, or the latter in preference to the former. Here, too, there must be a controlling kind.

CHAPTER 8

Political wisdom and practical wisdom are the same state of mind, but being them is not the same. Of the wisdom concerned with the city, the practical wisdom which plays a controlling part is legislative wisdom,   25 while that which is related to this as particulars to their universal is known by the general name 'political wisdom'; this has to do with action and deliberation, for a decree is a thing to be carried out in the form of an individual act. This is why the exponents of this art are alone said to take part in politics; for these alone do things as manual labourers do things.

Practical wisdom also is identified especially with that form of it   30 which is concerned with a man himself—with the individual; and this is known by the general name 'practical wisdom'; of the other kinds one is called household management, another legislation, the third politics, and of the last one part is called deliberative and the other judicial. Now knowing what is good for oneself will be one kind of knowledge, but is very different from the other kinds; and the man who knows and concerns himself with his own interests is thought to   1142ᵃ have practical wisdom, while politicians are thought to be busybodies; hence the words of Euripides,

> But how could I be wise, who might at ease,
> Numbered among the army's multitude,
> Have had an equal share? ...
> For those who aim too high and do too much. ...   5

Those who think thus seek their own good, and consider that one ought to do so. From this opinion, then, has come the view that such men have practical wisdom; yet perhaps one's own good cannot exist without household management, nor without a form of government. Further, how one should order one's affairs is not clear and needs inquiry.

What has been said is confimred by the fact that while young men become geometricians and mathematicians and wise in matters like these, it is thought that a young man of practical wisdom cannot be found. The cause is that such wisdom is concerned not only with universals but with particulars, which become familiar from experience, but a young man has no experience, for it is length of time that gives experience; indeed one might ask this question too, why a boy may become a mathematician, but not a wise man or a natural scientist. Is it because the objects of mathematics exist by abstraction, while the first principles of these other subjects come from experience, and because young men have no conviction about the latter but merely use the proper language, while the essence of mathematical objects is plain enough to them?

Further, error in deliberation may be either about the universal or about the particular; we may fail to know either that all water that weighs heavy is bad, or that this particular water weighs heavy.

That practical wisdom is not knowledge is evident; for it is, as has been said, concerned with the ultimate particular fact, since the thing to be done is of this nature. It is opposed, then, to comprehension; for comprehension is of the definitions, for which no reason can be given, while practical wisdom is concerned with the ultimate particular, which is the object not of knowledge but of perception—not the perception of qualities peculiar to one sense but a perception akin to that by which we perceive that the particular figure before us is a triangle; for in that direction too there will be a limit. But this is rather perception than practical wisdom, though it is another kind of perception.

CHAPTER 9

There is a difference between inquiry and deliberation; for deliberation is a particular kind of inquiry. We must grasp the nature of excellence in deliberation as well—whether it is a form of knowledge, or opinion, or skill in conjecture, or some other kind of thing. It is not *knowledge*; for men do not inquire about the things they know about, but good deliberation is a kind of deliberation, and he who deliberates inquires and calculates. Nor is it *skill in conjecture*; for this both involves no reasoning and is something that is quick in its operation, while men deliberate a long time, and they say that one should carry out quickly the conclusions of one's deliberation, but should deliberate slowly. Again, *readiness of mind* is different from excellence in deliberation; it is a sort of skill in conjecture. Nor again is excellence in deliberation *opinion* of any sort. But since the man who deliberates badly makes a mistake, while he who deliberates well does so correctly, excellence in deliberation is clearly a kind of correctness, but neither of knowledge nor of opinion; for there is no such thing as correctness of knowledge (since there is no such thing as error of knowledge), and correctness of opinion is truth; and at the same time everything that is an object of opinion is already determined. But again excellence in deliberation involves reasoning. The remaining alternative, then, is that it is *correctness of thinking*; for this is not yet assertion, since, while opinion is not inquiry but already assertion, the man who is deliberating, whether he does so well or ill, is searching for something and calculating.

But excellence in deliberation is a certain correctness of deliberation; hence we must first inquire what deliberation is and what it is about. And, there being more than one kind of correctness, plainly excellence in deliberation is not any and every kind; for the incontinent man and the bad man will reach as a result of his calculation what he sets himself to do, so that he will have deliberated correctly, but he will have got for himself a great evil. Now to have deliberated well is thought to be a good thing; for it is this kind of correctness of deliberation that is excellence in deliberation, viz. that which tends to attain what is good. But it is possible to attain even good by a false deduction and to attain what one ought to do but not by the right means, the middle term being false; so that this too is not yet excellence in deliberation—this state in virtue of which one attains what one ought but not by the right means. Again it is possible to attain it by long deliberation while another man attains it quickly. Therefore in the former case we have not yet got excellence in deliberation, which is rightness with regard to the expedient—rightness in respect both of the conclusion, the manner, and the time. Further it is possible to have deliberated well either in the unqualified sense or with reference to a particular end. Excellence in deliberation in the unqualified sense, then, is that which succeeds with reference to what is the end in the unqualified sense, and excellence in deliberation in a particular sense is that which succeeds relatively to a particular end. If, then, it is

characteristic of men of practical wisdom to have deliberated well,
excellence in deliberation will be correctness with regard to what
conduces to the end of which practical wisdom is the true apprehen-
sion.

CHAPTER 10

Understanding, also, and goodness of understanding, in virtue of
1143ᵃ which men are said to be men of understanding or of good understanding, are neither entirely the same as opinion or knowledge (for at
that rate all men would have been men of understanding), nor are they
one of the particular sciences, such as medicine, the science of things
connected with health, or geometry, the science of spatial magnitudes.
For understanding is neither about things that are always and are
5 unchangeable, nor about any and every one of the things that come
into being, but about things which may become subjects of questioning and deliberation. Hence it is about the same objects as practical
wisdom; but understanding and practical wisdom are not the same.
For practical wisdom issues commands, since its end is what ought to
be done or not to be done; but understanding only judges. (Under-
10 standing is identical with goodness of understanding, men of understanding with men of good understanding.) Now understanding is
neither the having nor the acquiring of practical wisdom; but as
learning is called understanding when it means the exercise of the
faculty of knowledge, so 'understanding' is applicable to the exercise
of the faculty of opinion for the purpose of judging of what someone
15 else says about matters with which practical wisdom is concerned—
and of judging soundly; for 'well' and 'soundly' are the same thing.
And from this has come the use of the name 'understanding' in virtue
of which men are said to be of good understanding, viz. from the
application of the word to learning; for we often call learning understanding.

CHAPTER 11

What is called judgement, in virtue of which men are said to be
20 forgiving[8] and to have judgement, is the right discrimination of the
equitable. This is shown by the fact that we say the equitable man is
above all others a man of forgiveness and identify equity with forgive-

---

[8] The Greek word for 'forgiveness' is cognate with that for 'judgement'.

ness about certain facts. And forgiveness is judgement which discriminates what is equitable and does so correctly; and correct judgement is that which judges what is true.

Now all the states we have considered converge, as might be expected, on the same point; for when we speak of judgement and understanding and practical wisdom and comprehension we credit the same people with possessing judgement and comprehension and with having practical wisdom and understanding. For all these faculties deal with ultimates, i.e. with particulars; and being a man of understanding and of good judgement or of forgiveness consists in being able to judge about the things with which practical wisdom is concerned; for the equities are common to all good men in relation to other men. Now all things which have to be done are included among particulars or ultimates; for not only must the man of practical wisdom know particular facts, but understanding and judgement are also concerned with things to be done, and these are ultimates. And comprehension is concerned with the ultimates in both directions; for both the primary definitions and the ultimates are objects of comprehension and not of argument, and in demonstrations comprehension grasps the unchangeable and primary definitions, while in practical reasonings it grasps the last and contingent fact, i.e. the second proposition. For these are the starting-points of that for the sake of which, since the universals are reached from the particulars; of these therefore we must have perception, and this is comprehension.

This is why these states are thought to be natural endowments—why, while no one is thought to be wise by nature, people are thought to have by nature judgement, understanding, and comprehension. This is shown by the fact that we think our powers correspond to our time of life, and that a particular age brings with it comprehension and judgement; this implies that nature is the cause. Therefore we ought to attend to the undemonstrated sayings and opinions of experienced and older people or of people of practical wisdom not less than to demonstrations; for because experience has given them an eye they see aright.

We have stated, then, what practical wisdom and wisdom are, and with what each of them is concerned, and we have said that each is the excellence of a different part of the soul.

CHAPTER 12

Difficulties might be raised as to the utility of these qualities of mind. For wisdom will contemplate none of the things that will make a man
20 happy (for it is not concerned with any coming into being), and though practical wisdom has *this* merit, for what purpose do we need it? Practical wisdom is the quality of mind concerned with things just and noble and good for man, but these are the things which it is the mark of a *good* man to do, and we are none the more able to act for *knowing*
25 them if the excellences are states, just as we are none the better able to act for knowing the things that are healthy and sound, in the sense not of producing but of issuing from the state of health; for we are none the more able to act for having the art of medicine or of gymnastics. But if we are to say that it is useful not for the sake of this but for the sake of becoming good, practical wisdom will be of no use to those who *are*
30 good; but again it is of no use to those who are not, for it will make no difference whether they have practical wisdom themselves or obey others who have it, and it would be enough for us to do what we do in the case of health; though we wish to become healthy, yet we do not learn the art of medicine. Besides this, it would be thought strange if practical wisdom, being inferior to wisdom, is to be put in authority over it, as seems to be implied by the fact that the art which produces
35 anything rules and issues commands about that thing.

These, then, are the questions we must discuss; so far we have only stated the difficulties.

1144ᵃ Now first let us say that in themselves these states must be worthy of choice because they are the excellences of the two parts of the soul respectively, even if neither of them produces anything.

Secondly, they do produce something, not as the art of medicine produces health, however, but as health produces health; so does
5 wisdom produce happiness; for, being a part of excellence entire, by being possessed and by actualizing itself it makes a man happy.

Again, the function of man is achieved only in accordance with practical wisdom as well as with moral excellence; for excellence makes the aim right, and practical wisdom the things leading to it. (Of the fourth part of the soul—the nutritive—there is no such excellence;
10 for there is nothing which it is in its power to do or not to do.)

With regard to our being none the more able to do because of our practical wisdom what is noble and just, let us begin a little further back, starting with the following principle. As we say that some people

who do just acts are not necessarily just, i.e. those who do the acts
ordained by the laws either unwillingly or owing to ignorance or for   15
some other reason and not for the sake of the acts themselves (though,
to be sure, they do what they should and all the things that the good
man ought), so is it, it seems, that in order to be good one must be in a
certain state when one does the several acts, i.e. one must do them as a
result of choice and for the sake of the acts themselves. Now excellence makes the choice right, but the question of the things which   20
should naturally be done to carry out our choice belongs not to excellence but to another faculty. We must devote our attention to these
matters and give a clearer statement about them. There is a faculty
which is called cleverness; and this is such as to be able to do the
things that tend towards the mark we have set before ourselves, and to   25
hit it. Now if the mark be noble, the cleverness is laudable, but if the
mark be bad, the cleverness is mere villainy; hence we call clever both
men of practical wisdom and villains. Practical wisdom is not the
faculty, but it does not exist without this faculty. And this eye of the
soul acquires its formed state not without the aid of excellence, as has   30
been said and is plain; for inferences which deal with acts to be done
are things which involve a starting-point, viz. 'since the end, i.e. what
is best, is of such-and-such a nature', whatever it may be (let it for the
sake of argument be what we please); and this is not evident except to
the good man; for wickedness perverts us and causes us to be deceived   35
about the starting-points of action. Therefore it is evident that it is
impossible to be practically wise without being good.

CHAPTER 13

We must therefore consider excellence also once more; for excellence   1144ᵇ
too is similarly related; as practical wisdom is to cleverness—not the
same, but like it—so is natural excellence to excellence in the strict
sense. For all men think that each type of character belongs to its possessors in some sense by nature; for from the very moment of birth we
are just or fitted for self-control or brave or have the other moral quali-   5
ties; but yet we seek something else as that which is good in the strict
sense—we seek for the presence of such qualities in another way. For
both children and brutes have the natural dispositions to these qualities, but without thought these are evidently hurtful. Only we seem to   10
see this much, that, while one may be led astray by them, as a strong
body which moves without sight may stumble badly because of its lack

of sight, still, if a man once acquires thought that makes a difference in action; and his state, while still like what it was, will then be excellence in the strict sense. Therefore, as in the part of us which forms opinions
15 there are two types, cleverness and practical wisdom, so too in the moral part there are two types, natural excellence and excellence in the strict sense, and of these the latter involves practical wisdom. This is why some say that all the excellences are forms of practical wisdom, and why Socrates in one respect was on the right track while in another he went astray; in thinking that all the excellences were forms
20 of practical wisdom he was wrong, but in saying they implied practical wisdom he was right. This is confirmed by the fact that even now all men, when they define excellence, after naming the state and its objects add 'that (state) which is in accordance with the right reason'; now the right reason is that which is in accordance with practical wisdom. All men, then, seem somehow to divine that this kind of state
25 is excellence, viz. that which is in accordance with practical wisdom. But we must go a little further. For it is not merely the state in accordance with right reason, but the state that implies the *presence* of right reason, that is excellence; and practical wisdom is right reason about such matters. Socrates, then, thought the excellences were forms of reason (for he thought they were, all of them, forms of knowledge), while we think they *involve* reason.
30   It is clear, then, from what has been said, that it is not possible to be good in the strict sense without practical wisdom, nor practically wise without moral excellence. But in this way we may also refute the dialectical argument whereby it might be contended that the excellences exist in separation from each other; the same man, it might be said, is not best equipped by nature for all the excellences, so that he
35 will have already acquired one when he has not yet acquired another. This is possible in respect of the natural excellences, but not in respect of those in respect of which a man is called without qualifica-
1145ᵃ tion good; for with the presence of the one quality, practical wisdom, will be given all the excellences. And it is plain that, even if it were of no practical value, we should have needed it because it is the excellence of the part of us in question; plain too that the choice will not be
5 right without practical wisdom any more than without excellence; for the one determines the end and the other makes us do the things that lead to the end.

But again it is not *supreme* over wisdom, i.e. over the superior part of us, any more than the art of medicine is over health; for it does not use

it but provides for its coming into being; it issues orders, then, for its
sake, but not to it. Further, to maintain its supremacy would be like   10
saying that the art of politics rules the gods because it issues orders
about all the affairs of the state.

BOOK VII.

CHAPTER 1

Let us now make a fresh beginning and point out that of moral states   15
to be avoided there are three kinds—vice, incontinence, brutishness.
The contraries of two of these are evident—one we call excellence, the
other continence; to brutishness it would be most fitting to oppose
superhuman excellence, something heroic and divine, as Homer has
represented Priam saying of Hector that he was very good,   20

> For he seemed not, he,
> The child of a mortal man, but as one that of God's seed came.

Therefore if, as they say, men become gods by excess of excellence, of
this kind must evidently be the state opposed to the brutish state; for   25
as a brute has no vice or excellence, so neither has a god; his state is
higher than excellence, and that of a brute is a different kind of state
from vice.

Now, since it is rarely that a godlike man is found—to use the
epithet of the Spartans, who when they admire any one highly call him
a 'godlike man'—so too the brutish type is rarely found among men; it   30
is found chiefly among foreigners, but some brutish qualities are also
produced by disease or deformity; and we also call by this evil name
those who surpass ordinary men in vice. Of this kind of disposition,
however, we must later make some mention, while we have discussed
vice before; we must now discuss incontinence and softness (or   35
effeminacy), and continence and endurance; for we must treat each of
the two neither as identical with excellence or wickedness, nor as a
different genus. We must, as in all other cases, set the phenomena   1145^b
before us and, after first discussing the difficulties, go on to prove, if
possible, the truth of all the reputable opinions about these affections   5
or, failing this, of the greater number and the most authoritative; for if
we both resolve the difficulties and leave the reputable opinions
undisturbed, we shall have proved the case sufficiently.

Now both continence and endurance are thought to be included among things good and praiseworthy, and both incontinence and softness among things bad and blameworthy; and the same man is thought to be continent and ready to abide by the result of his calculations, or incontinent and ready to abandon them. And the incontinent man, knowing that what he does is bad, does it as a result of passion, while the continent man, knowing that his appetites are bad, does not follow them because of his reason. The temperate man all men call continent and disposed to endurance, while the continent man some maintain to be always temperate but others do not; and some call the self-indulgent man incontinent and the incontinent man self-indulgent indiscriminately, while others distinguish them. The man of practical wisdom, they sometimes say, cannot be incontinent, while sometimes they say that some who are practically wise and clever *are* incontinent. Again men are said to be incontinent with respect to anger, honour, and gain.—These, then, are the things that are said.

CHAPTER 2

Now we may ask what kind of right belief is possessed by the man who behaves incontinently. That he should behave so when he has knowledge, some say is impossible; for it would be strange—so Socrates thought—if when knowledge was in a man something else could master it and drag it about like a slave. For *Socrates* was entirely opposed to the view in question, holding that there is no such thing as incontinence; no one, he said, acts against what he believes best—people act so only by reason of ignorance. Now this view contradicts the plain phenomena, and we must inquire about what happens to such a man; if he acts by reason of ignorance, what is the manner of his ignorance? For that the man who behaves incontinently does not, before he gets into this state, *think* he ought to act so, is evident. But there are *some* who concede certain of Socrates' contentions but not others; that nothing is stronger than knowledge they admit, but not that no one acts contrary to what has seemed to him the better course, and therefore they say that the incontinent man has not knowledge when he is mastered by his pleasures, but opinion. But *if* it is opinion and not knowledge, if it is not a strong belief that resists but a weak one, as in men who hesitate, we forgive their failure to stand by such convictions against strong appetites; but we do not forgive wickedness, nor any of the other blameworthy states. Is it then *practical wisdom* whose resistance is mastered? That is the strongest of all states. But this is absurd; the same man will be at once practically wise and incontinent, but *no one* would say that it is the part of a practically wise man to do willingly the basest acts. Besides, it has been shown before that the man of practical wisdom is one who will *act* (for he is a man concerned with the individual facts) and who has the other excellences.

Further, if continence involves having strong and bad appetites, the temperate man will not be continent nor the continent man temperate; for a temperate man will have neither excessive nor bad appetites. But the continent man *must*; for if the appetites are good, the state that restrains us from following them is bad, so that not all continence will be good; while if they are weak and not bad, there is nothing admirable in resisting them, and if they are weak and bad, there is nothing great in resisting these either.

Further, if continence makes a man ready to stand by any and every opinion, it is bad, i.e. if it makes him stand even by a false opinion; and if incontinence makes a man apt to abandon any and every opinion, there will be a good incontinence, of which Sophocles' Neoptolemus in the *Philoctetes* will be an instance; for he is to be praised for not standing by what Odysseus persuaded him to do, because he is pained at telling a lie.

Further, the sophistic argument presents a difficulty; for, because they want to produce paradoxical results to show how clever they are, when they succeed the resulting inference presents a difficulty (for thought is bound fast when it will not rest because the conclusion does not satisfy it, and cannot advance because it cannot refute the argument). There is an argument from which it follows that folly coupled with incontinence is excellence; for a man does the opposite of what he believes owing to incontinence, but believes what is good to be evil and something that he should not do, and in consequence he will do what is good and not what is evil.

Further, he who on conviction does and pursues and chooses what is pleasant would be thought to be better than one who does so as a result not of calculation but of incontinence; for he is easier to cure since he may be persuaded to change his mind. But to the incontinent man may be applied the proverb 'when water chokes, what is one to wash it down with?'. If he had been persuaded of the rightness of what he does, he would have desisted when he was persuaded to change his mind; but now he acts in spite of his being persuaded of something quite different.

Further, if incontinence and continence are concerned with any and every kind of object, who is it that is incontinent in the unqualified sense? No one has all the forms of incontinence, but we say some
5 people are incontinent without qualification.

CHAPTER 3

Of some such kind are the difficulties that arise; some of these points must be refuted and the others left in possession of the field; for the solution of the difficulty is the discovery of the truth. We must consider first, then, whether incontinent people act knowingly or not, and in what sense knowingly; then with what sorts of object the incontinent and the continent man may be said to be concerned (i.e.
10 whether with any and every pleasure and pain or with certain determinate kinds), and whether the continent man and the man of endurance are the same or different; and similarly with regard to the other matters germane to this inquiry. The starting-point of our investigation is the question whether the continent man and the
15 incontinent are differentiated by their objects or by their attitude, i.e. whether the continent man is incontinent simply by being concerned with such-and-such objects, or, instead, by his attitude, or, instead of that, by both these things; the second question is whether incontinence and continence are concerned with any and every object or not. The man who is incontinent in the unqualified sense is neither concerned with any and every object, but with precisely those with
20 which the self-indulgent man is concerned, nor is he characterized by being simply related to these (for then his state would be the same as self-indulgence), but by being related to them in a certain way. For the one is led on in accordance with his own choice, thinking that he ought always to pursue the present pleasure; while the other does not think so, but yet pursues it.

As for the suggestion that it is true opinion and not knowledge
25 against which we act incontinently, that makes no difference to the argument; for some people when in a state of opinion do not hesitate, but think they know exactly. If, then, it is owing to their weak conviction that those who have opinion are more likely to act against their belief than those who know, there will be no difference between
30 knowledge and opinion; for some men are no less convinced of what

they think than others of what they know; as is shown by the case of Heraclitus. But since we use the word 'know' in two senses (for both the man who has knowledge but is not using it and he who is using it are said to know), it *will* make a difference whether, when a man does what he should not, he has the knowledge but is not exercising it, or *is* exercising it; for the latter seems strange, but not the former.

Further, since there are two kinds of propositions, there is nothing 1147ª to prevent a man's having both and acting against his knowledge, provided that he is using only the universal and not the particular; for it is particular acts that have to be done. And there are also two kinds of universal; one is predicable of the agent, the other of the object; e.g. 'dry food is good for every man', and 'I am a man', or 'such-and-such 5 food is dry'; but whether this food is such-and-such, of this the incontinent man either has not or is not exercising the knowledge. There will, then, be, firstly, an enormous difference between these manners of knowing, so that to know in one way would not seem anything strange, while to know in the other way would be extraordinary.

And further the possession of knowledge in another sense than 10 those just named is something that happens to men; for within the case of having knowledge but not using it we see a difference of state, admitting of the possibility of having knowledge in a sense and yet not having it, as in the instance of a man asleep, mad, or drunk. But now this is just the condition of men under the influence of passions; for outbursts of anger and sexual appetites and some other such passions, 15 it is evident, actually alter our bodily condition, and in some men even produce fits of madness. It is plain, then, that incontinent people must be said to be in a similar condition to these. The fact that men use the language that flows from knowledge proves nothing; for even men under the influence of these passions utter scientific proofs and verses of Empedocles, and those who have just begun to learn can string 20 together words, but do not yet know; for it has to become part of themselves, and that takes time; so that we must suppose that the use of language by men in an incontinent state means no more than its utterance by actors on the stage.

Again, we may also view the cause as follows with reference to the facts of nature. The one opinion is universal, the other is concerned 25 with the particular facts, and here we come to something within the sphere of perception; when a single opinion results from the two, the soul must in one type of case affirm the conclusion, while in the case of opinions concerned with production it must immediately act (e.g. if

everything sweet ought to be tasted, and this is sweet, in the sense of
30   being one of the particular sweet things, the man who can act and is
not restrained must at the same time actually act accordingly). When,
then, the universal opinion is present in us restraining us from tasting,
and there is also the opinion that everything sweet is pleasant, and that
this is sweet (now this is the opinion that is active), and when appetite
happens to be present in us, the one opinion bids us avoid the object,
but appetite leads us towards it (for it can move each of our bodily
1147ᵇ parts); so that it turns out that a man behaves incontinently under the
influence (in a sense) of reason and opinion, and of opinion not
contrary in itself, but only incidentally—for the appetite is contrary
not the opinion—to right reason. It also follows that this is the reason
why the lower animals are not incontinent, viz. because they have no
5   universal beliefs but only imagination and memory of particulars.

The explanation of how the ignorance is dissolved and the incontinent man regains his knowledge, is the same as in the case of the
man drunk or asleep and is not peculiar to this condition; we must go
to the students of natural science for it. Now, the last proposition both
being an opinion about a perceptible object, and being what deter-
10   mines our actions, this a man either has not when he is in the state of
passion, or has it in the sense in which having knowledge did not mean
knowing but only talking, as a drunken man may utter the verses of
Empedocles. And because the last term is not universal nor equally an
object of knowledge with the universal term, the position that Socrates
sought to establish actually seems to result; for it is not what is thought
15   to be knowledge proper that the passion overcomes (nor is it this that
is dragged about as a result of the passion), but perceptual knowledge.

This must suffice as our answer to the question of whether men can
act incontinently when they know or not, and in what sense they know.

CHAPTER 4

20   We must next discuss whether there is any one who is incontinent
without qualification, or all men who are incontinent are so in a
particular sense, and if so, with what sort of objects. That both
continent persons and persons of endurance, and incontinent and soft
persons, are concerned with pleasures and pains, is evident.

Now of the things that produce pleasure some are necessary, while
25   others are worthy of choice in themselves but admit of excess, the
bodily causes of pleasure being necessary (by such I mean both those

concerned with food and those concerned with sexual intercourse, i.e.
the bodily matters with which we defined self-indulgence and
temperance as being concerned), while the others are not necessary
but worthy of choice in themselves (e.g. victory, honour, wealth, and　30
good and pleasant things of this sort). This being so, those who go to
excess with reference to the latter, contrary to the right reason which is
in themselves, are not called incontinent simply, but incontinent with
the qualification 'in respect of money, gain, honour, or anger',—not
simply incontinent, on the ground that they are different from incontinent people and are called incontinent by reason of a resemblance. (Compare the case of Man, who won a contest at the Olympic
games; in his case the general formula of man differed little from the　1148^a
one peculiar to *him*, but yet it *was* different.) This is shown by the fact
that incontinence, either without qualification or in some particular
respect, is blamed not only as a fault but as a kind of vice, while none
of these is so blamed.

But of the people who are incontinent with respect to bodily enjoy-　5
ments, with which we say the temperate and the self-indulgent man
are concerned, he who pursues the excesses of things pleasant—and
shuns those of things painful, of hunger and thirst and heat and cold
and all the objects of touch and taste—not by choice but contrary to
his choice and his judgement, is called incontinent, not with the　10
qualification 'in respect of this or that', e.g. of anger, but without
qualification. This is confirmed by the fact that men are called soft
with regard to these pleasures, but not with regard to any of the others.
And for this reason we group together the incontinent and the self-
indulgent, the continent and the temperate man—but not any of these
other types—because they are concerned somehow with the same　15
pleasures and pains; but although these are concerned with the same
objects, they are not similarly related to them, but some of them
choose them while the others do not choose them.

This is why we should describe as self-indulgent rather the man
who without appetite or with but a slight appetite pursues the excesses
and avoids moderate pains, than the man who does so because of his　20
strong appetites; for what would the former do, if he had in addition a
vigorous appetite, and a violent pain at the lack of the necessary
objects?

Now of appetites and pleasures some belong to the class of things
generically noble and good—for some pleasant things are by nature
worthy of choice—while others are contrary to these, and others are　25

intermediate, to adopt our previous distinction, e.g. wealth, gain, victory, honour. And with reference to all objects whether of this or of the intermediate kind men are not blamed for being affected by them, for desiring and loving them, but for doing so in a certain way, i.e. for going to excess. (This is why all those who contrary to reason either are mastered by or pursue one of the objects which are naturally noble
30   and good, e.g. those who busy themselves more than they ought about honour or about children and parents—for these too are goods, and those who busy themselves about them are praised; but yet there is an excess even in them—if like Niobe one were to fight even against the
1148ᵇ gods, or were to be as much devoted to one's father as Satyrus nick-named 'the filial', who was thought to be very silly on this point.) There is no wickedness, then, with regard to these objects, for the reason named, viz. because each of them is by nature a thing worthy of choice for its own sake; yet excesses in respect of them are bad and to be avoided. Similarly there is no incontinence with regard to them; for
5   incontinence is not only to be avoided but is also a thing worthy of blame; but owing to a similarity in the passion people apply the name incontinence, adding in each case what it is in respect of, as we may describe as a bad doctor or a bad actor one whom we should not call bad, simply. As, then, in this case we do not apply the term without
10   qualification because each of these conditions is not badness but only analogous to it, so it is clear that in the other case also that alone must be taken to be incontinence and continence which is concerned with the same objects as temperance and self-indulgence, but we apply the term to anger by virtue of a resemblance; and this is why we say with a qualification 'incontinent in respect of anger' as we say 'incontinent in respect of honour, or of gain'.

CHAPTER 5

15   Some things are pleasant by nature, and of these some are so without qualification, and others are so with reference to particular classes either of animals or of men; while others are not pleasant by nature, but some of them become so by reason of deformities, and others by reason of habits, and others by reason of bad natures. This being so it is possible with regard to each of the latter kinds to discover similar
20   states; I mean the brutish states, as in the case of the female who, they say, rips open pregnant women and devours the infants, or of the things in which some of the tribes about the Black Sea that have gone

savage are said to delight—in raw meat or in human flesh, or in
lending their children to one another to feast upon—or of the story of
Phalaris.

These states are brutish, but others arise as a result of disease (or, in　25
some cases, of madness, as with the man who sacrificed and ate his
mother, or with the slave who ate the liver of his fellow), and others are
morbid states resulting from custom, e.g. the habit of plucking out the
hair or of gnawing the nails, or even coals or earth, and in addition to
these paederasty; for these arise in some by nature and in others, as in
those who have been the victims of lust from childhood, from habit.　30

Now those in whom nature is the cause of such a state no one would
call incontinent, any more than one would apply the epithet to women
because of the passive part they play in copulation; nor would one
apply it to those who are in a morbid condition as a result of habit. To
have these various types of habit is beyond the limits of vice, as
brutishness is too; for a man who has them to master or be mastered by　1149ᵃ
them is not simply incontinence but that which is so by analogy, as the
man who is in this condition in respect of fits of anger is to be called
incontinent in respect of that feeling, but not incontinent.

For every excessive state whether of folly, of cowardice, of self-　5
indulgence, or of bad temper, is either brutish or morbid; the man who
is by nature apt to fear everything, even the squeak of a mouse, is
cowardly with a brutish cowardice, while the man who feared a weasel
did so in consequence of disease; and of foolish people those who by
nature are thoughtless and live by their senses alone are brutish, like　10
some races of distant foreigners, while those who are so as a result
of disease (e.g. of epilepsy) or of madness are morbid. Of these
characteristics it is possible to have some only at times, and not to be
mastered by them, e.g. Phalaris may have restrained a desire to eat the
flesh of a child or an appetite for unnatural sexual pleasure; but it is
also possible to be mastered, not merely to have the feelings. Thus, as　15
the wickedness which is on the human level is called wickedness
simply, while that which is not is called wickedness not simply but
with the qualification 'brutish' or 'morbid', in the same way it is plain
that some incontinence is brutish and some morbid, while only that
which corresponds to *human* self-indulgence is incontinence simply.　20

That incontinence and continence, then, are concerned only with
the same objects as self-indulgence and temperance, and that what is
concerned with other objects is a type distinct from incontinence, and
called incontinence by a metaphor and not simply, is plain.

CHAPTER 6

That incontinence in respect of anger is less disgraceful than that in
25 respect of the appetites is what we will now proceed to see. Anger
seems to listen to reason to some extent, but to mishear it, as do hasty
servants who run out before they have heard the whole of what one
says, and then muddle the order, or as dogs bark if there is but a knock
at the door, before looking to see if it is a friend; so anger by reason of
30 the warmth and hastiness of its nature, though it hears, does not hear
an order, and springs to take revenge. For reason or imagination
informs us that we have been insulted or slighted, and anger, reasoning as it were that anything like this must be fought against, boils up
straightway; while appetite, if reason or perception merely says that an
object is pleasant, springs to the enjoyment of it. Therefore anger
1149ᵇ obeys reason in a sense, but appetite does not. It is therefore more
disgraceful; for the man who is incontinent in respect of anger is in a
sense conquered by reason, while the other is conquered by appetite
and not by reason.

Further, we forgive people more easily for following natural desires,
5 since we forgive them more easily for following such appetites as are
common to all men, and in so far as they are common; now anger and
bad temper are more natural than the appetites for excess, i.e. for
unnecessary objects. Take for instance the man who defended himself
on the charge of striking his father by saying 'yes, but *he* struck *his*
10 father, and *he* struck *his*, and' (pointing to his child) 'this boy will
strike *me* when he is a man; it runs in the family'; or the man who when
he was being dragged along by his son bade him stop at the doorway,
since he himself had dragged his father only as far as that.

Further, those who are more given to plotting against others are
more unjust. Now a passionate man is not given to plotting, nor is
15 anger itself—it is open; but the nature of appetite is illustrated by what
the poets call Aphrodite, 'guile-weaving daughter of Cyprus', and by
Homer's words about her 'embroidered girdle':

And the whisper of wooing is there,
Whose subtlety stealeth the wits of the wise, how prudent soe'er.

Therefore if this form of incontinence is more unjust and disgraceful
than that in respect of anger, it is both incontinence without qualification and in a sense vice.

20   Further, no one commits wanton outrage with a feeling of pain, but

every one who acts in anger acts with pain, while the man who commits outrage acts with pleasure. If, then, those acts at which it is most just to be angry are more unjust, the incontinence which is due to appetite is the more unjust; for there is no wanton outrage involved in anger.

Plainly, then, the incontinence concerned with appetite is more disgraceful than that concerned with anger, and continence and incontinence are concerned with bodily appetites and pleasures; but we must grasp the differences among the latter themselves. For, as has been said at the beginning, some are human and natural both in kind and in magnitude, others are brutish, and others are due to deformities and diseases. Only with the first of these are temperance and self-indulgence concerned; this is why we call the lower animals neither temperate nor self-indulgent except by a metaphor, and only if some one kind of animals exceeds another as a whole in wantonness, destructiveness, and omnivorous greed; these have no power of choice or calculation, but they *are* departures from what is natural as, among men, madmen are. Now brutishness is less evil than vice, though more alarming; for it is not that the better part has been perverted, as in man,—they *have* no better part. Thus it is like comparing a lifeless thing with a living in respect of badness; for the badness of that which has no source of movement is always less hurtful, and thought is a source. Thus it is like comparing injustice with an unjust man. Each is in some sense worse; for a bad man will do ten thousand times as much evil as a brute.

CHAPTER 7

With regard to the pleasures and pains and appetites and aversions arising through touch and taste, to which both self-indulgence and temperance were formerly narrowed down, it is possible to be in such a state as to be defeated even by those of them which most people master, or to master even those by which most people are defeated; among these possibilities, those relating to pleasures are incontinence and continence, those relating to pains softness and endurance. The state of most people is intermediate, even if they lean more towards the worse states.

Now, since some pleasures are necessary while others are not, and are necessary up to a point while the excesses of them are not, nor the deficiencies, and this is equally true of appetites and pains, the man

25

30

1150ᵃ

5

10

15

who pursues the excesses of things pleasant, or pursues to excess
necessary objects, and does so by choice, for their own sake and not at
20   all for the sake of any result distinct from them, is self-indulgent; for
such a man is of necessity without regrets, and therefore incurable,
since a man without regrets cannot be cured. The man who is deficient
is the opposite; the man who is intermediate is temperate. Similarly,
there is the man who avoids bodily pains not because he is defeated by
them but by choice. (Of those who do not *choose* such acts, one kind of
25   man is led to them as a result of the pleasure involved, another
because he avoids the pain arising from the appetite, so that these
types differ from one another. Now anyone would think worse of a
man if with no appetite or with weak appetite he were to do something
disgraceful, than if he did it under the influence of powerful appetite,
and worse of him if he struck a blow not in anger than if he did it in
30   anger; for what would he have done if he *had* been strongly affected?
This is why the self-indulgent man is worse than the incontinent.) Of
the states named, then, the latter is rather a kind of softness; the
former is self-indulgence. While to the incontinent man is opposed
the continent, to the soft is opposed the man of endurance; for
endurance consists in resisting, while continence consists in conquer-
35   ing, and resisting and conquering are different, as not being beaten is
different from winning; this is why continence is also more worthy of
1150ᵇ choice than endurance. Now the man who is defective in respect of
resistance to the things which most men both resist and resist successfully is soft and effeminate; for effeminacy too is a kind of softness;
such a man trails his cloak to avoid the pain of lifting it, and plays the
5   invalid without thinking himself wretched, though the man he imitates
is a wretched man.

The case is similar with regard to continence and incontinence. For
if a man is defeated by violent and excessive pleasures or pains, there
is nothing wonderful in that; indeed we are ready to forgive him if he
has resisted, as Theodectes' Philoctetes does when bitten by the
10   snake, or Carcinus' Cercyon in the *Alope*, and as people who try to
restrain their laughter burst out in a guffaw, as happened to Xeno-
phantus. But it is surprising if a man is defeated by and cannot resist
pleasures or pains which most men can hold out against, when this is
not due to heredity or disease, like the softness that is hereditary with
15   the kings of the Scythians, or that which distinguishes the female sex
from the male.

The lover of amusement, too, is thought to be self-indulgent, but is really soft. For amusement is a relaxation, since it is a rest; and the lover of amusement is one of the people who go to excess in this.

Of incontinence one kind is impetuosity, another weakness. For some men after deliberating fail, owing to their passion, to stand by the conclusions of their deliberation, others because they have not deliberated are led by their passion; since some men (just as people who first tickle others are not tickled themselves), if they have first perceived and seen what is coming and have first roused themselves and their calculative faculty, are not defeated by their passion, whether it be pleasant or painful. It is keen and excitable people that suffer especially from the impetuous form of incontinence; for the former because of their quickness and the latter because of the violence of their passions do not wait on reason, because they are apt to follow their imagination.

CHAPTER 8

The self-indulgent man, as was said, has no regrets; for he stands by his choice; but any incontinent man is subject to regrets. This is why the position is not as it was expressed in the formulation of the problem, but the self-indulgent man is incurable and the incontinent man curable; for wickedness is like a disease such as dropsy or consumption, while incontinence is like epilepsy; the former is a permanent, the latter an intermittent badness. And generally incontinence and vice are different in kind; vice is unconscious of itself, incontinence is not (of incontinent men themselves, those who become beside themselves are better than those who possess reason but do not abide by it, since the latter are defeated by a weaker passion, and do not act without previous deliberation like the others); for the incontinent man is like the people who get drunk quickly and on little wine, i.e. on less than most people.

Evidently, then, incontinence is not vice (though perhaps it is so in a qualified sense); for incontinence is contrary to choice while vice is in accordance with choice; not but what they are similar in respect of the actions they lead to; as in the saying of Demodocus about the Milesians, 'the Milesians are not without sense, but they do the things that senseless people do', so too incontinent people are not unjust but they will do unjust acts.

Now, since the incontinent man is apt to pursue, not on conviction, bodily pleasures that are excessive and contrary to right reason, while the self-indulgent man is convinced because he is the sort of man to pursue them, it is on the contrary the former that is easily persuaded to change his mind, while the latter is not. For excellence and vice

15 respectively preserve and destroy the first principle, and in actions that for the sake of which is the first principle, as the hypotheses are in mathematics; neither in that case is it reason that teaches the first principles, nor is it so here—excellence either natural or produced by habituation is what teaches right opinion about the first principle. Such a man as this, then, is temperate; his contrary is the self-indulgent.

20   But there is a sort of man who is carried away as a result of passion and contrary to right reason—a man whom passion masters so that he does not act according to right reason, but does not master to the extent of making him ready to believe that he ought to pursue such pleasures without reserve; this is the incontinent man, who is better than the self-indulgent man, and not bad without qualification; for the

25 best thing in him, the first principle, is preserved. And contrary to him is another kind of man, he who abides by his convictions and is not carried away, at least as a result of passion. It is evident from these considerations that the latter is a good state and the former a bad one.

CHAPTER 9

Is the man continent who abides by any and every reasoning and any

30 and every choice, or the man who abides by the right choice, and is he incontinent who abandons any and every choice and any and every reasoning, or he who abandons the reasoning that is not false and the choice that is right? This is how we put it before in our statement of the problem. Or is it incidentally any and every choice but *per se* the true reasoning and the right choice by which the one abides and the other

1151ᵇ does not? If any one chooses or pursues this for the sake of that, *per se* he pursues and chooses the latter, but incidentally the former. But when we speak without qualification we mean what is *per se*. Therefore in a sense the one abides by, and the other abandons, any and every opinion; but without qualification, the true opinion.

5   There are some who are apt to abide by their opinion, who are called strong-headed, viz. those who are hard to persuade and are not easily persuaded to change; these have in them something like the continent man, as the prodigal is in a way like the liberal man and the rash man like the confident man; but they are different in many

respects. For it is to passion and appetite that the one will not yield, since on occasion the continent man *will* be easy to persuade; but it is to reason that the others refuse to yield, for they do form appetites and many of them are led by their pleasures. Now the people who are strong-headed are the opinionated, the ignorant, and the boorish—the opinionated being influenced by pleasure and pain; for they delight in the victory they gain if they are not persuaded to change, and are pained if their decisions become null and void as decrees sometimes do; so that they are more like the incontinent than the continent man.

But there are some who fail to abide by their resolutions, not as a result of incontinence, e.g. Neoptolemus in Sophocles' *Philoctetes*; yet it was for the sake of pleasure that he did not stand fast—but a noble pleasure; for telling the truth was noble to him, but he had been persuaded by Odysseus to tell the lie. For not every one who does anything for the sake of pleasure is either self-indulgent or bad or incontinent, but he who does it for a disgraceful pleasure.

Since there is also a sort of man who takes less delight than he should in bodily things, and does not abide by reason, he who is intermediate between him and the incontinent man is the continent man; for the incontinent man fails to abide by reason because he delights too much in them, and this man because he delights in them too little; while the continent man abides by it and does not change on either account. Now if continence is good, both the contrary states must be bad, as they actually appear to be; but because the other extreme is seen in few people and seldom, as temperance is thought to be contrary only to self-indulgence, so is continence to incontinence.

Since many names are applied analogically, it is by analogy that we have come to speak of the continence of the temperate man; for both the continent man and the temperate man are such as to do nothing contrary to reason for the sake of the bodily pleasures, but the former has and the latter has not bad appetites, and the latter is such as not to feel pleasure contrary to reason, while the former is such as to feel pleasure but not to be led by it. And the incontinent and the self-indulgent man are also like one another; they are different, but both pursue bodily pleasures—the latter, however, also thinking that he ought to do so, while the former does not think this.

Nor can the same man have practical wisdom and be incontinent; for it has been shown that a man is at the same time practically wise, and good in respect of character. Further, a man has practical wisdom not by knowing only but by acting; but the incontinent man is unable to act—there is, however, nothing to prevent a clever man from being
10 incontinent; this is why it is sometimes actually thought that some people have practical wisdom but are incontinent, viz. because cleverness and practical wisdom differ in the way we have described in our first discussions, and are near together in respect of their reasoning,
15 but differ in respect of their choice—nor yet is the incontinent man like the man who knows and is contemplating a truth, but like the man who is asleep or drunk. And he acts voluntarily (for he acts in a sense with knowledge both of what he does and of that for the sake of which he does it), but is not wicked since his choice is good; so that he is half-wicked. And he is not unjust; for he does not act of malice afore-thought; of the two types of incontinent man the one does not abide by the conclusions of his deliberation, while the excitable man does not
20 deliberate at all. And thus the incontinent man is like a city which passes all the right decrees and has good laws, but makes no use of them, as in Anaxandrides' jesting remark,

> The city willed it, that cares nought for laws;

but the wicked man is like a city that uses its laws, but has wicked laws to use.

25 Now incontinence and continence are concerned with that which is in excess of the state characteristic of most men; for the continent man abides by his resolutions more and the incontinent man less than most men can.

Of the forms of incontinence, that of excitable people is more curable than that of those who deliberate but do not abide by their decisions, and those who are incontinent through habituation are more curable than those in whom incontinence is innate; for it is
30 easier to change a habit than to change one's nature; even habit is hard to change just because it is like nature, as Evenus says:

> I say that habit's but long practice, friend,
> And this becomes men's nature in the end.

We have now stated what continence, incontinence, endurance, and softness are, and how these states are related to each other.

CHAPTER 11

The study of pleasure and pain belongs to the province of the political 1152^b
philosopher; for he is the architect of the end, with a view to which we
call one thing bad and another good without qualification. Further, it
is one of our necessary tasks to consider them; for not only did we lay it 5
down that moral excellence and vice are concerned with pains and
pleasures, but most people say that happiness involves pleasure; this is
why the blessed man is called by a name derived from a word meaning
enjoyment.

Now some people think that no pleasure is a good, either in itself or
incidentally, since the good and pleasure are not the same; others 10
think that some pleasures are good but that most are bad. Again there
is a third view, that even if all pleasures are goods, yet the best thing
cannot be pleasure. The reasons given for the view that pleasure is not
a good at all are (*a*) that every pleasure is a perceptible process to a
natural state, and that no process is of the same kind as its end, e.g. no
process of building is of the same kind as a house. (*b*) A temperate man 15
avoids pleasures. (*c*) A man of practical wisdom pursues what is free
from pain, not what is pleasant. (*d*) The pleasures are a hindrance to
thought, and the more so the more one delights in them, e.g. in sexual
pleasure; for no one could think of anything while absorbed in this. (*e*)
There is no art of pleasure; but every good is the product of some art.
(*f*) Children and the brutes pursue pleasures. The reasons for the view 20
that not all pleasures are good are that (*a*) there are pleasures that are
actually base and objects of reproach, and (*b*) there are harmful
pleasures; for some pleasant things are unhealthy. The reason for the
view that the best thing is not pleasure is that pleasure is not an end
but a process.

CHAPTER 12

These are pretty much the things that are said. That it does not follow
from these grounds that pleasure is not a good, or even the chief good, 25
is plain from the following considerations. First, since that which is
good may be so in either of two senses (one thing good simply and
another good for a particular person), natural constitutions and states,
and therefore also movements and processes, will be correspondingly
divisible. Of those which are thought to be bad some will be bad
without qualification but not bad for a particular person, but worthy of 30

his choice, and some will not be worthy of choice even for a particular person, but only at a particular time and for a short period, though not without qualification; while others are not even pleasures, but seem to be so, viz. all those which involve pain and whose end is curative, e.g. the processes that go on in sick persons.

Further, one kind of good being activity and another being state, the processes that restore us to our natural state are only incidentally pleasant; for that matter the activity at work in the appetites for them is the activity of so much of our state and nature as has remained un-impaired; for there are actually pleasures that involve *no* pain or appetite (e.g. those of contemplation), the nature in such a case not being defective at all. That the others are incidental is indicated by the fact that men do not enjoy the same things when their nature is in its settled state as they do when it is being replenished, but in the former case they enjoy the things that are pleasant without qualification, in the latter the contraries of these as well; for then they enjoy even sharp and bitter things, none of which is pleasant either by nature or without qualification. Nor, then, are the pleasures; for as pleasant things differ, so do the pleasures arising from them.

Again, it is not necessary that there should be something else better than pleasure, as some say the end is better than the process; for pleasures are not processes nor do they all involve process—they are activities and ends; nor do they arise when we are becoming some-thing, but when we are exercising some faculty; and not all pleasures have an end different from themselves, but only the pleasures of persons who are being led to the completing of their nature. This is why it is not right to say that pleasure is a perceptible process, but it should rather be called activity of the natural state, and instead of 'perceptible' 'unimpeded'. It is thought to be a process just because they think it is in the strict sense *good*; for they think that activity is a process, which it is not.

The view that pleasures are bad because some pleasant things are unhealthy is like saying that healthy things are bad because some healthy things are bad for the pocket; both are bad in the respect mentioned, but they are not *bad* for *that* reason—indeed, contempla-tion itself is sometimes injurious to health.

Neither practical wisdom nor any state is impeded by the pleasure arising from it; it is foreign pleasures that impede, for the pleasures arising from contemplation and learning will make us contemplate and learn all the more.

The fact that no pleasure is the product of any art arises naturally enough; there is no art of any other activity either, but only of the capacity; though for that matter the arts of the perfumer and the cook *are* thought to be arts of pleasure. 25

The arguments that the temperate man avoids pleasure and that the man of practical wisdom pursues the painless life, and that children and the brutes pursue pleasure, are all refuted by the same considera- tion. We have pointed out in what sense pleasures are good without qualification and in what sense some are not good; now both the brutes and children pursue pleasures of the latter kind (and the man of practical wisdom pursues tranquil freedom from that kind), viz. those which imply appetite and pain, i.e. the bodily pleasures (for it is these that are of this nature) and the excesses of them, in respect of which the self-indulgent man is self-indulgent. This is why the temperate man avoids these pleasures; for even he has pleasures of his own. 30

35

CHAPTER 13

But further it is agreed that pain is bad and to be avoided; for some pain is without qualification bad, and other pain is bad because it is in some respect an impediment to us. Now the contrary of that which is to be avoided, *qua* something to be avoided and bad, is good. Pleasure, then, is necessarily a good. For the answer of Speusippus, that pleasure is contrary both to pain and to good, as the greater is contrary both to the less and to the equal, is not successful; since he would not say that pleasure is essentially a species of evil. 1153^b

5

And if certain pleasures are bad, that does not prevent the best thing from being some pleasure—just as knowledge might be, though certain kinds of knowledge are bad. Perhaps it is even necessary, if each state has unimpeded activities, that whether the activity (if unimpeded) of all our states or that of some one of them is happiness, this should be the thing most worthy of our choice; and this activity is a pleasure. Thus the chief good would be some pleasure, though most pleasures might perhaps be bad without qualification. And for this reason all men think that the happy life is pleasant and weave pleasure into happiness—and reasonably too; for no activity is complete when it is impeded, and happiness is a complete thing; this is why the happy man needs the goods of the body and external goods, i.e. those of fortune, viz. in order that he may not be impeded in these ways. Those who say that the victim on the rack or the man who falls into great 10

15

20 misfortunes is happy if he is good, are, whether they mean to or not, talking nonsense. Now because we need fortune as well as other things, some people think good fortune the same thing as happiness; but it is not that, for even good fortune itself when in excess is an impediment, and perhaps should then be no longer called good fortune; for its limit is fixed by reference to happiness.

25 And indeed the fact that all things, both brutes and men, pursue pleasure is an indication of its being somehow the chief good:

No voice is wholly lost that many peoples. . . .

But since no one nature or state either is or is thought the best for all,
30 neither do all pursue the same pleasure; yet all pursue pleasure. And perhaps they actually pursue not the pleasure they think they pursue nor that which they would say they pursue, but the same pleasure; for all things have by nature something divine in them. But the bodily pleasures have appropriated the name both because we oftenest steer
35 our course for them and because all men share in them; thus because they alone are familiar, men think there are no others.

1154ᵃ It is evident also that if pleasure and activity is not a good, it will not be the case that the happy man lives a pleasant life; for to what end should he need pleasure, if it is not a good but the happy man may even live a painful life? For pain is neither an evil nor a good, if
5 pleasure is not; why then should he avoid it?

Therefore, too, the life of the good man will not be pleasanter than that of anyone else, if his activities are not more pleasant.

CHAPTER 14

With regard to the bodily pleasures, those who say that *some* pleasures are very much to be chosen, viz. the noble pleasures, but not the bodily
10 pleasures, i.e. those with which the self-indulgent man is concerned, must consider why, then, the contrary pains are bad. For the contrary of bad is good. Are the necessary pleasures good in the sense in which even that which is not bad is good? Or are they good up to a point? Is it that where you have states and processes of which there cannot be too much, there cannot be too much of the corresponding pleasure, and that where there can be too much of the one there can be too much of
15 the other also? Now there can be too much of bodily goods, and the bad man is bad by virtue of pursuing the excess, not by virtue of pursuing the necessary pleasures (for *all* men enjoy in some way or

other both dainty foods and wines and sexual intercourse, but not all men do so as they ought). The contrary is the case with pain; for he does not avoid the excess of it, he avoids it altogether; for the alterna- 20
tive to excess of pleasure is not pain, except to the man who pursues this excess.

Since we should state not only the truth, but also the cause of error—for this contributes towards producing conviction, since when a reasonable explanation is given of why the false view appears true, 25
this tends to produce belief in the true view—therefore we must state why the bodily pleasures appear the more worthy of choice. Firstly, then, it is because they expel pain; owing to the excesses of pain men pursue excessive and in general bodily pleasure as being a cure for the pain. Now curative agencies produce intense feeling—which is the 30
reason why they are pursued—because they show up against the contrary pain. (Indeed pleasure is thought not to be good for these two reasons, as has been said, viz. that some of them are activities belonging to a bad nature—either congenital, as in the case of a brute, or due to habit, i.e. those of bad men; while others are meant to cure a defective nature, and it is better to be in a healthy state than to be getting into it, but these arise during the process of being made complete and 1154^b
are therefore only incidentally good.) Further, they are pursued because of their violence by those who cannot enjoy other pleasures. At all events some people manufacture thirsts for themselves. When these are harmless, the practice is irreproachable; when they are hurtful, it is bad. For they have nothing else to enjoy, and, besides, a 5
neutral state is painful to many people because of their nature. For animals are always toiling, as the students of natural science also testify, saying that sight and hearing are painful; but we have become used to this, as they maintain. Similarly, while, in youth, people are, owing to the growth that is going on, in a situation like that of drunken 10
men, and youth is pleasant, on the other hand people of excitable nature always need relief; for even their body is ever in torment owing to its special composition, and they are always under the influence of violent desire; but pain is driven out both by the contrary pleasure, and by any chance pleasure if it be strong; and for these reasons they become self-indulgent and bad. But the pleasures that do not involve 15
pains do not admit of excess; and these are among the things pleasant by nature and not incidentally. By things pleasant incidentally I mean those that act as cures (for because as a result people are cured, through some action of the part that remains healthy, for this reason

the process is thought pleasant); things naturally pleasant are those
20   that stimulate the action of the healthy nature.

There is no one thing that is always pleasant, because our nature is
not simple but there is another element in us as well, inasmuch as we
are perishable creatures, so that if the one element does something,
this is unnatural to the other nature, and when the two elements are
evenly balanced, what is done seems neither painful nor pleasant; for
25   if the nature of anything were simple, the same action would always be
most pleasant to it. This is why God always enjoys a single and simple
pleasure; for there is not only an activity of movement but an activity of
immobility, and pleasure is found more in rest than in movement. But
'change in all things is sweet', as the poet says, because of some vice;
30   for as it is the vicious man that is changeable, so the nature that needs
change is vicious; for it is not simple nor good.

We have now discussed continence and incontinence, and pleasure
and pain, both what each is and in what sense some of them are good
and others bad; it remains to speak of friendship.

BOOK IX

CHAPTER 4

1166ᵃ   Friendly relations with one's neighbours, and the marks by which
friendships are defined, seem to have proceeded from a man's
relations to himself. For men think a friend is one who wishes and
does what is good, or seems so, for the sake of his friend, or one who
5   wishes his friend to exist and live, for his sake; which mothers do to
their children, and friends do who have come into conflict. And others
think a friend is one who lives with and has the same tastes as another,
or one who grieves and rejoices with his friend; and this too is found in
mothers most of all. It is by some one of these characteristics that
friendship too is defined.

10   Now each of these is true of the good man's relation to himself (and
of all other men in so far as they think themselves good; excellence and
the good man seem, as has been said, to be the measure of every class
of things). For his opinions are harmonious, and he desires the same
things with all his soul; and therefore he wishes for himself what is
good and what seems so, and does it (for it is characteristic of the good
15   man to exert himself for the good), and does so for his own sake (for he

does it for the sake of the intellectual element in him, which is thought to be the man himself); and he wishes himself to live and be preserved, and especially the element by virtue of which he thinks. For existence is good to the good man, and each man wishes himself what is good, while no one chooses to possess the whole world if he has first to become someone else (for that matter, even now God possesses the good); he wishes for this only on condition of being whatever he is; and the element that thinks would seem to be the individual man, or to be so more than any other element in him. And such a man wishes to live with himself; for he does so with pleasure, since the memories of his past acts are delightful and his hopes for the future are good, and therefore pleasant. His mind is well stored too with subjects of contemplation. And he grieves and rejoices, more than any other, with himself; for the same thing is always painful, and the same thing always pleasant, and not one thing at one time and another at another; he has, so to speak, nothing to regret.

Therefore, since each of these characteristics belongs to the good man in relation to himself, and he is related to his friend as to himself (for his friend is another self), friendship too is thought to be one of these attributes, and those who have these attributes to be friends. Whether there is or is not friendship between a man and himself is a question we may dismiss for the present; there would seem to be friendship in so far as he is two or more, to judge from what has been said, and from the fact that the extreme of friendship is likened to one's love for oneself. 1166

But the attributes named seem to belong even to the majority of men, poor creatures though they may be. Are we to say then that in so far as they are satisfied with themselves and think they are good, they share in these attributes? Certainly no one who is thoroughly bad and impious has these attributes, or even seems to do so. They hardly belong even to inferior people; for they are at variance with themselves, and have appetites for some things and wishes for others. This is true, for instance, of incontinent people; for they choose, instead of the things they themselves think good, things that are pleasant but hurtful; while others again, through cowardice and laziness, shrink from doing what they think best for themselves. And those who have done many terrible deeds and are hated for their wickedness even shrink from life and destroy themselves. And wicked men seek for people with whom to spend their days, and shun themselves; for they remember many a grievous deed, and anticipate others like them,

when they are by themselves, but when they are with others they forget. And having nothing lovable in them they have no feeling of love to themselves. Therefore also such men do not rejoice or grieve with themselves; for their soul is rent by faction, and one element in it by
20 reason of its wickedness grieves when it abstains from certain acts, while the other part is pleased, and one draws them this way and the other that, as if they were pulling them in pieces. If a man cannot at the same time be pained and pleased, at all events after a short time he is pained *because* he was pleased, and he could have wished that these things had not been pleasant to him; for bad men are laden with regrets.
25   Therefore the bad man does not seem to be amicably disposed even to himself, because there is nothing in him to love; so that if to be thus is the height of wretchedness, we should strain every nerve to avoid wickedness and should endeavour to be good; for so one may be both friendly to oneself and a friend to another.

CHAPTER 8

1168ᵃ The question is also debated, whether a man should love himself most, or some one else. People criticize those who love themselves
30 most, and call them self-lovers, using this as an epithet of disgrace, and a bad man seems to do everything for his own sake, and the more so the more wicked he is—and so men reproach him, for instance, with doing nothing of his own accord—while the good man acts for honour's sake, and the more so the better he is, and acts for his friend's sake, and sacrifices his own interest.
     But the facts clash with these arguments, and this is not surprising.
1168ᵇ For men say that one ought to love best one's best friend, and a man's best friend is one who wishes well to the object of his wish for his sake, even if no one is to know of it; and these attributes are found most of all in a man's attitude towards himself, and so are all the other
5 attributes by which a friend is defined; for, as we have said, it is from this relation that all the characteristics of friendship have extended to others. All the proverbs, too, agree with this, e.g. 'a single soul', and 'what friends have is common property', and 'friendship is equality', and 'charity begins at home'; for all these marks will be found most in a man's relation to himself; he is his own best friend and therefore
10 ought to love himself best. It is therefore a reasonable question, which of the two views we should follow; for both are plausible.

Perhaps we ought to mark off such arguments from each other and determine how far and in what respects each view is right. Now if we grasp the sense in which each party uses the phrase 'lover of self', the truth may become evident. Those who use the term as one of reproach ascribe self-love to people who assign to themselves the greater share of wealth, honours, and bodily pleasures; for these are what most people desire, and busy themselves about as though they were the best of all things, which is the reason, too, why they become objects of competition. So those who are grasping with regard to these things gratify their appetites and in general their feelings and the irrational element of the soul; and most men are of this nature (thus the epithet has taken its meaning from the prevailing type of self-love, which is a bad one); it is just, therefore, that men who are lovers of self in this way are reproached for being so. That it is those who give themselves the preference in regard to objects of this sort that most people usually call lovers of self is plain; for if a man were always anxious that he himself, above all things, should act justly, temperately, or in accordance with any other of the excellences, and in general were always to try to secure for himself the honourable course, no one will call such a man a lover of self or blame him.

But such a man would seem more than the other a lover of self; at all events he assigns to himself the things that are noblest and best, and gratifies the most authoritative element in himself and in all things obeys this; and just as a city or any other systematic whole is most properly identified with the most authoritative element in it, so is a man; and therefore the man who loves this and gratifies it is most of all a lover of self. Besides, a man is said to have or not to have self-control according as his intellect has or has not the control, on the assumption that this is the man himself; and the things men have done from reason are thought most properly their own acts and voluntary acts. That this is the man himself, then, or is so more than anything else, is plain, and also that the good man loves most this part of him. Whence it follows that he is most truly a lover of self, of another type than that which is a matter of reproach, and as different from that as living according to reason is from living as passion dictates, and desiring what is noble from desiring what seems advantageous. Those, then, who busy themselves in an exceptional degree with noble actions all men approve and praise; and if *all* were to strive towards what is noble and strain every nerve to do the noblest deeds, everything would be as it should be for the common good, and every one would secure for himself the goods that are greatest, since excellence is the greatest of goods.

Therefore the good man should be a lover of self (for he will both himself profit by doing noble acts, and will benefit his fellows), but the wicked man should not; for he will hurt both himself and his neighbours, following as he does evil passions. For the wicked man, what he does clashes with what he ought to do, but what the good man ought to do he does; for the intellect always chooses what is best for itself, and the good man obeys his intellect. It is true of the good man too that he does many acts for the sake of his friends and his country, and if necessary dies for them; for he will throw away both wealth and honours and in general the goods that are objects of competition, gaining for himself nobility; since he would prefer a short period of intense pleasure to a long one of mild enjoyment, a twelvemonth of noble life to many years of humdrum existence, and one great and noble action to many trivial ones. Now those who die for others doubtless attain this result; it is therefore a great prize that they choose for themselves. They will throw away wealth too on condition that their friends will gain more; for while a man's friend gains wealth he himself achieves nobility; he is therefore assigning the greater good to himself. The same too is true of honour and office; all these things he will sacrifice to his friend; for this is noble and laudable for himself. Rightly then is he thought to be good, since he chooses nobility before all else. But he may even give up actions to his friend; it may be nobler to become the cause of his friend's acting than to act himself. In all the actions, therefore, that men are praised for, the good man is seen to assign to himself the greater share in what is noble. In this sense, then, as has been said, a man should be a lover of self; but in the sense in which most men are so, he ought not.

CHAPTER 9

It is also disputed whether the happy man will need friends or not. It is said that those who are blessed and self-sufficient have no need of friends; for they have the things that are good, and therefore being self-sufficient they need nothing further, while a friend, being another self, furnishes what a man cannot provide by his own effort; whence the saying 'when fortune is kind, what need of friends?' But it seems strange, when one assigns all good things to the happy man, not to assign friends, who are thought the greatest of external goods. And if it is more characteristic of a friend to do well by another than to be well done by, and to confer benefits is characteristic of the good man and of excellence, and it is nobler to do well by friends than by strangers, the good man will need people to do well by. This is why the question is asked whether we need friends more in prosperity or in adversity, on the assumption that not only does a man in adversity need people to confer benefits on him, but also those who are prospering need people to do well by. Surely it is strange, too, to make the blessed man a solitary; for no one would choose to possess all good things on condition of being alone, since man is a political creature and one whose nature is to live with others. Therefore even the happy man lives with others; for he has the things that are by nature good. And plainly it is better to spend his days with friends and good men than with strangers or any chance persons. Therefore the happy man needs friends. 15

20

What then is it that the first party means, and in what respect is it right? Is it that most men identify friends with useful people? Of such friends indeed the blessed man will have no need, since he already has the things that are good; nor will he need those whom one makes one's friends because of their pleasantness, or he will need them only to a small extent (for his life, being pleasant, has no need of adventitious pleasure); and because he does not need *such* friends he is thought not to need friends. 25

But that is surely not true. For we have said at the outset that happiness is an activity; and activity plainly comes into being and is not present at the start like a piece of property. If happiness lies in living and being active, and the good man's activity is virtuous and pleasant in itself, as we have said at the outset, and if a thing's being one's own is one of the attributes that make it pleasant, and if we can contemplate our neighbours better than ourselves and their actions better than our own, and if the actions of virtuous men who are their friends are pleasant to good men (since these have both the attributes that are naturally pleasant)—if this be so, the blessed man will need friends of this sort, since he chooses to contemplate worthy actions and actions that are his own, and the actions of a good man who is his friend have both these qualities. 30

1170ᵃ

Further, men think that the happy man ought to live pleasantly. Now if he were a solitary, life would be hard for him; for by oneself it is not easy to be continuously active; but with others and towards others it is easier. With others therefore his activity will be more continuous, 5

being in itself pleasant, as it ought to be for the man who is blessed; for
a good man *qua* good delights in excellent actions and is vexed at
10   vicious ones, as a musical man enjoys beautiful tunes but is pained at
bad ones. A certain training in excellence arises also from the
company of the good, as Theognis remarks.

If we look deeper into the nature of things, a virtuous friend seems
to be naturally desirable for a virtuous man. For that which is good by
nature, we have said, is for the virtuous man good and pleasant in
15   itself. Now life is defined in the case of animals by the power of
perception, in that of man by the power of perception or thought; and
a power is referred to the corresponding activity, which is the essential
thing; therefore life seems to be essentially perceiving or thinking.
20   And life is among the things that are good and pleasant in themselves,
since it is determinate and the determinate is of the nature of the good;
and that which is good by nature is also good for the virtuous man
(which is the reason why life seems pleasant to all men); but we must
not apply this to a wicked and corrupt life nor to a life spent in pain;
for such a life is indeterminate, as are its attributes. The nature of pain
25   will become plainer in what follows. But if life itself is good and
pleasant (which it seems to be, from the very fact that all men desire it,
and particularly those who are good and blessed; for to such men life
is most desirable, and their existence is the most blessed); and if he
who sees perceives that he sees, and he who hears, that he hears, and
30   he who walks, that he walks, and in the case of all other activities
similarly there is something which perceives that we are active, so that
if we perceive, we perceive that we perceive, and if we think, that we
think; and if to perceive that we perceive or think is to perceive that we
1170^b exist (for existence was defined as perceiving or thinking); and if
perceiving that one lives is one of the things that are pleasant in themselves (for life is by nature good, and to perceive what is good present
in oneself is pleasant); and if life is desirable, and particularly so for
good men, because to them existence is good and pleasant (for they are
5   pleased at the consciousness of what is in itself good); and if as the
virtuous man is to himself, he is to his friend also (for his friend is
another self);—then as his own existence is desirable for each man, so,
or almost so, is that of his friend. Now his existence was seen to be
desirable because he perceived his own goodness, and such percep-
10   tion is pleasant in itself. He needs, therefore, to be conscious of the
existence of his friend as well, and this will be realized in their living
together and sharing in discussion and thought; for this is what living

together would seem to mean in the case of man, and not, as in the case of cattle, feeding in the same place.

If, then, existence is in itself desirable for the blessed man (since it is by its nature good and pleasant), and that of his friend is very much the same, a friend will be one of the things that are desirable. Now that which is desirable for him he must have, or he will be deficient in this respect. The man who is to be happy will therefore need virtuous friends.

BOOK X

CHAPTER I

After these matters we ought perhaps next to discuss pleasure. For it is thought to be most intimately connected with our human nature, which is the reason why in educating the young we steer them by the rudders of pleasure and pain; it is thought, too, that to enjoy the things we ought and to hate the things we ought has the greatest bearing on excellence of character. For these things extend right through life, with a weight and power of their own in respect both to excellence and to the happy life, since men choose what is pleasant and avoid what is painful; and such things, it will be thought, we should least of all omit to discuss, especially since they admit of much dispute. For some say pleasure is the good, while others, on the contrary, say it is thoroughly bad—some no doubt being persuaded that the facts are so, and others thinking it has a better effect on our life to exhibit pleasure as a bad thing even if it is not; for most people (they think) incline towards it and are the slaves of their pleasures, for which reason they ought to lead them in the opposite direction, since thus they will reach the middle state. But surely this is not correct. For arguments about matters concerned with feelings and actions are less reliable than facts: and so when they clash with the facts of perception they are despised, and discredit the truth as well; if a man who runs down pleasure is once seen to be aiming at it, his inclining towards it is thought to imply that it is all worthy of being aimed at; for most people are not good at drawing distinctions. True arguments seem, then, most useful, not only with a view to knowledge, but with a view to life also; for since they harmonize with the facts they are believed, and so they stimulate those who understand them to live according to them.

15

1172ᵃ
20

25

30

35

1172ᵇ

5

Enough of such questions; let us proceed to review the opinions that have been expressed about pleasure.

CHAPTER 2

Eudoxus thought pleasure was the good because he saw all things,
10   both rational and irrational, aiming at it, and because in all things that which is the object of choice is what is excellent, and that which is most the object of choice the greatest good; thus the fact that all things moved towards the same object indicated that this was for all things the chief good (for each thing, he argued, finds its own good, as it finds its own nourishment); and that which is good for all things and at
15   which all aim was *the* good. His arguments were credited more because of the excellence of his character than for their own sake; he was thought to be remarkably temperate, and therefore it was thought that he was not saying what he did say as a friend of pleasure, but that the facts really were so. He believed that the same conclusion followed no less plainly from a study of the contrary of pleasure; pain was in itself an object of aversion to all things, and therefore its contrary must
20   be similarly an object of choice. And again that is most an object of choice which we choose not because or for the sake of something else, and pleasure is admittedly of this nature; for no one asks to what end he is pleased, thus implying that pleasure is in itself an object of choice. Further, he argued that pleasure when added to any good, e.g. to just or temperate action, makes it more worthy of choice, and that it
25   is only by itself that the good can be increased.

This argument seems to show it to be one of the goods, and no more a good than any other; for every good is more worthy of choice along with another good than taken alone. And so it is by an argument of this kind that Plato proves the good *not* to be pleasure; he argues that the pleasant life is more desirable with wisdom than without, and that if
30   the mixture is better, pleasure is not the good; for the good cannot become more desirable by the addition of anything to it. Now it is clear that nothing else either can be the good if it is made more desirable by the addition of any of the things that are good in themselves. What, then, is there that satisfies this criterion, which at the same time we can participate in? It is something of this sort that we are looking for.

1173ª   Those who object that that at which all things aim is not necessarily good are talking nonsense. For we say that that which everyone thinks

really is so; and the man who attacks this belief will hardly have anything more credible to maintain instead. If it is senseless creatures that
desire the things in question, there might be something in what they
say; but if intelligent creatures do so as well, what sense can there be in
this view? But perhaps even in inferior creatures there is some natural
good stronger than themselves which aims at their proper good.   5

Nor does the argument about the contrary of pleasure seem to be
correct. They say that if pain is an evil it does not follow that pleasure
is a good; for evil is opposed to evil and at the same time both are
opposed to the neutral state—which is correct enough but does not
apply to the things in question. For if both belonged to the class of
evils they ought both to be objects of aversion, while if they belonged   10
to the class of neutrals neither should be or they should both be
equally so; but in fact people evidently avoid the one as evil and
choose the other as good; that then must be the nature of the opposition between them.

CHAPTER 3

Nor again, if pleasure is not a quality, does it follow that it is not a
good; for the activities of excellence are not qualities either, nor is   15
happiness.

They say, however, that the good is determinate, while pleasure is
indeterminate, because it admits of degrees. Now if it is from the
feeling of pleasure that they judge thus, the same will be true of
justice and the other excellences in respect of which we plainly say
that people of a certain character are so more or less, and act more or
less in accordance with these excellences; for people may be more   20
just or brave, and it is possible also to act justly or temperately more
or less. But if their judgement is based on the various pleasures,
surely they are not stating the cause, if in fact some pleasures are
unmixed and others mixed. Again, just as health admits of degrees
without being indeterminate, why should not pleasure? The same   25
proportion is not found in all things, nor a single proportion always in
the same thing, but it may be relaxed and yet persist up to a point, and
it may differ in degree. The case of pleasure also may therefore be of
this kind.

Again, they assume that the good is complete while movements and
comings into being are incomplete, and try to exhibit pleasure as being   30
a movement and a coming into being. But they do not seem to be right,

nor does it seem to be a movement. For speed and slowness are thought to be proper to every movement, if not in itself (as e.g. that of the heavens) then in relation to something else; but of pleasure neither of these things is true. For while we may *become* pleased quickly as we may become angry quickly, we cannot *be* pleased quickly, not even in relation to some one else, while we *can* walk, or grow, or the like, quickly. While, then, we can change quickly or slowly into a state of pleasure, we cannot quickly exhibit the activity of pleasure, i.e. be pleased. Again, how can it be a coming into being? It is not thought that any chance thing can come out of any chance thing, but that a thing is dissolved into that out of which it comes into being; and pain would be the destruction of that of which pleasure is the coming into being.

They say, too, that pain is the lack of that which is according to nature, and pleasure is replenishment. But these experiences are bodily. If then pleasure is replenishment with that which is according to nature, that which feels pleasure will be that in which the replenishment takes place, i.e. the body; but that is not thought to be the case; therefore the replenishment is not pleasure, though one might be pleased when replenishment was taking place, just as one would be pained if one was being operated on. This opinion seems to be based on the pains and pleasures connected with nutrition; on the fact that when people have been short of food and have felt pain beforehand they are pleased by the replenishment. But this does not happen with all pleasures; for the pleasures of learning and, among the sensuous pleasures, those of smell, and also many sounds and sights, and memories and hopes, do not presuppose pain. Of what then will these be the coming into being? There has not been lack of anything of which they could be the replenishment.

In reply to those who bring forward the disgraceful pleasures one may say that these are not pleasant; if things are pleasant to people of vicious constitution, we must not suppose that they are also pleasant to others than these, just as we do not reason so about the things that are wholesome or sweet or bitter to sick people, or ascribe whiteness to the things that seem white to those suffering from a disease of the eye. Or one might answer thus—that the pleasures are desirable, but not from *these* sources, as wealth is desirable, but not as the reward of betrayal, and health, but not at the cost of eating anything and everything. Or perhaps pleasures differ in kind; for those derived from noble sources are different from those derived from base sources, and

one cannot get the pleasure of the just man without being just, nor that   30
of the musical man without being musical, and so on.

The fact, too, that a friend is different from a flatterer seems to make
it plain that pleasure is not a good or that pleasures are different in
kind; for the one is thought to consort with us with a view to the good,
the other with a view to our pleasure, and the one is reproached for his
conduct while the other is praised on the ground that he consorts with
us for different ends. And no one would choose to live with the intel-   1174ᵃ
lect of a child throughout his life, however much he were to be pleased
at the things that children are pleased at, nor to get enjoyment by
doing some most disgraceful deed, though he were never to feel any
pain in consequence. And there are many things we should be keen
about even if they brought no pleasure, e.g. seeing, remembering,   5
knowing, possessing the excellences. If pleasures necessarily do
accompany these, that makes no odds; we should choose these even if
no pleasure resulted. It seems to be clear, then, that neither is pleasure
the good nor is all pleasure desirable, and that some pleasures *are*   10
desirable in themselves, differing in kind or in their sources from the
others. So much for the things that are said about pleasure and pain.

CHAPTER 4

What pleasure is, or what kind of thing it is, will become plainer if we
take up the question again from the beginning. Seeing seems to be at
any moment complete, for it does not lack anything which coming into   15
being later will complete its form; and pleasure also seems to be of this
nature. For it is a whole, and at no time can one find a pleasure whose
form will be completed if the pleasure lasts longer. For this reason,
too, it is not a movement. For every movement (e.g. that of building)
takes time and is for the sake of an end, and is complete when it has   20
made what it aims at. It is complete, therefore, only in the whole time
or at the final moment. In their parts and during the time they occupy,
all movements are incomplete, and are different in kind from the whole
movement and from each other. For the fitting together of the stones is
different from the fluting of the column, and these are both different
from the making of the temple; and the making of the temple is
complete (for it lacks nothing with a view to the end proposed), but the   25
making of the base or of the triglyph is incomplete; for each is the
making of a part. They differ in kind, then, and it is not possible to find
at any and every time a movement complete in form, but if at all, only

in the whole time. So, too, in the case of walking and all other movements. For if locomotion is a movement from here to there, it, too, has
differences in kind—flying, walking, leaping, and so on. And not only
so, but in walking itself there are such differences; for the whence and
whither are not the same in the whole racecourse and in a part of it,
nor in one part and in another, nor is it the same thing to traverse this
line and that; for one traverses not only a line but one which is in a
place, and this one is in a different place from that. We have discussed
movement with precision in another work, but it seems that it is not
complete at any and every time, but that the many movements are
incomplete and different in kind, since the whence and whither give
them their form. But of pleasure the form is complete at any and every
time. Plainly, then, pleasure and movement must be different from
each other, and pleasure must be one of the things that are whole and
complete. This would seem to be the case, too, from the fact that it is
not possible to move otherwise than in time, but it *is* possible to be
pleased; for that which takes place in a moment is a whole.

From these considerations it is clear, too, that these thinkers are not
right in saying there is a movement or a coming into being *of* pleasure.
For these cannot be ascribed to all things, but only to those that are
divisible and not wholes; there is no coming into being of seeing nor of
a point nor of a unit, nor is any of these a movement or coming into
being; therefore there is none of pleasure either; for it is a whole.

Since every sense is active in relation to its object, and a sense which
is in good condition acts completely in relation to the most beautiful of
its objects (for complete activity seems to be especially of this nature;
whether we say that *it* is active, or the organ in which it resides, may be
assumed to be immaterial), it follows that in the case of each sense the
best activity is that of the best-conditioned organ in relation to the
finest of its objects. And this activity will be the most complete and
pleasant. For, while there is pleasure in respect of any sense, and in
respect of thought and contemplation no less, the most complete is
pleasantest, and that of a well-conditioned organ in relation to the
worthiest of its objects is the most complete; and the pleasure
completes the activity. But the pleasure does not complete it in the
same way as the object perceived and the faculty of perception, if they
are good, do—just as health and the doctor are not in the same way the
cause of a man's being healthy. (That pleasure is produced in respect
to each sense is plain; for we speak of sights and sounds as pleasant. It
is also plain that it arises most of all when both the sense is at its best

and it is active in reference to an object which corresponds; when both object and perceiver are of the best there will always be pleasure, since 30 the requisite agent and patient are both present.) Pleasure completes the activity not as the inherent state does, but as an end which supervenes as the bloom of youth does on those in the flower of their age. So long, then, as both the intelligible or sensible object and the discriminating or contemplative faculty are as they should be, the pleasure will be involved in the activity; for when both the passive and 1175ᵃ the active factor are unchanged and are related to each other in the same way, the same result naturally follows.

How, then, is it that no one is continuously pleased? Is it that we grow weary? Certainly all human things are incapable of continuous activity. Therefore pleasure also is not continuous; for it accompanies activity. Some things delight us when they are new, but later do so less, 5 for the same reason; for at first the mind is in a state of stimulation and intensely active about them, as people are with respect to their vision when they look hard at a thing, but afterwards our activity is not of this kind, but has grown relaxed; for which reason the pleasure also is 10 dulled.

One might think that all men desire pleasure because they all aim at life; life is an activity, and each man is active about those things and with those faculties that he loves most; e.g. the musician is active with his hearing in reference to tunes, the student with his mind in reference to theoretical questions, and so on in each case; now 15 pleasure completes the activities, and therefore life, which they desire. It is with good reason, then, that they aim at pleasure too, since for everyone it completes life, which is desirable. But whether we choose life for the sake of pleasure or pleasure for the sake of life is a question we may dismiss for the present. For they seem to be bound up together and not to admit of separation, since without activity pleasure does not 20 arise, and every activity is completed by pleasure.

CHAPTER 5

For this reason pleasures seem, too, to differ in kind. For things different in kind are, we think, completed by different things (we see this to be true both of natural objects and of things produced by art, e.g. animals, trees, a painting, a sculpture, a house, an implement); 25 and, similarly, we think that activities differing in kind are completed by things differing in kind. Now the activities of thought differ from those of the senses, and among themselves, in kind; so, therefore, do the pleasures that complete them.

30 This may be seen, too, from the fact that each of the pleasures is bound up with the activity it completes. For an activity is intensified by its proper pleasure, since each class of things is better judged of and brought to precision by those who engage in the activity with pleasure; e.g. it is those who enjoy geometrical thinking that become geometers and grasp the various propositions better, and, similarly, those who 35 are fond of music or of building, and so on, make progress in their proper function by enjoying it; and the pleasures intensify the 1175ᵇ activities, and what intensifies a thing is proper to it, but things different in kind have properties different in kind.

This will be even more apparent from the fact that activities are hindered by pleasures arising from other sources. For people who are fond of playing the flute are incapable of attending to arguments if 5 they overhear someone playing the flute, since they enjoy flute-playing more than the activity in hand; so the pleasure connected with flute-playing destroys the activity concerned with argument. This happens, similarly, in all other cases, when one is active about two things at once; the more pleasant activity drives out the other, and if it is much more pleasant does so all the more, so that one even ceases from the other. This is why when we enjoy anything very much we do not throw 10 ourselves into anything else, and do one thing only when we are not much pleased by another; e.g. in the theatre the people who eat sweets do so most when the actors are poor. Now since activities are made 15 precise and more enduring and better by their proper pleasure, and injured by alien pleasures, evidently the two kinds of pleasure are far apart. For alien pleasures do pretty much what proper pains do, since activities are destroyed by their proper pains; e.g. if a man finds writing or doing sums unpleasant and painful, he does not write, or 20 does not do sums, because the activity is painful. So an activity suffers contrary effects from its proper pleasures and pains, i.e. from those that supervene on it in virtue of its own nature. And alien pleasures have been stated to do much the same as pain; they destroy the activity, only not to the same degree.

Now since activities differ in respect of goodness and badness, and 25 some are worthy to be chosen, others to be avoided, and others neutral, so, too, are the pleasures; for to each activity there is a proper pleasure. The pleasure proper to a worthy activity is good and that proper to an unworthy activity bad; just as the appetites for noble objects are laudable, those for base objects culpable. But the pleasures involved in activities are more proper to them than the desires; for the latter are separated both in time and in nature, while the former are close to the activities, and so hard to distinguish from them that it admits of dispute whether the activity is not the same as the pleasure. (Still, pleasure does not seem to *be* thought or perception—that would be strange; but because they are not found apart they appear to some people the same.) As activities are different, then, so are the corresponding pleasures. Now sight is superior to touch in purity, and hearing and smell to taste; the pleasures, therefore, are similarly superior, and those of thought superior to these, and within each of the two kinds some are superior to others.

Each animal is thought to have a proper pleasure, as it has a proper function; viz. that which corresponds to its activity. If we survey them species by species, too, this will be evident; horse, dog, and man have different pleasures, as Heraclitus says 'asses would prefer sweepings to gold'; for food is pleasanter than gold to asses. So the pleasures of creatures different in kind differ in kind, and it is plausible to suppose that those of a single species do not differ. But they vary to no small extent, in the case of men at least; the same things delight some people and pain others, and are painful and odious to some, and pleasant to and liked by others. This happens, too, in the case of sweet things; the same things do not seem sweet to a man in a fever and a healthy man—nor hot to a weak man and one in good condition. The same happens in other cases. But in all such matters that which appears to the good man is thought to be really so. If this is correct, as it seems to be, and excellence and the good man as such are the measure of each thing, those also will be pleasures which appear so to him, and those things pleasant which he enjoys. If the things he finds tiresome seem pleasant to someone, that is nothing surprising; for men may be ruined and spoilt in many ways; but the things are not pleasant, but only pleasant to these people and to people in this condition. Those which are admittedly disgraceful plainly should not be said to be pleasures, except to a perverted taste; but of those that are thought to be good what kind of pleasure or what pleasure should be said to be that proper to man? Is it not plain from the corresponding activities? The pleasures follow these. Whether, then, the complete and blessed man has one or more activities, the pleasures that complete these will be said in the strict sense to be pleasures proper to man, and the rest will be so in a secondary and fractional way, as are the activities.

CHAPTER 6

30   Now that we have spoken of the excellences, the forms of friendship,
and the varieties of pleasure, what remains is to discuss in outline the
nature of happiness, since this is what we state the end of human
nature to be. Our discussion will be the more concise if we first sum up
what we have said already. We said, then, that it is not a state; for if it
were it might belong to someone who was asleep throughout his life,
living the life of a plant, or, again, to someone who was suffering the
greatest misfortunes. If these implications are unacceptable, and we
1176ᵇ must rather class happiness as an activity, as we have said before, and
if some activities are necessary and desirable for the sake of something
else, while others are so in themselves, evidently happiness must be
placed among those desirable in themselves, not among those desirable for the sake of something else; for happiness does not lack any-
5   thing, but is self-sufficient. Now those activities are desirable in
themselves from which nothing is sought beyond the activity. And of
this nature excellent actions are thought to be; for to do noble and
good deeds is a thing desirable for its own sake.
        Pleasant amusements also are thought to be of this nature; we
10   choose them not for the sake of other things; for we are injured rather
than benefited by them, since we are led to neglect our bodies and our
property. But most of the people who are deemed happy take refuge in
such pastimes, which is the reason why those who are ready-witted at
them are highly esteemed at the courts of tyrants; they make them-
15   selves pleasant companions in the tyrant's favourite pursuits, and that
is the sort of man they want. Now these things are thought to be of the
nature of happiness because people in despotic positions spend their
leisure in them, but perhaps such people prove nothing; for excellence
and thought, from which good activities flow, do not depend on
despotic position; nor, if these people, who have never tasted pure and
20   generous pleasure, take refuge in the bodily pleasures, should these
for that reason be thought more desirable; for boys, too, think the
things that are valued among themselves are the best. It is to be
expected, then, that, as different things seem valuable to boys and to
men, so they should to bad men and to good. Now, as we have often
25   maintained, those things are both valuable and pleasant which are
such to the good man; and to each man the activity in accordance with
his own state is most desirable, and, therefore, to the good man that
which is in accordance with excellence. Happiness, therefore, does

not lie in amusement; it would, indeed, be strange if the end were
amusement, and one were to take trouble and suffer hardship all one's   30
life in order to amuse oneself. For, in a word, everything that we
choose we choose for the sake of something else—except happiness,
which is an end. Now to exert oneself and work for the sake of amusement seems silly and utterly childish. But to amuse oneself in order
that one may exert oneself, as Anacharsis puts it, seems right; for
amusement is a sort of relaxation, and we need relaxation because we
cannot work continuously. Relaxation, then, is not an end; for it is
taken for the sake of activity.   1177ᵃ

The happy life is thought to be one of excellence; now an excellent
life requires exertion, and does not consist in amusement. And we say
that serious things are better than laughable things and those
connected with amusement, and that the activity of the better of any
two things—whether it be two parts or two men—is the better; but the   5
activity of the better is *ipso facto* superior and more of the nature of
happiness. And any chance person—even a slave—can enjoy the
bodily pleasures no less than the best man; but no one assigns to a
slave a share in happiness—unless he assigns to him also a share in
human life. For happiness does not lie in such occupations, but, as we
have said before, in excellent activities.   10

CHAPTER 7

If happiness is activity in accordance with excellence, it is reasonable
that it should be in accordance with the highest excellence; and this
will be that of the best thing in us. Whether it be intellect or something
else that is this element which is thought to be our natural ruler and
guide and to take thought of things noble and divine, whether it be   15
itself also divine or only the most divine element in us, the activity of
this in accordance with its proper excellence will be complete happiness. That this activity is contemplative we have already said.

Now this would seem to be in agreement both with what we said
before and with the truth. For this activity is the best (since not only is   20
intellect the best thing in us, but the objects of intellect are the best of
knowable objects); and, secondly, it is the most continuous, since we
can contemplate truth more continuously than we can *do* anything.
And we think happiness has pleasure mingled with it, but the activity
of wisdom is admittedly the pleasantest of excellent activities; at all
events philosophy is thought to offer pleasures marvellous for their   25

purity and their enduringness, and it is to be expected that those who know will pass their time more pleasantly than those who inquire. And the self-sufficiency that is spoken of must belong most to the contemplative activity. For while a wise man, as well as a just man and the rest, needs the necessaries of life, when they are sufficiently

30   equipped with things of that sort the just man needs people towards whom and with whom he shall act justly, and the temperate man, the brave man, and each of the others is in the same case, but the wise man, even when by himself, can contemplate truth, and the better the wiser he is; he can perhaps do so better if he has fellow-workers, but

1177ᵇ   still he is the most self-sufficient. And this activity alone would seem to be loved for its own sake; for nothing arises from it apart from the contemplating, while from practical activities we gain more or less apart from the action. And happiness is thought to depend on leisure;

5   for we are busy that we may have leisure, and make war that we may live in peace. Now the activity of the practical excellences is exhibited in political or military affairs, but the actions concerned with these seem to be unleisurely. Warlike actions are completely so (for no one chooses to be at war, or provokes war, for the sake of being at war;

10   anyone would seem absolutely murderous if he were to make enemies of his friends in order to bring about battle and slaughter); but the action of the statesman is also unleisurely, and—apart from the political action itself—aims at despotic power and honours, or at all events happiness, for him and his fellow citizens—a happiness

15   different from political action, and evidently sought as being different. So if among excellent actions political and military actions are distinguished by nobility and greatness, and these are unleisurely and aim at an end and are not desirable for their own sake, but the activity of intellect, which is contemplative, seems both to be superior in worth

20   and to aim at no end beyond itself, and to have its pleasure proper to itself (and this augments the activity), and the self-sufficiency, leisureliness, unweariedness (so far as this is possible for man), and all the other attributes ascribed to the blessed man are evidently those connected with this activity, it follows that this will be the complete

25   happiness of man, if it be allowed a complete term of life (for none of the attributes of happiness is *in*complete).

But such a life would be too high for man; for it is not in so far as he is man that he will live so, but in so far as something divine is present in him; and by so much as this is superior to our composite nature is its activity superior to that which is the exercise of the other kind of

excellence. If intellect is divine, then, in comparison with man, the life 30
according to it is divine in comparison with human life. But we must
not follow those who advise us, being men, to think of human things,
and, being mortal, of mortal things, but must, so far as we can, make
ourselves immortal, and strain every nerve to live in accordance with
the best thing in us; for even if it be small in bulk, much more does it in
power and worth surpass everything. This would seem actually to 1178ᵃ
be each man, since it is the authoritative and better part of him. It
would be strange, then, if he were to choose not the life of himself but
that of something else. And what we said before will apply now; that 5
which is proper to each thing is by nature best and most pleasant for
each thing; for man, therefore, the life according to intellect is best and
pleasantest, since intellect more than anything else *is* man. This life
therefore is also the happiest.

CHAPTER 8

But in a secondary degree the life in accordance with the other kind of
excellence is happy; for the activities in accordance with this befit our 10
human estate. Just and brave acts, and other excellent acts, we do in
relation to each other, observing what is proper to each with regard to
contracts and services and all manner of actions and with regard to
passions; and all of these seem to be human. Some of them seem even
to arise from the body, and excellence of character to be in many ways
bound up with the passions. Practical wisdom, too, is linked to excel- 15
lence of character, and this to practical wisdom, since the principles of
practical wisdom are in accordance with the moral excellences and
rightness in the moral excellences is in accordance with practical
wisdom. Being connected with the passions also, the moral excellences must belong to our composite nature; and the excellences of 20
our composite nature are human; so, therefore, are the life and the
happiness which correspond to these. The excellence of the intellect
is a thing apart; we must be content to say this much about it, for to
describe it precisely is a task greater than our purpose requires. It
would seem, however, to need external equipment very little, or
less than moral excellence does. Grant that both need the necessaries, 25
and do so equally, even if the statesman's work is the more concerned
with the body and things of that sort; for there will be little difference
there; but in what they need for the exercise of their activities there
will be much difference. The liberal man will need money for the

doing of his liberal deeds, and the just man too will need it for the
30   returning of services (for wishes are hard to discern, and even people
who are not just pretend to wish to act justly); and the brave man will
need power if he is to accomplish any of the acts that correspond to his
excellence, and the temperate man will need opportunity; for how else
is either he or any of the others to be recognized? It is debated, too,
whether the choice or the deed is more essential to excellence, which
is assumed to involve both; it is surely clear that its completion
1178ᵇ   involves both; but for deeds many things are needed, and more, the
greater and nobler the deeds are. But the man who is contemplating
the truth needs no such thing, at least with a view to the exercise of his
activity; indeed they are, one may say, even hindrances, at all events to
5   his contemplation; but in so far as he is a man and lives with a number
of people, he chooses to do excellent acts; he will therefore need such
aids to living a human life.

But that complete happiness is a contemplative activity will appear
from the following consideration as well. We assume the gods to be
10   above all other beings blessed and happy; but what sort of actions
must we assign to them? Acts of justice? Will not the gods seem absurd
if they make contracts and return deposits, and so on? Acts of a brave
man, then, confronting dangers and running risks because it is noble
to do so? Or liberal acts? To whom will they give? It will be strange if
15   they are really to have money or anything of the kind. And what would
their temperate acts be? Is not such praise tasteless, since they have no
bad appetites? If we were to run through them all, the circumstances of
action would be found trivial and unworthy of gods. Still, every one
supposes that they *live* and therefore that they are active; we cannot
suppose them to sleep like Endymion. Now if you take away from a
20   living being action, and still more production, what is left but contemplation? Therefore the activity of God, which surpasses all others in
blessedness, must be contemplative; and of human activities, therefore, that which is most akin to this must be most of the nature of
happiness.

This is indicated, too, by the fact that the other animals have no
25   share in happiness, being completely deprived of such activity. For
while the whole life of the gods is blessed, and that of men too in so far
as some likeness of such activity belongs to them, none of the other
animals is happy, since they in no way share in contemplation. Happiness extends, then, just so far as contemplation does, and those to
30   whom contemplation more fully belongs are more truly happy, not

accidentally, but in virtue of the contemplation; for this is in itself precious. Happiness, therefore, must be some form of contemplation.

But, being a man, one will also need external prosperity; for our nature is not self-sufficient for the purpose of contemplation, but our body also must be healthy and must have food and other attention. Still, we must not think that the man who is to be happy will need many things or great things, merely because he cannot be blessed without external goods; for self-sufficiency and action do not depend on excess, and we can do noble acts without ruling earth and sea; for even with moderate advantages one can act excellently (this is manifest enough; for private persons are thought to do worthy acts no less than despots—indeed even more); and it is enough that we should have so much as that; for the life of the man who is active in accordance with excellence will be happy. Solon, too, was perhaps sketching well the happy man when he described him as moderately furnished with externals but as having done (as Solon thought) the noblest acts, and lived temperately; for one can with but moderate possessions do what one ought. Anaxagoras also seems to have supposed the happy man not to be rich nor a despot, when he said that he would not be surprised if the happy man were to seem to most people a strange person; for they judge by externals, since these are all they perceive. The opinions of the wise seem, then, to harmonize with our arguments. But while even such things carry some conviction, the truth in practical matters is discerned from the facts of life; for these are the decisive factor. We must therefore survey what we have already said, bringing it to the test of the facts of life, and if it harmonizes with the facts we must accept it, but if it clashes with them we must suppose it to be mere theory. Now he who exercises his intellect and cultivates it seems to be both in the best state and most dear to the gods. For if the gods have any care for human affairs, as they are thought to have, it would be reasonable both that they should delight in that which was best and most akin to them (i.e. intellect) and that they should reward those who love and honour this most, as caring for the things that are dear to them and acting both rightly and nobly. And that all these attributes belong most of all to the wise man is manifest. He, therefore, is the dearest to the gods. And he who is that will presumably be also the happiest; so that in this way too the wise man will more than any other be happy.

1179ᵃ

5

10

15

20

25

30

CHAPTER 9

If these matters and the excellences, and also friendship and pleasure, have been dealt with sufficiently in outline, are we to suppose that our programme has reached its end? Surely, as is said, where there are things to be done the end is not to survey and recognize the various things, but rather to do them; with regard to excellence, then, it is not enough to know, but we must try to have and use it, or try any other way there may be of becoming good. Now if arguments were in them-selves enough to make men good, they would justly, as Theognis says, have won very great rewards, and such rewards should have been provided; but as things are, while they seem to have power to encourage and stimulate the generous-minded among the young, and to make a character which is gently born, and a true lover of what is noble, ready to be possessed by excellence, they are not able to encourage the many to nobility and goodness. For these do not by nature obey the sense of shame, but only fear, and do not abstain from bad acts because of their baseness but through fear of punishment; living by passion they pursue their own pleasures and the means to them, and avoid the opposite pains, and have not even a conception of what is noble and truly pleasant, since they have never tasted it. What argument would remould such people? It is hard, if not impossible, to remove by argument the traits that have long since been incorporated in the character; and perhaps we must be content if, when all the influences by which we are thought to become good are present, we get some tincture of excellence.

Now some think that we are made good by nature, others by habituation, others by teaching. Nature's part evidently does not depend on us, but as a result of some divine causes is present in those who are truly fortunate; while argument and teaching, we may suspect, are not powerful with all men, but the soul of the student must first have been cultivated by means of habits for noble joy and noble hatred, like earth which is to nourish the seed. For he who lives as passion directs will not hear argument that dissuades him, nor under-stand it if he does; and how can we persuade one in such a state to change his ways? And in general passion seems to yield not to argu-ment but to force. The character, then, must somehow be there already with a kinship to excellence, loving what is noble and hating what is base.

But it is difficult to get from youth up a right training for excellence if one has not been brought up under right laws; for to live temperately and hardily is not pleasant to most people, especially when they are young. For this reason their nurture and occupations should be fixed by law; for they will not be painful when they have become customary. But it is surely not enough that when they are young they should get the right nurture and attention; since they must, even when they are grown up, practise and be habituated to them, we shall need laws for this as well, and generally speaking to cover the whole of life; for most people obey necessity rather than argument, and punishments rather than what is noble.

This is why some think that legislators ought to stimulate men to excellence and urge them forward by the motive of the noble, on the assumption that those who have been well advanced by the formation of habits will attend to such influences; and that punishments and penalties should be imposed on those who disobey and are of inferior nature, while the incurably bad should be completely banished. A good man (they think), since he lives with his mind fixed on what is noble, will submit to argument, while a bad man, whose desire is for pleasure, is corrected by pain like a beast of burden. This is, too, why they say the pains inflicted should be those that are most opposed to the pleasures such men love.

However that may be, if (as we have said) the man who is to be good must be well trained and habituated, and go on to spend his time in worthy occupations and neither willingly nor unwillingly do bad actions, and if this can be brought about if men live in accordance with a sort of intellect and right order, provided this has force,—if this be so, the paternal command indeed has not the required force or compulsive power (nor in general has the command of one man, unless he be a king or something similar), but the law *has* compulsive power, while it is at the same time an account proceeding from a sort of practical wisdom and intellect. And while people hate *men* who oppose their impulses, even if they oppose them rightly, the law in its ordaining of what is good is not burdensome.

In the Spartan state alone, or almost alone, the legislator seems to have paid attention to questions of nurture and occupations; in most states such matters have been neglected, and each man lives as he pleases, Cyclops-fashion, 'to his own wife and children dealing law'. Now it is best that there should be a public and proper care for such matters; but if they are neglected by the community it would seem right for each man to help his children and friends towards excellence, and that they should be able, or at least choose, to do this.

It would seem from what has been said that he can do this better if he makes himself capable of legislating. For public care is plainly effected by laws, and good care by good laws; whether written or unwritten would seem to make no difference, nor whether they are laws providing for the education of individuals or of groups—any more than it does in the case of music or gymnastics and other such pursuits. For as in cities laws and character have force, so in house-holds do the injunctions and the habits of the father, and these have even more because of the tie of blood and the benefits he confers; for the children start with a natural affection and disposition to obey. Further, individual education has an advantage over education in common, as individual medical treatment has; for while in general rest and abstinence from food are good for a man in a fever, for a particular man they may not be; and a boxer presumably does not prescribe the same style of fighting to all his pupils. It would seem, then, that the detail is worked out with more precision if the care is particular to individuals; for each person is more likely to get what suits his case.

But individuals can be best cared for by a doctor or gymnastic instructor or anyone else who has the universal knowledge of what is good for everyone or for people of a certain kind (for the sciences both are said to be, and are, concerned with what is common); not but what some particular detail may perhaps be well looked after by an un-scientific person, if he has studied accurately in the light of experience what happens in each case, just as some people seem to be their own best doctors, though they could give no help to anyone else. None the less, it will perhaps be agreed that if a man does wish to become master of an art or science he must go to the universal, and come to know it as well as possible; for, as we have said, it is with this that the sciences are concerned.

And surely he who wants to make men, whether many or few, better by his care must try to become capable of legislating, if it is through laws that we can become good. For to get anyone whatever—anyone who is put before us—into the right condition is not for the first chance comer; if anyone can do it, it is the man who knows, just as in medicine and all other matters which give scope for care and practical wisdom.

Must we not, then, next examine whence or how one can learn how to legislate? Is it, as in all other cases, from statesmen? Certainly it was

1180ᵇ

5

10

15

20

25

30

thought to be a part of statesmanship. Or is a difference apparent between statesmanship and the other sciences and faculties? In the others the same people are found offering to teach the faculties and practising them, e.g. doctors or painters; but while the sophists profess to teach politics, it is practised not by any of them but by the politicians, who would seem to do so by dint of a certain faculty and experience rather than of thought; for they are not found either writing or speaking about such matters (though it were a nobler occupation perhaps than composing speeches for the law-courts and the assembly), nor again are they found to have made statesmen of their own sons or any other of their friends. But it was to be expected that they should if they could; for there is nothing better than such a skill that they could have left to their cities, or could choose to have for themselves, or, therefore, for those dearest to them. Still, experience seems to contribute not a little; else they could not have become politicians by familiarity with politics; and so it seems that those who aim at knowing about the art of politics need experience as well.

But those of the sophists who profess the art seem to be very far from teaching it. For, to put the matter generally, they do not even know what kind of thing it is nor what kinds of thing it is about; otherwise they would not have classed it as identical with rhetoric or even inferior to it, nor have thought it easy to legislate by collecting the laws that are thought well of; they say it is possible to select the best laws, as though even the selection did not demand intelligence and as though right judgement were not the greatest thing, as in matters of music. For while people experienced in any department judge rightly the works produced in it, and understand by what means or how they are achieved, and what harmonizes with what, the inexperienced must be content if they do not fail to see whether the work has been well or ill made—as in the case of painting. Now laws are as it were the works of the political art; how then can one learn from them to be a legislator, or judge which are best? Even medical men do not seem to be made by a study of textbooks. Yet people try, at any rate, to state not only the treatments, but also how particular classes of people can be cured and should be treated—distinguishing the various states; but while this seems useful to experienced people, to the ignorant it is valueless. Surely, then, while collections of laws, and of constitutions also, may be serviceable to those who can study them and judge what is good or bad and what enactments suit what circumstances, those who go through such collections without a practised faculty will not have right

1181ᵃ

5

10

15

20

1181ᵇ

5

10 judgement (unless it be spon·aneous), though they may perhaps
become more intelligent in such matters.

Now our predecessors have left the subject of legislation to us un-
examined; it is perhaps best, therefore, that we should ourselves study
it, and in general study the question of the constitution, in order to
complete to the best of our ability the philosophy of human nature.

15 First, then, if anything has been said well in detail by earlier thinkers,
let us try to review it; then in the light of the constitutions we have
collected let us study what sorts of influence preserve and destroy
states, and what sorts preserve or destroy the particular kinds of
constitution, and to what causes it is due that some are well and others

20 ill administered. When these have been studied we shall perhaps be
more likely to see which constitution is best, and how each must be
ordered, and what laws and customs it must use. Let us make a beginning of our discussion.

EUDEMIAN ETHICS*

BOOK I

CHAPTER I

The man who, in the shrine at Delos, published his opinion by 1214ᵃ
composing an inscription on the propylaeum of the temple of Leto,
distinguished the good, the fine, and the pleasant as not all belonging
to the same thing. These were his verses:

> The most just is finest, being healthy is best; 5
> Most pleasant is to achieve one's heart's desire.

But we do not agree with him: for happiness, the finest and best thing
of all, is the most pleasant.

There are many inquiries concerning each object and each branch 10
of nature which pose problems and require investigation; some contribute only to the attainment of knowledge; some have to do also with
getting and doing. In regard to those things that belong solely to
theoretical philosophy, we must say, when the occasion arises, whatever is relevant to the discipline.

But first we must consider what living well consists in and how it is 15
to be attained: Is it by nature that all those become happy who win this
appellation at all—just as men are naturally tall, or short, or of
different complexions? Or is it through learning,—happiness being a
form of knowledge? Or again, is it through a kind of training? (Many
things come the way of human beings neither in the course of nature,
nor after learning, but after habituation—bad ᵗhings to those with the 20
wrong sort of habituation, good to those with the right sort.) Or is it in
none of *those* ways, but one of two further alternatives: either a divine
dispensation, as if by divine inspiration, like those possessed by a deity
or supernatural powers, or is it a matter of luck? After all, many say 25
that happiness and good fortune are the same thing.

That happiness comes to men either through all, or through some,

---

* *Translation*: M. J. Woods (Clarendon Aristotle series, 1982); *Text*: F. Susemihl
(Teubner Library, 1984), with emendations (see Woods pp. 199–221).

or through just one of these means is evident. For virtually all changes fall under these principles: actions resulting from thought may all be classed along with those resulting from knowledge.

30   But to be happy, and to live the fine and divinely-happy life, would seem to reside in three things above all, three things that seem to be the most worth having there are. For some say that wisdom is the greatest good, others virtue, others pleasure. And some enter into dispute about the importance of those in relation to happiness,

1214ᵇ   claiming that one contributes more than another to it: some hold wisdom to be a greater good than virtue, others the reverse; while others again believe pleasure a greater good than either. And again, some think that living happily is composed of all of these, some of two

5   of them, others that it consists in one of them in particular.

CHAPTER 2

Taking note of these things, everyone who can live according to his own choice should adopt some goal for the fine life, whether it be honour or reputation or wealth or cultivation—an aim that he will

10   have in view in all his actions; for, not to have ordered one's life in relation to some end is a mark of extreme folly. But, above all, and before everything else, he should settle in his own mind,—neither in a hurried nor in a dilatory manner—in which human thing living well consists, and what those things are without which it cannot belong to human beings.

For being healthy is not the same as the things without which it is

15   not possible to be healthy; and this holds likewise in many other cases too. So, living well also is not the same as the things without which living well is impossible. (Some things of this sort are not specific to health or to the good life, but are common to more or less everything, both dispositions and actions—for example, without our breathing or

20   being awake or sharing in movement, nothing either good or bad could belong to us; whereas other things are specific to each kind of thing. This is a point which must not be overlooked: the things just mentioned are not relevant to physical well-being in the same way as are the eating of meat and the taking of exercise after meals.) These are the reasons for the dispute over being happy—what it is and the means

25   by which it comes about: things without which it is not possible to be happy are thought by some to be parts of happiness.

CHAPTER 3

It would be superfluous to examine all the opinions about happiness
that find adherents. Many opinions are held by children and by the   30
diseased and mentally unbalanced, and no sensible man would concern himself with puzzles about them; the holders of such views are in
need, not of arguments, but of maturity in which to change their
opinions, or else of correction of a civil or medical kind (for medical
treatment is no less a form of correction than flogging is). Similarly,
neither need we examine the views of the many; they speak in an   1215ᵃ
unreflective way on almost any topic, most of all when they speak
about this; only the opinions of reasonable men should be examined;
it would be strange to present argument to those who need not
argument, but experience. But, as each inquiry has its own problems,
so, evidently, does that concerning the best and highest life. It is *these*   5
opinions, then, that it is right for us to investigate; for the refutation of
those who dispute a certain position is a demonstration of the
opposing view.

   Moreover, clarity about such matters is helpful, but above all for the
purpose that anyone must have who enquires how it is possible to live
a fine and happy life (if it is unacceptable to say 'divinely happy')—and   10
for the prospect that reasonable men would have, with each alternative, of achieving it. If living well is to be found among those things
which occur by luck or in the course of nature, for many it would be a
hopeless aspiration; for in that case its possession would not be by
their own efforts and in their own power, nor a matter of their own
enterprise. But if it consists in the having of a certain character by   15
oneself and one's actions, the good will be at once a more common
possession and a more divine one: more common because it will be
possible for more people to have a share in it, more divine because
happiness is there for those who cultivate a certain character in themselves and their actions.

CHAPTER 4

Most of the matters of controversy and puzzlement will become clear   20
if what happiness should be thought to be is properly defined. Should
we think that it consists only in the soul's having a certain character, as
some older philosophers thought? Or must a man, himself, or rather
his actions, also have a certain character?   25

Various lives are distinguished. Some do not even enter the contest for such good fortune, but are engaged in in order to provide for the necessities of life. I have in mind those devoted to vulgar trades, and to commerce, and the banal occupations (by 'vulgar trades' I mean those engaged in only to obtain reputation, by 'banal occupations', I mean those of a sedentary or wage-earning kind, and by 'commercial', those concerned with the marketing and selling of goods). Just as there are three things that are assigned to a happy conduc₁ of life—the goods that we have in fact already mentioned as the greatest available for human beings, virtue, wisdom, and pleasure—so too we see three lives which all who have the opportunity choose to live, the political, the philosophical, and the pleasure-loving.

Of these, the philosophical aspires to a concern with wisdom and speculation about truth, the political with fine actions,—actions that result from virtue—and the pleasure-loving with physical pleasures. And so, as we have said before, one man is called happy by one person, another by another. Anaxagoras of Clazomenae, when asked who was happiest said: 'None of the people you think; he would seem a strange person to you.' He answered in this fashion because he saw that his inquirer supposed that it was impossible for anyone who was not powerful and attractive, or rich, to win this appellation; whereas *he* perhaps thought that it was the man who led a life without pain and free from stigma in matters of justice, or participated in some divine speculation, who was, humanly speaking, divinely happy.

CHAPTER 5

About many things it is not easy to judge correctly, but it is especially difficult to do so in regard to that which everyone thinks is most easy and within anyone's capacity to know; namely, which of the things in life is worth choosing, and such that one who obtains it will have his desire fulfilled. After all, many things that happen are such as to induce people to abandon life—disease, extremes of pain, storms, for example; so that it is evident that, on account of those things at any rate, it would, given the choice, have been worth choosing not to be born in the first place. Again, there is the life which men lead while they are still children. For no one in his right mind would tolerate a return to that sort of existence. Moreover, many of the things that involve neither pleasure nor pain, or involve pleasure, but of a reprehensible sort, are enough to make not existing at all preferable to being alive. In general, if we put together all the things that everyone does or undergoes, but not voluntarily (because they are not done or undergone for their own sake), and an infinite stretch of time were provided in addition, no one would choose in order to have *them* to be alive, rather than not. Nor again would anyone, unless he were a complete slave, prefer to live solely for the pleasure associated with nutrition and sex, if all the pleasures were removed that knowing or seeing or any of the other senses bestow upon human beings; for it is evident that, for a man who made such a choice as *this* for himself, it would make no difference whether he were born a beast or a man. Certainly the ox in Egypt, which they honour as the god Apis, has a greater abundance of several of such things than many sovereigns. Similarly, no one would prefer life for the pleasure of sleep; for what difference is there between sleeping without ever waking from one's first day to one's last, over a period of ten thousand years—or however many one likes—and living the life of a plant? Certainly plants seem to have a share in some such sort of life, as do infants. Babies indeed when they first come to be inside the mother exist in their natural state, but asleep all the time. So all this makes it clear that what the well and the good is in life eludes those who investigate the subject.

They say that Anaxagoras, when someone raised just these puzzles and asked him what it was for which a person would choose to be born rather than not, answered that it would be 'in order to apprehend the heavens and the order in the whole universe'. So *he* thought that it was knowledge that made the choice of life worth making; on the other hand, those who admire Sardanapallus, or Smindurides of Sybara, or one or other of those who live the pleasure-loving life, all appear to place happiness in enjoyment; but others again would choose neither wisdom nor bodily pleasures of any kind in preference to virtuous actions. And certainly, they are done by some not only for a reputation but also when there is no prospect of fame. But in fact the majority of political men do not really win this appellation, for in reality they are not political men. For the political man is one who chooses to perform fine actions for their own sake, but the majority of them take up this sort of life for profit and personal advancement.

From what we have said it is clear that everyone attributes happiness to three lives, the political, the philosophical, and the pleasure-loving. In considering these, it is evident to all what pleasure is associated with the body and with physical enjoyments, what its

30

35

1216ᵃ

5

10

15

20

25

30

character is, and how it is produced; so we do not need to inquire what those pleasures are, but whether or not they contribute in any way to happiness, how they contribute to it, and whether, if we ought to allot some pleasures to the good life, it is *those* that we should allot, or whether, although the happy man must share in them in some *other*

35 way, it is on account of other pleasures that it is reasonable to think that the happy man lives a pleasurable and not merely a painless life.

We must investigate these matters further in due course; but first we must look into virtue and wisdom, and discover the nature of each. Are

40 they parts of the good life, either themselves or the actions resulting

1216ᵇ from them? For they are ascribed to happiness, if not by everyone, at any rate by all the people worth taking account of.

The elder Socrates thought that the end of life was to know virtue,

5 and used to inquire what justice is, and courage, and each of virtue's parts. It was understandable that he should have proceeded in this way, as he thought that the virtues were all forms of knowledge, and therefore once a man knew justice, he would be a just man. After all, as soon as we have learned geometry and building, we are geometricians

10 and builders. And so Socrates used to inquire what virtue is, rather than how it arises and from what. This approach holds good in the theoretical sciences: nothing belongs to astronomy or natural science or geometry except knowing and apprehending the nature of the

15 objects which fall under these sciences; though incidentally they may well be useful to us for many of the things we need.

Of the productive sciences, however, the end is distinct from the science itself and from understanding: health is the end of medicine, good social order—or something of the sort distinct from the science itself,—the end of political science. If something is fine, understanding

20 it is fine also; but still, in the case of virtue, the most valuable thing is not to have knowledge of it, but to know from what sources it arises. For what we wish is to be courageous, not to know what courage is; to be just, not to know what justice is; in the same way as we wish to be healthy rather than to know what being healthy is, and to be in a good

25 state, rather than to know what it is to be in a good state.

BOOK II

CHAPTER I

We must now make a fresh start, and turn to the next topic of 1218ᵇ
discussion. According to a distinction made also in the external
discussions, all goods are either in the soul or outside it, and it is those
in the soul that are more worthy of choice; for wisdom, virtue, and
pleasure are in the soul, and some or all of these seem to be an end for 35
everyone. Of things in the soul, some are states or capacities, others
activities and processes.

Let this be assumed; and about excellence, that it is the best
disposition, state, or capacity of anything that has some employment 1219ᵃ
or function. This is evident from induction: in all cases this is what we
suppose. For example, a cloak has an excellence—and a certain
function and employment also; and the best state of the cloak is its
excellence. Similarly too with a boat, a house, and other things. So the
same is true also of the soul; for there is something which is its 5
function.

Let us assume that a better state has a better function; and that as
the states stand in relation to one another, so do the functions deriving
from them; and each thing's function is its end. From these considerations, then, it is clear that the function is better than the state. For the
end, as it is the end, is best; for it is assumed that that which is best, 10
and which is the final thing for whose sake everything else is chosen, is
an end. So it is evident that the function is better than the state and the
disposition.

But a function is so called in two ways. In the case of some things,
the function is something distinct, over and above the employment, in
the way that the function of house-building is a house, not the building
of one, and of medicine health, not the act of curing or applying treat- 15
ment; but in some cases the employment is the function, in the way
that, for example, seeing is the function of sight, and speculation the
function of mathematical science. So it follows that, where a thing's
employment is its function, the employment is better than the state.

Having made these distinctions, let us say that a thing and its excellence have the same function, though in different ways. For example, a 20
shoe is the function of the art of shoe-making and the activity of shoe-
making. So if there is some excellence which is the excellence of shoe-
making and of a good shoe-maker, its function is a good shoe. The

same holds in the other cases also. Now let us assume that the function of the soul is to make things live, but that is an employment and a waking state, since sleep is an idle and inactive state.

25 So, as the function of the soul and of its excellence must be one and the same, the function of its excellence is a good life. This, then, is the final good, that we agreed to be happiness. It is evident from our assumptions: happiness was assumed to be the best thing, and ends,—

30 the best among goods—are in the soul; but things in the soul are states or activities, (since the activity is better than the disposition, and the best activity is of the best state, and virtue is the best state)—that the activity of virtue must be the best thing of the soul.

But happiness too was said to be the best thing: so happiness is

35 activity of a good soul. Now as happiness was agreed to be something complete, and life may be complete or incomplete—and this holds with excellence also (in the one case it is total, in the other partial)— and the activity of what is incomplete is itself incomplete, happiness must be activity of a complete life in accordance with complete virtue.

40 Evidence that we are giving the genus and definition of happiness

1219ᵇ correctly is provided by opinions that we all have: that both acting well and living well are the same thing as being happy, and each of these (both the living and the acting) is an employment and an activity (for the practical life is a life of employment: the copper-smith makes a bridle, but the horseman makes use of it); also that one cannot be

5 happy either for a single day, nor as a child, nor for a stage of one's life. (And so Solon's idea was right when he said that one should not felicitate a man on being happy when he is alive, only when his life attains completion; for nothing incomplete is happy, as it does not form a whole.)

Further, awards of praise for virtue are on account of deeds, and encomia are for deeds; and it is those who win that are crowned with

10 wreaths, not those who have the ability to win, but fail to do so. And there is the fact that one judges from deeds what sort of person someone is.

Again, why is happiness not praised? Because it is the reason for which other things are praised, either through being referred to it as a standard, or being parts of it. That is why felicitation and praise and

15 encomium are all different. An encomium speaks of a particular deed; praise of the agent's having that character generally; felicitation is of the end.

These considerations clear up the puzzle sometimes raised, why virtuous men are no better than the bad for half their life, since all men are alike when asleep; the reason is that sleep is not activity, but inactivity, of the soul. For this reason, too, if there is some other part of the soul, the nutritive, for example, its virtue is not a part of total virtue, any more than the body's is; for in sleep the nutritive is more active whereas the perceiving and desiring parts do not fulfil their function during sleep. However, in so far as they are involved in changes in a way, virtuous men have better dreams unless owing to disease or degeneration they do not.

We must now investigate the soul: because virtue belongs to the soul, and does so not incidentally. As it is human virtue that is the object of our inquiry, let us assume that there are two parts of a soul that share in reason, but that they do not both share in reason in the same way: one's nature is to prescribe, the other's to obey and listen; if there is something that is non-rational in a different way from this, let us disregard that part. It makes no difference if the soul is divided into parts or lacks parts, as it certainly has distinct capacities, including the ones mentioned—just as in a curve the concave and convex are inseparable, and the white and the straight may be, though the straight is not white, except incidentally, and it is not essentially the same.

Any other part of the soul that there may be, the vegetative for example, is removed from consideration. But the parts we have mentioned *are* peculiar to the human soul. (And so, the excellences of the nutritive and growing parts are not human virtues, either.) For, if virtue belongs to a human being *qua* human being, it necessarily includes reasoning, as a starting-point of action; but reasoning controls inclination and the affections, not reasoning itself, so the human soul must have those parts. And as physical well-being is made up of the virtues of the several parts, so is the virtue of the soul, in so far as it is a complete whole.

Virtue is of two forms, virtue of character, and intellectual virtue. For we praise not only the just, but also the intelligent and the wise. For virtue, or its function, was assumed to be commended, but those things are not actualizations, though there exist actualizations of them. The intellectual virtues, having, as they do, a rational principle, such virtues belong to the part that has reason and prescribes to the soul in so far as it possesses reason, whereas the virtues of character belong to the part that is non-rational, but whose nature is to follow the rational part; for we do not say what a man's character is like when we say that he is wise or clever, but when we say that he is gentle or daring.

We must next ask first what virtue of character is, and—since that is what this amounts to—what parts it has, and by what means it is

15 produced. Just as in other cases everyone goes in search with something in hand, we must so conduct our search that we try to arrive at what is said truly and clearly through things said truly but not clearly. At the moment we are placed as we should be if we knew that health was the best disposition of the body and that Coriscus was the

20 swarthiest person in the market-place; we do not know what either of these things is, but it is helpful, in order to know what each of them is, to be so placed.

Let it be laid down, first, that the best disposition is produced by the best things, and that, with each thing, the best things are done from that thing's excellence; for example, the best exertions and nourish-

25 ment are those from which physical well-being results, and it is from well-being that men best exert themselves; moreover that any disposition is produced and destroyed by the same things, applied in a certain way—as we see health is by nourishment, exercise, and time of life. These things are evident from induction.

Virtue, therefore, is the sort of disposition which is produced by the

30 best processes to do with the soul, and from which are produced the best functions of the soul and its best affections; and it is by the same things that it is, in one manner, produced, and in another destroyed, and its employment has to do with the same things as those by which it is promoted and destroyed: those in relation to which it disposes things in the best way. That is evidence that both virtue and vice have to do with pleasant and unpleasant things: for punishment operates

35 through these, being as it is a kind of therapy that works through opposites, as in other cases.

CHAPTER 6

1222^b Let us then take a new starting-point to the ensuing inquiry. All

15 substances are naturally starting-points of a sort, which is why each one can actually generate many things of the same sort—for a human being generates human beings, and, in general, an animal generates animals and a plant plants. A human being, moreover, is a starting-point of some actions, and he alone of animals; for of nothing else should we say that it *acted*.

20 Among starting-points, those that are of that sort—those from which changes first arise—are called *controlling* starting-points, and

most correctly those from which results what cannot be otherwise, the sort of control with which the god perhaps governs. In the case of unchanging starting-points, mathematical ones, for instance, there is no *controlling*, though they are called 'starting-points' on the strength of a similarity; with these, too, if the starting-point were different, everything demonstrated would change, though they do not change one another where one thing is refuted by another, except through refuting the hypothesis and demonstrating by means of it. A human being is the starting-point of a certain kind of change; for an action is a change.

Since, as in other cases, the starting-point is a cause of those things that are or come about because of it, we must understand it as we do in the case of demonstrations. For if it is necessary, if a triangle contains two right angles, that a quadrilateral has four, it is clear that the cause of this is that a triangle has two. If a triangle is different, the quadrilateral must be different too; if the triangle has three right angles, the quadrilateral has six, and if the triangle has four, the quadrilateral eight. And if a triangle is of such-and-such a character, and could not be different from that, the other must also be of such-and-such a character. It is evident from the *Analytics* that what we are attempting to show is necessarily the case; here we can say precisely neither that it is nor that it is not so, except this much: for if nothing else is the cause of a triangle's being so, this must be a sort of starting-point and cause of what follows.

So that if some of the things that are are capable of being in opposite states, their starting-points must also be of that kind. For, what follows from what holds of necessity must itself be necessary, whereas what results from these is capable of turning out in opposite ways,—and many of such things are in men's power and of such things they themselves are the starting-points. So it is clear that all those actions that man is a starting-point of, and controls, are capable of coming about or not, and, with those things at least that he controls whether they are or are not, it is in his own power whether they come about or not. All those things that are in his own power either to do or not do he himself is the cause of, and all those things that he is the cause of, are in his own power.

Now since virtue and vice and the resulting deeds are in some cases commended and in others blamed (for blame and commendation are given not to things that occur of necessity or by luck or in the course of nature, but to all the things we ourselves are a cause of; since for things

that someone else is the cause of, he gets the praise and blame), it is
evident that virtue and vice have to do with those things of which a
15 man himself is the cause, a starting-point of actions. So we must determine of which a man himself is the cause, and a starting-point. Now
we all agree that all those things that are voluntary and in accordance
with an individual's choice he is a cause of, while those that are
involuntary, he is not a cause of. And all the things that he does having
20 chosen to do them, he actually does voluntarily. So it is evident that
both virtue and vice must concern the things that are voluntary.

CHAPTER 7

So we must determine what the voluntary is and what the involuntary
is, and what choice is, since these set limits to virtue and vice. We must
first look into the voluntary and the involuntary. Now it would seem
that it is one of three things—either inclination or choice or thought—
25 the voluntary being in accordance with one of them, the involuntary
contrary to one of them. But inclination has three divisions—wish,
spirit, and desire. So these must be distinguished; we first consider
accordance with desire.

It would seem that everything in accordance with desire is
30 voluntary. For everything involuntary seems to be compelled, and
what is compelled is unpleasant, as is everything which men are forced
to do or undergo, as Evenus says:

> For everything unpleasant is,
> That men are forced to do.

So that if a thing is unpleasant, it is compelled, and if compelled,
unpleasant. But anything contrary to desire is unpleasant (because
35 desire is for the pleasant), so it must be compelled and involuntary.
Thus that which is in accordance with desire is voluntary, the
voluntary and the involuntary being opposed to one another.

Again, vice always makes a man less just; incontinence appears to
be a vice; the incontinent man is of a sort to act against reason, in
accordance with desire, and he acts incontinently when he is active in
accordance with desire; and unjust action is voluntary. So that the
1223ᵇ incontinent man will act unjustly through acting in accordance with
desire. So the incontinent man will act voluntarily, and what is in
accordance with desire will be voluntary. It would indeed be strange if
those who became incontinent thereby became more just.

In view of *those* considerations it would·seem that what is in accordance with desire is voluntary, but if we look at *these* the opposite appears to be the case. Anything which a man does voluntarily he does wishing to do it, and what he wishes to do he does voluntarily. But no one wishes for what he believes to be bad. But the man who acts incontinently does not do what he wishes to do, for to act, as a result of desire, against what one believes to be best is to act incontinently. So it will follow that the same man acts voluntarily and involuntarily at the same time; which is impossible.

Again, the continent man will act justly, and more so than the incontinent man. For continence is a virtue, and virtue makes men more just. A man acts continently when he acts in accordance with reasoning against desire. So, if acting justly is voluntary, as acting unjustly is (for both of these seem to be voluntary, and, if one is voluntary, the other must be also), but what is against desire is involuntary, the same man will at the same time be acting voluntarily and involuntarily.

The same argument holds for spirit also. For continence and incontinence seem to concern spirit, as well as desire; and what is contrary to spirit is unpleasant, and its suppression is compelled, so that if the compelled is involuntary, what is in accordance with spirit must all be voluntary. (It is likely that Heraclitus has in view the strength of spirit when he says that the restraining of it is unpleasant. 'For it's a hard thing', he says, 'to fight against spirit; for it buys victory at the price of life.') If it is impossible for the same man to do the same thing voluntarily and involuntarily at the same time in respect of the same aspect of the situation, what is in accordance with wish is voluntary rather than what is in accordance with spirit or desire. Evidence for that is that we do many things voluntarily without either anger or desire.

It remains therefore to investigate whether the wished for and the voluntary are the same thing. That too seems impossible, for it is our assumption, and seems to be the case, that vice makes people less just, and incontinence appears to be a form of vice, whereas on the assumption under discussion the opposite will follow. For no one wishes for things that he believes to be bad, yet a man who becomes incontinent does such things. If therefore acting unjustly is voluntary, and the voluntary is in accordance with wish, when a man becomes incontinent, he will no longer act unjustly, but be more just than he was before he become incontinent. And that is impossible.

CHAPTER 8

So it is clear that the voluntary does not consist in acting in accordance with inclination, nor is that which is against it involuntary; that it is not acting in accordance with choice either, is evident from the following considerations: what is in accordance with wish has not

1224ᵃ been shown to be involuntary; rather everything that is wished for is also voluntary. (It has been demonstrated only that it is *possible* to act voluntarily even in the absence of wish.) But many things that we wish to do, we do in a flash, yet no one chooses in a flash.

5   If it is necessary that the voluntary should be one of those three things, being in accordance either with inclination or choice or thought, but it is not two of them, it follows that the voluntary consists in action accompanied by thought of some kind. Now let us carry the discussion forward a little and complete the task of distinguishing the voluntary and involuntary; for it seems that the doing of something under compulsion and doing it not under compulsion are relevant to

10   what has been said: we say that what is compelled is involuntary and what is involuntary is always compelled. So we must first investigate what *under compulsion* is and how it is related to the voluntary and involuntary.

It appears that the compelled and the forced and compulsion and force are opposed in the case of action to the voluntary and to

15   persuasion; though quite generally we speak of compulsion and force also where inanimate things are concerned: after all, we say that under compulsion, and when forced, a stone travels upwards and fire downwards. When, however, they travel according to their nature and their essential impulse, they are not said to travel under compulsion though not voluntarily either; that term of the opposition lacks a name.

20   When they travel against that impulse, we say that they do so under compulsion. Similarly, with animate things, including animals, we see them doing and undergoing many things under compulsion, when something external moves them against their internal impulse. In inanimate things the starting-point is single, in animate things there is more than one; for inclination and reason are not always in harmony.

25   So, with animals other than human beings, the compelled is all of one kind, as it is with inanimate things (they do not have reason and inclination each opposed to the other—they live by inclination); in a man, however, both elements are present, at a certain age—that, in fact, to which action also is ascribed. For we do not say that a child

acts, or a brute either; only someone who is already doing things from
reasoning.   30

Now it appears that the compelled is always unpleasant: no one acts
under compulsion, but with enjoyment. That is why the most
controversy arises over the continent and the incontinent man. For
each of them acts with impulses contrary to himself; so that it is by
compulsion, as they say, that the continent man drags himself away
from desires for pleasant things (as he feels pain, when he drags   35
himself away, against the opposing inclination) and under compulsion
the incontinent goes against reasoning. The incontinent man seems to
suffer less pain, in that desire is for the pleasant, which he follows with
enjoyment, and thus the incontinent man acts voluntarily rather, and
not under compulsion, because it is not unpleasant. But persuasion is
opposed to compulsion and force. It is towards what he has already
been persuaded to do that the continent man proceeds, voluntarily,
not under compulsion. Desire, on the other hand, as it has no share in 1224^b
reason, drives one without having persuaded.

We have said that these men seem to be very close to acting under
compulsion and involuntarily, and the reason for that—a certain
similarity to that 'under compulsion' which we use of inanimate things   5
also; all the same, if the further element in the earlier definition is
added, the problem we have stated is solved. For when something is
moved or kept at rest by something external, against the internal
impulse, it is, we say, under compulsion, and when that is not so, it is
not under compulsion. Now within the continent and the incontinent
man it is his own impulse that drives him (for he has both tendencies);
so neither is under compulsion, but, as far as the above argument goes,   10
each would be acting voluntarily, and would not be forced to act. For
we call force that external starting-point of change which impedes or
generates change against impulse, as if a man seized another's hand
and struck him in opposition both to wish and desire; but when the
starting-point is within, it is not under compulsion.

Moreover, both pleasure and pain are present in both of them. The   15
man acting continently suffers pain in that he is even now acting
against his desire, and gets enjoyment from the expectation that he
will benefit in the future or from the fact that he is even now benefiting
from being healthy; while the incontinent man gets enjoyment from
getting what he desires when he acts incontinently, but suffers pain   20
from an expectation, as he thinks that he will fare ill.

Thus there is some reason to say that each of them acts under

compulsion, and that because of reasoning and because of inclination
each sometimes acts involuntarily; for each of those two, because they
are distinct, is overcome by the other. And so, they transfer it to the
25 whole soul when they see something of that sort among the soul's
elements. In the case of the parts it is possible to say this; but the
whole soul, both of the continent man and the incontinent, acts
voluntarily; neither acts under compulsion, though an element in
them does, given that by nature we possess both parts.

For reason is among the natural starting-points, since it will be
30 present if growth is allowed to proceed, and is not stunted; desire, too,
because it is there straightaway and present from birth. And it is more
or less by these two marks that we distinguish what belongs naturally:
everything that is there straightaway as soon as something comes to
be, and all that occurs to us if growth is allowed to proceed normally—
35 things such as greying hair, ageing, and the like. So that each of the
two men, in a way, does not act in accordance with nature, though,
without qualification, each *does* act in accordance with it, but not the
same nature in each case. These, then, are the problems over the
incontinent and the continent man—whether both act under compulsion or one of them does, with the consequence that either they do not
act voluntarily, or they act at the same time under compulsion and
voluntarily, and that if what occurs under compulsion is involuntary,
1225ᵃ they act at the same time voluntarily and involuntarily. It is pretty
evident from what has been said how we should deal with this.

In another way, men are said to act under compulsion and to be
forced to act though reason and inclination are *not* in disharmony, and
when they do what they take to be both unpleasant and bad, yet, if they
5 do not do it, flogging or imprisonment or death await them. They
certainly say they are forced to do these things. Or is that not so? Do
they all rather do the thing itself voluntarily. For it is open to them not
to do it, but to endure the other experience.

Alternatively, someone might assent to some of these things, but not
to others. All things of that kind that are such that it is within
10 someone's power whether they come about or not—even if he does
things that he does not wish to do—he does voluntarily and not under
compulsion; but things of that sort which are not within his power are,
in a way, under compulsion, though not so without qualification,
because he does not choose the actual thing that he does, but the thing
for the sake of which he does it; since in these, also, there is some
difference. If someone kills in order to prevent someone from catching

hold of him, it would be absurd if he said that he did so under compul- 15
sion, and because he was forced to do it; the evil which he is going to
suffer if he does not do the thing has to be greater and more unpleasant. For a man will, in this way, be acting because he is forced,
and under compulsion, or not naturally at any rate, whenever he does
evil for the sake of a good, or the removal of a greater evil, and he
will be acting involuntarily, as those things are not within his control.

That is why many classify even love as involuntary, and certain 20
cases of anger and certain natural states as being too strong for human
nature; and we regard them as being pardonable, as being of such a
nature as to constrain nature. And a man would appear to be acting
under compulsion and involuntarily more when he does so to avoid
suffering a severe pain than when he does so to avoid a slight one, and,
in general, more when he does so to avoid pain than when he does so
to get enjoyment. For what is in one's power, on which the whole issue 25
turns, is what one's nature is able to withstand. And what it is not able
to withstand, and is not within the scope of one's natural inclination or
reasoning, is not in one's power. That is why even with those who are
possessed by divine inspiration, and utter prophecies, though they
produce a work of thought, we say that it was not under their control to 30
say what they said or do what they did. Nor is it done as a result of
desire. Hence certain thoughts and certain affections—or rather the
actions that occur in accordance with such thoughts and calculations—
are not under our control. As Philolaos said, some reasonings are
stronger than we are. So, if it was necessary to examine the voluntary
and involuntary in relation to what is under compulsion, let them be 35
distinguished in this way.

CHAPTER 9

Now that that discussion is complete, and the voluntary has been
defined neither by inclination nor by choice, it remains to define what 1225ᵇ
in accordance with thought is. The voluntary seems to be the opposite of
the involuntary, and acting knowing either whom or with what or for
what result—thus sometimes a man knows that it is his father, but not
that he is aiming to kill him, but instead thinks that he is acting to save
him, as in the case of the daughters of Pelias, or he thinks that this is a
drink, but in fact it was a love potion, or that it is wine when it was 5
aconite—is opposed to acting in ignorance of whom and with what and
what, because of ignorance, not incidentally; but what is done because

of ignorance of what and with what and whom, is involuntary; so its opposite is voluntary.

So whatever a man does—not in ignorance, and through his own agency—when it is in his power not to do it, must be voluntary, and
10 that is what the voluntary is; but what he does in ignorance and because of ignorance, he does involuntarily. But since knowing and understanding is of two kinds, one *having* and the other *using* knowledge, the man who has knowledge but does not use it could in a way rightly be said to have acted in ignorance, but in another way not; for example, if he failed to use his knowledge because of negligence. Likewise, too, someone would be blamed even if he did not have it, if it
15 is what was easy or essential that he fails to have because of negligence or pleasure or pain. So let these things be added to the definition.

CHAPTER 10

Let this be enough on the distinction between the voluntary and the involuntary; let us now say something about choice, after raising problems in argument about it. For one might hesitate about the genus
20 in which it belongs and where to place it, and about whether the chosen is or is not the same as the voluntary. In particular, some people say—and on examination it would seem to be the case—that choice is one of two things, either opinion or inclination; for both of those things appear to accompany choice.

However, that it is not inclination is clear; for it would then be wish
25 or desire or spirit, since no one has an inclination without experiencing one of those. Now spirit and desire belong even to brutes, but choice does not. Further, even in the case of those to whom both these things belong, they make many choices without either spirit or desire; and when men are subject to affections, they are not choosing but are
30 resisting the affections. Again, desire and spirit are always accompanied by pain, but we make many choices without pain. Nor is wish the same thing as choice, either. For men knowingly wish for some things that are impossible, such as to rule over the whole of mankind and to be immortal, whereas no one chooses them unless he is
35 ignorant of their impossibility, nor, in general, those things that are possible, but which he does not believe are within his power to do or not to do. So one thing is clear, that the chosen must be one of the things within the agent's power.

1226ᵇ Similarly, it is evident that it is not opinion either, nor quite generally something that someone believes; the chosen was found to be something in one's own power, but we opine many things that are not in our power, for example that the diagonal is incommensurable. Again, choice is not true or false. Nor therefore is it an opinion about the things in one's own power, that whereby we in fact believe that we should or should not do something. 5

This point holds alike of opinion and of wish: no one chooses an end, only the things that contribute to the end. I mean, for example, no one chooses to be healthy, rather he chooses to walk or to sit with a view to health, nor again to be happy, but rather to engage in commerce or take a risk with a view to being happy; and in general a man evidently always chooses something, and chooses for the sake of something; and the second is that for the sake of which he chooses something else, and the first, what he chooses for the sake of another thing. It is the end, above all, that he wishes for, and he judges that he ought to be healthy and to act well. Thus it is clear from these considerations that choice is different both from opinion and from wish. For wish and opinion are pre-eminently of the end, choice is not. 10

It is evident, then, that choice is not wish or judgement or opinion of any kind. How does it differ from those, and how is it related to the voluntary? It will then be evident also what choice is. Among the things that can either be or not be, some are such that it is possible to deliberate about them; about some it is not possible. For some are capable either of being or not being, yet their coming to be is not in our power, but, some come to be naturally, others on account of other causes. About such things no one would attempt to deliberate unless in ignorance. Those things, however, which are such that not only can they either be or not be, but also men can deliberate about them, are those which are within our power to do or not do. 20

Thus we do not deliberate about affairs in India, nor how the circle is to be squared; for the former of those is not in our power, the latter not realizable by action at all, whereas things that are chosen and realizable are among those that are in our power. But nor do we deliberate about all the things that *are* in our power—and that makes it evident also that choice is not any sort of opinion either. This might lead someone to be puzzled about why doctors deliberate about things that fall under the science that they possess, but scribes do not. The reason is that errors occur in two ways (we err either in calculation or in perception when actually doing the thing); in medicine it is possible to make a mistake in both ways, whereas in the case of a scribe's skill, 30 35

1226^b it is possible only in perception and action, and if they reflect upon that, there will be no end to it.

Since, then, choice is not either opinion or wish, neither one of them nor both (no one chooses in a flash, but it seems that men act—and wish—in a flash), it must result from both of these; for both of them occur in one who chooses.

5 But we must investigate *how* it results from these. To some extent the word 'choice' itself shows us. Choice (*prohairesis*) is a taking (*hairesis*), but not without qualification—a taking of one thing before (*pro*) another; that is not possible without examination and deliberation. So choice comes from deliberative belief.

10 No one deliberates about the end—that is there for everyone; men deliberate about the things that lead towards it, whether this or that contributes to its attainment, or else, when that has been decided, how it will come about. We all continue deliberating until we carry the starting-point of the process of change back to ourselves. If, then, no one makes a choice without preliminary deliberation on whether it

15 would be better or worse to act thus, and one deliberates about the things, among those that are capable of being or not being, that are in our power and lead towards the end, it is evident that choice is deliberative inclination for that which is in our power. For we all deliberate about those things that we also choose, though we do not choose all the things that we deliberate about (by a 'deliberative'

20 inclination, I mean one whose starting-point and cause is deliberation, and our inclination results from deliberation).

So choice is not present in other animals, nor at every time of life, nor in a human being no matter what state he is in; for deliberation is not, either, nor an opinion about the why; an opinion about whether something should be done or not may well be present to many people,

25 though not through reasoning. For that part of the soul is deliberative which is capable of discerning a cause: the reason for the sake of which—which is one of the causes—'cause' being something because-of-which. And we say that that for the sake of which something is or comes to be is a cause—for instance, the carrying of goods is a cause of walking if it is for the sake of that that a man walks. That is why those who have no goal before them are not in a position to deliberate.

30 So that, since a man voluntarily does or abstains from doing that which is in his power to do or not to do if it is through his own agency and not in ignorance that he acts or abstains from acting—we do many

things of that sort not after deliberation and without premeditation—it follows that what is chosen is all voluntary, but what is voluntary is not all chosen, and everything done from choice is voluntary, but what is 35 voluntary is not all from choice. These considerations make this clear, and at the same time the fact that legislators are right to distinguish some deeds as voluntary and others as involuntary and others as premeditated; for even if they are not wholly correct, they are on to the 1227ᵃ truth in a way.

About this we shall be saying something in the examination of justice. But it is evident that choice is neither simply wish nor opinion, but opinion *together with* inclination, whenever as a result of delibera- 5 tion they are brought to a conclusion.

Since one who deliberates always deliberates with something in view, and there is always some goal with reference to which he inquires what is useful, no one deliberates about the end, this being a starting-point and hypothesis, like hypotheses in the theoretical sciences (a little was said about them at the start of our discussion, and 10 they are treated in detail in the *Analytics*), but everyone's investigation, whether he is using some expertise or not, is about what contributes to the end—for example, those deliberating whether to go to war or not.

But before the process begins there will be that because of which, i.e. *that for whose sake*—for example, wealth or pleasure or whatever else 15 of that kind happens to be *that for whose sake*. For one who deliberates, if he has carried his inquiry back from the end, deliberates about what contributes to it, in order to bring the process back to himself, or what he can do himself towards the end.

The end is naturally always good, the good they deliberate about in a particular application: the doctor would deliberate whether to administer a drug, and the general where to set up his camp, and to 20 them the end, what is best without qualification, is good; what is against nature, on the other hand, and involves corruption is not the good, but the apparent good. The reason is that it is not possible to use some of the things that there are except for what they naturally exist for—sight for example; it is not possible to see what is not an object of sight, nor hear what is not an object of hearing; but it *is* possible to 25 produce, by means of a science, that which is not what the science is a science of. For the same science is not a science of disease in the same way as it is the science of health; it is the science of one in accordance with nature, of the other against nature. Similarly, too, wish is naturally of the good, but also, against nature, of the bad, and one

30   naturally wishes for the good, but, against nature, and through corrup-
      tion, also for the bad.
            However, the destruction and corruption of anything is not into any
      arbitrary state, but into the opposite ones and the intermediates on
      the way to them. For it is impossible to get outside these, as error also,
      when it occurs, takes place into the opposite state, where there is one,
35   not into any arbitrary state, and to those opposite states that are
      opposed with respect to the knowledge. So both the error and the
      choice must be from the mean towards the opposites (and more and
      less are opposed to the mean). The cause is the pleasant and the
      unpleasant; for the situation is that the pleasant appears good to the
      soul, and the pleasanter better, the unpleasant bad, and the more
1227^b unpleasant worse. So from this, too, it is evident that virtue and vice
      have to do with pleasures and pains. They are in fact concerned wth
      things chosen, and choice has to do with the good and bad, and what
      appears thus, and such, naturally, are pleasure and pain.
5   So it follows, since virtue of character itself is a mean state and
      always concerned with pleasures and pains, while vice lies in excess
      and deficiency, and has to do with the same things as virtue, that virtue
      is that state of character which chooses the mean, relative to us, in
      things pleasant and unpleasant, all those in respect of which a man is
10   said to have a certain sort of character according as he enjoys them or
      suffers pain from them. (For the man who is fond of sweet things, or
      the one fond of bitter ones, is not said to be a certain sort of person in
      regard to *character*.)

BOOK VIII

CHAPTER 2

      Since not only do practical wisdom and virtue produce welfare, but we
1247^a say also that the fortunate prosper, as if good fortune produces welfare
      and the same things that knowledge does, we must inquire whether it
      is by nature that one man is unfortunate, another fortunate, and how
      the matter stands in regard to these men.
            For, that some people are fortunate we see: though foolish, many
5   people are successful in matters in which luck is decisive, others also in
      matters in which skill is involved, but there is a large element of luck,
      for example in generalship and navigation. Is it then because of some

state that these men are fortunate, or is it not through being them-selves of a certain kind that they score successes? For, as things are, that is what people think—as if some are fortunate by nature, and nature makes some people to be of a certain sort, and those are different right from birth and, just as some people are blue-eyed and others black-eyed through being necessarily thus because of being such-and-such a kind, so are people fortunate and unfortunate.

For that it is not by practical wisdom that they succeed, is evident. For practical wisdom is not irrational but has a principle on account of which it acts thus and so, but these people would not be able to say why they succeed; for if they could, it would be skill. For it is clear that, being foolish—not that they are so about other things—that would be not at all strange (Hippocrates, for example, was a geometer, but in other matters he seemed to be stupid and foolish, and when he sailed he was cheated of much money by the customs men in Byzantium, as a result of unworldliness, as they say)—but that they are foolish even about those matters in which they enjoy good fortune. For in navigation, it is not the most skilful who are fortunate, but, as in dice-throwing, one man scores nothing, another throws a naturally fortunate man's throw. Or is it through being favoured, as they say, by a god and because the source of success is external, in the way that a ship badly constructed often sails better, though not because of itself but because it has a good steersman? However, in that way the fortu-nate man has the divine being as a good steersman, but it is strange that a god or divine being should favour such a man, rather than the best and the wisest. So if success must come about either by nature or intelligence or some guidance, and it is not two of these, the fortunate must be so by nature.

Nature, however, is the cause of what occurs in the same way always or for the most part, whereas luck is the opposite. So if to prosper contrary to expectation seems to belong to luck—but if someone is fortunate, he is so by luck—the cause would not seem to be the sort of thing that is the cause of what is always, or usually, the same. Further, if it is because he is of such-and-such a sort that a man prospers or comes to grief, just as it is because a man is blue-eyed that he does not see clearly, then luck is not the cause, but nature; so he is not fortunate, but, as it were, naturally well endowed. Thus what we ought to say is that those whom we call fortunate are not so by luck. They are *not*, therefore, fortunate; it is those for whom good luck is a cause of goods that are fortunate.

10

15

20

25

30

35

If that is so, will luck not exist at all, or will it exist, but not be a cause? In fact, it must both exist and be a cause. It will therefore also be a cause of good things, or bad, for some people. Whether we must eliminate it altogether, and say that nothing happens by luck, though 5 we, when there is some other cause, because we do not see it, say that luck is a cause—that is why, when they define luck, they lay down that luck is a cause not open to reasoning by human calculation as if it were some nature—that, however, would be another problem.

Since we see some people enjoying good fortune once, why should 10 they not succeed again, for the same reason, and yet again? For the same thing has the same cause. So this will not belong to luck. But when the same thing results from causes that are indefinite and indeterminate, it may be a good thing or a bad thing for someone, but there will be no knowledge of it, knowledge from experience, as otherwise some people could learn to be fortunate, or indeed all forms of 15 knowledge would, as Socrates said, be forms of good fortune. What, then, prevents such things from befalling someone many times in succession, not because he is of such-and-such a sort, but as it would be always to make lucky throws of the dice?

What follows then? Are there not impulses in the soul, some issuing from reasoning, others from non-rational inclination, and are not 20 those, at least by nature, prior? For if by nature our desire is an inclination for the pleasant, by nature, at any rate, all our desires proceed towards the good. So, if some people are naturally well endowed (as untaught singers, who lack knowledge of how to sing, are well endowed in that respect) and, without reason, are impelled in accordance with nature, and desire both what they ought and when 25 they ought and as they ought—these people will succeed even if they are actually foolish and unreasoning, as men may actually sing well who are not capable of teaching it; but certainly it is such men who are fortunate—men who succeed most of the time without reasoning. It is therefore by nature that the fortunate are fortunate.

Or is good fortune so called in several ways? For some things are 30 done from impulse, and when people have chosen to do them, some are not—the opposite holds. And in *those* cases, if they succeed in circumstances in which they seem to reason badly, we say that they have had good fortune; and again in those cases, if they wanted another good, or a smaller one, than they got. With those people therefore, it is possible that they have good fortune as a result of nature; for the impulse and the inclination, being for what was

required, prospered, though the reasoning was idle. And these people, 35
when reasoning appears not to be correct, but in fact desire is the
cause of it, are rescued because the desire is correct. (And yet, on some
occasions, from desire a man reasoned thus—and came to grief.) But
in the other cases, how can there be good fortune in accordance with a
good natural endowment of inclination and desire? But then either 1248ᵃ
good fortune both in this case and in that are the same, or there is
more than one form of good fortune, and luck is of two kinds.

Since we see some people having good fortune contrary to every
sort of knowledge and correct reasonings, it is evident that something
else is the cause of the good fortune. But is that good fortune? Or is it 5
not, if a man desires the things he should and when he should, a man
for whom human calculation, at any rate, is not the cause of this? For
that for which indeed the desire is natural is not altogether without
reason, but it is distorted by something; however, he seems to have
good fortune, because luck is a cause of things contrary to reason, and
that is contrary to reason, since it is contrary to knowledge and the 10
universal. But, as it seems, it is not by luck, but appears to be for this
reason. So this argument does not demonstrate that people have good
fortune by nature, but that not all who seem to have good fortune
prosper by luck, and not through nature; nor that luck is not a cause of
anything, but that it is not a cause of all the things it seems to be.

The question might be raised 'Is luck the cause of this very thing— 15
desiring what one should or when one should?' Or will luck in that way
be the cause of everything? For it will be the cause both of thinking
and deliberating; for a man who deliberates has not deliberated
already before deliberating—there is a certain starting-point. Nor did
he think, after thinking already before thinking, and so on to infinity. 20
Intelligence, therefore, is not the starting-point of thinking, nor is
counsel the starting-point of deliberation. So what else is there save
luck? Thus everything will be by luck. Or is there some starting-point
beyond which there is no other, and this—because it is essentially of
such a sort—can have such an effect? But what is being sought is this:
What is the starting-point of change in the soul? It is now evident: as it 25
is a god that moves in the whole universe, so it is in the soul; for, in a
sense, the divine element in us moves everything; but the starting-
point of reason is not reason but something superior. What then could
be superior to knowledge and intelligence but a god? For virtue is an
instrument of intelligence.

And for that reason, as I was saying earlier, they are called fortunate 30 who succeed in what they initiate though they lack reason. And it is of no use for them to deliberate; for they possess such a starting-point as is superior to intelligence and deliberation (others have reason but do not have this), and a divine inspiration, but cannot do this; for, though unreasoning, they succeed . . . that the power of prophecy of those who

35 are wise and clever is swift, and, one should suppose, not only what results from reasoning. But some through experience, others through familiarity with employing the god in inquiry . . . see well what is to be and what is the case, and those whose reason is thus disengaged; thus those of a melancholic temperament also have vivid dreams. For the starting-point seems to be stronger when reason is disengaged, just as

1248ᵇ blind people remember better, because the remembering element is better when that concerned with visible things is disengaged.

It is clear, then, that there are two sorts of good fortune, the one divine—hence it actually seems that the fortunate man owes his

5 success to a god. This man is the one who is successful in accordance with impulse; the other is so contrary to impulse; but both are non-rational. It is this one form of good fortune rather, that is continuous; the latter form is not continuous.

CHAPTER 3

We have spoken earlier about each virtue individually; but since we have distinguished and separated their capacity, we must also

10 articulate the virtue that results from them, which we now call *nobility*. Now it is clear that the man who is truly to meet this appellation must have the individual virtues. For it cannot be otherwise in other cases, either. For no one is healthy in his body as a whole, yet not in any part

15 of it; rather, all parts, or most and the most important, must be in the same state as the whole.

Being good and being fine-and-good admit of distinction, not only in their names but also in themselves. For, of all goods, those are ends which are worth having for their own sake, while, of these, all that are

20 commended for themselves are fine. For of these things it is true that the actions from them are commended and they are themselves commended—justice, both itself and the actions from it, and those who are temperate; for temperance is also commended. But health is not something commended; for neither is its function. Nor is acting with strength, for strength is not, either. But, though they are not commended, they are goods.

Likewise, this is clear in other cases also, by induction. Now a good   25
man is one for whom the natural goods are goods. For the things that
are competed for and seem to be the greatest goods, honour and
wealth and bodily excellences and good fortune and capacities, are
naturally good, but may be harmful for some because of their states of   30
character. For neither a foolish nor an unjust or intemperate man
would get any benefit from using them, just as neither will the sick
man using the food of the healthy, nor would the weak and deformed
using the adornments of the sound and whole person. A person is fine-
and-good because, among goods, those that are fine for themselves   35
belong to him, and because he is a practiser of fine things, and for their
own sake. Fine things are the virtues and the deeds resulting from virtue.

There is a certain state of a citizen such as the Spartans have, or
other such people would have. This is a state of the following sort:
there are those who think that one should possess virtue, but for the   40
sake of the natural goods. They are therefore good men (for natural   1249ᵃ
goods are so for them), but they do not have nobility. For they do not
possess the things that are fine for themselves, but those who possess
them also choose things fine-and-good, and not only those things, but
also the things not fine by nature, but good by nature, are fine for   5
them. For they are fine when the things for whose sake they act and
choose are fine. So, for the fine-and-good man, the natural goods are
fine. For what is just is fine; and that is what is in accord with desert;
and this man deserves these things. And what is fitting is fine; and
these things befit this man,—wealth, noble birth, power. So, to the
fine-and-good man, the beneficial things themselves, too, are also   10
fine; but for the many there is a divergence here. For the things good
without qualification are not good also for them, but are good for the
good man. But to the fine-and-good man they are also fine. For he
does many fine actions because of them. But the man who thinks that   15
the virtues should be possessed for the sake of external goods, does the
fine things incidentally. So nobility is complete virtue.

Concerning pleasure, too, it has been said what sort of thing it is
and how it is a good, and that the things pleasant without qualification
are also fine, and the things good without qualification are pleasant.
But pleasure does not occur except in action; for that reason, the truly
happy man will also live most pleasantly, and it is not for nothing that   20
people believe this.

Now there is some limit also for the doctor, by reference to which he

judges what is healthy for a body and what is not, and by reference to which each thing is to be done up to a certain amount, and is healthy, but is not so if less or more is done. So too for the virtuous man, with
25 respect to his actions and choices of the things naturally good but not
1249ᵇ commended, there must be some limit both for the possession and the choice and avoidance of abundance and exiguousness of material goods and of successes. Now *as principle prescribes* is what was said earlier. But that is as if, in matters of nutrition, someone were to say, *as*
5 *medicine and its principle prescribes*. But that, though true, is not clear.

So it is needful, as in other cases, to live by reference to the governing thing, and by reference to the state and activity of what governs, as a slave to the rule of the master and each thing to its appropriate governing principle. But since a human being, also, is by nature
10 composed of a thing that governs and a thing that is governed, each too should live by reference to its own governing principle. But that is of two sorts; for medicine is a governing principle in one way, and health in another; for the first is for the sake of the second. Thus it is with the speculative part. For the god is a governor not in a prescrip-
15 tive fashion, but it is that *for* which practical wisdom prescribes (but *that for which* is of two sorts—they have been distinguished else-where—since the god is in need of nothing). So if some choice and possession of natural goods—either goods of the body or money or friends or the other goods—will most produce the speculation of the god, that is the best, and that is the finest limit; but whatever, whether
20 through deficiency or excess, hinders the service and speculation of the god, is bad. Thus it is for the soul, and this is the best limit for the soul—to be aware as little as possible of the non-rational part of the soul as such. But let what has been said be enough on the limit of
25 nobility, and what the goal is of things good without qualification.

POLITICS*

BOOK I

Observation tells us that every state is an association, and that every 1252ᵃ association is formed with a view to some good purpose. I say 'good', because in all their actions all men do in fact aim at what they think good. Clearly then, as all associations aim at some good, that association which is the most sovereign among them all and embraces all others will aim highest, i.e. at the most sovereign of all goods. This is 5 the association which we call the state, the association which is 'political'.

It is an error to suppose, as some do, that the roles of a statesman, of a king, of a household-manager and of a master of slaves are the same, on the ground that they differ not in kind but only in point of numbers of persons—that a master of slaves, for example, has to do with a few 10 people, a household-manager with more, and a statesman or king with more still, as if there were no differences between a large household and a small state. They also reckon that when one person is in personal control over the rest he has the role of a king, whereas when he takes his turn at ruling and at being ruled according to the 15 principles of the science concerned, he is a statesman. But these assertions are false.

This will be quite evident if we examine the matter according to our established method. We have to analyse other composite things till they can be subdivided no further; let us in the same way examine the 20 component parts of the state and we shall see better how these too differ from each other, and whether we can acquire any systematic knowledge about the several roles mentioned.

* *Translation*: T. A. Sinclair and T. J. Saunders (Penguin Classics, Harmondsworth, 1981); *Text*: W. D. Ross (Oxford Classical Texts, 1957).

CHAPTER 2

25 We shall, I think, in this as in other subjects, get the best view of the matter if we look at the natural growth of things from the beginning. The first point is that those which are incapable of existing without each other must be united as a pair. For example, the union of male and female is essential for reproduction; and this is not a matter of *choice*, but is due to the *natural* urge, which exists in the other animals 30 too and in plants, to propagate one's kind. Equally essential is the combination of the natural ruler and ruled, for the purpose of preservation. For the element that can use its intelligence to look ahead is by nature ruler and by nature master, while that which has the bodily strength to do the actual work is by nature a slave, one of those who are ruled. Thus there is a common interest uniting master and slave.

1252ᵇ   Nature, then, has distinguished between female and slave: she recognizes different functions and lavishly provides different tools, not an all-purpose tool like the Delphic knife; for every instrument will be made best if it serves not many purposes but one. But non-5 Greeks assign to female and slave exactly the same status. This is because they have nothing which is by nature fitted to rule; their association consists of a male slave and a female slave. So, as the poets say, 'It is proper that Greeks should rule non-Greeks', the implication being that non-Greek and slave are by nature identical.

Thus it was out of the association formed by men with these two, 10 women and slaves, that a household was first formed; and the poet Hesiod was right when he wrote, 'Get first a house and a wife and an ox to draw the plough.' (The ox is the poor man's slave.) This association of persons, established according to nature for the satisfaction of daily needs, is the household, the members of which Charondas calls 'bread-fellows', and Epimenides the Cretan 'stable-companions'.

15   The next stage is the village, the first association of a number of houses for the satisfaction of something *more* than daily needs. It comes into being through the processes of nature in the fullest sense, as offshoots of a household are set up by sons and grandsons. The members of such a village are therefore called by some 'homo-galactic'.[1] This is why states were at first ruled by kings, as are foreign 20 nations to this day: they were formed from constituents which were themselves under kingly rule. For every household is ruled by its

---

[1] I.e. 'sucklings of the same milk'.

senior member, as by a king, and the offshoots too, because of their blood relationship, are ruled in the same way. This kind of rule is mentioned in Homer: 'Each man has power of law over children and wives.' He is referring to scattered settlements, which were common in primitive times. For this reason the gods too are said to be governed by a king—namely because men themselves were originally ruled by kings and some are so still. Just as men imagine gods in human shape, so they imagine their way of life to be like that of men.

The final association, formed of several villages, is the state. For all practical purposes the process is now complete; self-sufficiency has been reached, and while the state came about as a means of securing life itself, it continues in being to secure the *good* life. Therefore every state exists by nature, as the earlier associations too were natural. This association is the end of those others, and nature is itself an end; for whatever is the end-product of the coming into existence of any object, that is what we call its nature—of a man, for instance, or a horse or a household. Moreover the aim and the end is perfection; and self-sufficiency is both end and perfection.

It follows that the state belongs to the class of objects which exist by nature, and that man is by nature a political animal. Anyone who by his nature and not simply by ill luck has no state is either too bad or too good, either subhuman or superhuman—he is like the war-mad man condemned in Homer's words as 'having no family, no law, no home'; for he who is such by nature is mad on war: he is a non-cooperator like an isolated piece in a game of draughts.

But obviously man is a political animal in a sense in which a bee is not, or any other gregarious animal. Nature, as we say, does nothing without some purpose; and she has endowed man alone among the animals with the power of speech. Speech is something different from voice, which is possessed by other animals also and used by them to express pain or pleasure; for their nature does indeed enable them not only to feel pleasure and pain but to communicate these feelings to each other. Speech, on the other hand serves to indicate what is useful and what is harmful, and so also what is just and what is unjust. For the real difference between man and other animals is that humans alone have perception of good and evil, just and unjust, etc. It is the sharing of a common view in *these* matters that makes a household and a state.

Furthermore, the state has priority over the household and over any individual among us. For the whole must be prior to the part. Separate

hand or foot from the whole body, and they will no longer be a hand or foot except in name, as one might speak of a 'hand' or 'foot' sculptured in stone. That will be the condition of the spoilt hand, which no longer has the capacity and the function which define it. So, though we may say they have the same names, we cannot say that they are, in that
25 condition, the same things. It is clear then that the state is both natural and prior to the individual. For if an individual is not fully self-sufficient after separation, he will stand in the same relationship to the whole as the parts in the other case do. Whatever is incapable of participating in the association which we call the state, a dumb animal for example, and equally whatever is perfectly self-sufficient and has no need to (e.g. a god), is not a part of the state at all.

Among all men, then, there is a natural impulse towards this kind of
30 association; but the first man to construct a state deserves credit for conferring very great benefits. For as man is the best of all animals when he has reached his full development, so he is worst of all when divorced from law and justice. Injustice armed is hardest to deal with; and though man is born with weapons which he can use in the service
35 of practical wisdom and virtue, it is all too easy for him to use them for the opposite purposes. Hence man without virtue is the most savage, the most unrighteous, and the worst in regard to sexual licence and gluttony. The virtue of justice is a feature of a state; for justice is the arrangement of the political association, and a sense of justice decides what is just.

CHAPTER 3

1253ᵇ Now that I have explained what the component parts of a state are, and since every state consists of households, it is essential to begin with household-management. This topic can be subdivided so as to correspond to the parts of which a complete household is made up, namely, the free and the slaves; but our method requires us to examine
5 everything when it has been reduced to its smallest parts, and the smallest division of a household into parts gives three pairs—master and slave, husband and wife, father and children. And so we must ask ourselves what each one of these three relationships is, and what sort of thing it ought to be. The word 'mastership' is used to describe the first, and we may use 'matrimonial' (in the case of the union of man and
10 woman), and 'paternal' to describe the other two, as there is no more specific term for either. We may accept these three; but we find that

there is a fourth element, which some people regard as covering the whole of household-management, others as its most important part; and our task is to consider its position. I refer to what is called 'the acquisition of wealth'.

First let us discuss master and slave, in order to see how they bear on the provision of essential services, and whether we can find a better way towards understanding this topic than if we started from the suppositions usually made. For example, some people suppose that being a master requires a certain kind of knowledge, and that this is the same knowledge as is required to manage a household or to be a statesman or a king—an error which we discussed at the beginning. Others say that it is contrary to nature to rule as master over slave, because the distinction between slave and free is one of convention only, and in nature there is no difference, so that this form of rule is based on force and is therefore not just.

CHAPTER 4

Now property is part of a household, and the acquisition of property part of household-management; for neither life itself nor the good life is possible without a certain minimum supply of the necessities. Again, in any special skill the availability of the proper tools will be essential for the performance of the task; and the household-manager must have his likewise. Tools may be animate as well as inanimate; for instance, a ship's captain uses a lifeless rudder, but a living man for watch; for a servant is, from the point of view of his craft, categorized as one of its tools. So any piece of property can be regarded as a tool enabling a man to live, and his property is an assemblage of such tools; a slave is a sort of living piece of property; and like any other servant is a tool in charge of other tools. For suppose that every tool we had could perform its task, either at our bidding or itself perceiving the need, and if—like the statues made by Daedalus or the tripods of Hephaestus, of which the poet says that

> self-moved they enter the assembly of the gods

—shuttles in a loom could fly to and fro and a plucker play a lyre all self-moved, then master-craftsmen would have no need of servants nor masters of slaves.

Tools in the ordinary sense are productive tools, whereas a piece of property is meant for action. I mean, for example, a shuttle produces

something other than its own use, a bed or a garment does not. More-over, since production and action differ in kind and both require tools,
5 the difference between their tools too must be of the same kind. Now life is action and not production; therefore the slave, a servant, is one of the tools that minister to action.

A piece of property is spoken of in the same way as a part is; for a
10 part is not only part of something but belongs to it *tout court*; and so too does a piece of property. So a slave is not only his master's slave but belongs to him *tout court*, while the master is his slave's master but does not belong to him. These considerations will have shown what the nature and functions of the slave are: any human being that by
15 nature belongs not to himself but to another is by nature a slave; and a human being belongs to another whenever, in spite of being a *man*, he is a piece of property, i.e. a tool having a separate existence and meant for action.

CHAPTER 5

But whether anyone does in fact by nature answer to this description, and whether or not it is a just and a better thing for one man to be a slave to another, or whether all slavery is contrary to nature—these are
20 the questions which must be considered next. Neither theoretical discussion nor empirical observation presents any difficulty. That one should command and another obey is both necessary and expedient. Indeed some things are so divided right from birth, some to rule, some to be ruled. There are many different forms of this ruler–ruled relationship, and the quality of the rule depends primarily on the
25 quality of the subjects, rule over man being better than rule over animals; for that which is produced by better men is a better piece of work; and the ruler–ruled relationship is itself a product created by the men involved in it.

For wherever there is a combination of elements, continuous or
30 discontinuous, and a common unity is the result, in all such cases the ruler–ruled relationship appears. It appears notably in living creatures as a consequence of their whole nature (and it can exist also where there is no life, as dominance in a musical scale, but that is hardly relevant here). The living creature consists in the first place of
35 mind and body, and of these the former is ruler by nature, the latter ruled. Now we must always look for nature's own norm in things whose condition is according to nature, and not base our observations

on degenerate forms. We must therefore in this connection consider the man who is in good condition mentally and physically, one in whom the rule of mind over body is conspicuous—because the bad and unnatural condition of a permanently or temporarily depraved person will often give the impression that his body is ruling over his soul. 1254^b

However that may be, it is, as I say, within living creatures that we first find it possible to see both the rule of a master and that of a statesman. The rule of soul over body is like a master's rule, while the rule of intelligence over desire is like a statesman's or a king's. In these relationships it is clear that it is both natural and expedient for the body to be ruled by the soul, and for the emotional part of our natures to be ruled by the mind, the part which possesses reason. The reverse, or even parity, would be fatal all round. This is also true as between man and the other animals; for tame animals are by nature better than wild, and it is better for them all to be ruled by men, because it secures their safety. Again, as between male and female the former is by nature superior and ruler, the latter inferior and subject. And this must hold good of mankind in general.

Therefore whenever there is the same wide discrepancy between human beings as there is between soul and body or between man and beast, then those whose condition is such that their function is the use of their bodies and nothing better can be expected of them, those, I say, are slaves by nature. It is better for them, just as in the cases mentioned, to be ruled thus. For the 'slave by nature' is he that can and therefore does belong to another, and he that participates in reason so far as to recognize it but not so as to possess it (whereas the other animals obey not reason but emotions). The use made of slaves hardly differs at all from that of tame animals: they both help with their bodies to supply our essential needs. It is then part of nature's intention to make the bodies of free men to differ from those of slaves, the latter strong enough to be used for necessary tasks, the former erect and useless for that kind of work, but well suited for the life of a citizen of a state, a life which is in turn divided between the requirements of war and peace.

But the opposite often occurs: people who have the right kind of bodily physique for free men, but not the soul, others who have the right soul but not the body. This much is clear: suppose that there were men whose bodily physique showed the same superiority as is shown by the statues of gods, then all would agree that the rest of

mankind would deserve to be their slaves. And if this is true in relation
to physical superiority, the distinction would be even more justly
made in respect of superiority of soul; but it is much more difficult to
see beauty of soul than it is to see beauty of body. It is clear then that
1255ª by nature some are free, others slaves, and that for these it is both just
and expedient that they should serve as slaves.

CHAPTER 6

On the other hand it is not hard to see that those who take opposing
views are also right up to a point. The expressions 'state of slavery' and
5   'slave' have a double connotation: there exists also a *legal* slave and
state of slavery. The law in question is a kind of convention which
provides that all that is conquered in war is termed the property of the
conquerors. Against this right many of those versed in law bring a
charge analogous to that of 'illegality' brought against an orator: they
hold it to be indefensible that a man who has been overpowered by the
10 violence and superior might of another should become his property.
Others see no harm in this; and both views are held by experts.

   The reason for this difference of opinion, and for the overlap in the
arguments used, lies in the fact that in a way it is virtue, when it
acquires resources, that is best able actually to use force; and in the
15 fact that anything which conquers does so because it excels in some
good. It seems therefore that force is not without virtue, and that the
only dispute is about what is just. Consequently some think that 'just'
in this connection is a nonsense, others that it means precisely this,
that 'the stronger shall rule'. But when these propositions are dis-
20 entangled, the other arguments have no validity or power to show that
the superior in virtue ought not to rule and be master.

   Some take a firm stand (as they conceive it) on 'justice' in the sense
of 'law', and claim that enslavement in war is just, simply as being
legal; but they simultaneously deny it, since it is quite possible that
25 undertaking the war may have been unjust in the first place. Also one
cannot use the term 'slave' properly of one who is undeserving of
being a slave; otherwise we should find among slaves and descendants
of slaves even men of the noblest birth, should any of them be
captured and sold. For this reason they will not apply the term slave to
such people but use it only for non-Greeks. But in so doing they are
30 really seeking to define the slave by nature, which was our starting-
point; for one has to admit that there are some who are slaves every-

where, others who are slaves nowhere. And the same is true of noble birth: noblesregard themselves as of noble birth not only among their own people but everywhere, and they allow nobility of birth of non-Greeks to be valid only in non-Greek lands. This involves making two grades of free status and noble birth, one absolute, the other con-   35
ditional. (In a play by Theodectes, Helen is made to say, 'Who would think it proper to call me a slave, who am sprung of divine lineage on both sides?') But in introducing this point they are really basing the distinction between slave and free, noble-born and base-born, upon virtue and vice. For they maintain that as man is born of man, and   1255ᵇ
beast of beast, so good is born of good. But frequently, though this may be nature's intention, she is unable to realize it.

It is clear then that there is justification for the difference of opinion: while it is not invariably true that slaves are slaves by nature   5
and others free, yet this distinction does in some cases actually prevail—cases where it is expedient for the one to be master, the other to be the slave. Whereas the one must be ruled, the other should exercise the rule for which he is fitted by nature, thus being the master. For if the work of being a master is badly done, that is contrary to the interest of both parties; for the part and the whole, the soul and the   10
body, have identical interests; and the slave is in a sense a part of his master, a living but separate part of his body. For this reason there is an interest in common and a feeling of friendship between master and slave, wherever they are by nature fitted for this relationship; but not when the relationship arises out of the use of force and by the law which we have been discussing.   15

CHAPTER 7

From all this it is clear that there is a difference between the rule of master over slave and the rule of a statesman. All forms of rule are not the same though some say that they are. Rule over naturally free men is different from rule over natural slaves; rule in a household is monarchical, since every house has one ruler; the rule of a statesman is rule over free and equal persons.

A man is not called master in virtue of what he knows but simply in   20
virtue of the kind of person he is; similarly with slave and free. Still, there *could* be such a thing as a master's knowledge or a slave's knowledge. The latter kind may be illustrated by the lessons given by a certain man in Syracuse who, for a fee, trained houseboys in their

25 ordinary duties; and this kind of instruction might well be extended to include cookery and other forms of domestic service. For the tasks of the various slaves differ, some being more essential, some more highly valued (as the proverb has it 'slave before slave, master before master').

30 All such fields of knowledge are the business of slaves, whereas a master's knowledge consists in knowing how to put his slaves to *use*; for it is not in his acquiring of slaves but in his use of them that he is master. But the use of slaves is not a form of knowledge that has any great importance or dignity, since it consists in knowing how to direct

35 slaves to do the tasks which they ought to know how to do. Hence those masters whose means are sufficient to exempt them from the bother employ an overseer to take on this duty, while they devote themselves to statecraft or philosophy. The knowledge of how to *acquire* slaves is different from both these, the just method of acquisition, for instance, being a kind of military or hunting skill.

So much may suffice to define master and slave.

BOOK III

CHAPTER I

1274ᵇ In considering now the varieties and characteristics of constitutions, we must begin by looking at the state and asking what it is. There is no unanimity about this; for example, some say that an action was taken

35 by the state, others that it was taken not by the state, but by the oligarchy or by the dictator. Now obviously the activities of statesman and legislator are wholly concerned with the state, and the constitution is a kind of organization of the state's inhabitants; but like any

40 other whole that is made up of many parts, the state is to be classed as a composite thing; so clearly we must first try to isolate the citizen, for

1275ᵃ the state is an aggregate of citizens. So we must ask, Who is a citizen? and, Whom should we call one?

Here too there is no unanimity, no agreement as to what constitutes a citizen; it often happens that one who is a citizen in a democracy is not a citizen in an oligarchy. (I think we may leave out of account those

5 who merely acquire the title indirectly, e.g. the 'made' citizens.) Nor does mere residence in a place confer citizenship: resident foreigners and slaves are not citizens, but do share domicile in the country.

Another definition is 'those who have access to legal processes, who may prosecute or be prosecuted'. But this access is open to any person 10 who is covered by a commercial treaty—at any rate partially open, for a resident foreigner is in many places obliged to appoint a patron, so that not even this degree of participation is open to him unqualifiedly. (Likewise boys not yet old enough to be enrolled, and old people who 15 have retired from duty, must be termed citizens in a sense, but only with the addition of 'not fully' or 'superannuated' or some such term— not that it matters which word we use since what we mean is clear enough). What we are looking for is the citizen proper, without any defect needing to be amended. Similar difficulties may be raised, and 20 solved, about persons exiled or with civic disqualifications.

What effectively distinguishes the citizen proper from all others is his participation in giving judgement and in holding office. Some offices are distinguished in respect of length of tenure, some not being tenable by the same person twice under any circumstances, or only 25 after an interval of time. Others, such as membership of a jury or of an assembly, have no such limitation. It might be objected that such persons are not really officials, and that these functions do not amount to participation in office. But they have the fullest sovereign power, and it would be ridiculous to deny their participation in office. In any case nomenclature ought not to make any difference; it is just that there is no name covering that which is common to a juryman and to a 30 member of an assembly, which ought to be used of both. For the sake of a definition I suggest that we say 'unlimited office'. We therefore define citizens as those who participate in this. Such a definition seems to cover, as nearly as may be, those to whom the term citizen is in fact applied.

On the other hand we must remember that in the case of things in which the substrata differ in kind, one being primary, another 35 secondary, and so on, there is nothing, or scarcely anything, which is common to all those things, in so far as they are the kind of thing they are. Thus we see the various constitutions differing from each other in 1275ᵇ kind, some being prior to others—since those that have gone wrong or deviated must be posterior to those which are free from error. I will explain later what I mean by 'deviated'. A citizen, therefore, will necessarily vary according to the constitution in each case.

For this reason our definition of citizen is best applied in a 5 democracy; in the other constitutions it *may* be applicable, but it need not necessarily be so. For in some constitutions there is no body

comprising the people, nor a recognized assembly, but only an occasional rally; and justice may be administered piecemeal. For
10 example, at Sparta contract cases are tried by the Ephors, one or other of them, cases of homicide by the Elders, and other cases doubtless by other officials. Similarly at Carthage all cases are tried by officials.

But our own definition of a citizen can be amended so as to apply to the other constitutions also. We simple replace our 'unlimited' office
15 of juror or member of assembly by 'limited'. For it is to all or some of these that the task of judging or deliberating is assigned, either on all matters or on some. From these considerations it has become clear who a citizen is: as soon as a man becomes entitled to participate in office, deliberative or judicial, we deem him to be a citizen of that
20 state; and a number of such persons large enough to secure a self-sufficient life we may, by and large, call a state.

CHAPTER 2

For practical purposes a citizen is defined as one of citizen birth on *both* his father's *and* his mother's side; some would go further and
25 demand citizen descent for two, three, or even more generations. But since these are only crude definitions, employed by states for practical purposes, some people pose the puzzle of how a great or great-great-grandfather's citizenship can itself be determined. Gorgias of Leontini, partly perhaps in puzzlement and partly in jest, said that, as mortars are what mortar-makers make, so Larissaeans are those made
30 by the workmen, some of whom were Larissaean-makers. The answer to such objectors is simple: if they participated in the constitution in the manner prescribed in our definition, they were citizens. Of course, the criterion of having citizen-parents cannot be applied in the case of the original colonists or founders.

I think however that there is perhaps a more important puzzle here,
35 namely about those who got a share in the constitution because it had changed—as for example after the expulsion of the tyrants from Athens, when Cleisthenes enrolled many foreigners and slaves in the tribes. The question here is not 'Are these persons citizens?', but whether they are citizens justly or unjustly. Some would go further
1276ᵃ and question whether anyone can be a citizen unless he is justly so, on the ground that unjust and false mean the same thing. But when persons exercise their office unjustly, we continue to say that they rule, though unjustly; and as the citizen has been defined by some

kind of office (i.e. if he shares in such-and-such an office, he is, as we said, a citizen), we cannot deny the propriety of using the term even in these cases.

CHAPTER 3

This question of justice or the lack of it cannot be separated from the dispute we have already mentioned, which arises from the difficulty some people raise as to whether it was or was not the state that acted— for example when a change takes place from oligarchy or tyranny to democracy. There are those who after such a change claim that they are no longer obliged to fulfil the terms of a contract; for it had been entered into, so they say, not by the state but by the tyrant. Similarly they would disown other obligations, if these have been incurred under one of those types of constitution which rest on force and disregard the common interest. It follows that if there is a democracy of this type, we must say that the acts of this constitution are acts of the state to the same degree as those flowing from the oligarchy or tyranny are.

And this topic seems to be part of yet another question—how are we to tell whether a state is still the same state or a different one? We might try to investigate this question using territory and inhabitants as criteria; but this would not carry us very far, since it is quite possible to divide both territory and population into two, putting some people in one part and some into the other. That is not a very serious difficulty: it arises from our use of the word *polis* in more than one sense. Such a puzzle is therefore resolved easily enough.

Another question is this: when a population lives in the same place, what is the criterion for regarding the state as a unity? It cannot be the walls, for it would be possible to put one wall round the whole Peloponnese. Babylon is perhaps a similar case, and any other state with a circumference that embraces a nation rather than a state. (It is said of Babylon that its capture was, two days later, still unknown to a part of the city.) These questions of the state's size—both how big it should be and whether it helps to have the population drawn from one nation or more than one—are problems to which it will be useful to return later, since the statesman has to keep them in mind.

But when the same population continues to dwell in the same territory, must we say that the state remains the same so long as there is continuity of race among that population, even though one generation of people dies and another is born—just as a river or spring is commonly said to be the same, although different water passes into and out of it all the time? Alternatively, ought we to speak of the *population* as being the same for the reasons stated, but say that the 1276ᵇ state is different? For the state is a kind of association—an association of citizens in a constitution; so when the constitution changes and becomes different in kind, the state also would seem necessarily not to be the same. We may use the analogy of a chorus, which may at one 5 time perform in a tragedy and at another in a comedy, so that we say it is different—yet often enough it is composed of the same persons. And the same principle is applicable to other associations and combinations, which are different if the combination in question differs in kind. For example, we say the same musical notes are fitted together differently, to produce either the Dorian or the Phrygian mode. If this 10 is right, it is clear that the main criterion of the continued identity of a state ought to be its constitution. This leaves it quite open either to change or not to change the *name* of a state, both when the population is the same and when it is different.

But whether, when a state's constitution is changed, it is just to 15 disown obligations or to discharge them—that is another question.

CHAPTER 4

Connected with the matters just discussed is the question whether we ought to regard the virtue of a good man and that of a sound citizen as the same virtue, or not. If this is a point to be investigated, we really must try to form some rough conception of the virtue of a citizen. 20   So then: we say a citizen is a member of an association, just as a sailor is; and each member of the crew has his different function and a name to fit it—rower, helmsman, look-out, and the rest. Clearly the most exact description of each individual will be a special description of his virtue; but equally there will also be a general description that 25 will fit them all, because there is a task in which they all play a part— the safe conduct of the voyage; for each member of the crew aims at securing that. Similarly the task of all the citizens, however different they may be, is the stability of the association, that is, the constitution. Therefore the virtue of the citizen must be in relation to the constitu- 30 tion; and as there are more kinds of constitution than one, there cannot be just one single *and perfect* virtue of the sound citizen. On the other hand we do say that the good *man* is good because of one single virtue which *is* perfect virtue. Clearly then it is possible to be a sound citizen without having that virtue which makes a sound man.

Look now at the problem from another angle and consider the same point in relation to the best constitution. That is to say, if it is impossible for a state to consist entirely of sound *men*, still each of them must do, and do well, his proper work; and doing it well depends on his virtue. But since it is impossible for all the *citizens* to be alike, there cannot be one virtue of citizen and good man alike. For the virtue of the sound citizen must be possessed by all (and if it is, then that state is necessarily best.) *But* if it is inevitable that not all the citizens in a sound state are good, it is impossible for all to have the virtue of the good man.

Again, a state is made up of unlike parts. As an animate creature consists of body and soul, and soul consists of reasoning and desiring, and a household consists of husband and wife, and property consists of master and slave, so also a state is made up of these and many other sorts of people besides, all different. The virtue of all the citizens cannot, therefore, be *one*, any more than in a troupe of dancers the goodness of the leader and that of the followers are one.

Now while all this shows clearly that they are not the same in general, the question may be asked whether it is not possible in a particular case for the same virtue to belong both to the sound citizen and the sound man. We would answer that there is such a case, since we maintain that a sound ruler is both good and wise, whereas wisdom is not essential for a citizen. Some say that from the very start there is a different kind of education for rulers. They instance the obvious training of the sons of royalty in horsemanship and war, and a saying of Euripides, which is supposed to refer to the education of a ruler: 'No frills in education please . . . only what the state doth need.' But though we may say that the virtue of good ruler and good man is the same, yet, since he too that is ruled is a citizen, we cannot say in general that the virtue of citizen and man are one, but only that they may be in the case of a particular citizen. For certainly the virtue of ruler and citizen are not the same. And that doubtless is the reason why Jason of Pherae said that he went hungry whenever he ceased to be tyrant, not knowing how to live as a private person.

But surely men praise the ability to rule and to be ruled, and the virtue of a citizen of repute seems to be just this—to be able to rule and be ruled well. If then we say that the virtue of the good man is to do with ruling, and that of the citizen to do with both ruling and being ruled, the two things cannot be praiseworthy to the same degree....

For there is such a thing as rule by a master which we say is concerned with necessary tasks; but the master has no necessity to
35 know more than how to *use* such labour. Anything else, I mean to be able actually to be a servant and do the chores, is simply slave-like. (We speak of several kinds of slave, corresponding to the several varieties of operation. One variety is performed by manual workers,
1277ᵇ who, as the term itself indicates, live by their hands; among these are the skilled mechanics.) Hence, in some places, only with the arrival of extreme democracies have workmen attained to participation in office. The work then of those who are subject to rule is not work which either the good statesman or the good citizen ought to learn,
5 except occasionally for the personal use he may require to make of it. For then the distinction between master and slave just ceases to apply.

But there is another kind of rule—that exercised over men who are free, and similar in birth. This we call rule by a statesman. It is this that a ruler must first learn through being ruled, just as one learns to
10 command cavalry by serving under a cavalry-commander and to be a general by serving under a general, and by commanding a battalion and a company. This too is a healthy saying, namely that it is not possible to be a good ruler without first having been ruled. Not that good ruling and good obedience are the same virtue—only that the good citizen must have the knowledge and ablity both to rule and be ruled. That is what we mean by the virtue of a citizen—understanding
15 the governing of free men from both points of view.

Returning now to the good *man*, we find the same two qualities. And this is true even though the self-control and justice exercised in ruling are not the same in kind. For clearly the virtue of the good man, who is free but governed, for example his justice, will not be always one and the same: it will take different forms according to whether he
20 is to rule or be ruled, just as self-control and courage vary as between men and women. A man would seem a coward if he had only the courage of a woman, a woman a chatterbox if she were only as discreet as a good man. Men and women have different parts to play in managing the household: his to win, hers to preserve. But the only
25 virtue special to a ruler is practical wisdom; all the others must be possessed, so it seems, both by rulers and by ruled. The virtue of a person being ruled is not practical wisdom but correct opinion; he is

rather like a person who makes the pipes, while the ruler is the one who can play them.

These considerations have made clear whether the virtue of the   30
good man and that of the sound citizen are the same or different, and
the sense in which they are the same and the sense in which they are
different.

BOOK VII

CHAPTER 1

If we wish to investigate the best constitution appropriately, we must   1323^a
first decide what is the most desirable life; for if we do not know that,   15
the best constitution is also bound to elude us. For those who live
under the best-ordered constitution (so far as their circumstances
allow) may be expected, barring accidents, to be those whose affairs
proceed best. We must therefore first come to some agreement as to   20
what is the most desirable life for all men, or nearly all, and then
decide whether it is one and the same life that is more desirable for
them both as individuals and in the mass, or different ones.

In the belief that the subject of the best life has been fully and
adequately discussed, even in the external discourses, I propose to
make use of this material now. Certainly nobody will dispute one
division: that there are three ingredients which must all be present to   25
make us blessed—our bodily existence, our intellectual and moral
qualities, and all that is external. (No one would call blessed a man
who is entirely without courage or self-control or practical wisdom or
a sense of justice, who is scared of flies buzzing past, who will stop at
nothing to gratify his desire for eating or drinking, who will ruin his   30
closest friends for a paltry profit, and whose mind also is as witless and
deluded as a child's or a lunatic's.) But while there is general
agreement about these three, there is much difference of opinion   35
about their extent and their order of superiority. Thus people suppose
that it is sufficient to have a certain amount of virtue, but they set no
limit to the pursuit of wealth, power, property, reputation, and the
like.

Our answer to such people will be twofold. First, it is easy to arrive
at a firm conviction on these matters by simply observing the facts: it is   40
not by means of external goods that men acquire and keep the virtues,

1323ᵇ but the other way round; and to live happily, whether men suppose it
to consist in enjoyment or in virtue or in both, does in fact accrue more
to those who are outstandingly well-equipped in character and intellect, and only moderately so in the possession of externally acquired
goods—more, that is, than to those who have more goods than they
5　 need but are deficient in the other qualities. Yet the matter can be
considered on the theoretical level too, and the same result will be
seen easily enough. External goods, being like a collection of tools
each useful for some purpose, have a limit: one can have too many of
them, and that is bound to be of no benefit, or even a positive injury, to
10　 their possessors. It is quite otherwise with the goods of the soul: the
more there is of each the more useful each will be (if indeed one
ought to apply to these the term 'useful', as well as 'admirable'). So
clearly, putting it in general terms, we shall maintain that the best
condition of anything in relation to the best condition of any other
thing is commensurate in point of superiority with the relationship
15　 between the things themselves of which we say these conditions are
conditions. Hence as the soul is a more precious thing (both
absolutely and relatively to ourselves) than both property and the
body, its best condition too will necessarily show a proportionate
relationship to that of each of the others. Moreover, it is for the sake
of our souls that these things are to be desired and all right-minded
20　 persons ought to desire them; it would be wrong to reverse this
priority.

　　Let this then be agreed upon at the start: to each man there comes
just so much happiness as he has of virtue and of practical wisdom,
and performs actions dependent thereon. God himself is an indication
of the truth of this. He is blessed and happy not on account of any of
25　 the external goods but because of himself and what he is by his own
nature. And for these reasons good fortune must be something
different from happiness; for the acquisition of goods external to the
soul is due either to the coincidence of events or to fortune, but no
man is just or restrained as a result of, or because of, fortune. A
connected point, depending on the same arguments, applies with
equal force to the state: the best and well-doing state is the happy
30　 state. But it is impossible for those who do not do good actions to do
well, and there is no such thing as a man's or a state's good action
without virtue and practical wisdom. The courage of a state, or its
sense of justice, or its practical wisdom, or its restraint have exactly the
same effect and are manifested in the same form as the qualities which

the individual has to share in if he is to be called courageous, just, 35
wise, or restrained.

These remarks must suffice to introduce the subject; it was
impossible to start without saying something, equally impossible to try
to develop every relevant argument, for that would be a task for
another session. For the present let this be our fundamental basis: the
life which is best for men, both separately, as individuals, and in the 40
mass, as states, is the life which has virtue sufficiently supported by
material resources to facilitate participation in the actions that virtue 1324ᵃ
calls for. As for objectors, if there is anyone who does not believe what
has been said, we must pass them by for the purposes of our present
inquiry and deal with them on some future occasion.

CHAPTER 2

It remains to ask whether we are to say that happiness is the same for 5
the individual human being and for the state, or not. The answer is
again obvious: all would agree that it is the same. For those who hold
the view that the good life of an individual depends on wealth will
likewise, if the whole state be wealthy, count it blessed; and those who
prize most highly the life of a tyrant will deem most happy that state 10
which rules over the greatest number of people. So too one who
commends the single individual on the basis of his virtue will also
judge the more sound state to be the happier.

But there are still these two questions needing consideration:
Which life is more desirable, the life of participation in the work of the 15
state and constitution, or one like a foreigner's, cut off from the
association of the state? What constitution are we to lay down as best,
and what is the best condition for the state to be in (whether we
assume that participation in the state is desirable for all or only for the
majority)? The first question was a matter of what is desirable for an
individual; the second belongs to political theory and insight, and we 20
have chosen to examine it now. The other question would be merely
incidental, this second one is the business of our inquiry.

Obviously the best constitution must be one which is so ordered
that any person whatsoever may prosper best and live blessedly; but it
is disputed, even by those who admit that the life of virtue is the most 25
desirable, whether the active life of a statesman is preferable to one
which is cut off from all external influences, i.e. the contemplative life,
which some say is the only life for a philosopher. Both in earlier and in

30 modern times men most ambitious for virtue seem generally to have preferred these two kinds of life, the statesman's or the philosopher's. It makes a considerable difference which of the two is correct, because we must, if we are right-minded people, direct ourselves to the better of the two aims, whichever it may be; and this equally as individuals and collectively as members of a constitution. Some hold that to

35 dominate neighbouring peoples in the manner of a slave-master involves the greatest injustice, but to do so in a statesmanlike way involves none, though it does mean making inroads on the comfort of the ruler. Others hold pretty well the opposite, namely that the life of

40 active statesmanship is the only one worthy of a man, and activity springing from each of the individual virtues is just as much open to those who take part in public affairs under the constitution as to

1324^b private persons. That is one view, but there is also a set of people who say that the only style of constitution that brings happiness is one modelled on tyranny and on mastery of slaves. And in some places the definitive purpose both of the laws and of the constitution is to facilitate mastery of the neighbouring peoples.

5 Hence, even though in most places the legal provisions have for the most part been established on virtually no fixed principle, yet if it is anywhere true that the laws have a single purpose, they all aim at domination. Thus in Sparta and Crete the educational system and the bulk of the laws are directed almost exclusively to purposes of war;

10 and outside the Greek peoples all such nations as are strong enough to aggrandize themselves, like the Scythians, Persians, Thracians, and Celts, have always set great store by military power. In some places there are also laws designed to foster military virtue, as at Carthage, where men reputedly receive decorations in the form of armlets to the

15 number of the campaigns in which they have served. There used also to be a law in Macedonia that a man had to be girdled with his halter until he had slain his first enemy; and at a certain Scythian feast when the cup was passed round only those were allowed to drink from it who had killed an enemy. Among the Iberians, a warlike race, the

20 tombs of their warriors have little spikes stuck around them showing the number of enemy slain. There are many other such practices, some established by law and some by custom, among different peoples.

Yet surely, if we are prepared to examine the point carefully, we shall see how completely unreasonable it would be if the work of a statesman were to be reduced to an ability to work out how to rule and

be master over neighbouring peoples, with or without their consent.   25
How could that be part of statecraft or lawgiving, when it is not even
lawful in itself? To rule at all costs, not only justly but unjustly, is
unlawful, and merely to have the upper hand is not necessarily to have
a just title to it. Nor does one find this in the other fields of knowledge:
it is not the job of a doctor or a ship's captain to persuade or to force   30
patients or passengers. Certainly most people seem to think that
mastery is statesmanship, and they have no compunction about
inflicting upon others what in their own community they regard as
neither just nor beneficial if applied to themselves. They themselves
ask for just government among themselves; but in the treatment of   35
others they do not worry at all about what measures are just. Of course
we may be sure that nature has made some things fit to be ruled by a
master and others not, and if this is so, we must try to exercise master-
like rule not over all people but only over those fit for such treatment—
just as we should not pursue human beings for food or sacrifice, but
only such wild animals as are edible and so suitable to be hunted for   40
this purpose.

Surely too a single state could be happy even on its own (provided of
course that its constitution runs well), since it is possible for a state to   1325ᵃ
be administered in isolation in some place or other, following its own
sound laws; the organization of its constitution will not be directed to
war or the defeat of enemies, for the non-existence of these is
postulated. The conclusion is obvious: we regard every provision   5
made for war as admirable, not as a supreme end but only as serving
the needs of that end. It is the task of a sound legislator to survey the
state, the clan, and every other association and to see how they can be
brought to share in the good life and in whatever degree of happiness   10
is possible for them. There will of course be different rules laid down
in different places; if there are neighbouring peoples, it will be part of
the legislative function to decide what sort of attitude is to be adopted
to this sort and that sort, and how to employ towards each the proper
rules for dealing with each. But this question, 'What end should the
best constitution have in view?', will be properly examined at a later   15
stage.

CHAPTER 3

We must now deal with those who, while agreeing that the life which is
conjoined with virtue is the most desirable, differ as to how it is to be

followed. Some reject altogether the holding of state-offices, regarding the life of a free man as different from that of a statesman, and as
20 the most desirable of all lives. Others say that the statesman's life is
best, on the grounds that a man who does nothing cannot be doing
well, and happiness and doing well are the same thing. To both parties
we may say in reply, 'You are both of you partly right and partly wrong.
Certainly it is true, as some of you maintain, that the life of a free man
25 is better than the life like that of a master of slaves: there is no dignity
in using a slave, *qua* slave, for issuing instructions to do this or that
routine job is no part of noble activity. But not all rule is rule by a
master, and those who think it is are mistaken. The difference between
ruling over free men and ruling over slaves is as great as the difference
between the naturally free and the natural slave, a distinction which
30 has been sufficiently defined in an earlier passage. And we cannot
agree that it is right to value doing nothing more than doing something. For happiness is action; and the actions of just and restrained
men represent the consummation of many fine things.'
    But perhaps someone will suppose that if we define things in this
35 way, it means that absolute sovereignty is best, because then one is in a
sovereign position to perform the greatest number of fine actions; and
so anyone who is in a position to rule ought not to yield that position
to his neighbour, but take and keep it for himself without any regard
for the claims of his parents or his children or friends in general,
40 sacrificing everything to the principle that the best is most to be
desired and nothing could be better than to do well. Perhaps there is
some truth in this, but only if we suppose that this most desirable of
1325^b things is in fact going to accrue to those who use robbery and violence.
But maybe this is impossible and the supposition is false. For a man
who does not show as much superiority over his fellows as husband
over wife, or father over children, or master over slave—how can his
5 actions be fine actions? So he who departs from the path of virtue will
never be able to go sufficiently straight to make up entirely for his
previous errors. As between similar people, the fine and just thing is to
take turns, which satisfies the demands of equality and similarity.
Non-equality given to equals, dissimilar positions given to similar
persons—these are contrary to nature and nothing that is contrary to
10 nature is fine. Hence it is only when one man is superior in virtue, and
in ability to perform the best actions, that it becomes fine to serve him
and just to obey him. But it should be remembered that virtue in itself
is not enough; there must also be the power to translate it into action.

If all this is true and if happiness is to be equated with doing well, then the active life will be the best both for any state as a whole community and for the individual. But the active life need not, as some suppose, be always concerned with our relations with other prople, nor is intelligence 'active' only when it is directed towards results that flow from action. On the contrary, thinking and speculation that are their own end and are done for their own sake are *more* 'active', because the aim in such thinking is to do well, and therefore also, in a sense, action. Master-craftsmen in particular, even though the actions they direct by their intellect are external to them, are nevertheless said to 'act', in a sovereign sense.

As for states that are set up away from others and have chosen to live thus in isolation, there is nothing in that to oblige them to lead a life of inaction. Activity too may take place as among parts: the parts of a state provide numerous associations that enter into relations with each other. The same is true of any individual person; for otherwise God himself and the whole universe would scarcely be in a fine condition, for they have no external activities, only those proper to themselves. It is therefore clear that the same life must inevitably be the best both for individuals and collectively for states and mankind.

CHAPTER 13

We must now discuss the constitution itself, and ask ourselves what people, and what kind of people, the state ought to be composed of if it is going to be blessed and have a well-run constitution. The well-being of all men depends on two things: one is the right choice of target, of the end to which actions should tend, the other lies in finding the actions that lead to that end. These two may just as easily conflict with each other as coincide. Sometimes, for example, the aim is well-chosen, but in action men fail to attain it. At other times they successfully perform everything that conduces to the end, but the end itself was badly chosen. Or they may fail in both, as sometimes happens in the practice of medicine, when doctors neither rightly discern what kind of condition a healthy body ought to be in, nor discover the means which will enable their goal to be attained. Wherever skill and knowledge come into play, these two must both be mastered: the end and the actions which are means to the end.

It is clear then that all men aim at happiness and the good life, but some men have an opporunity to get it, others have not. This may be due to their nature, or to some stroke of fortune, for the good life needs certain material resources (and when a man's disposition is comparatively good, the need is for a lesser amount of these, a greater amount when it is comparatively bad). Some indeed, who start with the opportunity, go wrong from the very beginning of the pursuit of happiness. But as our object is to find the *best* constitution, and that means the one whereby a state will be best ordered, and since we call that state best ordered in which the possibilities of happiness are greatest, it is clear that we must keep constantly in mind what happiness is.

We defined this in our *Ethics* (if those discussions were worth anything), and we here state, again, that happiness is an activity and a complete utilization of virtue, not conditionally but absolutely. By 'conditionally' in this connection I refer to things that are necessary, and by 'absolutely' I mean nobly. For example, actions relating to justice, the infliction of just chastisements and punishments, spring from virtue; but they are 'necessary' and whatever good is in them is there by necessity. (It is preferable to have a state of affairs in which such things would be *un*necessary both for state and for individual.) But actions directed towards honours and abundant resources are noblest actions, in an absolute sense. For the former actions are but the removal of some evil, the latter sort are not; they are on the contrary the creation and the begetting of positive goods.

A sound man will nobly utilize ill-health, poverty, and other misfortunes; but blessedness requires the opposite of these. (This definition too was given in our ethical discussions—that the sound man is the sort of man for whom things absolutely good are good, on account of his own virtue; and clearly his utilization of them must be sound and noble absolutely.) Hence men imagine that the causes of happiness lie in external goods. This is as if they were to ascribe fine and brilliant lyre-playing to the quality of the instrument rather than to the skill of the player.

From what has been said it follows that, while some things must be there from the start, others must be provided by a lawgiver. Ideally, then, we wish for the structure of our state all that Fortune has it in her sovereign power to bestow (that she *is* sovereign, we take for granted). But it is not Fortune's business to make a state sound; that is a task for knowledge and deliberate choice. On the other hand, a state's being sound requires the citizens who share in the constitution to be sound; and for our purposes *all* the citizens share in the

constitution. The question then is, 'How does a man become sound?' 35
Of course, even if it is possible for all to be sound, and not just each
citizen taken individually, the latter is preferable, since each entails
all.

However, men become sound and good because of three things.
These are nature, habit, and reason. First, nature; a man must be born, 40
and he must be born a man and not some other animal; so too he must
have body and soul with certain characteristics. It may be of no
advantage to be born with some of these qualities, because habits 1332^b
cause changes; for there are some qualities which by nature have a
dual possibility, in that subsequent habits will make them either better
or worse. Other creatures live mainly by nature, some by habit also to a
small extent. Man, however, lives by reason as well: he alone has
reason, and so needs all three working concertedly. Reason causes 5
men to do many things contrary to habit and to nature, whenever they
are convinced that this is the better course. In an earlier place we
described what men's nature should be if they are to respond easily to
handling by the legislator. After that it becomes a task of education, for 10
men learn partly by habituation and partly by listening.

CHAPTER 14

Since every association of persons forming a state consists of rulers
and ruled, we must ask whether those who rule and those who are
ruled ought to be different persons or the same throughout life; for the 15
education which will be needed will depend upon which way we make
this distinction. If one group of persons were as far superior to all the
rest as we believe gods and heroes to be superior to men, and if they
had both bodies and souls of such outstanding quality that the
superiority of the rulers were indisputable and evident to those ruled 20
by them, then it would obviously be better that the same set of persons
should always rule and the others always be ruled, once and for all.
But since this is not a condition that can easily be obtained, and since
rulers are not so greatly superior to their subjects as Scylax says the
kings are in India, it is clear that, for a variety of reasons, all must share 25
alike in the business of ruling and being ruled by turns. For equality
means giving the same to those who are alike, and the established
constitution can hardly be long maintained if it is contrary to justice.
Otherwise everyone all over the country combines with the ruled in a
desire to introduce innovations, and it is quite impossible for even a 30

numerous citizen-body to be strong enough to withstand such a combination.

Yet it cannot be disputed that rulers have to be superior to those who are ruled. It therefore becomes the duty of the lawgiver to consider how this is to be brought about and how they shall do the
35 sharing. We noted earlier that nature herself has provided one way to choose: that very element which in respect of birth is all the same she has divided into older and younger, the former being fit for ruling, the latter for being ruled. No one objects to being thus ruled on grounds of age, or thinks himself too good for it; after all, once he reaches the
40 required age, he will get back his contribution to the pool. There is then a sense in which we must say the 'same' persons rule and are ruled, and a sense in which we must say thay they are 'different'
1333ᵃ persons. So their education too must be in one sense the same, in another different; for, as is often said, one who is to become a good ruler must first himself be ruled. (Rule, as was said in our first discussions, is of two kinds, according as it is exercised for the sake of the
5 ruler, which we say is master-like rule, or for the sake of the ruled, which we say is rule over free men; and some instructions that are given differ not in the actual tasks to be performed, but in their purpose, which is why many jobs generally considered servile may be honourably performed even by free men, by the younger among them. For the question whether a job is honourable or not is to be decided
10 less with reference to the actions themselves than in the light of their end and purpose.) But since we hold that the virtue of citizen and ruler is the same as that of the best man, and that the same man should be first ruled and later ruler, it immediately becomes an essential task of the lawgiver to ensure that they both may become *good* men, and to
15 consider what practices will make them so, and what is the aim of the best life.

Two parts of the soul are distinguished, one intrinsically possessing reason, the other not possessing reason intrinsically but capable of listening to it. To these belong, we think, the virtues which qualify a man to be called in some sense 'good'. To those who accept our
20 division of the soul there is no difficulty in answering the question 'In which of the two parts, more than in the other, does the. *end* lie?' For what is inferior is always for the sake of what is superior; this is equally clear both in matters of skill and in those of nature; and the superior is that which is possessed of reason. There is a further twofold division,
25 which follows from our custom of making a distinction between

practical reason and theoretical reason; so clearly we must divide this part similarly. Actions, we shall say, follow suit: those of that which is by nature better must be regarded as preferable by those who are in a position to attain all three or two of them. For each man, that which is the very highest that he can attain is the thing most to be preferred.

Again, all of life can be divided into work and leisure, war and 30 peace, and some things done have moral worth, while others are merely necessary and useful. In this connection the same principle of choice must be applied, both to the parts of the soul and to their respective actions—that is to say, we should choose war for the sake of 35 peace, work for the sake of leisure, necessary and useful things for the sake of the noble. The statesman must therefore take into consideration the parts of the soul and their respective actions, and in making laws must have an eye to all those things, but more especially to the better ones and to the ends in view; and he must regard men's lives and their choice of what they do in the same light. For one must be 40 able to work and to fight, but even more to be at peace and have 1333^b leisure; to do the necessary and the useful things, yes, but still more those of moral worth. These then are the targets at which education should be aimed, whether children's education or that of such later age-groups as require it.

It is obvious however that those Greeks who have today a reputation 5 for running the best constitutions, and the lawgivers who drew up those constitutions, did not in fact construct their constitutional plans with the best possible aim, and did not direct their laws and education towards producing all the virtues; but instead, following the vulgar way of thinking, they turned aside to pursue virtues that appeared to 10 be useful and more lucrative. And in a similar manner to these some more recent writers have voiced the same opinion: they express their approval of the Lacedaemonians' constitution and admire the aim of their lawgiver, because he ordered all his legislation with a view to war and conquest. This is a view which can easily be refuted by reasoning, and already in our own day has been refuted by the facts. Just as most 15 men crave to be master of many others, because success in this brings an abundance of worldly goods, so the writer Thibron is clearly an admirer of the Laconian lawgiver, and so too is each of the others who, writing about the Spartan constitution, have stated that thanks to their 20 being trained to face dangers they came to rule over many others. But since today the Spartan rule is no more, it is clear that they are not happy and their lawgiver was not a good one. There is also something

laughable in the fact that, for all their keeping to his laws, and with no
25 one to stop them from using those laws, they have lost the good life.

They are also wrong in their notion of the kind of rule for which a
lawgiver ought to display admiration; for rule over free men is nobler
than master-like rule, and more connected with virtue. To say that a
state has trained itself in the acquisition of power with a view to ruling
30 its neighbours—that is no ground for calling it happy or applauding its
lawgiver. Such an argument may have dangerous consequences: its
acceptance obviously requires any citizen who can to make it his
ambition to be able to rule in his own city—the very thing that the
Lacedaemonians accuse King Pausanias of seeking, and that too
35 though he was already in a position of such high honour. So none of
these theories or laws is of any value for a statesman, and they are
neither useful nor true. The same things are best for a community and
for individuals, and it is these that a lawgiver must instil into the souls
of men.

And as for military training, the object in practising it regularly is
40 not to bring into subjection those not deserving of such treatment, but
to enable men (a) to save themselves from becoming subject to others,
(b) to win a position of leadership, exercised for the benefit of the
1334ᵃ ruled, not with a view to being the master of all; and (c) to exercise the
rule of a master over those who deserve to be slaves. The lawgiver
should make particularly sure that his aim both in his military
legislation and in his legislation in general is to provide peace and
5 leisure. And facts support theory here, for though most military states
survive while they are fighting wars, they fall when they have established their rule. Like steel, they lose their fine temper when they are
at peace; and the lawgiver who has not educated them to be able to
10 employ their leisure is to blame.

CHAPTER 15

Since it seems that men have the same ends whether they are acting as
individuals or as a community, and that the best man and the best
constitution must have the same definitive purpose, it becomes
evident that there must be present the virtues needed for leisure; for,
15 as has often been said, the end of war is peace and leisure is the end of
work. Of the virtues useful for leisure and civilized pursuits, some
function in a period of leisure, others in a period of work—because a
lot of essential things need to be provided before leisure can become

possible. Hence a state must be self-restrained, courageous, and steadfast; for as the proverb says, 'no leisure for slaves', and those who cannot bravely face danger are the slaves of their attackers. We need courage and steadfastness for our work, philosophy for leisure, and restraint and a sense of justice in both contexts; but particularly in times of leisure and peace. For war *forces* men to be just and restrained, but the enjoyment of prosperity, and leisure in peacetime, are apt rather to make them arrogant. Therefore a great sense of justice and much self-restraint are demanded of those who are thought to be successful and to enjoy everything the world regards as a blessing, men such as might be living, in the poets' phrase, in the Isles of the Blest. For these especially will need philosophy, restraint, and a sense of justice; and the greater the leisure that flows from an abundance of such blessings, the greater that need will be. Clearly then the state, too, if it is to be sound and happy, must have a share in these virtues. For if it is a mark of disgrace not to be able to use advantages, it is especially so in a period of leisure—to display good qualities when working or on military service, but in leisure and peace to be no better than slaves.

Training in virtue, therefore, should not follow the Lacedaemonian model. The difference between them and other nations lies not in any disagreement about what are the greatest goods but in their view that there is a certain virtue which will produce them with particular effectiveness.

We have already distinguished three essentials—nature, habit, and reason. Of these we have already dealt with the first, determining the qualities we should have by natural endowment; next we must ask whether education should first proceed by means of reason or by the formation of habits. Certainly these must chime in perfect unison; for it is possible to make an error of reason about the best principle, and to find oneself equally led astray by one's habits.

One thing is clear from the start: just as in everything else, so here too coming into being originates in a beginning, and the end which originates in some beginning is itself the beginning of another end; and for us, reason and intelligence are the end to which our nature tends. Thus it is to these that the training of our habits, as well as our coming into being, must be directed. Next, as soul and body are two, so also we note two parts of the soul, the reasoning and the unreasoning; and each of these has its own condition, of intelligence in the former case, of appetition in the latter. And just as the body comes into

being earlier than the soul, so also the unreasoning is prior to that which possesses reason. This is shown by the fact that, while passion and will as well as desire are to be found in children even right from birth, reasoning and intelligence come into their possession as they
25 grow older. Therefore the care of the body must begin before the care of the soul, then the training of the appetitive element, but this latter for the sake of the intelligence, and the body's training for the sake of the soul.

BOOK VIII

CHAPTER I

1337ᵃ No one would dispute the fact that it is a lawgiver's prime duty to arrange for the education of the young. In states where this is not done the quality of the constitution suffers. Education must be related to the particular constitution in each case, for it is the special character
15 appropriate to each constitution that set it up at the start and commonly maintains it, e.g. the democratic character preserves a democracy, the oligarchic an oligarchy. And in all circumstances the better character is a cause of a better constitution. And just as there must also be preparatory training for all skills and capacities, and a
20 process of preliminary habituation to the work of each profession, it is obvious that there must also be training for the activities of virtue. But since there is but one aim for the entire state, it follows that education must be one and the same for all, and that the responsibility for it must be a public one, not the private affair which it now is, each man looking after his own children and teaching them privately whatever
25 private curriculum he thinks they ought to study. In matters that belong to the public, training for them must be the public's concern. And it is not right either that any of the citizens should think that he belongs just to himself; he must regard all citizens as belonging to the state, for each is a *part* of the state; and the responsibility for each part
30 naturally has regard to the responsibility for the whole. In this respect the Lacedaemonians will earn our approval: the greatest possible attention is given to youth in Sparta, and all on a public basis.

CHAPTER 2

It is clear then that there should be laws laid down about education, and that education itself must be made a public concern. But we must not forget the question of what that education is to be, and how one ought to be educated. For in modern times there are opposing views about the tasks to be set, for there are no generally accepted assumptions about what the young should learn, either for virtue or for the best life; nor yet is it clear whether their education ought to be with more concern for the intellect than for the character of the soul. The problem has been complicated by the education we see actually given; and it is by no means certain whether training should be directed at things useful in life, or at those conducive to virtue, or at exceptional accomplishments. (All these answers have been judged correct by somebody.) And there is no agreement as to what in fact does tend towards virtue. For a start, men do not all prize the same virtue, so naturally they differ also about the training for it.

Then as to useful things: there are obviously certain essentials which the young must learn; but it is clear that they must not learn *all* useful tasks, since we distinguish those that are proper for a free man and those that are not, and that they must take part only in those useful occupations which will not turn the participant into a mechanic. We must reckon a task or skill or study as mechanical if it renders the body or intellect of free men unserviceable for the uses and activities of virtue. We therefore call mechanical those skills which have a deleterious effect on the body's condition, and all work that is paid for. For these make the mind preoccupied, and unable to rise above lowly things. Even in some branches of knowledge worthy of free men, while there is a point up to which it does not demean a free man to go in for them, too great a concentration on them, too much mastering of detail—this is liable to lead to the same damaging effects that we have been speaking of. In this connection the purpose for which the action or the study is undertaken makes a big difference. It is not unworthy of a free man to do something for oneself or for one's friends or on account of virtue; but he that does the same action on others' account may often be regarded as doing something typical of a hireling or slave. The established subjects studied nowadays, as we have already noted, have a double tendency.

35

40

1337^b

5

10

15

20

CHAPTER 3

Roughly four things are generally taught to children: reading and
25 writing, physical training, music, and, not always included, drawing.
Reading and writing and drawing are included as useful in daily life in
a variety of ways, gymnastics as promoting courage. But about music
there could be an immediate doubt. Most men nowadays take part in
music for the sake of the pleasure it gives; but originally it was
included in education on the ground that our own nature itself, as has
30 often been said, wants to be able not merely to work properly but also
to be at leisure in the right way. And leisure is the single fundamental
principle of the whole business, so let us discuss it again.

If we need both work and leisure, but the latter is preferable to the
former and is its end, we must ask ourselves what are the proper
35 activities of leisure. Obviously not play; for that would inevitably be to
make play our end in life, which is impossible. Play has its uses, but
they belong rather to the sphere of work; for he who toils needs rest,
and play is a way of resting, while work is inseparable from toil and
40 strain. We must therefore admit play, but keeping it to its proper uses
and occasions, and prescribing it as a cure; such movement of the soul
1338ᵃ is a relaxation, and, because we enjoy it, rest. But leisure seems in
itself to contain pleasure, happiness, and the blessed life. This is a
state attained not by those at work but by those at leisure, because he
that is working is working for some hitherto unattained end, and
5 happiness is an end, happiness which is universally regarded as
concomitant not with pain but with pleasure. Admittedly men do not
agree as to what that pleasure is; each man decides for himself following his own disposition, the best man choosing the best kind of enjoyment from the finest sources. Thus it becomes clear that, in order to
10 spend leisure in civilized pursuits, we do require a certain amount of
learning and education, and that these branches of education and
these subjects studied must have their own intrinsic purpose, as
distinct from those necessary occupational subjects which are studied
for reasons beyond themselves.

Hence, in the past, men laid down music as part of education, not as
15 being necessary, for it is not in that category, nor yet as being useful in
the way that a knowledge of reading and writing is useful for business
or household administration, for study, and for many of the activities
of a citizen, nor as a knowledge of drawing seems useful for the better
judging of the products of a skilled worker, nor again as gymnastics are

useful for health and vigour—neither of which do we see gained as a   20
result of music. There remains one purpose—for civilized pursuits
during leisure; and that is clearly the reason why they do introduce it,
for they give it a place in what they regard as the civilized pursuits of
free men. Thus Homer's line, 'to summon him alone to the rich   25
banquet'; and after these words he introduces certain other persons,
'who summon the bard whose singing shall delight them all'. And
elsewhere Odysseus says that the best civilized pursuit is when men
get together and 'sit in rows up and down the hall feasting and
listening to the bard'.

Clearly then there is a form of education which we must provide for   30
our sons, not as being useful or essential but as elevated and worthy of
free men. We must on a later occasion discuss whether this education
is one or many, what subjects it embraces, and how they are to be
taught. But as it turns out, we have made some progress in that direction: we have some evidence from the ancients too, derived from the   35
subjects laid down by them—as the case of music makes clear.

It is also clear that there are some useful things, too, in which the
young must be educated, not only because they are useful (for example
they must learn reading and writing), but also because they are often
the means to learning yet further subjects. Similarly they must learn   40
drawing, not for the sake of avoiding mistakes in private purchases,
and so that they may not be taken in when buying and selling
furniture, but rather because it teaches one to be observant of physical   1338ᵇ
beauty. But to be constantly asking 'What is the use of it?' is un-
becoming to those of broad vision and unworthy of free men.

Since it is obvious that education by habit-forming must precede
education by reasoned instruction, and that education of the body   5
must precede that of the intellect, it is clear that we must subject our
children to gymnastics and to physical training; the former produces a
certain condition of the body, the latter its actions.

POETICS*

CHAPTER I

1447ᵃ   The subject I wish to discuss is poetry itself, its species with their
respective capabilities, the correct way of constructing plots so that
10   the work turns out well, the number and nature of the constituent
elements [of each species], and anything else in the same field of
inquiry.

To follow the natural order and take first things first, epic and tragic
15   poetry, comedy and dithyrambic, and most music for the flute or lyre
are all, generally considered, varieties of *mimēsis*, differing from each
other in three respects, the media, the objects, and the mode of
mimēsis. ['Media' needs explaining]: in some cases where people,
20   whether by technical rules or practised facility, produce various
mimēseis by portraying things, the media are colours and shapes, while
in others the medium is the voice; similarly in the arts in question,
taken collectively, the media of *mimēsis* are rhythm, speech, and
harmony, either separately or in combination.

25   For example, harmony and rhythm are the media of instrumental
music, rhythm alone without harmony the medium of dancing, as
dancers represent characters, passions, and actions by rhythmic
movement and postures.

The art that uses only speech by itself or verse [that is, rhythmical
1447ᵇ   speech], the verses being homogeneous or of different kinds, has as yet
10   no name; for we have no common term to apply to the [prose] mimes
of Sophron and Xenarchus and to the Socratic dialogues, nor any
common term for *mimēseis* produced in verse, whether iambic
trimeters or elegiacs or some other such metre. True, people do attach
the making [that is the root of the word *poiētēs*] to the name of a metre
15   and speak of elegiac-makers and hexameter-makers; they think, no
doubt, that 'makers' is applied to poets not because they make
mimēseis but as a general term meaning 'verse-makers', since they call
'poets' or 'makers' even those who publish a medical or scientific

---

* *Translation*: M. E. Hubbard (in *Ancient Literary Criticism*, eds. D. A. Russell and
M. Winterbottom, Oxford, 1972). The words in square brackets, and the bracketed
numerals and letters, have been added by the translator to help the reader follow the
argument. *Text*: R. Kassel (Oxford Classical Texts, 1965).

theory in verse. But [this is open to two objections]: (1) as Homer and Empedocles have nothing in common except their metre, the latter had better be called a scientific writer, not a poet, if we are to use 'poet' of the former; (2) similarly, if we suppose a man to make his *mimēsis* in   20
a medley of all metres, as Chaeremon in fact did in the *Centaur*, a recitation-piece in all the various metres, we still have to call him a poet, a 'maker'.

So much for the simpler kinds. Some use all the media mentioned, rhythm, song, and verse: these are dithyrambic and nomic poetry,   25
tragedy, and comedy. But the two former use them all simultaneously, while the latter use different media in different parts. So much for the differentiae derived from the media.

CHAPTER 2

The objects of this *mimēsis* are people doing things, and these people   1448ᵃ
[as represented] must necessarily be either good or bad, this being, generally speaking, the only line of divergence between characters, since differences of character just are differences in goodness and badness, or else they must be better than are found in the world or worse or just the same, as they are represented by the painters,   5
Polygnotus portraying them as better, Pauson as worse, and Dionysius as they are; clearly therefore each of the varieties of *mimēsis* in question will exhibit these differences, and one will be distinguishable from another in virtue of presenting things as different in this way.

These dissimilarities can in fact be found in dancing and instru-   10
mental music, and in the arts using speech and unaccompanied verse: Homer for instance represents people as better and Cleophon as they are, while Hegemon of Thasos, the inventor of parodies, and Nicochares, the author of the *Deiliad*, represent them as worse . . .;   15
this is also the differentia that marks off tragedy from comedy, since the latter aims to represent people as worse, the former as better, than the men of the present day.

CHAPTER 3

There is still a third difference, the mode in which one represents each of these objects. For one can represent the same objects in the same   20
media

(i) sometimes in narration and sometimes becoming someone else, as Homer does; or

(ii) speaking in one's own person without change, or

(iii) with all the people engaged in the *mimēsis* actually doing things.

25   These three then, media, objects, and mode, are, as I said at the beginning, the differentiae of poetic *mimēsis*. So, if we use one of them [to separate poets into classes], Sophocles will be in the same class as Homer, since both represent people as good, and if we use another, he will be in the same class as Aristophanes, since they both represent people as actively doing things. . . .

1448ᵇ   So much for the number and nature of the differentiae of poetic *mimēsis*.

CHAPTER 4

5   Poetry, I believe, has two overall causes, both of them natural:

(a) *Mimēsis* is innate in human beings from childhood—indeed we differ from the other animals in being most given to *mimēsis* and in making our first steps in learning through it—and pleasure in instances of *mimēsis* is equally general. This we can see from the facts:

10   we enjoy looking at the most exact portrayals of things we do not like to see in real life, the lowest animals, for instance, or corpses. This is because not only philosophers, but all men, enjoy getting to understand something, though it is true that most people feel this pleasure

15   only to a slight degree; therefore they like to see these pictures, because in looking at them they come to understand something and can infer what each thing is, can say, for instance, 'This man in the picture is so-and-so.' If you happen not to have seen the original, the picture will not produce its pleasure *qua* instance of *mimēsis*, but because of its technical finish or colour or for some such other reason.

20   (b) As well as *mimēsis*, harmony and rhythm are natural to us, and verses are obviously definite sections of rhythm. . . .

1449ᵃ   To inquire whether even tragedy [as distinct from epic] is sufficiently elaborated in its qualitative elements, judging it in itself and in its relation to the audience, is another story. At any rate, after originating

10   in the improvizations of the leaders of the dithyramb, as comedy did in those of the leaders of the phallic songs still customary in many Greek

cities, tragedy gradually grew to maturity, as people developed the
capacities they kept discovering in it, and after many changes it
stopped altering, since it had attained its full growth. The main
changes were:

(i) in the number of actors, raised from one to two by Aeschylus,
who made the choral part less important and gave speech the
leading role; Sophocles added a third—and also scene-
painting;

(iii) in amplitude: as tragedy developed from the satyr-style, its
plots were at first slight and its expression comical, and it was a
long time before it acquired dignity;

(iii) in metre: the iambic trimeter replaced the trochaic tetrameter,
which had been used before as suitable for a satyr-style poetry,
that is, for productions involving more dancing; when verbal
expression came to the fore, however, nature herself found the
right metre, the iambic being the most speakable of all metres;
this we can see from the fact that it is the one we most often
produce accidentally in conversation, where hexameters are
rare and only occur when we depart from conversational tone;

(iv) in the increased number of episodes.

There is no need to say more of this or of the other developments that
gave it beauty; it would take too long to go through them in detail.

CHAPTER 5

Comedy is, as I said, a *mimēsis* of people worse than are found in the
world—'worse' in the particular sense of 'uglier', as the ridiculous is a
species of ugliness; for what we find funny is a blunder that does no
serious damage or an ugliness that does not imply pain, the funny face,
for instance, being one that is ugly and distorted, but not with pain.

. . .

CHAPTER 6

I shall deal later with the art of *mimēsis* in hexameters and with
comedy; here I want to talk about tragedy, picking up the definition of
its essential nature that results from what I have said.

Well then, a tragedy is a *mimēsis* of a high, complete action
('complete' in the sense that implies amplitude), in speech pleasurably
enhanced, the different kinds [of enhancement] occurring in separate

sections, in dramatic, not narrative form, effecting through pity and fear the *catharsis* of such emotions. By 'speech pleasurably enhanced' I mean that involving rhythm and harmony or song, by 'the different 30 kinds separately' that some parts are in verse alone and others in song.

One can deduce as necessary elements of tragedy (*a*) [from the mode] the designing of the spectacle, since the *mimēsis* is produced by people doing things; (*b*) [from the media] song-writing and verbal expression, the media of tragic *mimēsis*; by 'verbal expression' I mean 35 the composition of the verse-parts, while the meaning of 'song-writing' is obvious to anybody. [Others can be inferred from (*c*) the objects of the *mimēsis*:] A tragedy is a *mimēsis* of an action; action implies people engaged in it; these people must have some definite 1450ᵃ moral and intellectual qualities, since it is through a man's qualities that we characterize his actions, and it is of course with reference to their actions that men are said to succeed or fail. We therefore have (i) the *mimēsis* of the action, the plot, by which I mean the ordering of the particular actions; (ii) [the *mimēsis* of] the moral characters of the 5 personages, namely that [in the play] which makes us say that the agents have certain moral qualities; (iii) [the *mimēsis* of] their intellect, namely those parts [of the play] in which they demonstrate something in speech or deliver themselves of some general maxim.[1]

So tragedy as a whole will necessarily have six elements, the possession of which makes tragedy qualitatively distinct [from other literary kinds]: they are plot, the *mimēsis* of character, verbal 10 expression, the *mimēsis* of intellect, spectacle, and song-writing. The media of *mimēsis* are two, the mode one, the objects three, and there are no others. Not a few tragedians do in fact use these as qualitative elements; indeed virtually every play has spectacle, the *mimēsis* of character, plot, verbal expression, song, and the *mimēsis* of intellect.

15 The most important of these elements is the arrangement of the particular actions [as the following arguments show]:

(*a*) A tragedy is [by definition] a *mimēsis* not of people but of their actions and life. Both success and ill success are success and ill success in action—in other words the end and aim of human life is doing something, not just being a certain sort of person; and though we consider people's characters in deciding what sort of person they 20 are, we call them successful or unsuccessful only with reference to

---

[1] Throughout the rest of the treatise '*mimēsis* of character' and '*mimēsis* of intellect' are used without square brackets to translate *ēthos* and *dianoia* in this technical sense (translator's note).

their actions. So far therefore from the persons in a play acting as they do in order to represent their characters, the *mimēsis* of their characters is only included along with and because of their actions. So the particular actions, the plot, are what the rest of the tragedy is there for, and what the rest is there for is the most important.

(*b*) [By definition] a work could not be a tragedy if there were no action. But there could be a tragedy without *mimēsis* of character, and the tragedies of most of the moderns are in fact deficient in it; the same   25
is true of many other poets, and of painters for that matter, of Zeuxis, for instance, in comparison with Polygnotus: the latter is good at depicting character, while Zeuxis' painting has no *mimēsis* of character to speak of.

(*c*) If you put down one after another speeches that depicted character, finely expressed and brilliant in the *mimēsis* of intellect, that   30
would not do the job that, by definition, tragedy does do, while a tragedy with a plot, that is, with an ordered series of particular actions, though deficient in these other points, would do its job much better.

(*d*) The most attractive things in tragedy, *peripeteiai* and recognition scenes, are parts of the plot.

(*e*) Novices in poetry attain perfection in verbal expression and in   35
the *mimēsis* of character much earlier than in the ordering of the particular actions; this is also true of almost all early poets.

The plot therefore is the principle, or one might say the principle of life,[2] in tragedy, while the *mimēsis* of character comes second in importance, a relation similar to one we find in painting, where the   1450^b
most beautiful colours, if smeared on at random, would give less pleasure than an uncoloured outline that was a picture of something. A tragedy, I repeat, is a *mimēsis* of an action, and it is only because of the action that it is a *mimēsis* of the people engaged in it. Third comes the *mimēsis* of their intellect, by which I mean their ability to say what   5
the situation admits and requires; to do this in speeches is the job of political sense and rhetoric, since the older poets made their people speak as the former directs, while the moderns make them observe the rules of rhetoric. Of these two, the *mimēsis* of character is that [in the play] which makes plain the nature of the moral choices the personages make, so that those speeches in which there is absolutely

[2] The 'principle of life' renders *psychē* ('soul'), which stands to the living body in the same relation as plot to tragedy; it is 'what the rest is there for' as in argument (*a*), and it is what the living body essentially is as in argument (*b*). In traditional language it is both a 'final cause' and the 'formal cause'. Cf. *De Anima* 415^b 8ff. (translator's note).

10   nothing that the speaker chooses and avoids involve no *mimēsis* of character. By '*mimēsis* of intellect' I mean those passages in which they prove that something is or is not the case or deliver themselves of some general statement. Fourth comes the expression of the spoken parts, by which I mean, as I said before, the expression of thought in words;

15   the meaning is the same whether verse or prose is in question. Of the others, which are there to give pleasure, song-writing is the most important, while spectacle, though attractive, has least to do with art— with the art of poetry, that is; for a work is potentially a tragedy even without public performance and players, and the art of the stage-designer contributes more to the perfection of spectacle than the

20   poet's does.

CHAPTER 7

Now that these definitions are out of the way, I want to consider what the arrangement of the particular actions should be like, since that is the prime and most important element of tragedy.

Now, we have settled that a tragedy is a *mimēsis* of a complete, that

25   is, of a whole action, 'whole' here implying some amplitude (there can be a whole without amplitude).

By 'whole' I mean 'with a beginning, a middle, and an end'. By 'beginning' [in this context] I mean 'that which is not necessarily the consequent of something else, but has some state or happening naturally consequent on it', by 'end' 'a state that is the necessary or

30   usual consequent of something else, but has itself no such consequent', by 'middle' 'that which is consequent and has consequents'. Well-ordered plots, then, will exhibit these characteristics, and will not begin or end just anywhere.

35   It is not enough for beauty that a thing, whether an animal or anything else composed of parts, should have those parts well ordered; since beauty consists in amplitude as well as in order, the thing must also have amplitude—and not just any amplitude. Though a very small creature could not be beautiful, since our view loses all distinctness when it comes near to taking no perceptible time, an enormously ample one could not be beautiful either, since our view of

1451ᵃ   it is not simultaneous, so that we lose the sense of its unity and whole-ness as we look it over; imagine, for instance, an animal a thousand miles long. Animate and inanimate bodies, then, must have amplitude, but no more than can be taken in at one view; and similarly a plot must have extension, but no more than can be easily remembered. What is, for the poetic art, the limit of this extension? Certainly not that imposed by the contests and by perception. .... As the limit imposed by the actual nature of the thing, one may suggest 'the ampler the better, provided it remains clear as a whole', or, to give a rough specification, 'sufficient amplitude to allow a probable or necessary succession of particular actions to produce a change from bad to good or from good to bad fortune'.

CHAPTER 8

Unity of plot is not, as some think, achieved by writing about one man; for just as the one substance admits innumerable incidental properties, which do not, some of them, make it a such-and-such, so one man's actions are numerous and do not make up any single action. That is why I think the poets mistaken who have produced *Heracleids* or *Theseids* or other poems of the kind, in the belief that the plot would be one just because Heracles was one. Homer especially shows his superiority in taking a right view here—whether by art or nature: in writing a poem on Odysseus he did not introduce everything that was incidentally true of him, being wounded on Parnassus, for instance, or pretending to be mad at the mustering of the fleet, neither of which necessarily or probably implied the other at all; instead he composed the *Odyssey* about an action that is one in the sense I mean, and the same is true of the *Iliad*. In the other mimetic arts a *mimēsis* is one if it is a *mimēsis* of one object; and in the same way a plot, being a *mimēsis* of an action, should be a *mimēsis* of one action and that a whole one, with the different sections so arranged that the whole is disturbed by the transposition and destroyed by the removal of any one of them; for if it makes no visible difference whether a thing is there or not, that thing is no part of the whole.

CHAPTER 9

What I have said also makes plain that the poet's job is saying not what did happen but the sort of thing that would happen, that is, what can happen in a strictly probable or necessary sequence. The difference between the historian and the poet is not merely that one writes verse and the other prose—one could turn Herodotus' work into verse and it would be just as much history as before; the essential difference is that

5

10

15

20

25

30

35

1451ᵇ

the one tells us what happened and the other the sort of thing that
would happen. That is why poetry is at once more like philosophy and
more worth while than history, since poetry tends to make general
statements, while those of history are particular. A 'general statement'
means [in this context] one that tells us what sort of man would,
probably or necessarily, say or do what sort of things, and this is what
poetry aims at, though it attaches proper names; a particular statement
on the other hand tells us what Alcibiades, for instance, did or what
happened to him.

That poetry does aim at generality has long been obvious in the case
of comedy, where the poets make up the plot from a series of probable
happenings and then give the persons any names they like, instead of
writing about particular people as the lampooners did. In tragedy,
however, they still stick to the actual names; this is because it is what is
possible that arouses conviction, and while we do not without more
ado believe that what never happened is possible, what did happen is
clearly possible, since it would not have happened if it were not.
Though as a matter of fact, even in some tragedies most names are
invented and only one or two well known: in Agathon's *Antheus*, for
instance, the names as well as the events are made up, and yet it gives
just as much pleasure. So one need not try to stick at any cost to the
traditional stories, which are the subject of tragedies; indeed the
attempt would be absurd, since even what is well known is well known
only to a few, but gives general pleasure for all that.

It is obvious from all this that the poet should be considered a
maker of plots, not of verses, since he is a poet *qua* maker of *mimēsis*
and the objects of his *mimēsis* are actions. Even if it is incidentally true
that the plot he makes actually happened, that does not mean he is not
its maker; for there is no reason why some things that actually happen
should not be the sort of thing that would probably happen, and it is in
virtue of that aspect of them that he is their maker.

Of defective plots or actions the worst are the episodic, those, I
mean, in which the succession of the episodes is neither probable nor
necessary; bad poets make these on their own account, good ones
because of the judges; for in aiming at success in the competition and
stretching the plot more than it can bear they often have to distort the
natural order.

Tragedy is a *mimēsis* not only of a complete action, but also of things
arousing pity and fear, emotions most likely to be stirred when things
happen unexpectedly but because of each other (this arouses more

surprise than mere chance events, since even chance events seem 5
more marvellous when they look as if they were meant to happen—
take the case of the statue of Mitys in Argos killing Mitys' murderer by
falling on him as he looked at it; for we do not think that things like
this are merely random); so such plots will necessarily be the best. 10

CHAPTER 10

Some plots are simple, some complex, since the actions of which the
plots are *mimēsis* fall naturally into the same two classes. By 'simple
action' I mean one that is continuous in the sense defined and is a 15
unity and where the change of fortune takes place without *peripeteia* or
recognition, by 'complex' one where the change of fortune is
accompanied by *peripeteia* or recognition or both. The *peripeteia* and
recognition should arise just from the arrangement of the plot, so that
it is necessary or probable that they should follow what went before; 20
for there is a great difference between happening next and happening
as a result.

CHAPTER 11

A *peripeteia* occurs when the course of events takes a turn to the
opposite in the way described,[3] the change being also probable or
necessary in the way I said. For example, in the *Oedipus*, when the man
came and it seemed that he would comfort Oedipus and free him from 25
his fear about his mother, by revealing who he was he in fact did the
opposite. Again in the *Lynceus*, Lynceus was being led off and it
seemed that he would be put to death and that Danaus who was with
him would kill him, but the earlier actions produced Danaus' death
and Lynceus' release.

Recognition is, as its name indicates, a change from ignorance to 30
knowledge, tending either to affection or to enmity; it determines in
the direction of good or ill fortune the fates of the people involved.
The best sort of recognition is that accompanied by *peripeteia*, like that
in the *Oedipus*. There are of course other kinds of recognition. For a
recognition of the sort described can be a recognition of inanimate
objects, indeed of quite indifferent ones, and one can also recognize 35
whether someone has committed an act or not. But the one mentioned
has most to do with the plot, that is, most to do with the action; for a

[3] That is, in a way involving surprise.

recognition accompanied by *peripeteia* in this way will involve either
pity or fear, and tragedy is by definition a *mimēsis* of actions that rouse
these emotions; it is moreover such recognitions that lead to good or
bad fortune.

Since recognition involves more than one person, in some cases
only one person will recognize the other, when it is clear who the
former is, and sometimes each has to recognize the other: Orestes, for
example, recognized Iphigenia from her sending the letter, but a
second recognition was necessary for her to recognize him.

These then are two elements of the plot, and a third is *pathos*. I have
dealt with the first two, *peripeteia* and recognition. A *pathos* is an act
involving destruction or pain, for example deaths on stage and
physical agonies and woundings and so on.

So much for the parts of tragedy that one ought to use as qualitative
elements.

CHAPTER 13

What ought one to aim at and beware of in composing plots? And what
is the source of the tragic effect? These are the questions that naturally
follow from what I have now dealt with.

Well, the arrangement of tragedy at its best should be complex, not
simple, and it should also present a *mimēsis* of things that arouse fear
and pity, as this is what is peculiar to the tragic *mimēsis*.

So it is clear that one should not show virtuous men passing from
good to bad fortune, since this does not arouse fear or pity, but only a
sense of outrage. Nor should one show bad men passing from bad to
good fortune, as this is less tragic than anything, since it has none of
the necessary requirements; it neither satisfies our human feeling nor
arouses pity and fear. Nor should one show a quite wicked man
passing from good to bad fortune; it is true that such an arrangement
would satisfy our human feeling, but it would not arouse pity or fear,
since the one is felt for someone who comes to grief without deserving
it, and the other for someone like us (pity, that is, for the man who does
not deserve his fate, and fear for someone like us); so this event will not
arouse pity or fear. So we have left the man between these. He is one
who is not pre-eminent in moral virtue, who passes to bad fortune not
through vice or wickedness, but because of some piece of ignorance,
and who is of high repute and great good fortune, like Oedipus and
Thyestes and the splendid men of such families.

1452ᵇ

5

10

30

35

1453ᵃ

5

10

So the good plot must have a single line of development, not a double one as some people say; that line should go from good fortune to bad and not the other way round; the change should be produced not through wickedness, but through some large-scale piece of 15
ignorance; the person ignorant should be the sort of man I have described—certainly not a worse man, though perhaps a better one.

This is borne out by the facts: at first the poets recounted any story that came to hand, but nowadays the best tragedies are about a few families only, for example, Alcmaeon, Oedipus, Orestes, Meleager, 20
Thyestes, Telephus, and others whose lot it was to suffer or commit fearful acts.

Well then, the best tragedy, judged from the standpoint of the tragic art, comes from this sort of arrangement. That is why those who censure Euripides for doing this in his tragedies and making many of 25
them end with disaster are making just the same mistake. For this is correct in the way I said. The greatest proof of this is that on the stage and in the contests such plays are felt to be the most properly tragic, if they are well managed, and Euripides, even if he is a bad manager in the other points, is at any rate the most tragic of the poets. 30

Second comes the sort of arrangement that some people say is the best: this is the one that has a double arrangement of the action like the *Odyssey*, and ends with opposite fortunes for the good and bad people. It is thought to be the best because of the weakness of the audiences; for the poets follow the lead of the spectators and make plays to their 35
specifications. But this is not the pleasure proper to tragedy, but rather belongs to comedy; for in comedy those who are most bitter enemies throughout the plot, as it might be Orestes and Aegisthus, are reconciled at the end and go off and nobody is killed by anybody.

CHAPTER 14

Now though pity and fear can be elicited by the spectacle, they can 1453^b
also be elicited just by the arrangement of the particular actions [that make up the plot], and this is a prior consideration and the sign of a better poet. For the plot ought to be so composed that even without seeing the action, a man who just hears what is going on shudders and 5
feels pity because of what happens; this one would feel on hearing the plot of the *Oedipus*, for instance. But to produce this effect via the spectacle has less to do with the art of tragedy and needs external aids. To go further and use the spectacle to produce something that is

10   merely monstrous, instead of something that rouses fear, is to depart
entirely from tragedy. For one should look to tragedy for its own
pleasure, not just any pleasure; and since the poet's job is to produce
the pleasure springing from pity and fear via *mimēsis*, this clearly ought
to be present in the elements of the action.

What sort of events, then, do seem apt to rouse fear, or [rather] pity?
15   This is my next subject. In such actions, people must do something to
those closely connected with them, or to enemies, or to people to
whom they are indifferent. Now, if it is a case of two enemies, this
arouses no particular pity, whether the one damages the other or only
intends to; or at least, pity is felt only at the *pathos* considered in itself.
The same is true in the case when people are indifferent to each other.
20   The cases we must look for are those where the *pathos* involves people
closely connected, for instance where brother kills brother, son father,
mother son, or son mother—or if not kills, then means to kill, or does
some other act of the kind.

Well, one cannot interfere with the traditional stories, cannot, for
instance, say that Clytaemestra was not killed by Orestes or Eriphyle
25   by Alcmaeon; what one should do is invent for oneself and use the
traditional material well. Let me explain more clearly what I mean by
'well'. One can make the act be committed as the ancient poets did,
that is, with the agents knowing and aware [whom they are damaging];
even Euripides has the example of Medea killing her children with full
30   knowledge. [And they can have knowledge and not act.] Or they can
commit the deed that rouses terror without knowing to whom they are
doing it, and later recognize the connection, like Sophocles' Oedipus;
this indeed happens outside the play, but we have examples in the
tragedy itself, for example, Astydamas' *Alcmaeon* and Telegonus in
the *Wounded Odysseus*. Again, apart from these one might through
35   ignorance intend to do something irreparable, and then recognize the
victim-to-be before doing it. These are the only possible ways, as they
must either do it or not, and in knowledge or ignorance.

The worst of these is to have the knowledge and the intention and
then not do it; for this is both morally outraging and untragic—
1454ᵃ   'untragic' because it involves no *pathos*. That is why nobody does
behave in this way except very rarely, as Haemon, for example, means
to kill Creon in the *Antigone*. The second worst is doing it: the better
form of this is when the character does it in ignorance, and recognizes
his victim afterwards; for this involves no feeling of outrage and the
5   recognition produces lively surprise. But the best is the last, for

example, the case in the *Cresphontes* where Merope means to kill her son and does not, but recognizes him instead, and the case involving brother and sister in the *Iphigenia in Tauris*; again in the *Helle* the son recognized his mother when on the point of giving her up.

As I said before, this is why tragedies are about very few families. As it was not art but chance that led the poets in their search to the discovery of how to produce this effect in their plots, they have to go to the families in which such *pathē* occurred.

So much for the arrangement of the particular acts and the qualities required of plots.

CHAPTER 15

In the representation of character, there are four things that one ought to aim at:

(*a*) First and foremost, the characters represented should be morally good. The speech or action will involve *mimēsis* of character if it makes plain, as said before, the nature of the person's moral choice, and the character represented will be good if the choice is good. This is possible in each class: for example, a woman is good and so is a slave, though the one is perhaps inferior, and the other generally speaking low-grade.

(*b*) The characters represented should be suitable: for example, the character represented is brave, but it is not suitable for a woman to be brave or clever in this way.

(*c*) They should be life-like; this is different from the character's being good and suitable in the way I used 'suitable'.

(*d*) They should be consistent: for even if the subject of the *mimēsis* is an inconsistent person, and that is the characteristic posited of him, still he ought to be consistently inconsistent.

In the representation of character as well as in the chain of actions one ought always to look for the necessary or probable, so that it is necessary or probable that a person like this speaks or acts as he does, and necessary or probable that this happens after that. Clearly then, the dénouements of plots ought to arise just from the *mimēsis* of character, and not from a contrivance, a *deus ex machina*, as in the *Medea* and in the events in the *Iliad* about the setting off. The contrivance should be used instead for things outside the play, either all that happened beforehand that a human being could not know, or

5   all that happens later and needs foretelling and reporting; for we
    attribute omniscience to the gods. In the particular actions themselves
    there should be nothing irrational, and if there is it should be outside
    the tragedy, like that of Sophocles' *Oedipus*.

       Since a tragedy is a *mimēsis* of people better than are found in the
10 world, one ought to do the same as the good figure-painters; for they
    too give us the individual form, but though they make people lifelike
    they represent them as more beautiful than they are. Similarly the poet
    too in representing people as irascible and lazy and morally deficient in
    other ways like that, ought nevertheless to make them good, as Homer
    makes Achilles both good and an example of harsh self-will. . . .

                              CHAPTER 19

1456ᵃ As I have dealt with the other qualitative elements, I now have to talk
    about the representation of intellect and about verbal expression. The
35 representation of intellect we may take to be covered by the *Rhetoric*;
    for it does belong rather to that inquiry. What is involved in the
    representation of intellect is every effect to be produced by speech. Its
    sections are proof and disproof, rousing emotion (pity, fear, anger, and
1456ᵇ so on), making a thing look important or unimportant. Clearly in the
    plot too one ought to proceed from just these same main heads, when
    one needs to produce an effect of pity or fear, likelihood or impor-
5   tance. There is some difference, though; in the action these should be
    obvious without one's being told, whereas the other effects should be
    produced in words by the person using them and should result from
    his words, as the speaker would be quite unnecessary if the desired
    result were obvious without his saying anything.

       So far as verbal expression goes, one branch of inquiry is that into
10 the forms of speech. Knowledge of this really falls under the study of
    delivery and is the province of the expert in that subject. I mean such
    questions as 'What is a command, a wish, a statement, a threat, a
    question, an answer?' and so on. A poet's knowledge or ignorance in
    this sphere does not leave him open to any critical censure worth
    bothering about. For anyone would think pretty trivial the fault
15 censured by Protagoras, when he says: 'Homer thinks he is beginning
    with a prayer and in fact uses a command, when he says, "Sing of the
    wrath, goddess", since to tell somebody to do something or not is a
    command.' So let us leave that alone, since it belongs to another field
    and not to poetry.

CHAPTER 20

Verbal expression as a whole has the following parts: element,   20
syllable, linking word, articulatory word, noun, verb, termination,
statement.

An element is an indivisible sound, not any sound, but that capable
of producing intelligible utterance; for some animals produce
indivisible sounds, which I do not, however, call elements. This class
has three subdivisions: sounded, half-sounded, and soundless.[4] A   25
sounded element is that which has an audible sound without any
contact occurring. A half-sounded element is one that produces an
audible sound when contact does occur: such are *s* and *r*. A soundless
element is one where contact occurs without the element itself having
any audible sound, though it is audible when combined with elements
that have audible sound: such are *g* and *d*. The elements in these three   30
classes can be further classified, according to the shape of the mouth,
the place of contact, rough or smooth breathing, length or shortness of
quantity, and accent, acute, grave, or intermediate. One can investigate the subject further in works on metric.

A syllable is a composite non-significant sound made up of a voice-   35
less element and one with voice: *gr*, for example, is a syllable by itself
without *a*, and also if *a* is added to make *gra*. But the investigation of
this too is a matter of metric.

A linking word is (*a*) a non-significant sound which neither   1457ᵃ
prevents nor produces the formation from a number of sounds of one
significant utterance; it ought not to stand alone at the beginning of a
statement: examples are *men*, *toi*, *dē*, *de* [the linking particles]; (*b*) a
non-significant sound that naturally produces from a plurality of   5
sounds that nevertheless signify one thing a single significant
utterance: examples are *amphi*, *peri*, and the rest [of the prepositions].

An articulatory word (*arthron*) is a non-significant sound that
indicates the beginning or end or dividing point of a statement; it is
naturally put at either end (?) of a statement or in the middle.   10

A noun is a composite significant sound with no temporality, and
made up of parts not in themselves significant. For in compound
words we do not take the parts to be significant in themselves; in
Theodorus, for example, the *dōron* has no significance.

A verb is a composite significant sound with temporality, and, like a
noun, is made up of parts not in themselves significant; by 'with   15

---

[4] In modern terminology: vowels, fricatives, and stops.

temporality' I mean that, while 'man' and 'white' do not signify when, 'walks' and 'walked' do signify present and past time respectively.

Termination is the part of a noun or verb that signifies case and number and also the part concerned with delivery, for example, question and command: 'Did he walk?' and 'Walk' show terminations of the verb under the sections of this class.

A statement is a composite significant sound whose separate parts are themselves significant; I give this definition because not every statement is made up of nouns and verbs—the definition of man, for instance; one can, that is, have a statement with no verb, but it will always have a significant part. A statement is one statement in two senses: (*a*) as signifying one thing, (*b*) by being composed of a plurality of statements: the *Iliad*, for example, is one as being composite, and the definition of man as signifying one thing.

Topics

LIST OF TOPICS

Action
Akrasia
Being (Existence)
Biology
Categories
Causes
Change
Contradiction, Law of
[Cosmology: see God]
Definition
Deliberation and Choice
Determinism
Dialectic
[*Energeia* (Activity): see Change]
Essence
Eudaimonia (the Good for Man)
Form and Matter
Friendship
God (the Unmoved Mover)
Identity and Unity
Imagination
Individuation
Infinity
Justice
Knowledge
Matter
Meaning

Memory
Metaphysics
[Movement: see Action and
    Change]
Necessity and Possibility
Plato (Aristotle's Criticism of the
    Theory of Forms)
Pleasure
Poetry
Political Philosophy
Practical Wisdom
Predication
Responsibility (the Voluntary and
    Involuntary)
Science, Theory of
Sense-perception
Soul
Substance
Syllogism
Teleological Explanation
Thought
Time
Truth
Universals
Virtue
[Zeno's Paradoxes: see Infinity]

ABBREVIATIONS

AA (1, 2, 3, 4)	*Articles on Aristotle*, ed. Barnes, J., Schofield, M., and Sorabji, R., London, 1975–9. (Volumes 1–4)
AGP	*Archiv für Geschichte der Philosophie*
AJP	*American Journal of Philology*
Ar.Soc.Proc.	*Aristotelian Society Proceedings*
Ar.Soc.Sup.Vol.	*Aristotelian Society Supplementary Volume*
CQ	*Classical Quarterly*
J.H.Ideas	*Journal of History of Ideas*
J.H.Ph.	*Journal of History of Philosophy*
JHS	*Journal of Hellenic Studies*
J.Ph.Logic	*Journal of Philosophical Logic*
J.Ph.	*Journal of Philosophy*
OSAP	*Oxford Studies in Ancient Philosophy*
PQ	*Philosophical Quarterly*
PR	*Philosophical Review*
Ph.	*Philosophy*
Ph. of Sc.	*Philosophy of Science*
Rev. of Met.	*Review of Metaphysics*
Rev.Ph.	*Revue Philosophique*

TOPICS

Action

EN III. 1–5, VI. 2, 4, VII. 3; *MA* 6–7; *De An.* III. 9–11.

Milo, cc. 1 and 2; Hardie, c. 12; Cooper, c. 1; Kenny (3), Part Three; Nussbaum, Essays 4 and 5; Charles, c. 2.

D. J. Allan, 'The Practical Syllogism', in *Autour d'Aristote*.
G. E. M. Anscombe, 'Thought and Action in Aristotle', in *AA* 2.
M. Mothersill, 'Anscombe's Account of the Practical Syllogism', *PR* 1962.
J. L. Ackrill, 'Aristotle on Action', in Rorty.
M. T. Thornton, 'Aristotelian Practical Reason', *Mind* 1982.
D. Charles, 'Aristotle's Ontology and Moral Reasoning', *OSAP* 1986.

See also: Deliberation and Choice; Practical Wisdom.

Akrasia

EN VII. 1–10.

Hardie, c. 13; Milo, c. 3; Kenny (3), c. 14; Charles, c. 3; Dahl, Part Two.

R. Robinson, 'Aristotle on Akrasia', in *AA* 2.
G. Santas, 'Aristotle on Practical Inference, the Explanation of Action, and Akrasia', *Phronesis* 1969.
D. Davidson, 'How is Weakness of Will Possible?', in Feinberg and in Davidson.
D. Wiggins, 'Weakness of Will, Commensurability, and the Objects of Deliberation and Desire', in Rorty.
J. H. McDowell, 'Are Moral Requirements Hypothetical Imperatives?', *Ar.Soc.Sup.Vol.* 1978.
G. Watson, 'Skepticism about Weakness of Will', *PR* 1977.

See also: Action; Deliberation and Choice; Practical Wisdom.

Being (Existence)

Met. V. 7, VII. 1–2, VIII. 2; *De Int.* 16^{b}19–25, 21^{a}18–33.

Kahn, c. 2; Mansion, pp. 218–53.

G. E. L. Owen, 'Aristotle in the Snares of Ontology', in Bambrough.
M. J. Woods, 'Existence and Tense', in Evans and McDowell.

See also: Metaphysics; Categories.

Biology

PA (esp. I and II. 1); *GA*.

Peck (1), Introduction; Peck (2), Preface and Introduction; Balme; Boylan; Gotthelf; Gotthelf and Lennox.

D. M. Balme, 'Aristotle's Use of Differentiae in Zoology', in *AA* 1.

A. Preus, 'Science and Philosophy in Aristotle's *Generation of Animals*', *Journal of the History of Biology*, 1970.

D. M. Balme, 'Aristotle: Natural History and Zoology', in Gillispie.

[For animal movement see Nussbaum on *MA* 6–11.]

See also: Teleological Explanation; Definition; Soul.

Categories

Cat. 1–5; *Top.* I. 9; *Met.* V. 7, VII. 1. [*Cat.* 6–9; *An. Post.* I. 27.43ᵃ25–43.]

Ross (1), p. lxxxii–xc; Ackrill (1), pp. 71–91.

C. M. Gillispie, 'The Aristotelian Categories', in *AA* 3.

A. Kosman, 'Aristotle's First Predicament', *Rev. of Met.* 1967.

C. L. Stough, 'Language and Ontology in Aristotle's *Categories*', *J.H.Ph.* 1972.

J. L. Ackrill, 'Aristotle on "Good" and the Categories', in *AA* 2.

B. Jones, 'An Introduction to the First Five Chapters of Aristotle's *Categories*', *Phronesis* 1975.

G. E. L. Owen, 'The Platonism of Aristotle', in *AA* 1.

M. Frede, 'Categories in Aristotle', in O'Meara.

J. Malcolm, 'On the Generation and Corruption of the Categories', *Rev. of Met.* 1981.

See also: Predication; Substance.

Causes

Phys. II. 3–7; *Met.* VI. 2. [*Met.* I; *An. Post.* II. 11; *Met.* V. 2, V. 30.]

Ross (2), pp. 33–44; Charlton, pp. 98–120; Kirwan, pp. 124–8, 180–2; Ackrill (3), pp. 36–41; Sorabji (2), cc. 2–3.

D. J. Allan, 'Causality Ancient and Modern', *Ar.Soc.Sup.Vol.* 1965.

R. K. Sprague, 'The Four Causes: Aristotle's Exposition and Ours', *Monist* 1968.

M. Hocutt, 'Aristotle's Four Becauses', *Ph.* 1974.

J. Annas, 'Aristotle on Inefficient Causes' (part III), *PQ* 1982.

See also: Teleological Explanation; Necessity and Possibility; Science.

Change

Phys. III. 1–3; *Met.* IX. 6.1048ᵇ18–35. [*Phys.* V–VII, VIII. 4; *GC* I. 4–5.]

Ross (2), pp. 44–8; Hussey, pp. 57–72; Waterlow (1), c. 3; Sorabji (3), c. 26.

A. L. Peck, 'Aristotle on *kinesis*', in Anton and Kustas.

G. Boas, 'Aristotle's Presuppositions about Change', *AJP* 1947.

L. A. Kosman, 'Aristotle's Definition of Motion', *Phronesis* 1967.

J. Owens, 'Aristotle—Motion as Actuality of the Imperfect', *Paideia* 1978.

[On Aristotle's distinction between change (*kinēsis*) and activity (*energeia*) *see*:

J. L. Ackrill, 'Aristotle's distinction betweer. *Energeia* and *Kinesis*', in Bambrough.

T. Penner, 'Verbs and the Identity of Actions', in Pitcher and Wood.

Gosling and Taylor, c. 16.

Waterlow (1), pp. 183–203.]

See also: Matter; God; Time.

Contradiction, Law of

Met. IV. 3–6. [*Met.* XI. 5, 6.]

Ross (4), pp. 159–63; Kirwan, pp. 86–116; Anscombe and Geach, pp.39–45; Lear, c. 6.

J. Lukasiewicz, 'Aristotle on the Law of Contradiction', in *AA* 3.

J. Barnes, 'The Law of Contradiction', *PQ* 1969.

H. W. Noonan, 'An Argument of Aristotle on Non-contradiction', *Analysis* 1977.

H. Weidemann, 'In Defence of Aristotle's Theory of Predication', *Phronesis* 1980 (pp. 76–80).

[On Aristotle's argument against relativism in *Met.* IV *see*:

A. Kenny, 'The Argument from Illusion in Aristotle's *Metaphysics* (Γ.1009–10)', *Mind* 1967.

M. C. Scholar, 'Aristotle *Met.* 1010^{b}1–3', *Mind* 1971.

J. D. G. Evans, 'Aristotle on Relativism', *PQ* 1974.

F. C. T. Moore, 'Evans off Target', *PQ* 1975.]

See also: Dialectic.

Definition

An. Post. II. 1–13; *Top.* I. 5–6; *Met.* VII. 4,10–12; VIII. 2, 6; *PA* I. 2–3.

Ross (4), p. 49–54; Cherniss, pp. 27–63; Sorabji (2), cc. 12–13.

J. M. Le Blond, 'Aristotle on Definition', in *AA* 3.

R. Rorty, 'Genus as Matter: a Reading of *Metaphysics* Z. 11', in Lee, Mourelatos, and Rorty.

M. Grene, 'Is Genus to Species as Matter to Form?', *Synthese* 1974.

R. Sorabji, 'Definitions: Why Necessary and in What Way', in Berti.

J. L. Ackrill, 'Aristotle's Theory of Definition: Some Questions on *Posterior Analytics* II. 8–10', in Berti.

A. Gomez-Lobo, 'Definitions in Aristotle's *Posterior Analytics*' in O'Meara.
See also: Essence; Causes; Science; Biology.

Deliberation and Choice

EN III. 2–4; *EE* II. 6–10. [*Rhet*. I. 4–7.]

Hardie, c. 9; Kenny (3), Part Two; Cooper, c. 1.

G. E. M. Anscombe, 'Thought and Action in Aristotle', in *AA* 2.
R. Sorabji, 'Aristotle on the Role of Intellect in Virtue', in Rorty.
D. Wiggins, 'Deliberation and Practical Reason', in Rorty.
See also: Practical Wisdom; Action; *Akrasia*.

Determinism

De Int. 9; *GC* II. 11; *Met*. VI. 2–3.

Ackrill (1), pp. 132–42; Kneale and Kneale, pp. 46–54; Hintikka, c. 8; Sorabji (2), c. 5; Waterlow (2), c. 5; Williams, pp. 197–210; Kirwan, pp. 189–98.

G. E. M. Anscombe, 'Aristotle and the Sea-battle', in Moravcsik.
C. Strang, 'Aristotle and the Sea-battle', *Mind* 1960.
L. D. Harris, 'Solving the "Naval Battle"', *Ar.Soc.Proc.* 1977/8.
M. J. White, 'Fatalism and Causal Determinism', *PQ* 1981.
D. Frede, 'The Sea Battle Reconsidered: a Defence of the Traditional Interpretation', *OSAP* 1985.
See also: Necessity and Possibility; Causes.

Dialectic

Top. I; *Met*. IV. 2.1004^{b}17–26. [*Top*. II–VIII; *Soph. El*. 2, 11, 34; *Rhet*. I. 1–3.]

Hardie, pp. 37–45, 365–8; Ackrill (3), pp. 110–15; Evans, c. 2; Brunschwig, pp. xviii–lv.

G. E. L. Owen, '*Tithenai ta Phainomena*', in *AA* 1.
W. Wieland, 'Aristotle's Physics and the Problem of Inquiry into Principles', in *AA* 1.
F. Solmsen, 'Dialectic without the Forms', in Owen.
G. Ryle, 'Dialectic in the Academy', in Owen.
M. C. Nussbaum, 'Saving Aristotle's Appearances', in Schofield and Nussbaum (pp. 284–8).
T. H. Irwin, 'Aristotle's Methods of Ethics', in O'Meara.
M. Galston, 'Aristotle's Dialectic, Refutation, and Inquiry', *Dialogue* 1982.

Essence

Met. VII 4–6, 10–11, 17.

Ross (1), pp. xciv–c, cxi–cxiv; Hartman, c. 2.

I. M. Copi, 'Essence and Accident', in Moravcsik.

N. P. White, 'Origins of Aristotle's Essentialism', *Rev. of Met.* 1972.

M. J. Woods, 'Substance and Essence in Aristotle', *Ar.Soc.Proc.* 1974/5.

S. M. Cohen, 'Individual and Essences in Aristotle's *Metaphysics*', *Paideia* 1978.

M. Furth, 'Transtemporal Stability in Aristotelian Substances', *J.Ph.* 1978.

A. Code, 'Aristotle: Essence and Accident', in Grandy and Warner.

See also: Definition; Substance; Individuation.

Eudaimonia (the Good for Man)

EN I. 1–5, 7–12; X. 6–8; *EE* I. 1–5; II. 1; VIII. 3; *Pol.* VII. 1–3.

Cooper, c. 2; Hardie, c. 2 and pp. 359–65; Engberg-Pedersen, cc. 1, 4.

W. F. R. Hardie, 'The Final Good in Aristotle's Ethics', *Ph.* 1965.

A. Kenny, 'Aristotle on Happiness', in *AA* 2 and in Feinberg.

T. Nagel, 'Aristotle on *Eudaimonia*', in Rorty.

J. L. Ackrill, 'Aristotle on *Eudaimonia*', in Rorty.

D. Keyt, 'Intellectualism in Aristotle', *Paideia* 1978.

T. H. Irwin, 'The Metaphysical and Psychological Basis of Aristotle's Ethics', in Rorty.

R. Kraut, 'Two Conceptions of Happiness', *PR* 1979.

W. F. R. Hardie, 'Aristotle on the Best Life for a Man', *Ph.* 1979.

K. V. Wilkes, 'The Good Man and the Good for Man in Aristotle's Ethics', in Rorty.

J. H. McDowell, 'The Role of *Eudaimonia* in Aristotle's Ethics', in Rorty.

N. P. White, 'Goodness and Human Aims in Aristotle's Ethics', in O'Meara.

D. T. Devereux, 'Aristotle on the Essence of Happiness', in O'Meara.

M. V. Wedin, 'Aristotle on the Good for Man', *Mind* 1981.

See also: Virtue; Practical Wisdom.

Form and Matter

Met. VII. 7–9, 11, 17; VIII. 2–3; IX. 7; XII. 1–5. [For other texts and topics *see* Matter.]

Ross (4), pp. 167–76

D. C. Williams, 'Form and Matter', *PR* 1958.

H. Cartwright, 'Heraclitus and the Bath Water', *PR* 1965.

V. C. Chappell, 'Stuff and Things', *Ar.Soc.Proc.* 1970/1.

S. Mansion, 'The Ontological Composition of Sensible Substances in Aristotle', in *AA* 3.

V. Chappell, 'Aristotle's Conception of Matter', *J.Ph.* 1973.

E. Ryan, 'Pure Form in Aristotle', *Phronesis* 1973.

M. J. Loux, 'Form, Species and Predication in *Metaphysics* Z, H, and θ', *Mind* 1979.

G. E. L. Owen, 'Particular and General', *Ar.Soc.Proc.* 1978/9.
See also: Matter; Substance; Definition; Individuation.

Friendship

EN VIII–IX. [*EE* VII, *Rhet.* II. 4.]

Hardie, c. 15.

J. M. Cooper, 'Aristotle on Friendship', in Rorty.
E. Telfer, 'Friendship', *Ar.Soc.Proc.* 1970/1.
G. Vlastos, 'The Individual as an Object of Love in Plato', in Vlastos (p. 33).
J. Annas, 'Plato and Aristotle on Friendship and Altruism', *Mind* 1977.
W. W. Fortenbaugh, 'Aristotle's Analysis of Friendship: Function and Analogy, Resemblance, and Focal Meaning', *Phronesis* 1975.
C. H. Kahn, 'Aristotle and Altruism', *Mind* 1981.

God (the Unmoved Mover)

Met. XII. 6, 7, 9. [*Phys.* VII. 1; VIII. 4–5; *MA* 2–4.]

Guthrie (1), pp. xv–xxxvi; Ross (1), pp. cxxx–cliv; Ross (2), pp. 85–102; Ross (4), pp. 179–186; Ackrill (3), pp. 128–34; Clark, pp. 174–90; Waterlow (1), c. 5; Nussbaum, pp. 125–42.

G. Vlastos, 'A Note on the Unmoved Mover', *PQ* 1963.
R. Norman, 'Aristotle's Philosopher-God', in *AA* 4.
H. J. Easterling, 'The Unmoved Mover in Early Aristotle', *Phronesis* 1976.
J. Owens, 'The Relation of God to World in the *Metaphysics*', in Aubenque.
See also: Change; Thought.

Identity and Unity

De Int. 11; *Top.* 1. 7; *Met.* VI 2; X. 1.

N. P. White, 'Aristotle on Sameness and Oneness', *PR* 1971.
F. D. Miller, 'Did Aristotle have the Concept of Identity?', *PR* 1973.
A. Code, 'Aristotle's Response to Quine's Objections to Modal Logic', *J.Ph.Logic* 1976.
G. B. Matthews, 'Accidental Unities', in Schofield and Nussbaum.
See also: Essence.

Imagination

De An. III. 3,8, 10; *De Mem.* 1; *MA* 6–11. [*De Insomn.* 1.459^{a}8–22, 2.460^{b}2–27, 3.461^{a}25–462^{a}31.]

Beare, pp. 290–307; Hamlyn, pp. 129–35; Ross (6), pp. 32–3; Nussbaum, pp. 221–69.

K. Lycos, 'Aristotle and Plato on Appearing', *Mind* 1964.

D. A. Rees, 'Aristotle's Treatment of *Phantasia*', in Anton and Kustas.
M. Schofield, 'Aristotle on the Imagination', in Lloyd and Owen, and in *AA* 4.
J. Engmann, 'Imagination and Truth in Aristotle', *J.H.Ph.* 1976.

See also: Memory; Thought; Sense-perception.

Individuation

Met. V. 6.1016^{b}31–5; VII. 8.1034^{a}5–8, 10.1035^{b}27–1036^{a}25, 11.1037^{a}5–10, ^{a}25–^{b}7, 15.1039^{b}20–1040^{a}7; VIII. 1.1042^{a}26–31, 3.1043^{a}29–^{b}4; X. 9.1058^{b}5–12; XII. 3.1070^{a}9–13, 5.1071^{a}27–9, 8.1074^{a}31–8; *De An.* II. 1.412^{a}6–9; *De Caelo* I. 9.277^{b}27–278^{b}8.

Ross (1), pp. cxv–cxix; Ross (4), pp. 169–73; Hartman, c. 2.

G. E. M. Anscombe, 'The Principle of Individuation', in *AA* 3.
R. Albritton, 'Forms of Particular Substances in Aristotle's Metaphysics', *J.Ph.* 1957.
A. C. Lloyd, 'Aristotle's Principle of Individuation', *Mind* 1970.
W. Charlton, 'Aristotle and the Principle of Individuation', *Phronesis* 1972.
R. D. Sykes, 'Form in Aristotle: Universal or Particular', *Ph.* 1975.
E. Regis, 'Aristotle's Principle of Individuation', *Phronesis* 1976.
G. E. L. Owen, 'Particular and General', *Ar.Soc.Proc.* 1978/9.
D. K. Modrak, 'Forms, Types, and Tokens in Aristotle's *Metaphysics*', *Rev.of Met.* 1981.

See also: Matter; Form and Matter; Essence; Soul.

Infinity

Phys. III. 4–8; *De Caelo* I. 5–7.

Ross (2), pp. 48–53; Hussey, pp. 72–98.

J. Hintikka, 'Aristotelian Infinity', in *AA* 3 and in Hintikka (c. 6).
D. J. Furley, 'Aristotle and the Atomists on Infinity', in Düring.
D. Bostock, 'Aristotle, Zeno and the Potential Infinite', *Ar.Soc.Proc.* 1972/3.

[On Zeno's paradoxes *see*:

Phys. VI (especially c. 9); VIII. 8.

Ross (2), pp. 71–85; Sorabji (3) c. 21.

G. E. L. Owen, 'Zeno and the Mathematicians', *Ar.Soc.Proc.* 1957/8.
G. Vlastos, 'Zeno's Race-course', *J.H.Ph.* 1966.
G. Vlastos, 'A Note on Zeno's Arrow', *Phronesis* 1966.
G. Vlastos, 'Zeno', in Edwards vol. 8.
R. Sorabji, 'The Instant of Change', in *AA* 3.]

See also: Change; Time.

Justice

EN V. [*Rhet.* I. 13; *Pol.* III. 10.]

Ross (4), pp. 209–15; Hardie, c. 10; Hamburger, Part II; Leyden.

D. J. Allan, 'Individual and State in Aristotle's *Ethics* and *Politics*', in Fondation Hardt.

H. Kelsen, 'Aristotle's Doctrine of Justice', in Walsh and Shapiro.

R. Bambrough, 'Aristotle on Justice, a Paradigm of Philosophy', in Bambrough.

B. A. O. Williams, 'Justice as a Virtue', in Rorty.

M. I. Finley, 'Aristotle and Economic Analysis', in *AA* 2.

See also: Virtue; Political Philosophy.

Knowledge

Met. XIII. 10.1087ᵃ10–25; *De An.* II. 5.417ᵃ21–9. [*Met.* III. 4.999.ᵃ24–1000ᵃ4; 6.1003ᵃ5–17.]

Ross (1), pp. cviii–cx; Annas, pp. 190–2.

W. Leszl, 'Knowledge of the Universal and Knowledge of the Particular in Aristotle', *Rev.of. Met.* 1972.

J. Owens, 'The Grounds of Universality in Aristotle', in Owens (2).

See also: Thought; Science.

Matter

Phys. I. 5–9; *GC* I. 3–4; *Met.* VII. 3. [*De Caelo* IV. 5.312ᵃ30–ᵇ1. *GC* II. 1–5.]

Charlton, pp. 63–87; McMullin, pp. 79–101, 173–217; Ackrill (3), pp. 24–33; Williams, pp. 211–19.

H. R. King, 'Aristotle without Prime Matter', *J.H.Ideas* 1956.

F. Solmsen, 'Aristotle and Prime Matter: a reply to King', *J.H.Ideas* 1958.

V. Chappell, 'Aristotle's Conception of Matter', *J.Ph.* 1973.

H. M. Robinson, 'Did Aristotle believe in Prime Matter?', *Phronesis* 1974.

B. Jones, 'Aristotle's Introduction of Matter', *PR* 1974.

P. Suppes, 'Aristotle's Concept of Matter and its Relation to Modern Concepts of Matter', *Synthese* 1974.

J. Brunschwig, 'La Forme, Prédicat de la Matière?', in Aubenque.

F. D. Miller, 'Aristotle's Use of Matter', *Paideia* 1978.

D. Bostock, 'Aristotle on the Principles of Change in *Physics* I', in Schofield and Nussbaum.

See also: Change; Form and Matter; Substance; Definition; Individuation.

Meaning

Cat. 1; *De Int.* 1–4, 8; *Top.* I. 15; *Met.* IV. 2.1003ᵃ33–ᵇ15. [*Soph. El.* 1.]

Robins, c. 2; Ackrill (1), pp. 71–3, 113–25, 130–2; Kirwan, pp. 79–80.

J. Hintikka, 'Aristotle and the Ambiguity of Ambiguity', in Hintikka.

N. Kretzmann, 'Aristotle on Spoken Sound Significant by Convention', in Corcoran.

T. Irwin, 'Aristotle's Concept of Signification', in Schofield and Nussbaum.

T. Irwin, 'Homonymy in Aristotle', *Rev.of Met.* 1981.

See also: Categories; Predication; Metaphysics; Definition.

Memory

De Mem.

Ross (5), pp. 32–7; Sorabji (1); Beare, pp. 307–25.

J. Annas, 'Aristotle on Memory and the Self', *OSAP* 1986.

See also: Imagination; Sense-perception.

Metaphysics

Met. I. 1–2; IV. 1–3; VI. 1; XII. 1. [*Met.* XI. 3, 4, 7.]

Ross (1), pp. lxxvii–lxxix; Kirwan, pp. 76–90, 183–9; Owens (1), c. 7.

G. Patzig, 'Theology and Ontology in Aristotle's *Metaphysics*', in *AA* 3.

G. E. L. Owen, 'Logic and Metaphysics in Some Earlier Works of Aristotle', in *AA* 3.

T. H. Irwin, 'Aristotle's Discovery of Metaphysics', *Rev.of Met.* 1977–8.

P. Merlan, 'On the terms "Metaphysics" and "Being-qua-Being"', *Monist* 1968.

See also: God.

Necessity and Possibility

De Int. 12–13; *An.Pr.* A. 3, 13; *De Caelo* I. 12.

Ross (3), pp. 40–7; Ackrill (1), pp. 149–53; Kneale and Kneale, pp.81–96; Lukasiewicz, cc. 6–8; Patzig, c. 2; Hintikka, cc. 2–5, 7; Waterlow (2), cc. 1–4, 6–8.

R. Bluck, 'On the Interpretation of Aristotle, *De.Int.* 12–13', *CQ* 1963.

C. J. F. Williams, 'Aristotle and Corruptibility', *Religious Studies* 1965.

L. Judson, 'Eternity and Necessity in *De Caelo* I. 12', *OSAP* 1983.

C. A. Kirwan, 'Aristotle on the Necessity of the Present', *OSAP* 1986.

See also: Syllogism; Determinism.

Plato (Aristotle's Criticisms of the Theory of Forms)

Met. XIII. 4–5. [*Met.* I. 9. *On Ideas* fragments 3–4 in Ross (7), revised Oxford translation vol. II, pp. 2435–440.]

Annas, pp. 152–62; Cherniss, pp. 226–305.

G. E. L. Owen, 'A Proof in the *Peri Ideōn*', *JHS* 1957.

G. Fine, 'Aristotle and the More Accurate Arguments', in Schofield and Nussbaum.

G. E. L. Owen, 'The Platonism of Aristotle', in *AA* 1 (pp. 21–5).

A. Code, 'On the Origins of some Aristotelian Theses about Predication', in Bogen and McGuire.

G. Fine, 'Owen, Aristotle, and the Third Man', *Phronesis* 1982.

[On the Form of Good *see*

EN I. 6 and *EE* I. 8, with Hardie (c. 4), Woods (pp. 66–92), and J. L. Ackrill, 'Aristotle on "Good" and the Categories' (in *AA* 2).]

Pleasure

EN VII. 11–14; X. 1–5. [*Rhet.* I. 11.]

Hardie, c. 14; Kenny (1), c. 6; Gosling and Taylor, cc. 11–17.

J. O. Urmson, 'Aristotle on Pleasure', in Moravcsik.

G. E. L. Owen, 'Aristotelian Pleasures', in *AA* 2.

J. C. B. Gosling, 'More Aristotelian Pleasures', *Ar.Soc.Proc.* 1973/4.

J. Annas, 'Aristotle on Pleasure and Goodness', in Rorty.

See also: Change [on the distinction between change and activity].

Poetry

Poetics. [*Politics* VIII. 7.1341ᵇ32–1342ᵃ16].

Russell and Winterbottom, c. 3 (esp. pp. 85–9); Russell, pp. 91–3, c. 7; House.

J. Bernays, 'Aristotle on the Effect of Tragedy', in *AA* 4.

N. Gulley, 'Aristotle on the Purposes of Literature', in *AA* 4.

R. S. Yanal, 'Aristotle's Definition of Poetry', *Nous* 1982.

I. Smithson, 'The Moral View of Aristotle's *Poetics*', *J.H.Ideas* 1983.

See also: Imagination.

Political Philosophy

Politics.

Sinclair and Saunders (good translation with extremely useful chapter-analyses).

Mulgan (concise introduction to the *Politics* and the problems it raises, with a useful bibliography).

Robinson (on books III–IV); Ross (4), c. 8; Bodéüs (on the relation between ethics and politics in Aristotle).

See also: Justice; Friendship.

Practical Wisdom

EN VI.

Hardie, c. 11; Milo, c. 3; Cooper, c. 3; Greenwood, Introduction and Section II, esp. pp. 37–73; Engberg-Pedersen, cc. 7–8; Dahl, Part One.

D. J. Allan, 'Aristotle's Account of the Origin of Moral Principles', *Actes du XIe. Congrès International de Philosophie*, XII, 1953.

T. H. Irwin, 'Aristotle on Reason, Desire, and Virtue', *J.Ph.* 1975.

T. H. Irwin, 'First Principles in Aristotle's Ethics', *Midwest Studies in Philosophy* III, 1978.

See also: Deliberation and Choice; Action; *Eudaimonia*.

Predication

Cat. 1–5; *Met.* V. 7; VII. 1. [*An.Post.* I. 22.]

Ackrill (1), pp. 71–6, 82–8.

G. E. L. Owen, 'The Platonism of Aristotle', in *AA* 1 (pp. 21–6).

H. Weidemann, 'In Defence of Aristotle's Theory of Predication', *Phronesis* 1980.

A. Code, 'On the Origins of some Aristotelian Theses about Predication', in Bogen and McGuire.

[On problems arising from *Cat.* 2 *see*:

G. E. L. Owen, 'Inherence', *Phronesis* 1965.

J. M. E. Moravcsik, 'Aristotle on Predication', *PR* 1967.

G. B. Matthews and S. M. Cohen, 'The One and the Many', *Rev.of Met.* 1967–8.

R. E. Allen, 'Individual Properties in Aristotle's *Categories*', *Phronesis* 1969.

B. Jones, 'Individuals in Aristotle's *Categories*', *Phronesis* 1972.

J. Annas, 'Individuals in Aristotle's *Categories*: two Queries', *Phronesis* 1974.

R. E. Allen, 'Substance and Predication in Aristotle's *Categories*', in Lee, Mourelatos, and Rorty.

R. Heinaman, 'Non-substantial Individuals in the *Categories*', *Phronesis* 1981.]

See also: Categories; Meaning; Universals.

Responsibility (the Voluntary and Involuntary)

EN III. 1, 5; V. 8.; *EE* II. 6–9.

Hardie, c. 8; Kenny (3), Part 1; Sorabji (2), cc. 14–17.

J. L. Austin, 'A Plea for Excuses', in Austin.

F. A. Siegler, 'Voluntary and Involuntary', *Monist* 1968.
D. J. Furley, 'Aristotle on the Voluntary', in *AA* 2.
W. F. R. Hardie, 'Aristotle and the Freewill Problem', *Ph.* 1968.
T. H. Irwin, 'Reason and Responsibility in Aristotle', in Rorty.
J. L. Ackrill, 'An Aristotelian Argument about Virtue', *Paideia* 1978.
R. Hursthouse, 'Acting and Feeling in Character: *Nicomachean Ethics* III. 1', *Phronesis* 1984.

See also: Action; Deliberation and Choice.

Science (Theory of)

An.Post. I. 1–3, 10, 13; II. 19.

Ackrill (3), cc. 7–8; Barnes (1) pp. 248–60; Ross (3), 51–75, 84–6; Ross (4), pp. 41–9, 54–4; Gotthelf and Lennox, Part II.

J. H. Lesher, 'The Meaning of *Nous* in the *Posterior Analytics*', *Phronesis* 1973.
L. A. Kosman, 'Understanding, Explanation and Insight in the *Posterior Analytics*', in Lee, Mourelatos, and Rorty.
H. Scholz, 'The Ancient Axiomatic Theory', in *AA* 1.
J. Barnes, 'Aristotle's Theory of Demonstration', in *AA* 1.
B. A. Brody, 'Towards an Aristotelian Theory of Scientific Explanation', *Ph. of Sc.* 1972.
M. C. Nussbaum, 'Saving Aristotle's Appearances', in Schofield and Nussbaum.
G. E. L. Owen, 'Aristotle: Method, Physics, and Cosmology', in Gillispie, pp. 250–8.
M. F. Burnyeat, 'Aristotle on Understanding Knowledge', in Berti.
C. H. Kahn, 'The Role of *nous* in the Cognition of First Principles in *Posterior Analytics* II. 19', in Berti.
J. Barnes, 'Proof and the Syllogism', in Berti.
B. C. van Fraassen, 'A Re-examination of Aristotle's Philosophy of Science', *Dialogue* 1980.

See also: Causes; Definition; Biology.

Sense Perception

(a) *General*
De An. II. 5–III. 2; *De Insomn.* 2–3.

Beare, pp. 215–49, 325–36; Ross (6) pp. 24–37; Ackrill (3) pp.63–8; Clarke, c. 3.
D. W. Hamlyn, 'Aristotle's Account of *Aesthesis* in the *De Anima*'. *CQ* 1959.
I. Block, 'Truth and Error in Aristotle's Theory of Sense-Perception', *PQ* 1961.
T. Slakey, 'Aristotle on Sense-Perception', *PR* 1961.
R. Sorabji, 'Aristotle on Demarcating the Five Senses', in *AA* 4.

J. Owens, 'The University of the Sensible in the Aristotelian Noetic', in Anton and Kustas, and in Owens (2).

A. Ben-Zeev, 'Aristotle on Perceptual Truth and Falsity', *Apeiron* 1984.

(b) *The 'common sense', and 'incidental sensibles'*

De An. II. 6; III. 1.425ᵃ14–ᵇ11, 3.428ᵇ18–30; *De Mem.* 1.499ᵇ30–450ᵃ25; *De Somno* 2; *De Iuv.* 3. [*De Sensu* 1.437ᵃ3–12, 4.441ᵇ4–10, 7.499ᵃ2–20.]

Beare, pp. 276–90; Ross (6), pp. 33–6.

D. W. Hamlyn, '*Koine Aesthesis*', *Monist* 1968.

C. H. Kahn, 'Sensation and Conciousness in Aristotle's Psychology', in *AA* 4.

S. Cashdollar, 'Aristotle's Account of Incidental Perception', *Phronesis* 1973.

L. A. Kosman, 'Perceiving that We Perceive', *PR* 1975.

A. Graeser, 'On Aristotle's Framework of *Sensibilia*' in Lloyd and Owen.

Soul

De An. I. 1, 4. 408ᵃ34–ᵇ29; II. 1–4.

Ackrill (3), c. 5; Wilkes, c. 7; Nussbaum, pp. 146–58; Hartman, c. 4.

W. F. R. Hardie, 'Aristotle's Treatment of the Relation between the Soul and the Body', *PQ* 1964.

C. H. Kahn, 'Sensation and Consciousness in Aristotle's Psychology', in *AA* 4.

J. Barnes, 'Aristotle's Concept of Mind', in *AA* 4.

J. L. Ackrill, 'Aristotle's Definitions of *Psuche*', in *AA* 4.

R. Sorabji, 'Body and Soul in Aristotle', in *AA* 4.

W. F. R. Hardie, 'Concepts of Consciousness in Aristotle', *Mind* 1976.

H. M. Robinson, 'Mind and Body in Aristotle', *CQ* 1978.

W. Charlton, 'Aristotle's Definition of Soul', *Phronesis* 1980.

H. M. Robinson, 'Aristotelian Dualism', *OSAP* 1983.

M. Nussbaum, 'Aristotelian Dualism: Reply to Howard Robinson', *OSAP* 1984.

B. Williams, 'Hylomorphism', *OSAP* 1986.

See also: Sense-perception; Thought; Form and Matter; Individuation.

Substance

Cat. 5; *Met.* VII (esp. 1, 16, 17).

Ross (1), pp. xci–cxxiv; Hartman, c. 1.

S. Mansion, 'The Ontological Composition of Sensible Substances in Aristotle (*Met.* VII. 7–9)', in *AA* 3.

G. E. L. Owen, 'Particular and General', *Ar.Soc.Proc.* 1978/9.

J. A. Driscoll, 'ΕΙΔΗ in Aristotle's Earlier and Later Theories of Substance', in O'Meara.

L. A. Kosman, 'Substance, Being, and Energeia', *OSAP* 1984.
See also: Categories; Form; Essence; Metaphysics; Predication; Individuation.

Syllogism

An.Pr. I. 1–7.

Kapp, cc. II–IV; Ross (3), pp. 23–40; Lukasiewicz, c. 1; Kneale and Kneale, pp. 67–81; Patzig, c. 1; Ackrill (3), c. 6; Lear, c. 1.

E. Kapp, 'Syllogistic', in *AA* 1.

M. Thompson, 'On Aristotle's Square of Opposition', in Moravcsik.

T. Smiley, 'What is a Syllogism?', *J.Ph.Logic* 1973.

J. Barnes, 'Proof and the Syllogism', in Berti.

See also: Necessity and Possibility.

Teleological Explanation

Phys. II. 8–9; *PA* I. 1; *GA* V. 8.

Charlton, pp. 120–6; Balme, pp. 93–100; Ackrill (3), pp. 41–54; Sorabji (2), cc. 9–11; Edel, c. 5; Gotthelf and Lennox, Part III.

D. M. Balme, 'Greek Science and Mechanism', *CQ* 1939 and 1941.

W. Wieland, 'The Problem of Teleology', in *AA* 1.

D. M. Balme, 'Aristotle's Use of Teleological Explanation' (Inaugural Lecture, London, 1965).

A. Gotthelf, 'Aristotle's Conception of Final Causality', *Rev. of Met.* 1976.

J. M. Cooper, 'Aristotle on Natural Teleology', in Schofield and Nussbaum.

See also: Causes; Biology.

Thought

De An. III. 4–8; *EN* VI; X. 7–8; *Met.* XII. 7, 9; *GA* II. 3.736^{a}24–737^{a}34; *De Mem.* 1.449^{b}30–450^{a}14; *An.Post.* II. 19.

Hardie, c. 16; Clark, c. V.3; Cooper, c. 3.

R. Sorabji, 'Myths about Non-propositional Thought', in Schofield and Nussbaum.

A. C. Lloyd, 'Non-discursive Thought—an Enigma of Greek Philosophy', *Ar.Soc.Proc.* 1969/70.

S. H. Rosen, 'Thought and Touch: a note on Aristotle's *De Anima*', *Phronesis* 1961.

J. M. Rist, 'Notes on Aristotle *De Anima* III. 5', in Anton and Kustas.

J. Owens, 'A Note on Aristotle *De Anima* III. 4.429^{b}9', in Owens (2).

R. Norman, 'Aristotle's Philosopher-God', in *AA* 4.

M. F. Lowe, 'Aristotle on Kinds of Thinking', *Phronesis* 1983.

See also: God; Truth; Imagination.

Time

Phys. IV. 10–14.

Ross (2), pp. 63–9; Callaghan, c. 2; Hussey, pp. 138–75; Sorabji (3), esp. cc. 2, 4.

F. D. Miller, 'Aristotle on the Reality of Time', *AGP* 1974.

G. E. L. Owen, 'Aristotle on Time', in *AA* 3.

J. Annas, 'Aristotle, Number and Time', *PQ* 1975.

D. Corish, 'Aristotle's Attempted Derivation of Temporal Order from that of Movement and Space', *Phronesis* 1976.

J. Moreau, 'Le Temps et l'Instant selon Aristote', in Düring.

W. Kneale, 'Time and Eternity in Theology', *Ar.Soc.Proc.* 1960/1.

W. von Leyden, 'Time, Number and Eternity in Plato and Aristotle', *PQ* 1964.

S. Waterlow, 'Aristotle's Now', *PQ* 1984.

See also: Change.

Truth

Cat. 5.4ᵃ10–ᵇ19; *De Int.* 1–6; *Met.* VI.4; IX. 10; *De An.* III. 6.

Ackrill (1), pp. 90–1, 114–15; Kirwan, pp. 198–200.

J. Hintikka, 'Time, Truth and Knowledge in Aristotle and Other Greek Philosophers', in Hintikka.

E. Berti, 'The Intellection of Indivisibles according to Aristotle *De Anima*, III. 6', in Lloyd and Owen.

P. Aubenque, 'La Pensée du Simple dans *Met.* Z. 17 et θ. 10', in Aubenque.

F. Brentano, 'On the Concept of Truth', in Brentano (I. 1).

M. Matthen, 'Greek Ontology and the "Is" of Truth', *Phronesis* 1983.

See also: Thought.

Universals

De Int. 7.17ᵃ38–41; *Met.* VII. 13.

Ross (1), pp. cvii–cxi.

M. J. Woods, 'Problems in *Metaphysics* Z. 13', in Moravcsik.

J. H. Lesher, 'Aristotle on Form, Substance, and Universals', *Phronesis* 1971.

J. Engmann, 'Aristotle's Distinction between Substance and Universal', *Phronesis* 1973.

R. Elugardo, 'Woods on *Metaphysics* Z. 13', *Apeiron* 1975.

A. Code, 'No Universal is a Substance', *Paideia* 1978.

G. E. L. Owen, 'Particular and General', *Ar.Soc.Proc.* 1978/9.

D. K. Modrak, 'Forms, Types, and Tokens in Aristotle's *Metaphysics*', *Rev.of Met.* 1981.

See also: Knowledge; Substance.

Virtue

EN I. 13; II; VI. 1.1138^{b}18–34. [*EN* III. 6–IV. *EE* II. 1–5; III; VIII. 1–3.]

Hardie, cc. 6–7; Engberg-Pedersen, c. 3; Fortenbaugh, c. 4.

W. F. R. Hardie, 'Aristotle's Doctrine that Virtue is a "Mean"', in *AA* 2.

J. O. Urmson, 'Aristotle's Doctrine of the Mean', in Rorty.

L. A. Kosman, 'Being Properly Affected: Virtues and Feelings in Aristotle's Ethics', in Rorty.

D. F. Pears, 'Courage as a Mean', in Rorty.

W. F. R. Hardie '"Magnanimity" in Aristotle's Ethics', *Phronesis* 1978.

R. Hursthouse, 'A False Doctrine of the Mean', *Ar.Soc.Proc.* 1980/1.

J. D. Wallace, 'Excellences and Merit', *PR* 1974.

M. F. Burnyeat, 'Aristotle on Learning to be Good', in Rorty.

R. Sorabji, 'Aristotle on the Role of Intellect in Virtue', in Rorty.

J. H. McDowell, 'Virtue and Reason', *Monist* 1979.

See also: *Eudaimonia*; Practical Wisdom; Responsibility.

LIST OF BOOKS

This list is meant only to facilitate reference, and does not aim at completeness.

Ackrill, J. L. (1) *Aristotle's Categories and De Interpretatione*, trans. with notes, Oxford, 1963.

—— (2) *Aristotle's Ethics*, London, 1973.

—— (3) *Aristotle the Philosopher*, Oxford, 1981.

Allan, D. J. *The Philosophy of Aristotle*, 2nd edn., Oxford, 1970.

Annas, J. *Aristotle's Metaphysics M and N*, trans. with notes, Oxford, 1976.

Anscombe, G. E. M. and Geach, P. *Three Philosophers*, Oxford, 1961.

Anton, J. P. and Kustas, G. L., eds. *Essays in Ancient Greek Philosophy*, New York, 1971.

Aubenque, P. *Etudes sur la Metaphysique d'Aristote*, Paris, 1979.

Austin, J. L. *Philosophical Papers*, Oxford, 1961.

Autour d'Aristote (Recueil d'Etudes offert à Mgr. A. Mansion), Louvain, 1955.

Balme, D. M. *Aristotle's De Partibus Animalium I and De Generatione Animalium I*, trans. with notes, Oxford, 1972.

Bambrough, R., ed. *New Essays on Plato and Aristotle*, London, 1965.

Barnes, J. (1) *Aristotle's Posterior Analytics*, trans. with notes, Oxford, 1975.

—— (2) *Aristotle*, Oxford, 1982.

Beare, J. I. *Greek Theories of Elementary Cognition*, Oxford, 1906.

Berti, E. *Aristotle on Science: The Posterior Analytics*, Padua, 1981.

Bodéüs, R. *Le Philosophe et la Cité*, Paris, 1982.

Bogen, J. and McGuire, J. E., eds. *How Things Are: Studies in Predication and the History of Philosophy and Science*, Dordrecht, 1985.

Boylan, M. *Method and Practice in Aristotle's Biology*, Washington DC, 1983.

Brentano, F. *The True and the Evident*, London, 1966.

Brunschwig, J., ed. *Aristote: Topiques I—IV*, Paris, 1967.

Callaghan, J. F. *Four Views of Time in Ancient Philosophy*, Cambridge, Mass., 1948.

Charles, D. *Aristotle's Philosophy of Action*, London, 1984.

Charlton, W. *Aristotle's Physics I and II*, trans. with notes, Oxford, 1970.

Cherniss, H. F. *Aristotle's Criticism of Plato and the Academy*, Baltimore, 1944.

Clark, S. R. L. *Aristotle's Man*, Oxford, 1975.

Cooper, J. M. *Reason and Human Good in Aristotle*, Cambridge, Mass. and London, 1975.

Corcoran, J., ed. *Ancient Logic and its Modern Interpretations*, Dordrecht, 1974.

Dahl, N. O. *Practical Reason, Aristotle, and Weakness of the Will*, Minneapolis, 1984.

Davidson, D. *Essays on Actions and Events*, Oxford, 1980.

Düring, I., ed. *Naturphilosophie bei Aristoteles und Theophrast*, Heidelberg, 1969.

Edel, A. *Aristotle and his Philosophy*, Chapel Hill, 1982.

Edwards, P., ed. *The Encyclopaedia of Philosophy*, London, 1967.

Engberg-Pedersen, T. *Aristotle's Theory of Moral Insight*, Oxford, 1983.

Evans, J. D. G. *Aristotle's Concept of Dialectic*, Cambridge, 1977.

Evans, G. and McDowell, J., eds. *Truth and Meaning*, Oxford, 1976.

Feinberg, J., ed. *Moral Concepts*, Oxford, 1969.

Fondation Hardt, Entretiens XI, *La 'Politique' d'Aristote*, Geneva, 1965.

Fortenbaugh, W. W. *Aristotle on Emotion*, London, 1975.

Gillispie, C. C., ed. *Dictionary of Scientific Biography*, vol. I, New York, 1970.

Gosling, J. C. B. and Taylor, C. C. W. *The Greeks on Pleasure*, Oxford, 1982.

Gotthelf, A., ed. *Aristotle on Nature and Living Things*, Pittsburgh and Bristol, 1985.

—— and Lennox, J., eds. *Philosophical Issues in Aristotle's Biology*, Cambridge, 1987.

Grandy, R. and Warner, R., eds. *Philosophical Grounds of Rationality: Intentions, Categories, and Ends*, Oxford, 1985.

Grant, A. *The Ethics of Aristotle illustrated with Essays and Notes*, 4th edn., London, 1885.

Greenwood, L. H. G. *Aristotle's Nicomachean Ethics VI*, Cambridge, 1909.

Guthrie, W. K. C. (1) *Aristotle: On the Heavens*, London, 1939.

—— (2) *A History of Greek Philosophy*, vol. VI (Aristotle), Cambridge, 1981.

Hamburger, M. *Morals and Law: the Growth of Aristotle's Legal Theory*, New Haven, 1951.

Hamlyn, D. W. *Aristotle's De Anima II and III*, Oxford, 1968.

Hardie, W. F. R. *Aristotle's Ethical Theory*, 2nd (enlarged) edn., Oxford, 1980.

Hartman, E. *Substance, Body and Soul*, Princeton, 1977.

Hintikka, J. *Time and Necessity*, Oxford, 1973.

House, H. *Aristotle's Poetics*, London, 1956.

Hussey, E. *Aristotle's Physics III and IV*, trans. with notes, Oxford, 1983.

Irwin, T. *Aristotle's Nicomachean Ethics*, trans. with notes, Indianapolis, 1985.

Kahn, C. H. *The Verb 'Be' in Ancient Greek*, Dordrecht, 1973.

Kapp, E. *Greek Foundations of Traditional Logic*, New York, 1942.

Kenny, A. (1) *Action, Emotion and Will*, London, 1963.

—— (2) *The Aristotelian Ethics*, Oxford, 1978.

—— (3) *Aristotle's Theory of the Will*, London, 1979.

Kirwan, C. A. *Aristotle's Metaphysics, Books Γ, Δ, E*, trans. with notes, Oxford, 1971.

Kneale, W. and Kneale, M. *The Development of Logic*, Oxford, 1962.

Lear, J. *Aristotle and Logical Theory*, Cambridge, 1980.

Lee, E. N., Mourelatos, A. P. D., and Rorty, R. M., eds. *Exegesis and Argument*, Assen, 1973.

Leyden, W. von, *Aristotle on Equality and Justice*, London, 1985.

Lloyd, G. E. R. *Aristotle: The Growth and Structure of his Thought*, Cambridge, 1968.

—— and Owen, G. E. L., eds. *Aristotle on Mind and the Senses*, Cambridge, 1978.

Lukasiewicz, J. *Aristotle's Syllogistic*, 2nd (enlarged) edn., Oxford, 1957.

McMullin, E., ed. *The Concept of Matter in Greek and Medieval Philosophy*, Notre Dame, 1963.

Mansion, S. *Le Jugement d'Existence chez Aristote*, 2nd edn., Louvain, 1976.

Milo, R. D. *Aristotle on Practical Knowledge and Weakness of Will*, The Hague, 1966.

Moravcsik, J. M. E., ed. *Aristotle*, New York, 1967.

Mulgan, R. G. *Aristotle's Political Theory*, Oxford, 1977.

Nussbaum, M. C. *Aristotle's De Motu Animalium*, Princeton, 1978.

O'Meara, D. J., ed. *Studies in Aristotle*, Washington, DC, 1981.

Owen, G. E. L., ed. *Aristotle on Dialectic*, Oxford, 1968.

Owens, J. (1) *The Doctrine of Being in the Aristotelian Metaphysics*, 2nd edn., Toronto, 1963.

—— (2) *Aristotle*, collected papers ed. J. R. Catan, Albany, 1981.

Patzig, G. *Aristotle's Theory of the Syllogism*, trans. J. Barnes, Dordrecht, 1968.

Peck, A. L. (1) *Aristotle: Parts of Animals*, London, 1937.

—— (2) *Aristotle: Generation of Animals*, London, 1953.

Pitcher, G. and Wood, O. P., eds. *Ryle*, New York, 1970.

Robins, R. H. *Short History of Linguistics*, London, 1967.

Robinson, R. *Aristotle's Politics III and IV*, trans. with notes, Oxford, 1962.

Rorty, A. O., ed. *Essays on Aristotle's Ethics*, Berkeley and Los Angeles, 1980.

Ross, W. D. (1) *Aristotle's Metaphysics*, 2 vols., Oxford, 1924.

—— (2) *Aristotle's Physics*, Oxford, 1936.

—— (3) *Aristotle's Prior and Posterior Analytics*, Oxford, 1949.

—— (4) *Aristotle*, 5th (revised) edn., London, 1953.

—— (5) *Aristotle's Parva Naturalia*, Oxford, 1955.

—— (6) *Aristotle's De Anima*, Oxford, 1961.

—— (7) *The Works of Aristotle*, vol. XII, *Select Fragments*, Oxford, 1952.

Russell, D. A. *Criticism in Antiquity*, London, 1981.

—— and Winterbottom, M., eds. *Ancient Literary Criticism*, Oxford, 1972.

Schofield, M. and Nussbaum, M., eds. *Language and Logos*, Cambridge, 1982.

Sinclair, T. A. and Saunders, T. J. *Aristotle: the Politics*, Penguin Classics, Harmondsworth, 1981.

Sorabji, R. (1) *Aristotle on Memory*, London, 1972.

—— (2) *Necessity, Cause, and Blame*, London, 1980.

—— (3) *Time, Creation and the Continuum*, London, 1983.

Vlastos, G. *Platonic Studies*, Princeton, 1973.

Walsh, J. J. and Shapiro, H. H., eds. *Aristotle's Ethics: Issues and Interpretations*, Belmont, 1967.

Waterlow, S. (1) *Nature, Change, and Agency in Aristotle's Physics*, Oxford, 1982.
—— (2) *Passage and Possibility*, Oxford, 1982.
Wilkes, K. V. *Physicalism*, London, 1978.
Williams, C. J. F. *Aristotle's De Generatione et Corruptione*, trans. with notes, Oxford, 1982.
Woods, M. J. *Aristotle's Eudemian Ethics I, II, and VIII*, trans. with notes, Oxford, 1982.